THE

LABOR RELATIONS PROCESS

Fourth Edition

WILLIAM H. HOLLEY, JR.
Auburn University

KENNETH M. JENNINGS
University of North Florida

The Dryden Press
Chicago Fort Worth San Francisco Philadelphia
Montreal Toronto London Sydney Tokyo

Acquisitions Editor: Robert Gemin
Developmental Editor: Kathi Erley
Project Editor: Paula Dempsey
Art and Design Director: Jeanne Calabrese
Production Manager: Bob Lange
Permissions Editor: Doris Milligan
Director of Editing, Design, and Production: Jane Perkins

Cover Illustration: Bob Conge
Copy Editor: Alison Shurtz
Compositor: Pam Frye Typesetting, Inc.
Text Type: 10/12 Times Roman

Library of Congress Cataloging-in-Publication Data

Holley, William H.
The labor relations process / William H. Holley, Kenneth M. Jennings. – 4th ed.
p. cm.
Includes bibliographical references.
ISBN 0-03-033062-9
1. Industrial relations–United States. I. Jennings, Kenneth M. II. Title.
HD8072.5.H64 1991
658.3'15'0973–dc20 90-30233
CIP

Printed in the United States of America
012-015-987654321

Address orders:
The Dryden Press
Orlando, FL 32887

Address editorial correspondence:
The Dryden Press
908 N. Elm Street
Hinsdale, IL 60521

The Dryden Press
Holt, Rinehart and Winston
Saunders College Publishing

To Ali and Bret, who unsuccessfully argued
that the word processor is better than the pencil,
and to Betty and Jackie, who gave the pencils
a reason for moving.

The Dryden Press Series in Management

Bartlett
Cases in Strategic Management for Business

Bedeian
Management
Second Edition

Bedeian and Zammuto
Organizations: Theory and Design

Boone and Kurtz
Contemporary Business
Sixth Edition

Bowman and Branchaw
Business Report Writing
Second Edition

Bracker, Montanari, and Morgan
Cases in Strategic Management

Cullinan
Business English for Industry and the Professions

Czinkota, Rivoli, and Ronkainen
International Business

Daft
Management
Second Edition

Efendioglu and Montanari
The Advantage Ski Company: A Strategic Simulation

Gaither
Production and Operations Management: A Problem-Solving and Decision-Making Approach
Fourth Edition

Foegen
Business Plan Guidebook with Financial Spreadsheets

Forgionne
Quantitative Management

Gatewood and Feild
Human Resource Selection
Second Edition

Greenhaus
Career Management

Higgins
Strategy: Formulation, Implementation, and Control

Higgins and Vincze
Strategic Management: Text and Cases
Fourth Edition

Hills
Compensation Decision Making

Hodgetts
Modern Human Relations at Work
Fourth Edition

Holley and Jennings
The Labor Relations Process
Fourth Edition

Huseman, Lahiff, and Penrose
Business Communication: Strategies and Skills
Fourth Edition

Jauch, Coltrin, and Bedeian
The Managerial Experience: Cases, Exercises, and Readings
Fifth Edition

Kemper
Experiencing Strategic Management

Kuehl and Lambing
Small Business: Planning and Management
Second Edition

Kuratko and Hodgetts
Entrepreneurship: A Contemporary Approach

Lee
Introduction to Management Science
Second Edition

Luthans and Hodgetts
Business

Montanari, Morgan, and Bracker
Strategic Management: A Choice Approach

Northcraft and Neale
Organizational Behavior: A Management Challenge

Tombari
Business and Society: Strategies for the Environment and Public Policy

Varner
Contemporary Business Report Writing
Second Edition

Vecchio
Organizational Behavior
Second Edition

Wolters and Holley
Labor Relations: An Experiential and Case Approach

Zikmund
Business Research Methods
Third Edition

Preface

When preparing to write the fourth edition of *The Labor Relations Process,* we focused our attention on our original objective in writing the book: to provide students with a text that will generate an understanding of and appreciation for union-management relationships. We have attempted to involve the student with the subject matter and to create an interest in related issues that will continue after the course is completed. A model of the labor relations process (Exhibit 1.1) is presented in the first chapter and extended in subsequent chapters through extensive references to academics and practitioners that focus on real-world situations and concerns. This provides a balance between concepts and applications for the reader. As with the first edition and all subsequent editions, the fourth edition of *The Labor Relations Process* continues to be the most comprehensive text on the market.

Features of the Fourth Edition

The fourth edition enhances our original objective through overall and chapter-specific changes. Some of the primary features of this edition include the following:

- **Currency.** There are many opportunities for the reader to become involved with the current applications of this subject. For example, recent collective bargaining occurring with the Screen Writers Guild, the Greyhound Bus Lines strike, football players, Pittston mine workers' strike, the baseball lock-out, and the ongoing labor problems at Eastern Airlines are among the topics covered in this edition.
- **Ethics.** Ethical issues and situations are integrated throughout the text and highlighted with marginal logos. Issues such as ethical considerations in bargaining behavior, union organizing, and termination of union advocates are discussed.
- **International Labor.** The international chapter (Chapter 15) has been updated and expanded to include the changes in Eastern Europe (including the Soviet Union) and the implications of the 1992 European Community (EC) agreement.
- **Labor Relations in Action.** The Labor Relations in Action boxes integrate current events in labor relations and have been updated with almost 60 percent new applications.

- **Epilogue.** New to the fourth edition, the epilogue discusses the future of labor and some possibilities for the direction labor may take through the 1990s and beyond.
- **Cases.** This edition also features new cases from the National Labor Relations Board courts and various arbitrators. The cases appear at the end of each part and focus on a variety of concepts.

Major Changes in the Fourth Edition

Each chapter has been extensively updated in terms of sources, studies, and statistics. The following subjects have also been added:

- **Chapter 1:** New work rule considerations and applications (AIDS and drug testing), current union membership trends, and the "Union Yes" campaign.
- **Chapter 2:** Violent labor-management episodes and related media coverage, concession bargaining since World War II, and organized labor and the 1988 presidential campaign.
- **Chapter 3:** Assessment of the National Labor Relations Board, including "Labor Relations in Action: Justice Delayed," plant closing legislation (Worker Adjustment and Retraining Notification Act—WARN), and Racketeering Influenced and Corrupt Organizations Act (RICO).
- **Chapter 4:** Strategic planning and structure of unions and management (additional emphasis from previous editions) and the associate membership program.
- **Chapter 5:** Macro and micro explanations of why employees join unions; greater coverage of management's activities in unionization campaigns, including employers' statements (Labor Relations in Action); and analysis of union election voting practices.
- **Chapter 6:** Additional pre-negotiation activities and strategic approaches during negotiations, application of the bargaining power model to the entertainment industry (Labor Relations in Action), and ethical considerations in bargaining behavior.
- **Chapter 7:** Mediators' behavior (Labor Relations in Action), labor-management cooperative programs (expanded coverage from previous editions), and employee participation programs in the nonunion setting.
- **Chapter 8:** Research considerations of employee grievances (Labor Relations in Action), and nonunion grievance procedures.
- **Chapter 9:** Arbitrator's role in hearings and arbitration and public policy, including comments from the arbitrator of the *Misco* decision (Labor Relations in Action).
- **Chapter 10:** Employment at will challenges and witness credibility.
- **Chapter 11:** Voting trends in right-to-work law referendums and minority/female union officers.
- **Chapter 12:** Technological issues (additional emphasis from previous editions) and contemporary safety and health issues such as chemical hazards, VDT disease, and smoking.

- **Chapter 13:** Health care containment, family issues such as child-care and parental leave, and ESOPs (additional emphasis with a related Labor Relations in Action).
- **Chapter 14:** Inclusion of public sector labor relations in one chapter, the air traffic controllers controversy (Labor Relations in Action), and inclusion of various groups: elementary and secondary teachers, higher education, police, fire fighters, and postal service employees.
- **Chapter 15:** Multinational corporations (additional emphasis and integration from previous editions), coverage of the European Community (EC) by 1992, and changes in Eastern Europe with highlights of *glasnost* and *perestroika* in the Soviet Union and Solidarity in Poland.
- **Chapter 16:** Relationship between performance measures and salaries in professional sports, the National Labor Relations Board's policies concerning health care employees and HMO physicians, and farm workers' concerns with illegal aliens and pesticides.
- **Epilogue:** Discusses both the financial and political direction labor may take in the 1990s as well as labor's impact on society.

Ancillary Materials

The new *Instructor's Manual* will include chapter outlines, answers to end-of-chapter discussion questions, case notes, suggested student readings and term projects, and both instructors' and students' instructions for the Collective Bargaining Negotiations Exercise. The *Test Bank* has been revised, updated, and expanded. The number of transparency masters has been increased.

A Computerized Test Bank, designed for the IBM microcomputer, is also available free to adopters. The Computerized Test Bank allows instructors to select, edit, and add test items and print tests for classroom use.

A new bargaining simulation is available as a supplement for the fourth edition, as well as a variety of videotapes.

Acknowledgments

We are especially grateful to the following professors for their reviews of the fourth edition and earlier editions:

James F. Byers, Indiana University of Pennsylvania; James B. Dworkin, Purdue University; Denise Tanguay Hoyer, Eastern Michigan University; Philip Kienast, University of Washington; Howard T. Ludlow, Seton Hall University; Marick Masters, University of Pittsburgh; Dane M. Partridge, Virginia Polytechnic Institute; Richard L. Rowan, University of Pennsylvania; Peter Sherer, University of Illinois; Herman A. Theeke, Central Michigan University; Elizabeth Wesman, Syracuse University; and Roger S. Wolters, Auburn University.

Thanks are extended to other professors who made valuable suggestions to previous editions: John C. Bird, Mollie Bowers, Joseph M. Cambridge, Anthony

Campagna, William Chase, Milton Derber, Geraldine Ellerbrock, Paul Gerhart, Carol L. Gilmore, Thomas P. Gilroy, David Gray, Charles R. Greer, Marvin Hill, Jr., H. Roy Kaplan, Kenneth A. Kovach, Charles Krider, Douglas McCabe, Karl O. Magnusen, William Maloney, Pamela Marett, Jonathan Monat, Roy Moore, William L. Moore, Thomas Noble, Robert Penfield, Roy R. Reynolds, Robert Rodgers, David Shulenberger, Susanne M. Vest, and William Werther.

Similar appreciation is extended to many individuals who have read portions of this book and have contributed their expertise in specialized areas: Dawn Bennett-Alexander, Gwynne Berry, Bruce Fortado, Marc Grossman, Alexander Hadden, Dan C. Heldman, Robert Helsby, Eileen Hoffman, Wayne Howard, Truly Kincey, Terry Leap, Jim McCollum, Marvin Miller, Ed Perron, Steve Shapiro, William Simkin, Ron Smith, Hans Stadtlander, and Albert Zack.

We are grateful to A. Dale Allen, Jr., Milden J. Fox, Jr., Paul Gerhart, and James P. O'Grady for furnishing an excellent selection of arbitration cases.

We also wish to thank those individuals who have either directly or indirectly aided in the preparation of this book: Anne Davis, Marion Gay, and Betty Geitz.

Special thanks is extended to those who helped along the way: John Abernathy, Achilles Armenakis, Art Bedeian, Ernie Brown, Cliff Carter, Margaret Chaplan, Boyd Childress, Kathy Cohen, Jack Davis, Hubert Feild, William Giles, Amit Goela, Langston Hawley, Harold D. Janes, Ed Johnson, Yvonne Kozlowski, Don Mosley, Steve Oehler, Joseph Schussler, Jay Smith, Linda Smoak, Lorna Wiggins, Rudy White, and Steve Williamson.

Finally, we would like to thank the Dryden staff for their fine work on this book. We are grateful to Butch Gemin, Bob Lange, Diane Tenzi, Rita Madsen, Katie Mattingly, and Doris Milligan at Dryden; and to Alison Shurtz and Marcia LaBrenz for copyediting and proofreading. A special "thank you" is extended to Kathi Erley and Paula Dempsey.

William H. Holley, Jr.
Auburn University

Kenneth M. Jennings
University of North Florida

June 1990

About the Authors

William H. Holley, Jr., is an Edward L. Lowder Professor at Auburn University, where he teaches labor relations, collective bargaining and arbitration, and human resource management. He received his B.S. and M.B.A. from Mississippi State University and his Ph.D. from the University of Alabama. He has been active in the Southern Management Association, a division of the Academy of Management, where he has served as Secretary and President, and on the editorial board of the *Journal of Management* for three terms. He is a coauthor of *Personnel/Human Resource Management* with Ken Jennings and of *Labor Relations: An Experiential and Case Approach* with Roger Wolters. His research has been published in a wide range of journals, such as the *Academy of Management Journal, Labor Law Journal, Personnel Psychology,* and others. As a member of the National Academy of Arbitrators, he serves on its Research and Continuing Education Committees. He also serves on the editorial boards of the *Journal of Collective Negotiations in the Public Sector* and *Employee Rights and Responsibilities Journal.*

Kenneth M. Jennings, Jr., is a Business Affiliates Professor at the University of North Florida, where he teaches undergraduate and graduate courses in labor relations and human resource management. After receiving his B.S. from Knox College and M.S. from the University of Illinois, he spent four years with Union Carbide in various industrial relations assignments. He then received a Ph.D. from the University of Illinois, and he has been at the University of North Florida for 18 years. He has written numerous books (*Balls and Strikes: The Money Game in Professional Baseball* being his latest) and articles in journals such as *Industrial and Labor Relations Review, Industrial Management, Personnel Journal, Employee Relations Law Journal,* and *Transportation Journal.* A Chicago Cubs fan and collector of jazz recordings and baseball cards, he lives with his wife, Jackie; daughter, Allison; and son, Bret.

Contents in Brief

Contents

Chapter 3
Legal Influences 59

Chapter 4
Unions and Management: Key Participants in the Labor Relations Process 87

Recognizing Rights and Responsibilities of Unions and Management

Part 1 introduces the labor relations process that will be discussed throughout the book, placing it in historical and legal perspectives. It also examines how employees become unionized and the relationships between the various organizational components of labor.

Union-Management Relationships in Perspective

As the United States faces unprecedented economic change and international challenges, an increasing number of companies and unions are rethinking their assumptions about work and how it is organized. In order to respond to rapidly changing market conditions, companies must . . . operate as efficiently as possible and . . . adapt quickly to new demands without continually looking to their workers for sacrifices.

Labor Management Cooperation: 1989 State-of-the-Art Symposium (Washington, D.C.: U.S. Department of Labor, 1989).

American business is faced with many urgent, strategic choices and challenges. This situation often includes employees who are involved in the labor relations process, in which management and the union (the exclusive bargaining agent for the employees) jointly decide upon and administer terms and conditions of employment (work rules).

This chapter places the labor relations process into an analytical perspective (Exhibit 1.1). It also introduces the elements and steps of this process, which are discussed in the book's remaining chapters.

Elements in the Labor Relations Process

Exhibit 1.1 provides a framework for the **labor relations process.** The elements shown can be applied to the labor relations activities at a single manufacturing facility, at some or all of the facilities owned by a single company, or in an entire industry. The exhibit cites three major categories: (1) the focal point of labor relations, which is the work rules; (2) the participants in the process, which are the union and management organizations, employees, third-party neutrals, and the government; and (3) constraints or influences affecting the parties in their negotiation and administration of the work rules.

These categories are interrelated (as is shown by Case 4.1, about Eastern Airlines). They will be discussed separately, however, to reflect their unique dimensions and considerations.

Focal Point of Labor Relations: Work Rules

Any academic discipline needs a focal point so that research, investigation, and commentary can generate applicable insights. "Labor" or "industrial" relations can become a very broad topic including many academic concerns. Sociologists have examined employee alienation, psychologists have investigated causes of job satisfaction, economists have studied wage determination, and political scientists have assessed the structural relationships of the internal union organization and its members and leaders.

In 1958 John Dunlop's book *Industrial Relations Systems* provided a useful focal point for the diverse academic approaches. Dunlop suggested that the center of attention in labor relations should be the work rules negotiated between management and union officials. It is important to understand the influences determining whether a work rule exists and, if so, its particular content.[1] **Work rules** can be placed in two general categories: (1) rules governing compensation in all its forms—overtime payments, vacations, holidays, shift premiums, and so on, and (2) rules specifying the employees' and employers' job rights and obligations, such as performance standards, promotion qualifications and procedures, job specifications, and layoff procedures. Additional examples of work rules are furnished in Exhibit 1.2.

Compensation work rules such as negotiated wages are often publicized because they are easily understood by the public. Union and management officials, however, can attach equal or greater significance to the second work rule category, job rights and obligations. Managers, for example, might be most concerned with obtaining a contract provision whereby production employees can be required to perform "minor repairs," instead of requiring higher-paid maintenance employees to do them. Also, at least one major union has been successful in negotiating a "justice and dignity" work rule whereby an employee who is suspended or discharged remains on the job until the disciplinary decision is reached (usually by an arbitrator, as discussed later in this chapter).[2]

Finally, many employees are currently concerned about work rules that require employees to work overtime, especially when some of their co-employees are unemployed on layoff. Longer hours increase fatigue along with earnings. Also, overtime pay can lead employees to take on payments for cars and other items that they cannot afford when they go back to 40 hours. One auto worker experiencing

Exhibit 1.1 **Elements in the Labor Relations Process**

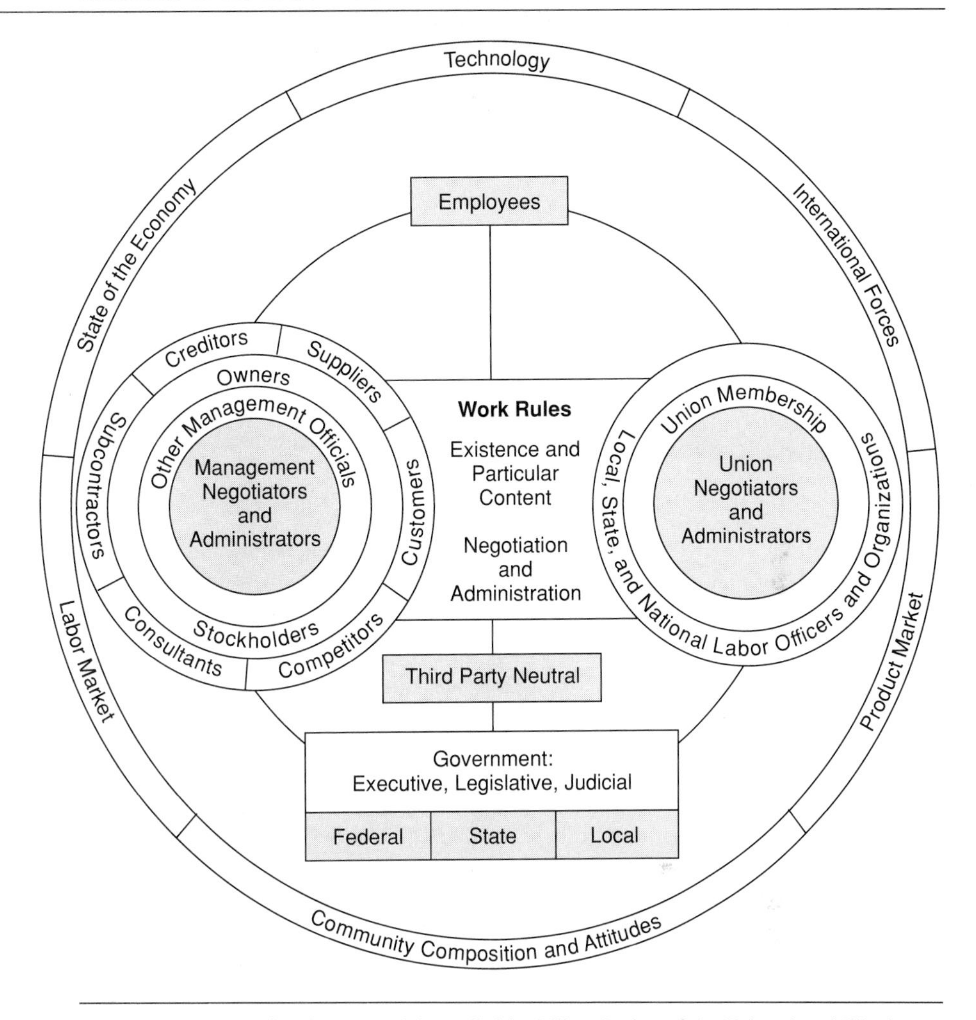

Source: Slightly modified from material supplied by Milton Derber of the University of Illinois.

this situation commented, "It is not the American dream . . . We're going into the twenty-first century,and we are working the same hours our grandfathers worked."[3]

Some work rules, such as the first one in Exhibit 1.2, are common to many occupations or industries. Others may be unique to a particular job classification, such as those for baseball players and cemetery employees. Work rules likewise may vary according to their vague or specific nature; for example, consider the provision for "Clerical and Technical Employees at a College" cited in Exhibit 1.2. This rule at first appears rather insignificant; yet unions and management could easily become heatedly involved over the meaning and intent of the word *democracy.* For example, a professor, discharged because of poor teaching evaluations, might con-

Exhibit 1.2 **Examples of Work Rules**

Job or Industry Classification	Work Rule
Government Installation	The Employer agrees to furnish adequate protective clothing for employees required to work outside during rain, sleet, snow, hail, or other atmospheric conditions detrimental to health or safety; provided the employee subjected to such assignments normally and historically performs the majority of his work assignment indoors. Employees who normally perform a majority of their work outdoors shall furnish their own protective clothing . . .
Professional Baseball	The Player and the Club recognize and agree that the Player's participation in certain other sports may impair or destroy his ability and skill as a baseball player. Accordingly, the Player agrees that he will not engage in professional boxing or wrestling; and that, except with the written consent of the Club, he will not engage in skiing, auto racing, motorcycle racing, sky diving, or in any game or exhibition of football, soccer, professional league basketball, ice hockey, or other sport involving a substantial risk of personal injury.
Television	The latest version of the script will be made accessible to the Player in the casting office twenty-four hours in advance of a scheduled reading or immediately after the scheduling of the interview, whichever last occurs.
Steel Industry	An employee reporting to work on his regularly-scheduled shift, unless he is notified by the Company not to report at least sixteen (16) hours prior to the scheduled starting time, shall be given work which is available, but in the event he is not permitted to start work, or works less than one hour, he shall be given four (4) hours' pay. In the event that an employee works more than one hour of his regular shift before being sent home because of lack of work, he will receive eight (8) hours' pay. This provision shall not apply in the event that an employee refused available work which he is physically able to perform or in the event that catastrophes, failures of utilities, or acts of a public enemy interfere with work being provided.
Clerical and Technical Employees at a College	The Board and the Union recognize and agree that while democratic principles should prevail in every American school system, urban colleges in a city as diverse in population as is Chicago must be exemplary in their expression and practice of the democratic ideal.
Cemeteries	In all cases where a grave is dug straight down, a second man shall be assigned to assist the digger after a depth of five feet is reached.

Sources: Various collective bargaining agreements in the United States.

tend this decision violated the "democratic ideal" cited in the labor agreement since he or she also supported an unpopular political cause.

One empirical study of labor agreement provisions found that the rank-and-file union members would need a college degree and 2 years of graduate school to understand a typical union-management agreement, because of its legalistic, technical language.[4] This situation can make the members suspicious, angry, and unsure of the labor agreement they have ratified.

An analysis of work rules helps us understand the complex output of the labor relations process. The formal labor agreement in this sense represents a compilation of jointly negotiated work rules. However, as discussed in Chapter 8, labor relations activities are not limited to those involving the establishment and content of the work rule; it is also appropriate to examine how the particular rule is administered between union and management officials.

Work rules also respond to changing workplace conditions and societal values over time. For example, the contemporary work rules for airline flight attendants would most certainly differ from the following three work requirements formulated in the 1930s: (1) swat flies in the cabin after takeoff, (2) prevent passengers from throwing lighted cigar butts out the windows, and (3) carry a railroad timetable in case of plane trouble.

In the 1980s, Acquired Immune Deficiency Syndrome, or AIDS, represented a dramatic new working condition that has commanded union concern and shaped work rules. The Screen Actors Guild (SAG), for example, has responded to members' concerns about AIDS transmission through open-mouth kissing. SAG maintains that a member actor or actress has the individual right to determine what constitutes a personal hazard on the movie set under Section 28 of its Basic Labor Agreement, which indicates an actor will not be placed in dangerous circumstances, even though the union agrees with medical evidence suggesting that the risk of transmitting the AIDS virus through kissing is remote. SAG now requires the producer to notify the actor-union member in advance if an open-mouth kissing scene is required in the movie. If this notice is not given, the producer may not require the player to perform in such a scene.[5]

Participants in the Labor Relations Process

Management Officials Through the corporation structure managers represent the stockholders. The negotiated and administered work rules involve managers at several organizational levels and functions. Labor relations managers and representatives are typically found at corporate, divisional, and plant levels. Labor relations objectives are developed and coordinated at the corporate and divisional levels to ensure that a particular work rule, such as a wage rate for a particular job classification, does not adversely alter precedents or conditions at another production facility.

Labor relations representatives at the plant level implement these directives, but they must also deal with other managers at the location, particularly first-line supervisors, who direct the daily work activities of hourly employees. As will be further discussed in Chapter 8, management's first-line supervisors typically hear and attempt to resolve employees' grievances on the production floor. In some cases,they are surprised to learn that higher-level management officials have overturned their decisions. Alert union leaders may use dissension among management officials to influence labor relations activities and the company's position toward unions.

Union Officials Union leaders, usually elected by the members, represent the membership, but they do not necessarily represent a consensual group since unions experience internal differences of view. Members and officers do not completely agree on priorities; sometimes conflict occurs over specific tactics to be used in accomplishing commonly shared bargaining objectives.

Recently, the United Auto Workers Union (UAW) has had some difficulty in resolving bargaining priorities among its different locals. Some local union officials urge the national union to seek higher wages while other local union officials stress job security. Victor Reuther, brother of the legendary UAW founder, the late Walter Reuther, has charged that current UAW leadership has lost touch with its members and is too cozy with management. Five former UAW officials responded with a scathing 13-page statement branding Reuther as an irresponsible, out-of-touch troublemaker.

In some cases different labor relations priorities or beliefs can occur between two labor organizations. PATCO, the Professional Air Traffic Controllers Organization (further discussed in Chapter 14), claimed in its dramatic strike that replacements coupled with extended working schedules would increase the likelihood of aircraft crashes. The president of the Airline Pilots Association, however, declared during this period that "without equivocation the air traffic control system in this country is safe."[6]

Other cases have witnessed strong, even essential support between two unions. One highly publicized example occurred when Eastern Airline pilots refused to cross a picket line established by the International Association of Machinists. This backing meant that Eastern could not initially run its operations, and bankruptcy proceedings resulted. (See Case 4.1 for an update of this situation.)

The outer circle surrounding both management and union negotiators (see Exhibit 1.1) demonstrates external pressures and potential influences. Management consultants' activities in the labor relations process are varied, ranging from restructuring personnel practices in nonunion firms (without any organizing campaign) to designing and presenting the employer's response throughout the campaign and representation election. Controversy occurs over the consultants' effectiveness and ethics. One union estimate found that consultants were involved in over 90 percent of the representational elections lost by unions.[7] However, another research effort found that the impact of consultants on union victories in representation elections was not very great.[8]

Management must be conscious of its competitors, who may challenge the company's product in quality, price, and/or service; at the same time, it must provide a return to the owners (stockholders) by operating in such a way as to retain its customers, pay its creditors, and maintain its supply of raw materials and parts. A company must consider its competitors when negotiating terms of the labor agreement. In some cases (the airline industry, for example) a strike can result in customers and revenues being transferred to competitors.

A recent advertisement of Ford Motor Products stressed that its particular labor-management relationship gives it a competitive edge. The advertisement was titled, "A Breakthrough in Labor Relations Has Helped Create the Highest Quality Vehicles Made in America." It referred to a new era of commitment and mutual respect between union and management.[9]

Unions at each level must operate within the policies and rules of their local and national unions as well as those of the AFL-CIO if they affiliate with this federation. Moreover, since union officers are elected, they must continue to provide those services and benefits that members believe are important. Thus, both union and management negotiators have pressures, policies, and rules that guide their behavior.

Employees Employees represent perhaps the most significant participant category since they often determine whether a union is even present in an organization (representation elections and union organizing drives are discussed in Chapter 5). Employees also determine whether a negotiated labor agreement is accepted or rejected and whether a threatened strike is actually carried out (Chapter 7).

Employees are treated here as a separate category because they may have loyalties to both management and union organizations.[10] This situation is found in both the private and public sectors; for example, public employees such as fire fighters, police, and teachers may feel torn between the critical or professional nature of their jobs and the strategic advantages of a strike. Employees want their organizations to thrive and prosper; at the same time, they want to share in the rewards of success. Since their desires may shape the existence and content of particular work rules, employees can be considered the third participant in the labor relations process.

In many instances, the employees' racial or ethnic backgrounds may shape work rules' negotiation and content. For example, an employer recently violated the National Labor Relations Act when it insisted that the union bargain in English only. The union's chief negotiator spoke limited English, and two members of management's bargaining team could negotiate in his native language (Spanish), so the union proposed that a neutral translator be assigned to the bargaining sessions.

In other cases, the age of the employees might affect the content of the work rules. If the average age of employees at a facility is 50, there will probably be more emphasis on pension plan improvements, whereas a younger work force might stress maternity benefits or higher hourly wages.

Third-Party Neutrals Often differences of opinion between management and union officials are revealed in contract administration through the grievance procedure (discussed in Chapter 8) or in negotiations (discussed in Chapters 6, 7, and 14). Third-party neutrals are available to assist the parties in settling their differences.

An **arbitrator** is a third-party neutral selected by union and management officials to resolve a grievance; an arbitrator's decision is binding. Arbitration is discussed in more detail in Chapter 9.

In a very few instances arbitrators might also resolve an impasse during the negotiation of the labor agreement. However, the **mediator** (discussed in Chapters 7 and 14) is the most frequently involved third-party neutral if a collective bargaining impasse occurs. The mediator only offers advice and does not have binding decision-making authority.

The Government The government participates through three activities: executive, legislative, and judicial, occurring at federal, state, and local levels. In the public sector, government officials also serve as management officials in the labor relations process. This situation can become complicated when it cuts across other government activities. In the PATCO example, the federal government filed at least 104 civil actions in 85 federal district courts seeking injunctions ordering the air traffic controllers back to work. When the employees violated court orders, the government sought and obtained civil and criminal contempt citations against many strikers.[11]

In the private sector the federal government has traditionally played an indirect role at the bargaining table. A mediator from the Federal Mediation and Conciliation Service can assist union and management officials in reaching an agreement. The mediator's advice, however, can be refused; this individual can also be asked by one or both parties to leave the negotiations. One government official has recently explained,

> [I]t is not the government's job to ensure anything when it comes to what I continue to call the miracle of collective bargaining. Industry . . . and labor . . . know better their own needs and their own limits than any Federal Government does. Collective bargaining has served this country well and it will continue to.[12]

Although the federal government does not dictate the terms of a negotiated labor agreement, laws, judicial decisions, and administrative agencies (local, state, or federal) can influence or restrict work rules. For example, union and management officials cannot negotiate a mandatory retirement age of 60 years since this would conflict with the Age Discrimination in Employment Act. Or, although coal miners have long believed that if females worked in the mines, bad luck would result, union and management officials would be violating the Equal Employment Opportunity Act if they negotiated a provision prohibiting female employees from working in the mines. Perhaps more widespread is the controversy over negotiated seniority provisions that are used for administration decisions, such as promotions and layoffs, and affirmative action programs monitored by the government. This issue will be discussed in more detail later in this text.

Influences Affecting Participants' Negotiation and Administration of Work Rules

Thus far we have suggested that the desires and composition of the labor relations participants can affect the development of work rules. However, these participants are in turn influenced by several variables or constraints (see the outer circle of Exhibit 1.1) in their labor relations activities. These influences may relate to the particular firm, the local community, or society in general. The following discussion furnishes a few illustrations of how these influences can affect the existence and content of work rules.

Technology Perhaps the most immediate and persistent influence on work rules is the technology of the particular workplace. **Technology** is defined to include the equipment used in the operation, the pace and scheduling of work, and characteristics of the work environment and tasks to be performed. Consider, for example, the major equipment found at a steel mill, blast furnaces, which require very high temperatures for operation. These furnaces cannot be simply turned on and off like a household oven. Often several days are required for either reaching these high temperatures or for cooling the furnaces for repairs. This equipment characteristic affects the facility's work rules. In essence, steel mills must be operated 24 hours a day, 7 days a week—a situation prompting related work rules such as wage premiums for working the night shift, weekends, and holidays.

In some cases the introduction of equipment reduces or eliminates employees in a particular job classification.[13] This situation occurs when industrial robots handle tasks formerly performed by employees. A rather common application occurs in the auto industry, where mechanically joined arms perform spot welding, spraying, machine unloading, and assembly. Unions faced with having membership replaced by robots have increased related bargaining demands (such as more paid time off and the 4-day week) for its members' job security.

However, unions might not face as strong a challenge from robotics as was initially anticipated. Orders for American-made robots have been falling since their peak of $504 million in 1984. A current estimate suggests that less than 5 percent of American companies have installed even one robot. Managers have found that robots are expensive to make and often shut down, requiring human attention.[14]

The pace and scheduling of the workday also affect the work rules of certain occupations. For example, bus companies optimizing their productivity and revenue would concentrate on rush hour traffic (6:00–9:00 a.m., 3:00–7:00 p.m.), when buses would be likely to be filled with passengers. But problems would remain in scheduling work because many bus drivers might have a daily work schedule of 3 hours on, 3 hours off, 1 hour on, 2 hours off, 4 hours on. Because of the nature of the work, most labor agreements in related industries have provisions pertaining to the permissible number, length, and possible compensation of intervals (times off) between daily work assignments.

The work environment and tasks to be performed can also influence work rules; for example, particular safety equipment is required on certain jobs in the manufacturing and construction industries. A more specific example relates to actors performing at dinner theatres. The lights in dinner theatres are usually turned off between the acts of a play, and the actors retire to their dressing rooms while the stage crew changes the stage scenery for the next act. The actors then return to the stage via aisles that are commonly surrounded by dinner tables before the lights are turned back on for the new act. Those who have attended a dinner theatre might wonder how the actor safely walks to the stage in virtual darkness. This concern has been shared by union officials, and the Actors' Equity Association labor agreement governing employment in dinner theatres includes a detailed provision requiring proper spacing and placement of guide-lights.

Finally, computer operations can help both union and management officials in their daily labor relations activities. Union officers can use computer applications to maintain membership and dues records as well as word processing for communication to the membership. Union and management officials can also use computer applications in the areas of contract negotiations (costing the various proposals) and administration (maintenance and research of grievances and arbitration decisions).[15]

International Forces The international influence on the labor relations process was most vividly reflected in U.S. involvement in World War I and World War II. The impact of these wars on domestic labor relations activities will be described in Chapter 2. However, it should be noted that President Franklin Roosevelt, realizing that U.S. production output could not be jeopardized during World War II, established a War Labor Board, which encouraged union and management officials to negotiate provisions in their labor agreement for the administration of work rules.

In 1973–1974, the Arab oil embargo increased gasoline prices and consumer preference for fuel-efficient automobiles. This situation resulted in the layoffs of several hundred thousand automotive employees who manufactured large, low-mileage cars. More recently, there has been a major reduction in traditional animosities between the United States and other countries such as China, the Soviet

Union, Poland, and East Germany. These changes are unclear, but related new business opportunities will raise exciting problems and prospects for unionized firms in the United States.

Product Market The **product market** is where the company either sells its product or purchases key elements for manufacture of its product. In respect to the first element, management would be more vulnerable if a strike occurred at a time when major customer sales were anticipated. For example, management at a brewery would prefer to avoid a labor agreement expiring, possibly leading to a strike, during the summer months. Indeed, one major brewery has been successful in changing the contract expiration date from June 1 to March 1.

The second dimension of the product market is illustrated by the UAW's deep concern over the fact that many of the parts for U.S. automobiles are being manufactured in foreign countries. It is likely that a provision in the labor agreement will eventually be negotiated to restrict the use of foreign-made parts.[16]

Community Composition and Attitudes The influence of community composition and attitudes can be examined from two perspectives: (1) influential individuals and/or organizations, such as the media, within the community; and (2) cultural values, traditions, and public opinion, which are reflected in the community's population. *Community* can represent the local municipality or a broader geographical region. This variable can even be extended to include societal differences in labor relations patterns (Chapter 15). Consider, for example, the goals of a prominent Japanese union leader whose standard of living goals for his members include:[17]

- The square footage of a member's apartment (for example, 154 square feet for a union member in his or her twenties).
- The age (36) at which a member first owns golf clubs and a piano.
- The formal education of the member's children—a private university for the son and a junior college for the daughter.

These values would not likely be imported into the U.S. labor movement. However, Japanese managerial philosophies have affected the labor relations process when joint Japanese-American business ventures have operated in the United States (for example, the GM-Toyota joint venture in Fremont, California, discussed in Chapter 7).[18]

The very existence of a labor union can be largely determined by community influences. For example, the Economic Development Council of Richmond, Virginia, recently placed a full-page ad in *The Wall Street Journal* that urged firms to relocate and join Richmond's 14 corporate headquarters. Among the sales points: "There isn't a single office union in the Richmond area. In fact, there haven't been any attempts to organize one."[19]

If a facility becomes unionized, community attitudes can shape the work rules desired by management or union officials, especially when union and management officials reach an impasse over an issue. Chapter 7 describes various strategies used by management and labor to resolve a negotiations impasse. One related tactic involves soliciting support from community residents. For example, teachers desiring limits on the number of students allowed in a classroom might stress to the community that increased class size would lower educational quality. Educational administrators, on the other hand, would probably indicate to the community that a teachers' strike over this issue would place educational funding in jeopardy.

The mass media often serve as both generator and conduit of community opinion. Unfortunately, few empirical studies have investigated the effects of the mass media on labor relations participants and work rules in the United States.

One of the few such studies that have been done examined the editorials of five major newspapers on the air traffic controllers' strike. Nearly two-thirds of the editorials indicated that the strikers were "lawbreakers" who "withheld vital services."[20] The news media are profit-making businesses, and at least one prominent union official contends that this orientation biases the reporting of labor relations activities:

> The media tend to cover collective bargaining as if it were a pier six brawl. The intricate moves and tradeoffs that really make up bargaining aren't as newsy as impassioned rhetoric or a picket line confrontation.
>
> Reporters are given little training in covering collective bargaining. They are told to look for the "news"—the fist fight, the walkout, the heated exchange—and, as a result, frequently miss the "story," which is the settlement. . . .
>
> Every union proposal is a "demand," every management proposal is an "offer."[21]

Public opinion is more directly gauged by various surveys conducted by the media and other organizations. One recent poll found that 55 percent of the public approves of unions; 37 percent disapproves; and 8 percent has no opinion. Union approval ratings were higher among Democrats versus Republicans (67 percent versus 44 percent) and union versus nonunion households (77 percent versus 49 percent).[22]

Unions have attempted to moderate public opinion. See Exhibit 1.3 for a related effort by the Teamsters Union, for example. Two major, recent attempts have been the "associate member" drive and the "Union Yes" campaign. Some 16 national unions affiliated under the AFL-CIO offer members and their dependents lower-cost legal services, lower credit card interest charges, group insurance, and educational programs. Under an associate member approach, "associate" members participating in these programs might not be fully enrolled dues-paying members of a national union. Some union strategists maintain this approach would enhance public opinion by convincing many people not heretofore involved with unions that a labor organization could effectively represent and obtain their goals. However, not all unions are in favor of the associate member approach. The American Federation of Teachers conducted an associate member drive in 1989 with 976 of the 20,000 contacted joining as associate members for one-fourth the cost of full AFT membership.

The AFL-CIO also recently unveiled its $13 million "Union Yes" campaign that is based on the premise that unions can and do help resolve conflicts between work and family and can help find positive solutions to workplace issues. The effort represents a long-range image change that will attract new employees by indicating the good things unions stand for such as a voice on the job. However, this attempt to change public opinion has had its problems, such as actors refusing to participate in the endorsement because of insufficient remuneration or the concern that subse-

Exhibit 1.3 **Example of an Effort by the Teamsters Union to Enhance Public Opinion**

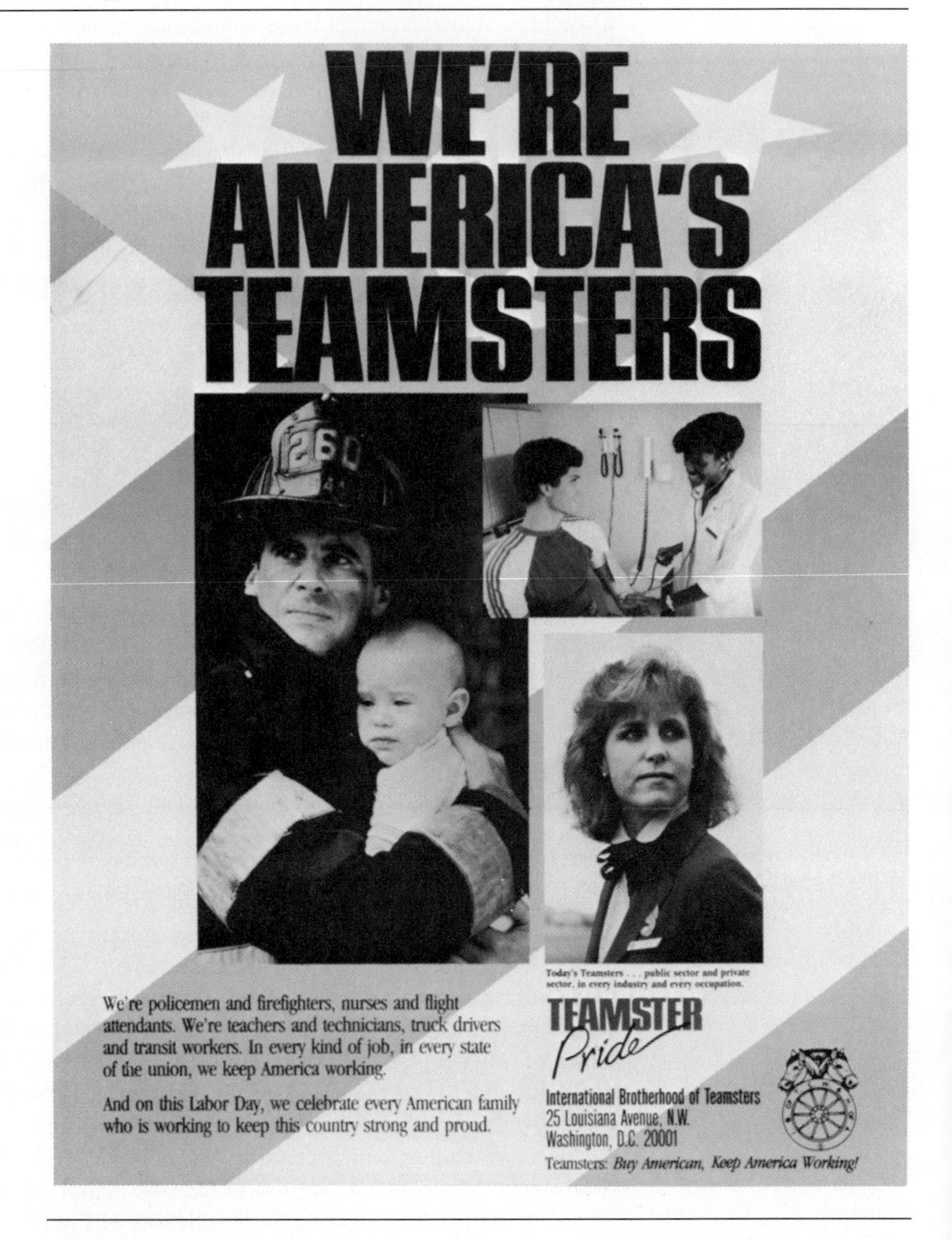

quent involvement with a nonunion entity such as dinner theatre would appear hypocritical.

Unions have also organized protest against unfair portrayals of union members and organizations. For example, the Association of Flight Attendants criticized NBC and a comedienne on the "Tonight Show" in 1981 for labeling flight attendants "high-altitude hookers."[23]

Labor Market The skills and wage levels of employees in the local **labor market** can affect negotiated work rules. Management is often concerned with the skill levels of employees in the particular community. For example, a firm needing skilled employees from a relatively unskilled labor market would probably wish to negotiate work rules regarding apprenticeship programs. Management would also consider negotiating a 90-day probationary period within which it could terminate the employment of an unskilled or nonproductive employee, and the union could not protest the action through the grievance procedure.

Both management and union representatives are also interested in the compensation rates for comparably skilled employees in the labor market. Certainly, the wages paid by other companies in the local area affect negotiated wage rates. In some cases, particularly in the construction trades, some unions have had to reduce their wages to counter nonunion competition.

A recent major shift of skills involves some 20 million members of the Baby Boom generation who mostly work in service jobs that are neither blue-collar nor white-collar. These "new-collar" employees include insurance agents, keypunch operators, loan officers, and salespeople. They typically do not have a full college education, and "they use their heads on the job, but probably are not asked to take a great deal of intellectual initiative."[24] Unions are interested in organizing new-collar employees and are emphasizing skill-related concerns such as career development, professional autonomy, dealing with technological change, and stress management.

State of the Economy: National, Industrial, and Firm-Specific Indicators The state of the **economy** is usually referred to by indicating movement among such quantitative indicators as inflation, unemployment, and productivity. During the late 1960s and through the 1970s, the United States witnessed a rising inflation rate, which influenced the negotiation of work rules—notably, union insistence that a labor agreement include provisions to increase the wages if there are increases in the cost of living (see Chapter 13).[25] Similarly, an increase in interest rates could retard home and industrial construction projects. Under these circumstances, work rules might be negotiated to ensure that construction workers are not laid off and/or that they receive some compensation for the reduced work load.

The unemployment rate, another key economic indicator of the state of the economy, affects work rules providing job protection. Chapter 6 discusses ways in which the unemployment rate can affect the bargaining power of union and management officials. If this and other economic measures pertaining to the Gross National Product, productivity, cost of living, compensation at all employee levels, and exports and imports are unfavorable, unions will be more likely to accept bargaining concessions (see Chapter 6).

Economic characteristics of a particular industry or organization also can significantly affect the labor agreement. The steel industry represents one of the more dramatic declines found in American industries today. In 1959 U.S. Steel Corporation and other steelmakers were involved in a strike that involved the Supreme Court and idled one million blue-collar employees. However, a strike at the same organization in 1986 did not raise any nationwide concern. This reduced impact was largely due to the following industrial trends.

By the late 1970s, several developing countries enjoyed both more advanced steel-making technology and lower labor costs than their American competitors. Domestically, "mini-mills," using scrap inputs, could underprice the big integrated manufacturers in several product lines. At precisely the same historical moment, autos were getting smaller, economic growth was slowing, and new plastics and composite products were cutting into steel markets, irrevocably reducing steel demand.[26]

Unions bargaining with employers in this and other economically distressed industries modify traditional bargaining tactics and goals. Between 1947 and 1979 there were typically between 200 and 400 strikes/lockouts each year involving 1,000 employees or more in the private sector. This number dropped to 187 in 1980 and continued to decline to a record low of 40 strikes/lockouts in 1988. Also, annual wage settlements covering 1,000 employees or more in the private sector had averaged between 5.1 percent and 7.9 percent increases for the years 1972 through 1981. Comparable wage settlements for 1982 through 1987 averaged much less—between 1.6 percent and 3.8 percent increases.[27]

Tradeoffs between layoff protections and wage and work rule concessions have frequently occurred in the tire industry. A recent settlement at a Uniroyal facility, for example, promised to avoid layoffs and plant closings. In exchange, the union and its members agreed to a 63-cent-an-hour reduction in pay, one less vacation week, three fewer annual holidays, no cost-of-living increases, and extensive work-rule changes. A union spokesman justified the new settlement: "It's not the kind of agreement we cherish, but there's no point in negotiating a huge agreement and then having the plants close."[28]

Phases in the Labor Relations Process

The labor relations process is comprised of three phases:

1. *Recognition of the legitimate rights and responsibilities of union and management representatives.* This phase includes the legal right of employees to join unions (see Chapter 3), union-organizing drives (see Chapter 5), and the rights of management and union officials, as well as their responsibilities to abide by related laws and labor agreement provisions.
2. *Negotiation of the labor agreement, including appropriate strategies and tactics and impasse-resolution techniques.* Strikes and mediation are examples of the latter (discussed in Chapter 7). This phase is usually the most publicized by the media, even though phases 1 and 3 are equally essential.
3. *Administration of the negotiated labor agreement—applying and enforcing the terms of the agreement on a daily basis.* This phase of the process (discussed in detail in Chapters 8 and 9) accounts for the most time and energy spent by union and management officials and usually involves a larger number of these officials than the preceding phases.

Clearly, the sequence of the labor relations process is cumulative. Seldom do formal negotiations occur if the parties have not first recognized each other's legitimate rights and responsibilities. Similarly, the first two phases are necessary for the existence of the third phase—administration of the labor agreement. This sequence is applied to an increasingly significant topic, employee drug testing, in the "Labor Relations in Action" box.

Of course, not all labor-management relationships have focused on these three phases. Indeed, employees and their representative unions at some public and private sector facilities are still striving to accomplish the first phase of the process.[29]

The phases of the labor relations process are subject to qualitative variation as well. In the first phase, for example, organizations vary in the amount of respect union and management officials have for each other's goals. In the second phase, negotiations are carried out with different levels of intelligence, preparation, and sincere desire to achieve results. The third phase may vary as to how well the negotiated labor agreement is understood and effectively administered in good faith by both parties.[30] There are probably as many different relationships as there are union and management officials negotiating labor agreements.

Current Status of Labor Unions

Labor unions' status can be assessed from both statistical and general or philosophical standpoints. Exhibit 1.4 reflects a nearly 30-year drop in the proportion of employees who are unionized. There are three general explanations for this reduction: employment shifts, organizational practices, and legal alterations.

Employment has shifted from traditionally unionized industries (manufacturing, railroads, mining) to high-technology industries (computers, scientific instruments) that are difficult to organize. There has also been a shift in the occupational mix toward more professional, technical, and service (white-collar) employees, who are also traditionally difficult to organize. Employment has also been growing faster in small businesses than in larger ones. Data show that 80 percent of the new jobs have been created in firms with 100 or fewer employees, where fewer than 9 percent of the employees are members of unions.[31] There has also been a demographic shift of those who are employed. Many new entrants are female, better educated, and younger employees, who have traditionally been more difficult to organize.

More organizations are learning how to operate their businesses on a nonunion basis. Sometimes this entails moving some or all operations to less unionized sections of the United States (the West and South). Managers are also adopting personnel practices including antiunion campaigns (see Chapter 5) to keep their firms nonunion. They have become more sophisticated in understanding the reasons employees organize unions and more aggressive within the legal framework in presenting the firm's viewpoint to the employees.

Some union officials indicate that employers often use labor law loopholes to forestall or negate free employee union choices through secret-ballot elections. For example, pre-election time delays, contested elections, lengthy appeals, and stalled labor agreement negotiations are possible under the National Labor Relations Act (see Chapter 3).

Legal alterations that have expanded employees' legal rights[32] through the Equal Employment Opportunity Act, Occupational Safety and Health Act, Employee Retire-

Labor Relations in Action

Drug Testing and the Labor Relations Process

Drug testing has been called the "Jar Wars" of the 1980s, and the controversy shows no sign of solution as we enter the 1990s. A nationwide concern over drug use and its accompanying problems has resulted in many businesses taking measures against drug use. In 1982, only 3 percent of Fortune 500 companies were involved in employee drug testing; 3 years later, 30 percent were involved. Whether for altruistic reasons—social responsibility or concern for employee welfare—or for monetary advantages—lower insurance rates, increased productivity, or reduction of property damage—concern has been translated into controversy.

The desire for a drug-free workplace appears to be a legitimate one, which would attract opposition only from drug users, pushers, or radical subversives. Yet organized labor is the most formidable opponent of the current drug testing movement, contending that random or mandatory testing assumes its members are guilty and must prove their innocence.

Drug testing involves the major participants and the three phases of the labor relations process. The government has partially resolved the first phase. Unions have contended in various legal suits that management's unilateral imposition of employee drug testing ignores the legal rights of their members and organizations and violates Fourth Amendment strictures regarding search and seizure.

The Supreme Court has not held private employers accountable to constitutional restraints. However, government agencies have formulated guidelines that can apply to both private and public sector employees. A recent Supreme Court decision, *Skinner* v. *Railway Labor Executives' Association,* ruled that post-accident drug and alcohol testing required by the Federal Railroad Administration did not violate rail employees' Fourth Amendment rights even though the regulations did not "individualize" suspicion of drug or alcohol use prior to testing. The court contended that the government's compelling public safety interest in ensuring that rail workers are not impaired on the job outweighed the "minimal" employee rights intrusion.

Another Supreme Court decision, *National Treasury Employees Union* v. *Von Raab,* upheld the U.S. Custom Service's policy of testing applicants for promotion for illegal drug use. The majority contended: "Employees involved in drug interdiction reasonably should expect effective inquiry into their fitness and probity."

Unions want to subject employee drug testing issues to the second phase in the labor relations process, negotiation of the labor agreement. The National Labor Relations Board (NLRB) is a government agency (discussed in more detail in Chapter 3) charged with adjudicating the National Labor Relations Act (NLRA), which affects most private-sector employees. The NLRB has made it clear that employee drug testing is a mandatory bargaining issue. In order to avoid an unfair labor practice charge, the details of such a program should be bargained for with the union until agreement or impasse. In the case of impasse, an employer may proceed with implementation of the program unless limited by other contract language. This ruling was in answer to unions' contention that drug testing is a change in conditions of employment and therefore cannot be unilaterally imposed by management.

Even in the case of impasse an employer can expect a fight based on the contract language limitation. A blanket management rights clause (Chapter 11) does not seem to afford much protection to employers. NLRB General Counsel Rosemary M. Collyer reads such clauses "narrowly" and insists on "clear and unmistakable waiver of the union's right to bargain."

The past practice of "for-cause" drug testing, also, does not give management the go-ahead to implement a change in the existing program such as a switch to random testing or testing as an addition to routine physicals. Unions must protest at the outset of such a program, however, or their lack of immediate response may be interpreted as a waiver of their rights. Even when a current program for routine physicals includes urinalysis, any change in the use of the samples should be an immediate matter of union interest.

Management also cannot assume that an agreement

in principle with the union on drug testing constitutes any waiver of the union's right to be included in outlining the specifics of the actual program. Subsequent union challenges can be filed with an arbitrator, who resolves agreement disputes (grievances), and the courts.

These situations refer to the third phase of the labor relations process, administering the labor agreement on a daily basis. Unions might challenge management's decision to unilaterally establish a drug-testing rule or to discipline an employee who either refuses to take the test or is found by the test to have drugs in his or her system. Arbitrator decision making, discussed in Chapters 9 and 10, is not completely predictable. Yet these individuals and judges often take the following labor relations aspects of employee drug testing into account:

Employee Privacy Rights Although many employees' constitutional rights do not block drug testing, arbitrators also maintain that employees are not without common law of the shop protections from management's arbitrary or capricious actions. Thus, a unilaterally imposed random drug-testing policy is likely to be viewed as unreasonable unless the company produces evidence of reasonable cause (existence of previous drug problems in the particular work force; safety or product damage concerns; and/or drug symptomatic behavior of the employee who was tested).

Test Procedures and Results The accuracy of drug tests is often subject to union challenge through the courts or through the labor agreement's grievance procedure. Related concerns focus on the proper identification and security of the drug test sample. There is also a high degree of errors in drug testing; some studies have found an error rate of 67 percent. Errors are high for false positives (stating that employees have drugs in their systems when they do not) and even higher for false negatives (overlooking employees with drugs in their systems). Some companies have strengthened their programs by having all employees who have tested positive take a second test. Even if the results are accurate there is no agreed-upon standard similar to blood-alcohol level that indicates the employee's drug ingestion adversely affects his or her job performance. Lacking this standard or evidence suggesting drug use on company premises, some arbitrators will overturn the discipline contending that the employee has some rights in determining his or her off-the-job conduct.

Program Implementation Considerations Any company implementing a drug-testing program needs to seriously consider the possible ramifications. Unions, too, have a responsibility to their membership to support and represent them in the best possible manner, which does not stop with the formulation of an acceptable program. The details, procedures, and goals of the program must be effectively communicated to the employees. Employees should have an opportunity to ask questions and have any fears about the program dispelled. A confirmation that the employee has been made aware of the program, or any changes in a program, should be recorded by obtaining each employee's signature. Updates and positive benefits of the program should be communicated to the employees as well as problems and their subsequent solutions. The employees need to feel that the union and management are concerned with employee welfare. The goal should be to have a drug-free workplace and to focus on positives, not on negatives such as discharging drug users.

Presently, the drug-testing controversy shows no signs of letting up. This issue, with its accompanying questions and problems, will continue to be an important one in labor-management relations.

Source: We are grateful to Sandra Wood, who researched and wrote much of this material.

Exhibit 1.4

National Union and Employee Association Membership, Totals and Proportion of Employed Workers, 1960–1989

	Union Membership	Total Labor Force	
		Number	Percentage
1960	17,049,000	72,142,000	23.6%
1970	19,381,000	85,903,000	22.6
1978	20,238,000	102,537,000	19.7
1983	17,717,000	88,290,000	20.1
1984	17,340,000	92,194,000	18.8
1985	16,996,000	94,521,000	18.0
1986	16,975,000	96,903,000	17.5
1987	16,913,000	99,303,000	17.0
1988	17,002,000	101,407,000	16.8
1989	16,960,000	103,480,000	16.4

Source: U.S. Department of Labor, Bureau of Labor Statistics, *News* (Washington, D.C.: Government Printing Office, September 18, 1981); "Union Membership Dips Again as Proportion of the Employed," *Daily Labor Report,* February 12, 1986, p. B-2; "Union Membership Decline Eases Somewhat in 1986 as Proportion Reaches 17.5 Percent," *Daily Labor Report,* February 23, 1987, p. B-7; Bureau of National Affairs Inc., *Daily Labor Report,* no. 18 (January 30, 1989), p. B-14.

ment and Income Security Act, and other legislation have helped make union organizing more difficult. These legal rights give employees a "free ride" in areas for which the union once was the primary protector and provider, and the increasing costs of these programs to employers have caused them to stiffen their resistance to unions, to be more cost-conscious, and to increase their managerial sophistication in personnel practices.

Some would suggest that union membership decline or stagnation reflects a broader insight into organized labor's social significance. A related question is, Have unions become obsolete? David Lipsky, Dean of Cornell University's School of Industrial and Labor Relations, suggests that organized labor's "corpse is still moving," as no other American institution can claim such a membership following today.[33] Lane Kirkland, president of the AFL-CIO, contends labor organizations' success cannot be measured solely in membership statistics, since unions are not economic institutions competing for market shares. This argument is strengthened when we realize that many parts of the labor force (managers and the unemployed, for example) do not join unions.

Indeed, many unions appear to be committing more of their resources to serving the needs of their current members rather than organizing new members. As unions mature and have organized a major portion of the workers within their jurisdictions, their expenditures, time, and efforts focus on representation services, such as negotiating contracts, research on wages and benefits, preparation for arbitration, processing grievances, and so on. In fact, organizing new employees may not be in the interests of the present union membership if these efforts would siphon funds earmarked for present members' services. Because unions are political organizations and the leaders are elected by the membership, the incentive to organize new members is frequently less than the incentive to provide services to current members.[34]

Unions' social significance can also be assessed in general terms by considering what the consequences would be if they were absent from our society. Some would argue that unions' previous bargaining gains, coupled with current legislation aimed at protecting employees' welfare, make unions obsolete. Others have suggested that unions must remain to ensure that employers do not reduce previously negotiated working conditions. This belief likens organized labor to the military in peace-time—a strong, countervailing power needed to preserve the existing situation.[35] In other words, unions are necessary to maintain some balance between employer and employee rights and responsibilities.

Summary

The labor relations process occurs when management and the exclusive bargaining agent for the employees (the union) jointly decide upon and enforce terms of the labor agreement. Work rules constitute the focal point of the labor relations process and pertain either to compensation in all its forms or to the employees' and employers' job rights and obligations.

At first glance, it might appear that union and management officials are the only participants in the labor relations process. Complexities arise with the realization that it is difficult to speak of *the* management or *the* union position on a particular issue. Instead, union and management officials are members of their respective organizations and subject to internal conflicts and external pressures. Employees represent a third participant category in the labor relations process since they can have loyalties to both union and management officials. Various sociodemographic characteristics of the employee group (race, age, and sex) can exert a strong influence on the existence and content of work rules. Other participants are third-party neutrals (arbitrators and mediators) and the government, with its executive decisions, legislative action, and judicial decisions. The participants in the labor relations process are influenced in their rule-making efforts by several variables or constraints, such as technology, international forces, the product market, community composition and attitudes, the labor market, and the state of the economy.

The labor relations process consists of three sequential phases: (1) recognition of the legitimate rights and responsibilities of union and management representatives, (2) negotiation of the labor agreement, and (3) applying and enforcing the terms of the agreement on a daily basis.

The current status of labor unions can be assessed from both statistical and general standpoints. A nearly 30-year drop in the proportion of employees who are unionized has occurred in the United States. However, this change and related general explanations (employment shifts, organizational practices, and legal alterations) do not indicate that unions have lost their societal significance.

Key Terms

labor relations process
work rules
arbitrator
mediator
technology
product market
labor market
economy

Discussion Questions

1. Exhibit 1.1 establishes the focal point of the labor relations process and many variables that affect the process. Select an academic discipline such as political science, economics, or sociology, and indicate three specific ways the discipline could add insights into the labor relations process.
2. Discuss the different dimensions of technology, indicating how this variable might contribute to two unique and specific work rules for unionized employees at a grocery store. Also indicate with examples how two other external constraints or influences (see the outer circle of Exhibit 1.1) could affect the work rules at a grocery store.
3. "The 'Labor Relations in Action' concerning employee drug testing illustrates the focal point but not the phases of the labor relations process." Is this statement true or false? Explain your answer.
4. "The rather consistent 30-year drop in the proportion of employees who are unionized reflects organized labor's lack of societal significance." Is this statement true or false? Explain your answer.

References

1. John Dunlop, *Industrial Relations Systems* (New York: Henry Holt, 1958), pp. 13-16.
2. Elliot I. Beitner, "Justice and Dignity: A New Approach to Discipline," *Labor Law Journal* 35 (September 1984), pp. 500–504. See also Ronald L. Miller, "Worker Privacy and Collective Bargaining," *Labor Law Journal* 33 (March 1982), pp. 154–168.
3. Gregory Stricharchuk and Ralph E. Winter, "Worked Up: As the Recovery Gains, Compulsory Overtime Becomes a Rising Issue," *The Wall Street Journal,* June 20, 1984, pp. 1, 14.
4. James Suchan and Clyde Scott, "Unclear Contract Language and Its Effect on Corporate Culture," *Business Horizons* 29 (January–February 1986), pp. 20–25.
5. "To Kiss Or Not to Kiss—The Choice Is Yours," *Screen Actor News,* January 1986, p. 9.
6. "Skies Are Safe, Pilots Declare," Bureau of National Affairs Inc., *Daily Labor Report,* no. 160 (August 19, 1981), p. 1. See also Dale D. Buss, "UAW's Chrysler Canada Strike Creates Further Strains with U.S. Auto Workers," *The Wall Street Journal,* November 11, 1982, p. 4.
7. Bureau of National Affairs Inc., *Daily Labor Report,* no. 37 (February 25, 1985), p. F-1; Jules Bernstein, "The Evolution of the Use of Management Consultants in Labor Relations: A Labor Perspective," *Labor Law Journal* 36 (May 1985), p. 296.
8. John J. Lawler, "The Influence of Management Consultants on the Outcome of Union Certification Elections," *Industrial and Labor Relations Review* 38 (October 1984), pp. 38–51. See also Bureau of National Affairs Inc., Special Report, *Labor Relations Consultants: Issues, Trends, and Controversies* (Washington, D.C.: Bureau of National Affairs Inc., 1985); and Terry A. Bethel, "Profiting from Unfair Labor Practices: A Proposal to Regulate Management Representatives," *Northwestern University Law Review* 79 (1984), pp. 506–565.
9. *Newsweek,* May 3, 1983, pp. 77–78.
10. For an early study of employee dual loyalty, see Theodore V. Purcell, *Blue Collar Man: Patterns of Dual Allegiance in Industry* Cambridge: Harvard University Press, 1960). See also Cynthia V. Fukami and Erik W. Larson, "Commitment to Company and Union: Parallel Models," *Journal of Applied Psychology* 69 (August 1984), pp. 367-371; and James L. Angle and Perry L. Harold, "Dual Commitment and Labor-Management Relationship Climates," *Academy of Management Journal* 29 (March 1986), pp. 31–50.
11. Neil Fox, "PATCO and the Courts: Public Sector Labor Law as Ideology," *University of Illinois Law Review,* 1985, pp. 245–314.
12. "Excerpts from Interview with Labor Secretary Donovan," Bureau of National Affairs Inc., *Daily Labor Report,* no. 7 (January 12, 1982), p. G-1.
13. See, for example, Paul Osterman, "The Impact of Computers on the Employment of Clerks and Managers," *Industrial and Labor Relations Review* 39 (January 1986), pp. 175–186. See also Michael Wallace and Arne L. Kallenberg, "Industrial Transformation and the Decline of Craft: The Decomposition of Skill in the Printing Industry, 1931–1978," *American Sociological Review* 47 (June 1982), pp. 307–324. For further related implications of technology, see the entire issue of *Scientific American* (September 1982); and Peter Rachleff, "Working the Fast Lane," *Radical America* (Spring 1982), pp. 79–96.
14. Catherine Dressler, "Demand for Robotics Dwindles," *Miami Herald,* March 6, 1989, p. 5-B.
15. Neil De Clereq, Alec Meiklejohn, and Ken Mericle, "The Use of Microcomputers in Local Union Administration," *Labor Studies Journal* 10 (Spring 1985), pp. 3–45.
16. Michael J. Piore and Charles F. Sabel, *The Second Industrial Divide* (New York: Basic Books Inc., 1984), pp. 198–199.
17. "Five Ages of Man," *Newsweek,* May 24, 1976, pp. 42–43.
18. John Holusha, "No Utopia, But to Workers It's a Job," *New York Times,* January 29, 1989, sec. 3-10.
19. *The Wall Street Journal,* October 18, 1988, p. A-13.
20. Lynne L. Ashmead, "An Analysis of Editorial Opinion and Public Opinion as Expressed in Letters to Editors Concerning the PATCO Strike" (1981), unpublished paper. This study performed a content analysis of 34 editorials from the following papers: *Chicago Tribune, Miami Herald, Washington Post, New York Times,* and *Los Angeles Times.*
21. Lane Kirkland, "Labor and the Press," *American Federationist* 82 (December 1975), p. 3. See also John A. Grimes, "Are the Media Short Changing Organized Labor?" *Monthly Labor Review* 110 (August 1987), pp. 53–54.
22. NBC News, "Poll Results," no. 122 (January 16, 1987), p. 14.

23. Bureau of National Affairs Inc., *Daily Labor Report,* no. 196 (October 9, 1981), p. 3.
24. Cathy Trost, "New-Collar Jobs: Unions Court People in Service Type Work to Stem Fall in Ranks," *The Wall Street Journal,* September 19, 1986, p. 1. See also Kenneth A. Kovach, "Organized Labor's Deteriorating Condition," *Labor Law Journal* 36 (November 1985), p. 851.
25. For related considerations, see Wayne Vroman, "Cost-of-Living Escalators and Price-Wage Linkages in the U.S. Economy, 1968–1980," *Industrial and Labor Relations Review* 38 (January 1985), pp. 225–235.
26. Robert Kuttner, "Steel: A Troubled Union and Its New Leader," *Dissent* 32 (Spring 1985), p. 172. For further discussion of the steel industry's decline and related collective bargaining efforts see John P. Hoerr, *And The Wolf Finally Came* (Pittsburgh: University of Pittsburgh Press, 1988); John Strohmeyer, *Crisis in Bethlehem* (Bethesda: Alder and Alder, 1986); and William Scheuerrman, *The Steel Crisis* (New York: Praeger, 1986).
27. George Ruben, "Collective Bargaining and Labor-Management Relations, 1988," *Monthly Labor Review* 112, no. 1 (1989), pp. 25-39; *The Wall Street Journal,* February 24, 1989, p. A5A.
28. Albert R. Karr, "Striking Out: Labor Unions' Chance for Gains in '88 Hits a Wall of Resistance," *The Wall Street Journal,* June 29, 1988, p. 7.
29. See, for example, William N. Cooke, "The Failure to Negotiate First Contracts: Determinants and Policy Implications," *Industrial and Labor Relations Review* 38 (January 1985), pp. 162–178.
30. James E. Martin and Lawrence L. Bisatti, "A Hierarchy of Important Elements Has Potential to Measure Success of Relationship," *Personnel Administrator* 29 (January 1984), p. 64.
31. *The State of Small Business* (Washington, D.C.: U.S. Government Printing Office, 1984), pp. xv, 9.
32. Milton Derber, "Changing Values in American Industrial Relations," Occasional Publication No. 156, Industrial Relations Center, University of Hawaii at Manoa, pp. 52, 53.
33. David B. Lipsky, "About the 'L' in ILR," *ILR Report* 26 (Spring 1989), p. 3.
34. Richard N. Bloch, "Union Organizing and the Allocation of Union Resources," *Industrial and Labor Relations Review* 34 (October 1980), pp. 101–112; Paula B. Voos, "Union Organizing Expenditures: Determinants and Their Implications for Union Growth," *Journal of Labor Research* 8 (Winter 1987), pp. 19–30.
35. Kenneth A. Kovach, "Do We Still Need Labor Unions?" *Personnel Journal* 58 (December 1979), p. 850.

CHAPTER 2

Evolution of Labor-Management Relationships

"The history of the trade union movement has shown that when organized workers were a very, very tiny percentage of the work force, they still accomplished and did things that were important for the entire work force."

George Meany

The American labor movement as we know it has adjusted to changing societal events, employers' attitudes and actions, and employee preferences for more than 100 years. A historical perspective is necessary to better understand current union behavior and helps us predict how most unions might react to sudden and dramatic change.

There is no best way to obtain this perspective.[1] Insights from many academic disciplines (sociology, economics, political science, and so forth) have to be considered, and many focal points can be assessed. Our discussion focuses on two interrelated historical dimensions: (1) relationships between labor and management organizations; and (2) organizational characteristics of labor organizations.

This second dimension is important to labor relations' students and practitioners because the current American Federation of Labor–Congress of Industrial Organizations (AFL-CIO, which represents 89 national and international unions and 14 million affiliated union members) has been historically affected by four major labor organizations: the Knights of Labor (KOL), the Industrial Workers of the World (IWW), the American Federation of Labor (AFL), and the Congress of Industrial Organizations (CIO).

The strength of any labor organization depends on four criteria:

- Its structural and financial stability.
- Its ability to work within established political and economic systems, particularly the wage system.
- Supportive or disruptive features of the broader social environment such as legislation, media, and public opinion.
- The ability of union leaders to identify and satisfy members' goals and interests.

Readers can use these criteria to assess why some labor organizations failed in the past and to predict the likelihood of current unions posing a strong challenge to management.

The historical dimensions are organized into three time periods: 1869 to World War I; World War I to World War II; and World War II to the present.

1869 to World War I

Unions as we know them today did not exist before 1800. There were small guilds, joint associations of employers and craftspeople that pressed for professional standards and restriction of outside competition.[2] These guilds pressed for concerns that typically benefited employees and employers alike. By 1820 there had been only a few scattered strikes, usually over wages, since only two industries, shoemaking and printing, had even the semblance of collective bargaining. There was also no general labor philosophy or labor movement in the United States at this time,[3] as the unions were limited to local geographical regions.

The 1850s and 1860s saw development of the U.S. factory system, improved transportation, and product mobility, factors that extended a company's (and potential unionized employees') organization beyond the local community.

The Civil War (1861–1865) refined and encouraged mass-production techniques, concentrating large numbers of semiskilled and unskilled employees under one factory roof—a situation that attracted organized labor.

The period of 1869 to World War I saw the formation of three national labor organizations: the Knights of Labor (Knights or KOL), the American Federation of Labor (AFL) under Samuel Gompers, and the Industrial Workers of the World (IWW). Each of these organizations will be discussed in terms of its orientations and goals, organizational structure, and strategies and tactics. Reasons suggested for the demise of the KOL and the IWW and other items discussed illustrate the previously mentioned criteria for a labor organization's strength. Three prominent labor episodes of this period are also discussed: the drive for an 8-hour workday (including the Haymarket Riot of 1886), the Homestead strike (1892), and the Pullman strike (1894).

These three events and other union-management confrontations through the 1930s reflect a degree of unbridled violence that has been unmatched in contemporary times. The "Labor Relations in Action" on pages 28–29 gives brief examples of steps companies would take to keep out unions and what employees were willing to do to force management to recognize their working concerns and unions. One way to gauge this historical difference is to imagine how these events would be covered on a national evening news program today.

The Knights of Labor (KOL)

Goals and Organizations of the KOL Founded by Uriah S. Stephens as a secret society in 1869, the Knights of Labor (KOL) maintained secrecy until 1882 so that the members would not be discharged by their employers for participating in a labor organization.

There are two major reasons for discussing the KOL. First, it was a union national in scope, larger than any previous union in American history. In the early 1880s, it had a steady growth, reaching over 100,000 members in 1885. Between 1885 and 1886, the organization's membership increased sharply, to 700,000. The KOL achieved more power, prestige, and notoriety than any other previous labor organization.[4] However, its goals and strategies also contributed to its demise as an effective organization. So the Knights served as an important negative lesson to the American Federation of Labor and more contemporary labor organizations in establishing and achieving their objectives.

The Knights strongly objected to the method of industrial organization and operation that began during the Civil War. This view led them to establish two major interrelated goals:

1. Change the existing labor-management relationships so that the depersonalized and specialized aspects of mass production can be avoided.
2. Attain moral betterment for employees and society.

The KOL's goals can best be grasped through the views of Terence V. Powderly, its leader and chief spokesman from 1879 to 1883. Powderly felt that mass production reduced the employees' feelings of pride and personal accomplishment.[5] In previous times, employees could be satisfied with their craftsmanship, a sense of skilled accomplishment in fashioning high-quality products from beginning to end. Mass production created several specialized employee classifications, each contributing to the completed product. Powderly placed this situation in perspective by considering the shoemakers' situation:

> The man who was called a shoemaker thirty years ago made shoes; the man who claims to be a shoemaker today makes only part of a shoe. What was once a trade in itself is a multiplicity of trades. Once there were shoemakers, now we have Beaters, Binders, Bottomers, Buffers, Burnishers, Channellers, Crimpers, Cutters, Dressers, Edge Setters . . . and several other workers at the shoe trade, and they all consider themselves shoemakers.[6]

Employees working in these specialized classifications could not obtain meaning or satisfaction from their fragmented work tasks, according to Powderly. He also felt that bankers and owners of gold were the villains of industrial society, causing higher taxes for employees and the creation of monopolies that further depersonalized the individual employee.[7]

The Knights believed that changing the existing industrial and societal system would help accomplish their second goal, moral betterment and increased dignity for their members. Powderly claimed that members must place their concerns on a "higher" ground than material working conditions, as these physical effects were but stepping stones to "a higher cause, of a nobler nature . . . the more exalted and divine nature of man, his high and noble capabilities for good."[8] The leadership of the KOL was continually concerned that its members would devote too much attention to improving working conditions and ignore the goal of moral betterment—to make every man his own master.[9]

The moralistic overtones of the Knights guided their membership policies, organizational structure, and strategies and tactics. Since moral betterment affected all members of society, the Knights encouraged people of all callings to join their organization except professional gamblers, stockbrokers, lawyers, bankers, and those who lived in whole or in part by the sale or manufacture of intoxicating liquors.[10] Employers were also encouraged to join the KOL, the rationale being that they along with employees were being duped by financiers and lawyers and once educated to this fact would join hands with the employees in improving society.

Thus, the *local assembly,* the basic unit in the KOL, could consist of employers and employees from several different trades. There were 1,100 KOL local assemblies in 1886; the purpose of these organizations was to educate members on KOL principles. However, authority and power of the Knights was very centralized, resting

Labor Relations in Action

Labor, Violence, and Related Media Coverage

Bitter, bloody violence has beset the American labor movement since its beginnings. Compared to nineteenth century and pre–World War II events, company and union actions are polite and well-mannered today, far removed from the death and slaughter perpetrated by both parties in earlier times. While corporate management did whatever it could to destroy unions and disrupt strikes (hiring "goon" squads and replacements, for example) usually with the support of local, state, and federal authorities, employees had no compunction about fighting back as viciously as they could and used particular venom against strikebreakers. Following the breakup of the Molly Maguires in the coal fields of Pennsylvania in 1877, and the great railway strikes of the same year, labor unrest continued and increased into the next century. Listed below is a chronology of some of the worst incidents of violence, with excerpts from the *New York Times.*

July 1892 Coeur d'Alene, Idaho – The Bunker Hill & Sullivan Company's determination to keep the mines open with strikebreakers precipitated violence from the striking miners. "Western Miners At War . . . [they] load 750 pounds of giant powder . . . sent it down the track toward the Frisco Mine." The resulting explosion killed one guard and injured 20. (*New York Times,* July 12, 1892, p. 1) Idaho Attorney General George Roberts stated "the mob must be crushed by overwhelming force. We can't retreat now." (*New York Times,* July 14, 1892, p. 1) Continuing the battlefield imagery, the paper reported the next day "Union Miners of the Coeur d'Alene District Disperse . . . State Authorities, Aided by The Federal Troops, In Full Possession of The Field." (*New York Times,* July 15, 1892, p. 3)

February 24, 1912 Textile workers' strike, Lawrence, Mass. – Due to their poor living conditions during the strike, which had begun the previous month, the workers began to send their children to other cities. The police intervened because the mill owners complained that sending these children away would engender sympathy for the strikers in other cities. "Police Clubs Keep Lawrence Waifs In . . . Head Broken Over An Order to Prevent Strikers Shipping Their Children Away." The police prevented about 40 children from boarding a train for Philadelphia and took them to the police headquarters. "Fifty arrests were made, many of them women who had fought the police savagely and several heads were broken by the clubs of the officers . . . four companies of infantry and a squad of cavalry surrounded the railroad station." As the police led the children from the police station to waiting cabs to transport them to the municipal home for neglected children, "a crowd of 500 foreigners [assembled] and a riotous scene followed . . . such a stubborn fight was made by the ex-

with the General Executive Board headed by Powderly.[11] As will be seen later in this section, the structure of the KOL differed dramatically from that of the AFL.

Strategies to Accomplish the KOL's Goals The Knights used at least four strategies to accomplish their goals. First, political action was viewed as important, particularly since the Knights felt that previous legislation had led society down the wrong road. The Knights believed that politicians were motivated by self-interest and therefore required careful watching. However, the Knights believed in operating through the existing party. They also actively lobbied against importation of foreign labor and for appropriations to public school systems.

cited crowd . . . [that] a squad of militia was called . . ." (*New York Times,* February 25, 1912, p. 2)

April 20, 1914 Ludlow Massacre—When the Colorado Fuel and Iron Company refused to recognize a miners' union, the miners struck. The United Mine Workers Union established a tent colony for the miners and their families at Ludlow. Frequent clashes between the miners and mine guards caused the Colorado governor to call out the National Guard, which attacked the tent camp and set fire to the tents, burning 11 children and 2 women. The "war" lasted 10 days and resulted in at least 46 deaths, and in the midst of the Mexican invasion President Wilson had to send in federal troops to stop the bloodshed. "The bodies of eleven children and two women have been recovered at Ludlow . . . union officials said . . . that the troops surrounding Ludlow had used dynamite in the ruins of the colony for destruction of the bodies of the dead . . ." in an attempt to hide evidence of how many had died. (*New York Times,* April 23, 1914, p. 22)

June 22, 1922 Herrin Massacre—When John L. Lewis, leader of the United Mine Workers, called a coal strike, the Illinois Coal Company in Herrin hired strikebreakers, which enraged the union miners. "5,000 Strikers Storm Illinois Mine . . . 14 Reported Killed, Score Wounded . . . Passing Train Crew See Heap of Bodies Lying in a Pit on a Hillside." (*New York Times,* June 22, 1922, p. 1) The next day the paper reported "29 to 40 Killed by Mine Strikers . . . Massacred While Bound . . . Eyewitnesses of Both Factions Describe Slaughter by Crazed Strikers . . . 15 Bodies Thrown in Pond . . . Some Hanged to Roadside Trees . . ." (*New York Times,* June 23, 1922, p. 1)

May 26, 1937 Battle of the Overpass—Richard T. Frankensteen and Walter Reuther attempted to organize the Ford Motor Company in Dearborn, Michigan for the United Auto Workers. Company agents reacted immediately. "An outburst of violence, in which union organizers were beaten, kicked and driven away, marked the first attempt to organize the employees of the Ford Motor Company." The *New York Times* quoted Frankensteen, "They bounced us down the concrete steps of the overpass . . . Then they would knock us down, stand us up, and knock us down again." (*New York Times,* May 27, 1937, p. 1)

May 30, 1937 Memorial Day Massacre—During a strike at the Republic Steel Plant, strikers marched on the plant. "4 Killed, 84 Hurt as Strikers Fight Police in Chicago . . . Crowd Uses Guns and Rocks, Police Employ Clubs, Tear Gas, and Bullets." (*New York Times,* May 31, 1937, p. 1)

Source: We are grateful to Kathy Cohen for preparing this discussion. The Haymarket Riot and Homestead Incident are described in some detail in the text and are therefore not covered here.

A second strategy was the encouragement of producer and consumer cooperatives. Unlike the socialists, the Knights did not want the cooperatives to be owned by the state. Instead, they wanted current employees to save enough from their wages to either purchase the operation or establish a new cooperative. Since factories would then be owned by the employees, conflict between labor and capital would cease.[12] Cooperatives would also enable the employees to become their own masters; they would have a voice in decision making, including the determination of a fair distribution of profits.

The Knights' leadership believed cooperatives would affect the established wage-profits system most directly; yet they made little attempt to establish a cooperative or to financially aid approximately 100 cooperatives established at the local or district level during the mid-1880s. Most of the cooperatives failed because of "inefficient managers, squabbles among shareholders, lack of capital, and injudicious borrowing of money at high rates of interest."[13]

The KOL pursued a third strategy when it actively avoided the use of strikes to obtain its goals. Indeed, the leadership often actively discouraged strikes and, in some cases, demoralized strikers with their statements.[14] Some leaders viewed strikes as a last resort, feeling they would distract members from the major goal of moral betterment and lessen the common interests of employers and employees. The General Executive Board set up a complicated procedure that local assemblies had to follow before they could obtain strike funds.[15] Powderly believed that no employees should be able to enter a strike that would result in other employees losing their jobs; therefore, a procedure was needed to ensure that every employee possibly affected by a strike would have a voice in the strike decision.[16] Yet the red tape involved in obtaining strike funds caused a great amount of dissension between the KOL leaders and members. Local assemblies that conducted strikes were left on their own financially, and the members bitterly resented the lack of support from the board.[17] It became common for local assemblies to conduct strikes without support from the Executive Board—in 1886, there were at least 538 local assemblies participating in either a strike or a boycott of an uncooperative employer's products.

The Knights' leadership preferred a fourth strategy to the strike; namely, the education of the members and citizens as to the perceived evils of the existing industrial system as well as the Knights' goals for societal improvement. Usually the leaders would meet with members of local assemblies in private sessions to inform them of the organization's goals and objectives. The emphasis on education instead of job action efforts (strikes and boycotts) will be further discussed in the next section.

Reasons for the KOL's Failure and Demise Despite tremendous growth, the KOL experienced a sudden demise. One reason for its growth must be the successful strike taken by the local assemblies against Jay Gould's railroads in 1885, in which the Knights showed the public that an aggressive, well-disciplined group could take on one of the most powerful financiers and win. Yet the effect of this strike may have been limited because neither the Knights nor the newspapers publicized the events. Another reason for the KOL's growth is its identification with the 8-hour workday, an issue that was important to the nation's work force.[18] However, as discussed in the next section, the KOL's endorsement of the 8-hour workday was rather weak.

Faulty Assumptions in the KOL's Orientation The Knights were reform-oriented, interested in changing existing aspects of society. With the advantages of hindsight, it becomes clear that the KOL erred in assuming that technological advancement could be halted and possibly reversed. The KOL also overestimated the extent to which employers and employees shared common interests. While there are some common grounds, each group is motivated by self-interest. Employers are concerned about increased efficiency and profitability of the operation, while employees are concerned about job security and improvement of working conditions.

The organization's third faulty assumption was that all categories of employees would have identical interests. The KOL was ahead of its time in its attempt to organize unskilled employees—a goal eventually accomplished by the Congress of Industrial Organizations (CIO) in the late 1930s. However, as further discussed in Chapter 11, employees do not all have the same interests, particularly if they have different skills and work classifications. The "one big union" approach (enrolling nearly anyone who expressed an interest in the Knights) was further complicated by many immigrant members whose differences in race, language, and religion presented barriers.[19]

A Lack of Legislation Protecting the Rights of Employees to Join Unions and Engage in Collective Bargaining This point will be further discussed in the next chapter. Suffice it to say that the Knights, as well as other labor organizations before 1935, did not have the full force of the law on their side.

Inability of the KOL's leadership (Particularly Powderly) to Identify with Members' Goals The Knights insisted upon adopting a middle-class program for the American labor force, which they refused to contemplate in industrial, working-class terms. Many of the members showed little, if any, interest in the Knights after they joined. Almost all local assembly meetings required the members to dress up after a day's work to engage in intellectual discourse. In essence, the members had nothing to do except "ceremonialize, play politics, and study."[20] Powderly felt his position was above the membership. Instead of understanding members' needs, he imposed his goals, on his terms:

> I will talk at no picnics. . . . When I speak on the labor question I want the individual attention of my hearers and I want that attention for at least two hours and in that two hours I can only epitomize. At a picnic where . . . the girls as well as the boys swill beer I cannot talk at all.[21]

The preference for intellectual deliberation over immediate, gut-level response is perhaps best viewed through Powderly's approach to the 8-hour workday movement.

The 8-Hour Workday Movement and the Haymarket Riot One of the more important reforms desired by many employees in the late 1800s was reducing the prevalent 10-hour workday to 8 hours. Samuel Gompers, who was a Knights member and an official of other labor organizations (Federation of Organized Trades and Labor Unions, and Cigar Makers' Union), pressed Powderly to support a nationwide general strike on May 1, 1886 for the 8-hour workday. Powderly was receptive to the 8-hour day, as it would give employees more leisure time to pursue intellectual activities. However, he did not join with Gompers since he did not believe the length of the workday was the major problem: "To talk of reducing the hours of labor without reducing the power of machinery is a waste of energy."[22]

Supporters of the 8-hour workday believed that, if instituted, it would result in more people working, thereby reducing the unemployment problem. On May 3, 1886, some workers striking over this issue in Chicago became involved in a skirmish with the police, and at least four strikers were killed. A leader of this dispute published an inflammatory circular urging "Revenge!" and "Workingmen to Arms!" The circular also indicated that a mass rally would be held the next day at Haymarket Square in Chicago. The stage was set for an event (known later as the **Haymarket Riot**) that virtually eliminated the effectiveness of the KOL.

A mass rally by strikers supporting the 8-hour workday movement began peacefully but ended in violence and death in Chicago's Haymarket Square.

Source: Reproduced from the collection of the Library of Congress.

On May 4, 1886, approximately 3,000 people attended the scheduled meeting, which began peacefully, for the police who monitored the meeting were ordered by their chief to return to the station. However, Police Captain Bonfield, whom the governor of Illinois later charged as being responsible for the incident, ordered them back to the meeting. During a speech a bomb was thrown into the gathering of police, killing 7 and wounding 60. What happened next is uncertain. The *Chicago Tribune* reported that "anarchists and rioters poured in a shower of bullets before the first action of the police was taken."[23] Yet another report in the same article stated the police opened fire on the crowd immediately after the bomb exploded. Regardless of the order of events, the police did shoot into the crowd, killing several and wounding 200.

Eight individuals allegedly responsible for the incident were arrested. Four of the eight were hanged, one committed suicide in prison, and three were eventually pardoned by the governor of Illinois after serving some of their sentence. Their trial was at best shoddy; for example, the hand-picked jury included a relative of one of the bombing victims.[24] The trial never did establish who threw the bomb; however, the accused were judged guilty by the *Chicago Tribune* before the trial took place. More specifically, the paper stressed that the "mob" was led by "two wirey whiskered foreigners,"[25] who were "Nihilistic Agitators."[26]

The Knights were not directly labeled in the immediate press accounts of the strike or in the subsequent series of unsuccessful strikes over the 8-hour workday, which involved nearly 340,000 employees. However, the strikes contributed to the organization's demise for at least two paradoxical reasons. A substantial body of public opinion labeled the Knights as being involved in the strikes. Yet many of the Knights' members criticized the leadership for not participating enough in the related events during and after Haymarket.[27] Indeed, Powderly strongly discouraged strikes over the 8-hour workday, believing instead that members should write essays on the subject. Thus, the Haymarket Riot dramatically reflected the split between the KOL and the newly-formed American Federation of Labor, under Gompers, an organization that was to flourish and endure.

The American Federation of Labor (AFL)

Origin and Goals of the AFL An outgrowth of the Federation of Organized Trades and Labor Unions of the United States and Canada, the **American Federation of Labor (AFL)** was formed in 1886 after some of its member national unions (most notably the Cigar Makers) were expelled from the Knights.[28] As previously mentioned, Samuel Gompers, a major founder of the AFL, was a member of the Knights but became disenchanted with the leadership's long-range social reform philosophy. Gompers was also upset about KOL activities involving the cigar makers – in particular, KOL's raiding of its members and supplying strikebreakers when the cigar makers struck firms.

He met with the Knights in December 1886 to discuss these problems, but the meeting did not resolve the situation. Indeed, Gompers became incensed when a pamphlet was circulated among KOL representatives that attacked Gompers personally by indicating "the General Executive Board has never had the pleasure of seeing Mr. Gompers sober."[29] Also, in retrospect, KOL leaders blundered when they concentrated on influencing craft employees, a move that resulted in bitter reactions from the trade unions. The Knights would have been better off (and still consistent with their goals) if they had devoted more attention to the unskilled employees where the trades did not have any argument.[30]

Unlike the KOL, the AFL was not established as one big union. (This is discussed more fully in Chapter 4.) It represented a federation or organization that many national unions could join while each national union maintained its separate union status. Craft unions, such as the Cigar Makers, dominated the early stages of the AFL. The AFL influenced its member unions through its services, particularly organizing activities, philosophies, and strategies.

It is impossible to discuss the AFL apart from Gompers since "in the early years, the A.F. of L. existed only in the person of Gompers and in the annual conventions."[31] With the exception of 1895, Gompers was president of the AFL from its founding in 1886 until his death in 1924. Therefore, much of the discussion of the goals, strategies, and organization of the AFL will be from the perspective of Gompers, a point of view that relates strongly to the current thinking of organized labor; there has been relatively little change in orientation, strategies, and organization since the time of Gompers.

Gompers placed little emphasis on intellectual betterment, and he scorned other union leaders' pretensions to show labor union members the course of action they should pursue.[32] He criticized the KOL as representing "a hodgepodge with no basis for solidarity with the exception of a comparatively few trade assemblies."[33] Gompers believed that the goals and organization of unions should flow directly and naturally from the members' needs, not from the pronouncements of top leaders who structured unions based on their views of what should have been, rather than what was.

Gompers particularly scorned those union leaders who tried to change the existing social system through revolutionary means.[34] Although he was a socialist in his early years, he grew to despise this philosophy, contending that it was economically unsound, socially wrong, and impossible to apply in an industrial setting.[35] He also believed that union members should work for the development of, not the overthrow or destruction of, the society in which they lived and for the most part enjoyed.[36]

Thus, the AFL's major if not sole goal was to improve the material conditions of members through the existing capitalistic system. This goal was attacked by the critics of the AFL as representing pure and simple unionism. Gompers embraced this intended insult; indeed, he seemed to devote most of his attention to ensuring that the AFL's "pure and simple" approach to collective bargaining successfully differentiated it from other labor organizations.

"Pure and simple unionism" had two major objectives. The primary objective was economic betterment of the organization's members; Gompers believed the "truth," or essence, of labor unions should be measured in terms of their economic accomplishments:

> Economic betterment–today, tomorrow, in home and shop, was the foundation upon which trade unions have been built. Economic power is the base upon which may be developed power in other fields. It is the foundation of organized society. Whoever or whatever controls economic power directs and shapes development for the group or the nation.[37]

Thus, the AFL's notion of "employee dignity" equated with measured economic gains. This view differed from the KOL's contention that employee dignity is attained by participation as equals in meaningful work and in other societal concerns.[38]

Gompers also stressed a second objective of pure and simple unionism–the enhancement of the capitalistic system, which can benefit both employees and employers. Workers can obtain more only if capitalism continues to flourish. Without capitalism neither employees nor employers receive revenues. The AFL therefore believed labor and management shared some similar interests. However, Gompers did not agree with Powderly that this situation would lead to complete employer-employee agreement on all issues. He realized that major differences of opinion would occur over the distribution of revenues and that employees would probably have to pressure employers in order to receive their fair share.

Strategies and Tactics of the AFL This realization prompted the AFL to rely on one of its three major tactics–the strike. Unlike the Knights, Gompers believed the strike was a viable collective bargaining alternative:

> A workman must convince his employer that he is entitled to an advance in wages. . . . Why should the wage-earner work for less than living wages, which he would have to do if he could not strike? The worker is expected to continue to work at whatever wages his employer is willing to give in order to save the public from inconvenience.[39]

A second AFL tactic (particularly when its headquarters moved to Washington, D.C.) was that of involvement in the political arena. Gompers, an aggressive lobbyist, attempted to translate election votes of AFL members into "rewards" for political friends of labor and "punishments" for political enemies of labor. However, political efforts during Gompers's leadership were neither intense nor widespread throughout the AFL.[40]

AFL political efforts were directed at influencing the existing two-party system instead of forming a third political party. Gompers felt that establishing a third party would divert too much time away from fundamental collective bargaining efforts. He also felt that any new political party would fall into the socialists' control.[41]

The third AFL tactic was to secure increased status for organized labor and collective bargaining. Gompers devoted much attention to the National Civic Foundation, formed in 1899 to promote industrial peace through collective bargaining. This organization, composed of prominent labor, management, and political officials, attempted to guide public opinion toward the positive aspects of collective bargaining. However, at least one observer of industrial relations has questioned the success of this tactic, believing that "its rhetoric surpassed its performance."[42]

Organization of the AFL The AFL's organizational structure was based on two related principles: exclusive jurisdiction and decentralized authority. The AFL avoided the concept of "one big union"—which proved to be ineffective for the KOL—and insisted on the principle of exclusive jurisdiction. This principle rested on the twofold observation that (1) each craft or trade had unique working conditions and job interests and (2) combining members of different trades into one organization would jeopardize those interests and cause unnecessary dissension. The AFL thus believed in one union representing a particular craft; for example, separate unions would represent carpenters, painters, and cigar makers.

Gompers also strongly believed the AFL was a voluntary organization held together by the mutual self-interests of members. Unlike Powderly, who believed that centralized authority was necessary to achieve the Knights' objectives, Gompers viewed the central AFL as a "rope of sand," dependent entirely on the acceptance of its members. Thus, the real authority rested with various national unions and their member locals. As will be further discussed in Chapter 4, these principles continue to influence contemporary union organizations.

The organizational activity as well as the organizational structure of the AFL must be considered. Gompers was a most active union organizer; he claimed to have helped in organizing 28 unions representing different crafts such as painters, paper makers, firefighters, and post office clerks.[43] Much of this effort was due to Gompers's view of himself as "one of the boys"—he took pride in his ability to socialize with the members on their own terms.

In spite of Gompers's efforts, the AFL's early growth was not spectacular. Its original membership of 150,000 had increased to only 250,000 six years later. The initial slow growth was due to the counterattack of industry (discussed in the section on World War I to World War II), the generally repressive attitude of the government and the courts, and the difficulties raised by the depression of 1893. Yet Gompers could view these modest membership gains as a tribute to the AFL's powers of "stability and permanency."[44]

From its formation until World War I, the AFL was directly or indirectly involved in three prominent events: the Homestead and Pullman incidents and the formation and demise of the Industrial Workers of the World (IWW).

The Homestead Strike

The Carnegie Steel Works, located in Homestead, Pennsylvania, was ironically the scene of one of the more violent episodes in labor history. The founder of these operations, Andrew Carnegie, was a renowned philanthropist who gave every indication of being receptive to organized labor. In one article, written before the Homestead incident, he stated that a strike or a lockout was a "ridiculous affair" since it only represented a test of strength instead of determining what was "fair and just."[45] Carnegie also believed that labor-management problems would occur in large firms run by salaried managers instead of owners, because the former group had no permanent interest in the desires of the workmen.

Carnegie's remarks proved prophetic in the **Homestead Incident** of July 6, 1892. Although many have labeled the incident a strike, one labor historian has noted that no strike vote was ever taken by the membership,[46] and the employer prohibited the employees from working. During negotiation between the mill and the Amalgamated Association of Iron, Steel, and Tin Workers (an affiliate of the AFL), a 15-foot-high solid board fence, topped with barbed wire, was constructed around the building. Andrew Carnegie was vacationing in Scotland during negotiations and had delegated these duties to a management official named Henry Clay Frick. The union labeled the structure around the steel mill "Fort Frick." Members were also undoubtedly aware that Frick was negotiating with Pinkerton detectives while labor-management negotiations were being conducted. Frick intended to use Pinkerton detectives inside the facility to protect the company's property and as strikebreakers.

On June 30, 1892, the company made its last offer, which represented a substantial reduction of previous wages,[47] and locked out its 4,000 employees. Workmen then began an around-the-clock surveillance of the plant. One newspaper account indicated, "The line of pickets covers the river, roads, and railways so tightly that no stranger can enter the town without being known to the strikers."[48] On the morning of July 5, 300 Pinkertons gathered at Ashtabula, Ohio, and proceeded by rail to Youngstown, Ohio. They then traveled up the Monongahela River by barge. On July 6, word had reached the townspeople that the Pinkertons would be entering the plant from the river. Six thousand people lined the river banks at 2:00 A.M., and employees prepared two small cannons, one on each side of the river, to be used on the Pinkertons.[49]

The Pinkertons attempted to land by the company's beach at 5:00 A.M.; shots were exchanged, and three Pinkertons were killed. Shooting by both sides continued for 12 hours, with an additional 7 townspeople being killed and 50 wounded. The Pinkertons surrendered to the townspeople and were forced to run a bloody gauntlet before being locked up for their protection. The townspeople had taken the weapons from the Pinkertons, a situation that resulted in 8,700 National Guard militiamen being sent to secure the town.There were few further incidents, particularly since union leaders believed the troops would discourage further attempts by Pinkertons or strikebreakers.[50] The incident ended for all purposes some 5 months later (November 20, 1892) when the Amalgamated lifted its prohibition against returning to work.

The bloody confrontation between Pinkerton agents and employees of the Carnegie Steel Works in Homestead, Pennsylvania, in 1892 was one of the most violent in labor history and actually set back the cause of unions in the steel industry.

Source: Courtesy of the AFL-CIO.

Homestead has been labeled the Waterloo of unions in the steel industry. National membership in the Amalgamated dropped from 24,000 in 1892 to 8,000 in 1894. On the local level, only 800 of the original Homestead employees were reinstated. Carnegie's mills showed a dramatic increase in profits when the union was eliminated,[51] a message that must have encouraged other employers to take an antiunion stance.

While Homestead represented a victory for management, the AFL and organized labor did benefit to some extent from the situation. First, Gompers demonstrated to existing and potential union members his very real concern about the Homestead situation.[52] The funds contributed by the AFL to help defray the workers' legal expenses also demonstrated that the AFL was interested in helping its member unions in a material sense.[53] Finally, the Homestead situation received more sympathetic newspaper accounts than did the Haymarket Riot. The press charged Carnegie with provoking the situation. For example, the *Chicago Tribune* criticized the company's use of Pinkertons strongly and contended that Carnegie's company as well as any large industrial organization "has duties and obligations toward society which it must not forget, and not the least of them is to do all in its power, and make all of the concessions it can, to preserve civil and industrial peace."[54] At a minimum, the press could not continually criticize the involved union or employees in this incident, especially since no individual was found guilty of participating in the incident.

The Pullman Strike

Strikes were common in the railroad industry; for example, the Great Upheaval of 1877 involved independent railroad employee associations protesting wage cuts. It was a bitter and violent confrontation in which more than one hundred employees were killed and several hundred were badly wounded.[55]

Yet the **Pullman Strike** of 1894 assumes significance because of the principal personalities involved (Eugene Debs and George Pullman) and an organization (the American Railway Union, or ARU) that had the potential to challenge the AFL for union members. It also approached being the only revolutionary strike in the United States; it became a nationwide strike in one industry and came near to involving all industries.[56]

As a result of the 1893 depression, the Pullman Company laid off 3,000 of its 5,800 employees and cut wages 25 to 40 percent. Both actions were important since they occurred in the milieu of George Pullman's company town. This town represented a social, paternalistic experiment by the owner of the Pullman Palace Car Company. The company owned all of the houses, buildings, and services in the town; employees were not allowed to own their own homes.[57] Pullman did not correspondingly reduce rents and charges for other services; thus, the wage cuts resulted in some employees having a net 2-week pay of $1 to $6 during the winter of 1893 to 1894.

This situation generated much hostility among employees, many of whom were members of the American Railway Union (ARU), formed in 1893. The ARU was completely independent from the AFL; indeed, it competed for members with the AFL-affiliated railway brotherhoods. The ARU accepted any white employee, regardless of specific job classification, so that railroad employees could present a unified front to the railroad companies.[58] It was attractive to many employees because employers previously had been able to create dissension among the different craft unions by playing one off against the other in wage negotiations.

The ARU's local unions had sole authority to call a strike, and the Pullman strike began on May 11, 1894. Debs, the union leader, informed the strikers that the strike should represent a protest against philosophical issues instead of mere material betterment: "The paternalism of Pullman is the same as the interest of a slave holder in his human chattels. You are striking to avert slavery and degradation."[59]

At first the strikers followed Debs's orders not to damage railroad property. The ARU instead adopted a strategy of not operating any train that included a Pullman sleeping car—the common practice was to cut these cars from the train and move them to the side tracks. If any employee was discharged for this action, then the entire crew would quit, leaving the train immobilized. This tactic, employed in 27 states and territories, was intended to make railroad carriers put pressure on Pullman to agree with the ARU's bargaining position.

However, the railroad employers rallied behind Pullman and countered the union's strategy by hiring strikebreakers. They also decided to include federal mail on nearly every train and were able to obtain an injunction on July 2, 1894 (subsequently upheld by the Supreme Court) to prevent any employee from interfering with the delivery of the mail. Employees could no longer engage in their strike strategy of rendering the trains inoperative. Some 16,000 troops, dispatched by President Cleveland to enforce the injunction, either delivered the mail and operated the trains or protected strikebreakers so that food and other perishable items could be delivered throughout the country.

The strike then took a particularly ugly turn; employees burned at least 700 railroad cars in Chicago on July 7, 1894. Interestingly, management was also criticized for this incident, at the least for failing to take minimum security measures such as guarding or locking the railroad cars. At a maximum, some management officials may have provoked the incident to receive additional support from the government. This possibility is suggested because all of the burnt cars were old (the more expensive Pullman cars were not on the property), and very few of the cars were loaded with any product.[60]

The resulting negative public opinion and increased action by the federal troops forced Debs to seek Gompers's cooperation. Debs wanted Gompers to call a national strike to enforce Debs's last offer, which was simply management's reinstatement of the striking employees. Gompers refused to support Debs, contending that he did not have authority to call a general strike. Gompers also believed that the proposed settlement would, in effect, admit to the public that the ARU had failed to win material benefits for its members. Much of Gompers's reluctance was due to his view of Debs as being "a leader of irregular movements and lost causes."[61] However, Gompers's inaction might have also been due to his desire to eliminate a potential rival to the AFL and bolster his reputation in the business community.

Debs was eventually convicted and sentenced under the Sherman Antitrust Act of 1890; and the ARU, which had grown to 150,000 members in one year, quickly faded from existence. Organized labor did learn an important lesson from this strike; namely, it would be difficult to alter the existing system against the wishes of a persistent, if not exceptionally stubborn, owner (Pullman), the federal government (troops, injunctions, legislation), the AFL (which supported this system), and negative public opinion (fueled by exaggerated and dramatic newspaper articles).

The Industrial Workers of the World (IWW)

The **Industrial Workers of the World (IWW)** was formed as an alternative to the AFL on June 27, 1905. "Big Bill" Haywood, initial organizer of the IWW, originated the organization's goals in calling the convention of 209 delegates to order with the following remarks:

> Fellow Workers . . . We are here to confederate the workers of this country into a working class movement that shall have for its purpose the emancipation of the working class from the slave bondage of Capitalism. . . . The aims and objects of this organization should be to put the working class in possession of the economic power, the means of life, in control of the machinery of production and distribution without regard to capitalist masters.[62]

The initial goal of the IWW was to overthrow the existing capitalistic system by any means, since it felt that employers and employees had nothing in common. The IWW and the Knights agreed on one point: the existing wage and profit system had to be changed. The Knights, however, stressed that employees and employers had common interests and that change must be peaceful and gradual. The IWW, on the other hand, had no reservations about using any method that would result in the quick destruction of capitalism.

The IWW also wanted to remove any societal aspect or group that supported capitalism. This approach placed the IWW in direct opposition to the AFL. The IWW regarded the AFL as an "extension of the capitalist class"[63] since it advocated "pure and simple unionism," which was dependent on capitalism. Haywood believed that Gompers had sold out the ARU when he had not supported Debs in the Pullman strike, and he viewed Gompers as an arrogant, power-hungry leader.[64] Thus, the IWW appeared to have two general enemies: capitalism and the AFL, which did not recognize a working-class movement of hourly employees as being a class-conscious group apart from the rest of society. An analysis of the IWW reveals that establishing goals can be an easier task than accomplishing them.

The IWW never did establish an effective organization; in fact, its leaders never made up their minds about precisely what kind of organizational structure it should adopt.[65] Most of the IWW officials agreed with Haywood's objective of organizing "every man that earns his livelihood either by his brain or his muscle."[66] But major differences arose over how to organize one big union into an effective organization. Some members felt that the IWW should work slowly; for example, infiltrate the established AFL unions and gradually persuade members that the IWW cause was best. Others felt that this temporary acceptance of collective bargaining with the capitalists only made employees "better paid slaves" and would hinder the quick and necessary overthrow of the capitalistic system.[67]

In addition to organizational differences, there were at least four reasons for the demise of the IWW, reasons that served as negative lessons for contemporary organized labor.

1. **Lack of permanent membership and financial base.** A large proportion of the IWW consisted of itinerants – individuals who were either unemployed or traveled from job to job, particularly in the agriculture, mining, and lumber industries. This contributed to an unstable financial base. Many IWW leaders thought the members' dues should not be mandatory; instead, they should be paid out of a voluntary "inner conviction." Apparently, many members did not share this "inner conviction"; for example, in 1907 only 10,000 members out of the total 31,000 members paid any dues. The lack of revenues resulted in meager strike funds, and by 1909 the organization was deeply in debt.
2. **Inability of the IWW to appeal to members' interests.** The IWW did not consider the short-run material interests of its members. Its major emphasis on long-term philosophical goals and its concern with propaganda as a means to achieve these goals failed to demonstrate tangible signs of success on a continuous basis.[68] The average trade unionist, in or outside the IWW, had no desire to help the underdog. Indeed, it was all he could do to look out for himself.[69]
3. **Identification of the IWW with sabotage and violence.** The relationship between the IWW and sabotage and violence was ambiguous. The IWW in 1914 became the only labor organization to ever officially endorse sabotage at its convention. Yet no local, state, or federal authority could ever establish legal proof of any IWW-instigated violence. A strike in 1917 closed the logging camps and sawmills of the Pacific Northwest but did not record any violent

acts of sabotage by the IWW.[70] The IWW often stated that sabotage does not equal destruction of equipment. For example, employees could "sabotage" the company by "malicious obedience" (following the work rules to the letter, thereby creating a slowdown) and by informing customers that the company's product was of inferior quality. However, at least one article in the IWW's paper, the *Industrial Worker,* indicated how emery dust and ground-up glass could cause the destruction of machinery.

Evidence suggests that the IWW's leadership denounced any type of physical violence.[71] Yet there are also some accounts of incidents in which IWW members and leaders pledged a "life for a life" or "an eye for an eye."[72] At a minimum, it appears that the IWW did not actively discourage its link with violence.

4. **Alienation of the news media and government officials.** The newspapers enhanced the IWW's reputation for violence by labeling members as "desperate villains who set fire to wheat fields, drove spikes into sawmill-bound logs, derailed trains, destroyed industrial machinery, and killed policemen."[73] Part of this negative image was enhanced by leaders of IWW factions who would damn each other in the press. The IWW also engaged in several "free speech fights"—soap box speeches in local communities. This strategy, which has since been copied by various protest groups, including students, relied on there being more participants than there were available jail spaces. City officials, faced with this situation, typically allowed the "unlawful" demonstration to continue.[74] In many of these speeches, the IWW would shout antisocial comments such as "there is no God."[75]

The press, never enthusiastic about unions in general, reserved a special hatred for the IWW. One editorial against the IWW stated:

> They would be much better dead, for they are absolutely useless in the human economy; they are the waste material of creation and should be drained off into the sewer of oblivion there to rot in cold obstruction like any other excrement.[76]

The IWW also remained alienated from the government. It did not actively use the existing political system because many of its transient members could not meet voter registration requirements. It also incurred the wrath of the federal government when it refused to support involvement in World War I, proclaiming instead that the war represented a capitalistic plot. The government responded to the IWW's antiwar stance by arresting over 100 leaders and sentencing most of them to prison terms ranging from 5 to 20 years. In effect, the IWW went out of existence in 1918, even though the organization remains today with a handful of members.

The onset of World War I found the AFL on unfirm ground. It had been the first nationally organized labor movement to withstand a severe economic depression, a hostile press, reluctant or hostile employers, and three rival labor organizations (KOL, ARU, and IWW). Yet the AFL had internal pressures from at least three sources: (1) socialists and other related political groups that advocated independent political action and the organization of unskilled industrial employees; (2) pacifist members who wanted the AFL to remain neutral or take a stand against the war;[77] and (3) member unions that became involved in jurisdictional problems caused by increased specialization and technological change (for example, the plumber was no longer responsible for the complete installation of the water and heating system for a building). Perhaps the most lingering concern of the AFL was that the largest proportion of the organizable labor force, the unskilled industrial employees, remained essentially outside the ranks of organized labor.[78] This concern and its eventual resolution are discussed more in the following section.

World War I to World War II

The period from World War I to World War II witnessed several important phenomena:

1. The inability of unions, particularly the AFL, to make substantial membership gains in the 1920s.
2. The development of employer strategies to retard union growth.
3. Increased union concern over organizing the unskilled industrial employees, which led to a bitter rivalry between the AFL and CIO (Congress of Industrial Organizations).

Some union organizing drives in various industries will be cited briefly to give a further indication of the problems and prospects facing organized labor in this period.

Union Organizing after World War I: Problems and Prospects

The AFL overcame its initial reluctance toward participating in World War I and eventually pledged its cooperation when the United States became directly involved in the war. The government, aware of the necessity of uninterrupted production during wartime, responded by attempting to meet labor's concerns. Government agreements with the AFL provided for the enforcement of trade union standards in all government contracts; labor representatives were appointed to all government agencies, including the War Labor Board; and Gompers was made a member of the Advisory Commission of the National Council of Defense. In short, organized labor was elevated to a more prominent status than had theretofore been seen. Accordingly, the AFL had a sizable growth in membership during this period (an increase from 2,370,000 members in 1917 to 3,260,000 members in 1919). Legislative interests were also met; a long-time AFL goal of severely restricting immigrants, a strongly competitive labor source, was accomplished.

The rather sharp increase in the cost of living that followed World War I, coupled with the newly recognized status of labor, resulted in an unprecedented number of strikes. For example, the Seattle General Strike occurred in 1919, along with other strikes by actors, New York waterfront employees, and coal miners. The most widespread strike occurred in 1919 in the steel industry, where some 367,000 employees walked off the job in 70 major cities.

This strike actually resulted in a setback to organized labor in the steel industry. Many possible factors contributed to the setback; some were notably similar to those found in the Homestead and Pullman incidents, while others reflected a typical situation unions faced in the 1920s and early 1930s. Of crucial importance were internal union difficulties: an organizing campaign conducted by 24 unions instead of one common industrial union, improvised leadership rather than a consistent union approach to the issue, and poor financial resources. U.S. Steel was also successful in withstanding the strike by using strikebreakers and maintaining strong ties with other companies and social institutions like the press and the pulpit. Thus, the strike was terminated without a labor agreement, and it would take another 15 years before organized labor would make inroads into the steel industry.[79]

Although the steel industry did not reflect all industrial reactions to collective bargaining, apparently many other unions were similarly powerless to organize companies that, like U.S. Steel, firmly believed unions were not in the firm's best interests. For example, another 1919 strike almost paralyzed the coal industry when no miners returned to work until President Wilson persuaded them to accept a temporary wage increase and submit all other issues to a newly appointed Bituminous Coal Commission. In 1920 the commission awarded increases ranging from 20 to 30 percent; but this was the last victory for mine workers for several years.

In spite of increased status and militancy, something went wrong for organized labor in the 1920s; the "Golden Twenties" for the majority in the United States was a dreary decade for labor—both for hourly employees in terms of real income[80] and for labor unions in terms of membership. Between 1920 and 1924, total union membership declined from 5,110,000 to 3,600,000; membership in AFL unions dropped from 4,078,000 to 2,866,000. By 1930 total union membership dropped to 3,400,000, and AFL membership dropped to 2,700,000.[81] This decline was due to at least two major factors: (1) aggressive counteractions by employers and (2) organized labor's inability to overcome antiunion sentiment among potential union members.[82]

Counteractions by Employers Concerned with the increased status given labor during the war, employers actively engaged in efforts to roll back gains in union membership, beginning in the 1920s and continuing through the 1930s. These tactics took the form of either (1) aggressive opposition toward labor unions or (2) formation of an acceptable alternative to unions.

Employers actively opposed unions throughout the *open-shop movement,* which is discussed in more detail in Chapter 11. The alleged purpose of this movement was to ensure that employees had the freedom to determine whether they would choose to join a union. Rationale for this movement was found in its companion name, the **American Plan**—employers felt that employees should adhere to the traditional American value of "rugged individualism" instead of the "foreign," "subversive," and "corrupt" principles of labor unions.

Many employers equated the open shop—the right to join or not to join unions—with no unionized employees. Steps were taken to prevent employees from joining a union. For example, some employers would hire industrial spies to determine which employees had pro-union sentiments.[83] These employees would then be discharged and possibly *blacklisted,* meaning that their names would be given to other employers, who would refuse to hire them. Employer violence against participants in union organizing drives was also a potential strategy to counter unions during this period.[84]

A variation of the open shop, or American Plan, occurred in the 1930s, with the development of the Mohawk Valley Formula. This approach was used when a union attempted to organize or strike a facility in the community. The Mohawk Valley Formula would then be implemented with the following steps:

> Form a citizens' committee in the community, label the union leaders as outside agitators, stir up violence or the fear of violence, have a "state of emergency" declared, organize a back-to-work movement, and finally have the back-to-work employees march into the plant protected by armed police.[85]

Employers also countered unions by providing an alternative model to unionism. The 1920s saw widespread employer *paternalism,* which assured that the employer had a superior wisdom and knew what was best for the employees. Paternalistic practices included free lunches, baseball fields, vacations, pensions, and employee counseling.[86] Employers felt that employees receiving these benefits would be indebted to the employer and realize that unions would be unnecessary since they could not bargain for what the employees already had.

Employee Representation Plans Company-established unions represented another substitute model for unions. Called **Employee Representation Plans** (ERPs), they included as many as 1.5 million employees, and appeared superficially similar to unions since selected employee representatives would discuss working conditions with management officials. But ERPs differed from unions in two major respects. First, unions had more autonomy than ERPs. Employers could strongly influence the selection of ERP officers, and could also veto any decision made by the joint labor-management committee. Second, ERPs were usually limited to a single facility, and employees under ERPs could neither press for work rules that would remove unfair competition from other facilities nor push for legislation at the local, state, or federal level.[87]

Labor's Inability to Overcome Antiunion Sentiment The lack of organizing gains during the 1920s also has to be attributed to the antiunion sentiment of potential union members and the activities and attitudes of organized labor. Part of this problem may have been due to the relatively good economic conditions that prevailed:

> While job insecurity may have deterred some employees from joining unions in the face of employer opposition, many of them apparently felt that unions were no longer as necessary as they had formerly believed them to be. What profit strikes or other agitation for collective bargaining when the pay envelope was automatically growing fatter and a more abundant life seemed to be assured with our rapid approach to the final triumph over poverty?[88]

Many potential members also believed that much of organized labor was corrupt and subject to control by the socialists and communists. Racketeering had become a feature of some local union-employer relationships. For example, in one incident a union official signed a two-paragraph agreement with three major employers guaranteeing no wage increase for 3 years and requiring all employees to join the union or be discharged. None of the employees had ever solicited the union, nor did they ever see a union official during the life of the contract. This "sweetheart" arrangement or contract was often coupled with financial kickbacks to the union official, meaning the employer paid the union official a portion of the wage savings.[89]

Some labor unions had also been accused of harboring communists and other political radicals. Many prominent union leaders would occasionally accept help from almost any group that would devote time and effort in organizing employees, believing that they could control these political elements once the local union had been established. However, they overestimated their controlling ability in some instances. One former president of the Steelworkers Union recalled how communists could dominate local union meetings by using the *V technique,* where the leader would find a seat in the center of the auditorium about the second or third row. Then the following would ensue:

> A few rows back, two of his associates would locate about ten seats apart, and this same pattern would be followed all the way to the rear of the hall. When the chief spokesman opened debate, his line would then be parroted all the way through the V behind him, giving an illusion of widespread strength. They would also wait until other union members, tired and bored, had gone home before trying to push through their own proposals.[90]

Thus, labor, particularly the AFL, devoted much of its attention during the 1920s to overcoming its negative public image.[91] These efforts detracted from active organizing efforts, particularly since Gompers had lost much of his former physical enthusiasm for this activity. In 1924 Gompers died, and his successor, William Green, did not revive any major organizing activities, as he had to maintain the AFL's existing organization in an adverse atmosphere.[92] This situation eventually led to the formation of the Congress of Industrial Organizations (CIO).

Rise of the CIO and Industrial Unionism

There was major disagreement within the AFL over organizing the large ranks of unskilled and semiskilled employees. Tremendous technological shifts occurring during and after World War I reduced the demand for highly skilled employees; hence, an increasing percentage of the labor force consisted of production workers. In 1926, for example, 85 percent of the hourly employees at Ford Motor Company required less than 2 weeks of training.[93] Since craft employees no longer dominated the industrial scene, the AFL needed to organize the industrial employees.

Many of the AFL unions did not want to bring industrial employees into their organizations. Some AFL leaders believed these employees were inferior to craft employees and possessed less bargaining power, while others thought their inclusion would confuse and distort the AFL's organization. William Green himself did not view industrial employees as being compatible with the AFL's organizational principle of exclusive jurisdiction.

Some leaders thought that a separate union would be needed for each company's or industry's products. Thus, if General Electric had 50 different products, then 50 different AFL unions (each having exclusive jurisdiction over its members' interests) would be needed for effective collective bargaining. In other words, at least 50 separate collective bargaining agreements could be negotiated by GE and its unions. Other leaders believed that industrial unionism would at least weaken the AFL's concept of organized labor. The president of one AFL union urged his members to stamp out "the awful serpent of industrial trade unionism that would destroy this International and weaken the entire structure of the Labor Movement."[94]

The issue came to a head in 1935 under the direction of John L. Lewis, president of the AFL's United Mine Workers Union. The AFL rejected the concept of industrial unionism through three separate votes at its 1935 convention.[95] On November 9, 1935, the Committee for Industrial Organizations (CIO) was formed. Its purpose was allegedly "educational and advisory"; in reality, it was intended to promote organizing the unorganized, particularly those in the mass-production industries.[96]

In January 1936 AFL leaders were shocked to find that the Committee for Industrial Organizations had been formed among AFL unions. They had thought the industrial unionism issue had been buried once and for all at the 1935 convention. The Committee not only discussed the industrial union concept but also requested the immediate granting of industrial union charters to a number of industries such as the rubber workers and the auto workers. The Committee further insisted that an organizing campaign be started at once in the steel industry.

The AFL, confronted with the most serious challenge in its history, ordered the Committee to disband or get out. Personalities intensified the issue. John L. Lewis, a powerful man in voice and action, sought and obtained power and publicity in his union activities.[97] Lewis managed to provoke AFL leaders into a confrontation while at the same time whipping his United Mine Workers members into a "lather of rage" against the AFL.[98] The split over the industrial unionism issue resulted in seven unions with almost a million members forming a rival and completely independent labor federation, the **Congress of Industrial Organizations (CIO),** in 1938.[99]

The development of the CIO coincided with a significant upsurge in union membership. By November 1937, the CIO's affiliated unions had organized 75 percent of the steel industry, 70 percent of the automobile industry, 65 percent of the rubber industry, and about one-third of the maritime and textile industries.[100] The AFL also saw rapid growth in membership during the late 1930s and the 1940s. It organized the mass-production employees into local labor unions and national councils assigned to various craft unions. The steady growth of the AFL during the late 1930s was also aided by employers' preference to deal with the more conservative organization instead of taking their chances with the new and unpredictable CIO.[101]

Why did union membership increase dramatically in the 1930s and 1940s? This question is particularly important since the CIO, like the unsuccessful Knights and IWW before it, organized employees of different crafts into one union for each industry. There appear to be at least five reasons for the growth in unionism during this period.

Strong CIO Leadership The aggressive and effective CIO leaders (John L. Lewis, Sidney Hillman, and David Dubinsky, among others) infused new life into a movement previously content with resting on its laurels. Most of the CIO union leaders had extensive organizing experience and prided themselves on keeping in touch with their membership.[102] Union leaders' accomplishments should not be overstated, however, since organizing drives involved the tireless efforts of many individuals who typed up circulars, contacted prospective members, and provided routine services that assured union election victories. In fact, one biographer of John L. Lewis indicated his lack of involvement in the many organizing chores by noting that he preferred "arriving only in time for the triumphant finale."[103]

Much organization effort in the steel, mining, automobile, and other industries was effectively directed toward second generation immigrants. Some 30 percent of the CIO leadership came from a "new immigrant" background. One historian notes, "The success of the CIO was based on the mobilization of ethnic workers and on their willingness to join unions."[104]

Realistic Goals The CIO shared only a superficial similarity with the KOL in respect to grouping employees with different job interests, believing that organizing along industrial lines would still consider the common interests of employees. More importantly, the CIO dramatically differed from the Knights and the IWW in its goals—short-run gains instead of long-range reform—which paralleled the AFL's "pure and simple unionism" approach, including support of the established economic order, as illustrated in Lewis's remarks:

> I think most people have come to realize, that we cannot progress industrially without real cooperation between workers and management, and that this can only be brought about by equality in strength and bargaining power of labor and management. Labor is sincere in its desire to help. It looks forward to an industrial procedure which will increase productive efficiency and lower prices to the consumer.[105]

The Effective Use of Sit-Down Strikes The CIO also developed a most successful tactic for heightening employer recognition of its unions—the *sit-down strike,* in which employees stayed inside the plant instead of picketing outside. This technique was very successful since employers were reluctant to physically remove the employees from the plant for fear that their equipment could be damaged in the confrontation.

The tactic was initially applied by the IWW at a General Electric facility in 1906, but the most famous of these strikes occurred in December 1936 at a General Motors facility in Flint, Michigan. At one time, 26,000 General Motors employees had belonged to a union; in early 1936, there were only 122 union members, many of whom were management spies.[106] A local grassroots organization was secretly established to build up the union at Flint. The sit-down strike was locally planned; Lewis and the CIO preferred to organize the steel industry before attempting major organizing drives in the automobile industry. The CIO, however, did lend its active support once the strike was under way.

The sit-down strike at Flint lasted 44 days and received widespread community support, while hindering GM's efforts to reverse its negative profit situation of previous years.[107] The strike resulted in employer recognition of the union, a fact that was noticed by many employees in other trades. Between September 1936 and June 1937, some 500,000 employees in the rubber, glass, and textile industries put the technique to use. Although effective, the sit-down strike was short-lived, because public opinion eventually frowned on this tactic, and a subsequent decision by the Supreme Court declared such strikes illegal.

Passage of the Wagner Act Another (and perhaps the most significant) reason for the increased number of union members was the passage of the Wagner Act in 1935 (discussed in more detail in Chapter 3). The federal government indicated through this law that collective bargaining was in the national interest. More important were the provisions establishing the National Labor Relations Board to administer union representation elections, define employer unfair labor practices, and enforce the legal rights of employees to join unions.

Changes in Employees' Attitudes Many employees' previously negative attitudes toward organized labor changed dramatically. They had experienced the Great Depression of the 1930s and realized that job security could not be achieved solely through hard work and loyalty to the employer. These employees now viewed unions as a mechanism to promote job security as well as provide other material benefits.

By the onset of World War II, organized labor had reversed its membership decline of the 1920s, rising to almost 9 million members in 1940. Yet the rivalry between the CIO and the AFL was intense and violent as AFL and CIO organizers often physically clashed over the right to represent factory employees. James Hoffa, a former president of the International Brotherhood of Teamsters (then an AFL union), recalled violent organizing drives of 1941 between the CIO and his union:

> Through it all the members wore two pins, putting on a Teamster button when we were around and switching to a CIO button when those guys showed up. They were waiting to see which union was going to win the battle. You couldn't really blame them. They were scared out of their britches because they didn't want to get caught in the bloody middle.[108]

The CIO-AFL rivalry existed in almost every industry[109] and extended to the local level, where it was common for an employer to have both AFL and CIO unions representing the same employees. Even employers with the best intentions could not build an effective labor-management relationship in this environment.

World War II to the Present

The AFL at first did not want the United States to become involved in World War II; however, this attitude changed after the bombing of Pearl Harbor. Concern over the nation's defense prompted union-management cooperation. For example, both union and management officials participated on War Production Board subcommittees. Such panels weighed employee suggestions, which saved 31 million man-hours and $44 million during World War II.[110]

The cooperative spirit was not total, particularly from the standpoint of strikes taken during wartime. In February 1943 organized labor complained to President Roosevelt that the cost of living during wartime had increased far beyond wage increases permitted by the government under the 1942 "Little Steel Formula."[111] The United Mine Workers conducted a series of strikes to obtain wage increases of $2 a day in 1943. These actions resulted in President Roosevelt seizing the mines, but eventually a compromise wage settlement was obtained.

The public viewed these and other strikes with anger and alarm, considering them violations of the no-strike pledge announced by organized labor in 1941. Negative public sentiment increased when labor strikes continued and, after 1942, increased every year of the war. The number of employee days lost to strikes was estimated to be the equivalent of no more than 1 day per year per worker for the 4 war years.[112] Yet the mere act of participating in a strike was viewed by some as unpatriotic.

Labor's collective bargaining concerns shifted at the end of the war to the issues of full employment and further wage increases in order to sustain national purchasing power and thereby create an expanding market for industrial goods. Labor, remembering the reconversion period of World War I, was also concerned about employer policies aimed at restricting union growth and wage gains.

Unions backed their postwar concerns with strikes. "During no period in the history of the United States did the scope and intensity of labor-management conflicts match those recorded in the year following VJ Day, August 14, 1945."[113] In this 1-year period, over 4,600 strikes, involving 5 million workers and resulting in almost 120 million man-days of idleness, affected almost every major industry. They were basically nonviolent, representing essentially economic tests of strength and endurance. Generally, both labor and management wanted to be free to resolve their differences at the bargaining table without the government interference and wage restrictions that were present during World War II.

Developments in Organized Labor Since World War II

Three major developments have occurred in organized labor since World War II: increased concern over new collective bargaining issues, organizing drives aimed at white-collar and public-sector employees, and the merger of the AFL and CIO.

New Collective Bargaining Issues The return to peacetime after World War II and, particularly, the Korean War saw increased efforts to extend the provisions of the labor agreement to include all aspects of the collective bargaining relationship. In the late 1950s and early 1960s, the relative scarcity of jobs coincided with the need for price stability to ease the deficit in international payments.

Unions directed their collective bargaining efforts toward guaranteeing members job security in the face of possible technological advances, and wages that would compensate for inflation. Organized labor's response toward technological change (discussed in more detail in Chapter 12) brought notable results during this period, including the Automation Fund Agreement between Armour and Company and the Packinghouse Workers and Meat Cutters' unions (1959), the Mechanization and Modernization Agreement in the Pacific Coast longshore industry (1960), and the Long-Range Sharing Plan negotiated between Kaiser Steel and the United Steelworkers (1962).

Employee benefits represented a second new bargaining area. Before World War II, labor cost was overwhelmingly straight-time pay for time actually worked.[114] Subsequent bargaining efforts by labor unions (and personnel policies of nonunion firms) have resulted in a substantial increase in employee benefits (pensions, insurance plans, and so forth), which are currently estimated at 38 percent of payroll costs.[115]

The trend in multiyear labor agreements after World War II put pressure on union leaders to safeguard wage increases against the possibilities of inflation. In 1948 General Motors and the United Auto Workers negotiated a long-term agreement with a cost-of-living provision that adjusted wages for inflationary changes during the life of the contract. This contract provision spread to other labor-management negotiations. In 1952 almost 3 million workers (approximately 20 percent of the employees covered by labor agreements) had cost-of-living provisions in their contracts.[116]

Recent competition from foreign companies and nonunion organizations in the United States has resulted in **concession bargaining,** in which management seeks to obtain from the union work-rule modifications and flexible/reduced wages. Work-rule modifications include scheduling changes, fewer rest breaks, and combining job classifications to give management more flexibility in employee work assignments.

Wage concessions represent the most significant organized labor development since World War II. Audrey Freeman of the Conference Board notes that, "wages, even under union bargaining pressures, are far more responsive to economic conditions at the industry and firm level and even the product level. . . ."[117] Examples of wage flexibility include:

- "Two-tiered wage plans," where employees hired after the negotiated labor agreement have a lower hourly pay rate than their counterparts.
- "Lump sum" wage increases directly associated with a firm's economic performance for a given time period. This wage payment does not continue, as the employee's wage rate remains the same after the bonus is given.

Organization of White-Collar and Public-Sector Employees The second major development in organized labor since World War II involves the organization of different types of employees. More specifically, white-collar and public (government) employees (discussed in Chapters 14 and 15) have received increased attention from union organizers.

Merger of the AFL and CIO Perhaps the most dramatic postwar development in organized labor was the merger of the AFL and CIO. The intense rivalry between the AFL and CIO did not end after World War II. However, the presence of three influences during the 1950s resulted in the eventual merger of these organizations in 1955.[118]

First was the change in the presidents of the AFL and CIO. Phillip Murray became president of the CIO when Lewis resigned in 1940, and continued the verbal feud against the AFL and its president, William Green. In November 1952, however, both Green and Murray died. Their successors (Walter Reuther of the CIO and George Meany of the AFL) had no particular fondness for each other; but unlike Green and Murray, they had not previously gone on record against each other. Therefore, a merger could occur without either president losing face.

Another influence contributing to the AFL-CIO merger was the recognized ineffectiveness of union raiding. The two labor organizations investigated employee representation elections in which the AFL tried to organize CIO employees, and vice versa. During a 2-year period (1951–1952), 1,245 such elections involved some 366,740 employees, with only 62,000 employees changing union affiliation. This figure overestimates the number affected, because it does not consider the offsetting nature of elections. An AFL union could organize a CIO factory of 1,000 employees only to have a CIO union organize an AFL factory of 1,000 employees—the net change would be zero. In fact, the extensive raiding during 1951 and 1952 resulted in a net gain for the AFL of only 8,000 members, or only 2 percent of the total number of employees involved.[119]

Both the AFL and the CIO finally realized that organized labor would benefit if the energies devoted to raiding each other were spent on organizing nonunion employees. Accordingly, many of the AFL and the CIO unions signed a no-raiding agreement in 1954. Instead of concentrating on differences emphasized in raiding activities, the two major federations could now look at similar goals that might be more easily attained by a merger.

One similar goal was the desire of both organizations to reward their political friends and punish their political enemies.[120] In many instances, the independent organizations failed to achieve this goal. For example, they were unable to defeat Senator Taft (one of the authors of the Taft-Hartley Act who was perceived as being antilabor) and failed to elect Adlai Stevenson (supporter of organized labor) over Dwight D. Eisenhower. Both organizations felt that a merger might increase their effectiveness in the political arena.

The AFL-CIO merger on December 12, 1955, involved 15,550,000 members, making the new organization the largest trade union center in the world. The president of the AFL-CIO, George Meany, believed this merger would lead to more employees becoming unionized and to a greater political influence for labor within the American two-party system.[121]

The merger resulted in the continued reduction of union raiding. It also reduced the influence of union locals within the national unions, since they could no longer threaten to affiliate with the rival national organization.[122] However, as will be further discussed in the next section, the AFL-CIO merger has not resulted in a tremendous increase in union membership or political influence. It did reduce the former divisiveness within organized labor, but it cannot be concluded that the merger was a significant impetus for growth and change.

Aspects of Organized Labor Unchanged Since World War II

Organized labor as it existed at the end of World War II compared to its present state appears to have more similarities than differences:[123]

- Exclusive representation, in which one union is given a job territory selected by a majority of employees who vote.
- Collective bargaining agreements that embody a sharp distinction between negotiation and interpretation of contract provisions. Once the contract is negotiated, the no-strike, no-lockout, and grievance procedures assure that the parties will use an arbitrator instead of job action to resolve any disputes over the labor agreement's meaning.
- The government's role has been basically passive in industrial relations, with most of its attention focused on procedural aspects of the process.

Three major labor relations similarities from World War II to the present are organized labor's political ineffectiveness, difficulty in achieving consensus among unions and union members, and emphasis on short-run bargaining goals.

1. Limited Effectiveness in Political Efforts Organized labor has remained a minority movement since World War II, and union membership has never exceeded 28 percent of eligible workers. It has seldom if ever mobilized its members into a unified public voice. Union influence in American politics has unfortunately received little systematic empirical research,[124] although some observations can be made from available non-quantitative accounts.

Since World War II, the relationship between organized labor and the Democratic and Republican political parties has been largely unpredictable.[125] In 1976 organized labor helped President Carter win key political victories in New York and Ohio. However, subsequent disappointment with the Carter administration translated into insufficient union votes in Carter's reelection bid against President Reagan in 1980.

Determined to bolster the AFL-CIO's political influence, Lane Kirkland, who became president of the AFL-CIO after George Meany's death in 1980, endorsed Walter Mondale *before* the Democratic primaries and convention of 1984. This unprecedented event was dramatized by the fact that Mondale's stance on many labor issues was very similar to that expressed by four other Democratic candidates. Yet Kirkland felt a major shift in the AFL-CIO's previous political involvement was needed to stop Ronald Reagan, who, Kirkland maintained, "sold out his talents many years ago to the forces of greed and privilege in our society."[126]

The AFL-CIO's efforts were not greatly rewarded; 45 percent of union households voted against Mondale. Some serious lessons were learned as the AFL-CIO leadership realized that many of the rank and file were not reached in the election campaign. Also, future presidential candidates might not regard a union endorsement as being a strong plus.

Organized labor appeared even more unsuccessful in the 1988 presidential campaign between George Bush and Michael Dukakis. Its lack of political unity and concentrated influence was illustrated in the Iowa primary, where many Democratic candidates received fragmented support. There was a record number of union delegates at the Democratic presidential convention; however, some of these delegates angrily felt that Dukakis ignored unions in public while privately sending urgent appeals for labor's help.

Lack of enthusiasm, even disunity characterized labor's role in post-convention proceedings as well. The Teamsters, who last endorsed a Democratic presidential candidate (Hubert Humphrey) in 1968, endorsed George Bush; yet the National Education Association endorsed Dukakis. The AFL-CIO mounted a major literature distribution drive extolling Dukakis's presidential qualifications some 4 days before the election. Many union leaders felt that union members were more enthusiastic for Dukakis than they had been for Mondale in 1984, and that they would vote for the Democratic presidential candidate if they went to the polls. Concentrated last-minute efforts were placed in key states (California, Illinois, New York, Ohio, Pennsylvania, and Texas) that organized labor felt could elect Dukakis.

Dukakis and organized labor lost these states and the election. AFL-CIO president Lane Kirkland sent Bush a congratulatory telegram saying the AFL-CIO "stands ready to assist you in constructive efforts to build a better nation and better lives for all Americans."[127]

There are two general barriers to organized labor's political efforts. First, elected candidates must consider a wide range of programs, some of which might ignore or even contradict union goals. Active political support does not ensure complete cooperation from the elected government official. Perhaps the most dramatic example of this barrier is found with the Professional Air Traffic Controllers Organization (PATCO), whose president endorsed Reagan in the 1980 election, believing that Carter was not sympathetic to union members' concerns. Reagan informed the PATCO president that he would devote attention to the air controllers.

A subsequent nationwide strike by air traffic controllers prompted his administration to fire nearly 12,000 controllers and decertify PATCO.

Second, union voters are concerned about more issues than those pertaining to organized labor. Labor's political strength depends on persuading its members that its self-interest is at stake and that they should act to defend it.[128] However, union members have preferences that extend beyond the work situation. Even former AFL-CIO president George Meany viewed one such issue, support of the Vietnam War, as being significant enough to withhold political support of the Democratic presidential candidate (George McGovern) in 1972. It would be difficult to predict whether a union member who was strongly against abortion would vote for a pro-labor political candidate in favor of abortion. Additional problems in mobilizing political support are discussed in the following second similarity.

2. Difficulty in Achieving Consensus among Unions and among Members Understandably, agreement among the diverse national unions within the AFL-CIO federation and members within national and local unions is rare. This problem occurs in any large organization, particularly one that grants a large amount of autonomy to its members. The AFL-CIO is always subject to national unions withdrawing from it. The federation also realizes that many national unions can get along quite well without its support. For example, the expulsion of the Teamsters and the United Auto Workers from the federation did not hinder these organizations' ability to increase their membership, grow in influence, and engage in collective bargaining. (Both the Teamsters and the UAW have since returned to the AFL-CIO.)

Lack of consensus is also found at the local union level, especially when younger employees become members. Most labor unions have a long tradition of struggle and sacrifice; their leaders have risked physical hardships merely to gain employer recognition of their union. However, many of the younger members are now asking the leaders, "What have you done for me lately?"

3. Pursuit of Short-Range Material Goals Instead of Long-Range Reform The Knights of Labor appeared to teach organized labor a permanent lesson—that goals should relate to members' needs instead of being abstract attempts to change the existing societal system. The period since World War II has witnessed tremendous economic growth and technological change; therefore, union leaders believe these issues deserve more attention than other societal concerns.

Labor's priorities have been often challenged by members of the academic and intellectual community, who claim that labor should use its strength to press for progressive social change and legislation. Some hostility exists between organized labor and members of the intellectual community. Many intellectuals believe that the labor movement is "facing dynamic new challenges with old leaders and old ideas."[129] Many union leaders reply that intellectuals, in their work and in their surroundings, are out of touch with the everyday struggles faced by union members. Union leaders have also contended that the ivory tower views of academicians have been blurred by their stereotypic view of union members' behaviors and hopes, and that academicians need to "get their hands dirty" on the line so they will make a more accurate assessment of unionism.[130] Even when unions make bargaining concessions, as they sometimes might, due to recessionary economic conditions, the concessions are viewed as short-term and material—less wages in exchange for job security, for example.

Summary

In obtaining a contemporary perspective of organized labor, one must be aware of the evolution of labor-management relationships as well as of various labor organizations that have attempted to influence those relationships. Current labor organizations have learned important lessons from their historical counterparts. Criteria for success for comparing the effectiveness of various labor organizations are their structural/financial stability; ability to work within established political and economic systems; and supportive or disruptive features of the social environment such as mass media, legislation, and the ability of union leaders to identify and satisfy members' goals and interests. Organized labor did not exert much of an influence before 1869, although employees became increasingly concerned with working and market conditions associated with mass production. The active years of organized labor can be grouped into three time periods: 1869 to World War I, World War I to World War II, and World War II to the present.

Three major labor organizations developed in the period from 1869 to World War I: the Knights of Labor (KOL), the American Federation of Labor (AFL) under Gompers, and the Industrial Workers of the World (IWW). These organizations had different goals, strategies, and organizational characteristics, which in part furnished reasons for the demise of the KOL and IWW. The Haymarket Riot and the Homestead and Pullman strikes hurt organized labor although Gompers managed to derive some benefit from each of these events.

The period immediately following World War I saw limited growth in union membership. Factors contributing to this situation included several strategies used by employers to counter union organizing campaigns. Internal differences occurred within the AFL regarding the advantages of organizing the heretofore nonunion unskilled and semiskilled employees working in the nation's factories. This disagreement led to the formation of a rival union organization,the Congress of Industrial Organizations (CIO), whose major objective was to organize industrial employees. The CIO achieved substantial membership gains in the late 1930s and 1940s.

Three major developments have occurred in organized labor since World War II. There has been increased concern over new collective bargaining issues; organizing drives have been aimed at public and white-collar employees; and the AFL and CIO have merged. Although several influences prompted the AFL-CIO merger, the impact of this event on contemporary union-management relationships is difficult to assess. There appear to be more similarities than differences when the state of organized labor at the end of World War II is compared to its present state. Organized labor remains a minority, yet influential, movement in our society. It has continued to have a minimal effectiveness in the political community, possibly because of the difficulty of mobilizing younger union members. Also, the short-range, material collective bargaining goals are basically unchanged since World War II.

Key Terms

Haymarket Riot
American Federation of Labor (AFL)
Homestead Incident
Pullman Strike
Industrial Workers of the World (IWW)
American Plan
Employee Representation Plans
Congress of Industrial Organizations (CIO)
concession bargaining

Discussion Questions

1. "Strive for the better day" was stated by Gompers (AFL); however, the remark could have just as easily been stated by Powderly (KOL) or Haywood (IWW)—but with entirely different meanings. Explain.
2. Considering the criteria for labor organization strength mentioned on page 25, why did the AFL survive and the IWW fade into obscurity?
3. Briefly explain how the Haymarket, Homestead, and Pullman incidents helped as well as hurt the AFL.
4. Discuss the various employer tactics used to thwart union growth in the 1920s and 1930s.
5. Why was the CIO successful in organizing members in the late 1930s when it had the same "one big union" approach that proved unsuccessful for the KOL in the 1880s?
6. What were several reasons behind the merger of the AFL and the CIO? To what extent will these or other reasons continue this merger into the near future—say, the next 10 years?
7. Discuss two similarities of organized labor as it existed at the end of World War II and as it does in the present. Speculate as to how these similarities might be modified in the near future.

References

1. Robert Ozanne, "Trends in American Labor History," *Labor History* (Fall 1980), p. 521. See also Barry Goldberg, "A New Look at Labor History," *Social Policy* 12 (Winter 1982), pp. 54–63; and Robert H. Zieger, "Industrial Relations and Labor History in the Eighties," *Industrial Relations* 22 (Winter 1983), pp. 58–70.
2. Henry Pelling, *American Labor* (Chicago: University of Chicago Press, 1960), pp. 12–13.
3. Edward B. Mittelman, "Trade Unionism 1833–1839," in John R. Commons et al., eds. *History of Labour in the United States* (1918; reprint ed. New York: Augustus M. Kelly, Publishers, 1966), vol. 1, p. 430.
4. William C. Birdsall, "The Problems of Structure in the Knights of Labor," *Industrial and Labor Relations Review* 6 (July 1953), p. 546.
5. For a discussion of how the expansion of the markets affected unionization among the shoemakers, see John R. Commons, *Labor and Administration* (New York: Macmillan, 1913), pp. 210–264.
6. T. V. Powderly, *Thirty Years of Labor: 1859–1889* (Columbus, Ohio: Excelsior Publishing House, 1889), p. 21.
7. Ibid., pp. 58–59.
8. Ibid., p. 163.
9. Philip Taft, *Organized Labor in American History* (New York: Harper and Row, 1964), p. 90.
10. Gerald N. Grob, *Workers and Utopia* (Evanston, Ill.: Northwestern University Press, 1961), p. 35. Powderly was most concerned about the evils of drinking; for example, he spent almost 50 pages of his autobiography, *Thirty Years of Labor,* discussing this issue.
11. Birdsall, "The Problems of Structure," p. 533.
12. Melton Alonza McLaurin, *The Knights of Labor in the South* (Westport, Conn.: Greenwood Press, 1978), p. 39.
13. Joseph G. Rayback, *A History of American Labor* (New York: Macmillan, 1968), p. 174.
14. Joseph R. Buchanan, *The Story of a Labor Agitator* (1903: reprint ed. Westport, Conn.: Greenwood Press, 1970), pp. 318–323.
15. For details of these procedures, see Taft, *Organized Labor,* p. 91.
16. Powderly, *Thirty Years of Labor,* pp. 151–157.
17. It should be noted that local assemblies were somewhat responsible for this situation, as they contributed only $600 to the General Assembly's strike funds in 1885–1886 (McLaurin, *The Knights of Labor,* p. 54). For more details of KOL's strike activities see Norman J. Ware, *The Labor Movement in the United States, 1860–1895* (1929; reprint ed. Gloucester, Mass.: Peter Smith, 1959), pp. 117–154. It should be further noted that the Knights made more effective use of boycotts than any previous union. However, as was true with strikes, the boycott was instigated by the local assemblies and forced on the Knights' national leaders (Grob, *Workers and Utopia,* p. 61).

18. Donald L. Kemmerer and Edward D. Wickersham, "Reasons for the Growth of the Knights of Labor in 1885–1886," *Industrial and Labor Relations Review* 3 (January 1950), pp. 213–220.
19. Foster Rhea Dulles, *Labor in America: A History,* 3d ed. (New York: Thomas Y. Crowell, 1966), p. 127.
20. Ware, *The Labor Movement,* p. 96.
21. Dulles, *Labor in America,* p. 135.
22. Powderly, *Thirty Years of Labor,* p. 514. It should also be noted that Powderly believed Gompers misled employees by advocating the 8-hour workday without telling them that their wages would be proportionately reduced. Most workers thought they would receive 10 hours payment for 8 hours of work.
23. "A Hellish Deed!" *Chicago Tribune,* May 5, 1886, p. 1.
24. For additional details of the rigged nature of the trial, see Samuel Yellen, *American Labor Struggles* (1936; reprint ed. New York: Arno Press, 1969), pp. 60–65.
25. "A Hellish Deed!"
26. "Their Records," *Chicago Tribune,* May 5, 1886, p. 1. See also Paul Avrich, *The Haymarket Tragedy* (New Jersey: Princeton University Press, 1984).
27. Sidney Lens, *The Labor Wars: From the Molly Maguires to the Sitdowns* (Garden City, N.Y.: Doubleday, 1973), p. 67.
28. The origination of the AFL was changed to 1881 in 1889 to include activities under the Federation of Organized Trades and Labor Unions. At least one historian has claimed that the revised date is regrettable since the parent organization (Federation of Organized Trades and Labor Unions) had little similarity to the AFL in terms of effective organization and broad-based support (Ware, *The Labor Movement,* p. 251). See also Glen A. Gildemeister, "The Founding of the American Federation of Labor," *Labor History* 22 (Spring 1981); and Harold C. Livesay, *Samuel Gompers and Organized Labor in America* (Boston: Little, Brown and Company, 1978), pp. 75–86.
29. Samuel Gompers, *Seventy Years of Life and Labor* (New York: E. P. Dutton, 1925), p. 266.
30. Ware, *The Labor Movement,* pp. 70–71.
31. Norman J. Ware, *Labor in Modern Industrial Society* (1935; reprint ed. New York: Russell & Russell, 1968), p. 262.
32. Dulles, *Labor in America,* p. 155.
33. Gompers, *Seventy Years of Life and Labor,* p. 245.
34. Samuel Gompers, *Labor and the Employer* (1920; reprint ed. New York: Arno Press, 1971), pp. 33–34.
35. Stuart Bruce Kaufman, *Samuel Gompers and the Origins of the American Federation of Labor: 1848–1896* (Westport, Conn.: Greenwood Press, 1973), p. 173. For details of this relationship, see Gompers, *Seventy Years of Life and Labor,* pp. 381–427.
36. Louis Reed, *The Labor Philosophy of Samuel Gompers* (1930; reprint ed. Port Washington, N.Y.: Kennikat Press, 1966), p. 20. See also an editorial by Gompers in the *American Federationist,* June 1924, p. 481.
37. Gompers, *Seventy Years of Life and Labor,* pp. 286–287, 381–427.
38. Alice Kessler-Harris, "Trade Unions Mirror Society in Conflict between Collectivism and Individualism," *Monthly Labor Review* 110 (August 1987), p. 33.
39. Gompers, *Labor and the Employer,* p. 202.
40. Marc Karson, *American Labor Unions and Politics: 1900–1918* (Carbondale, Ill.: Southern Illinois University Press, 1968), p. 29.
41. Reed, *The Labor Philosophy of Samuel Gompers,* pp. 106–110.
42. Milton Derber, *The American Idea of Industrial Democracy: 1865–1965* (Urbana: University of Illinois Press, 1970), p. 117.
43. Gompers, *Seventy Years of Life and Labor,* p. 342. For additional details regarding early AFL organizing see Philip Taft, *The AF of L in the Time of Gompers* (1957; reprint ed. New York: Octagon Books, 1970), pp. 95–122.
44. Dulles, *Labor in America,* pp. 163–164.
45. Andrew Carnegie, "An Employer's View of the Labor Question," in *Labor: Its Rights and Wrongs* (1886; reprint ed. Westport, Conn.: Hyperion Press, 1975), pp. 91, 95.
46. Yellen, *American Labor Struggles,* p. 81.
47. For details of the wage package, see Ibid., pp. 77–80. See also E. W. Bemis, "The Homestead Strike," *Journal of Political Economy* 2 (1894), pp. 369–396; and Linda Schneider, "The Citizen Striker: Workers' Ideology in the Homestead Strike of 1892," *Labor History* 23 (Winter 1982), pp. 47–66.
48. "Surrounded by Pickets," *New York Times,* July 4, 1892, p. 1.
49. "Mob Law at Homestead," *New York Times,* July 7, 1892, p. 1.
50. "Leader O'Donnell Is Glad," *New York Times,* July 12, 1892, p. 2; "Bayonet Rule in Force," *New York Times,* July 13, 1892, p. 1.
51. Lens, *The Labor Wars,* p. 77.
52. "A Talk with Gompers," *New York Times,* July 7, 1892, p. 2; and "Provoked by Carnegie," *New York Times,* July 7, 1892, pp. 2, 5.
53. Taft, *AF of L in the Time of Gompers,* p. 136.
54. "Arbitrate the Homestead Strike," *Chicago Tribune,* July 8, 1892, p. 4. See also "The Origin of the Trouble," *New York Times,* July 8, 1892, p. 2.
55. Yellen, *American Labor Struggles,* p. 3.
56. Lens, *The Labor Wars,* p. 81. See also Susan Kay Morrison's unpublished paper, "Eugene V. Debs: His Ride on the Pullman," 1981.
57. For additional details about the town, see Almont Lindsay, *The Pullman Strike* (Chicago: University of Chicago Press, 1967), pp. 38–60.
58. For more details regarding ARU's organization, see Philip S. Foner, *History of the Labor Movement in the United States,* vol. II (New York: International Publishers, 1955), p. 256.
59. Lindsay, *The Pullman Strike,* p. 124.
60. Ibid., p. 215.
61. Gompers, *Seventy Years of Life and Labor,* p. 403.
62. *Proceedings of the First Convention of the Industrial Workers of the World* (New York: Labor News Company, 1905), p. 1.
63. Ibid., p. 143.
64. Bill Haywood, *Bill Haywood's Book: The Autobiography of William D. Haywood* (New York: International Publishers, 1929), p. 73.
65. Melvyn Dubofsky, *We Shall Be All: A History of the Industrial Workers of the World* (Chicago: Quadrangle Books, 1969), p. 481.
66. Haywood, *Bill Haywood's Book,* p. 181.
67. For additional details pertaining to these differences, see Dubofsky, *We Shall Be All,* pp. 105–119; and Joseph Robert Conlin, *Bread and Roses Too* (Westport, Conn.: Greenwood Publishing, 1969), pp. 97–117; and Lens, *The Labor Wars,* pp. 154–155.
68. David J. Saposs, *Left-Wing Unionism* (1926: reprint ed. New York: Russell & Russell, 1967), p. 148.
69. Louis Adamic, *Dynamite: The Story of Class Violence in America* (1934; reprint ed. Gloucester, Mass.: Peter Smith, 1963), p. 174.
70. Robert E. Ficken, "The Wobbly Horrors, Pacific Northwest Lumbermen, and the Industrial Workers of the World, 1917–1918," *Labor History* 24 (Summer 1983), p. 329.
71. Conlin, *Bread and Roses Too,* pp. 97–117. See also Fred Thompson, *The IWW: Its First Fifty Years* (Chicago: Industrial Workers of the World, 1955), pp. 80–87.
72. Adamic, *Dynamite,* pp. 163–164.

73. Conlin, *Bread and Roses Too,* p. 96.
74. Philip S. Foner, ed., *Fellow Workers and Friends: I.W.W. Free Speech Fights as Told by Participants* (Westport, Conn.: Greenwood Press, 1981), p. 15.
75. Foner, *History of the Labor Movement,* vol. III, p. 465.
76. Conlin, *Bread and Roses Too,* p. 68.
77. For additional details, see Frank L. Grubbs, Jr., *The Struggle for Labor Loyalty: Gompers, the AFL, and the Pacifists, 1917–1920* (Durham, N.C.: Duke University Press, 1968).
78. James O. Morris, *Conflict within the AFL: A Study of Craft versus Industrial Unionism, 1901–1938* (1958; reprint ed. Westport, Conn.: Greenwood Press, 1974), pp. 9–10.
79. Taft, *Organized Labor,* pp. 355–358; and Francis Fox Piven and Richard A. Cloward, *Poor People's Movements* (New York: Pantheon Books, 1977), p. 104. For details of this strike, see Lens, *The Labor Wars,* pp. 196–219.
80. Frank Stricker, "Affluence for Whom? Another Look at Prosperity and the Working Classes in the 1920s," *Labor History* 24 (Winter 1983), pp. 5–34.
81. Lens, *The Labor Wars,* pp. 222, 296, 312.
82. Derber, *The American Idea,* p. 246. For an application of these reasons to a specific industrial situation during this time period, see Stephen L. Shapiro, "The Growth of the Cotton Textile Industry in South Carolina: 1919–1930" (Ph.D. diss., University of South Carolina, 1971), pp. 168–171.
83. For additional details regarding this tactic, see Clinch Calkins, *Spy Overhead: The Story of Industrial Espionage* (1937; reprint ed. New York: Arno Press, 1971).
84. Violence was limited neither to this time period nor to the employer. One of the more publicized episodes of employer violence was the Ludlow Massacre of 1914. The mining camps in Colorado were involved in a strike for union recognition when, on April 20, militiamen opened fire on a tent colony, killing two strikers and one boy. They then set fire to the tents, killing two women and eleven children. For more details of this event, see Leon Stein, ed., *Massacre at Ludlow: Four Reports* (reprint ed.; New York: Arno Press, 1971). Perhaps one of the more vivid examples of union violence occurred in Herrin, Illinois (1922), where miners tortured and killed at least 26 management officials and strikebreakers. For details of this episode, see Saul Alinsky, *John L. Lewis: An Unauthorized Biography* (New York: Vintage Books, 1970), pp. 43–50.
85. Richard C. Wilcock, "Industrial Management's Policies toward Unionism," in Milton Derber and Edwin Young, eds., *Labor and the New Deal* (Madison: University of Wisconsin Press, 1957), p. 293.
86. For a case study of paternalism, see "Welfare Work in Company Towns," *Monthly Labor Review* 25 (August 1927), pp. 314–321. For a more thorough discussion of employer counteractions during this time period, see Larry J. Griffin, Michael E. Wallace, and Beth A. Rubin, "Capitalist Resistance to the Organization of Labor Before the New Deal: Why? How? Success?" *American Sociological Review* (April 1986), pp. 147–67.
87. Derber, *The American Idea,* pp. 220–221; Morris, *Conflict within the AFL,* pp. 40–41. For more details on ERPs, see Ware, *Labor in Modern Industrial Society,* pp. 414–435. For a contemporary assessment of the problems and prospects facing the single-firm, independent union, see Arthur B. Shostak, *America's Forgotten Labor Organization* (Princeton: Industrial Relations Section, Department of Economics, Princeton University, 1962).
88. Dulles, *Labor in America,* p. 245.
89. This example was drawn from a more detailed account of racketeering during this period found in Sidney Lens, *Left, Right, and Center: Conflicting Forces in American Labor* (Hinsdale, Ill.: Henry Regnery, 1949), pp. 86–108.
90. David J. McDonald, *Union Man* (New York: E. P. Dutton, 1969), p. 185. See also Max Gordan, "The Communists and the Drive to Organize Steel, 1936," *Labor History* 23 (Spring 1982), pp. 226–245. For further historical insights into the relationship between organized labor and communism, see Harvey A. Levenstein, *Communism, Anticommunism and the CIO* (Westport, Conn.: Greenwood Press, 1981).
91. James O. Morris, "The AFL in the 1920s: A Strategy of Defense," *Industrial and Labor Relations Review* 11 (July 1958), pp. 572–590
92. See, for example, "William Green: Guardian of the Middle Years," *American Federationist* 88 (February 1981), pp. 24–25.
93. Bruce Minton and John Stuart, *Men Who Lead Labor* (New York: Modern Age Books, 1937), pp. 14–15.
94. Morris, *Conflict within the AFL,* p. 216.
95. For additional details pertaining to the background of this historic convention, see Herbert Harris, *Labor's Civil War* (1940; reprint ed. New York: Greenwood Press, 1969), pp. 22–60.
96. Lens, *The Labor Wars,* p. 284.
97. Cecil Carnes, *John L. Lewis: Leader of Labor* (New York: Robert Speller Publishing, 1936), p. 299.
98. David Dubinsky and A. H. Raskin, *David Dubinsky: A Life with Labor* (New York: Simon and Schuster, 1977), p. 226.
99. The seven unions were the United Mine Workers; the Amalgamated Clothing Workers; the International Ladies Garment Workers Union; United Hatters; Cap and Millinery Workers; Oil Field, Gas Well and Refinery Workers; and the International Union of Mine, Mill, and Smelter Workers.
100. Benjamin Stolberg, *The Story of the CIO* (1938; reprint ed. New York: Arno Press, 1971), p. 28.
101. Milton Derber, "Growth and Expansion," in Derber and Young, *Labor and the New Deal,* p. 13.
102. See, for example, John Hutchinson, "John L. Lewis: To the Presidency of the UMWA," *Labor History* 19 (Spring 1978), pp. 185–203.
103. James Arthur Wechsler, *Labor Baron: A Portrait of John L. Lewis* (New York: William Morrow, 1944), p. 71.
104. Thomas Gobel, "Becoming American: Ethnic Workers and the Rise of the CIO," *Labor History* 29 (Spring 1988), p. 174.
105. S. J. Woolf, "John L. Lewis and His Plan," in Melvyn Dubofsky, ed., *American Labor since the New Deal* (Chicago: Quadrangle Books, 1971), pp. 110–111.
106. Lens, *The Labor Wars,* p. 295.
107. Sidney Fine, *Sit-Down: The General Motors Strike of 1936–1937* (Ann Arbor: The University of Michigan Press, 1969), pp. 156–177. For another perspective of the sitdown strike, see Daniel Nelson, "Origins of the Sit-Down Era: Worker Militancy and Innovation in the Rubber Industry, 1934–38," *Labor History* 23 (Winter 1982), pp. 198–225.
108. James R. Hoffa and Oscar Fraley, *Hoffa: The Real Story* (New York: Stein and Day Publishers, 1975), p. 65.
109. For a detailed account of the AFL-CIO rivalries in several industries see Walter Galenson, *The CIO Challenge to the AFL* (Cambridge, Mass.: Harvard University Press, 1960).
110. Richard B. Morris, ed., *The U.S. Department of Labor Bicentennial History of the American Worker* (Washington, D.C.: U.S. Government Printing Office, 1976), p. 236.
111. For details of this formula and the extent that cost of living

estimates exceeded this formula see Taft, *Organized Labor in American History,* pp. 549–553 and 557–559.
112. Dulles, *Labor in America: A History,* p. 334.
113. Arthur F. McClure, *The Truman Administration and the Problems of Postwar Labor, 1945–1948* (Cranburry, N.J.: Associated University Presses, 1969), p. 45.
114. George H. Hildebrand, *American Unionism: An Historical and Analytical Survey* (Reading: Addison-Wesley, 1979), pp. 36–37.
115. *Policies and Practices, Personnel Management* 267 (January 1982), p. 188. Copyright 1982 by Bureau of National Affairs Inc., Washington, D.C.
116. Robert M. MacDonald, "Collective Bargaining in the Postwar Period," *Industrial and Labor Relations Review* 20 (July 1967), p. 568.
117. Audrey Freeman, "How the 1980's Have Changed Industrial Relations," *Monthly Labor Review* (May 1988), p. 37.
118. For a more detailed discussion of historical attempts at the merger of the AFL and CIO, see Joel Seidman, "Efforts toward Merger 1935–1955," *Industrial and Labor Relations Review* 9 (April 1956), pp. 353–370.
119. "Document: AFL-CIO No-Raiding Agreement," *Industrial and Labor Relations Review* 8 (October 1954), p. 103.
120. "A Short History of American Labor," *American Federationist* 88 (March 1981), p. 14.
121. George Meany, "Merger and the National Welfare," *Industrial and Labor Relations Review* 9 (April 1956), p. 349.
122. Richard A. Lester, *As Unions Mature* (Princeton, N.J.: Princeton University Press, 1958), p. 25.
123. John T. Dunlop, "Have the 1980s Changed Industrial Relations?" *Monthly Labor Review* 111 (May 1988), pp. 29–33.
124. For problems and prospects associated with this research see Marick F. Masters and John Thomas Delaney, "Union Political Activities: A Review of the Empirical Literature," *Industrial and Labor Relations Review* 40 (April 1987), pp. 336–353.
125. Max M. Kempelman, "Labor in Politics," in George W. Brooks, et al., eds., *Interpreting the Labor Movement* (Ann Arbor, Mich.: Industrial Relations Research Association, 1967), p. 188; and Dick Bruner, "Labor Should Get Out of Politics," in Charles M. Rehmus and Doris B. McLaughlin, eds., *Labor and American Politics: A Book of Readings* (Ann Arbor: University of Michigan Press, 1967), p. 430. For an assessment of organized labor's limited effectiveness in the political arena since the 1930s, see Piven and Cloward, *Poor People's Movements,* pp. 161–172; Graham K. Wilson, *Unions in American National Politics* (New York: St. Martin's Press, 1979), p. 36; David Montgomery, *Workers' Control in America: Studies in the History of Work, Technology, and Labor Struggles* (New York: Cambridge University Press, 1979), p. 170; David Brody, *Workers in Industrial America* (New York: Oxford University Press, 1980), p. 243; and Marick F. Masters and John Thomas Delaney, "The AFL-CIO's Political Record, 1974–1980," in Barbara D. Dennis, ed.; *Proceedings of the 34th Annual Meeting of The Industrial Relations Research Association* (Madison, Wisconsin: Industrial Relations Research Association, 1982), pp. 351–359.
126. "Kirkland Hopeful on Mondale Prospects Despite the Polls," Bureau of National Affairs Inc., *Daily Labor Report,* October 26, 1984, p. 2.
127. "Bush Victory Came Despite Massive AFL-CIO Effort for Governor Dukakis," Bureau of National Affairs Inc., *Daily Labor Report,* no. 218 (November 10, 1988), p. A-9.
128. Patricia Cayo Sexton and Brendan Sexton, *Blue Collars and Hard Hats: The Working Class and the Nature of American Politics* (New York: Random House, 1971), p. 307. See also David Halle, *America's Working Man* (Chicago: University of Chicago Press, 1984), pp. 190–191.
129. A. H. Raskin, "The Fat Cats of Labor," in David Boroff, ed., *The State of the Nation* (Englewood Cliffs, N.J.: Prentice-Hall, 1965), p. 50. For a further related discussion, see Harold L. Wilensky, *Intellectuals in Labor Unions* (Glencoe, Ill.: The Free Press, 1956).
130. Brendan Sexton, "The Working Class Experience," *American Economic Review* 62 (May 1972), p. 152.

CHAPTER 3

Legal Influences

"Born in a period of extreme economic disruption, the National Labor Relations Act brought the rule of law to American labor relations. It established a legal framework for labor relations that for 50 years has fostered industrial peace and has been a key factor in our country's immense economic growth.

More importantly, the Act has enriched our democracy by ensuring the right of self-determination in the workplace for employees."

Rosemary M. Collyer, General Counsel of the National Labor Relations Board from 1984 to 1989, *NLRB: The First 50 Years*, Washington, D.C.: U.S. Government Printing Office, 1986, p. viii.

Labor relations law serves as the framework for most of our labor relations activities. This chapter establishes a foundation for such subjects as organizing unions, negotiating labor agreements, and assuring employee rights. Further, it is essential today not only to know the law but to understand and appreciate the interrelationships between the law and the labor relations process.

This chapter logically follows the one on historical development of unions in the United States because labor relations law and union development go hand in hand. Law as it pertains to labor is traced from the first major court case involving union activities through the development of common law and the use of antitrust legislation that inhibited the growth of unions to the laws that pertain to most private firms: the Norris–La Guardia, Wagner, Taft-Hartley, and Landrum-Griffin Acts. Since these acts cover the major portion of U.S. industries and businesses, a substantial amount of space is devoted to their content. The Railway Labor Act, which principally covers railroads and airlines, is also explained and assessed. A final section briefly considers several other laws that can affect the labor relations process.

Origin of Labor Relations Law

Labor relations law in the United States is derived from statutory law, judicial decisions and interpretations, constitutional rights, and administrative decisions by agencies of the executive branch. Likewise, at the state and local government levels, law is developed and established by analogous documents and actions.

Statutory law can be created and amended by legislative enactment at the federal, state, or local levels of government. Congress has enacted numerous labor relations laws in the interest of employees and employers, public welfare, and interstate commerce. Three major ones – the Norris–La Guardia Act, the National Labor Relations Act, as amended, and the Railway Labor Act – are discussed at length later in the chapter. State legislatures may pass laws and local municipalities pass ordinances to fill voids in the federal laws or to cover issues not covered by federal laws, such as the right of city employees to engage in collective bargaining.

The judicial branch of government, with its accompanying court system at the federal, state, and local levels, functions to determine a law's constitutionality and conformity to legal standards, to assess the accuracy of interpretations by administrative agencies, and to issue injunctions that restrict or require certain activities. In addition, the courts must decide issues not covered by laws and make rulings under the general guides of "equity." These decisions and rulings constitute *case*, or *common law*, which has developed over the years, setting precedents and providing guidance for future decisions.

One example of the common law doctrines that has created much controversy in recent years is the **employment at will** doctrine. This doctrine simply means that an employer may terminate an employee for any reason, good or bad. While the doctrine has been modified in many state courts, it remains intact in many others. (This doctrine is more thoroughly discussed in Chapter 10.)

Several provisions of the U.S. Constitution have been interpreted as applying to labor relations activities. For example, Article I, Section 8, which authorizes Congress to regulate commerce, has been used to determine the constitutionality of several statutory enactments. The First Amendment, which assures the rights of peaceful assembly and free speech, usually has been interpreted as allowing employees to form and join unions and has provided the justification for union picketing (to communicate information to possible union members and union supporters). The Fifth and Fourteenth Amendments contain due process provisions, and the Fourteenth Amendment provides equal protection under law. These amendments have been used for employment protection in discharge decisions, refusal-to-hire cases, and discrimination cases regarding equal employment opportunity where either state or federal employees are involved.

The executive branch includes the administrative agencies responsible for administration of applicable laws. These government agencies establish policies and make rules to guide the administration of these laws. They make decisions within the framework of the statutes or laws that are legal and binding, although they are subject to appeal to the courts. As long as the decisions are within the authority of the administrative agency and are accurate interpretations of its delegated authority, they have the same effect as law.

Some of the more important administrative agencies mentioned include:

- **National Labor Relations Board (NLRB):** Administers the National Labor Relations Act as amended by the Taft-Hartley and Landrum-Griffin acts, conducts union representation elections, and adjudicates unfair labor practice complaints.
- **Federal Mediation and Conciliation Service (FMCS):** Provides mediation services to unions and management in collective bargaining and assists these parties in selecting arbitrators in grievance administration.
- **U.S. Department of Labor (DOL):** Performs many employment-related services, such as research and data-collecting functions; administers federal wage and safety laws; and enforces federal contract compliance under equal employment opportunity requirements. In addition, its secretary serves as the president's cabinet member responsible for employment-related matters.
- **National Mediation Board:** Handles union representation issues under the Railway Labor Act, provides mediation services to parties in negotiations, assists in disputes over contract interpretation, and in cases involving emergency disputes proposes arbitration and certifies the dispute to the president as an emergency.
- **National Railroad Adjustment Board:** Hears and attempts to resolve railroad labor disputes growing out of grievances and interpretation or application of the labor agreements.
- **State and local administrative agencies:** Numerous agencies at the state and local levels of government are responsible for the enforcement and administration of state laws and local ordinances involving labor relations topics.

Early Legal Interpretations Involving Labor-Management Relationships (1806–1931)

As the previous chapter demonstrated, in earlier times labor unions in the United States had to struggle for their existence. With the absence of legislative direction, the judiciary system not only controlled the relationships between labor unions and employers but also played a key role in limiting the organization of unions for many years, especially from the early 1800s to the 1930s.

Criminal Conspiracy

The first major labor relations case in the United States, known as the "Cordwainers case," occurred in 1806, when a group of journeymen shoemakers in Philadelphia were indicted, convicted, and fined $8 each for forming an illegal criminal conspiracy. The shoemakers had joined together in an attempt to raise their wages and refused to work with nonmembers or at a wage rate less than they demanded. Twelve jurors (all businessmen) found the shoemakers guilty of forming an illegal coalition for the purpose of raising their own wages while injuring those who did not join the coalition.[1]

The prosecutor in the trial stated:

> Our position is that no man is at liberty to combine, conspire, confederate and unlawfully agree to regulate the whole body of workmen in the city. The defen-

> dants are not indicted for regulating their own individual wages but for undertaking by a combination, to regulate the price of labour of others as well as their own.
>
> It must be known to you, every society of people are affected by such confederacies; that are injurious to the public good and against the public interest.[2]

The application of the criminal conspiracy doctrine to attempts by employees to organize unions aroused much public protest, not only from employees but also from factory owners who feared the closing of their factories if the workers' feelings grew too strong. These feelings were undoubtedly considered in 1842 when the Supreme Judicial Court of Massachusetts *(Commonwealth* v. *Hunt)* set aside the conviction for criminal conspiracy of seven members of the Journeymen Bootmakers Society who refused to work in shops where nonmembers were employed at less than their scheduled rate of $2 per pair of boots. While not rejecting the criminal conspiracy doctrine, Justice Shaw cut the heart from it by insisting that the purpose of the concerted activity must be considered, not just the fact that the activity occurred. His decision stated that an association of workers could be established for "useful and honorable purposes" as well as for purposes of "oppression and injustice"; however, the means of achieving these purposes could also be legal or illegal. Therefore, to determine its legality, an investigation must be made of the objectives of the particular labor union involved and of the means used to achieve its objectives.[3]

Civil Conspiracy

The *Commonwealth* v. *Hunt* decision virtually ended the use of the criminal conspiracy doctrine in labor relations. However, the courts developed the civil conspiracy doctrine, which holds that a group involved in concerted activities can inflict harm on other parties even though it is pursuing a valid objective in its own interest.[4] In the *Vegelahn* v. *Guntner* case, an injunction was issued against a union that was picketing for higher wages and shorter hours. While the court agreed that the purposes were legitimate, it concluded that the picketing and a refusal to work would lead to more serious trouble, and employers could seek injunctive relief.[5]

Breach of Contract (Contractual Interference)

Breach of contract, a common-law rule, was used by employers in restricting union membership and union-organizing activities. For example, an employer would require its employees to sign a **yellow-dog contract**—an agreement stating that they would neither join a union nor assist in organizing a union. Since this contract would be a condition of continued employment, any violation would allow the company to discharge the employee. More importantly, if any union organizers who were not employees of the company, but of the national union, attempted to solicit union members among those who had signed yellow-dog contracts, they would be interfering with a legal contractual relationship between the employer and its employees. Thus, the employer could go to court and secure an injunction against the union organizers and any union-related activities. Union organizers who violated the court order then could be charged with contempt of court and possibly fined and imprisoned.[6]

Application of Antitrust Legislation to Labor Unions

In the late 1800s an attempt was made to guard against increasing business monopolies, concentration of ownership, and business combinations that eliminated competition. One such attempt was the passage of the Sherman Antitrust Act of 1890, whose coverage neither specified nor excluded labor unions. Section I of this act states that "every contract, combination in the form of trust or otherwise, or conspiracy, in restraint of trade or commerce among the several states . . . is hereby declared to be illegal."[7] Such wording made it debatable whether Congress had intended labor unions to be covered.

The answer was not given until 1908 in the landmark decision, *Loewe* v. *Lawlor* (better known as the *Danbury Hatters case*). The United Hatters of America, having organized 70 of 82 firms in the industry, wanted to organize Loewe and Company, a nonunion employer. They sought to have their union recognized and to have only union members employed (a closed shop). When the company refused, the union struck. However, strikers were replaced, and operations were continued. Recognizing the strike failure, the United Hatters organized a nationwide boycott assisted by the American Federation of Labor and directed toward all retailers, wholesalers, and customers. The boycott was successful; the employer thereupon went to court and eventually appealed to the Supreme Court. The high court ruled that unions were covered under the Sherman Act. The end result was that the union owed the company $250,000 (treble damages), and the membership was responsible for payment.[8]

Once the *Loewe* decision was publicized, organized labor concluded that it must seek changes in the act. An aggressive campaign led to the enactment of the Clayton Act of 1914. Included among its provisions were the following:

> [The] labor of a human being is not a commodity or article of commerce. Nothing contained in the antitrust laws shall be construed to forbid the existence and operation of labor [unions] . . . nor shall such organizations . . . be held or construed to be illegal combinations or conspiracies in restraint of trade.
>
> No restraining order or injunction shall be granted . . . in any case between an employer and employees . . . growing out of a dispute concerning terms or conditions of employment, unless necessary to prevent irreparable injury to property. . . .
>
> No such restraining order . . . shall prohibit any person or persons . . . from ceasing to perform work . . . recommending, advising, or persuading others by peaceful means so to do, . . . peacefully persuading any person to work or abstain from working, . . . peacefully assembling in a lawful manner, and for lawful purposes.[9]

When Samuel Gompers, president of the American Federation of Labor, read the provisions of the act, he proclaimed it U.S. labor's Magna Charta. Gompers's joy, however, was short-lived; a series of Supreme Court decisions in the 1920s left no doubt that the Clayton Act was not labor's Magna Charta. In fact, the Clayton Act hurt union growth and development more than it helped, because under the act employers could seek injunctions on their own, whereas only the U.S. district attorneys could seek injunctions under the Sherman Act.

The first major case occurred in 1921 and involved the printing press industry. The machinists union had been successful in organizing all of the four major manufacturers of printing presses except Duplex Printing Press. While the three unionized companies operated under an 8-hour day and union wage scale, Duplex continued a 10-hour day and paid below the union scale. Failing to unionize Duplex, the union organized a strike, which was also unsuccessful. Because Duplex was operating at a lower cost than the other companies and posed an economic threat to them, the machinists union formed a boycott, refusing to install or handle Duplex products and warning users against operating Duplex equipment. The company petitioned for an injunction under the Clayton Act. The case was appealed to the Supreme Court, which ruled that unions were not exempt from antitrust legislation when they departed from normal and legitimate union activities. Therefore, the Clayton Act restricted injunctions only when a boycott involved an employer and its own employees. Since many of the boycott activities were conducted by sympathetic union members, not employees of Duplex, the use of the injunction was legal.[10]

Another Supreme Court decision in the same year defined "peaceful picketing" as a single representative at each employer entrance announcing that a strike was occurring and trying to peacefully persuade employees and others to support the strike.[11] With only one person on the picket line, the unions would obviously be unable to demonstrate their strength and unity in the strike.

With injunctions easier to obtain, a series of devastating Supreme Court decisions, absence of favorable labor legislation, use of antiunion tactics such as "goon squads," blackmail, and blacklisting, and the U.S. economy beginning a period of economic prosperity in the 1920s, the labor movement entered a comparatively static period. Although the Railway Labor Act (covered later in this chapter) was passed in 1926, this was primarily a time of regrouping, self-analysis, and establishment of new strategies.

The Norris–La Guardia Act

In the early 1930s, with the beginning of the country's most severe economic depression, political pressure on Congress mounted, and there was general dissatisfaction with judicial restrictions in labor relations. In 1932 Congress passed the Norris–La Guardia Act (also called the Federal Anti-Injunction Act). Marking a change in U.S. policy in labor relations, the act allowed employees "full freedom of association, self-organization, and designation of representatives of (their) own choosing, negotiation of terms and conditions of . . . employment" and "freedom from employer interference, restraint, or coercion." Further, it recognized employees' right to freedom from employer interference in their efforts of "self-organization and other concerted activities for the purpose of collective bargaining or other mutual aid or protection."[12]

The act restricted the role of the federal courts in labor disputes. Foremost was the restriction of issuance of any injunction, temporary or permanent, in any case involving or growing out of a labor dispute,[13] except where the employer, in open courts and under cross-examination, could prove the following conditions:

1. Unlawful acts had been threatened or committed.
2. Substantial and irreparable injury to the employer's property would follow.

3. Greater injury would be inflicted upon the employer by denial of an injunction than upon the union by granting injunction.
4. The employer had no adequate remedy at law.
5. Public officers were unable or unwilling to furnish adequate protection.
6. The employer had made every effort to settle the dispute through collective bargaining (including mediation, voluntary arbitration, and so on) before going to court.

If an injunction was issued, it must be directed toward stopping specific acts; thereby the general, all-encompassing injunctions that had become customary were prohibited. In addition, individuals held in contempt of court (usually labor leaders who violated a court injunction) would be provided a trial by jury.

The Norris–La Guardia Act also declared that the yellow-dog contract was unenforceable in federal courts.[14] This provision allowed union organizers more freedom in contacting employees about joining unions with less fear of a breach of contract violation, a tactic that had been used successfully against them. However, many companies continued to discharge employees for union activities.

Although the passage of the Norris–La Guardia Act noted a change in U.S. policy in labor relations, the act did not establish an administrative agency to enforce this policy or the act's provisions. This meant that organized labor had to pursue enforcement through the judicial system, which had not been responsive to labor's interests and needs.

Historical Development of the National Labor Relations Act and Its Amendments

In addition to the Norris–La Guardia Act, 1932 witnessed a new president, Franklin Roosevelt, who was backed strongly by labor unions, and a new Congress receptive to labor legislation as a means of ending a long depression. One of the first acts of this new administration was to encourage Congress to pass the National Industrial Recovery Act—a law designed to stabilize economic activity by allowing businesses to form associations drawing up codes of fair competition to standardize marketing, pricing, financial, and other practices. Upon approval of the codes by the National Recovery Administration, firms could display the "Blue Eagle" symbol that supposedly signified compliance and identified firms from which customers should purchase their goods and services. Section 7 of the act required the codes to guarantee employees the right to unionize without employer interference, and a National Labor Board was later established to help settle disputes and to determine violations under Section 7.

Because the act did not require employers to deal with unions, and because the National Labor Board could not enforce its orders effectively, many employers chose to create their own company unions. Prompted by the board's failure, increasing employer resistance, and growing strike activity, in 1934 Congress issued a joint resolution calling for the president to establish a National Labor Relations Board to investigate violations under Section 7 and to hold elections to determine whether the employees would choose a union to represent them.[15] This board, created like its predecessor by executive order of the president, had trouble enforcing its orders and determining employee organizational units for conducting elections. Then, in 1935, the Supreme Court ruled the codes of fair competition unconstitutional, invalidating the National Labor Relations Board.

Senator Robert Wagner, chairman of the National Labor Relations Board and an active participant in labor law matters, in 1935 steered through Congress a separate labor relations law—the *Wagner Act,* or National Labor Relations Act (NLRA). It established a new national policy that encouraged collective bargaining, guaranteed certain employee rights, detailed specific employer unfair labor practices, and established the National Labor Relations Board to enforce its provisions. The board would adjudicate unfair labor practices and conduct representation elections (other provisions are covered later in the chapter).

For the next 2 years, significant employer resistance to the act mounted because most employers believed it would be ruled unconstitutional like the National Industrial Recovery Act.[16] However, in 1937 the Supreme Court decided five labor relations cases—the most publicized, *NLRB* v. *Jones & Laughlin Steel Corporation* [301 U.S. 1(1937)]—and declared the Wagner Act constitutional.

With Supreme Court recognition of the Wagner Act and the improvement of economic conditions in the United States, unions experienced tremendous growth and power.[17] In fact, for the next 10 years, union activities caused many to believe that the labor relations pendulum had swung too far toward unions. Examples that precipitated much public antagonism were strikes over union representation rights between CIO and AFL unions, boycotts that hurt innocent bystanders, union walkouts over bargaining issues, refusal to negotiate in good faith with employers, and pressure on job applicants to become members of unions before qualifying for employment.

As a reaction to organized labor's actions, in 1947 Congress amended the National Labor Relations Act by enacting the *Taft-Hartley Act,* or Labor Management Relations Act. Calling it a "slave labor act," labor groups immediately mounted a successful campaign to have President Truman veto the bill; however, Congress easily overrode Truman's veto. Regaining greater balance in labor relations legislation, the act reorganized the NLRB and included union unfair labor practices covering such topics as union membership, bargaining requirements, boycotts by unions not involved in the dispute, and strikes over work assignments.

In the late 1950s, a special Senate committee headed by John McClellan vigorously pursued the abuses of power and corruption of union leaders, particularly those of the Teamsters and specifically of Dave Beck and James Hoffa.[18] Exposing shocking examples of union corruption and abuses of power, Congress reacted in 1959 by passing the Landrum-Griffin Act, also called the Labor-Management Reporting and Disclosure Act. Its first six titles pertain mostly to union internal affairs and government (covered in Chapter 4), and Title VII further amends the National Labor Relations Act.

Since 1959, there have been two successful legislative attempts to enact major modifications in the NLRA. First, the NLRA was extended to cover the postal service in 1970 (see Chapter 15) and to the private health-care industry in 1974 (see Chapter 16). The most widely publicized unsuccessful attempt occurred in 1978 when a bitter battle for labor law reform was launched. The bill was designed to require representation elections within a month from the date the NLRB received the petition for an election. Also, it called for compensation for employees whose employer refused to bargain in good faith in initial negotiations and included double back pay for employees who were unfairly discharged by employers for union activities. Further, it authorized the withdrawal of federal government contracts from employers who continued to commit flagrant unfair labor practices. Strongly backed by the Carter administration and passed in the House by a strong majority, the bill met its death by a successful Senate filibuster. However, labor law reform remains at the top of organized labor's legislative agenda.

The National Labor Relations Act: The Wagner Act of 1935 as Amended by the Taft-Hartley Act in 1947 and the Landrum-Griffin Act in 1959

The National Labor Relations Act is discussed here primarily from a contemporary perspective. The origins of each specific provision are only briefly discussed where appropriate to avoid confusion.

Statement of Public Policy

The United States was in the midst of its most severe economic depression when the Wagner Act was passed. The act established a new U.S. labor relations policy of encouraging collective bargaining and gave some indication of the federal government's more active role in national economics. It recognized that employer denials of the employees' right to organize and employer refusal to accept collective bargaining had previously led to strikes and industrial conflict. It also acknowledged that inequality of bargaining power between employees and employers affected the flow of commerce and aggravated recurring economic depressions by depressing wages and purchasing power and thereby prevented the stability of wages and working conditions. Further, it recognized that protection by law of the right of employees to organize and bargain collectively would promote the flow of commerce, restore equality of bargaining power, and encourage friendly adjustment of industrial disputes.[19]

The Taft-Hartley amendments added that industrial strife could be minimized if employees and labor unions, as well as employers, recognized one another's rights and declared that no party had the right to engage in activities or practices that jeopardized the national health or safety.

Rights of Employees (Section 7)

Under Section 7 of the NLRA (see Exhibit 3.1) employees were assured certain rights: (1) to form and organize their own labor organizations, (2) to become members of labor unions or to refuse to join (unless there is a valid contractual requirement to join), (3) to bargain collectively through representatives of their own choosing, and (4) to engage in other concerted activities for the purpose of collective bargaining or other forms of mutual aid or protection, such as strikes, picketing, and boycotts.

Exhibit 3.1 **Rights of Employees**

Sec. 7. Employees shall have the right to self-organization, to form, join, or assist labor organizations, to bargain collectively through representatives of their own choosing, and to engage in other concerted activities for the purpose of collective bargaining or other mutual aid or protection, and shall also have the right to refrain from any or all of such activities except to the extent that such right may be affected by an agreement requiring membership in a labor organization as a condition of employment as authorized in section 8(a)(3).

Source: Labor-Management Relations Act, 1947, as amended.

These rights are not unlimited; they can be restricted. For example, the right to strike can be limited by a strike's objective, its timing, and the conduct of the strikers. If a strike's purpose is to achieve a contract provision forcing the employment of only union members, its purpose is illegal; therefore, the strike is illegal. If a strike occurs in violation of a no-strike provision in the contract, the timing of the strike is inappropriate, and all striking employees may be disciplined. Further, strikers do not have the right to threaten or engage in acts of violence. For example, neither sit-down strikes nor refusals to leave the plant are protected strike activities. Strikers also exceed their rights when they physically block persons from entering a struck plant or when threats of violence are made against workers not on strike. Picketing and boycott activities are likewise limited. (These activities are further explained in Chapter 7.)

Collective Bargaining and Representation of Employees

The NLRA specifies important elements of collective bargaining. (Because representational procedures and elections are nearly always prerequisites to collective bargaining, they are explained in detail in Chapter 5.) Collective bargaining requires both the employer and the representative of the employees to meet at reasonable times and confer in good faith with respect to wages, hours, and other terms and conditions of employment. While the act does not compel either party to agree to a proposal from the other party or to make a concession, it does require the good faith negotiation of an agreement. If an agreement is reached, it must be reduced to writing and executed in good faith.

Other procedural requirements cover those times when either party may desire to change an existing contract. First, the party requesting a change, usually the union, must notify the other party in writing 60 days before the expiration date of the existing agreement of a desire to change it. Upon receipt of the request, the other party, usually management, must offer to meet and negotiate a new contract. Within 30 days after notifying the other party, the initiating party must notify the Federal Mediation and Conciliation Service if no agreement has been reached on the proposed change. Both parties are required to continue to negotiate without a strike or lockout until 60 days after the first notice or until the contract expires, whichever is later. Only when the contract expires and other procedural obligations have been fulfilled is the union allowed to strike or the company to lockout.

Unfair Labor Practices

While unfair labor practices of employers were included in Section 8 of the Wagner Act of 1935 to protect employees from employer abuse, unfair labor practices of labor organizations were added in 1947 and 1959 for employer, employee, and union member protection.

Unfair Labor Practices: Employer First, the employer is forbidden to interfere with, restrain, or coerce employees in the exercise of the rights in Section 7. Violations include employer threats to fire workers if they join a union, threats to close the plant if the union is organized—especially when other plants owned by the employer are located in the same area—or questioning employees about their union activities. If such violation does occur, the employee or the union may file an unfair labor practice charge with the NLRB, which then initiates its enforcement procedure (covered later in the chapter). Employees are also protected in pursuing their joint working condition concerns even if they do not belong to a labor organization. [*8(a)(1)*]

The NLRB at first was excessively restrictive in its rulings on employer expressions about unionism and ruled that most employer speeches to employees about unionism were unlawful interference with union activities. However, in 1947 restrictions were eased. Employers were given the right to explain their labor policies, present the advantages and disadvantages of unions, and communicate orally and in writing their arguments and opinions as long as they contained no threats or promises of benefits.[20] (Current application and interpretation of this provision as it pertains to union election campaigns will be covered in Chapter 5.)

Attempting to dominate, interfering with the formation of, and financing and supporting a labor union are all prohibited employer activities. For instance, the existence of a **company union,** one which receives financial help from the company, is illegal. Nor are companies allowed to pressure employees into joining a particular union, to take an active part in organizing a union, to promote one union over a rival union during a representation election campaign, or to otherwise engage in "sweetheart" arrangements with union officials. [*8(a)(2)*]

Employer discrimination against employees in terms of hiring, tenure of employment, or terms and conditions of employment for the purpose of encouraging or discouraging union membership constitutes an unfair labor practice. However, if the labor agreement requires union membership as a condition of employment and the employee does not pay (or offer to pay) the required union initiation fees and membership dues in accordance with the agreement, the employee may be discharged (see Chapter 11). [*8(a)(3)*]

Another unfair labor practice pertains to discharge of or discrimination against an employee because he or she had filed charges or given testimony in an NLRB investigation, hearing, or court case under the act. Employers may not refuse reinstatement to, demote, or lay off employees because they have filed charges with the NLRB or testified at NLRB hearings. [*8(a)(4)*]

Employers may not refuse to bargain in good faith about wages, hours, and terms and conditions of employment with the representative chosen by the employees. Employer obligations include the duty to supply relevant economic information, to refrain from unilateral action, and to negotiate with employees after purchasing a unionized plant. (For a more thorough discussion, see Chapter 6.) Refusing to meet with the union for purposes of negotiation, refusing a union request for cost data concerning an insurance plan, and announcing a wage increase without consulting the union are unfair labor practices. [*8(a)(5)*]

Unfair Labor Practices: Labor Union Unfair labor practices committed by unions were included in both major amendments in 1947 [Section 8(b)] and 1959. The first forbids a union or its agents to restrain or coerce employees in the exercise of their rights guaranteed under the act. Examples include mass picketing that prevents entrance to the plant by nonstriking employees, threats to employees for not supporting the union, refusal to process a grievance because the employee has criticized the union officers, and refusal to refer an employee to a job based on such considerations as race or lack of union activities. [*8(b)(1)*]

A second union unfair labor practice pertains to actions that cause an employer to discriminate against an employee with regard to wages, hours, and conditions of employment or for the purpose of encouraging or discouraging union membership. For example, the company may be forced to assign better jobs to union members. Or, when two unions compete to represent the same workers, the company may be forced to side with the more aggressive union by assigning better jobs to its members. Such prohibited practices include causing an employer to discharge employees who circulate a petition challenging a union practice or who make speeches against a contract proposal. [*8(b)(2)*]

A third provision imposes on unions the same duty as employers to bargain in good faith. Refusing to negotiate with the employer's attorney, refusing to process a grievance of a bargaining unit employee, and striking a company to compel it to leave a multi-employer bargaining unit are some activities illegal under the amended act. [*8(b)(3)*]

The fourth unfair labor practice includes four prohibited activities. The union may not:

- Force an employer or self-employed person into entering into a **hot-cargo agreement** (a signed agreement stating that union members will not be required to handle "hot cargo"—goods made by nonunion labor and workers at a struck plant except in the garment industry).
- Restrict any person from using, selling, handling, and transporting goods of a producer, processor, or manufacturer that is directly involved in a labor dispute (secondary boycott—covered in more detail in Chapter 7).
- Force any employer to recognize or bargain with a particular labor organization if another labor organization has already been certified by the NLRB.
- Cause any employer to assign certain work to employees in a particular labor union, trade, or craft rather than another. [*8(b)(4)*]

Unions are prohibited from charging excessive or discriminatory membership fees. Any discrepancy would be investigated by the NLRB in accordance with the practices and customs of other unions in the particular industry and wages paid to the affected employees. For example, if a union raises its initiation fee from $75.00 to $250.00, an amount equal to 4 weeks' pay, when other unions charge only $12.50, the practice would be declared illegal. Also prohibited is charging black or female employees higher fees so as to discourage their membership. Labor unions are also forbidden to cause or attempt to cause an employer to pay for services that are not performed or not to be performed; this practice, known as *featherbedding*, is discussed further in Chapter 12. [*8(b)(5)*] [*8(b)(6)*] Another union unfair labor practice covers organizational and recognition picketing [*8(b)(7)*], which is covered in Chapter 5.

Other legal issues addressed in later chapters include:

- Chapter 4: Rights and obligations of unions and employers.
- Chapter 5: Representation elections, composition of bargaining units, and the decertification process.
- Chapter 6: Bargaining in good faith.
- Chapter 7: Strikes, boycotts, and pickets; national emergency work stoppages.
- Chapter 8: Duty of fair representation.
- Chapter 9: Legal aspects of arbitration.
- Chapter 10: Employee right to representation.
- Chapter 11: "Right-to-work" and union security; rights of minorities.
- Chapter 12: Jurisdictional work disputes and safety issues.
- Chapter 13: Pay discrimination, wage-price controls, and ERISA.

Enforcement of the Act

National Labor Relations Board Because the rights of employees provided by the act are not self-enforcing, and because guaranteeing the rights through the court system would be cumbersome and time-consuming, an independent federal agency was established to administer the act. The National Labor Relations Board (NLRB) includes a five-member board that is recommended by the President and confirmed by the U.S. Senate; the general counsel; and 50 regional and field offices. While the general counsel has final authority to investigate unfair labor practice (ULP) charges and issue complaints and general supervisory responsibilities over the regional and field offices, the board establishes policy, supervises administrative law judges, and decides final appeals within the NLRB structure. In ULP charges, the general counsel's role is like that of a prosecutor, and the board's like that of a judge.

The agency has two major functions: (1) supervising and conducting representation elections (covered in Chapter 5) and (2) adjudicating employer and union unfair labor practices. The NLRB processes are set in motion only when requested in writing and filed with the proper NLRB office. Such requests are called petitions in the case of elections and charges in the case of unfair labor practices.

While the NLRB has authority to administer the act in all cases involving interstate commerce, it has exercised its discretion and established jurisdictional standards for those cases it will accept, which are those it believes have a substantial effect on commerce. For example, a gas station, hotel, retail store, or apartment complex must gross $500,000 in annual volume before the NLRB will accept its petition or charge, whereas gross annual receipts of private colleges and universities must reach $1 million.

NLRB Procedure Regarding Unfair Labor Practices The procedure for an unfair labor practice complaint (see Exhibit 3.2) starts when an employee, employer, labor union, or individual files a charge with an NLRB office. The party that is charged is then notified that an investigation of the alleged violation will be conducted, and the charge is investigated by an NLRB representative from a nearby regional or field office. Interviews are conducted, documents studied, and other necessary steps taken. At each step the charge may be settled or withdrawn, or the NLRB may dismiss the case due to lack of evidence. (In cases of an unlawful boycott or strike, the NLRB may request a federal district court to issue a temporary restraining order.) If the investigation confirms the charge, the regional director of the NLRB issues a complaint and provides notice of a hearing. The charged party must then respond in 10 days to the complaint.

In many cases, the parties themselves may agree to a resolution before the investigation, and no further steps are needed. However, if no settlement is reached, an unfair labor practice hearing is conducted before an administrative law judge, who presents findings and recommendations to the board based on the evidence presented at the hearing. All parties are authorized to appeal the administrative law judge's decision directly to the board. The board considers the evidence, and if it believes an unfair labor practice has occurred, it issues an order to cease and desist such practices and to take appropriate affirmative action. Parties may appeal the board's decision as shown in Exhibit 3.2.

Cease and desist orders simply direct the violators to stop whatever activities were deemed unfair labor practices. The board exercises some discretion in determining **appropriate affirmative action,** and typical orders to employers include

- Disestablish an employer-dominated company union.
- Offer employees immediate and full reinstatement to their former positions, and pay them back wages plus interest.
- Upon request, bargain collectively with the exclusive bargaining representative of the employees.

Orders to unions include

- Refund excessive or illegally collected dues plus interest.
- Upon request, bargain collectively in good faith with the prescribed employer.

In fiscal year 1988, the NLRB found probable cause that an unfair labor practice had occurred in 35.3 percent of the cases where charges had been filed. In 92.7 percent of these cases, a voluntary resolution was reached.[21]

The Role of the Judiciary The courts under the enforcement provisions of the act serve two major purposes: (1) provide injunctive relief where appropriate and (2) review appealed decisions and orders of the NLRB. As part of the enforcement procedure, the act authorizes the NLRB to petition for an injunction in connection with unfair labor practices where either an employer or a union fails to comply with a board order. It also provides that any person aggrieved by a board order may appeal directly to an appropriate court of appeals for a review. Upon reviewing the order, the court of appeals may enforce the order, return it for reconsideration, alter it, or set it aside. The final appeal, of course, is to the U.S. Supreme Court, which may be asked to review a decision, especially where several federal courts of appeal have differed in their interpretations of the law.

The board's record of enforcement before the federal courts of appeal was impressive in the 1980s, when about 80 percent of its orders were enforced by the

Exhibit 3.2 Basic Procedures in Cases Involving Charges of Unfair Labor Practices

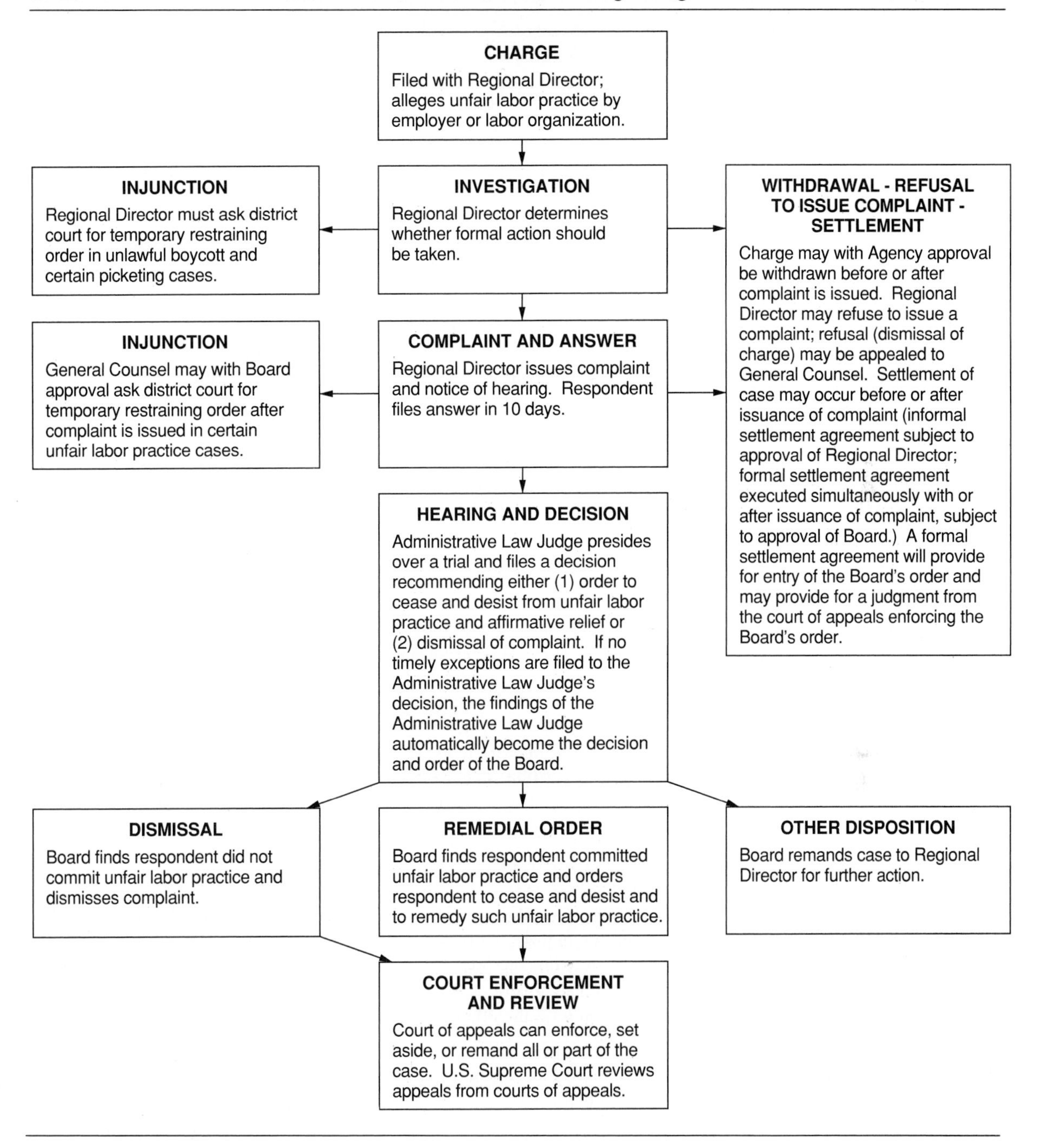

Source: National Labor Relations Board, December 13, 1984.

courts. The board's record with the U.S. Supreme Court was equally impressive; the high court agreed with the board's decision in about 80 percent of the cases.[22]

Assessment of the Administration of the NLRB

Using overall statistics, the administration of the NLRB, the Office of the General Counsel, and the regional offices have improved their performance in recent years. In fiscal 1988, unfair labor practices were investigated, and formal complaints, if warranted, were issued on average in approximately 45 days; representation elections usually were held on average about 45 days after the petition for election was filed. NLRB Chairman James Stephens reported in July 1989 that the NLRB had reduced the number of cases pending before the board to 449, as compared to a record high of 1,647 in February 1984. Still, 64 of the cases pending before the board were more than 2 years old, including 11 that were over 5 years old. As a comparison of progress, in July 1988 there were 178 cases over 2 years old, including 36 that were more than 5 years old.[23]

In fiscal 1988, the 50th year of the NLRB, the agency received 39,225 cases, of which 31,373 (80 percent) were unfair labor practices, 7,307 (19 percent) were union representation election cases, and 545 (1 percent) other matters. About $34.8 million was recovered for workers who suffered monetary losses as a result of unfair labor practices; 4,299 offers of reinstatement were made; and 4,132 representation elections were held, totaling more than 350,000 elections and more than 35 million votes cast since 1935.[24]

One of the NLRB's greatest critics has been Congress. In a report entitled "Delay, Slowness in Decisionmaking, and Case Backlog at the National Labor Relations Board," a congressional committee concluded:

> The National Labor Relations Board is in a crisis. Delays in decisionmaking at the Board level and a staggering and debilitating case backlog have resulted in workers being forced to wait years before cases affecting their livelihood and the economic well-being of their families are decided. We have reached a point where legal rights given to employees under the National Labor Relations Act are in jeopardy because of the Board's failure to issue timely decisions. Delays by the Board in deciding cases also impact adversely on employers since a company's potential monetary liability rises while the case is pending before the Board.[25]

Former NLRB Chairman John Fanning explained:

> It should be remembered that there is a basic dynamism to labor law, a dynamism that exists because of the strong competing interests of labor, on the one hand, and management, on the other. The tension is such that the sum total of potential disputes in our industrial life is probably twice the sum total of individuals involved in it. As someone who has participated in well over 25,000 decisions of the National Labor Relations Board, I can assure you that the one thing every case has in common with the others is at least two people who see things completely differently.[26]

While the board has continually faced new problems, such as union officers' failure to carry out the duty of representing their members fairly, deferral to arbitration of certain statutory rights, and preplanned and repetitive violations of the act, the subject that has caused the most criticism has been the inadequacy of the board's remedial powers. At present, it has no constitutional penal powers; it cannot award damages; it cannot impose severe penalties even when the violations are flagrant and repetitive. For individuals who have been discriminatorily discharged and deprived of employment for improper reasons, reinstatement with back pay plus interest rarely covers the real costs that accompany the period of unemployment.[27]

The board's record of obtaining reinstatement for unfairly discharged employees has not been impressive either. Approximately 95 percent of all 8(a)(3) violations entail some form of employment loss; about 90 percent occur during organizing drives, just prior to elections, and during first-contract negotiations. In determining the merits of the complaints, the board attempts to determine the employer's motive in the treatment of an employee. Criteria used include: (1) whether the employer acted in a coercive manner, (2) whether the employee had a poor work record, and (3) whether the employer had an economic necessity for displacing the employee. Most illegally discharged employees who are reinstated by the NLRB receive their back pay but choose not to return to work.

In past years, delay in discharge cases involving alleged violations of 8(a)(3) was a problem. It took the NLRB 50 days to settle an 8(a)(3) charge before it issued a complaint, 240 days to settle after issuance of a complaint. It took a total of 551 days for cases decided by the board, and if appealed to the courts, the number of days increased to 860. Therefore, employers could effectively prevail in use of the law, and union activists, if terminated in violation of 8(a)(3), were permanently displaced or not reinstated in sufficient time to assist in an organizing campaign.[28]

An example of the use (or misuse) of the legal procedure is highlighted in the 15-year case involving the discharge of employees in an organizing campaign, which was finally concluded in 1989 (see "Labor Relations in Action"). This atypical case highlights not only illegal and expensive behavior by an employer, but more importantly, it raises the ethical questions of why the U.S. Congress continues to tolerate such an imbalance of an employer's potential use of the legal procedure under present law and those rights provided to employees.

The commitment of unfair labor practices, litigation costs, and potential remedial decisions of the NLRB have become considerable influences in the strategic choices of labor and management. For example, an employer may knowingly commit an unfair labor practice and incur the litigation and remedial costs in the anticipation that these costs will be less than the cost of compliance with the law. Likewise, the incentive for either the union or management to commit an unfair labor practice that will cause the other party to file a charge depends on the expected costs and gains in terms of the litigation and remedial costs and the probability of a favorable NLRB ruling.[29]

Nonpartisan analysts have agreed that the board's remedies for serious unfair labor practices regarding refusal to bargain in good faith in the initial contract have been woefully deficient. Several attempts have been made to broaden the NLRB's authority, but none have succeeded thus far.[30] For example, when the NLRB attempted to assert itself by imposing a checkoff provision on an employer who had not bargained in good faith[31] and requiring the company to compensate its employees for monetary losses incurred as a result of the company's unlawful refusal to bargain with the certified union, the courts overruled the NLRB, stating that it had gone beyond its statutory authority.[32]

It is even debatable whether stricter, harsher, and costlier remedies would reduce the number of unfair labor practice charges filed or defer illegal behavior. Al-

Labor Relations in Action

Justice Delayed

At the Lundy Packing Co. in Clinton, North Carolina, two employees were terminated during a 1974 union organizing drive and 44 workers struck in protest. The workers unconditionally offered to return to work, but the company refused to reinstate them. The union filed an unfair labor practice charge and the NLRB ordered the company to reinstate the workers with back pay in 1976. The company appealed the decision and the Fourth Circuit Court of Appeals upheld the NLRB decision. The company appealed to the U.S. Supreme Court, which refused to review the case.

A 6-month hearing was held before an administrative law judge (ALJ) of the NLRB in 1979 to resolve the back pay award. A decision was issued in September 1981 and the company appealed the decision to the board. It was not until September 1987 that the board made its decision to uphold the ALJ's decision. Then the company appealed this NLRB decision to the Fourth Circuit Court. On September 7, 1988, the appeals court upheld the NLRB order.

On February 6, 1989, individual checks ranging from $11,000 to $57,000, totaling $1.7 million, were mailed to the affected workers. These payments came nearly 15 years after the union had initiated the organizing campaign.

During the interim years, the union was never able to win union representation rights, but represented the affected workers throughout the nearly 15 years of legal proceedings. A union spokesperson revealed that the union received no money for its legal work, although its costs were substantial.

Source: "Discharged Lundy Packing Workers Share $1.7 Million Backpay Award," *Daily Labor Report,* February 24, 1989, pp. A-4 to A-5.

though several unions, former board members, and at least one circuit court of appeals have endorsed financial reparations to employees in specific refusal to bargain cases, it is important to recognize that the intent of the act is not to reduce the intake of cases, but to promote collective bargaining as a method for management officials and union representatives to jointly determine their working conditions.[33] Some have suggested that the board should press more vigorously to fully realize its present enforcement authority in the courts.

Orders of the NLRB are not self-enforcing; the NLRB applies to the appropriate court of appeals for enforcement. If the NLRB order is enforced by the court, it becomes a lawful decree of that court, requiring compliance and backed with civil contempt sanctions. If court-enforced orders are violated, the violator can be held in contempt of court and subject to more serious penalties. On the other hand, contempt of court actions were not effective in the Pittston Coal–Mine Workers strike when the union was fined millions of dollars and several union leaders were jailed.[34]

Not to be overlooked is the fact that the members of the NLRB are presidential appointees. The appointment process has a substantial influence on the philosophy and direction of the NLRB and its decisions. "Interpretations of the facts and law governing union-management relations is . . . dependent in part on the makeup of the board."[35] During the 1980s, for example, the board appointed by Presi-

Labor Relations in Action

Controversial Reversals by the Reagan Board

Meyer Industries[a]
Previous rulings: An individual employee is protected from discipline for participating in a concerted activity of concern to other employees.
New Ruling: For an individual employee to be protected for participating in a concerted activity, he/she must have authority of other employees to act on their behalf.

Milwaukee Springs[b]
Previous ruling: Relocation of unit work for labor costs not only required bargaining but because it occurred during the term of a contract, required the union's consent before relocation.
New ruling: Union consent is required only when there is language in the contract specifically prohibiting the employer from relocating the work.

Indianapolis Power & Light Company[c]
Previous ruling: Despite a no-strike clause, employees may honor another union's picket line.
New ruling: A broad no-strike clause in the contract waives the employees' right to engage in a sympathy strike, thus permitting employers to discipline sympathy strikers.

Sears Roebuck & Co.[d]
Previous ruling: Employees who are not represented by unions have the right to representation during an interview that they believe could lead to discipline.
New ruling: Employees who are not represented by a union have no right to have a representative at an investigatory interview.

Olin Corp.[e]
Previous ruling: An arbitrator's decision can be overturned if it is not consistent with the key concepts of the NLRA as interpreted by the board.
New ruling: An arbitrator's decision will not be overturned if the arbitrator had decided essentially the same issue a party tries to present to the NLRB, assuming that the arbitrator was presented essentially the same facts that would be relevant to resolving the case if the board were to consider it again.

Rossmore House[f]
Previous ruling: Virtually all interrogation of employees who are union supporters is prohibited.
New ruling: Employers may, in certain circumstances, interrogate union supporters without committing an unfair labor practice.

Otis Elevator Division of United Technologies[g]
Previous ruling: The company must bargain with the union before it can transfer work normally performed by bargaining unit employees to another facility.
New ruling: The union does not have the right to bargain over an employer's decision to transfer production work from one facility to another where such management's decision is based on considerations other than labor cost, which might be amenable to resolution through the negotiation process.

Source: "Remarks on Recent Developments in NLRB Case Law by William Kocol, Deputy Regional Attorney for NLRB Region 13," *Daily Labor Report,* March 18, 1985, pp. E-1–E-4; "Remarks of Former NLRB Chairman Edward B. Miller on Recent Board Cases," *Daily Labor Report,* June 4, 1984, p. E-1; and Peter Walther, "The NLRB Today," *Labor Law Journal* 36 (November 1985), pp. 803–816.

[a]268 NLRB 73 (1984); 281 NLRB 118 (1986)
[b]268 NLRB 87 (1984)
[c]273 NLRB 211 (1985)
[d]274 NLRB 55 (1985)
[e]268 NLRB 86 (1984)
[f]269 NLRB 198 (1984)
[g]269 NLRB 891 (1984)

dent Reagan overturned many decisions that had existed for as long as 20 years. Similarly, during their tenure in office, members of the board appointed by Presidents Kennedy and Johnson reversed 31 previous decisions. Some of these reversals, shown in the "Labor Relations in Action," demonstrate the importance of presidential appointments to the board.

The NLRA is now half a century old, and it has prompted the following pessimistic views by two authorities on the act.

> If there is any one observation that one can make with some degree of confidence during this, the fiftieth anniversary year of the National Labor Relations Act, it is that the authors of the Act would be mightily surprised to hear who is saying what about their offspring. The business community, which excoriated the Wagner Act as the most radical feature of the New Deal, now praises the balanced and constructive character of our legislation. The ". . . damned Labor Board," to use Fortune Magazine's sobriquet of 1938, is now applauded by management attorneys for its moderate and even-handed jurisprudence. Meanwhile, the Democratic supporters of the union movement in Congress have just issued a report entitled "Has Labor Law Failed?": their answer to their question is, most emphatically, "Yes!" More and more union leaders—up to and including Lane Kirkland, President of the AFL-CIO—are saying that labor would be better off if the Board were disbanded, the Act repealed, and we were all "to return to the law of the jungle."[36]

> The NLRB has never known peace in its time. At different stages of its history, the Board's antagonists have included not only management but also organized labor (at one point in the 1930s both the otherwise mutually hostile AFL and CIO), the president of the United States, Congress, the federal judiciary, and the press. Although the charges brought against the NLRB over the years have been many and varied, every Board from Madden's to Dotson's—that is, from the first to today's—has been accused of exceeding its statutory authority by making labor law instead of merely administering the law passed by Congress. More significant, every Board has been accused of making a labor policy inconsistent with congressional intent.[37]

Transportation-Related Labor Relations Laws (Railway and Airlines)

Rail and air transportation labor relations are covered by the Railway Labor Act and deregulation legislation has had dramatic effects on them. Although the Railway Labor Act was passed in 1926 to apply only to the railway industry, it was actually the first comprehensive labor relations law. Like other labor laws, the Railway Labor Act did not develop overnight; it resulted from years of union activity and attempts to pass laws accommodating railway labor relations.[38] The act relies almost entirely on collective bargaining for settling labor disputes, but it has established mandatory mediation by the National Mediation Board (NMB). If mediation fails, the NMB must recommend arbitration. To assist in dispute resolution, the president has authority to appoint an emergency board composed of neutrals to investigate the dispute and recommend procedures and terms for agreement. This approach was designed to arouse public opinion, which would pressure the parties to arrive at terms of agreement on their own. (More detailed discussion of dispute resolution under the Railway Labor Act can be found in Chapter 7.)

Although the Railway Labor Act has been amended several times, its purposes remain largely the same:

- To avoid interruptions of commerce.
- To forbid any limitation on employees' rights to organize and join labor unions.
- To provide complete independence for both parties in carrying out purposes of the act.
- To provide prompt and orderly settlement of disputes over pay, work rules, and working conditions.
- To provide prompt and orderly settlement of disputes over grievances and contract interpretation.

The first major amendment to the Railway Labor Act occurred in 1934. It provided assistance to unions by barring employers from attempting to influence employees in selecting their bargaining representatives. Further, employers were directed to bargain collectively with certified labor representatives, and company-dominated unions and yellow-dog contracts were forbidden. The National Railroad Adjustment Board, a bipartisan group of 18 union and 18 management representatives, was established to assist in resolving grievances and interpreting provisions of the labor agreements. Where the board could not agree to a settlement, the amendment provided that the grievance be settled by an arbitrator selected by the parties. The National Mediation Board was empowered to conduct representation elections and to help resolve conflicts in negotiating new labor agreements. In 1936, the act was amended again, and coverage was extended to a new and developing industry—air transportation—although the airlines continued their local system boards for grievance resolution.[39]

Deregulation Legislation

The **Airline Deregulation Act of 1978** ended government controls of fares and routes, and the Motor Carrier Act of 1980 reduced the amount of economic regulation of the industry by the Interstate Commerce Commission. The Staggers Rail Act of 1980 gave railroads more flexibility in setting rates and service levels.

Since the enactment of these laws, employment has remained relatively unchanged in the airline and trucking industries but has continued to decline in the railroads. Relative wages have remained constant in airlines while declining in trucking and rising in railroads. Labor costs have increased at a slower pace in airlines and trucking while they have declined in railroads.[40]

Other effects have been wage concessions, breakup in industrywide standards, increased mergers and acquisitions, fragmentation of national agreements, greater hostility at the bargaining table, two-tier wage systems, compensation tied to company stock, and more nonunion companies.[41]

Airline deregulation prompted the introduction of 128 nonunion carriers; by 1987, only 37 had survived. Their introduction sparked a wave of mergers by the major airlines, ticketing agreements between major carriers and regional and commuter airlines, hub-and-spoke airports, and frequent flier programs to promote airline allegiance.[42] Deregulation also brought about the benefits of price competition, with 90 percent of passengers traveling at discount prices averaging 60 percent below the coach price. During the same time accident rates have not increased and service to small communities has not deteriorated; however there have been increased congestion at airports and in the airways, delays in departures and arrivals, threats to safety, and a general decline in the quality of air service.[43]

Assessment of the Railway Labor Act

Faced with such problems as changing markets for freight transportation, severe competition, government regulation, and public interest in uninterrupted railroad service, labor relations in the railway industry are unique. Complicating the situation further are the chronic financial instability of the numerous independent railroads, the presence of strong, competing craft unions, and tradition-bound work rules. These factors affect labor relations in the following ways: (1) Because the public depends on railroad transportation for many essential goods, there has been much effort to avoid strikes (five interventions by Congress). (2) With the "fractionated" craft unions, the labor relations process takes much time and creates many opportunities for disputes. (3) The tradition-bound work rules of the operating crafts strictly control not only how a particular job will be performed, but also which craft will be assigned the job. These work rules postpone the introduction of new technology and magnify the problems of a declining industry.[44] Any assessment of the Railway Labor Act must be kept in proper perspective. There are over 7,000 labor agreements in the railroad and airline industries, and about 1,000 railroad and 200 airline agreements (mostly local) are in negotiations during any given year.[45] Further, any measure of its effectiveness must be made with reference to the act's objectives—to promote free collective bargaining and protect the public from interrupted flows of commerce.[46]

Regarding negotiations, mediation has been the most important method of intervention under the act; however, few nationwide railroad wage cases have been settled by mediation since 1936. Its greatest success has been in settling minor controversies after the major issues have been resolved. This does not mean that mediation is unimportant—minor disputes left unresolved could easily lead to major strikes in future negotiations.

Since its inception, the NMB has successfully resolved 5,500 representation worries, largely without incident or challenge. The mediation staff has handled nearly 12,000 negotiations with only 350 (or 3 percent) unsuccessful—a record unmatched by almost any other major industry. Only 17 emergency boards have been appointed over the last 10 years, well below the 4-per-year average of earlier decades. Also, compared with the 1930s and 1940s, when about 80 percent of all railroad grievances were resolved by the NLRB, now over 90 percent of the 1,000 each year are resolved by neutral referees. Congress was forced to intervene in labor disputes under the Railway Labor Act in 1962, 1966, 1967, 1971, and 1972; however, since 1972 the parties have been able to resolve their differences through the procedures of the RLA.[47]

Promising Developments Regarding the Railway Labor Act

Despite the prolonged strike at Eastern Airlines (covered in detail in Case 4.1), which highlights the interrelations of various laws, financial manipulations, and company and union strategies and actions, several recent events and developments provide the basis for some optimism:

- The most recent national railroad agreements have included a fixed term, a no-strike clause, and common expiration dates.
- Recent negotiations have also been characterized by union-management cooperation, which has resulted in fewer conflicts and outside interventions.

- Emergency board procedures have been drastically improved, and the ritualism and legalism so prevalent in the 1960s have been reduced.
- Encouraging progress has been made on some long-standing manning and work-rule issues, such as the fireman on diesel trains, combined road and yard service, and interdivisional runs.
- New leadership has had a positive influence on both management and unions, and neutrals and government officials have provided capable assistance in the bargaining and dispute-resolution processes.

Critical issues remain to be resolved, including secondary picketing, endless stalling, restrictive work rules in some agreements, intercraft wage structure problems, and crew size disputes.[48] But there is still reason to be optimistic if the recent trend can be sustained. As one authority has said:

> No labor law can ensure peaceful and constructive labor relations. Although specific amendments to the Railway Labor Act may be desirable—notably, in connection with representational questions—we should be careful about casting into oblivion a law that both parties, on balance, seemingly want to retain.[49]

Other Laws That Affect Labor Relations

Other statutes and executive orders, more narrow in scope, influence labor relations either directly or indirectly. The following section only highlights their major provisions; however, practitioners find that detailed knowledge of them is essential to most business operations. (Related legislation is summarized here, but its specific implications for labor relations activities and unions are discussed in the appropriate chapters.)

Bankruptcy Act

Bankruptcy legislation enacted in 1984 includes standards for the rejection of collective bargaining agreements by companies filing for bankruptcy. The act includes detailed procedures for companies in their preparation for obtaining modifications in labor agreements. It requires the company to provide relevant information to the union and good-faith efforts to reach an agreement. In cases where no agreement can be reached, the act specifies the requirements for terminating or altering provisions of the agreement.[50]

Worker Adjustment and Retraining Notification Act (WARN)

Triggered by major plant closings without notification, the Worker Adjustment and Retraining Notification Act (WARN) was passed in 1988. WARN requires employers with 100 or more employees to give 60 days advance notice to employees (excluding those employed less than 20 hours per week) who will be affected by a plant closing or major layoff. Also, the union, the chief elected local government official, and the state government must be notified. The law also allows the union and companies to negotiate a clause in their collective bargaining agreement which requires advance notice of more than 60 days.

The situations covered include

- "plant closing" resulting in an employment loss for 50 or more workers at one site within a 30-day period

- "mass layoff" of at least 33 percent of the work force (minimum of 50 employees) within any 30-day period
- "mass layoff" involving at least 500 employees within any 30-day period

Remedies to affected employees for employer violations include back pay and benefits for up to 60 days and payments (maximum of $500 per day) to local communities for a period of up to 60 days. Enforcement will be via a lawsuit in a federal district court by aggrieved employees, the union, or the local government.

WARN ties in closely with the Job Training Partnership Act (JTPA), which provides funds to state and local governments for training and retraining. In cases of plant closing and mass layoff, state "rapid response" teams are available to work with labor and management officials to set up retraining and re-employment programs for the affected workers.

Racketeering Influenced and Corrupt Organizations Act (RICO)

RICO, part of the Organized Crime Control Act, forbids anyone involved in racketeering from investing in or controlling through racketeering activity any enterprise (businesses or labor unions) engaged in interstate commerce. The law provides for penalties of up to $25,000, twenty years of imprisonment, and forfeiture of all relevant property. If found guilty, the convicted person may be required to divest himself of all interests in the organization and restricted from any future activities in that or related organizations. In addition, any persons who suffered damages from the prohibited activities are entitled to threefold recovery of damages.[51] In 1988–1989, the Justice Department used RICO against the International Brotherhood of Teamsters and the Teamsters were placed under a court-appointed trustee.

Employment Discrimination Laws and Executive Orders

The **Equal Employment Opportunity Act of 1972,** which amended Title VII of the Civil Rights Act of 1964, prohibits any form of employment discrimination by companies, labor unions, and employment agencies on the basis of race, color, religion, sex, or national origin. By creating the Equal Employment Opportunity Commission, the act provided an enforcement procedure that includes investigations, attempts at conciliation, and suits filed on behalf of the complainant.

The **Age Discrimination in Employment Act of 1967,** as amended in 1978, 1984, and 1986, prohibits employment discrimination against those over the age of 40, permits compulsory retirement for executives who are entitled to pensions of $44,000 per year or more, and authorizes jury trials in covered cases.

Executive Order 11246, as amended by Executive Order 11375, prohibits employment discrimination in the federal government and by federal government contractors and subcontractors receiving $50,000 or more. Those having contracts of $50,000 or more and employing 50 people or more are required to establish affirmative action plans that prescribe specific goals and procedures for increasing the percentage of minority employees. Firms that fail to comply could lose part or all of their contracts.

The **Vocational Rehabilitation Act of 1973** (Section 503) requires holders of federal government contracts in excess of $2,500 to take affirmative action to employ and advance in employment qualified physically and mentally handicapped individuals. Further, if any handicapped individual believes that a federal contractor has failed or refused to comply with the act, he or she may file a complaint with the Department of Labor, which will investigate the complaint and take any warranted action. In addition, Section 504 extends coverage to organizations receiving federal financial assistance and is enforced by the Department of Health and Human Services.

Related Labor Relations Laws

The **Military Selection Act of 1967** requires employers to restore veterans (those whose total military service time does not exceed 4 years) to the positions they held before entering the armed services or to similar positions of like seniority, status, and pay.

Also, the **Vietnam Era Veteran Readjustment Assistance Act** requires employers with government contracts of $10,000 or more to take affirmative action to employ and advance disabled veterans and qualified veterans of the Vietnam War.

The **Social Security Act of 1935,** as amended, established two national systems of social security for protection against loss of income due to unemployment, old age, disability, and death: (1) retirement, survivors and disability insurance, and health insurance for persons over age 65 and (2) unemployment insurance, which operates under a state-administered, federal-state plan whose operating costs are paid by the federal government.

Other important laws include the Wage Laws and Employee Retirement and Income Security Act of 1974 (covered in Chapter 13), the Occupational Safety and Health Act (covered in Chapter 12), and state laws and local ordinances that pertain to public-sector labor relations and equal employment opportunity.

Summary

This chapter has presented the major provisions of federal labor relations laws in the United States. These legal influences must be understood in order to fully appreciate the remaining chapters in this book, because nearly all issues in labor relations are either directly or indirectly influenced by labor relations law.

While many think of law in terms of statutes passed by the U.S. Congress or state legislatures, labor relations and other types of law proceed not only from statutes but also from the U.S. Constitution, judicial decisions, and administrative decisions of government agencies. Similar laws and decisions develop at the state and local government levels.

Developing the legal influences historically, this chapter began with the early struggles of labor unions to exist as they faced unsympathetic judiciary and lack of any permissive legislation. Several hurdles included the criminal conspiracy and civil conspiracy doctrines as well as the breach of contract rulings. Then the Sherman Act, passed primarily to control business monopolies, was applied to labor unions also. With support of labor, the Sherman Act was amended by the Clayton Act; however, this act also proved unfavorable to unions.

While the 1920s did bring passage of the Railway Labor Act, little legislative action occurred in other sectors. However, the 1930s, with the country's most severe economic depression, brought about major changes. The enactment of the Norris–La Guardia Act changed the public policy toward labor relations. Not only did it recognize employees' rights to various freedoms, such as freedom of association and self-organization, it also restricted the role of the federal courts in labor disputes.

Recognizing several deficiencies in the Norris–La Guardia Act, Congress passed the National Labor Relations Act in 1935. This act dealt with employer unfair labor practices, established an administrative agency, the NLRB, and guaranteed a number of employee rights, such as the right to form and join unions and to participate in concerted actions. Then, in 1947 and again in 1959, Congress amended the National Labor Relations Act, with passage of the Taft-Hartley Act and the Landrum-Griffin Act, respectively. The 1947 amendments added union unfair labor practices and restrictions on union security clauses, and the 1959 act added regulations of government and internal operations of unions and amended strike, picketing, and boycott activities.

Starting in 1863, union activity in the railroad industry played a key role in the legislative arena. The Railway Labor Act of 1926, whose major purpose is to provide for stable and effective labor relations without major interruptions in commerce, established procedures for resolving labor disputes and created the National Mediation Board and National Railroad Adjustment Board to accomplish the act's purposes. While the assessment of these measures may seem less than optimistic, several recent developments give some evidence of success: acceptance of negotiations and responsibilities by the parties, recent no-strike clauses, improved employer-union cooperation on important issues, new leadership in both unions and management, and improved emergency board procedures.

Key Terms

employment at will
yellow-dog contract
company union
hot-cargo agreement
cease and desist order
appropriate affirmative action

Discussion Questions

1. How have the major labor relations laws helped or hindered the development of unions?
2. How were yellow-dog contracts used to limit activities of union organizers? How were they used to slow union growth?
3. Why did the 1914 Clayton Act, called U.S. labor's Magna Charta by AFL president Samuel Gompers, prove to be less than a benefit to unions?
4. What was missing in the Norris–La Guardia Act (regarding administration of the law) that was present in the National Labor Relations Act? Why was its absence important?
5. Although the National Labor Relations Act gives employees certain rights, these rights are not unlimited. Discuss.
6. The NLRB has been criticized for its lack of success in the reinstatement and continued employment of discharged employees under the NLRA. What could be changed in the NLRA or its administration that would improve its record on reinstatement?
7. Why is there still a separate labor relations law for the railway and airline industries?
8. Project the effects of the bankruptcy and deregulation laws on labor relations, then on society in general.

References

1. J. R. Commons and E. A. Gilmore, *A Documentary History of American Industrial Society* (Cleveland, Ohio: A. H. Clark, 1910), p. 68.
2. Quoted by John Fanning in "The Balance of Labor-Management Economic Power under Taft-Hartley," *Proceedings of the 40th Annual Meeting of the Industrial Relations Research Association*, ed. Barbara D. Dennis (Madison, Wis.: IRRA, 1988), p. 70.
3. *Commonwealth* v. *Hunt*, 45 Mass. 4 (1842).
4. E. E. Herman and G. S. Skinner, *Labor Law* (New York: Random House, 1972), p. 21.
5. *Vegelahn* v. *Guntner*, 44 N.E. 1077 (1896). See Herbert L. Sherman, Jr., and William P. Murphy, *Unionization and Collective Bargaining*, 3d ed. (Washington, D.C.: Bureau of National Affairs Inc., 1975), p. 3.
6. *Hitchman Coal & Coke Company* v. *Mitchell*, 245 U.S. 229 (1917).
7. 26 Stat. 209 (1890).
8. *Loewe* v. *Lawlor*, 208 U.S. 274 (1908).
9. 38 Stat. 731 (1914).
10. *Duplex Printing Press Co.* v. *Deering*, 254 U.S. 443 (1921).
11. *Truax* v. *Corrigan*, 257 U.S. 312 (1921).
12. 47 Stat.70 (1932).
13. A labor dispute was defined as "any controversy concerning terms or conditions of employment, or concerning the association or representation of persons in negotiating, fixing, maintaining, changing, or seeking to arrange terms or conditions of employment regardless of whether or not the disputants stand in the proximate relation of employer and employee." 47 Stat.70 (1932).
14. Ibid.
15. Alvin L. Goldman, *The Supreme Court and Labor-Management Relations Law* (Lexington, Mass.: D. C. Heath, 1976), pp. 26–28; and Sherman and Murphy, *Unionization and Collective Bargaining*, pp. 7–9.
16. Goldman, *The Supreme Court*, pp. 28–31.
17. Sherman and Murphy, *Unionization and Collective Bargaining*, p. 9
18. Goldman, *The Supreme Court*, pp.31–39.
19. This section was taken from the Wagner Act, 49 Stat. 449 (1935); Labor Management Relations Act, 61 Stat. 136 (1947); Landrum-Griffin Act, 73 Stat.519 (1959); Office of General Counsel, National Labor Relations Board, *A Guide to Basic Law and Procedures under the National Labor Relations Act* (Washington, D.C.: Government Printing Office, 1976), unless otherwise noted.
20. "NLRB General Counsel's Quadrennial Report for FY 1985 through FY 1988," *Daily Labor Report*, April 10, 1989, pp. D-1–D-6.
21. Ibid.
22. Ibid.
23. Ibid.
24. "NLRB Reports Case Backlog at Lowest Level Since 1978," *Daily Labor Report*, July 28, 1989, p. A-4.
25. *Delay, Slowness in Decisionmaking, and Case Backlog at the NLRB* (Washington, D.C.: U.S. Government Printing Office, 1984), p. 4.
26. Fanning, "Balance of Labor-Management Economic Power," pp. 72–73.
27. John H. Fanning, "We are Forty—Where Do We Go?" *Labor Law Journal* 27 (January 1976), pp. 5–6.
28. William N. Cooke, "The Rising Toll of Discrimination against Union Activists," *Industrial Relations* 24 (Fall 1985), p. 438.
29. Robert J. Flanagan, "Remedial Policy and Compliance with the NLRA," *Proceedings of the 39th Annual Meeting of the Industrial Relations Research Association*, ed. Barbara D. Dennis (Madison, Wis.: IRRA, 1987), pp. 21-27.
30. Frank W. McCulloch and Tim Bornstein, *The National Labor Relations Board* (New York: Praeger Publishers, 1974), p. 180.
31. *H. K. Porter Co.* v. *NLRB*, 73 LRRM 2561 (1970).
32. *Auto Workers* v. *NLRB*, 76 LRRM 2573 (1971); *Ex-Cell-O Corp.* v. *NLRB*, 77 LRRM 2547 (1971).
33. Bernard Samoff, "The Case of the Burgeoning Load of the NLRB," *Labor Law Journal* 22 (October 1971), pp. 264-265.
34. Douglas S. McDowell and Kenneth Huhn, *NLRB Remedies for Unfair Labor Practices* (Philadelphia:Industrial Research Unit, University of Pennsylvania, 1976), pp. 245-246.
35. William N. Cooke and Frederick H. Gautschi III, "Political Bias in NLRB Unfair Labor Practice Decisions," *Industrial and Labor Relations Review* 35 (July 1982), p. 549.
36. "Speech by Paul C. Weiler Before the National Academy of Arbitrators," *Daily Labor Report*, June 11, 1986, p. E-1.
37. James A. Gross, "Complicating Statutory Purposes: Another Look at Fifty Years of NLRB Law Making," *Industrial and Labor Relations Review* 39 (October 1985), p. 8.
38. Charles M. Rehmus, "Evolution of Legislation Affecting Collective Bargaining in the Railroad and Airline Industries," in Charles M. Rehmus, ed., *The Railway Labor Act at Fifty* (Washington, D.C.: U.S. Government Printing Office, 1977), p. 4.
39. Rehmus, "Collective Bargaining," pp. 14–15. The remaining amendments were comparatively minor; the 1940 amendment clarified the coverage of rail operations in coal mines; 1951, the closed shop was prohibited, but the union shop was allowed; 1964, the terms of office for members of the National Mediation Board were classified; 1966, special adjustment boards were authorized to hear and resolve grievances on local properties; 1970, membership on the National Railroad Adjustment Board was reduced to 34—half management-appointed and half union-appointed.
40. "Deregulation in Three Transport Industries Has Produced Widely Diverse Labor Market Results," *Daily Labor Report*, May 13, 1986, p. A-13.
41. William J. Curtin, "Airline Labor Relations Under Deregulation," *Proceedings of the 38th Annual Meeting of the Industrial Relations Research Association* (Madison, Wis.: Industrial Relations Research Institute, 1986), pp. 158–162.
42. Mark Kahn, "Introduction," *Cleared for Takeoff: Airline Labor Relations Since Deregulation*, ed. Jean T. McKelvey (Ithaca, N.Y.: ILR Press, 1988), p. 3.
43. Alfred Kahn, "In Defense of Deregulation," *Cleared for Takeoff: Airline Labor Relations Since Deregulation*, ed. Jean T. McKelvey (Ithaca, N.Y.: ILR Press, 1988), pp. 344–345. For a legal analysis, see Beth Adler, "Comment: Deregulation in the Airline Industry: Toward a New Judicial Interpretation of the Railway Labor Act," *Northwestern University Law Journal* 80 (Winter 1986), pp. 1003–1006.
44. Douglas M. McCabe, "The Railroad Industry's Labor Relations Environment: Implications for Railroad Managers," *ICC Practitioners' Journal* 49 (September–October 1982), pp. 592–602.
45. Charles M. Rehmus, "The First Fifty Years—And Then," in Rehmus, ed., *Railway Labor Act at Fifty*, p. 246.
46. Beatrice M. Burgoon, "Mediation under the Railway Labor Act," in Rehmus, ed., *Railway Labor Act at Fifty*, p. 23.
47. Charles M. Rehmus, *The National Mediation Board at Fifty* (Ithaca, N.Y.: Cornell University, 1984), pp. 1–20.
48. Cullen, "Emergency Boards," pp. 176–183. Also see "The Rail-

roads Lose Their Bargaining Unity," *Business Week,* April 10, 1978, pp. 31–32.

49. Mark L. Kahn, "Labor-Management Relations in the Airline Industry," in Rehmus, ed., *Railway Labor Act at Fifty,* p. 128.

50. "The Bankruptcy Act," *Labor Law Journal* 35 (September 1984), p. 593. For more thorough coverage of the bankruptcy issues, see George S. Roukis and Bruce H. Charnov, "Section 1113 of the Bankruptcy Amendments and Federal Judgeship Act of 1984: A Management-Labor Compromise That Will Not Work," *Labor Law Journal* 37 (May 1986), pp. 273–281; and William A. Wines, "An Overview of the 1984 Bankruptcy Amendments: Some Modest Protections for Labor Agreements," *Labor Law Journal* 36 (December 1985), pp. 911–918.

51. Garth Mangum, "RICO versus Landrum-Griffin as Weapons against Union Corruption: The Teamsters Case," *Labor Law Journal* 40 (February 1989), pp. 94–98.

Unions and Management: Key Participants in the Labor Relations Process

"What does labor want? It wants the earth and the fullness thereof. There is nothing too precious, there is nothing too beautiful, too lofty, too ennobling unless it is within the scope and comprehension of labor's aspirations and wants. . . . We want more schoolhouses and less jails; more books and less arsenals; more learning and less vice; more justice and less revenge; in fact, more of the opportunities to cultivate our better natures, to make manhood more noble, womanhood more beautiful and childhood more happy and bright."

Samuel Gompers, Founder and President of the American Federation of Labor

As noted in Chapter 1, two key participants in the labor relations process are the union, which as the exclusive bargaining agent represents employees in the bargaining units, and management, which represents the owners or stockholders of the company. This chapter first provides a general explanation of the goals, strategies, and organizational structure of the company and the union for labor relations purposes. Because companies and unions are organized differently to meet different purposes, explanations of basic goals, strategies, and organizational structures will be presented that may be adjusted to meet individual differences. The second part of the chapter focuses on union governance and structure by describing the characteristics of unions, government at the various levels, organizational structure, and problems with corruption and misuse of power within a few unions.

Goals and Strategies: Management and Unions

Unions and management of companies have goals that are similar and goals that may at times conflict. Their goals provide direction and serve as the basis for their organization's strategies, plans, and organizational structure. Exhibit 4.1 displays some major goals for companies and for unions, which in several cases are similar and consistent and in others have potential for conflict. The areas of potential conflict create possibilities for an adversarial relationship, and the areas of agreement create possibilities for cooperation and labor peace. As will be noted, most of the time unions and management are able to settle their differences without resorting to a work stoppage (less than 1 percent of total man-days are lost to work stoppages). The collective bargaining process itself is a mechanism designed by the parties and confirmed by the U.S. Congress as the preferred method for resolving differences between unions and management.

Both the company and the union want the company to survive and remain competitive. It would not make any sense for the union to disagree with this goal because the employees would lose their jobs and the union would not survive. Likewise, the union wants to survive as the representative of the employees of the company and will take steps to retain this designation. When a company wishes to remain nonunion or to have the union decertified, an inevitable conflict occurs.

The company wants to grow and prosper—a sign of success of its management and a greater return for the owners or stockholders. The union agrees with this goal and supports it because it creates more opportunities and benefits for employees, adds union members, allows more funds for union activities, and strengthens the union as an institution. Likewise, both company and union want the company to achieve a favorable return on its investment. While there may be disagreements on what is meant by favorable, both parties understand the mechanics of the financial side of the business. However, the union also wants to achieve a favorable or "fair" return for the workers' efforts, input, and contribution. Here, there may be a disagreement over what is a favorable return to the investors and a "fair" return to the workers.

Two related goals of the company are to achieve the effective utilization of its human resources and to attract, retain, and motivate employees. The union accepts these goals for the company as long as the company abides by the provisions that were negotiated and included in the collective bargaining agreement. For example, the company may wish to have the most productive employee work on an overtime assignment to be able to ship a rush order; however, the agreement may require that overtime assignments be made on a rotating basis. The presence of the union does not prevent making overtime assignments to the most productive employee; however, the overtime provision is a negotiable subject and the parties must live by the provisions that they agree on.

The company wants to protect its right to make decisions and retain the flexibility to operate the business. The union accepts the philosophy that some decisions are best made by management; these include the type of product, the price of products, financial policies, customer relations, advertising and promotion decisions, product design, and plant layout. At the same time, the union represents the interests of employees and attempts to provide protection and guarantee job opportunities

Exhibit 4.1 **Goals of the Company and Union**

The Company Wants:	The Union Wants:
To survive and remain competitive	The company to survive and remain competitive as well as for the union to survive and remain secure
To grow and prosper	The company to grow and prosper as well as the union
To achieve a favorable return on its investment	The company to achieve a favorable return on its investment and return "fair" wages to employees
To effectively use human resources	The company to effectively use human resources within the rules and policies of the agreement and to achieve job security and employment opportunities for members
To attract, retain, and motivate employees	The company to attract, retain, and motivate employees within the rules and policies of the agreement
To protect management's rights to make decisions and retain flexibility	To protect union and employee rights that were negotiated and included in the labor agreement
To obtain commitment from the union that there will be no strike for the duration of the agreement	To obtain commitment from the company that there will be no lockout for the duration of the agreement

for them, and it does this by negotiating provisions in the labor agreement such as contracting out work, use of seniority, and promotions and transfers to provide for these rights.[1]

The company wants a union commitment to have no work stoppage for a specified period of time; this guarantees a stable work force and allows production promises to customers. This commitment comes in the form of a "no-strike" clause in the labor agreement. As well, the union may want a commitment from the company that the workers have the right to have their grievances heard by management and may appeal them to a third-party neutral (arbitrator) when necessary to resolve differences over the grievances.

Once the union and the company decide on their respective goals, they determine the appropriate strategies to reach these goals. Companies have been involved in strategic planning much longer than unions, and their strategic plans are usually more detailed and sophisticated. Only in recent times have unions started to think and operate in terms of strategic planning.

Company Strategic Planning

A company's strategy in labor relations is determined by its managerial philosophy, the ethics of its management, its economic condition, the composition of the work force, competition in the industry, the time in the life of the company, and the capabilities of management. Management has choices about the strategy it may take. Management may believe that the company is better off remaining nonunion and devote much time and effort to assuring positive human resources management. Management members who are in a highly competitive industry may be willing to do almost anything to keep unions out. Management at other companies may choose to change from a hard-bargaining approach to one of labor-management cooperation after it has finally accepted the philosophy that both parties would gain more by cooperating than by conflicting. Exhibit 4.2 shows the range of company strategies in labor relations from union suppression to labor-management cooperation.

Nonunion Companies' Strategies Some authorities believe that labor relations underwent profound changes in the 1980s brought on by forces external to union-management relationships. These forces include competition from abroad, deregulation, and competition from nonunion companies. More and more companies are finding that their labor relations strategies are driven by economic choices and their need to adapt to new, more competitive business conditions. Because union suppression, union avoidance, and union substitution strategies have existed in different forms since the Industrial Revolution, a company may choose to attempt to maintain its nonunion status by preventing or supplanting unions. Another company may choose one of the nonunion strategies as a legitimate response that has been forced on it to cut costs, innovate, enter new markets, and devise flexible labor force strategies. This latter approach focuses on costs and productivity of human resources and the management of human resources.[2]

A company may use the *union suppression* strategy to maintain its nonunion status or to destroy the union. As noted in Chapter 3, Lundy Packing Company used the legal procedures of the National Labor Relations Act for 15 years to suppress the union. It fired employees who had shown interest in the union during an organizing campaign and were able to use the appellant system for 15 years to keep the union out.

Continental Airlines through hard bargaining caused a strike, declared bankruptcy, voided its labor agreement, and replaced the strikers. Today, Continental Airlines operates primarily as a nonunion, low-cost carrier. More recently, Eastern Airlines demanded concessions from its unions that resulted in a strike by the machinists that was honored by the other unions. Then Eastern declared bankruptcy, continued to sell its assets, and operated with striker replacements (see Case 4.1).

Exhibit 4.2 Company Strategies in Labor Relations

Union Suppression	Union Avoidance	Union Substitution	Codified Business-Like	Accommodation or Labor-Management Cooperation
Union busting Illegal acts Refusal to bargain Decertification Filing for bankruptcy Encouraging strikes	Positive human resources management Double-breasting	Company paternalism Company-sponsored employee organizations Forms of worker participation and employee involvement	Neutral in union campaign Straightforward approach	Gain-sharing Union involvement ESOPs Joint planning

More extreme tactics are used by some companies to avoid unionization:

- Developing a spy network (tattletales) to identify union supporters.
- Refusing to hire former employees of unionized companies (but giving the applicant a reason other than prior union affiliation for employment denial).
- Establishing a case for discharge (including documentation) of known union advocates.
- Seeking to determine prospective employees' attitudes toward unions from interviews, references, and so on, then refusing to hire them (again giving another reason) if they are pro-union.
- Giving psychological tests (job-interest questionnaires) to determine the likelihood that an applicant will be interested in a union.
- Locating new plants in areas where union membership is low and expanding the company's nonunion plants.
- Using a standard application form of a State Employment Service that asks applicants whether they have been a member of a union and using the application form as part of the pre-employment inquiry.[3]

Some employers facing union-organizing campaigns have committed unfair labor practices deliberately, with the expectation of economic returns to them. A recent research study demonstrated that "under realistic conditions it is economically feasible for employers to secure economic gains by violating the National Labor Relations Act."[4] Even more disappointing was this conclusion:

> [I]n the past, the compliance system [of the National Labor Relations Act] has been inadequate to the extent that some employers have found it profitable to commit unfair labor practices in order to forestall unionization. Those employers obeying the law because "it's the law" have faced a greater probability of incurring costs of unionization and may have been at a competitive disadvantage to employers who violated the law. Such inequities do not encourage compliance with the law and provide evidence of the need for labor law reform.[5]

When illegal practices yield economic returns to the violators, ethical questions are raised as to the fairness of the law and its application. Companies that select the *union avoidance* strategy take a strong stance against union representation, even in facilities where unions already exist. They open nonunion facilities and attempt to keep them nonunion. They shift their capital investments away from the unionized facilities and make plant improvements in the nonunion plants. Where the union represents the employees, they attempt to reduce the labor costs by lowering wages and benefits, moderating traditional work practices, and encouraging decertification to the point of committing illegal actions. In these situations, the labor relations environment is highly adversarial, and union-management collaboration is not considered an option.[6]

Some companies adopting the *union avoidance* strategy practice *positive human resources management* or operate *double-breasted.* Company officials who adopt positive human resources management subscribe to the following beliefs:

> Unions exist as a reflection of management failures. Unions are able to organize only where an employer is insensitive to the needs and desires of the workforce. Where managers are insensitive, the workers will vote for a union, and the managers deserve it. Where managers are alert and sensitive, employees will not want a

> third party (that is a union) in the relationship between the company and the employees. Furthermore, where managers are sensitive, employees have no need for a union.[7]

Companies such as IBM, Texas Instruments, Eastman Kodak, and Delta Airlines have essentially adopted this strategy. These companies have developed a positive human resources management program including the following elements:

- The absence of symbols of rank and status such as parking spaces, company cars, or country club memberships for managers.
- Carefully considered surroundings—locating where high-quality schools and universities are near and keeping individual facilities small.
- Overall corporate strength—high profits, fast growth, high technology, or dominant market position.
- Programs to promote employment security, such as work sharing or overall reduction in pay to avoid layoffs in hard times.
- Promotion from within—job posting, career development, training and education programs.
- Influential personnel programs, for example, having the personnel director report directly to top management.
- Competitive pay and benefits, especially having compensation that is equitable externally and internally and comparable to the pay at unionized companies.
- Management that listens—using systematic approaches such as attitude surveys and open-door policies and appeal procedures.
- Careful grooming of managers—focusing on long-term results, using assessment centers, and appraising in terms of competence and employee relationships.[8]

Double-breasting exists when one company has two or more subsidiaries, one unionized and the others nonunion or open shop. These arrangements take several forms: (1) a holding company has financial control of one or more operating subsidiaries, (2) a unionized company buys a nonunion subsidiary and continues to operate it nonunion, and (3) a nonunion company buys a unionized subsidiary and continues to operate it unionized. At present, the law requires the open shop and unionized units of a holding company to be separately managed and operated as distinct entities. The NLRB determines whether too seemingly separate companies should be treated as one by considering the following guidelines: interrelation of operations, centralization of control of labor relations, common management, and common ownership or financial control.[9] The board stated:

> No one of these factors has been held to be controlling, but the Board opinions have stressed the first three factors, which go to show "operational integration," particularly centralized control of labor relations. The Board has declined in several cases to find integration merely upon the basis of common ownership or financial control.[10]

A third company strategy to maintain nonunion status is the *union substitution* strategy. This strategy originated in the company paternalism and company unions of the 1920s, and still exists today in the form of employee committees and other forms of worker participation. Although the NLRA has outlawed company unions and unlawful assistance to unions affiliated with national organizations, some companies have organized and supported employee committees for the purpose of discussing and resolving grievances.[11] Even though these committees differ from traditional unions because they do not negotiate labor agreements, they could subsequently come under the provisions of the National Labor Relations Act if their discussions over wages and employment conditions are interpreted as negotiations by the NLRB. Further, the employer could be directed to recognize and bargain with committee members as a labor union.[12]

Many nonunion companies have initiated employee-involvement programs to restore the sense of working in a small business, to gain worker commitment to the enterprise, to dissuade union organizing, and to provide feedback to enhance motivation and productivity. Over 85 percent of companies in a Conference Board survey have a system for giving nonunion employees information about the competitive conditions or economic circumstances of their company. The majority have employee participation programs such as quality circles and small-group discussions of production and quality of work and have provided formal complaint and grievance systems.[13]

During recent years nonunion companies have become more concerned about employee terminations, which are estimated to be about three million each year in the United States. At least half of these terminations occur without the employee being protected by either law or contract. In other words, the employee is terminated under the *employment-at-will doctrine* that states that either the employer or employee is free to terminate the employment relationship "at will" (at any time, for any reason or no reason). There are laws that prohibit discrimination on the basis of race, sex, color, religion, age, national origin, and union activities, and a collective bargaining agreement usually protects employees against termination without "just cause" (see Chapter 10).

Employers are concerned about unfavorable court decisions and enormous sums awarded by juries; however, a recent survey of 78 nonunion companies ranging in size from 40 to 40,000 employees revealed that managers are still not inclined to relinquish control over the resolution of employee grievances. Even though all companies surveyed had a grievance appeal system, less than 8 percent provided arbitration of unresolved employee grievances, and these companies limited the types of grievances that could be appealed to arbitration.

The most common system for resolving employee grievances was the "open door" policy, wherein employees may present their grievances to management representatives. The success of this system depends on how conscientious managers at all levels are in fulfilling this policy and whether employees fear that presenting their grievances to managers above their immediate supervisor will have undesirable consequences. The second most common system is the grievance appeal board, wherein employees present their grievances to a board for a final decision. In this system, three management members and two employees might hear the grievance and decide the outcome. Although the system is sometimes called a "jury of one's peers," management representation is usually greater than that of employees and can outvote employee board members if necessary.[14]

Unionized Companies' Strategies A strategy adopted by unionized companies is the *business-like, codified* strategy. These companies accept unions as the legitimate representative of the employees and conclude that if the employees want a union, they will deal with it. They do not attempt to have the union decertified, do not commit flagrant unfair labor practices, and do not try to substitute participative groups for unions. The managers of these companies respect and trust their union counterparts, and they expect respect and trust in return. For the relationship to last, both parties must realize that respect and trust are fundamental to both of their futures. The approach of these companies is to deal directly and bargain with the union over wages, hours, and terms and conditions of employment at the appropriate times. When the negotiations of the labor agreement are complete, managers of these companies administer the agreement as they interpret it. In other words, they "go by the book." Although General Electric was known in the 1950s for its "take-it-or-leave-it" approach to labor negotiations, its strategy today can be categorized as a business-like approach. The remaining chapters explain this approach to labor relations. Also, as noted previously, strategies of companies and unions change during their lifetimes and with economic conditions, changes in leadership, and personalities of participants.

The fifth strategy is one of *accommodation and labor-management cooperation.* This strategy entails the union participating with management, rather than the parties having an adversarial relationship. Management and unions actively work together to create an organizational climate and a way of operating that will allow employees to participate directly in decisions in their work areas as members of task teams and as members of problem-solving groups. Unions represent their members in decision making as well as in collective bargaining.[15]

In some cases, management may even seek union leaders' input into strategic business decisions. The goal is to reduce labor costs by increasing productivity and efficiency and to improve sales by improving product quality and customer service. This strategy does not preclude an exercise in managerial prerogatives. On occasion, management may be required to engage in concessionary bargaining or to request a change in restrictive work rules. However, management never engages in aggressive union avoidance tactics and never attacks the legitimacy of the union as the representative of the employees.[16]

This relationship ensures that unions and management focus on common goals, which include the health of the business in a changing economic environment, and new issues, such as adopting new technology to assure competitiveness and business survival. Management accepts unions as stakeholders in an ongoing complex, multi-stakeholder organization designed to ensure survival and provide an equitable return for all involved in the process. Several companies and unions have already proceeded in this new direction. General Motors and the United Auto Workers have included cooperation, gain-sharing, and teamwork in the new GM Saturn plant. The Amalgamated Clothing and Textile Workers and Xerox have organized Horizon Study Teams to investigate and make recommendations on a wide range of strategic business decisions. (Other examples will be discussed in Chapter 7.)

To achieve this new union role, management and union leaders must develop different skills. Union leaders need business decision making skills: they must understand the business and the problem-solving process. At the same time, they must maintain contact with the membership to better represent their interests. Management must take steps to reorient its views; from viewing unions and labor agreements as constraints to recognizing a more cooperative union-management relationship. Management must provide the union and its leadership with a secure position as the legitimate, permanent representative of the bargaining unit employees. This means abandoning efforts to decertify the union or to reduce the union's importance at the workplace. It means developing a mutual trust between parties at every level of the organization.[17]

Companies may choose a mixed strategy, which encompasses union avoidance, union substitution, or labor-management cooperation, at various sites in a multiplant operation. For example, it may operate double-breasted as a company and strongly oppose the union at one of its nonunion plants. At the same time, it may engage in labor-management cooperation at another plant. Such strategic choices are made at the highest levels of the organization, and the advantages and disadvantages of each strategy are seriously debated and deliberated before any strategy is adopted by the company.

Upper management considers the market pressures, operational and financial factors, and collective bargaining relationships in its deliberations. If the market pressures are intense due to import penetration, management may be inclined to choose union avoidance in the nonunion sector. However, if a high proportion of the plants are unionized, management may choose the labor-management cooperation strategy. Researchers continue to examine which factors lead to certain strategies.[18]

Union Strategic Planning

Labor unions, like other organizations, define their operational goals, determine their organizational strategies and plans, develop policies and procedures, and manage their resources to reach their goals and maximize their performance. Unions also are involved in long-range planning, establishing procedures for budgeting, attracting able staff members, communicating with members to provide information and to obtain reliable feedback, and establishing controls for financial accountability.[19]

Labor unions in the United States have been involved in strategic planning for only a short time. For years, unions as a rule reacted to managerial decisions with little concern for long-range implications. Today, more and more unions are finding it essential to become involved in strategic planning. Such planning activities seem to be taking three forms: (1) *proactive/growth* strategies, (2) *defensive* strategies, and (3) *environmental modification* or *"change the game"* strategies. The *proactive/growth* strategies are designed to increase membership by such actions as organizing new jurisdictions and expanding the union's boundaries. The unions in this group have witnessed membership growth and an enlarged membership base. For example, the United Food and Commercial Workers (UFCW) have steadily increased in membership although overall union membership in the United States has stagnated. The UFCW has invested increased time, effort, and resources in union organizing activities, and its strategy appears to be working. The *defensive* strategies are attempts to preserve the union's present position by providing services to present members, preventing decertification, pursuing mergers with other unions, and preventing further declines in membership. The *"change the game"* strategies involve actions to modify the environment by changing the traditional adversarial relationship with management and pursuing a positive approach through labor-management cooperation efforts. Other attempts to "change the game" include modifying public policy and legislation through lobbying and political actions and use of corporate campaigns to achieve more financial leverage with employers.[20] Some unions, like the United Auto Workers, have established internal commissions to participate in strategy planning. The report of the Commission on the Future of the UAW, entitled "A Strong Union in a Changing World," was completed in 1989. Excerpts from the report are included in "Labor Relations in Action" on pages 98–99.

Additional items in UAW's strategic plan are:

- *Improving union image and communication* through media portrayals that identify UAW's diverse membership, characterized by pride in their union and progressive beliefs and attitudes that represent a part of the solution to America's problems. Communication might be enhanced through a new weekly bulletin, scientific polling, and "town meetings" held with members across the country.
- *Organizing new members* by training local union officials and members in successful organizing techniques that in turn are targeted to the most promising fields, such as white-collar, government, health care, and the service and repair employees of automobile dealerships. The union also seeks expansion of modern techniques such as polling, video, and computers to identify issues in organizing companies and to help project a positive image of the union.
- *Education for the future,* including fair and adequate treatment of labor issues in the school curriculum as well as training for labor relations officials and union awareness programs as part of the members' employment orientation.

In 1982, the AFL-CIO Executive Council established the Committee on the Evolution of Work to review and evaluate changes that were occurring within unions and in the labor force, occupations, industries, and technology. This committee in 1985 produced a report entitled *The Changing Situation of Workers and Their Unions,* which provides strategic plans in several areas of union activities. Exhibit 4.3 outlines these plans.

Exhibit 4.3

Recommendations of the AFL-CIO Committee on the Evolution of Work

1. New methods of advancing the interests of workers, which include associate union membership, expanded use of the electronic media, and corporate campaigns to secure neutrality of employers in organizing efforts.
2. Increasing members' participation in their unions, which includes increased interaction between local union members and national union leaders, orientation of new members, and greater resources devoted to training officers, stewards, and members.
3. Improving the labor movement's communications, training for union spokespersons in media techniques, efforts to better inform reporters about unions and trade unionism, and advertising to improve the public's understanding of labor.
4. Improving organizing activity by carefully choosing and training organizers, better use of modern technology, greater involvement of union members in organizing campaigns, experimenting with new organizing techniques, and attracting workers who are covered under contracts but who have not joined unions (estimated to be 2 million employees).
5. Structural changes to enhance the labor movement's overall effectiveness by adopting guidelines and providing assistance for union mergers, resolving organizing disputes among unions, modern budgeting, program analysis, and planning techniques to improve the administration of unions.

Source: *The Changing Situation of Workers and Their Unions* (Washington, D.C.: AFL-CIO), 1985.

Significant changes in the operational and financial structure of U.S. corporations that have occurred in the 1980s and that are intertwined with labor relations have caused unions to change their existing strategies and assume new roles. For example, in 1985 alone there were 3,001 acquisitions and divestitures. Firms such as Continental Airlines and Wilson Foods used Chapter 11 of the bankruptcy law to facilitate business reorganizations. Continental and Eastern Airlines, both of which were headed by Frank Lorenzo, engaged in negotiations that led to strikes, then declared bankruptcy, hired striker replacements, and began operating as nonunion airlines. Wheeling-Pittsburgh and LTV made wage cuts during bankruptcy that placed much pressure on USX to follow suit in order to remain competitive. Others such as Goodyear and Westinghouse have used company repurchase of stock from shareholders to ward off takeovers. The result has been greater centralization of management, a reduction in employment, and a more aggressive stance toward unions.[21] As a result, unions are learning to use their financial clout and expertise either directly by the purchase of stock or indirectly by participating in corporate takeovers.

Unions in the airline industry have taken the lead in many corporate reorganizations and takeover battles. They have negotiated special contingent agreements with contenders for corporate control and have negotiated "poison pills" to ward off takeovers. "Poison pills" involve issuing stockholders the right to purchase stock at discounted prices in the event that a "corporate raider" attempts a hostile takeover of the corporation. Although these rights are not redeemable, current stockholders are able to increase their share of the corporation's stock, thereby making it more difficult for the corporate raider to buy controlling interest in the corporation. When Carl Icahn conducted a hostile takeover of TWA, the unions had to provide concessions to allow the financing of the debt. Then, in 1989, a management-labor committee (primarily the pilots' union) participated in an attempt to purchase United Airlines. Unions became involved in bankruptcy proceedings in order to protect their pension plans and negotiated with creditors, lenders, management, and shareholders about how to restructure the business.

Unions have made labor concessions as a quid pro quo for debt restructuring. They have increased the frequency of union representation on corporate boards of directors, usually in exchange for wage concessions (in the automobile, airline, trucking, and food processing industries). Unions have obtained direct ownership in corporations through employee stock ownership plans (ESOPS, covered in more detail in Chapter 13) and have attempted direct buyouts of several companies. These forms of union involvement have come about not by virtue of the union's statutory rights, but by virtue of the union's accumulation of market and financial power.[22]

Company Organization for Labor Relations Activities

There are many different organizational structures for labor relations activities in U.S. companies. Therefore, the following discussion introduces some of the basic organizational structures, although different company characteristics will alter these designs.[23]

In larger corporations, the labor relations function is usually highly centralized, with policy, strategic planning, and bargaining decisions made at the corporate level. In fact, the final economic decisions are usually made by the chief operating

Labor Relations in Action

Our Changing World (Strategic Considerations)

While we recognize the reality that social transformation is a long-term process, we think it is urgently necessary for the UAW to maintain its leadership role in that process and to advance the following specific ideas and programs that will contribute to social progress:

The union's central economic message – concern about erosion of the nation's industrial base and related problems of corporate flight and disinvestment – is on target. We suggest that these issues will continue to have great economic importance and political appeal and should be further reinforced in union communications. Traditional economic concerns like full employment are closely related, and remain important in their own right.

The union must continue developing and projecting a positive vision for America's future, including alternatives that would allow labor, government, and business to focus on a common social commitment that would benefit all of society. Our vision contrasts sharply with the unregulated free market "vision" of most of the business community, which is based fundamentally on private greed rather than social need and includes using our human resources to fulfill our social needs. Our nation has a growing backlog of unmet needs in areas such as health care, education, infrastructure and the environment which can only be met through increased public investment. We must recognize the importance of the media and "think tanks" in shaping public debate, and we need to make more effective use of both in developing and disseminating our message.

The issue of tax policy and tax fairness will be increasingly important in the years ahead. Many workers are convinced that their tax burden is unfair, and they are right. Corporations and wealthy individuals do not pay their fair share of taxes. We need to cultivate the view that everyone in society, including corporations, should pay a fair share of the cost of government, and likewise that the payers are entitled to get their money's worth from high-quality governmental programs and services.

Problems of dislocated workers deserve greater priority and attention. It is important for trade unionists to become active in Private Industry Councils (PICs), and to pursue other avenues for helping dislocated workers.

The workforce will be changing substantially in the years ahead, as women, minorities and immigrants make up a growing proportion of new workers. The nature of work is also changing, as more and more jobs come to be performed by temporary part-time,

Source: *A Strong Union in a Changing World: The Report of the Commission on the Future of the UAW 1989* (Detroit, Mich.: United Auto Workers, 1989), pp. 19–20.

executive with the advice of corporate-level labor relations managers. In smaller companies with only one or a few facilities, these decisions are made at the plant level and shared with plant management with advice from the plant labor relations manager.

In larger companies, at the operations or plant level the plant manager and plant labor relations manager play the key roles in certain labor relations activities such as administration of the contract, grievance handling, and monitoring union activities. In smaller companies, activities at the plant level also include bargaining, strategic planning, and policy formulation.[24]

The duties and responsibilities of all labor relations managers and specialists are determined in large part by the organizational structure and its degree of cen-

subcontracted and other "contingent" workers. In our collective bargaining, organizing and political action programs, we must take these changes in the nature of work and the make-up of the workforce fully into account.

Rapid change in technology and methods of work organization will continue in UAW workplaces. The union must develop and implement a positive program that steers technology in ways that are beneficial to workers, and away from directions that are harmful to them. Job content, ergonomics, and the potential increase of monitoring in the workplace are among the many issues that will need to be addressed. Reduced worktime without reduction in pay, and reduction of overtime, will also be increasingly important goals in the years ahead; we must develop a comprehensive educational program to reach our members about these issues, and we must continue to support our trade union colleagues in other countries who are struggling to win improvements in these areas.

We face major challenges in UAW industries, including imports of vehicles and parts, transplants, outsourcing, and new methods of manufacture. Particular attention is needed to the parts supplier industry, where there has been tremendous growth of non-union competition in recent years. International labor solidarity will be increasingly important as we move forward to meet our collective bargaining and organizing challenges.

Declining political participation is a serious national problem. Among all major American institutions, the labor movement is uniquely positioned to make a meaningful contribution toward reversing this disturbing trend. The UAW should review this matter, and lead the initiative for increasing the political participation of American citizens.

We must encourage and create more opportunities for rank-and-file involvement and participation in political action within the union. In keeping with our tradition as a socially-conscious union, it will be important to continue to stress social solidarity rather than purely self-centered political action.

Racism and sexism continue to be cancers on American life. The UAW must continue its proud tradition of leadership on civil rights and struggle against all forms of bigotry and intolerance.

Political action is vital, but we must also do a more effective job of helping *ourselves*. Examples include improving the effectiveness of our Buy Union/Buy UAW campaigns and increased use of pension fund investments to create union jobs while preventing the use of such investments to harm workers' interests.

---

tralization or decentralization of authority. The duties typically include corporatewide responsibility for policies, procedures, and programs ranging from union organizing drives at nonunion facilities to negotiations with the union at others.

Exhibit 4.4 shows the organization chart for the labor relations function in this large, complex company. As shown in the organization chart, the vice president of personnel and industrial relations reports directly to the president and has the director of labor relations reporting to him or her. Each of the company's six product lines has its own labor relations organization.

Plant personnel and industrial relations managers are involved in many previously mentioned activities as well as in administering the terms of the labor agreement and resolving related grievances (see Exhibit 4.5). Exhibit 4.6 shows that the

Exhibit 4.4 Labor Relations Organization: Dotted-Line Relationships

Note to Organizational Chart: Note that each respective Group Personnel and Industrial Relations Manager has a direct reporting relationship to his or her respective group management while maintaining a "dotted-line" relationship to the corporate staff, which has the responsibility for the formulation of corporatewide labor relations policies and procedures.

As each group is dependent upon the corporate function as the formulator of this policy, the lines of communication and working relationships are strong and the level of communication very frequent.

Their function is to administer corporate policies and procedures as formulated by the Vice President of Personnel and Industrial Relations and his or her staff.

Source: Audrey Freedman, *Managing Labor Relations* (New York: The Conference Board, 1979), p. 28.

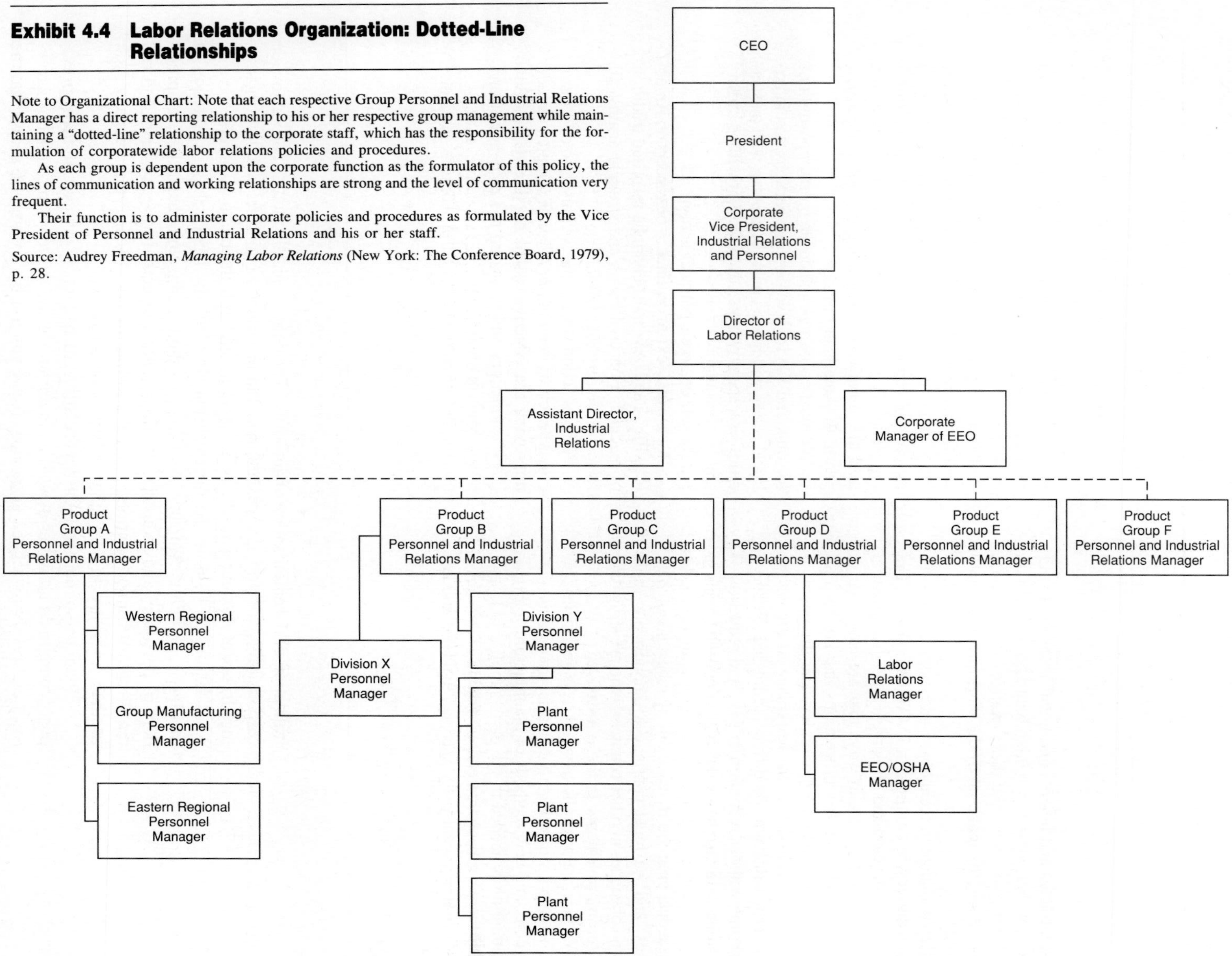

CEO

President

Corporate Vice President, Industrial Relations and Personnel

Director of Labor Relations

Assistant Director, Industrial Relations

Corporate Manager of EEO

Product Group A Personnel and Industrial Relations Manager

Western Regional Personnel Manager

Group Manufacturing Personnel Manager

Eastern Regional Personnel Manager

Product Group B Personnel and Industrial Relations Manager

Division X Personnel Manager

Division Y Personnel Manager

Plant Personnel Manager

Plant Personnel Manager

Plant Personnel Manager

Product Group C Personnel and Industrial Relations Manager

Product Group D Personnel and Industrial Relations Manager

Labor Relations Manager

EEO/OSHA Manager

Product Group E Personnel and Industrial Relations Manager

Product Group F Personnel and Industrial Relations Manager

Exhibit 4.5 **Plant Personnel and Industrial Relations Manager**

Responsible, in conjunction with their corporate personnel and industrial relations staff, for the day-to-day administration of corporate labor relations policies and programs.
Responsible, in conjunction with their corporate personnel and industrial relations staff, for day-to-day contract administration and application of collective bargaining agreements at plant.
Responsible, in conjunction with their corporate personnel and industrial relations staff, for the maintenance of relationships with union and nonunion employees.
Assist personnel and industrial relations managers and the corporate staff in union organizing drives at other plants.
Responsible for handling first- and second-step grievances at the local plant level.
Responsible for the day-to-day administration of grievance procedures for nonunion employees.
Works with the corporate staff in conducting the corporatewide personnel and labor relations audit program within the corporation.

Source: Audrey Freedman, *Managing Labor Relations* (New York: The Conference Board, 1979), pp. 15–16.

organization chart for the labor relations function at the plant level is much more direct in dealing with employees than at the corporate level. The number of staff members depends on the size of the plant and the services performed by the labor relations function.

Position descriptions of employee relations managers in nonunion companies reflect differences in activities from those in unionized companies. Exhibit 4.7 shows that the duties and responsibilities do not include dealing with unions, but focus on

Exhibit 4.6 **Organization Chart for the Labor Relations Function at the Plant Level**

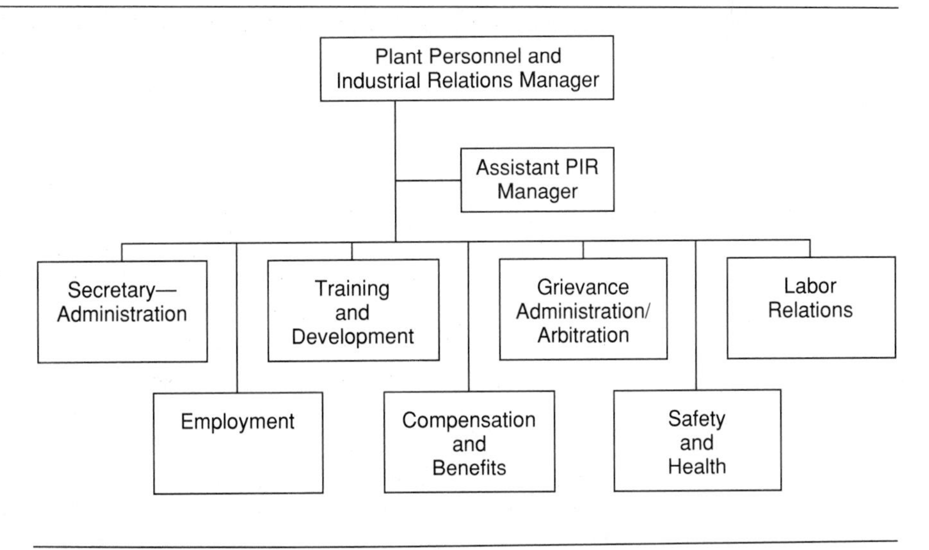

Exhibit 4.7 **Position Description for Employee Relations Manager, Nonunion Soft Goods Firm**

Duties and Responsibilities	The Employee Relations Manager will: ▪ provide liaison and communications with a group of facilities to which assigned. ▪ conduct action for prevention of union petitions, card signing, unfair labor practices, EEO charges. ▪ act as conduit to and from assigned locations for all personnel and labor activities and policies. ▪ deal directly with plant personnel managers and, where applicable, plant managers. ▪ develop a working knowledge of assigned locations. ▪ recommend policy changes. ▪ train personnel managers. Reports to Corporate Director, Employee Relations.
Background and Experience	Five years' experience in the area of personnel management. Exposure to a preventive labor environment in nonunion company especially desirable. If a law graduate, 1 to 3 years' experience in labor law. Desirable to have been an Employee Relations Manager previously, but not required.

Source: Adapted from Audrey Freedman, *Managing Labor Relations* (New York: The Conference Board, 1979), p. 16.

human resource management practices and administering the employee relations program, which includes avoidance of unions in this case.

Union Governance and Structure

Unions as organizations are fundamentally different from business organizations. Business organizations are built on the assumption that power, authority, and legitimacy flow downward from the owner or stockholders through management. Union organizations, on the other hand, have mechanisms such as a written constitution and by-laws that ensure an opportunity for members to participate in the governance of the organization—hold office, attend meetings, vote in elections, or express dissatisfaction with the leadership. Thus, in the democratic organization of a union, power, authority, and legitimacy ultimately flow upward from the consent of the governed. If the leadership of a union wishes to move in a new direction, such as greater union-management cooperation, the new direction ultimately depends on the approval of the membership. If elected leaders do not consider new initiatives in terms of the political realities, they will be rejected by the vote of the members. For example, in cases where the members do not trust management's actions in a joint cooperative effort, the leadership must put forth the appropriate effort to build a trusting relationship before developing the joint effort.[25]

There are about 100 different international and national unions and over 60,000 local unions in the United States, whose governance will be discussed in this chapter following a brief description of their organizational structure. As with companies, unions' organizational structure reflects their activities. Exhibit 4.8 shows the organizational structure of an international union, which includes the various officers, operational departments and staff, regions, and local unions. In this case, the basic functions include financial activities handled by the Secretary-Treasurer, research, administration, education, organizing, political action, and international affairs. These activities will usually be carried out at the union's national headquarters, with some headquarters staff members possibly working in the field. The regional offices are headed by a vice president, who has an advisory relationship with the local unions in the region. Regional offices are established to better serve the needs of the local unions and to represent the national office in the region.

At the local union level, the organizational structure is fairly simple. Exhibit 4.9 shows the officers and the shop stewards. In small unions, all of these are part-time positions; only in the larger unions does the financial support allow full-time union leaders. Most local unions have at least one vice president, a secretary, and a treasurer. The addition of any other officer, such as the sergeant-at-arms in Exhibit 4.9, will depend on the needs of the union. Shop stewards are usually elected to represent the membership in their respective departments. The following section explains how unions are governed at the different levels and presents some of the major problems in the governing process.

To understand union governance, one can compare the union with a unit of state or federal government. There are executive, legislative, and judicial activities at various levels. The local union meetings and national conventions are the legislative bodies; the officers and executive boards comprise the executive bodies; and the various appeal procedures serve the judicial function. A union can also be compared to a private organization because it is a specialized institution having a primary purpose of improving the economic conditions of its members.

Unions claim the democratic ideal, but realistically they must rely on a representative form of government. On the whole they seem to be as democratic as local, state, and federal governments. In fact, the union membership has more of a say in the way the union operates than most citizens have in their governments or most stockholders in their corporations.[26]

To appreciate unions as organizations, one must recognize their wide diversity, the organizational relationships of the various levels, the functions of the officers, and the varying degrees of control. This section explores the characteristics of craft and industrial unions, the functions of local union officers, and the government and operations of local unions. The national or international union,[27] which is composed of the local unions within a craft or industry, is explained in a similar framework. Not to be overlooked are the various intermediate levels of union organizations that provide specific functions for their affiliated unions. A fourth level for many union organizations is the federation, or the AFL-CIO, whose organizational structure, functions, and officer responsibilities are also discussed.

The Local Union

Although there are generally four levels of unions—local, national (or international), intermediate, and the federation of unions—the local union is the main point of contact for the individual employee. The typical union member often identifies more closely with the local union than with the other union levels. He or she attends and sees local officers at the local meetings and workplace. When the union member

Exhibit 4.8 **Organization Chart of an International Union**

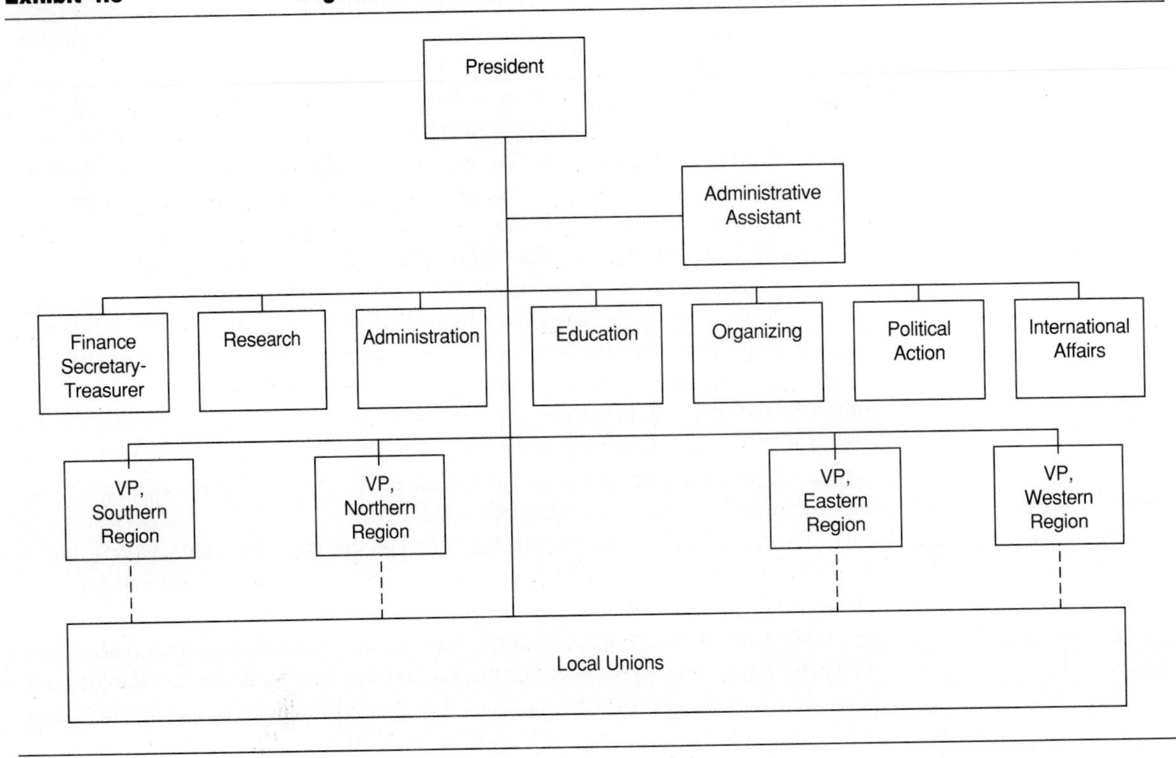

has a grievance, the local union officers are the first to assist. When a strike occurs, the local union officers are the ones who make continuous contact with the strikers on the picket line. Although the national union may negotiate the master labor agreement under which the local union member works, and the AFL-CIO may deal with the president and Congress on certain issues facing the nation, the local union serves as the vital link between the individual union member and the national union, which in turn might link with the AFL-CIO.

Organizationally, the local union is a branch of the national union. It receives its charter from the national union, and it operates under the national union's constitution, bylaws, and rules. The constitution of the national union prescribes the number and types of officers, their duties and responsibilities, and the limits of their authority. Although union constitutions vary in length and content, they often mandate certain financial reports and require that a certain number of meetings be held, that the local labor agreement conform to the master labor agreement negotiated by the national union if there is companywide bargaining, and that approval to call a strike be obtained by the local union. With the trend toward greater centralization of authority by the national union, the local union over the years has lost much of its operational flexibility.

Local Craft versus Industrial Unions The operation of the local union in large part depends on the type of workers making up its membership. Although there is

Exhibit 4.9 **Organization Chart for a Local Union**

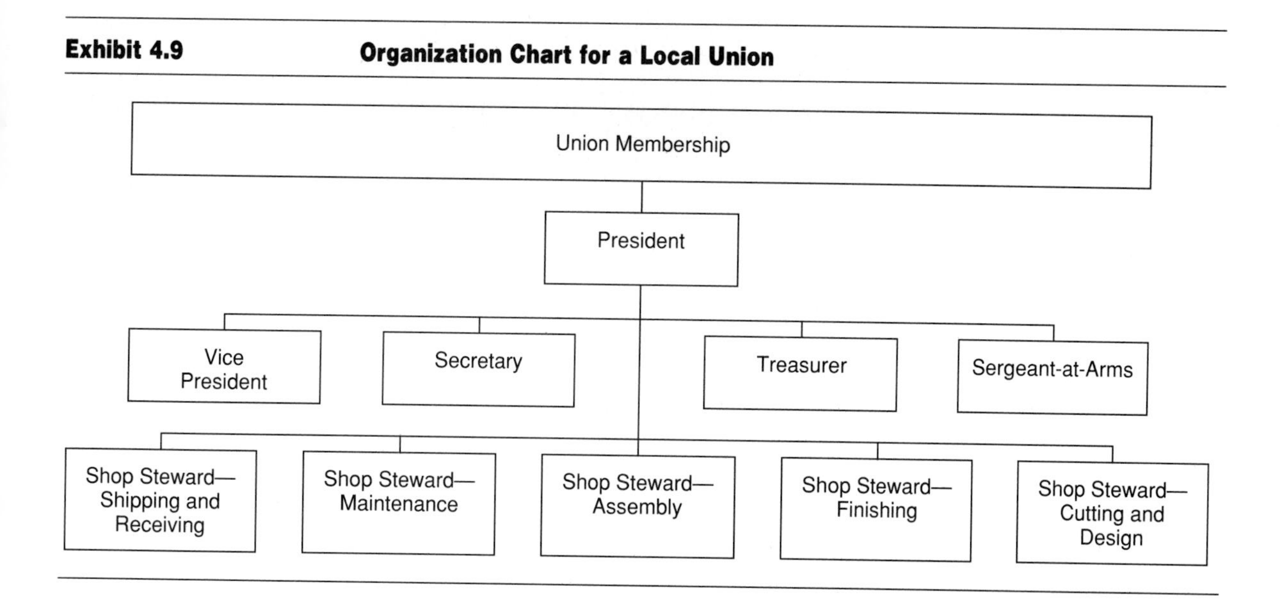

not a clear-cut division between them, unions can be divided generally into two groups: craft and industrial.

Differing Union Organizations The **craft unions** are composed of members who have been organized in accordance with their craft or skill, for example, bricklayers, electricians, carpenters, or ironworkers. **Industrial unions** have been organized on an industry basis, for example, the Steelworkers, Auto Workers, Rubber Workers, Mine Workers, Textile Workers, and so on. This, of course, does not mean that there are no skilled workers in the steel, auto, rubber, or textile industries; but it does mean the electricians in a steel plant would likely be members of the Steelworkers.

Differing Scope of the Labor Agreement The craft and industrial unions differ in other ways that have an effect on their operations. First, the craft unions, which frequently represent the building trades, usually negotiate short labor agreements (supplemented by detailed agreements on special topics, such as apprenticeship programs and safety) that cover a small geographic region, and each has considerable independence from the national union compared to industrial unions. Because of the nature of their work, craft union members may work on several different job sites for several different employers in a given year, still working under the same labor agreement. The labor agreement covers the construction companies and a number of the building trades unions in the particular geographic area.

The industrial union, on the other hand, may be covered by a national labor agreement negotiated between the company and the national union, which covers all of the company's unionized plants. For example, General Motors plants in Atlanta, Detroit, and Los Angeles are covered by the same master agreement. Well over 100 pages long, it explains in detail the wage plan, transfers, pensions, layoffs, etc. A separate local agreement is negotiated to cover matters of concern to the specific local plant and its employees, which must be consistent with the master agreement.

Differing Skills Types of skills help demonstrate another difference in local union operations. The craft members are highly skilled artisans who have completed formal training, usually in a formal apprenticeship program. Many industrial employees, on the other hand, do not require much prior job training. Therefore, the craft union members often feel that they have higher status than their industrial counterparts. The training programs available for the industrial union members are usually offered by the company, whereas the training received by members of craft unions is jointly controlled and operated by the unions. So craft unions select those who will be offered the apprenticeship training, while companies alone select the trainees in the plants. Such an arrangement has allowed the craft unions to limit the numbers in the craft, sometimes only to their families and friends. In addition, the administration of these apprenticeship programs may adversely affect minority group members, a situation discussed in Chapters 11 and 12.

Differing Job Characteristics The nature of their work creates a unique opportunity for craft unions to operate under conditions that approximate a closed shop. Since many of the work assignments last only a short period, the craft members, such as electricians on a building project, return to the union hiring hall for their next assignment after their part of a project is completed. Upon receiving the assignment, the union members could report to another job site and work, possibly for another company. Usually, these arrangements are worked out in advance by the business agent of the craft union and the companies who agree to operate under the existing labor agreement. In other words, the union hiring hall serves as a clearinghouse or placement office for the construction companies as well as the union members. Since the hiring hall must be operated in a nondiscriminatory manner, nonunion workers may also use its services; however, use by nonunion employers is still quite rare. In comparison, the typical member of the industrial union is hired by the company and will work for the same employer—usually at the same facility—until employment is terminated.

Differing Leadership Roles Another difference between craft and industrial unions pertains to the roles of the business agent and shop stewards of the craft union and the local union officials of the industrial unions. The **business agent,** the full-time administrator of the local craft union, provides many of the same services as the local union president of a large industrial union. Both are considered the key administrative officials of their respective local union halls, and they lead the local union negotiations and play a key role in grievance administration. However, the business agent has additional duties, such as administering the union hiring hall, serving as the chief "watchdog" over the agreement at the various work sites, and appointing an employee on each job site to serve as the shop steward. The **shop steward,** who may be the first person on the job or a senior employee, handles employee grievances, represents the business agent on the job, and contacts the business agent if anything goes wrong.

In local industrial unions, the president may or may not serve full time. If the position is full-time, the salary comes from union dues. If the position is part-time, the president is compensated from the union treasury only for the time taken off the company job (at the regular rate of pay). The presidential duties include participating in local negotiations, maintaining the local lodge, assisting in grievance administration, and assuring that management abides by the agreement. On many occasions, a staff member of the national union (usually the national union representative) assists local officers in negotiations and in administering the labor agreement and makes sure that the local's activities conform to the national constitution and directives. The shop steward, the elected representative in each department in the plant or facility, represents the members at local union meetings, handles grievances at the shop level, and collects dues, if necessary.[28]

Union officers may be granted preference in shift assignment and protected from layoffs; however, they must be involved in the day-to-day administration of the collective bargaining agreement. (See Exhibit 4.10 for the shop steward's organizational relationship.)

Government and Operation of the Local Union There are several common ways for union members to participate in union activities: holding office, participating in meetings, attending conventions, voting (elections, ratification, and strike vote), and helping with the monthly newsletter.

Union members whose growth needs are not fulfilled on their job are usually more willing to become involved in union administration. Also, individuals are usually more willing to participate in union administration when their values are closely aligned with their role in the union.[29]

Participation in Meetings Attendance at local union meetings often varies between 5 and 10 percent of the membership; attendance is higher, however, among union members who perceive a potential payoff for participation.[30] When the union is con-

Exhibit 4.10 **An Example of the Organizational Relationship between Union Officials and Management Officials at a Local Plant**

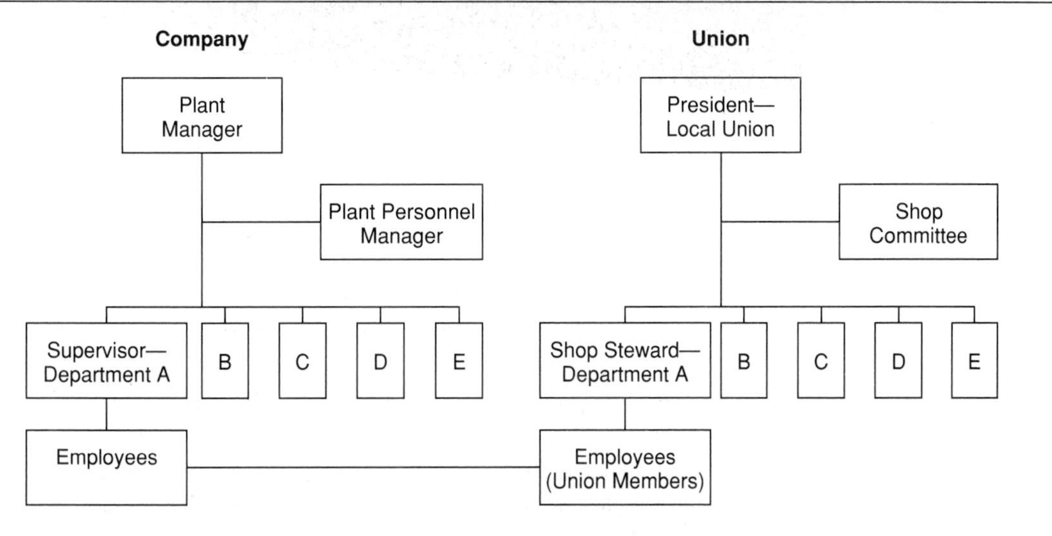

fronted with important business or a crisis, such as during union elections, taking a strike vote, negotiations, or ratifying the negotiated agreement, attendance also rises. Unions and their members have been criticized for their lack of attendance, but formal attendance cannot be taken as the real measure of membership participation. Much membership participation takes place on an informal basis at the plant level between employees, among friends during lunch, or between shop stewards and members during rest breaks. Concerns are channeled to the union leadership through these stewards, who regularly attend local meetings. The influence of these informal channels over union policies and actions should not be underestimated.

The union leaders almost always attend local union meetings, as do departmental representatives, "hard-core" members, pressure groups, social groups, and aspirants to union leadership positions. Union stewards are expected to attend local union meetings and represent the interests of those in their units. Although direct votes occur only on major issues, the union steward can usually reflect the membership views.[31]

Locals have tried a number of techniques to increase attendance of regular members, such as providing beer and sandwiches, showing movies, fining members who miss a specified number of meetings or refusing to let them seek an elected office, and providing door prizes. While some gimmicks may increase the attendance in the short run, many members still feel the meetings are "long, boring, and frustrating affairs."[32]

Local meetings are held at a time that meets the approval of the majority. While they often start late and last too long, the average length is about 2 hours. The content inspires little attendance because much of the time is devoted to reading reports from the treasurer, project leaders, and committee chairpersons. Opportunities are provided for members to discuss these reports, but this procedure itself takes time, especially when a grievance involving someone in attendance is presented or when a controversial issue is raised before the meeting as a whole. Parliamentary procedure is used at times to excess by quasi-parliamentary experts who may want to tie up the meeting. Although the meeting may stray from the ideal, generally the business of the local is accomplished.

Functions of the Meeting While the local union meeting may seem boring and not well attended, it serves several vital functions in the local union government. First, the meeting is the union's single most important governmental activity, and all authority at the local level is derived from it. Second, the meeting provides an opportunity for members to communicate with union leaders, express gripes directly, and call attention to their concerns. Likewise, it is an opportunity for leaders to give information to members, present results of activities, seek union support, and give direction to the membership. Last, the meeting is the supreme legislative body; this is where decisions are made on such items as disposition of grievances and approval of expenses and constitutional changes, election of officers, and ratification of the contract.[33]

The National or International Union

The national or international (these terms are used interchangeably in this chapter) union in the United States occupies the "kingpin" position in organized labor "because of its influence in collective bargaining—the core function of American unions."[34] Size alone (see Exhibit 4.11) indicates the magnitude of the influence of national unions–millions of members work under labor agreements that are directly or indirectly the result of national union actions. The local union operates under its constitution and directives, and the federation (AFL-CIO) derives its influence, prestige, and power from the affiliated national unions.

The national union operates under a **constitution** adopted in a convention by representatives from locals. These constitutions have evolved over time through three stages: first, the locals were initially careful to restrict the power of the national union; second, as national unions became more active in collective bargaining, political action, and so on, the locals became subordinate bodies; and third and presently, the constitution includes provisions that not only authorize the major national union functions but also protect individual rights and rights of locals in relation to the national union.[35]

The Convention The supreme governing body of the national union is its **convention,** which is usually held annually or biennially.[36] It serves the national union in many ways: as the constitutional assembly, the legislature of the national union, the final court for union decisions, and the means for nominating officers (and the elec-

Exhibit 4.11 **International Unions**

Organization	Members
Teamsters (IBT)	1,161,000
National Education Association (NEA) (Ind.)	2,000,000
Steel Workers (USW)	494,000
Auto Workers (UAW)	917,000
Food and Commercial (UFCW)	999,000
State, County (AFSCME)	1,090,000
Electrical (IBEW)	744,000
Service Employees (SEIU)	762,000
Carpenters (CJA)	613,000
Machinists (IAM)	517,000
Communications Workers (CWA)	492,000
Teachers (AFT)	544,000
Laborers (LIUNA)	406,000
Clothing and Textile Workers (ACTWU)	180,000
Hotel and Restaurant (HERE)	278,000
Plumbers (PPF)	220,000
Operating Engineers (IUOE)	330,000
Ladies' Garment Workers (ILGWU)	153,000
Paper Workers (UPIU)	210,000
Retail (RWDSU)	137,000
Postal Workers (APWU)	213,000
Government Workers (AFGE)	156,000

Note: All organizations not identified as independent (Ind.) are affiliated with the AFL-CIO.

Source: Courtesy D. Gifford, *Directory of U.S. Labor Organizations, 1988–89* (Washington, D.C.: The Bureau of National Affairs, Inc., 1988), pp. 59–65; "AFL-CIO Membership Hits 14.1 Million," *Daily Labor Report,* December 8, 1989, pp. A-8–E-4.

tion in many cases). The convention provides the time and place for national officers to report to the members their accomplishments and failures. It provides the agenda for policy formulation, program planning, and rule making. It represents the time in which the voice of the membership holds leaders accountable for their actions. However, not all activities are official; the convention provides a reward for drudgery work at the local, an opportunity for politicking and public relations, and a time and place for the members to "let their hair down."

The convention makes use of the *delegate system* in which the number of delegates allowed depends on the number of members in the local. Since even the smallest union is allowed one delegate, the number of delegates is not in direct proportion to the size of the local, although larger locals usually have more delegates. The convention conducts its business similarly to Congress and various state legislatures in that much committee work (including the possible holding of hearings) is performed prior to debate and vote on the convention floor. However, much discussion takes place in the convention hotel bars and smoke-filled rooms.[37]

Although many subjects may go before the convention, several continue to emerge year after year.

- Internal government: dues, financial matters, authority of the president, executive board, and locals.
- Collective bargaining: problems with current agreements, membership requests for future negotiations, establishment of bargaining priorities, determination of strategy for next negotiations.
- Resolutions in support of or against domestic and international public policies: labor law reform, inflation, interest rates, unemployment, international balance of payments, loss of jobs to foreign countries.[38]

Leadership and Administration Between conventions, the national union is led by its executive board, whose members are elected by the membership. In some cases, executive board members are elected on a regional basis, and they are responsible for regional intermediate organizations that maintain contact between the locals in the region and the national. The relationship between the executive board and the national union president is usually specified in the constitution. For example, some national union presidents primarily carry out the policies of the executive board; others direct the affairs of the national union, subject to the approval of the board. However, the largest group of presidents has virtually unrestricted authority to appoint its staff, regulate locals, and direct the activities of the national union. The rationale for allowing such great authority to be vested in the chief executive is that the union frequently finds itself in struggles with employers or in other situations where it must act decisively and quickly. Thus, a strong executive is needed and a single spokesperson for the union is required. However, the concentration of power creates opportunities for misuse of power, and an internal system of checks and balances must be devised to assure democracy and adequate representation. Experiences that brought on the passage of Titles I to VI of the Landrum-Griffin Act have shown that internal control often does not work effectively, and government regulation is essential.

A major and difficult reason for abuse of leadership is member apathy. For example, only 33 percent of the members of the International Union of Electrical

Workers (IUE) voted in one of its last elections of national union officers, and only 193 of the 600 local unions were represented at the national union convention. In response to this apathy and lack of participation, the delegates to the convention voted to have the officer elections conducted at the convention rather than by direct vote of the rank and file, further removing the individual member from a role of active participation in union decisions.[39]

One slight sign of improved democracy and active participation by members has been the increased turnover rates of national union presidents. Although some former international union leaders maintained their positions for extended periods of time (Dan Tobin, Teamsters, 45 years; John L. Lewis, Mine Workers, 39 years), about one in ten presidencies changes hands each year. While turnover is not the necessary prerequisite for union democracy, the general rule is that the union leader must be responsive to the membership and satisfy the membership's objectives to remain in office.[40] The president's tenure in office tends to be longer in larger unions, with formalized communication networks, centralized bargaining, and heterogeneous rank-and-file members.[41]

The operational departments of nationals vary in kind and number, but the typical national union will have at least the following departments: (1) executive and administration; (2) financial and auditing; (3) organizing and servicing; and (4) technical staff, which includes research, education, economics, law, publications, and public relations.

Likewise, the international unions create operating departments to serve various special interests among their membership. For example, in 1989 the United Auto Workers established the Transnational and Joint Ventures Department for the 8,000 UAW members who are employed by three Japanese-managed vehicle makers at U.S. sites. These include the Toyota-General Motors, Ford-Mazda, and Chrysler-Mitsubishi joint ventures (Nissan remains nonunion).

The executive and administrative group includes the president, vice president(s), secretary-treasurer, and their assistants. This group will be chiefly responsible for the activities of the overall union. In some cases the vice president may concentrate on organizing or collective bargaining, whereas the secretary-treasurer will focus on financial matters.

The organizing and service functions are usually handled by international union representatives employed by the national but assigned to a regional office to assist the locals in that geographic area. In addition, if there are unorganized workers in the area, this representative usually devotes some efforts to organizing these workers. The technical staff departments may be one-person shops that provide expert assistance to locals on a broad range of subjects, such as selecting arbitrators, carrying out economic research, and writing news releases.[42]

National unions have traditionally selected their staff through political processes by rewarding demonstrated leadership and loyalty at the local level. Union officers generally have been suspicious of college-educated persons and believed that the staff should work their way up the ranks. More recently, national unions are using personnel practices used by business and government. With the election of more college-educated persons to national offices, much of the resistance to college education has declined. For example, both the president and secretary-treasurer of the AFL-CIO have college degrees, and an attorney was elected president of the United

Mine Workers. Today, it is still common to employ international union representatives and organizers from the ranks, but almost all unions fill their technical positions with college-educated outsiders. Another personnel activity within unions that is growing is training and staff development. There are labor education centers at many universities; over 3,000 union staff members from nearly 100 national unions took courses from the George Meany Center for Labor Studies, and a college degree program has been established with the cooperation of Antioch College.[43]

Services to and Control of Locals As indicated earlier, the locals are constitutionally subordinated to the national union, but the degree of subordination varies with the union. The national provides services to the local union in several ways while at the same time controlling local union leaders. For example, where a national product market exists, a master labor agreement with one firm might be negotiated to cover all its facilities (such agreements have been negotiated in the steel, auto, rubber, aircraft, and electrical appliance industries). Also, a union such as the United Rubber Workers may negotiate an agreement with a company like Goodyear at the national level, and this agreement may establish a pattern for negotiating with other rubber companies such as Uniroyal, Goodrich, and Firestone. Following the negotiations of the master agreement between the national and each company, the local union will negotiate a local agreement with officials at each plant, covering local rules, policies, and benefits. Deviations from the master agreement are possible, but they must be okayed by the national union. (See Chapter 6 for further coverage.)

The national union assists locals in collective bargaining, grievance administration, strike activities, and internal financial administration. These services also provide an opportunity for national union staff members to make sure that the local unions are conforming to national policies.

The international union representative, in addition to organizing new unions, also helps the local unions in grievance administration and labor arbitration. The national supports the local in strike situations, but the local must get approval in order to qualify for strike benefits. The national union provides counseling and consultation for internal financial administration (bookkeeping, dues collection, purchases, financing union lodges, and so on), but trusteeship (receivership) procedures are available whereby the national union can set aside the local for abuses such as malfeasance, corruption, and misuse of funds in favor of a trustee under national direction.

Dues, Fees, and Distribution of Funds Although all union members pay dues or fees to their national unions, the amount and form vary considerably. Such fees are the chief source of revenue for unions. Typically, the monthly dues are about $20, and the initiation fee is about $40. Some unions set a single rate, but most allow the local some flexibility in making the final determination. Frequently, dues are collected via a dues checkoff system (discussed in more detail in Chapter 11). The member agrees to a payroll deduction of union dues, which are collected by the employer and paid directly to the union.

Several specialized unions with small memberships, such as the Director's Guild, Football Players, Mine Workers, and Iron Workers, charge over $100 for an initiation fee, and the Radio Association charges $2,000. Usually when dues are higher than average, the payments include premiums for insurance, pension payments, and other benefits.

The local unions forward a portion of the monthly dues for each member to the national union. The nationals use these funds for various purposes beneficial to the membership. While the largest percentage of funds goes to the general fund, which covers administrative and operational costs and salary expenses, allocations are also made to accounts such as a strike fund, a convention fund, union publications, educational activities, and a retirement fund.[44]

Use of union dues and fees for political purposes and non–collective bargaining activities has come under fire in the last few years. Union members who disagree with the manner in which their unions contribute or use their funds have challenged their unions. Recent court decisions have caused several unions, such as the Machinists, Auto Workers, Communications Workers, and American Federation of State, County, and Municipal Employees, to adopt dues rebate plans. These plans allow a rebate of a portion of member dues spent on political activities if the member requests it in advance (usually annually).

The U.S. Supreme Court has ruled that if a union uses dues and fees of protesting employees for non–collective bargaining activities and purposes, it breaches its fiduciary duty of fair representation. In addition, a district court judge listed 12 activities, including political ones, that were considered non–collective bargaining activities.[45] While unions can continue to solicit volunteer contributions through such units as the AFL-CIO Committee on Political Education (COPE), the UAW's Community Action Program (CAP), and the UMW's Coal Miners' Political Committee (COMPAC), collections may be more difficult.

Mergers of National Unions Encouraged by the AFL-CIO merger, but mostly spurred by rising costs, the need for stronger bargaining positions, expensive jurisdictional disputes, decline of some U.S. industries, economies of scale, avoidance of external controls, and the need for self-preservation, mergers of national unions have occurred at a quickening pace, especially after 1968. Between 1890 and 1984, there were 183 union mergers, with half of them (92) occurring after 1955.[46]

In recent years, important union mergers have occurred in the paper, clothing and textiles, railroad industries, the postal service, and among state government employees unions. The merger of the Retail Clerks and the Meat Cutters and Butchers created the United Food and Commercial Workers, with 1 million members—one of the largest unions in the United States.

These mergers occur through **amalgamation,** which is the joining together of two or more unions, or through **absorption,** which occurs when a large union takes over a smaller union. These mergers do not always produce a complete fusion or a total submergence of the absorbed unions. Occasionally there is a strong membership resistance to the merger, and the larger union may establish a division within its union to allow members of the former union to have a separate voice in the policy of the larger union after the merger. Other causes of resistance stem from membership interest in preserving their craft identity, desire to carry on their union's historical traditions, and membership identity with a small geographic region.[47]

Typically, mergers have not succeeded immediately in welding together functions, organizational units, and staff members. They have required the time, patience, and good will of all parties, as officers and staff members who have different personalities and modes of operation are meshed. The local unions must be accommodated as well as the employers and the collective bargaining relationships. Mergers have been particularly difficult when one of the unions feels a loss of its autonomy and when the merger occurs between unions whose prior dealings have been characterized by intense rivalry. Often members' pride is hurt, and fear surfaces when they find out that their union may be submerged by another.

In a more positive vein, the resulting larger unions gain more clout with industrial giants and can negotiate more as equals. The greater size generates resources to provide better training in collective bargaining, grievance administration, and steward leadership; to offer greater strike benefits; to lobby more effectively for legislation; and to maintain a staff to combat unfair labor practices. Moreover, successful mergers reduce the risks to smaller unions from technological change, economic recessions, declines in membership, unemployment, and financial strains.[48]

Most officers of unions with 50,000 or less members (includes more than half of AFL-CIO affiliates) believe that mergers have the best prospects of providing and maintaining member services. The benefits include more effective lobbying, increased bargaining power, expertise, economies of scale, and more effective strikes. The trade-offs are reduction in membership participation and less attention to needs of special interest groups. The potential advantages of a merger coupled with the risks of not merging suggest that mergers of national unions will be continued in the future.[49]

Intermediate Organizational Units

Within the union structure between national headquarters and the locals lie the intermediate organizational units—regional or district offices, trade conferences, conference boards, and joint councils. These units usually operate under the guidance of their various national units, but their activities are important to the union members and employers in their areas.

The regional, or district, offices house the regional or district officers, the staff, and the international union representatives for the geographic area served. For example, Michigan has a number of Auto Workers' district offices; the Steel Workers have district offices in Pittsburgh, Birmingham, and elsewhere. The offices are established to better serve locals from their respective national unions.

Trade conferences are set up within national unions to represent a variety of industrial groups. For example, the Teamsters union has established 11 trade conferences for such groups as freight, laundry, airlines, and moving and storage. These groups meet to discuss various mutual problems and topics of interest.

Conference boards are organized within national unions in accordance with the company affiliation to discuss issues that pertain to the union and the particular company. For instance, each of the national unions within the steel, auto, rubber, and electric industries has established conference boards that meet to discuss negotiations and related problems. Delegates are chosen from the local unions to represent the interests of their constituents at meetings, to plan the next negotiations, and then to relay these plans to the local union members.

Joint councils involve groupings of local unions that have common goals, employers, and interests. Examples are the building trades councils established in most metropolitan areas in the United States. They negotiate with the association of construction employers in the area, coordinate their activities, and assist in resolving jurisdictional disputes between unions.

The American Federation of Labor and Congress of Industrial Organizations (AFL-CIO)

The American Federation of Labor and Congress of Industrial Organizations (AFL-CIO), while not including all U.S. labor unions, is composed of 89 national and international unions that have 60,000 local unions and just over 14 million members. In addition, there are 32 directly affiliated local unions. Members represent a wide diversity of occupations, such as actors, construction workers, barbers and hairdressers, steelworkers, bus drivers, railroad workers, telephone operators, newspaper reporters, sales clerks, garment workers, engineers, schoolteachers, and police. These AFL-CIO affiliates maintain day-to-day relationships with several thousands of employers and administer more than 160,000 labor agreements. Most (over 99 percent) of these agreements are negotiated without strikes or other forms of conflict and serve as the basis of employment conditions under which many work.

Established in 1955 when the American Federation of Labor and the Congress of Industrial Organizations merged, the AFL-CIO recognized the principle that both craft and industrial unions are appropriate, equal, and necessary parts of U.S. organized labor. The federation accepts the principle of *autonomy*—each affiliated union conducts its own affairs; has its own headquarters, offices, and staff; decides its own economic policies; sets its own dues; carries out its own contract negotiations; and provides its own services to members.

No national union is required to affiliate with the AFL-CIO. About 60 unions remain outside the AFL-CIO. Member unions are free to withdraw at any time; however, their voluntary participation plays an essential role that advances the interest of every union. National unions continue their membership because they believe that a federation of unions serves purposes their own individual unions cannot serve as well.

Examples of the AFL-CIO services include

- Speaking for organized labor before Congress and other branches of government.
- Representing U.S. labor in world affairs, keeping in direct contact with labor unions throughout the free world.
- Coordinating activities such as community services, political education, lobbying, and voter registration with greater effectiveness.
- Helping to coordinate efforts to organize nonunion workers throughout the United States.

Another vital service enhances the integrity and prestige of AFL-CIO unions—they must operate under established ethical practice codes covering union democracy and financial integrity. The federation also assists in minimizing conflicts that cause work interruptions by mediating and resolving disputes between national unions, such as organizing disputes and conflicts over work assignments.[50]

Organizational Structure The AFL-CIO organizational structure, shown in Exhibit 4.12, illustrates the importance of the convention. Meeting every 2 years and at times of particular need, delegates decide on policies, programs, and direction for AFL-CIO activities. Each national or international union is authorized to send

Exhibit 4.12 **Structural Organization of the American Federation of Labor and Congress of Industrial Organizations**

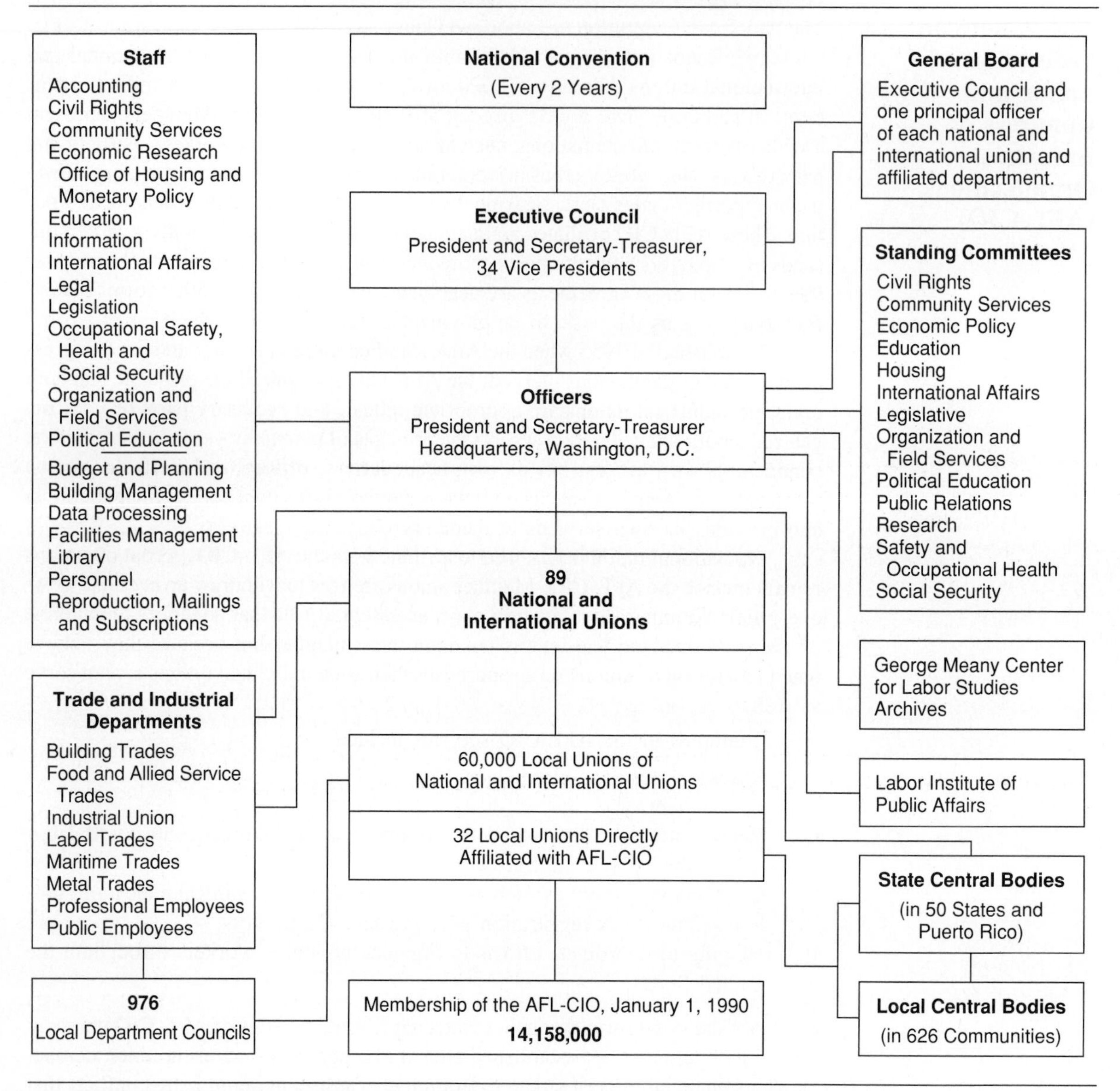

Source: AFL-CIO.

delegates to the convention. Each union's representation of delegates at the convention is determined by the number of dues-paying members. In addition, other affiliated organizations, such as state labor councils, are represented by one delegate each.

Between conventions, the governing body is the Executive Council, composed of the president (currently Lane Kirkland), secretary-treasurer (currently Thomas

R. Donahue), and 34 vice presidents elected by majority vote at the convention. The Executive Council meets at least three times a year and handles operational duties involving legislative matters, union corruption, charters of new internationals, and judicial appeals from member unions.

The AFL-CIO has been criticized for its lack of minorities in its 36-member Executive Council. While it now has three black members, it has only three female members, even though women make up 34 percent of the unionized workers and 44 percent of the total civilian labor force.[51]

Between meetings of the Executive Council, the president, who is the chief executive officer, has authority to supervise the affairs of the federation and to direct its staff, and the secretary-treasurer handles all financial matters. To assist in his administration, the president has appointed 15 standing committees on various subjects, which, with the assistance of the AFL-CIO staff, provide related services to member unions. The staff, located at headquarters in Washington, D.C., corresponds closely to these standing committees in order to better serve the member unions. (See Exhibit 4.12 for a listing of standing committees and staff divisions.) The General Board, composed of the Executive Council and one officer from each member union, is available to act on matters referred to it by the Executive Council.

The AFL-CIO has established 50 state central bodies (plus one in Puerto Rico) to advance the statewide interests of labor through political, lobbying, and organizing activities, which involve attempts to elect friends of labor, to have favorable legislation passed, and to organize nonunion workers, respectively. Each local union of the AFL-CIO–affiliated unions in a particular state may join the state organization and participate in and support its activities. In addition, 626 *local central bodies* have been formed by local unions of the national affiliates to deal with civic and community problems and other matters of local concern.

To accommodate and serve the interests and needs of various trade and industrial unions, the AFL-CIO has established eight *trade and industrial departments.* The Industrial Union Department represents the interests of industrial unions, mostly members of the former CIO. Another department, the Union Label Department, promotes the purchases and sales of union-made goods and services. The remaining departments represent the interests of such union groups as the building trades, food and beverage trades, maritime employees, metal trades, public employees, and professional employees. In addition, throughout the United States where there is sufficient interest and support, 976 *local department councils* have been organized.[52]

The AFL-CIO's operations are financed through regular member dues, called *per capita taxes,* which are paid by affiliated unions on behalf of their members. Currently, the per capita tax is $.31 per month or $3.72 per year for each member. Thus, the AFL-CIO's operating budget is $52.1 million, of which nearly all covers regular operating expenses. A major portion of the budget goes to the salaries of the staff. The detailed financial report of the AFL-CIO is submitted to the delegates at each convention.[53]

The AFL-CIO recently recognized the potential of maintaining contact with employees who are not members of unions by establishing an associate membership program. They include those who voted for the union in elections where the union did not win, employees in nonunion companies who would vote for the union if given a choice, and employees who are represented by the union but have not joined it. There were 300,000 associate union members by 1989 and the number continues to grow steadily. This program helps the AFL-CIO maintain contact with these employees and provides benefits for a nominal fee. The benefits of the program include life insurance, prescription drug coverage, travel services, legal services, and a credit card program[54] (see Exhibit 4.13).

Other AFL-CIO activities are educational and informational, presenting the federation's stance on a variety of issues. For example, the AFL-CIO publishes a weekly *AFL-CIO News* that keeps members up-to-date on current events that pertain to them and presents various reports on problems and policies of organized labor. The AFL-CIO maintains the George Meany Center for Labor Studies, which offers short courses in union leadership development and a Speaker's Bureau to provide labor speakers for high school and college classes and makes educational films available to interested groups for a nominal fee.

In the political arena, the AFL-CIO receives much attention. The representative of organized labor, it serves as the focal point of political activities. Not only does it lobby aggressively for favorable legislation, but it publishes the voting records of each senator and representative at both federal and state levels. It attempts to influence appointments, such as Supreme Court judges, the Secretary of Labor, and National Labor Relations Board members, who are important to organized labor. Its policy of "reward your friends, punish your enemies" has not changed much since Samuel Gomper's day. The AFL-CIO's Committee on Political Education (COPE) has a network in each state and in most large communities. COPE seeks voluntary contributions to provide funds for its activities, which include voter registration, "get-out-the-vote" campaigns, preparation of leaflets and posters, and research on behalf of its candidates.[55]

Although the Federal Election Campaign Act of 1971, amended in 1974, has restricted financial contributions to federal candidates, the AFL-CIO, COPE, and state and local bodies can still amass amazing support to help their candidates for office, especially when the candidate is clearly the choice of organized labor. Or-

Exhibit 4.13 **Union Privilege Benefit Program**

1. Life insurance: rates 25 percent lower than comparable plans, no medical exam required, guaranteed coverage for senior citizens (more than $1 billion in policies already issued)
2. Prescription drug coverage: pays 30 percent on prescriptions, toll-free hotline for questions, all family members eligible
3. Travel services: 5 percent cash back on travel expenditures, short-notice vacation hotline, free travel insurance, guaranteed lowest airfare, hotel and car rental discounts
4. Legal services: free consultation by phone or in person for up to 30 minutes, free follow-up services, 30 percent discount on complex matters, over 650 participating offices of attorneys
5. MasterCard program: no annual fee, lower rates, no check fees (over $150 million in interest and fees saved by participants by 1989)

Source: *AFL-CIO News,* August 19, 1989.

ganized labor and corporations have become major players in the funding of political campaigns at the federal level, primarily through Political Action Committees.

While organized labor has played a major role in U.S. politics, it retains independence of a national political party. Over the years it has been more closely aligned with the Democratic party, both philosophically and politically. It has become perhaps the single most important political force that has supported government programs to help the socially and economically disadvantaged. It has supported consumer and environmental protection and safety and health legislation that has benefited all workers, not only union members.

Organized labor has accumulated much power and influence through its own established network and has also been instrumental in organizing other politically active groups with socially oriented objectives, such as minorities and senior citizens. However, organized labor's overall political strength and actual effectiveness should not be exaggerated. In some states and municipalities, union membership is so negligible that its influence is inconsequential. In others, where union membership is high, its influence is significant, and political candidates must actively solicit its support.[56] The AFL-CIO does not control the membership's votes; however, members are an independent lot, and there are other reasons why union members vote for candidates.

New Leadership Style Lane Kirkland, AFL-CIO president, is projecting a new, modern style of directing the federation. He participates in discussions at regional meetings with rank-and-file union members, projects an image of an intelligent, articulate leader, and directs the AFL-CIO's Executive Council by consensus, with every member being given an opportunity to express an opinion.[57]

As A. H. Raskin, long-term labor analyst for the *New York Times,* has stated:

> In Kirkland the Federation has a leader of supreme intelligence and sophistication, who has also shown subtlety and skill in building consensus. His command is firm, his recognition of the need for change clear. If anyone can restore the movement to its indispensable place as an effective countervailing force in the American economy and public life, he is the one to do it.[58]

Union Corruption and the Landrum-Griffin Act

Unethical and illegal practices, including corruption, racketeering, and embezzlement have been discovered in some local and national unions. Union abuses of power were exposed by the McClellan hearings of the late 1950s. Large amounts of Teamsters pension funds have been misused. Union officials have been indicted for conspiracy to bribe a U.S. senator and for embezzlement. Indictments have been rendered where "ghost workers" were maintained on payrolls even though no services were performed.

In 1986, the President's Commission on Organized Crime reported that organized crime dominated four major American unions: the Teamsters, Longshoremen, Hotel Employees and Restaurant Employees, and Laborer's International. These unions were accused of violence and threats of violence against union members, misuse of pension and welfare funds, and pressuring employers to make payoffs for "sweetheart contracts" and "strike insurance."[59] It is important to note that many of these violations require a co-partner on the company side to participate in the illegal transactions.

In 1989, the Teamsters and the federal government settled charges that the union was under the influence of organized crime. The settlement occurred just before the scheduled opening of a trial of alleged violations under the Racketeer Influenced and Corrupt Organizations Act (RICO). The settlement barred persons allegedly involved in organized crime from participating in union activity and provided for three persons, jointly selected by the parties and acting separately from each other, to temporarily oversee union activities and supervise secret-ballot elections of union officers.[60]

Other unions have been investigated recently for corruption and racketeering. In the New York City area, members of both labor unions and construction companies were alleged to have participated in illegal activities in the construction and shipping industries. Opportunities for corruption and misuse of power are created by the unique characteristics and complexities of these industries. In construction in the New York City area, there are over 100,000 workers, hundreds of contractors, over $20 billion of construction work, over 30,000 building permits per year, over 100 building trades locals, and about 50 contractor associations. Because construction companies can be ruined by strikes, delays, and sabotage, union officers have leverage potentially to extort money from them. As well, companies often derive benefits from payoffs to union officials by having them ignore fringe benefits payments due union members, disregard union shop provisions, and show preferential treatment in securing adequate workers in time of need. Thus, opportunities for labor racketeering and union corruption are made available by corrupt business persons as well as corrupt union officials.

ETHICS

Possible resolutions to these problems include long-term commitment by law enforcement officials to ensure company and union compliance with existing laws and the guarantee of union democracy in union operations and elections of union officials. While union corruption and racketeering have received much national attention, the major portion of these activities has been centered in specific geographic areas involving only a few unions, most of which are not in the AFL-CIO or were not in the AFL-CIO at the time of these activities. At the same time, when these activities are coupled with the corruption in savings and loans institutions, the insider trading of investment bankers, and the national scandal of the federal Housing and Urban Development agency, it is clear that much work needs to be done in terms of ethical practices in business, unions, and government.[61]

It should also be noted that one review of public documents revealed that only 300 of the 75,000 local unions—less than one-half of one percent—had been found to be involved in illegal activities.[62] In fact, unions compare favorably with other sectors of the U.S. society. They certainly fare better than the banking industry, which in a single year reported 100 bank presidents, 65 vice presidents, 145 managers, 345 cashiers, and 490 other employees on embezzlement charges. Therefore, one must conclude that "the overwhelming majority of labor leaders are honest men who take seriously their obligations to represent the interest of the members who have elected them to office."[63]

The AFL-CIO established the **Ethical Practices Committee** in its efforts to control corrupt practices and racketeering of its member unions, and its Executive

Council was given the authority to suspend any affiliated union with corrupt practices.[64] Then, in 1959, the U.S. Congress showed its concern with union abuse and the potential misuse of union power by amending the National Labor Relations Act through passage of the Landrum-Griffin Act (the Labor-Management Reporting and Disclosure Act), which has several provisions governing union operations and government. For example, it governs the following:[65]

- Disclosure by union officers and employees (and employers and their agents) about financial dealings, trusteeships, and any private arrangements made with any employees.
- Regulation of union trusteeships, including rules for their establishment and maintenance, and the protection of the rights of members of unions under trusteeship.
- Fiduciary responsibilities of union officers and representatives. It also disqualifies criminals and former communists from holding union offices, and it requires certain union officers to be bonded to assure the faithful discharge of their duties and responsibilities.
- Rights to participate in union elections and governance, such as the right to nominate candidates in elections, to vote in elections, to attend membership meetings, to participate in the deliberations, and to vote on the business, such as setting dues and assessments.[66]

The law was intended to promote union democracy and financial integrity. Success in the administration of the law requires initiative on the part of union members and availability of necessary information for interested union members.

In 1984, the Comprehensive Crime Control Act, containing the Labor Racketeering Amendments, was passed. These amendments, backed by the AFL-CIO, closed the loopholes in the existing laws against labor malfeasance. Convicted labor officials cannot hold any union position for up to 13 years if they are convicted; previous law allowed for elongated appeals during which the officials might remain in office. Any convicted management official must be transferred outside of labor relations and cannot serve as a consultant or advisor in labor relations.[67]

Summary

This chapter discussed two of the major participants in the labor relations process: unions and management. First, the goals of unions and management were presented, with emphasis on where the goals are the same and where they have potential for conflict. Companies' labor relations strategies ranging from union suppression to labor-management cooperation were explained.

Union strategic plans, which are at the embryonic stages in most unions, were discussed, and examples from the AFL-CIO and United Auto Workers were presented. Companies and unions are structured according to their goals; typical examples of company labor relations organizations and organizations at various levels of unions were displayed.

The last part of the chapter focused on union governance. First, general characteristics of craft and industrial unions were explained. Then, the government and organizational activities of the local union, the national or international union, the intermediate bodies, and the federation (the AFL-CIO) were discussed. Because unions, like business and government, have experienced corruption and misuse of power and authority, examples of these problems and steps that have been taken to seek a resolution were provided.

Key Terms

craft unions
industrial unions
business agent
shop steward
constitution
convention
amalgamation
absorption
conference boards
joint councils
Ethical Practices Committee

Discussion Questions

1. Compare the steps companies may take to implement a positive human resources management program with principles of effective management.
2. What suggestions can you offer to emphasize common goals of companies and unions as opposed to conflicting goals?
3. Analyze the dilemma of nonunion companies in terms of employee termination under the employment-at-will doctrine.
4. Assess the strategic plans of the AFL-CIO and United Auto Workers and determine whether these plans provide direction for growth.
5. Locate a local union and/or a local plant and draw an organization chart for each.
6. Select a craft union and an industrial union and point out differing characteristics of these two types of unions.
7. Compare the government of the local union to student governments and municipal governments, with special attention to participation by members.
8. Explain why and how national unions presidents have been able to accumulate so much authority and power.
9. Differentiate among the business agent of a local union, a shop steward, and an international union representative. How do their roles differ?
10. Since the AFL-CIO does not negotiate labor agreements on behalf of national unions, how can it claim to be the "spokesperson for organized labor" in the United States?
11. Compare the requirements for union democracy to any student organization with which you are familiar.

References

1. Audrey Freedman, "How the 1980's Have Changed Industrial Relations," *Monthly Labor Review* 111 (May 1988), pp. 35–39.
2. Martin M. Perline and David J. Poynter, "Union Orientation and Perception of Managerial Prerogatives," *Labor Law Journal* 40 (December 1989), p. 781.
3. Alan Balfour, "The Unenforceability of the UAW's 'Neutrality Pledge' from General Motors," paper presented at the Second Annual Meeting of the Southern Industrial Relations Association, 1981.
4. Charles R. Greer and Stanley A. Martin, "Calculative Strategy Decisions during Organization Campaigns," *Sloan Management Review* 19 (Winter 1978), p. 73.
5. Ibid.
6. William N. Cooke and David G. Meyer, "Structural and Market Predictors of Corporate Labor Relations Strategies," *Industrial and Labor Relations Review* 43 (January 1990), pp. 280–282.
7. D. Quinn Mills, "Management Performance," in Jack Stieber, ed., *U.S. Industrial Relations 1950-1980: A Critical Assessment* (Madison, Wis.: Industrial Relations Research Association, 1981), p. 112.
8. Fred K. Foulkes, "How Top Nonunion Companies Manage Employees," *Harvard Business Review* 59 (September–October 1981).
9. Herbert R. Northrup, "Construction Doublebreasted Operations and Pre-Hire Agreements: Assessing the Issues," *Journal of Labor Research* 10 (Spring 1989), pp. 219–227.

10. *Twenty-First Annual Report of the NLRB* (Washington, D.C.: U.S. Government Printing Office, 1956), pp. 14–15.
11. Sherman and Murphy, *Unionization and Collective Bargaining*, p. 47.
12. *NLRB* v. *Cabot Cargon Co.*, 360 U.S. 203 (1959). The union challenged a General Foods job-enrichment program that divided employees into work groups for the purpose of working job assignments, scheduling overtime, and discussing job-related concerns with a consultant (with management representatives in attendance on occasion). While the NLRB ruled that no union existed, it could raise interesting issues in the future. *General Foods Corporation and American Federation of Grain Millers, AFL-CIO and Its Local 70,* 231 NLRB 122 (1977). Also see Donna Sockell, "The Legality of Employee-Participation Programs in Unionized Firms," *Industrial and Labor Relations Review* 37 (July 1984), pp. 541–556.
13. Audrey Freedman, *The New Look in Wage Policy and Employee Relations* (New York: The Conference Board, Inc., 1985), pp. 16–18.
14. Douglas M. McCabe, "Corporate Nonunion Grievance Arbitration Systems: A Procedural Analysis," *Labor Law Journal* 40 (July 1989), pp. 432–438.
15. William N. Cooke and David G. Meyer, "Structural and Market Predictors," pp. 280–282.
16. Edward E. Lawler, III and Susan A. Mohrman, "Unions and the New Management," *The Academy of Management Executive* 1 (no. 3, 1987), pp. 293-300.
17. Ibid.
18. William N. Cooke and David G. Meyer, "Structural and Market Predictors," pp. 292–294.
19. John T. Dunlop, *The Management of Labor Unions* (Lexington, Mass.: Lexington Books, 1989), pp. xii–7.
20. Kay Stratton and Robert B. Brown, "Strategic Planning in U.S. Labor Unions," in Barbara D. Dennis, ed., *Proceedings of the Forty-First Annual Meeting of the Industrial Relations Research Association* (Madison, Wis.: Industrial Relations Research Association, 1989), pp. 523–524.
21. Phillip K. Way, "American Enterprise in a Time of Change: Implications for Industrial Relations," in Barbara D. Dennis, ed., *Proceedings of the 40th Annual Meeting of the Industrial Relations Research Association* (Madison, Wis.: Industrial Relations Research Institute, 1988), pp. 183–188.
22. Katherine Van Wezel Stone, "Labor and the Corporate Structure: Challenging Conceptions and Emerging Possibilities," *The University of Chicago Law Review* 55 (Winter 1988), pp. 76–78.
23. John T. Dunlop, "Have the 1980's Changed U.S. Industrial Relations?" *Monthly Labor Review* 111 (May 1988), p. 33.
24. Audrey Freedman, *Managing Labor Relations* (New York: The Conference Board, Inc., 1979), pp. 7–33.
25. Bert Spector, "Transformational Leadership: The New Challenge for U.S. Unions," *Human Resource Management* 26 (Spring 1987), pp. 3–11.
26. Alice H. Cook, *Union Democracy: Practice and Ideal* (Ithaca, N.Y.: Cornell University, 1963), pp. 19–26.
27. National and international unions are nearly synonymous; the small difference is that internationals may have locals outside the United States. Thus, in this book, the terms will be used interchangeably.
28. Allan Nash, *The Union Steward: Duties, Rights and Status* (Ithaca, N.Y.: New York State School of Industrial and Labor Relations, 1977), pp. 20–22.
29. Steven L. McShane, "A Path Analysis of Participation in Union Administration," *Industrial Relations* 25 (Winter 1986), pp. 72–78.
30. John C. Anderson, "Local Union Participation: A Reexamination," *Industrial Relations* 18 (Winter 1979), p. 30.
31. James E. Martin and John M. Magenau, "An Analysis of Factors Related to the Accuracy of Steward Predictions of Membership Views," *Labor Law Journal* 35 (August 1985), pp. 490–494.
32. Leonard R. Sayles and George Strauss, *The Local Union,* rev. ed. (New York: Harcourt, Brace & World, 1967), pp. 96–100.
33. Ibid., pp. 93–105.
34. Jack Barbash, *American Unions* (New York: Random House, 1967), p. 69.
35. Ibid., pp. 71–72.
36. The Landrum-Griffin Act requires a convention at least every 5 years, and some unions, such as the Teamsters, take the limit of 5 years.
37. George Strauss, "Union Government in the U.S.: Research Past and Future," *Industrial Relations* 16 (Winter 1977), p. 234.
38. Barbash, *American Unions,* pp. 76–80.
39. John Hoerr, "Union Democracy and Apathy Don't Mix," *Business Week,* October 2, 1979, p. 28.
40. Shulamit Kahn, Kevin Long, and Donna Kadev, "National Union Leader Performance and Turnover in Building Trades," *Industrial Relations* 25 (Fall 1986), pp. 276–289.
41. Lawrence French, David A. Gray, and Robert W. Brobst, *Political Structure and Presidential Tenure in International Unions: A Study of Union Democracy,* paper presented at the annual meeting of the Academy of Management, Detroit, 1980, p. 16.
42. Barbash, *American Unions,* pp. 81–88.
43. Lois S. Gray, "Union Implementing Managerial Techniques," *Monthly Labor Review* 104 (June 1981), pp. 3–8.
44. Charles W. Hickman, "Labor Organizations' Fees and Dues," *Monthly Labor Review* 100 (May 1977), pp. 19–24.
45. Examples include recreation, social and entertainment activities, organization and recruitment of new members, convention attendance, general news publications, support of pending legislation, and contributions to charity. Ibid., pp. 117–118.
46. John L. Conant and David Kaserman, "Union Merger Incentives and Pecuniary Externalities," *Journal of Labor Research* 10 (Summer 1989), pp. 243–246.
47. Gary N. Chaison, "Union Mergers and Integration of Union Governing Structures," *Journal of Labor Research* 3 (Spring 1982), p. 139.
48. Charles J. Janus, "Union Mergers in the 1970s: A Look at the Reasons and Results," *Monthly Labor Review* 101 (October 1978), pp. 13–15.
49. "Officers of Small Unions Found Receptive to Concept of Merger," *Daily Labor Report,* February 13, 1986, pp. A-8–A-9. Also see Gary N. Chaison, "Union Merger Outcomes: The View from the Smaller Unions," unpublished paper, Clark University, pp. 1–26.
50. *This is the AFL-CIO* (Washington, D.C.: American Federation of Labor and Congress of Industrial Organizations, 1986), pp. 1–2.
51. Cathy Trost, "To the Union Chiefs, It's Still a Brotherhood," *The Wall Street Journal,* November 20, 1985, p. 30
52. U.S. Department of Labor, Bureau of Labor Statistics, *Directory of National Unions and Employee Associations, 1975* (Washington, D.C.: Government Printing Office, 1977), pp. 1–4.
53. *This Is the AFL-CIO,* pp. 8–10.
54. "Solidarity, New Initiatives by Unions Mark Labor Day 1989, Kirkland Says," *Daily Labor Report,* September 1, 1989, p. A-9.
55. *This Is the AFL-CIO,* pp. 10–12.
56. David Greenstone, *Labor in American Politics* (Chicago: University of Chicago Press, 1977), pp. xiii–xxix.

57. Robert S. Greenberger, "Kirkland Alters Style at AFL-CIO, Stresses Politics, Organizing Moves," *The Wall Street Journal,* June 18, 1982, p.27.
58. A. H. Raskin, "The Road to Solidarity: Labor Enters a New Century," *The New Leader,* November 30, 1981, p. 13.
59. "Crime Panel Releases Final Report on Union Corruption," *Daily Labor Report,* March 10, 1986, p. A-7.
60. George Ruben, "Developments in Industrial Relations," *Monthly Labor Review* 112 (May 1989), p. 58.
61. James B. Jacobs and Thomas D. Thacher II, "Attacking Corruption in Union-Management Relations: A Symposium," *Industrial and Labor Relations Review* 42 (July 1989), pp. 501-507.
62. "Union Corruption:Worse than Ever," *U.S. News and World Report,* September 8, 1980, p. 33.
63. Derek Bok and John T. Dunlop, *Labor and the American Community* (New York: Simon & Schuster, 1970), pp. 67-69.
64. Woodrow Ginsburg, "Review of Literature on Union Growth, Government, and Structure: 1955-1969," *A Review of Industrial Relations Research,* vol. 1 (Madison, Wis.: Industrial Relations Research Association, 1970), pp. 232-233.
65. George W. Bohlander and William B. Werther, Jr., "The Labor-Management Reporting and Disclosure Act Revisited," *Labor Law Journal* 30 (September 1979), pp. 582-589.
66. Marick F. Masters, Robert S. Atkin, and Gary W. Florkowski, "An Analysis of Union Reporting Requirements Under Title II of the Landrum-Griffin Act," *Labor Law Journal* 40 (November 1989), pp. 713-722.
67. "President Signs Funding Bill That Includes Labor Racketeering Amendments," *Daily Labor Report,* October 15, 1984, p. A-11.

CHAPTER 5

How Unions Are Organized

As we examine the gaps in the public's understanding of trade unionism and attempt to fill those gaps with convincing evidence, perhaps it is the experience of our own members—their satisfaction in membership, the benefits of unionism they see in their daily working lives, the kinds of problems unions have helped them manage and solve—that will best tell the story. These are the types of messages [that] will be invaluable as we try to help nonmembers grasp the full meaning of union representation.

Carol Keegan, "How Union Members and Nonmembers View the Role of Unions," *Monthly Labor Review* 110 (August 1987), p. 51.

This chapter focuses on the essential elements of unionization: why unions are formed, the procedures for organizing employees into unions, new union strategies for obtaining union recognition, and union decertification.

Why Unions are Formed

Unions are not present in every organization; in many instances, employees have chosen to remain nonunion. In some countries, workers have formed independent labor political parties, and in others they have begun even broader social movements, seeking to establish employee rights through a variety of strategies. This section provides explanations of employees' collective behavior that cut across many organizations; the following section attempts to explain what propels employees at a particular facility to vote for a union.

Work and Job Conditions Explanation

Alienation Theory Karl Marx is identified as the creator of the **alienation theory.** He maintained that employees might seek collective action to relieve their feelings of alienation, which have resulted from the extensive use of machinery in manufacturing operations. According to Marx, employees became alienated from the work as they[1]

- lost contact with their own labor as the products they created were taken away from them, thereby reducing their spirit and stature.
- lost involvement in their work as the machine dominated, separating the work of the hand from the work of the brain.
- became estranged from fellow employees as their work made them so tired and competitive that they were incapable of having authentic relationships.

Marx believed that employees would become aware of their common plight and that class-consciousness would compel them to join together in a union or to engage in collective activities to improve their working situation. Unions can and do address a possible aspect of employee alienation, namely the employees' desire to speak their minds without fear of management reprisal. In other words, "intertwined with the motives for union membership is the almost universal desire to tell the boss to 'go to hell.' "[2] A union typically indicates to its potential members that the employees' rights to voice their opinions regarding a managerial action are protected by negotiated grievance procedures and disciplinary policies (see Chapters 8 and 10).

Employees might be dissatisfied with some aspects of their jobs while not being alienated from their work. Some research has shown that employees might join unions if they (1) are dissatisfied with physical characteristics of the workplace, low wages, or lack of benefits and (2) believe that a union will help them achieve the job-related conditions important to them.[3]

Scarcity Consciousness Theory—The Need for Job Security Selig Perlman suggested that employees are attracted to unions on the assumption that unions will protect their jobs. Many employees, particularly manual workers, strongly believe they are living in a country of limited opportunity and become **scarcity conscious**—the employees collectively believe that jobs are difficult to obtain and retain. This belief is particularly true today for some industries, such as steel and coal. Thus, employees turn to unions to solve these perceived difficulties.[4]

Unions therefore are attractive to the many employees concerned about job security, regardless of their skill or occupational level. Few employees are currently immune from the possibility of a layoff. And unions do offer several ways of strengthening the employees' job security: *They can negotiate work rules,* which prescribe procedures for performing a job, thereby ensuring that a certain number of employees will be assigned work. *They can negotiate apprenticeship programs,* which ensure that qualified people are available for certain skilled jobs. *They can negotiate seniority and layoff provisions,* which require the company to lay off employees by their seniority and to recall the most senior ones first. *They can negotiate grievance procedures,* which include a final step of arbitration to protect them against unjust discharges, unfair treatment, and violations of the labor agreement. *They can lobby for legislation protecting employees' job rights,* which has been a viable alternative used by unions throughout the years. Here, unions attempt to strengthen job security by pressing for restrictions against cheap labor—foreign citizens, child labor, prison labor—quotas or restrictions against imported products such as steel, automobiles, and textiles, and adjustment assistance to employees who are displaced as a result of foreign competition.

Employees' Backgrounds and Personal Desires Explanation

Employees' previous experiences with a union can strongly affect their attitudes toward unions and decision to join one. Many might even be influenced by parental attitudes and family experiences regarding unions. One active union member stated, "I attended union meetings with my father before I was ever inside a church."[5] Another commented, "My dad was a great union man and that's where I got it—if it wasn't union, it wasn't no good."[6] Of course, parental comments regarding unions may be unfavorable as well.

Studies have shown that employees' characteristics such as age, sex, education, and prior union experience are not closely associated with favorable union votes or attitudes.[7] Race appears to be the one exception, as several studies have suggested that more black employees have positive attitudes toward potential union advantages than their white counterparts.[8]

One recent study of over 1,200 employees during union-organizing campaigns only partially confirmed the offsetting nature of personal experiences and the opinions of employees' relatives. For example, the employees' decisions to vote for a union were not significantly correlated with members of their families being union members. Similarly, prior union membership was not significantly associated with a vote for the union in the campaign, suggesting that many members who had been union members elsewhere were not entirely satisfied with union representation. In short, it appears that employees' backgrounds do not explain group voting behavior; that is, what influences an individual might not be characteristic of the group. This lack of explanation is probably due to a combination of complex, potentially offsetting relationships among all the variables found in employees' backgrounds.

Unions as well as all formal organizations potentially satisfy the members' needs by providing "a means of developing, enhancing, or confirming a sense of identity and maintaining self-esteem."[9] Thus, unions can appeal to two interrelated social needs of members, the need for affiliation, or belonging, and the need for status. One prominent observer of industrial relations has noted that unions restore an employee's social ties to his or her work environment, a situation that also assumes moral significance.

> If there is any meaning that can be derived from the persistent grouping of men about their tools or within their industry, it is that work must fill a social and moral as well as an economic role. The vacuum created between the job and the man has proved intolerable; and it cannot be filled by higher wages, shorter hours, better conditions of labor, music in the shops, or baby clinics. Man has to belong to something real, purposeful, useful, creative; he must belong to his job and his industry, or it must belong to him. . . . what gnaws at the psychological and moral roots of the contemporary world is that most urban people, workers and owners, belong to nothing real, nothing greater than their own impersonal pecuniary interests. . . . For the worker the trade-union has represented an unwitting attempt to escape from this dilemma.[10]

The union's possible benefit of social affiliation is strengthened or weakened by the degree of prestige or self-esteem it offers its members. Some employees join a union for the same reason they would join any social organization, namely, to enjoy the responsibility and status associated with being a member of that organization. This feature can be particularly attractive to employees whose jobs are basically interchangeable and carry very few elements of prestige or room for advancement.

Employees who become union officers can often attain prestige or self-esteem in their dealings with management officials:

> As a shop steward or union officer or member of the grievance committee, a worker can become "a fellow your buddies look to." Such positions give him the opportunity to win other workers' approval by being "a fellow who stands up to the boss" with impunity. The role of "a fellow who stands up to the boss" is made more significant because the definition of the boss has been enlarged to include not merely the foreman but "the head office in Pittsburgh." He can win prestige as "a guy that gets results" in such matters as the distribution of work, assignment to jobs, seniority policy, and protection from discrimination.[11]

Chapter 8 discusses the notion that union officers and management officials are equals in their day-to-day administration of the labor agreement. However, as the preceding quotation suggests, the union steward can often emphatically disagree with a management official six levels above the steward on the organization chart. This ability to challenge without fear or reprisal is not usually afforded nonunion employees or even management officials when they deal with their organizational superiors.

Procedures for Organizing Unions

In forming and joining a union, employees mainly consider whether it will improve their personal situations in terms of wages and benefits, promotional opportunities, and job security. Can the employees expect to satisfy their job-related goals and needs by supporting a union? Will the union provide the means for achieving these goals? If employees perceive that a union will help them attain their goals, they will likely vote for it in an election and support its activities afterwards. If they are not convinced, they will not vote for the union and will not support its activities.

The union's campaign to secure employee support may contribute to a union vote, especially among those who are familiar with the union's positions and who attend union campaign meetings. Employees who are satisfied with the working conditions are less likely to attend union campaign meetings, but if they attend, they often become more favorable toward the union.

The company's campaign can affect the vote because it affects employees' belief in the anticipated influence of the union. If the company campaigns hard, some employees will believe that the employer has "seen the light" and will now improve conditions without the union. Further, a strong antiunion campaign may convince some employees that the employer is so antiunion that the union cannot improve working conditions.[12]

While there may be many reasons why a particular group of employees votes for or against the union in a specific election,[13] several influences have been identified that affect union votes generally. Exhibit 5.1 shows the relationships among the general influences on employees. The work context includes specific work-related influences such as supervisory effectiveness and style, job dissatisfaction, and inability to influence management to change working conditions, pay, and benefits. Attitudes toward unions include the beliefs that employees have prior to the vote about unions as institutions and their role in society and in organizations.[14] Economic considerations include such factors as wage levels of other firms, level of unemployment in the industry, economic activity and forecasts, and growth rates.[15] These influences interact with **union instrumentality,** which is the employees' perception of whether the union will be instrumental in attaining desired outcomes, such as higher wages, improved working conditions, job security, and protection from arbitrary treatment by management.[16] In general if these interactions are positive, the employee will vote for the union; if not, the employee will vote against union representation.[17] For the individual worker, any one of the influences may cause the employee to vote a certain way. For example, if an employee believes his or her supervisor is considerate and supportive, this belief may be enough to cause a vote against union representation.[18]

An individual's decision on whether to vote for union representation depends on his or her subjective assessment of the expected benefits to be obtained as weighed against the subjective assessments of the costs.[19] If the expected benefits of being represented by the union are higher than the cost, the employee will vote for the

Exhibit 5.1 **Influences on Employees on Whether to Vote For or Against Unions**

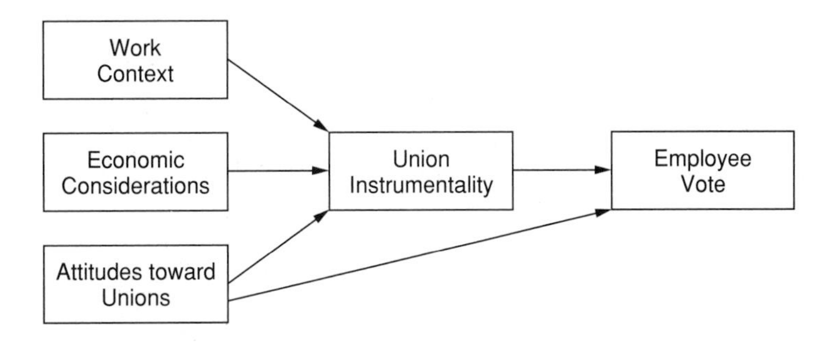

union. Otherwise, the vote will be against representation. If employees have a good chance of promotion, can expect a higher wage based on their present level of effort, and are pleased with their supervisor, they probably will not vote for representation.[20]

Four job characteristics are significantly related to positive attitudes toward union representation: (1) lack of autonomy, (2) lack of job security, (3) inadequate pay, and (4) a high degree of danger associated with work. Experience in the union is important, because 87 percent of workers between the ages of 28 and 38 who are union members said they would vote for a union; only 27 percent of the nonunion workers would.[21]

Studies of union election voting patterns have identified four categories of voters:

1. Employees who have pro-union attitudes, who perceive the union as a positive change agent, and who vote for the union in an attempt to improve an unsatisfactory work relationship.
2. Employees who vote for the union because they hold pro-union beliefs and attitudes irrespective of work context and union instrumentality perceptions.
3. Employees who vote against the union or abstain from voting because the union is not perceived as instrumental in bringing positive change.
4. Employees who vote against the union or abstain from voting because they hold antiunion beliefs or attitudes, irrespective of the perception of the work context and union instrumentality.

In addition, research has identified a positive correlation between the number of workers in the organizing drive and the amount of difference between union and nonunion wages. Negative correlations have been found between the length of the organizing campaign and the percentage of local jobs concentrated among a few employers.[22]

Role of the Union in Organizing Unions

Employees' initial interest in unionization is usually based on their dissatisfaction with some work-related situation (see Exhibit 5.2) coupled with a feeling that each of them acting alone cannot change the situation. Most managers of nonunion companies incorrectly believe that labor unions initiate union organization drives; however, it is usually the employees themselves who begin the process by contacting the union. This contact with union organizers usually occurs after employees believe that there is sufficient support for the union and that the union's expertise and representation will help them.[23]

Union organizers enter the campaign by playing three general roles that influence employees' decisions on whether to vote for unionization. First, organizers try to *educate* the workers on the benefits of the union, the labor movement traditions, and protections afforded by union representation and the present laws. Next, union organizers attempt to *persuade* workers to vote for unionization and respond to statements and allegations made by management during the organizing campaign. Third, organizers try to *support* workers in their individual and collective actions.[24] In order to ensure that these roles are carried out capably, unions recruit and select union organizers with the appropriate education, competencies, and personality characteristics.

Exhibit 5.2 **Seven Warning Signals of a Union Organizing Drive**

Wage below the market
Failure to have one person responsible for personnel matters
No complaints
Weak supervisors
Perception of unfair treatment
Nonminority supervision of a minority work force
Failure to recognize leaders among employees

Source: Joseph Al Latham, Jr., "Susceptibility to a Successful Union Organizing Campaign—The Seven Warning Signals," *Employee Relations Law Journal* 6 (Autumn 1980), pp. 228–238.

The union organizer does not create job dissatisfaction but rather assists in transforming this employee dissatisfaction into collective action. The union organizer tailors the organizing approach to employee concerns and problems and focuses on the special needs of various groups, such as older workers, female or minority workers, or white-collar workers. The organizer tries to sell the idea that group action via the union provides the instrument through which employee concerns and dissatisfaction can be most effectively addressed.[25]

The influence of union organizers should never be underestimated by a company. The union organizers may be first seen distributing handbills to employees as they leave the company parking lots. They dress like the workers so that the workers will identify with them. While their dress may be misleading, management should realize that union organizers are professionals at what they do.[26] Like their counterparts in management, contemporary union organizers must understand the psychology of the workplace and the labor relations climate in which employees work. The union organizers must be able to (1) sort out these complex factors for the employees on a group or individual basis and (2) communicate in the employees' language how the union can assist in fulfilling their needs in the specific work environment.

As an example, Exhibit 5.3 lists a number of work-related concerns and problems. To the right of each is a possible course of action the union could take to satisfy the concern or alleviate the problem. The union organizer would bring to the employees' attention outcomes that could result from such activities by the union on their behalf.

The union enters the organizing campaign knowing that it must convince the uncommitted employees that the union is composed not of outsiders but of concerned fellow employees, that the changes that the union proposes are worth fighting for, that the union will be able to protect employees against reprisals, and that the union officials can be trusted. The union realizes that its success depends on the development of a strong inside organizing committee to convey the message directly to employees who do not attend union meetings and the ability of the union organizer to convey his or her own personal commitment and concern, get to know the employees, listen to employees about their job concerns, and have employees themselves speak at public meetings to express their feelings and their commitment to the cause.

Exhibit 5.3

Union's Strategy and Courses of Action to Achieve Employee Goals and Resolve Job-Related Problems

Examples of Work-Related Problems and Employee Concerns	What the Union Could Negotiate with the Company
Desire for improvement of present fringe benefits	Negotiate better benefits for bargaining unit employees
Desire for additional fringe benefits	Negotiate new benefits, such as dental insurance and legal aid, which would not be provided on the company's initiative
Earns less than deserved compared to others doing similar work	Emphasize comparable wages (local, regional, national, industry); provide data from other unions, Department of Labor, and wage surveys
Exposed to one or more safety and health hazards	Highlight the role of union safety committees and the responsibilities of the company and rights of the union under OSHA
Difficult to get work days and hours changed	Negotiate work schedule procedures with rules and policies which are administered fairly and in accordance with the contract
Inconvenient or excessive hours	Negotiate hours and days of work with advance notice to employees when they work at inconvenient times, call-in pay, overtime, flexitime systems, and so on
Difficult to get duties changed	With job content declared as a *mandatory* negotiable issue, the union could present alternative job descriptions, combine tasks, and so on
Inadequate time for leisure activities	Attempt to obtain shorter hours and workweek, more holidays, and longer vacations for time worked
Skills underutilized in present job	Negotiate promotion policies and procedures, institute a job bidding plan
Unpleasant work environment	Negotiate working conditions and transfer opportunities; institute safety and health committee

Source for work-related problems: Graham L. Staines and Robert P. Quinn, "American Workers Evaluate the Quality of Their Jobs," *Monthly Labor Review* 102 (January 1979), pp. 3–12. Survey data courtesy of the Center for Political Studies, University of Michigan.

Role of the Company in Organizing Unions

The employer realizes that the keys to its success are whether it is able to sustain and increase the employees' concern about how the union would perform if chosen and whether it can convince employees that the employer's past record shows that it deserves their support or at least a second chance. The employer enters the campaign with three advantages: (1) it has instant and prolonged access to the employees; (2) although it can make no promises during the election campaign, it informs the employees of the possibility of improvement without cost and without the creation of a new bureaucracy, and (3) it can take advantage of the fact that most people find the thought of substantial change in their lives frightening.[27]

Employer campaign strategies attempt to avert an employee vote in favor of unionization. However, usually more than one campaign activity must be used. Alone, each activity has only a modest effect; however, combined activities can have a pronounced effect. Exhibit 5.4 shows the frequency of use of various employer campaign activities; literature distribution and speeches to employees during working hours ("captive audience") are used most frequently. Exhibit 5.5 lists certain employer practices and their effect on the election. For example, the employer has much influence on changing the election unit composition and the date of the election but only modest influence on the outcome of the election through such activities as publicizing the disadvantages of the union, displaying posters, and making campaign speeches. Companies must be cautious in election campaigns because they may overdo their resistance and cause a negative reaction from employees, especially when both attorneys and management consultants are used.[28]

The use of consultants in organizational campaigns has increased dramatically. One study reported that 70 percent of the elections studied were directed by consultants. In these campaigns, employer unfair labor practices were committed in over half of the elections, and companies actively resisted the union by making captive audience speeches and writing letters to employees in over 90 percent of the cases.[29] Use of consultants to advise employers how to persuade employees not to vote for a union requires reports to be filed with the Secretary of Labor, even though the consultants have no direct contact with employees.[30]

Illegal discharge and other forms of discrimination against union activists, used by employers to effect the outcome of the election, have increased dramatically in the last several years. Such discrimination reduces the probability of an organizing success by 17 percent and nearly cuts in half the likelihood of the first contracts being obtained. About 90 percent of these illegal activities occur during an organizing drive, just prior to an election, or during the first-contract negotiations. Such violations generally occur when employers perceive the financial gains of keeping

Exhibit 5.4 **Frequency of Employer Campaign Activities**

Campaign Activities	Reported Frequency
Literature distribution	70%
Captive audience speeches	65
Supervisor training	38
Small group meetings	36
Employee surveillance	34
Employment discrimination	24
Directed election	22
Management consultant used	20
Wage increase during campaign	16
Administration of surveys	11
Voter list irregularities	11
Threats of reprisals	10
Promises of gains/inducements	4

Source: John J. Lawler and Robin West, "Impact of Union-avoidance Strategy in Representation Elections," *Industrial Relations* 24 (Fall 1985), p. 412.

Exhibit 5.5

Election Campaign Practices and Activities Used by Employer to Effect the Outcome of an Election

Employer Practices	Effect on Election Outcome
Changing election unit composition	Fairly strong
Changing election date	Fairly strong
Publicizing disadvantages of unions (other than strikes)	Modest
Displaying posters on bulletin boards	Modest
Making campaign speeches	Modest
Employing outside consultants	Some
Restricting employee solicitation	Some
Sending personal letters	Some
Holding small group meetings	Some
Giving handbills to employees	Some
Sending messages in payroll envelopes	Some
Showing movies	Some
Publicizing negative image of unions	Some
Publicizing employer good points	Some
Warning of results of potential strikes	Some

Fairly strong = Correlation with election outcome, .55 to .68

Modest = Correlation with election outcome, .35 to .39

Some = Correlation with election outcome, .23 to .30

All correlations were statistically significant.

Source: Kent F. Murrmann and Andrew A. Porter, "Employer Campaign Tactics and NLRB Outcomes: Some Preliminary Evidence," *Proceedings of the Thirty-fifth Annual Meeting: Industrial Relations Research Association,* ed. Barbara D. Dennis (Madison, Wis.: Industrial Relations Research Association, 1983), p. 67.

unions out as far greater than the costs of back-pay awards and reinstatement of union advocates. And such is often the case. One study reported that only 39 percent of illegally discharged workers were offered reinstatement and only 69 percent of those ever returned to work. Since it takes so long to settle a case and reinstatement comes so long after the organizing drive, some employers have been able to frustrate the legal process and use the legal process against the union and employees interested in the union.[31]

One must wonder how employers reconcile their personal ethics when either they or their representatives knowingly commit illegal practices by discharging an employee or a group of employees for exercising their legal right to support a union. Moreover, one must wonder why the U.S. Congress continues to tolerate such an imbalance in the legal procedures governing the exercise of statutory rights, which have existed in the United States since 1935.

Methods for Organizing Unions

There are three ways for unions to be recognized: (1) employer's voluntary recognition, (2) secret-ballot election, and (3) NLRB directive. Voluntary recognition is the simplest and may be the appropriate alternative for the employer if the union is acceptable and there is no doubt that the union represents the majority of employees. Since voluntary recognition does not include a campaign against unionization, it eliminates any costs of conducting a campaign. Also, it does not involve negative comments made by the parties during a typical organizing campaign, thereby increasing the chances of a cooperative relationship. In most cases, unions attain exclusive bargaining agent status through secret-ballot elections conducted by the NLRB. Most of the following discussion will focus on this process in some detail.

In rare cases, the NLRB may direct the employer to recognize and bargain with the union. While the NLRB considers secret-ballot elections superior, it has discretionary authority to use alternative means to determine the majority interests of employees. In the landmark *Gissel* case, the NLRB decided (and the Supreme Court agreed) that a company may be ordered to recognize and bargain with a union under the following conditions:

1. Evidence reveals that a fair, impartial election would be impossible because of flagrant employer unfair labor practices.
2. Wording on the authorization cards[32] is clear and unambiguous (see Exhibit 5.6).
3. Employee signatures on the cards were obtained without threat or coercion.
4. A majority of employees in the bargaining unit had indicated their interest in having the union represent them by signing the authorization cards.[33]

In essence, the NLRB and the courts have concluded that holding another election in certain situations where the employer had made a fair and impartial election impossible would not be a realistic remedy because a rerun election would favor the party that had interfered with the first election.[34]

In a few cases the union may request employer recognition and then offer to prove that a majority of employees want to join the union. The union may offer to submit signed authorization cards to an impartial third party (arbitrator, mediator, or member of the clergy) who will check the signatures on the cards against payroll signatures. If the employer agrees to this process, the majority status can be affirmed and union recognition extended.[35]

There has been strong employer opposition to granting union recognition based on signed cards. Employers allege that employees were pressured or forced into signing cards. Examples of extreme cases include the refusal of union organizers to leave employees' houses until the cards are signed, obtaining signatures after drinking parties, and threatening injury to or perpetrating violence against employees who refuse to sign. These extremes reveal obvious violations of employees' rights, but they occur in very few cases.[36] Another reason for opposition to union recognition without elections is that signed authorization cards are relatively poor predictors of union success in elections. In a study of 1,174 elections, where over 75 percent of the employees had previously signed the cards, the union won only 70 percent of the elections.[37]

Initiation of Campaigns for Organizing Unions

The union pre-election campaign is not a simple process of exchanging letters and handbills and then holding an election. The campaign usually goes through several stages.[38]

1. Initial contacts between employees and union organizers either by employee requests for help or distribution of union literature (handbilling) at the workplace.

Exhibit 5.6 **Example of a Union Authorization Card**

United Food & Commercial Workers International Union

Affiliated with AFL-CIO-CLC

AUTHORIZATION FOR REPRESENTATION

I hereby authorize the United Food & Commercial Workers International Union, AFL-CIO-CLC, or its chartered Local Union(s) to represent me for the purpose of collective bargaining.

(Print Name) (Date)

(Signature) (Home Phone)

(Home Address) (City) (State) (Zip)

(Employer's Name) (Address)

(Hire Date) (Type Work Performed) (Department)

(Hourly Rate) (Day Off) Day Shift ____ Night Shift ____ Full Time ____ Part-Time ____

Would you participate in an organizing committee? Yes ____ No ____

Source: Courtesy of the United Food and Commercial Workers International Union.

2. Determining interest by calling meetings, visiting homes, and counting responses to handbills. (See "Labor Relations in Action" for a good array of responses received by union organizers who were seeking support from fellow employees.)
3. Setting up an organizing committee by identifying leaders and educating them as to the benefits and procedures of the union, the law, and the issues likely to be raised by management.
4. Building interest by soliciting signatures on authorization cards. (Most organizers will wait to announce that the union represents a majority until over 50 percent, and usually 60 to 80 percent, have signed cards.)

During this time the union discovers and highlights employees' problems, compares wages at their facility to wages at unionized facilities, and explains the role of the union in helping to satisfy their job-related needs. In other words, the union will attempt to convince the workers that they need a union and then that they should sign union authorization cards (see Exhibit 5.6) and should support the forthcoming organizing campaign by wearing union buttons, attending meetings, and signing up members. While various means are available to gain support, research indicates that one-to-one contact, peer contact and persuasion, and high-quality, professionally designed written communications are most effective.[39] Other efforts used by unions include television and radio advertising, "hotline" telephone numbers, group meetings, and handbilling.

Labor Relations in Action

Objections to Joining the Union

"Why should I join the union when I get exactly the same wages and benefits without joining?"

"I can't afford to join. I've got a family to support, and my check just isn't big enough [to cover union dues]."

"I don't believe in unions. They are too strong and powerful now to suit me."

"I don't need a union. My employer is fair and will take care of me. What could the union get for me that I wouldn't have gotten anyway?"

"My husband (or other relative) doesn't like unions."

"The union does not do anything for you [grievances are not settled satisfactorily]. I don't like the people who are running things in the union."

"I can handle my own affairs. I can take care of myself. I'll make my own decisions. I do not intend to stay on this job forever; I'm looking for a promotion."

"My religion doesn't permit me to belong to any outside organizations."

"My boss doesn't believe in unions. I've seen what happens to union members."

"I don't want anything to do with unions. They are all corrupt."

"I don't know enough about the local or the union movement."

"I'm not interested. I just don't want to join."

"I'll think about it. Maybe I'll join someday."

Source: Organizing Committee, AFSCME Council 24, WSEU, 5 Odana Court, Madison, Wisconsin 53719.

Organizing new locals is costly. Evidence shows that the cost of each additional union member is about $600.[40] These costs include direct, out-of-pocket expenditures for such items as the printing and mailing of leaflets and other literature, rent for office space, salaries for staff hired, and legal fees. These efforts take time from the union staff that could be devoted to providing services to present union members (handling grievances, arbitration, and negotiating).

The costs of organizing new members must be compared to the returns:

- Extra compensation made possible by increased bargaining power.
- Additional dues and fees paid by new members.
- Enhanced political influence.
- Social benefits and satisfaction derived from extending membership to others.[41]

Because present members pay dues and because unions are democratic institutions, the union's priority is to provide services first to its membership, then to attempt to organize new members when it promises a return on its investment. In other words, organizing new unions may not be a high-priority item for unions when the costs do not justify the expected returns to the union.[42]

Companies often learn of union-organizing attempts from supervisors or rank-and-file employees and through observing handbilling at the work site before they receive official notification (by letter or telegram) from the union demanding recognition. Some companies react vigorously, while others do little to acknowledge any union's attempt to organize the employees. Some employers tell their employees about their opposition and urge them not to sign union authorization cards. Because the cards may specifically state that the signee favors union representation, any employee signature assists the union in establishing itself in the company. Some employers publish no-solicitation rules that apply to all nonemployees and are specifically designed to curtail unionization efforts.[43] If posted, these rules must have been in effect prior to the organizing campaign.[44] Typical employer statements during a union campaign can be found in "Labor Relations in Action."

Filing a Petition for the Election Prior to 1935, in order to obtain recognition the union usually had to show its strength and employee interest in representation by such actions as strikes. The Wagner Act and the NLRB changed this situation by developing procedures and guidelines for peacefully determining the majority interest of employees through elections or some other comparable demonstration. The procedure is initiated when the potential bargaining representative for the employees files a petition for an election.

The NLRB is authorized to conduct an election only when a valid petition has been filed by an employee, group of employees, an individual or labor organization, or an employer. Usually the petition is filed by the union after it has requested union recognition from the employer and the request is denied. The petition must be supported by evidence (usually authorization cards) that a substantial interest in union representation (30 percent of the bargaining unit) exists. Further, it must show that the employer has declined a request by the union to be recognized as the exclusive bargaining agent.[45] An employer cannot petition for an election until the union seeks recognition. If the employer could, it would petition at the time when the union's support was weakest. After receiving a petition, the NLRB will first determine whether it has jurisdiction and the petition is valid. If so, it will promptly notify the company and request a listing of employees. Companies are not required to submit this list but usually comply with the request as an act of good faith. Next, the NLRB will arrange a conference with the company and union to discuss the possibility of a consent election. Here, if both sides agree to the appropriate bargaining unit, voter eligibility, ballot, date, time and place for the election, a *consent election* will be held. If either party refuses to agree on any of these items, a formal hearing to settle these matters will be conducted.[46]

Election Investigation and Hearing If the union and management officials cannot agree to a consent election, the NLRB will investigate the petition, hold a hearing, and then direct an election if it finds that there is substantial interest in union representation. This investigation will secure answers to the following questions.[47]

1. What is an appropriate bargaining unit?
2. Does substantial interest in representation (30 percent) exist among employees in the unit?
3. Are there any barriers to an election in the form of existing unions, prior elections, or present labor agreements?

Labor Relations in Action

Examples of Employer Statements during Union Campaigns

Things are not so bad now and they could easily get worse with the selection of the union.

The Company has provided the wage increases and fringe benefits it could afford and still stay competitive.

The Company has provided good jobs and wages to you voluntarily without you having to pay any outsider (the union) one cent or having to strike.

We want this to be as good a place for you to work as this company's financial ability and business will permit us.

Wages and working conditions will not be improved by collective bargaining; the union can guarantee nothing; the law does not require the Company to agree to any of the union's proposals.

Strikes are a brutal and unpleasant experience; you get no wages and no unemployment compensation; the Company can hire permanent replacements for the strikers.

During strikes, everybody loses except the union organizer; he/she continues to receive his/her pay.

The union organizers are outsiders; they have no stake in the company or the community; they are only interested in your dues and initiation fees.

The Unions did a lot of good once, but they are no longer needed; they have become too big, too rich; they are removed from the true interests of the working people.

Check your next pay envelope; there will be two sample checks—one with the union dues deducted and another without any dues. Which one will you be voting for?

Source: Julius G. Getman, "Ruminations on Union Organizing in the Private Sector," *The University of Chicago Law Review* 53 (Winter 1986), pp. 48–53.

Appropriate Bargaining Unit An appropriate bargaining unit is a grouping of jobs or positions in which two or more employees share common employment interests and conditions (community of interests) and which may reasonably be grouped together for collective bargaining purposes. Determination of an appropriate bargaining unit is left to the discretion of the NLRB, which decides in each representation case how employee rights can best be protected under the act. The board's discretion has, however, been limited by law in several ways.[48] The statute includes the following:

- Professional employees cannot be included in a unit composed of both professional and nonprofessional employees, unless a majority of the professional employees vote to be included in a mixed unit.
- A proposed craft unit cannot be ruled inappropriate simply because a different unit has been previously approved by the NLRB unless a majority of employees in the proposed craft unit vote against being represented separately.
- Plant guards cannot be included in any bargaining unit that has nonguard employees in the unit.
- Supervisors and managers are not considered employees covered under the act and may not be in any bargaining unit.

- Excluded are agricultural laborers, public employees (except postal employees), and independent contractors, although some of these may be covered in separate state statutes.

The NLRB's determination of the appropriate bargaining unit strongly influences whether the union will win the election, whether one union will prevail in an interunion contest, whether craft employees will have their own union or be included in a plantwide unit, or whether the union will include key employees who could give direction and leadership for the bargaining-unit employees. Thus, the composition of the bargaining unit is important to the employer, the union, and the public.

Some companies pay attention to these considerations and take preventive steps regarding the management structure, employee interactions, and personnel policies and practices. For example, if the company prefers a large multi-unit bargaining unit, it will retain centralized control on management practices and decisions. If it prefers smaller, independent units, it will decentralize decision making in these independent units. Since the union has no control over management structure and the authority-responsibility relationship, it can only try to convince the NLRB that the bargaining unit should be composed of those employees who are supporting the union.[49]

Should a plant have several small bargaining units, the employer may face different unions in negotiations several times throughout the year, which could cause continuous instability in labor relations. Separate units concerned with similar jobs may cause disputes over rights to jobs, leading to strikes or slowdowns. Should a small bargaining unit be merged with a nationwide bargaining unit, any confrontation that resulted in a strike could cause a nationwide shutdown and complications for customers in need of the companies' products.[50] Chapter 6 will cover the various bargaining structures and their implications.

The bargaining unit itself may cover employees in one plant or in two or more facilities of the same employer. The NLRB considers a number of relevant guidelines in determining the composition of an appropriate bargaining unit:

- Interests of employees and employers.
- Community of interests, such as wages, working conditions, training, and skill.
- History of collective bargaining either at the location in question or another facility owned by the company.
- Transfers of employees among various facilities.
- Geography and physical proximity of the workplaces.
- Employer's administrative or territorial divisions.
- Degree of separation (or distinctiveness) of work or integration (or interrelatedness) of work.[51]

Where the relevant factors do not give a clear indication for the composition of an appropriate bargaining unit, an election (commonly called a *Globe* election, from the original NLRB case) may be held to determine employee interests. For example, one group of electricians in a steel plant might wish to be represented by the International Brotherhood of Electrical Workers (IBEW) instead of the United Steel Workers of America (USWA). The USWA wants to include all electricians in a bargaining unit composed of all production and maintenance workers in the plant. Under such circumstances, the electricians' vote will determine whether they will be members of the Steel Workers, a separate electricians' union (IBEW), or no union.[52]

Eligibility of Voters Before an election is conducted, voter eligibility must be determined. The general rule is that employees on the payroll before the date of the election are eligible. An employee must be employed in the unit on the date of the election. However, employees who are on sick leave, vacation, temporary layoff, or temporary leave, such as military duty, may vote in the election. In addition, the NLRB will occasionally consider irregularity of employment, such as in the construction, food processing, and longshoring industries. Economic strikers who have been replaced by permanent employees are allowed to vote in any election within 12 months after the strike begins. This policy ensures that management does not provoke a strike and hire replacements who could vote out the union. Employees hired after the union files its petition but before the election may be challenged as eligible voters by the union.

Untimely Petitions There are several rules that make a petition for a representation election untimely. The first is a legal requirement that prohibits any NLRB representation election where one has been held in the last 12 months and where a petition for election covers a group of employees who are already covered by an existing contract and already members of a legally certified union.

The second barrier to elections is an administrative determination that was made in the interest of stable and effective labor relations. The NLRB rule, called the **contract bar doctrine,** specifies that a valid signed agreement for a fixed period of 3 years or less will bar any representation election for the life of the agreement (a longer contract is still limited to 3 years). Thus, the contract bar doctrine could extend the 12-month statutory limitation on elections to 3 years. To do otherwise would be unfair to union and management officials who have negotiated a multiyear labor agreement in good faith.[53]

"Names and Addresses" (Excelsior) Rule Within 7 days after the regional director of the NLRB has approved a consent election or after an election has been directed, the employer must file a list of names and addresses of all eligible voters with the regional director. This information is then made available to the union. Refusal to comply could be identified as a bad faith act on the part of the employer and cause the election to be set aside or the NLRB to seek the names and addresses by subpoena. The purpose of this disclosure rule is to give the unions access to employees that management already possesses.[54]

The Election The representation election, acclaimed as one of the great innovations of American labor law, is conducted by NLRB officials. Over 80 percent are consent elections and are held within about 45 days (median) of the initial request. After a pre-election hearing, elections are held in about 75 days. NLRB data show that 90 percent of the eligible voters in NLRB elections, as compared to about 50 percent in major political elections, choose to vote.

The high voter turnout in union representation elections might be due to the convenient voting procedure (usually carried out on company property) and the belief of many employees that their vote more directly affects their lives (at least their working conditions) than do political elections. Finally, both unions and management realize that an employee could express union preference to a union representative and an opposite preference to the management representative to avoid a confrontation during the election campaign. Neither side is sure of employee voting preferences when faced with a secret ballot; therefore, union and management officials actively work to get out the vote.

Voter participation tends to decline the longer it takes for the NLRB to conduct the election. Thus, some employers are motivated to refuse a consent election in hopes of increasing the chances of the union losing the election. Also, because most single-unit elections are close, the number of nonparticipants affects the outcome of many elections.[55] Also, a small number of votes greatly influences the outcome of the election; research shows that a switch of eight votes would have changed the outcome of half the elections.[56] Furthermore, small increases in the time to process cases are important; a delay of 10 days has proven to be a significant factor in differentiating employer wins from employer losses. The number of pre-election days has also been linked to union losses. During the first 6 months of delay, there is an average drop-off in union victories of 2.5 percent per month. Consent elections have the highest union victory rate; however, there has been a decided downward trend in these types of elections.[57]

The size of the election unit has tended to be negatively related to union victories. The larger election unit is closely related to delay because it takes longer to process and is more likely to result in a hearing than in a voluntary settement.[58] Recent research has also revealed that success in union organizing has been influenced positively by the size of the union and democracy within the union, and negatively influenced by the union's propensity to strike and centralization of the union's decision making.[59]

Using a ballot with the appropriate company and union designations (see Exhibit 5.7) a secret-ballot election is conducted under NLRB supervision usually during working hours on payday at the employer's location. However, the NLRB has discretionary authority to conduct it by mail ballot if a regular election would not be fair and reasonable. For example, if it is physically impractical for eligible voters to cast their ballots at a centralized location for such reasons as widely scattered work, adverse weather conditions, or excessive travel required, the regional director of the NLRB may allow an election by mail balloting.[60]

The NLRB must determine whether the majority of the employees in an appropriate bargaining unit want to be represented by a union for collective bargaining purposes. It defines *majority* as the simple majority rule generally accepted in democratic elections, which means that those choosing not to vote in the election have decided to assent to the wishes of the majority who did vote. Therefore, a majority of the employees who vote (50 percent plus one of those voting) in the election must favor representation before a union will be certified by the NLRB.[61]

If two or more choices are placed on the ballot, a runoff election may be necessary between the choices receiving the two highest numbers of votes in the initial election. If the majority votes "no union," no representation election can be held

Exhibit 5.7 **Examples of Secret Ballots for Union Representation Elections**

UNITED STATES OF AMERICA
National Labor Relations Board
OFFICIAL SECRET BALLOT
FOR CERTAIN EMPLOYEES OF
CONTAINER CORPORATION

Do you wish to be represented for purposes of collective bargaining by:

METAL PRODUCTS, MACHINERY AND RELATED EQUIPMENT WORKERS OF AMERICA, AFL-CIO

SAMPLE

MARK AN "X" IN THE SQUARE OF YOUR CHOICE

YES	NO
☐	☐

DO NOT SIGN THIS BALLOT. Fold and drop in ballot box.
If you spoil this ballot return it to the Board Agent for a new one.

UNITED STATES OF AMERICA
National Labor Relations Board
OFFICIAL SECRET BALLOT
FOR CERTAIN EMPLOYEES OF
CONTAINER CORPORATION

This ballot is to determine the collective bargaining representative, if any, for the unit in which you are employed.

MARK AN "X" IN THE SQUARE OF YOUR CHOICE

SAMPLE

[Name of Union A]	NEITHER	[Name of Union B]
☐	☐	☐

DO NOT SIGN THIS BALLOT. Fold and drop in ballot box.
If you spoil this ballot return it to the Board Agent for a new one.

for 12 months. If a union receives the majority of the votes, the NLRB will certify it as the exclusive bargaining agent of the employees in the bargaining unit. Interestingly, where more than one union has vied for representation rights in the same election, unions have fared extremely well. Between 1977 and 1985, unions have won between 70 and 91 percent of such elections.[62] The major reason for this positive vote is that two unions would have to gain support from a sufficient number of the bargaining unit's employees to be placed on the ballot. Such support usually indicates that the employees have already decided to vote for the union; the election is conducted to determine which union will receive the majority vote.

After the votes have been counted, either party has 5 days to file objections alleging misconduct or to challenge the ballots of voters whom one party believes should not have voted in the election.[63] This part of the representation process receives considerable criticism because the delay in assessing the ballot challenges and objections concerning misconduct seems excessive.

In 1988, the NLRB conducted 3,506 representation elections; the percentage of elections won by the union remained relatively stable at 48.6 percent, where it has been since 1984, an increase from averages of less than 45 percent between 1980 and 1983. Although the number of elections were not many, unions won the majority of elections held in the service, health care, finance, insurance, real estate, and construction industries in 1988.[64]

As noted in Chapter 1, the first step of the labor relations process, the recognition of legitimate rights and responsibilities of unions and management representatives, includes more than the representation election. After unions win bargaining rights in a representation election they attempt to negotiate a labor agreement; however, they fail to secure the first contract 25 to 30 percent of the time. Several factors increase the likelihood of reaching agreement: existence of relatively high wages already at the company, presence of other bargaining units within the company, large election victories, and active participation of international union representatives. Factors that reduce the chances of attaining the first contract include location in a southern state with right-to-work laws, the national union having to approve the local union contracts, presence of outside labor-management consultants hired by the company,[65] NLRB delays in resolving employer objections and challenges to election results, employer refusal to bargain in good faith, and discrimination against employees after the election.[66]

Delays associated with filing objections to campaign conduct have increased threefold over the last 20 years, and the median amount of delay time is now about 210 days. Then, employers fail or refuse to bargain in good faith 13 percent of the time. This unfair labor practice adds approximately 140 more days. Additional delay can occur if appeals are made to the full board in Washington or to the Court of Appeal or Supreme Court.

In addition to the delays, there has been a sixfold increase in the number of unfair labor practices charges for firing union supporters and an elevenfold increase in the number of back pay awards. Research has discovered that employers discharge union activists or union supporters for two main reasons: (1) to get the key union organizers out of the facility, and (2) to send a chilling message to the rest of the work force.[67] With such trends in statistics, it does not appear that ethical considerations prevent all employers from breaking the law.

Duties of the Exclusive Bargaining Agent and Employer The exclusive bargaining representative (the union) chosen by the majority of the employees in the appropriate unit has the duty to represent equitably and fairly all employees in the unit regardless of their union membership and to bargain in good faith with the employer. The employer has a comparable obligation, that is, to bargain in good faith with the exclusive bargaining agent and to refuse to bargain with any other union seeking to represent the employees. Further, any negotiated labor agreement will cover all employees in the bargaining unit, regardless of their union membership status.

Conduct of the Representation Election Campaign

All elections are conducted according to NLRB standards, which are designed to assure that employees in the bargaining unit can indicate freely whether they want to be represented by a union for collective bargaining purposes. However, election campaigns differ substantially, and the strategies of individual unions and employers vary widely. For example, handbills similar to those in Exhibit 5.8 are frequently used in addition to speeches, informal talks, interviews, and films. Thus, the election campaign, one of the most interesting and controversial activities in labor relations, has led to a body of doctrines and rules. Due to changes in the board's philosophy, those doctrines and rules are subject to change.

Campaign Doctrines and NLRB Policies

The **totality of conduct doctrine** guides the NLRB interpretations of unfair labor practice behavior. This doctrine essentially means that isolated incidents such as campaign speeches must be considered within the whole of the general circumstances of the campaign and with the possibility that other specific violations have occurred.

Employer statements to employees may seem harmless on the surface, but under the circumstances that exist at the time of the statements, they may carry implied threats. For example, if an employer stated that a third-party intervention could make it economically impossible for it to continue in business, it would be making an illegal statement during a union election campaign. However, if the employer made the same statement during an attempted leveraged buyout, there would be no legal violation.

One of the more enduring doctrines has been the **laboratory conditions doctrine** established in the *General Shoe* decision in 1948. In this case, the NLRB clearly specified that its function was as follows:

> [T]o provide a laboratory in which an experiment may be conducted, under conditions as nearly ideal as possible, to determine the uninhibited desires of the employees. It is our duty to establish these conditions; it is our duty to determine whether they have been fulfilled. . . . [If]the standard drops too low [and] the requisite conditions are not present, . . . the experiment must be conducted over again.[68]

In 1962 the NLRB established further campaign standards concerning preelection campaigns and held that it would overturn an election whenever an unfair labor practice occurred during a critical phase of the campaign. It concluded that conduct that interferes with the employees' exercise of "a free and untrammeled choice" in an election is cause to set aside the outcome of an election.[69] In the same year, the NLRB, in setting aside an election, established guidelines to determine

Exhibit 5.8 **Examples of Handbills Distributed during Representation Election Campaigns**

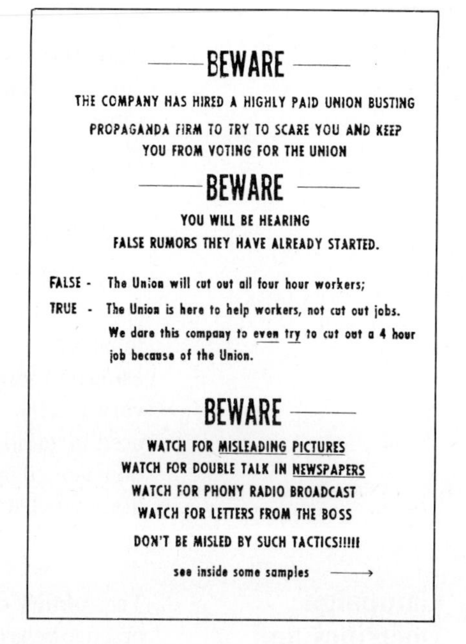

whether employer or union speeches constituted interference with employee rights to a fair election.[70] Subjects covered in these guidelines include the following:[71]

1. Misrepresentation of material facts or other similar trickery.
2. Presentation of information by a person known by employees to have special knowledge about the information presented.
3. Presentation of information so close to the election that the other party or parties have no opportunity to make an effective reply.
4. A reasonable probability that the misrepresentation may have a significant effect upon the election.
5. Lack of qualification to evaluate the statements.

Because the members of the National Labor Relations Board are appointed by the president and confirmed by the Senate, the political philosophy of the president and Senate is reflected in the board's composition. As a result, the board in office may exercise its discretion and change previous policies. In 1982, most of the board members had been appointed by former President Reagan, and the board rejected the laboratory of conditions doctrine as unrealistic in response to research showing that employees are well able to assess misleading campaign propaganda. In a 3-to-2 vote, the majority made this statement:

> We will no longer probe into the truth or falsity of the parties' campaign statements, and that we will not set elections aside on the basis of misleading campaign statements. We will, however, intervene in cases where a party has used forged documents which render the voters unable to recognize propaganda for what

> it is. Thus, we will set an election aside not because of the substance of the representation, but because of the deceptive manner in which it was made, a manner which renders employees unable to evaluate the forgery for what it is. . . .
>
> American employees may be better educated, in the formal sense, than those of previous generations, and may be in certain respects more sophisticated. We do not honor them by abandoning them utterly to the mercies of unscrupulous companies, including the expert cadre of professional opinion molders who devise campaigns for many of our representation elections.[72]

The NLRB was influenced by a research study involving over 1,000 employees in 31 elections in five states. This study cast doubt on the previously held assumption that employees are unsophisticated about labor relations and are swayed easily by campaign propaganda. In fact, votes of 81 percent of the employees could have been predicted from their pre-campaign intent and their attitudes toward working conditions and unions in general. The study concluded that employees' votes appeared to be the product of attitudes that resulted from their everyday experiences in the industrial world and not from the campaign itself.[73]

The data used in the study were later reanalyzed, and additional (some different) conclusions were made:[74]

- Worker predisposition toward the union is a very important determinant of voting behavior.
- Written communications distributed late in the campaign and meetings held early in the campaign most probably have an effect.
- Threats and actions taken against union supporters are effective in discouraging support for the union.

Thus far, these later analyses have not influenced the board's position on election campaigns.

Captive Audience—24-Hour Rule

One legal approach, usually taken by management, includes presenting "captive audience" speeches, which are delivered to employees during working time. The speeches, authorized by the Taft-Hartley amendments in 1947, must not be presented within 24 hours of an election, and the speech's content must not include threats of reprisal or promises of benefits. But if the union has no acceptable means of communicating with the employees, as in the lumber and logging industry where employees live on company property, and if the employer's unfair labor practices have created a serious election campaign imbalance, the NLRB and the courts may grant the union access to plant bulletin boards, parking lots, and entrances so that it may communicate with the employees.[75] Still, it is extremely difficult for the union to respond effectively by using its traditional means of contacting employees, such as plant employee solicitations, distribution of literature before or after work, house calls, and union meetings.[76]

Polling or Questioning Employees

Polling employees or asking questions about their interest in unions was considered unlawful interference with employee rights in earlier days. In 1984, the National Labor Relations Board announced that it would no longer automatically consider an employer interrogation about an employee's union sentiment an unlawful inquiry in violation of section 8(a)(1). It announced that it would examine the totality of the circumstances surrounding such interrogations in light of:

1. The background of the interrogation.
2. The nature of the information sought.
3. The identity of the questioner.
4. The place and method of the interrogation.

Therefore, an employer's questioning of open and active union supporters and other employees about their union sentiments in the absence of threats or promises does not necessarily violate the law. However, NLRB decisions since 1984 reveal that employers are still at risk in these interrogations because it is necessary only to establish that the questions asked may reasonably be said to have a tendency to interfere with the free exercise of an employee's rights under the act.[77]

Distribution of Union Literature and Solicitation by Employees on Company Property

The NLRB and the courts have long held that except in special circumstances employees may not be prohibited from distributing union organizing materials or soliciting union support in nonworking areas on their own time[78] unless the employer can show that such activity would disrupt production, employee work, and plant discipline. For example, employees of restaurants and retail establishments cannot distribute union materials in customer areas, and employees of health care institutions cannot distribute materials in areas designated strictly for patients.[79] However, distributing materials in such places as hospital cafeterias predominantly patronized by hospital employees cannot be prohibited.[80] In addition, the employer cannot prohibit distribution of union material if the basis for the prohibition is that part of its content includes political issues, such as right-to-work laws and minimum wages.[81] Nor can the employer prohibit employees from wearing buttons, hats, or T-shirts promoting the union.

The employer may limit the type of information distributed to employees by classifying company data as "confidential." The NLRB has upheld the discharge of five employees who distributed wage data comparing the company's wage scale with that of other plants in the area. The NLRB found that the company had declared this wage information to be confidential, and that it had not been obtained in the normal course of employment.

Showing of Films during Election Campaigns

Films presented to discourage workers from joining unions have taken on new dimensions, especially since the 1950s when the movie *And Women Must Weep* was produced by the National Right to Work Committee. This movie portrays union violence, strikes, vandalism, phone threats, a house bombing, and even the shooting of a baby of a dissident union member. Frequent use of the film by employers prompted the International Association of Machinists to produce a rebuttal film, entitled *Anatomy of a Lie,* which claims no evidence exists of a connection between the shootings and other misconduct and the union's activities. On-site interviews with persons involved in the strike are shown to reveal an opposite view of the employer film, and the president of the union is filmed stating that nearly 99 percent of the union members voted to strike. The NLRB's position regarding the showing of these films has varied; its current position is that their showing alone does not constitute an unfair labor practice and is not sufficient cause to have the results of an election set aside.[82]

New Union Strategies

In response to employers' strategies in maintaining nonunion status, unions have been forced to return to the drawing board to design new strategies. Some well-publicized corporate campaigns by unions include the following strategies:[83]

- Withholding use of union pension funds from investment in companies whose behavior is deemed antiunion and where organizing efforts are restricted.
- Pressuring the company's bank and creditors.
- Challenging company applications for industrial revenue bonds, zoning variances, and so forth.
- Embarrassing company directors and officers by picketing their homes, opposing management in proxy battles, and communicating directly with stockholders.
- Suing the company or officers for breach of fiduciary duty, fraud, or racketeering.
- Extending boycotts to health and life insurance, bank accounts, and stock purchases.
- Offering concessions to one corporate buyer to favor a corporate takeover.
- Offering seminars to union members on the internal operations of banks and corporations.
- Attending stockholder meetings and making stockholders aware of managerial attitudes toward employees and unions in hopes that adverse publicity and embarrassment will change management's behavior.

The AFL-CIO has also assisted in organizing efforts through its "Union Yes" and associate membership campaigns, covered in Chapters 1 and 4. It has also:

- Published two manuals, *The Inside Game: Winning with Workplace Strategies* and *Developing New Tactics: Winning with Coordinated Corporate Campaigns,* which "help unions persuade employers to deal fairly and equitably with workers through the application of pressures beyond the workplace."
- Opened an office of **Comprehensive Organizing Strategies and Tactics (COST)** to train union leaders to conduct corporate campaigns to combat employer resistance to union organizing. Tactics include electronic media, pickets, direct mailing, pressure on banks, creditors, customers, and board members, and purchase of stock.[84]
- Launched a Union Privilege Benefit Program with a discount credit card and legal services to employees. This program is available for current members, retains ties with former members, and attracts new members.[85]

Unions have tried to improve their public image by increasing their visibility through the news media, involving their leaders in education programs, identifying unions with positive activities and programs, improving their organizational effectiveness, and seeking to accomplish their bargaining and organizing objectives, such as labor-management cooperation, enhanced productivity, and so on.[86] Some specific strategies are as follows:

- Using a telephone taped speech in which an employee may call a well-publicized number and receive the "union message" for the day or week during an organizing campaign. These messages range from benefits of joining unions and anticompany messages to personal testimony of popular, well-known plant employees.

- Attempting to develop acceptance of unions in the community by allying with church groups or civil rights organizations as a way to address social, economic, and personal needs of the people.
- Coordinating organizing activities and combining resources of several groups in large metropolitan areas to promote unionization in that area.
- Negotiating a neutrality agreement that includes a clause stating that if the union seeks to organize employees in nonunion plants, management will remain neutral and a statement defining the limits of acceptable union organizing behavior. If management signs the agreement, the union will have to behave in a manner that neither demeans nor ridicules the company or its management.[87]

Decertification Procedure

Whenever employees believe that the union is not representing their interests, they may turn to a decertification procedure. In the last decade, decertification elections have nearly doubled. Researchers have identified a variety of reasons for this:

- Fair treatment of employees by employers.
- Poor job by unions (especially smaller unions) in providing services to members.
- Inability of unions to negotiate an effective first contract after winning bargaining rights.[88]
- Striking employees having skills that can be readily replaced,[89] so that when a strike occurs, the employer hires replacements.

Any employee, group of employees, or employee representative may file a petition for a decertification election 12 months after the union has been certified or upon expiration of the labor agreement (see "contract bar doctrine" above). This petition must be supported by at least 30 percent of the bargaining-unit employees.[90]

While employers cannot initiate the petition or assist in filing a petition for a decertification election, they can question the union's majority status and petition the NLRB for a representation election. This petition must be supported by objective evidence to show that the union no longer represents the majority of the bargaining-unit employees.[91] Examples of objective data include employee reductions, high employee turnover, changes in the composition of the bargaining unit, requests from employees to discontinue bargaining, statements from employees that they wish to discontinue union representation, and a downward trend in employees authorizing dues deductions. If the employees choose to decertify their union, there cannot be another representation election for 12 months.[92] However, after a valid petition is filed with the NLRB, but before the election, the employer must still bargain with the union until the question of union representation is resolved.[93]

Although employers must be careful of their role in the decertification process, they have exhibited growing interest in it.[94] For example, a 1-day seminar offered for $450 per person is designed to teach management representatives about the entire process of decertification.[95] Many employers have concluded that they should become more involved, especially since they are becoming aware that they do not necessarily have to play a passive role in the decertification process.

When management chooses to become involved in the decertification campaign, activities are limited to:

- Meeting with employees, either one-to-one, in small groups, or with the entire unit, in which management responds to questions.
- Using legal or expert assistance for advice in the campaign.
- Sending letters to employees at their homes.
- Improving employment climate at the workplace by developing more effective performance-appraisal and employee development programs and improved communication.[96]
- Providing employees with information about the mechanics of the decertification process if they have already initiated the process.[97]
- Answering employee inquiries on how to decertify unions by referring the employees to the NLRB.
- Responding to specific employee questions about the decertification process in a manner that conveys no coercion or other unfair labor practice.
- Furnishing an employee or any representative of a group of employees with a current list of employee names and addresses.

Yet the employer must be aware of related unlawful activities, such as the following:

- Obtaining NLRB forms for employees who may be interested in union decertification.
- Providing services such as typing, assistance in phrasing the petition for decertification, and use of company stationery by employees who are interested in launching a decertification campaign.
- Initiating discussions on how or whether to decertify the union.
- Allowing supervisors or any other persons identified with management to promote the decertification process.[98]

Unions respond to any challenge to their existence as the certified representative of the bargaining unit employees. They attempt to convince the employees that there are reasons to continue their union membership and representation and not to seek decertification. They do this by improving the level of services to the employees and by attempting to gain improvements in benefits through negotiation.[99]

The number of decertification elections has increased sixfold since the 1950s (there were 783 in 1986). Unions are losing as much as 75 percent of the elections. Nevertheless, only 0.2 percent (one in 500) of the estimated 14 million or more union members under the NLRB's jurisdiction have voted to decertify their unions, and the average size of the bargaining units that have lost their certification remains at less than 40 employees.[100]

Factors that influence the outcome of decertification elections follow:[101]

- Size of employer. Decertified units tend to be small. After the smaller local unions win elections, the international union finds it difficult and costly to serve these smaller locals.
- Socio-demographic composition of work force. Chances of decertification are greater when the work force is homogeneous.

- Type of industry. Decertification elections are more common in manufacturing and the retail and wholesale trades than other industries.
- Type of union. Seven national unions were involved in 45 percent of the decertification elections. The largest national union, the Teamsters, was involved in the most.
- Length of union representation. Votes to decertify occur most often after the first year of representation, and decline thereafter.
- Relationship between employees and management. Decertification is more likely when the employee-management relationship is extremely good (employees are happy with management) and management is trusted and credible.
- Degree of union participation. The vote for decertification declines when union involvement is intense. The percentage of employees who vote to decertify is directly related to the percentage of employees who had signed the decertification petition.
- Union leadership. The presence of an active, credible, informed leader or leaders who are able to convince the membership either to support the union or to vote for no union representation.
- Salient issue. The presence of a salient issue, such as pension payments by younger employees, union security, or unsafe working conditions.
- Incidents. The occurrence of an event or series of events, such as a strike or a number of grievances not processed, that causes employees to start the decertification process.[102]

While management must consider the economic costs of a decertification campaign, it must also consider the implications of both possible election outcomes and the legal issues involved in its participation. For example, if management campaigns vigorously for decertification but the union wins, what type of relationships will result? If the results are close, will the relationship be unstable in the future? Should the union lose, will a more militant union seek representation after a year? These factors and others should play an important role in determining the specific strategy of the employer.[103]

The employees, like the employer, must be aware of possible consequences of their activities attempting to decertify the union. Decertification advocates must be prepared for pressure from union officials and isolation from fellow employees who are pleased with the union. The NLRB has upheld the union's right to discipline union members who actively participate in the campaign to decertify the union, as long as the disciplinary action does not affect the employees' employment status.[104]

Summary

This chapter provides insights into reasons unions are formed. It discusses the most important theories and explanations ranging from alienation and class consciousness to the employees' background and personal desires. The role of a union is to fulfill employees' perceived needs and answer job-related concerns. Unionization efforts progress from first contacts with employees to the signing of authorization cards, petition for election, hearings, determination of the appropriate bargaining unit, and the eventual representation election. Within this framework numerous rules, regulations, and legal requirements govern the union certification process. The procedures by which employees can be formed into unions through voluntary recognition, NLRB directives, and secret ballot elections are explained.

In recent times, unions have launched new strategies to organize nonunion employees. The AFL-CIO has taken the lead with the introduction of several programs under its auspices. Finally, in those cases where the union is judged by employees as not representing their interests, a decertification procedure is available through the election process. Generally, only a few employees and only small bargaining units have been involved in decertification elections.

Key Terms

alienation theory
scarcity consciousness theory
union instrumentality
contract bar doctrine
totality of conduct doctrine
laboratory conditions doctrine
Comprehensive Organizing Strategies and Tactics (COST)

Discussion Questions

1. Refer to the reasons why employees become members of unions to assess the means used by union organizers to meet these needs.
2. Select an organization with which you are familiar, and determine the number of bargaining units that would be appropriate for its structure.
3. Explain the contract bar doctrine. How would it influence the negotiation of the first labor agreement?
4. Discuss the shifting position of the NLRB regarding representation election campaigning. Appraise each position.
5. Prescribe a "do" and "don't" list for supervisors involved in unionization campaigns so they will not commit any unfair labor practices.
6. Why do you believe employers are becoming more interested in decertification elections?
7. Explain the following statement: "It is not the union that organizes the workers; it is management."
8. What would be a good response from a union organizer for each statement in the "Labor Relations in Action" on page 139?
9. What new strategies have unions used to counter employer efforts to maintain nonunion status? Appraise the effectiveness of these strategies.

References

1. Kai Erikson, "On Work and Alienation,"*American Sociological Review* 51 (February 1986), p. 2. For examples of this situation, see Michael Hanagan and Charles Stephenson, *Confrontation, Class Consciousness, and the Labor Process* (New York: Greenwood Press, 1986).
2. Clinton S. Golden and Harold Ruttenberg, "Motives for Union Membership," in E. Wight Bakke, Clark Kerr, and Charles W. Anrod, eds., *Unions, Management, and the Public* (New York: Harcourt, Brace, 1948), p. 49.
3. M. D. Dunnette and W. K. Kirchner, *Psychology Applied to Industry* (New York: Appleton-Century-Crofts, 1965), pp. 199–200; and Henry S. Farber and Daniel H. Saks, "Why Workers Want Unions: The Role of Relative Wages and Job Characteristics" (working paper, Cambridge, Mass.: M.I.T., 1978), pp. 27–28. See also W. Clay Hamner and Frank J. Smith, "Work Attitudes as Predictors of Unionization Activity," *Journal of Applied Psychology* 63 (1978), p. 415; William J. Bigoness, "Correlates of Faculty Attitudes toward Collective Bargaining," *Journal of Applied Psychology* 63 (1978), pp. 228-233; Chester A. Schreisheim, "Job Satisfaction, Attitudes toward Unions, and Voting in a Union Representation Election," *Journal of Applied Psychology* 63 (1978), pp. 548–552; J. G. Getman, S. B. Goldberg, and J. B. Herman, *Union Representation Elections: Law and Reality* (New York: Russel Sage Foundation, 1976); Edward L. Harrison, "Employee Satisfaction and Voting Behavior in Union Representation Elections," in Dennis F. Ray and Thad B. Green, eds., *Toward Renewal of Management Thought and Practice* (State College, Miss.: Southern Management Association, Mississippi State University, 1978), p. 169.
4. Selig Perlman, *A Theory of the Labor Movement* (1928; reprinted New York: Augustus M. Kelley, 1968), p. 242.
5. Joel Seidman, Jack London, and Bernard Karsh, "Why Workers

Join Unions," *Annals of the American Academy of Political and Social Sciences* 274 (March 1951), pp. 775-784.
6. Ibid.
7. J. G. Getman, S. B. Goldberg, and J. B. Herman, *Union Representation Elections: Law and Reality* (New York: Russel Sage Foundation, 1976). See also Henry S. Farber and Daniel H. Saks, "Why Workers Want Unions: The Role of Relative Wages and Job Characteristics," *Journal of Political Economy* 88 (April 1980), pp. 349-369; and Jack Fiorito and Charles R. Greer, "Gender Differences in Union Membership, Preferences, and Beliefs," *Journal of Labor Research* (Spring 1986), pp. 145-164.
8. Farber, *Why Workers;* and Stephen M. Hills, "The Attitudes of Union and Nonunion Male Workers toward Union Representation," *Industrial and Labor Relations Review* (January 1985), pp. 179-194.
9. Edgar H. Schein, *Organizational Psychology,* 2d ed. (Englewood Cliffs, N.J.: Prentice-Hall, 1965).
10. Chamberlain and Cullen, *The Labor Sector,* p. 282.
11. E. Wight Bakke, "Why Workers Join Unions," *Personnel* 22 (July 1947), p. 3.
12. J. M. Brett and T. J. Hammer, "Organizational Behavior and Industrial Relations," in T. A. Kochan, et al., eds. *Industrial Relations Research in the 1970s: Review and Appraisal* (Madison, Wis.: Industrial Relations Research Association, 1982), pp. 245-251.
13. For review of reasons workers join unions, see Jack Fiorito, Daniel G. Gallagher, and Charles R. Greer, "Determinants of Unionism: A Review of the Literature," in Kendrith M. Rowland and Gerald R. Ferris, eds. *Research in Personnel and Human Resource Management* (Greenwich, Conn.: JAI Press, 1986), pp. 269-305.
14. Thomas A. DeCottis and Jean-Yves Le Lovarn, "A Predictive Study of Voting Behavior in a Representation Election Using Union Instrumentality and Work Perceptions, " *Organizational Behavior and Human Performance* 27 (February 1981), pp. 103-118. Also see Stuart A. Youngblood, Angelo S. DeNisi, Julie L. Molleston, and William H. Mobley, "The Impact of Work Environment, Instrumentality Beliefs, Perceived Labor Union Image, and Subjectivity Norms on Union Voting Intentions," *Academy of Management Journal* 27 (December 1984), pp. 576-590.
15. Thomas Hyclak, "Union-Nonunion Wage Changes and Voting Trends in Union Representation Elections," in B. D. Dennis, ed., *Proceedings of the Thirty-Fourth Annual Meeting: Industrial Relations Research Association* (Madison, Wis.: Industrial Relations Research Association, 1982), p. 350; William J. Bigoness and Henry L. Tosi, "Correlates of Voting Behavior in a Union Decertification Election," *Academy of Management Journal* 27 (September 1984), pp. 654-659.
16. DeCottis and Lovarn, "A Predictive Study of Voting Behavior," p. 109.
17. Stuart A. Youngblood, William H. Mobley, and Angelo S. DeNisi, "Attitudes, Perceptions, and Intentions to Vote in a Union Certification Election: An Empirical Investigation," in B. D. Dennis, ed., *Proceedings of the Thirty-Fourth Annual Meeting: Industrial Relations Research Association* (Madison, Wis.: Industrial Relations Research Association, 1982), pp. 244-253.
18. Edward L. Harrison, Douglas Johnson, and Frank M. Rachel, "The Role of the Supervisor in Representation Elections," *Personnel Administration* 26 (September 1981), pp. 69-70.
19. Orley Ashenfelter and John H. Pencaval, "American Trade Union Growth: 1900-1960," *Quarterly Journal of Economics* 83 (August 1969), pp. 434-448.
20. Henry S. Farber and Daniel H. Saks, "Why Workers Want Unions: The Role of Relative Wages and Job Characteristics," *Journal of Political Economy* 88 (April 1980), pp. 349-369.
21. Stephen M. Hills, "The Attitudes of Union and Non-Union Male Workers Toward Union Representation," *Industrial and Labor Relations Review* 38 (January 1985), pp. 192-193.
22. William T. Dickens, Douglas R. Wholey, and James C. Robinson, "Correlates of Union Support in NLRB Elections," *Industrial Relations* 26 (Fall 1987), pp. 240-252. A study of 11,899 NLRB certification elections during the years of 1977, 1978, and 1979.
23. John J. Hoover, "Union Organization Attempts: Management's Response," *Personnel Journal* 61 (March 1982), pp. 214-215.
24. Thomas F. Reed, "Do Union Organizers Matter? Individual Differences, Campaign Practices, and Representation Election Outcomes," *Industrial and Labor Relations Review* 43 (October 1989), pp. 102-117.
25. James A. Craft and Marian M. Extejt, "New Strategies in Union Organizing," *Working Paper Series* (Pittsburgh, Penn.: University of Pittsburgh, 1982), p. 304.
26. Hoover, "Union Organizing Attempts," pp. 214-215.
27. Julius G. Getman, "Ruminations on Union Organizing in the Private Sector," *The University of Chicago Law Review* 53 (Winter 1986), p. 59.
28. John J. Lawler and Robin West, "Impact of Union-Avoidance Strategy in Representation Elections," *Industrial Relations* 24 (Fall 1985), pp. 406-420.
29. Donna Sockell, "Contemporary Challenges of Labor Law," in Barbara D. Dennis, ed., *Proceedings of the Fortieth Annual Meeting of the Industrial Relations Research Association* (Madison, Wis.: Industrial Relations Research Association, 1988), pp. 85-90.
30. *United Autoworkers* v. *Secretary of Labor,* 678 F. Supp. 4 (D.C., 1988).
31. William N. Cooke, "The Rising Toll of Discrimination Against Union Activists," *Industrial Relations* 24 (Fall 1985), p. 437.
32. An authorization card signifies that the employee desires to be represented by the union in collective bargaining. The employee thereby authorizes the union to represent him with his employer. The signed card may be used later by the union as proof of majority representation, as support to demand recognition, and as evidence that there is "substantial interest" among the bargaining unit to support a petition to the NLRB for representation election. Schlossberg and Sherman, *Organizing and the Law,* p. 50.
33. *NLRB* v. *Gissel Packing Co.*, 395 U.S. 575 (1969).
34. Herbert L. Sherman, Jr., and William P. Murphy, *Unionization and Collective Bargaining,* 3d ed. (Washington, D.C.: Bureau of National Affairs, Inc., 1975), pp. 69-70.
35. Stephen I. Schlossberg and Frederick E. Sherman, *Organizing and the Law* (Washington, D.C.: Bureau of National Affairs, Inc., 1971), pp. 97-99.
36. Robert Lewis, "The Law and Strategy of Dealing with Union Organizing Campaigns," *Labor Law Journal* 25 (January 1974), p. 45.
37. Marcus H. Sandver, "The Validity of Union Authorization Cards as a Predictor of Success in NLRB Certification Elections," *Labor Law Journal* 28 (November 1977), pp. 698-701.
38. William E. Fulmer, "Step by Step through a Union Campaign," *Harvard Business Review* 59 (July-August 1981), pp. 94-95. For a review of the research literature on union certification elections, see Herbert G. Heneman, III and Marcus H. Sandver, *Industrial and Labor Relations Review* 36 (July 1983), pp. 537-559.
39. David B. Stephens and Paul R. Timm, "A Comparison of Campaign Techniques in Contested Faculty Elections: An Analysis of

the Florida Experience," *Journal of Collective Negotiations in the Public Sector* 7 (1978), pp. 167–177.
40. Paula B. Voos, "Does It Pay to Organize? The Cost to Unions," *Monthly Labor Review* 107 (June 1984), pp. 43–44.
41. Paula Voos, "Union Organizing: Costs and Benefits," *Industrial and Labor Relations Review* 36 (July 1983), pp. 576–580. Also see Paula Voos, "Trends in Union Organizing Expenditures, 1953–1977," *Industrial and Labor Relations Review* 38 (October 1984), pp. 52–66.
42. Richard N. Block, "Union Organizing and the Allocation of Union Resources," *Industrial and Labor Relations Review* 34 (October 1980), pp. 101–113.
43. This rule must be applied equally to all forms of solicitation, such as politicians seeking votes and charitable organizations seeking contributions.
44. Lewis, "Law and Strategy," pp. 42–48.
45. National Labor Relations Board, *Guide to Basic Law*, pp. 11–16.
46. Lewis, "Law and Strategy," pp. 45–47.
47. National Labor Relations Board, *Guide to Basic Law*, p. 11.
48. Ibid., pp. 9–11.
49. Robert Sebris, Jr., and Robert D. McDonald, "Bargaining Unit Determination Case Trends of the NLRB," *Labor Law Journal* 37 (June 1986), pp. 378–382.
50. Schlossberg and Sherman, *Organizing and the Law*, p. 60.
51. John E. Abodeely, *The NLRB and the Appropriate Bargaining Unit* (Philadelphia: Industrial Research Unit, University of Pennsylvania, 1971), pp. 7–86.
52. Sherman and Murphy, *Unionization and Collective Bargaining*, pp. 60–61.
53. National Labor Relations Board, *Guide to Basic Law*, pp. 13–14. There are exceptions, such as when the agreement is not in writing, has not been signed, or has not been ratified.
54. *Excelsior Underwear, Inc.*, 156 NLRB 1236 (1966).
55. Richard N. Block and Myron Roomkin, "Determinants of Voter Participation in Union Certification Elections," *Monthly Labor Review* 105 (April 1982), pp. 45–47.
56. Myron Roomkin and Richard N. Block, "Case Processing Time and the Outcome of Representation Elections: Some Empirical Evidence," *University of Illinois Law Review*, 1981, reprinted in *Oversight Hearings on the Subject "Has Labor Law Failed?"* (Washington, D.C.: Committee on Education and Labor, 1984), pp. 844–845.
57. Marcus H. Sandver and Herbert G. Heneman III, "Union Growth through the Election Process," *Industrial Relations* 20 (Winter 1981), pp. 109–115.
58. William N. Cooke, "Determinants of the Outcomes of Union Certification Elections," *Industrial and Labor Relations Review* 36 (April 1983), pp. 402–414.
59. Cheryl L. Maranto and Jack Fiorito, "The Effect of Union Characteristics on the Outcome of NLRB Elections," *Industrial and Labor Relations Review* 40 (January 1987), pp. 225–238.
60. Williams, Janus, and Huhn, *NLRB Regulation*, pp. 371–372.
61. Ibid., pp. 391–395. Between 1977 and 1981, under the NLRB simple majority rule, unions won 24 percent of the decertification elections and 46 percent of the certification elections. If the NLRB required that a majority of the unit must vote for the union, the union would have won only 19 percent of the decertification elections and 38 percent of the certification elections—an additional loss of 18,400 decertification elections and 162,000 certification elections. Also see Dennis A. Ahlburg, "Majority Voting Rules and the Union Success Rate in National Labor Relations Board Representation Elections," *Journal of Labor Research* 5 (Summer 1984), pp. 231–232.
62. James B. Dworkin and James R. Fain, "Success in Multiple Union Elections: Exclusive Jurisdiction vs. Competition," *Journal of Labor Research* 10 (Winter 1989), pp. 91–100. For multiunion elections involving incumbent unions and raids from another union, see Charles Odewahn and Clyde Scott, "An Analysis of Multi-Union Elections Involving Incumbent Unions," *Journal of Labor Research* 10 (Spring 1989), pp. 197–205; Clyde Scott and Charles Odewahn, "Multi-Union Elections Involving Incumbents: The Legal Environment," *Labor Law Journal* 40 (July 1989), pp. 403–410.
63. National Labor Relations Board, *Guide to Basic Law*, p. 17.
64. "Despite Declining Number of NLRB Elections, Union Win-Loss Ratio Held Steady in 1988," *Daily Labor Report*, April 7, 1989, pp. B-1–B-3.
65. "Study Calls for Labor Law Reform to Aid Unions Seeking First Contracts," *Daily Labor Report*, July 10, 1985, p. A-10.
66. William N. Cooke, "The Failure to Negotiate First Contracts: Determinants and Policy Implications," *Industrial and Labor Relations Review* 38 (January 1985), pp. 163–178.
67. Testimony of William Cooke, *National Labor Relations Act Practices and Operations*, Hearings Before the Subcommittee on Labor of the Committee on Labor and Human Resources, U.S. Senate, January 29 and February 5, 1988, pp. 288–290.
68. *General Shoe Corp.*, 77 NLRB 124 (1948).
69. *Dal-Tex Optical Co.*, 137 NLRB 1782 (1962).
70. *Hollywood Ceramics*, 140 NLRB 221 (1962).
71. Cindy M. Hudson and William B. Werther, Jr., "Section 8(c) and Free Speech," *Labor Law Journal* 28 (September 1977), p. 611.
72. *Midland National Life Insurance Company*, 110 LRRM 1489 (1982).
73. *Shopping Kart Food Market*, 94 LRRM 1705 (1977). Julius G. Getman, Stephen B. Goldberg, and Jeanne B. Herman, *Union Representation Elections: Law and Reality* (New York: Russell Sage Foundation, 1976).
74. William T. Dickens, "The Effect of Company Campaigns on Certification Elections: *Law and Reality* Once Again," *Industrial and Labor Relations Review* 36 (July 1983), pp. 574– 576.
75. Max Zimny, "Access of Union Organizers to Private Property," *Labor Law Journal* 25 (October 1974), p. 624.
76. Richard N. Block, Benjamin W. Wolkinson, and James W. Kuhn, "Some Are More Equal Than Others: The Relative Status of Employers, Unions and Employees in the Law of Union Organizing," *Industrial Relations Law Journal* 10 (no. 2, 1989), p. 220.
77. David P. Brenskelle, "Questioning Employees Concerning Union Sentiment Remains a Risky Proposition," *Employee Relations Law Journal* 13 (Summer 1987), pp. 141–147.
78. *Republican Aviation Corp.* v. *NLRB*, 324 U.S. 793 (1945).
79. "Justices Twice Back Right to Distribute Union Literature on Company Property," *The Wall Street Journal*, June 23, 1978, p. 6; Peter G. Kilgore, "No-Solicitation/No-Distribution Rules: The Word Battle of 'Time' Versus 'Hours' Continues," *Labor Law Journal* 35 (November 1984), pp. 671–672.
80. *Beth Israel* v. *NLRB*, 46 U.S.L.W. 4765 (June 22, 1978).
81. *Eastex, Inc.* v. *NLRB*, 46 U.S.L.W. 4783 (June 22, 1978).
82. Joseph A. Pichler and H. Gordon Fitch, "And Women Must Weep: The NLRB as Film Critic," *Industrial and Labor Relations Review* 28 (April 1975), pp. 395–410.
83. Aaron Bernstein and Michael A. Pollock, "The Unions Are Learning to Hit Where It Hurts," *Business Week*, March 17, 1986, pp. 112–114.
84. "AFL-CIO Soon to Open New Office to Develop Organizing Strategies," *Daily Labor Report*, April 3, 1986, p. A-1.
85. Gene Zack, "Credit Card Legal Services Plan Offered," *AFL-CIO News*, July 5, 1986, p. 1.
86. James A. Craft and Suhail Abboushi, "The Union Image: Con-

cept, Programs, and Analysis," *Journal of Labor Research* 4 (Fall 1983), pp. 300–311.
87. James A. Craft and Marian M. Extejt, "New Strategies in Union Organizing," *Working Paper Series* (Pittsburgh, Penn.: University of Pittsburgh, 1982), pp. 5–17; James A. Craft, "The Employer Neutrality Pledge: Issues, Implications, and Prospects," *Labor Law Journal* 31 (December 1980), pp. 753–754.
88. James B. Dworkin and Marian Extejt, "Why Workers Decertify Their Unions: A Preliminary Investigation," paper presented at the Annual Meeting of the Academy of Management, August 1979.
89. T. Chafetz and C. R. P. Fraser, "Union Decertification: An Exploratory Analysis," *Industrial Relations* 18 (Winter 1979), p. 68.
90. Mark Z. Sappir, "The Employer's Obligation Not to Bargain When the Issue of Decertification is Present," *Personnel Administrator* 27 (February 1982), pp. 41–45.
91. Lisa M. Lynch and Marcus H. Sandver, "Determinants of the Decertification Process: Evidence from Employer-Initiated Elections," *Journal of Labor Research* 8 (Winter 1987), p. 87.
92. Kenneth C. McGuiness and Jeffrey A. Norris, *How to Take a Case before the National Labor Relations Board,* 5th ed. (Washington, D.C.: Bureau of National Affairs, Inc., 1986), p. 66.
93. *Dresser Industries,* 111 LRRM 1436 (1982).
94. Ibid., p. 10; and Woodruff Imberman, "How to Win a Decertification Election," *Management Review* 66 (September 1977), pp. 26–28, 37–39.
95. Executive Enterprises, *The Process of Decertification.*
96. William E. Fulmer, "When Employees Want to Oust Their Union," *Harvard Business Review* 56 (March–April 1978), pp. 163–170. Also see William T. Downey, "The *Mar-Jac* Rule Governing the Certification Year," *Labor Law Journal* 29 (September 1978), pp. 608–614.
97. Robert Lewis, "Union Decertification: A New Look at Management's Role," *Labor Law Journal* 37 (February 1986), pp. 115–122.
98. William A. Krupman and Gregory I. Rasin, "Decertification: Removing the Shroud," *Labor Law Journal* 30 (April 1979), pp. 234–235.
99. Trevor Bain, Clyde Scott, and Edwin Arnold, "Deauthorization Elections: An Early Warning Signal to Decertification?" *Labor Law Journal* 39 (July 1988), pp. 432–36.
100. Marvin J. Levine, "Double-Digit Decertification Election Activity: Union Organizational Weakness in the 1980s," *Labor Law Journal* 40 (May 1989), pp. 311–315.
101. William E. Fulmer and Tamara A. Gilman, "Why Do Workers Vote for Union Decertification?" *Personnel* 58 (March–April 1981), pp. 29–32.
102. John C. Anderson, Gloria Busman, and Charles A. O'Reilly III, "The Decertification Process: Evidence from California," *Industrial Relations* 21 (Spring 1982), pp. 193–195.
103. Fulmer, "When Employees Want to Oust Their Union," pp. 167–169.
104. *Tawas Tube Production, Inc.,* 151 NLRB 9 (1965).

Cases for Part 1

CASE 1.1 Atlas Towers: Composition of Bargaining Unit

The Atlas Towers is a 30-story hotel in Atlantic City, New Jersey. The hotel derives approximately 83 percent of its gross revenues from its convention business. It has 1,250 rooms and employs about 832 regular full-time nonsupervisory employees. It has 4 restaurants, 3 cocktail lounges, a nightclub, recreational facilities, 52 meeting rooms, and an exhibition hall.

Because it is mainly a convention hotel, its facilities and organizational structure have been designed specifically for the purpose of serving convention business, and its operations are closely coordinated and functionally integrated. The conventions require each department to cooperate with the others to provide the promised services. Thus, the front office, sales, catering, reservations, food and beverage, and communications employees are involved in selling conventions to prospective customers and in an effort to ascertain customers' needs during their stay.

Atlas Towers has an extensive internal communications and record-keeping system. This consists of a MICOR computer system,[1] a pneumatic tube system linking the front desk and other parts of the facility, communications (PBX) and food and beverage outlets, a beeper paging system, and a walkie-talkie system.

The booking, planning, and execution of conventions require close coordination among all hotel areas. Preconvention meetings are held to review a convention resumé that outlines the convention functions and roles of each area. The convention resumé is circulated to approximately 40 different departments and contains instructions for each.

General Manager Ussery sends numerous memoranda to the department heads, assistant department heads, and assistant area managers. These memoranda demonstrate Ussery's close involvement in minor details of the hotel's day-to-day operation and reflect management's highly centralized control.[2] Individual department heads oversee routine operations in their areas but do not establish basic work policies or have final control over department functions.

The hotel's human resources department establishes

[1]The MICOR system is used by employees in accounting (cashiers), housekeeping, front desk, and communications. MICOR's information includes guest names, guest room locations, guest conventions, and room status.

[2]Some examples of the day-to-day issues with which Ussery has been involved include the policy regarding furnishing meals to police officers, cleaning guest elevator doors, availability of rollaway beds, the purchase of a knife for the dessert wagon, use of employee name tags, the maintenance and cost of shower curtains, approval of a front office clerk's vacation period, guest entrapment in elevators, and cleaning the lower ground floor area.

uniform personnel policies, including wages and benefits,[3] which apply to all hotel employees except property operations employees, whose terms and conditions of employment have been specified in a collective bargaining agreement. Human resources screens all applicants and refers qualified applicants to the department managers for interviews.[4] The director of human resources must approve all personnel decisions, including any discipline supervisors recommend. Hotel employees have an employee cafeteria, employee locker rooms, and a recreation program. There are employee training programs throughout the hotel in which employees of different departments participate. Some employees receive cross-training in other departments. For example, some communications employees received training to make them more aware of what goes on in the front office. There is also a "priority one" training program that covers any employee who has face-to-face contact with guests.

The hotel has a uniform transfer policy. The human resources department posts openings, and employees from any area may apply. The employee's current supervisor must sign a form, and the human resources department must approve the transfer. There have been numerous transfers among departments, including approximately 27 transfers in 2 years from housekeeping to other departments. There have also been transfers from the food and beverage and stewards area to housekeeping, and from communications to housekeeping, secretary, front office, and accounting. Other transfers have occurred from food and beverage to sales, front office, and accounting; from office to food and beverage; from housekeeping to the front desk; from greeter to catering; from bellstand to food and beverage; from communications to accounting; from room service to secretary; from personnel to catering; from public facilities to security; and from stewards to bellstand.

Employees from different areas have frequent contact with each other. Contacts between accounting personnel and other employees include the following: Front office cashiers issue keys to food and beverage employees, restaurant cashiers, housekeeping, engineering, and laundry employees. Shipping and receiving employees deal with engineering, food and beverage, laundry, and housekeeping employees in handling goods to be picked up by other departments or delivered. Night auditors have contact with restaurant employees when they pick up reports and read registers in the restaurant outlets. Accounts payable clerks obtain approvals for payments of invoices from every department.[5] Restaurant cashiers occasionally assist the hostesses or greeters in the dining rooms.

Laundry employees have contact with buspersons, banquet employees, kitchen employees, the storeroom clerk, shipping and receiving, communications, catering, and room service, and the bellstand. Employees from other departments bring laundry to be cleaned and pick up clean laundry and uniforms.

Housekeeping employees maintain contact with the front desk cashiers through the MICOR system regarding all room status changes. The front desk provides house counts to housekeeping for budgeting and scheduling purposes. Housekeeping employees have contacts with food and beverage employees when they clean restaurant outlets and work with public facilities employees in cleaning areas around the meeting rooms.

Food and beverage employees keep contact with the front office or house count and the pay-in-advance guest list. They have contact with restaurant cashiers and night auditors and work closely with the inventory control office. The convention services department advises food and beverage as to the services each convention requires. Food and beverage employees work with housekeeping employees in setting up VIP rooms.

Communications employees assist cashiers regarding guest telephone charges (using the pneumatic tube system). Operators take restaurant reservations when

[3]A hotelwide wage and salary program sets pay rates for each job classification, including the hiring rates and frequency and amounts of pay increases. Individual supervisors and department heads do not determine when their employees receive a pay increase. Among other hotelwide personnel policies the human resources department formulates with Ussery's approval are work hours, disciplinary procedures, dress standards, holidays, night differential pay rates, benefit improvements, funeral leave, vacation policy, jury duty, overtime pay, and probation periods. All hotel employees except property operations employees receive the same fringe benefits.

[4]Each manager makes the final hiring decision from among those human resources refers.

[5]Generally, rank-and-file employees in other departments are not involved with this function unless there is a question about receipt of merchandise.

food and beverage receptionists are not available. Restaurant cashiers call operators to verify guest room numbers, and operators call outlets to locate guests and give out information regarding the hours of the food and beverage outlets. Housekeeping employees call operators if a message light is left on in a vacant room or if a telephone is missing or damaged. Public facilities employees notify operators when a telephone needs to be removed from a meeting room. All departments notify communications when repairs are necessary.

There is some interchange of employees between departments, mainly under emergency situations. Accounting employees have worked as bartenders, and credit employees as hostesses. During an ice storm, accounting employees assisted housekeeping. Catering, sales, and accounting employees have been used as bar cashiers. Housekeeping employees sometimes fill in at the laundry and uniform room. A housekeeping employee fills in for the restroom attendant. Housekeeping employees have filled in as waitresses or buspersons, and they help in shipping and receiving when a large order arrives. They also occasionally substitute for lobby porters (bellstand).

The union had proposed that the appropriate bargaining unit should consist of all full-time and regular part-time housekeeping, laundry, public facility, and exhibit employees, as follows:

> All full-time and regular part-time housekeeping, laundry and public facility and exhibit employees employed by the Employer at its Atlantic City facility, including aides, on-call aides, turn-down aides, attendants, the payroll clerk, dispatchers, night cleaners, stockroom attendant, locker room attendant, drapery attendant, washman, chuteman, laundry attendant, linen runner, seamstress, uniform room attendant, meeting room attendant, banquet houseman and assistant team leaders, *excluding* office clerical employees, secretaries, property operations employees, front office employees, food and beverage employees, steward employees, room service employees, communication employees, the hostesses, guest greeters, purchasing employees, human resources employees, the tower clerk, marketing and sales employees, accounting employees, security employees, guards and supervisors as defined in the Act.

The employer proposed a unit consisting of all employees employed at the facility, excluding only property operations department employees, confidential employees, security officers, guards/watchmen and supervisors as defined in the NLRA.

The regional director of the NLRB had determined the unit to be all full-time and regular part-time food and beverage employees. This unit would include the following:

> All full-time and regular part-time food and beverage employees, steward employees, room service employees, guest services employees, bellmen, cashiers, and stockroom attendant; *excluding* office clerical employees, secretaries, property operations employees, communication employees, housekeeping, laundry and public facility and exhibit employees, human resources employees, purchasing employees, the Tower clerk, marketing and sales employees, accounting employees, security employees, guards and supervisors as defined by the Act.

The decision of the regional director has now been appealed to the board in Washington for a decision.

Questions

1. Explain the importance of the union's and employer's position regarding the composition of the appropriate bargaining unit.
2. What are the criteria that should be used in this determination?
3. Considering the views of the employer and the union and the decision of the regional director, what should the NLRB decide to be the appropriate unit?
4. Justify this decision.

References

Arlington Hotel Co., 126 NLRB 400 (1960).
77 Operating Co., 160 NLRB 927 (1966).
Regency Hyatt Hotel, 171 NLRB 1347 (1968).
Holiday Inn, Alton, 270 NLRB 199 (1984).
Holiday Inn, Southwest, 202 NLRB 781 (1973).
Holiday Inn, 214 NLRB 651 (1974).
Days Inn of America, 210 NLRB 1035 (1974).
Ramada Inn v. *NLRB*, 487 F.2d 1334 (1973).
Westward-Ho Hotel, 437 F.2d 1110 (1971).

CASE 1.2 Employer Formation of a President's Advisory Council

The company manufactures and services recreational vehicles in three plants in Jackson Center, Ohio. The union filed a certification petition with the National Labor Relations Board on January 21, 1985, to represent the production and maintenance employees at the three plants. In late February 1985, the company president announced the formation of the President's Advisory Council (PAC), which formalized an arrangement that had existed within the company for the last 4 years. This arrangement included monthly "rap sessions" with employees on a rotating basis, attended by the company president, where employees could ask any questions and make any suggestions they wished.

On March 1, each department was asked to vote for three representatives to sit on the PAC. At the first meeting of the PAC a few days before the union election, the president discussed the comparative merits of an attendance bonus program favored by management versus a personal sick day program favored by employees. He agreed to review the attendance/sick leave policy, but said no changes could be made until after the union election. On March 15, the election was held and the union lost by a vote of 106 to 181.

A week after the election a second meeting of the PAC was held and the president announced the reinstatement of the personal sick day program preferred by employees. At the third meeting of the PAC, the job bidding system was discussed and, again, changes were made in accordance with the suggestions of employee representatives at the meetings.

The union filed charges of unfair labor practices with the National Labor Relations Board and claimed that the PAC was an employer-dominated labor organization intended to undermine support for the union. In addition, the union charged that the company had unlawfully interfered with the election by holding meetings with the PAC members and discussing terms and other conditions of employment.

The company responded that it had only formalized an arrangement that had lasted for 4 years and it was careful not to discuss matters that would have been discussed with the union if it had won the election. Likewise, the company was careful not to take any action as a result of discussions with the PAC members until after the union election. Further, since the union lost the election, the company practiced good management by continuing the PAC meetings and responding affirmatively to employee suggestions and recommendations.

Questions

1. Is the PAC a labor organization? Why or why not?
2. Have the company actions violated the National Labor Relations Act?
3. Should the company be directed to recognize the union since it has already begun to hold meetings with employee representatives and to discuss and act on proposals on terms and conditions of employment?
4. How should the National Labor Relations Board decide this case? Explain and justify your reasons.

CASE 1.3 Socializing on the Job

Nina Bloomstein and Lisa Coe were employed as proofreaders at the document processing center for ABC Management Consulting Company. In November 1986, ABC hired two new proofreaders at salaries higher than those paid to Bloomstein and Coe, who had 6 and 2 years seniority, respectively. When Bloomstein and Coe found out about the new employees' salaries, they complained to their supervisors and then to a personnel specialist. The following day, both women received written warnings for past instances of tardiness.

On January 12, 1987, Bloomstein and Coe met with the human resources manager, and she indicated that she would get back with them. Five weeks later, she rejected their complaints. During the interim time period, Bloomstein and Coe met with other proofreaders for dinner and discussed their working conditions and job-related concerns.

One of the proofreaders who did not attend the dinner complained to her supervisor that she was being harassed by her coworkers to join them. The following day, the proofreaders were told that it was not proper to encourage other employees to complain and that the company would not tolerate strong-arm or union-like tactics. The human resources manager stated that she was aware of the salary problems and that the company was working to correct them.

On February 27, one of the proofreaders complained to management that Bloomstein had made offensive racial and ethnic comments to her and that Coe was considered the "Norma Rae" of the workplace. Upon hearing these complaints, the company immediately fired Bloomstein and implemented a new work rule that prohibited "socializing" and "congregating at each others' work stations." A week later, the company decided to terminate Coe.

After their termination, both Bloomstein and Coe filed charges with the National Labor Relations Board and alleged that the company had committed unfair labor practices by terminating their employment.

Questions

1. Were the actions of Bloomstein and Coe considered protected concerted activities under Section 7 of the National Labor Relations Act?
2. Does it matter that neither Bloomstein or Coe was a member of a labor union?
3. Assess the company reactions to the employee complaints.
4. Was the company guilty of violating the National Labor Relations Act? If so, what would be the appropriate remedy? Explain.

CASE 1.4 Free Medical Screening 2 Days before an Election

The company is a mailing services firm, and 280 production and maintenance employees were being organized by the United Food and Commercial Workers. The union has a health and welfare trust fund that owns two vans bearing the union's logo. The vans serve as mobile medical units and are used to provide health screening to employees in bargaining units represented by the union. Three days before the end of a vigorous election campaign, the union announced that it would make available free medical screenings to all employees at the company's factory. The heading of the announcement read: "First Union Benefit." Then it stated: "Please take advantage of your first union benefit. It's for your health."

The following day, only 2 days before the election, the two vans were stationed across from the employee entrance to the company's factory. An estimated 80 employees took advantage of the medical screenings for high blood pressure, lung functioning, cholesterol level, and diabetes. There was no requirement to demonstrate any pre-election support for the union to qualify for the screenings. However, the union logo was prominently displayed on the two vans.

The election was held, and the results were 157 for the union, 113 against the union, and 10 challenged ballots. The company filed a complaint with the National Labor Relations Board and alleged that the union had unlawfully interfered with the election. The company alleged that the union's announcement of the free medical screenings as the first union benefit 3 days before the election linked the granting of this benefit to the union's success in the pending election. Also, the company asserted that the actual provision of medical screening 2 days before the election maximized the impact of an illegal inducement to vote for the union, and thus, that the union had committed an unfair labor practice by illegally interfering with the election.

The union responded that the medical screening was provided to all employees and union support was not required. The union contended that it had not unlawfully interfered with the election and that the results of the election accurately reflected the interests of the bargaining unit employees.

Questions

1. Does it matter whether the free medical screening was offered to all employees?
2. Does it matter whether there was no requirement for any employee to show support before using the free medical screening?
3. Does the union's logo link the free medical screening with the union?
4. How important was the message, "First Union Benefit," provided to employees the day before the presence of the vans for free medical screening?
5. Did the union unlawfully interfere with the outcome of the election? Explain your reasons.

CASE 1.5 Providing Union Information in a Hospital Cafeteria

The incident started with a campaign by the Hospital Workers of America to organize the employees of First Methodist Hospital. As soon as the hospital administration heard about the organizing campaign, it issued a rule that prohibited employees from soliciting or distributing literature during working time or in patient areas at any time. The rule also provided that "visitors, patients, and other non-employees may not solicit or distribute literature on any hospital property for any purpose at any time."

On December 10, two union organizers accompanied by three off-duty employees went to the hospital's cafeteria, which was open to the general public as well as to all employees, and set up a union information table. The off-duty employees distributed union literature supplied by the union organizers while the union organizers simply remained seated at a table answering any questions directed toward them by employees. At no time did the union organizers distribute any union literature or sign up employees for the union.

After the union organizers had been in the cafeteria for less than an hour, the human resources director for the hospital went to the table and told the organizers that they were violating the hospital's rule against non-employee solicitation and distribution. At first, the union organizers balked and explained that they were only answering questions from interested employees. They claimed that they did not interfere with the operations of the hospital, did not adversely affect anyone's performance, and did not have any contact with any patient of the hospital. They argued that they were only providing information to those employees who requested it so that they would be better informed about the programs and activities of the union and better able to determine whether they wanted to be represented by the union.

The human resources director then threatened to have the union organizers arrested; the organizers then left the cafeteria voluntarily. However, when the union officers were informed of the hospital's actions, the union filed unfair labor practice charges with the National Labor Relations Board.

Questions

1. Does the hospital have the right to establish rules that prohibit solicitation and distribution "on any hospital property for any purpose at any time"?
2. May employees or union organizers provide union information to other employees in a public-access hospital cafeteria?
3. What are some guidelines that would be appropriate to employee solicitation and distribution?
4. Reconcile the conflicts between employer rights and union or employee rights with regard to solicitation and distribution.
5. How should the National Labor Relations Board rule in this case? Explain your reasoning.

CASE 1.6 Closing a Plant after a Successful Union Election

Mid-South Packing Company was formed in 1982 as a holding company by the leveraged buyout of several packing and distribution centers in Arkansas, Mississippi, Louisiana, and Tennessee. In all, Mid-South operates over 20 units in four states, including the Clarksdale, Mississippi plant. In 1986, Mid-South transferred the Clarksdale, Mississippi plant from its Tennessee division to its new Mississippi-Arkansas division and considered making substantial repairs to the 60-year-old plant, which was in poor condition.

On January 17, 1986, Mid-South was informed that a sufficient number of employees at the Clarksdale plant had signed authorization cards with the International Union of Electronic Workers (IUE) to require a representation election. During the union organizing campaign, Mid-South threatened to close the plant should the union emerge victorious in the election, among other antiunion tactics.

The union won the election and the company filed objections. The union responded to the objections and filed several unfair labor practice charges as well. During negotiations initiated by the company, the union agreed to drop the charges in exchange for the company's promise to recognize the union and bargain in good faith. The company agreed to withdraw its objection to the election and the IUE was certified as the bargaining representative for the Clarksdale plant employees on April 28, 1986.

On May 5, 1986, the company informed the union that it was shutting down the Clarksdale, Mississippi plant and actually shut the doors 4 days later. The union filed a new set of unfair labor practice charges with the National Labor Relations Board, alleging that the company had violated the National Labor Relations Act by shutting down the plant and by refusing to bargain with the union about the plant closure.

Mid-South claimed that the Clarksdale plant was not a profitable operation despite its showing a net profit in 1986 and the second-highest production level among the six plants in the Mississippi-Arkansas division. The company claimed reopening this plant would not only impose an undue or unfair burden on the company but would threaten the continued viability of its entire operation. Company officials concluded that the plant would require $150,000 in repairs merely to reopen, and that the plant would have closed regardless of how the employees had voted in the representation election.

The union charged that the reason for the shutdown was the successful union election campaign. The union was certified as the legal bargaining agent for the Clarksdale plant employees and the company had agreed to bargain in good faith with the union. Instead, the company shut down the plant and did not bargain in good faith. The union also claimed that among the unfair practices committed by the company during the organizing campaign the company had threatened to close the plant, and then after the union won the election the company did in fact close the plant.

Questions

1. Does the National Labor Relations Board have authority to require a company to re-open a plant?
2. Did the company commit an unfair labor practice?
3. Should the National Labor Relations Board consider the cost of $150,000 to reopen the plant?
4. What should be the National Labor Relations Board's decision? Justify your answer.

Negotiating and Administering the Labor Agreement

Part 2 pertains to key activities in the labor relations process: the negotiation and administration of the work rules. These topics are approached from the vantage point of legal and quasi-legal (labor agreement) proscriptions on related behavior as well as with an eye to the practical realities forged out of the relationships between union and management officials.

CHAPTER 6

Negotiating the Labor Agreement

Keep in mind that a labor contract is a political document more than a legal one—all of its legal language is worthless if the contract doesn't reflect the realities of the workplace.

Fritz Ihrig, "Labor Contract Negotiations: Behind the Scenes," *Personnel Administrator* 31 (April 1986), p. 59.

Negotiation, or collective bargaining, is a common feature of everyday life. While this chapter covers negotiations between union and management officials over conditions of employment, many aspects of negotiations have broader applications to other bargaining activities in our society.

This chapter first defines collective bargaining, then explains initial influences affecting this activity. Subsequent sections consider pre-negotiation activities such as bargaining team selection, proposal formulation and assessment, and collective behavior (situations, tactics, and communication style). The next section places these diverse collective bargaining considerations in perspective by describing the "bargaining power model," a likely resolution framework. Ethical and legal considerations affecting collective bargaining conclude this chapter.

Collective Bargaining: Definition and Structure

Collective bargaining is an activity whereby two groups, union and management officials, attempt to resolve conflicting interests by exchanging commitments in a manner that will sustain and possibly enrich their continuing relationship. Negotiation or collective bargaining is characterized by the following:

- *Interdependence*—union and management officials need each other to complete a labor agreement or contract.
- *Alteration of the other group's perceptions* to obtain a favorable settlement.
- *Subjectivity*—Imprecise bargaining procedures and values that each group assigns to bargaining issues and outcomes.

Attitudes of union and management officials toward collective bargaining and the negotiated settlement influence their relationships during the length of the labor agreement. A successful collective bargaining settlement occurs when both parties believe they have gained something, even if that gain is simply maintaining the status quo. Collective bargaining is more easily defined than explained, however, as this activity often involves more than just the appropriate bargaining unit discussed in Chapter 5.

Meaning and Dimensions

Bargaining structure has two general meanings: (1) employee groupings that can affect the collective bargaining outcome and (2) the employees and employers who are subject to the provisions of the negotiated labor agreement.

Unions are responsive to several groups within and outside their organizations. Every organization has *informal work groups* (the night shift crew or the company bowling team, for example) that have unique preferences and place pressures on union officers to achieve their preferences in collective bargaining.

In some cases union and management officials are influenced by other collective bargaining settlements. For example, a labor settlement between city government and the police might influence subsequent negotiations between city government and the firefighters. In the private sector, the United Rubber Workers' union has on occasion struck for cost-of-living labor agreement provisions similar to those obtained previously by the United Auto Workers' union.

A related concept is **pattern bargaining,** which can take the following forms:

- Unions focus their bargaining and strike threats on one company (Ford Motors, for example), then attempt to negotiate a similar settlement with another company that manufactures a similar product (such as General Motors).
- A settlement obtained for one segment of the industry (interstate truck drivers, for example) is passed on to related companies (such as local delivery and food wholesaling concerns).

Pattern bargaining strongly influenced wage settlements in the 1970s, although this activity was less popular in the 1980s. Competitive pressures on management have brought the realization that prices cannot always be increased to accommodate higher wages.[1] Pattern bargaining does remain today, however, particularly in the automobile industry. In 1987, Ford Motors obtained a settlement with these significant job security provisions:

- With the exception of an industrywide sales slump, the company would not lay off any of its 104,000 Auto Workers during the agreement's 3-year life.
- The company would also replace at least one of every two workers who departed.

The same provisions were then essentially included in General Motor's labor agreement, which was settled approximately 1 month later.

The Negotiating Unit The second dimension of the bargaining structure, the **negotiating unit,** refers to the employees and employers who will be bound by the negotiated labor agreement. There are three possible negotiating units:

1. The negotiating unit may be the same as the *appropriate bargaining unit* (ABU) determined by the National Labor Relations Board for representation election purposes and is the *minimal* collective bargaining component.
2. The negotiation unit may represent more than one ABU. This is called **centralized bargaining,** of which there are two major types. *Single employer–multi-plant bargaining* may be used when one company has several separate facilities, each having a separate ABU. The employer and union representatives at these facilities might combine into one negotiating unit for collective bargaining purposes.

   In *multi-employer bargaining,* more than one employer and the corresponding union or unions form one negotiating unit each at the bargaining table. This type of centralized bargaining is common in the trucking, construction, longshore, and newspaper industries.
3. The negotiating unit may be a combination of the preceding arrangements. ABUs might be combined for certain issues (pension plans, for example) that are equally applied to employees throughout the industry, while working conditions specific to the individual ABU are resolved at the local facility. In many cases the local negotiations can run counter to centralized bargaining.

Centralized Bargaining One or both parties might consider centralized bargaining because of product interdependence, market factors, or legal considerations. For example, a company may have three manufacturing facilities, each having a separate ABU. If the products at the facilities are interdependent (Facility A's product is needed for Facility B, whose product is in turn completed with products at Facility C), then management would probably prefer centralized bargaining—a common expiration date and one possible strike at all facilities—instead of three different contract expiration dates and possible separate strikes at each of the facilities. Separate bargaining could in effect shut down manufacturing operations three times compared to one shutdown under centralized bargaining.

If the three facilities are independent of each other—each facility can produce a completed product without parts or products from other facilities (for example, three steel mills, each completing a similar product, or three facilities having unrelated products such as baseball gloves, cereal, and marbles), management would probably prefer to negotiate separately with each facility's ABU. Separate negotiations would probably result in different contract expiration dates for the three facilities. If one facility went out on strike, the others could still continue production, and in the case of facilities that produce similar products, management could transfer some of the orders from the struck facility to the other two facilities where the contracts had not expired.

Some believe that conglomerate companies with a wide range of different products have too much bargaining power over unions. One sample of nine conglomerates revealed 846 different manufacturing products sold. A union threatening a strike to shut down one of these manufacturing facilities or even an entire product line will not be able to put sufficient pressure on a conglomerate to reach a bargaining settlement.[2] The union therefore prefers centralized bargaining in this situation, realizing that a strike could effectively shut down the company's entire operations, thereby increasing union bargaining strength.

Market factors also influence the degree of centralization of the bargaining unit. In a highly competitive market, a multi-employer (centralized) negotiating unit would be desirable to employers who fear being placed at a competitive disadvantage if other employers subsequently negotiate lower wage rates. Combining with other employers into a multi-employer negotiating unit alleviates this fear while minimizing another problem—the loss of customers to competitors during a strike.

Unions are also concerned about market problems in some industries (construction, coal, trucking, ladies' garment, longshore, and others) and attempt to extend the negotiating unit to include the entire geographic area in which the product is competitively produced. This is to prevent a few employers from separately negotiating lower wages, which would allow production at lower costs, thereby attracting customers from the other firms and resulting in employee layoffs. In essence, the unions are attempting to standardize wages, hours, and other terms of employment in order to exclude them as competitive factors and force the employers to compete on the basis of factors such as product design, service, marketing, and so on instead.

Multi-employer bargaining also has other advantages and disadvantages. A union engaged in multi-employer bargaining has a powerful advantage over rival unions because the NLRB holds that while a multi-employer negotiating unit is intact it is the only appropriate bargaining election unit. Thus, the NLRB will dismiss a rival union's petition for an election in a single firm as long as the incumbent union and the firm are engaged in multi-employer negotiations or are parties to a multi-employer agreement. "The rival union can only obtain an election that covers all the employees in the multi-employer unit."[3]

Both labor and management can pool their respective negotiation expenses by hiring a few experts to negotiate an agreement covering several firms. Yet a corresponding disadvantage of centralized bargaining is that the hired negotiators usually do not have extensive knowledge of the parties' attitudes and strategies. Centralized bargaining tends to become more formal and less flexible in terms of meeting employee and employer concerns at the individual workplace.[4] Finally, multi-employer bargaining can create tensions among the member employers, as evidenced in a recent coal negotiation—an employer might pull out of the association if it feels it can get a better deal negotiating separately with the union.

The decision to engage in centralized bargaining can also be affected by legal guidelines. Currently, the union can have representatives from other unions (desiring a centralized negotiating unit) at the bargaining table as negotiating team members. If the employer only wishes to negotiate with the single union, however, that union cannot delegate its authority to accept or reject the employer's settlement to the representatives of the other unions. The courts have also ruled out as unlawful a "lock-in" agreement between unions, which deprives individual unions of the right to sign a contract until all other unions have agreed to sign.

Pre-Negotiation Activities

Selection of Negotiating Team and Related Bargaining Responsibilities

Union and management negotiators often prepare well in advance of contract negotiations, although many of the activities discussed in this section continue throughout collective bargaining. Several considerations face the chief negotiators in selecting their respective negotiating teams. Personal attributes are a major factor in the selection process. Both chief negotiators desire members who can keep their emotions and opinions in check. An indiscreet negotiating team member can unintentionally reveal confidential settlement points and strategies to the other team.

The individual's experience and background are also considered in the selection process. Management wants at least one line manager who supervises bargaining-unit employees on its team to either interpret or answer related negotiating issues. Unions also prefer to select team members from a variety of operating departments to ensure membership representation and the discussion of working concerns that might be uniquely related to a particular department.

Finally, political or organizational considerations are also involved in the selection of negotiating team members. In many cases, the union negotiating team is elected by the members, and the union's chief negotiator has little input into the selection process. If discretion is allowed, the chief negotiator will at least think twice before appointing a political rival or member of an opposing faction to the negotiating team.

One study has isolated specific roles typically performed by one or more members on each bargaining team.

> The first, the *leader* (or chief negotiator) will normally be the most senior member of the team and in a management team may be empowered to make unilateral decisions without reference to outsiders. (Union officials, on the other hand, are usually delegates and have to seek approval of their decisions.) The leader's role is to do most of the speaking and, generally, to lead the negotiation toward a conclusion.
>
> The role of the *summarizer* is to follow the argument closely and to buy thinking time for the leader by intervening at the appropriate stage. The most constructive way to do this is to ask for clarification of a point or to summarize the negotiation to date. He or she should avoid making concessions unless this is previously agreed. Some people choose to have a "hard man" and a "soft man" in their team. This, however, needs careful planning.
>
> The role of the *recorder* is to remain silent throughout the negotiation unless called upon to answer a direct question. The recorder is often the legal or technical specialist. His or her job is to observe the people on the other team carefully and to watch for clues, both verbal and visual, that might reveal their inner thinking—or, indeed, the presence of "allies" among the opposition. The recorder writes down the terms of offers made and received and generally keeps minutes of the meeting. He or she should report to colleagues during adjournments.[5]

There are usually more members of the negotiating teams who act as silent observers presenting information and advice when each side meets in private. Also, some or all of these individuals might form subcommittees with members of the other bargaining team to resolve a particular bargaining issue and/or review final contract language before the labor agreement is printed. Management's chief negotiator in single-plant bargaining is often the labor relations manager at the plant level, although in a large, multi-plant organization, this individual might be another management official in the organization.

Estimating the Other Negotiator's Bargaining Behaviors and Perspective

The chief union and management negotiators assess each other in the context of their organizations. Each negotiator initially assesses the other's interpersonal characteristics as a major, possibly controlling influence in his or her organization. Opponent negotiators can be assessed according to their

- Collective bargaining experience.
- Temperament (volatile versus low-keyed).
- Sense of humor.
- Approachability for off-the-record discussions.
- Honesty and the reliability of his or her word.

Each negotiator knows that the other is also guided or limited by broader organizational constraints. The management negotiator, for example, estimates the likelihood that the national union will back a particular bargaining issue, and the strike funds available if agreement cannot be reached. The union negotiator assesses the company's profits, demand for its products and amount of inventory, and degree of employee layoffs.

Employees, as noted in Chapter 1, are independent, unpredictable participants who belong neither to the management nor the union organization entirely. Both chief negotiators therefore attempt to estimate employees' views on bargaining issues, their acceptance of a strike, and, based on previous strikes, whether they could be replaced if a strike occurred.[6]

Proposal Determination and Assessment

Management relies on several sources in anticipating what the union will seek in collective bargaining. A review of recent contract settlements negotiated by the company's competitors and by other local firms may suggest issues that will be raised by the union. The company and union may have negotiated settlements at other facilities that might also be used as a starting point in the current negotiations. Some management officials obtain bargaining insights by reviewing the proceedings of the national union's convention.

Much attention should be given to the previous negotiation, particularly to those issues that the union actively sought and reluctantly dropped. Compromise settlements on previous issues also generate valuable clues since compromise does not mean permanent resolution of the issue.

An analysis of previous grievances at the facility can also illustrate certain trouble spots. General Motors, for example, uses a computerized analysis of number, type, and resolution status of grievances in their negotiations preparation. However, caution has to be taken not to overemphasize these grievances. Unions often step up grievance activity just before negotiations to dramatize widespread concern over certain bargaining issues—a concern perhaps more tactical than real.

Formulating Proposals and the Bargaining Range Many management negotiators, unlike their union counterparts, do not formulate bargaining proposals to discuss with the union. Managers might be reluctant to formulate proposals because that will "tip their hand" to the union, revealing management's weaknesses. A recession, however, might prod management to formulate proposals and bargain accordingly.

Managers who do formulate proposals often perform a close analysis of the labor agreement to determine desirable changes in contract language that will reduce labor costs and give management more discretion in operations. Assume, for example, that the current provision restricts supervisors entirely from performing any bargaining-unit work. Management would probably seek to change this language to allow supervisors to perform bargaining-unit work under at least three conditions: (1) when training new employees, (2) in emergency situations (usually interpreted to mean when employees' lives or production equipment are jeopardized), and (3) when experimental production efforts are involved.

Both management and union officials are concerned about the legal implications of current contractual language, particularly in terms of recent decisions by the National Labor Relations Board and the courts (such as the *Milwaukee Springs* decision of the NLRB discussed later in this chapter). Management and union officials would also like to nullify the impact of adverse arbitration decisions. This can be accomplished by inserting contract language contradictory to the arbitrator's decision into the subsequent labor agreement.

Both parties would also be interested in knowing if various administrators of the labor agreement (union stewards and first-line supervisors) have difficulties in implementing certain labor agreement provisions on the shop floor. Management should contact first-line supervisors before and during the negotiation process because these individuals know the existence and magnitude of employee workplace concerns and must administer the negotiated provisions.

Efforts will also be made to research data from government reports, especially from the Departments of Commerce and Labor, and from various labor relations services such as the Bureau of National Affairs, Inc., Commerce Clearing House, and Prentice-Hall. Data from these and other sources give both parties substantial information with which to prepare for negotiations.

Unions often have an added consideration in proposal formulation—their members' expectations. The union generally encourages its members to present issues they feel are important in the upcoming negotiations, which, on the surface, reinforces the democratic principle that union officers are guided by members' input. Yet this activity can raise members' expectations and even antagonisms, which in turn pose political problems for officers in current negotiations or in subsequent elections.

Exhibit 6.1 represents an abbreviated bargaining issue questionnaire sent by a faculty union to its members. Expectations and subsequent antagonisms can be raised if the union fails to obtain any or all of these issues, or even if the union

Exhibit 6.1

Partial Bargaining Priorities Survey for Faculty Union Members of a Statewide University Bargaining Unit

Here are some questions about issues that will be raised in this year's negotiations. For each indicate whether you feel it should be:

5 Top priority to get this
4 High priority to get this
3 Moderate priority to get this
2 Low priority to get this
1 Against this, do not try to get it
DK Don't know, no opinion on this

Issue						
1. Tuition waivers for faculty members' spouse/children (they do not have to pay for the classes in which they are enrolled).	5	4	3	2	1	DK
2. Guaranteed summer supplements (a minimum payment for teaching and/or conducting research).	5	4	3	2	1	DK
3. Disputes over the amount of individual faculty merit wages that are eligible for the grievance procedure.	5	4	3	2	1	DK

does obtain the requested items. The member preference scale (1 through 5) on the questionnaire probably should not be averaged in a statistical sense. For example, an average score of 4.00 on tuition waivers for spouse/children might encourage the union to obtain this issue. Yet, this score could reflect that 25 percent of the respondents are against this issue and do not want the union to pursue it. This rejection percentage could pose problems for the union negotiation team, particularly if it includes many active union officials and potential political rivals.

Also, many of the faculty members might be disillusioned if they find out that the "summer supplements" obtained through negotiations are only $1,000, and are given only to faculty at the associate or full professor level. Obtaining grievability of merit raises does not mean that the union will subsequently take a professor's grievance concerning merit pay to arbitration or that the arbitrator will decide the grievance in the professor's favor.

The Bargaining Range Union and management officials both enter collective bargaining with their own ideas of an acceptable settlement, although both parties know the other will not agree entirely with their position. Therefore, both parties usually enter negotiations with a variety of acceptable positions, which gives them some room for maneuvering.

These positions are given priorities and grouped into two **bargaining ranges,** one for management, the other for the union. Exhibit 6.2 illustrates bargaining ranges for a few issues; however, it is common for the parties to negotiate a hundred or more bargaining issues. (See Exhibit 6.3 for a general list of issues that may be included in the bargaining range.)

Both management and union representatives have upper and lower limits on their respective ranges. Management's upper limit is usually determined by its objectives, such as profitability and growth. A settlement above this perceived upper

Exhibit 6.2 **Bargaining Ranges for Union and Management Negotiators**

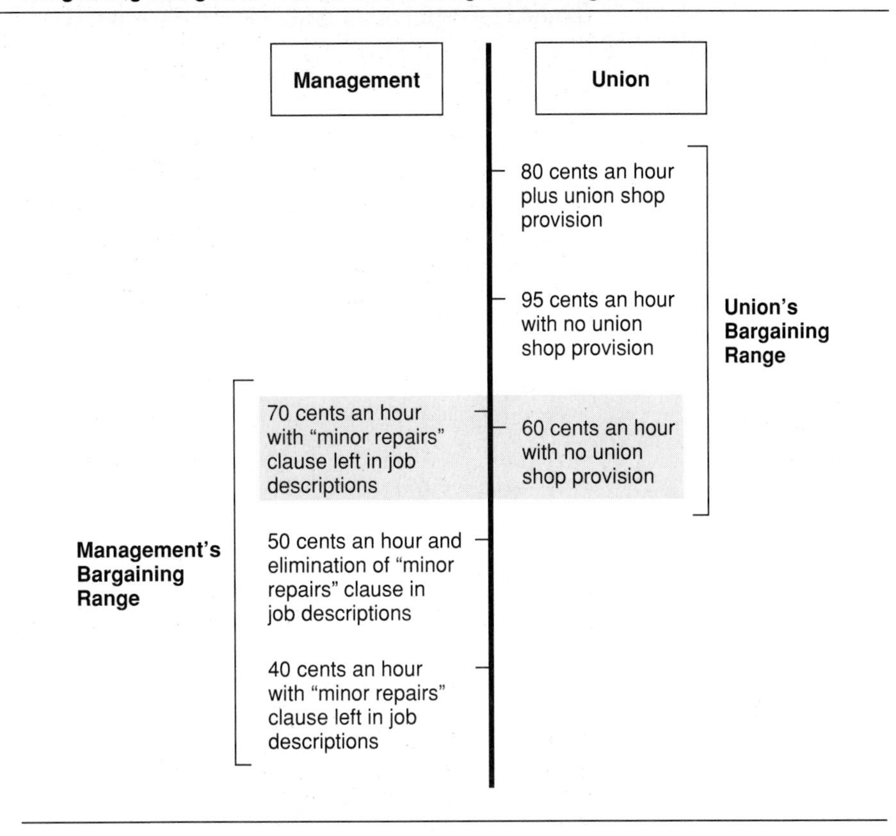

limit would be incompatible with the company's objectives. For example, management would close, move its operations, or bring new employees into its existing facility rather than agree to a settlement that would make operating unprofitable. On the other hand, management would not like to be known as the cheapest employer in the area, nor would it want to be unable to recruit, retain, and reward its employees. These concerns help place a lower limit on management's bargaining range—a minimum offer management feels is necessary to maintain employee morale and output.

The union's upper limit is usually shaped by two factors: (1) employment levels and (2) ability to promote and sustain a strike. The union realizes that there can be a tradeoff between a high economic settlement and total number of jobs at a facility—employers might offset their newly negotiated labor costs by laying off some employees. To some extent, the union's upper limit is governed by its desire to maintain the existing labor force or dues-paying membership.

The union also realizes that its members might not want to strike over an unrealistic, pie-in-the-sky proposal presented by the union. Some individuals believe that unions do not have upper limits on their bargaining range, that union leaders will press for outrageous proposals on the rationale that "it does not hurt to ask,"

Exhibit 6.3

Representative Issues That Might Appear in a Collective Bargaining Agreement and/or Bargaining Range

Ability, Definition of
Absence
Reporting of
With Leave
Without Leave
Arbitration
Bargaining Unit
Definition of
Benefits, Employee
Funeral Pay
Glove, Hat, and Shoe Allowance
Jury Duty
Layoff Allowance
Nonoccupational Disability Pay
Occupational Disability Pay
Pension and Insurance
Vacation
Bidding
Bulletin Boards
Call-out
Definition of
Holiday
Regular
Seventh Consecutive Day, in P/R
Sixth Day Worked in Holiday Week
Change of Rate
Permanent
Temporary
Company Service Credit Rules
Contract
Duration
Purpose of Termination
Differentials, Shift
Disability Pay Plans
Nonoccupational
Occupational
Discipline
Discharge
Unsatisfactory Attendance
Dues Deduction
Authorization Form
Duration
Withdrawal, Method and/or Date of
Funeral Pay
Grievances
General Committee
Procedure—General
Other
Discharge and Suspension
Job Rate Establishment
Handicapped Employees
Health and Safety
Holidays and Holiday Pay
Hospitalization Agreement
Hours of Work
Insurance Plan
Interchange of Work
Job Classifications and Rate Schedule
Job Rate Establishment
Job Sequence Charts
Jury Duty Allowance
Layoff
Allowance Plan
Procedure
Recall after
Seniority Rights during
Temporary
Leave-of-Absence
General
Military
Seniority, Accumulation of
Service Credit, Accumulation of
Union Business
Lunch, Overtime
Maintenance of Union Membership
Management Rights
Master Overtime Agreement
Military Service
Nonoccupational Disability Pay
Occupational Disability Pay
Overtime
Daily
Distribution of
Lunch
Pyramiding of
Weekly
Pay
Call-out
For Grievance Meetings
Hiring
Holiday
Overtime
Progression
Rate Schedule
Report-in
Seventh Consecutive Day in Workweek
Shift Differential
Sixth Consecutive Day in Workweek
Sunday Premium
Pension Plan
Probationary Period
Progression
Rate Schedule
Recall
Recognition, Union
Rehire and Reinstatement
Company Service Credit
Rate of Pay
Seniority Rights
Vacation Eligibility
Safety and Heatlh
Safety Shoes
Seniority
Application of
Bidding in
Curtailment in
Definition of
Departmental
Equality of
Handicapped Employees
Layoff during
Loss of
Plant
Recall after
Rehire after
Reinstatement after
Strike Notice during
Supervisors
Types of
Veterans
Seventh Day, Overtime Pay for
Shift Differential
Shoe Allowance
Sixth Day, Overtime Pay for
Stewards
Strikes and Lockouts
General Provisions

(continued)

Exhibit 6.3 *(continued)*

Suspension
Temporary Change of Rate
Termination of Contract
Time and One-Half Pay
Transfers (Vacancies)
Out of Bargaining Unit
Pay Changes Because of Temporary
Within Bargaining Unit
Transportation
Union
Bulletin Boards
Officials, Leave-of-Absence
Plant Visit of Business Representative
Recognition
Security
Vacancies
Permanent
Temporary
Vacation Plan
Voting Time
Wages (Pay)
Hiring Rate
Progression
Rate Schedule
Work
Conditions
Day, Basic
Hours of
Supervisors
Week, Basic

Source: Union contract.

and "nothing ventured, nothing gained." These unrealistic proposals can backfire on the union leaders if they raise membership desires. Assume, for example, that the union anticipates the employer's upper limit at a total settlement cost of $1.25 an hour per employee. The union could hold firm to an upper limit of $2.50 an hour per employee; however, it would incur tremendous risks. First, it would be difficult to motivate employees to go out on strike, particularly if they were satisfied with the $1.25 package. Even if it succeeded in calling a strike, the union would later have difficulty convincing employees to return to work on terms similar to management's prestrike offer. Union leaders who raised members' expectations would be placed in the awkward position of having to convince their members that the strike had not been in vain.

On the other hand, union leaders realize that there is a lower limit on the bargaining range and that a settlement below this limit would result in membership dissatisfaction. Because union leaders are strongly influenced by their desire to assure the survival of the union and their continued roles as union officers, they would seldom accept a settlement below this minimum, except in extreme cases. Members might angrily "accept" such a settlement but subsequently express their dissatisfaction by (1) voting in new union officers, (2) withdrawing their membership from the union, (3) reducing their support for the current officers through wildcat strikes or the formation of uncontrollable factions, or (4) voting out the existing union.

The bargaining ranges, while bounded by upper and lower limits, represent a multitude of issues. The assigning of priorities to these issues and their possible combinations produces bargaining ranges of an almost infinite number of possibilities. Bargaining ranges can also change over time, usually becoming finalized as the contract expiration date approaches. During the course of negotiations, management and union officials may receive additional information that causes them to alter their upper and lower limits.

Costing Proposals Management's overriding concern in negotiation preparations is the eventual cost of the union's proposals. Related activities occur both before and during negotiations. Costing proposals can become a very involved process. Unfortunately, there has been little published research into costing practices. One notable exception has suggested that many management officials do not use sophisticated costing practices in labor-management negotiations, because management negotiators fail to take into account the following:

- The precise financial impact of the labor agreement on corporate profits, as well as on operating costs.
- The opportunity costs of new contract provisions in terms of lost production (for example, the effect of a proposed 10-minute cleanup time provision).
- Expertise and figures from financial managers, because they usually do not sit in on formal negotiations and do not consult with industrial relations managers on a regular basis.

Yet, management negotiators include at least some costing considerations in their labor negotiations efforts. Two such methods are preparation of employee background data and the calculation of the cost of a cent-per-hour wage increase. Management usually obtains statistical summaries of employees cross-tabulated by several variables (age, sex, marital status, seniority, job classification). These summaries provide immediate information necessary to cost out a variety of union negotiation proposals such as vacations, funeral pay, and pensions.

A most significant calculation is the cost of a cent-per-hour wage increase. Since wages are inevitably discussed in negotiations, a cost figure is needed to formulate management's bargaining range and to determine whether a union's wage proposal is excessive. An illustrative calculation of a cent-per-hour wage increase for a bargaining unit of 1,000 employees follows:

$20,800	Straight time pay (1,000 employees × 40 hours a week × 52 weeks × $.01)
900	Premium pay related to wages (1,000 employees × estimated 60-hours-per-year overtime, holiday, and call-out premium worked × $.015)
5,200	"Roll up," or benefits directly affected by the wage increase (profit sharing, pensions, life insurance, employer contributions to social security, shift differential if paid on a percentage basis, unemployment insurance, workmen's compensation, and so on),[7] estimated for illustrative purposes at 25 percent of the straight time wage rate
$26,900	Cost of a cent-per-hour wage increase

The wage total calculated in this example does not take into account opportunity costs or the spillover effect on wages of nonunion company employees, who will probably receive the negotiated wage increase as a minimum in their subsequent salary increases.[8] Additionally, many cost categories, such as overtime and holidays worked, have to be estimated from past payroll records and future production and manning requirements.

Unions often pursue two general negotiating strategies to counter management's costing activities. Union officials often submit proposals that are difficult to cost, thereby weakening management's related statistical objections during negotiations. Assume, for example, a current contract provision provides a Sunday work premium of 75¢ an hour if the employees have no absences during their regularly scheduled work week. The union proposes that employees working on Sunday receive this premium regardless of their attendance record during the week. Management can examine past payroll records to estimate the added cost of this proposal, a difficult task if there are thousands of employees involved, and an uncertain indicator of extra absences that might occur if this proposal is accepted.

Other proposals are almost impossible to cost out because no records have been kept and there is no way to obtain accurate data, as in the case of a union's proposal to include deaths of employees' first cousins for the 3-day paid funeral leave provision. Management should maintain accurate and separate cost categories on benefits paid during the previous year.

Unions also formulate proposals that provide costly benefits to members and save management money at the same time. This accomplishment is difficult and depends on the abilities and imagination of union negotiators. One example of it is a proposal to allow police to keep a squad car for personal use after their workday. Although this benefit appears costly, it can deter crimes and thereby reduce crime statistics and related expenses.

Another example is paid time off (sabbaticals) for public university professors. Say, for example, a university agrees to pay half of the professor's salary and benefits ($48,000), and the professor is released from teaching obligations (six courses) for a 9-month period. It appears, at first glance, that the university pays $24,000 to the professor and receives nothing in return. However, a closer examination reveals the university has received funding from the state for the $48,000 salary, and retains $24,000 after paying the professor for his or her sabbatical. The six courses can be assigned to "adjunct" (part-time) professors or to teaching assistants for a total cost of $12,000. This often means that the university can divert the $12,000 salary savings to other expenses, and both administration and faculty have received financial benefit from this proposal.

Collective Bargaining Behavior

Bargaining Situations

It is impossible to describe a "typical" labor-management negotiation because there are over 100,000 labor agreements in the United States, involving virtually unlimited negotiators' personalities, bargaining relationships, and tactics. This quagmire can at least be approached by identifying four collective bargaining situations: distributive, integrative, and intra-organization bargaining and attitudinal structuring.[9]

Distributive Bargaining When the two parties' goals conflict, **distributive bargaining** may be employed. Certain issues, particularly wages, heighten conflict of interest in that resources are limited and one party tends to gain at the other party's expense. Each negotiator tries to discover and modify the opponent's position and values assigned to these issues. This approach encourages threats, bluffs, and secrecy as each party tries to keep the upper hand.[10]

Integrative Bargaining For the negotiation of issues that are not in conflict or when both parties attempt to resolve a common problem or concern to their mutual benefit, they use **integrative bargaining.** This approach encourages trust, an understanding of the other negotiator's real needs and objectives, and emphasis on commonalities between the parties instead of differences.[11] Related bargaining issues can include employee alcoholism treatment programs, and training or other assistance for union members whose jobs have been eliminated by technological change, foreign competition, or other external influences. Health care cost containment is another possible integrative bargaining issue, as discussed in the next section.

Mixing Distributive and Integrative Bargaining: The Case of Health Cost Containment Distributive bargaining over an issue can shift to integrative bargaining from one negotiated contract to the next or even within a particular labor agreement negotiation. Health care cost containment often reflects this overlap between distributive and integrative bargaining, although health insurance has been traditionally regarded as an economic benefit like wages, subject to distributive bargaining.

Health care costs are the fastest-growing industrial expense today. Management and union officials now often approach this issue from an integrative bargaining standpoint, attempting to jointly resolve this issue so that there are not corresponding reductions in wages or other benefits, or increased health care costs to union members. Approaches to this problem have included:

- Obtaining second opinions when surgery is involved.
- Establishing a Health Maintenance Organization (HMO).
- Designing wellness programs such as exercise, weight reduction, and no smoking classes.

Recent negotiations between American Telephone and Telegraph (AT&T) and the Communication Workers of America focused on health cost containment. AT&T maintained that union members should share at least some of the cost of health care increases. Management considered this situation serious because the company spent $1 billion on health care the year before the contract expired and forecasted a 10 percent annual increase for the next several years unless it revised its health benefits program. The settlement reflects a combination of distributive and integrative bargaining. The health plan premiums remain fully paid by the company. However, related provisions also

- Make it likely that more employees will reach the existing $150 annual deductible by exempting more medical services from so-called "first dollar" coverage.
- Make employees pay higher deductibles and fees if they choose a physician who charges more than "preferred providers" who agree to a fee structure negotiated with the company.
- Form a joint union-management committee that will lobby for legislative action to curb health care costs.

Attitudinal Structuring

Activities aimed at attaining a desired relationship between the parties are involved in **attitudinal structuring.** This process does not pertain to particular issues; instead, each party attempts to change the opponent's attitudes and the relationships that affect the negotiation process and subsequent administration of the labor agreement. These activities may be based on the assumption that a good relationship influences concessions. Related dimensions can include:

> [B]ehaving in a warm and friendly fashion, doing favors for the other so as to enhance the other's liking of and dependence on oneself, seconding the other's attitudes, behaving in accordance with the other's values, sending a representative who is similar to the other, encouraging the other to engage in role reversal, and choosing a pleasant setting (such as a bar or nice restaurant) for the conduct of business.[12]

Attitudinal structuring can also be harsh. During one contract negotiation involving a steel manufacturer, management officials emphasized declining economic conditions to the union negotiators by calling in laid-off employees to empty their lockers. The local union president and prominent bargaining team member noted, "That scares the hell out of them. These [management officials] have no finesse."[13] Management by these actions has communicated to the union bargaining team that labor agreement negotiations are occurring in an atmosphere of economic doom, which may convince them that their initial bargaining expectations were unrealistic. Attitudinal structuring can be used to accomplish either integrative (problem-solving) or distributive (competitive) bargaining, and can contribute to *intra-organizational* bargaining.

Intra-organizational Bargaining Activities employed by management and union negotiators to achieve consensus within their respective organizations are involved in **intra-organizational bargaining.** However, bargaining teams are seldom successfully unified by means of this approach; in fact, union and management negotiators often have more difficulty with members of their respective negotiating teams than with each other.[14]

Management's chief negotiator sometimes takes a back seat to other management officials, particularly lawyers, at the bargaining table. When a settlement is reached, it is also subject to second-guessing by other officials, who usually contend that management negotiators could have obtained a better deal. The union is not exempt from internal disputes either, particularly since its chief negotiator is seldom given a free hand in selecting the negotiating committee. In many cases, at least one member of the union's negotiating team is a political rival of the chief negotiator. More prevalent are factions that attempt to obtain various bargaining demands regardless of the chief negotiator's preferences.

Management and union negotiators spend much time resolving differences within their respective organizations. One observer of labor-management negotiations observed the following:

> [A] large share of collective bargaining is not conflict but a process by which the main terms of the agreement, already understood by the negotiators, are made acceptable, not to those in charge of the bargaining but to those who will have to live with its results.[15]

Bargaining Tactics and Approaches

Bargaining tactics are found in each of the preceding bargaining situations (see Exhibit 6.4 for specific examples). Many times these tactics are combined to form a broader strategic approach. Exhibit 6.5 illustrates four such approaches, which are paraphrased from an influential book on bargaining tactics, *Getting to Yes.*

Exhibit 6.4

Number of Negotiators Reporting Use of Specific Tactics in Recent Negotiation, in Order of Frequency of Use (N = 61)

Specific Tactic	Used	Didn't Use
Making information available to the other side	60	1
Identifying problem situation	59	2
Persuading other side of joint need for focusing on problem	59	2
Probing for other side's target and resistance points	56	5
Using clear hints and signals	56	3
Remaining flexible on team's position	54	7
Focusing upon long-term bargaining relationship	53	7
Allowing other side to "save face"	51	10
Withholding commitment while discussing problems and exploring solutions	51	10
Having frequent contact between bargaining teams	49	12
Persuading other side of minimal cost to them of your proposal	44	16
Holding back on responses to other side's proposals	26	33
Holding information close to the belt	24	36
Reminding the other side of your side's bargaining power	24	37
Maintaining freedom from constituents	22	34
Holding off final offer until deadline	21	39
Taking an early firm commitment	21	39
Keeping the other side off balance	21	38
Presenting a large number of bargaining demands	18	43
Withholding information from the other side	16	45
Using overt threats in bargaining	15	46
Dominating discussion of agenda items	14	46

Source: Richard B. Peterson and Lane Tracy, "Preferences, Bargaining Tactics and Goals of Union and Management Negotiators," paper presented at the 1981 Academy of Management Meeting (San Diego, California), p. 7.

Negotiation Communication Style

Bargaining behavior is reflected through messages transmitted between union and management negotiators. Most of this communication is channeled into three general directions: language analysis; package discussion of proposals; and argumentation.

Language Analysis In many cases union and management negotiators have to convey their preferences and positions to each other while at the same time giving their fellow bargaining team members a slightly different impression. This requires skill at **language analysis** on the part of the listener. For instance, consider the following situation. The chief union negotiator discusses the company's latest negotiation proposal with the union members, who in turn feel that the negotiator should go back to the table and press management for a more favorable settlement. Believing that the company's proposal was reasonable, the union negotiator must communicate this preference (to accept the proposal) to management and at the same time convince the bargaining committee that he or she fought for their rights. Confronted with this difficult situation, the union negotiator might open the next bargaining ses-

Exhibit 6.5 **Strategic Approaches to Negotiation**

1. *Understand the other side's participants* because bargaining differences occur between your thinking and theirs. Bargaining conflict lies in people's heads and not in objective reality. Therefore, the negotiator needs to see the situation from the other side's perspective. Includes several specific tactics such as making bargaining proposals consistent with opponents' values. This tactic enhances "face-saving," or a person's need to reconcile a negotiation stand or settlement with his or her past words and deeds.
2. *Focus on concerns and interests rather than on positions.* A negotiator's ego is often identified with convincing the other negotiator that her or his position is correct, which makes agreement less likely. "Any agreement reached may reflect a mechanical splitting of the difference between final positions rather than a solution carefully crafted to meet the legitimate interests of the parties."
3. *Invent and broaden bargaining options for mutual gains,* which includes considering and implementing "brainstorming" techniques.
4. *Use objective criteria.* Standards of fairness, efficiency, and scientific merit applied to a negotiation problem will increase the likelihood of a settlement that both parties can live with. Similarly, the more both sides refer to precedent and community practice, the greater the chance of benefiting from past experience.

Source: Roger Fisher and William Ury, *Getting to Yes* (Boston: Houghton Mifflin, 1981).

sion with, "The membership disagreed [with the company's economic proposal]. The present contract will not extend beyond 12 o'clock tonight."

At first glance, the union negotiator's statement seems strong and unyielding. However, a skilled management negotiator would analyze it through three questions:[16]

1. How final is the statement?
2. How specific is the statement?
3. What are the consequences associated with the statement?

At second glance, the statement appears neither final nor specific. In fact, management could interpret it to mean the union negotiator is relatively satisfied with the proposal, particularly if no specific recommendations for improvement follow. Finally, the union negotiator, by stating "the present contract will not extend," does not give a clear indication that a strike will occur if the offer is not changed.

Package Discussion of Proposals Since maintaining communication between parties during negotiations is essential to the bargaining process, negotiating several issues (a *package*) at the same time is preferable to the item-by-item, or "yes-no," approach. The item-by-item negotiations technique does not allow the parties to communicate their preferences realistically and at the same time maintain flexibility in their decision making.

In the package approach, each party combines several bargaining issues for discussion purposes. For example, the union might propose dropping issues 2 (union shop), 7 (birthday off), and 9 (voluntary overtime) from its bargaining list if management would agree to issues 3 (eliminating subcontracting) and 10 (optional retirement after 30 years). Management might then present the following counterproposal: agree to issues 3 and 10 if the union drops issues 2, 7, 9, and 11 (free dental care). This process would be repeated until the parties resolve the issues.

Exhibit 6.6

Checklist for Arguing in Collective Bargaining

Avoid:	Practice:
Interrupting	Listening
Point-scoring	Questioning for clarification
Attacking	Summarizing issues neutrally
Blaming	Challenging opponent to justify his case on an item-by-item basis (watch for signals)
Being "too clever"	Being noncommittal about his proposals and his explanations
Talking too much	Testing his commitment to his positions (looking for clues about his priorities)
Shouting your opponent down	Seeking and giving information (be careful about unintended signals)
Sarcasm	
Threats	

Source: Gavin Kennedy, John Benson, and John McMillan, *Managing Negotiations* (Englewood Cliffs, N.J.: Prentice-Hall, 1982), pp. 46–47.

The advantage of this approach is that both parties indicate which issues they are willing to concede; and, if agreement is not reached, these issues are still considered negotiable. Moreover, both parties keep track of these proposals because they offer insights into their opponent's bargaining preferences.

Argumentation In essence there are three bargaining positions: "Yes," "Maybe—keep on talking," or "No." When one negotiator has adopted a "Maybe" or "No" position, the other negotiator has to use arguments.

> Arguments are the justifications, explanations, rationalizations, or legitimizations that parties give for the positions they take in bargaining. Arguments are an instance of tactical dramaturgy, directed at recasting the opponent's definition of the bargaining situation. The objective validity of any redefinition is irrelevant as long as the opponent accepts its validity.[17]

Effective arguments depend on avoiding some interpersonal strategies while achieving others (see Exhibit 6.6).

Resolution Framework: The Bargaining Power Model

Applications of the Bargaining Power Model

Thus far bargaining situations and behaviors have been described. A framework is needed to place these behaviors in perspective. One such framework suggests that both parties arrange their strategies and tactics in a manner that will enhance their **bargaining power** and eventual settlement. One of the better-known models based on this framework was suggested by Chamberlain and Kuhn,[18] a model expressed in two equations presented in Exhibit 6.7. These equations can apply to individual issues or to the eventual package settlement. Although the bargaining power model is presented as an equation, it is an imprecise formula based on two major assumptions:

Exhibit 6.7 **Bargaining Power Equations for Union and Management**

$$\text{Union's Bargaining Power} = \frac{\text{Management's Cost of Disagreeing with the Union}}{\text{Management's Cost of Agreeing with the Union}}$$

$$\text{Management's Bargaining Power} = \frac{\text{Union's Cost of Disagreeing with Management}}{\text{Union's Cost of Agreeing with Management}}$$

Source: Equations are modified slightly from Allan M. Cartter and F. Ray Marshall, *Labor Economics*, rev. ed. (Homewood, Ill.: Richard D. Irwin, 1972), p. 283. © 1972 by Richard D. Irwin, Inc. Used by permission.

1. Union and management negotiators are rational individuals.
2. If it costs more for a party to disagree than to agree with the other, then the party will agree to the other's position.

Therefore, each side can increase its bargaining power by reducing the cost to the other of agreement or increasing the cost to the other of disagreement.

This strategic framework can be illustrated with a union bargaining proposal for 10 minutes cleanup time before the end of the work shift. Management would probably refuse this item unless the union presented arguments relating to the bargaining power model. First, the union could reduce management's cost of agreeing with the cleanup time proposal by eliminating some of its other bargaining proposals in exchange. The union negotiator might also reduce management's agreement costs with an argument along the following lines:

> There are currently many different cleanup practices at our facility. Some departments do not have cleanup time while other departments let their employees stop work a half hour early to clean up. If you calculated the total cleanup time in the plant, it would probably amount to 15 minutes per employee. Worse yet, you cannot currently discipline employees who are abusing cleanup time since there are so many different practices in the plant. This contract provision would enable management to wipe the past practice slate clean. Management could instruct the supervisors to rigidly enforce this provision, which could actually save the company money.

If management does not accept this argument, the union could follow the second strategic approach—increasing management's cost of disagreeing with the union. The ultimate argument would be to threaten a strike unless the cleanup time provision was granted. This threat might carry some weight if management knew there was widespread dissatisfaction over this issue. Otherwise, chances are that management would view this as an idle threat and would not believe its disagreement cost had increased.

Another threat, however, could raise management's cost of disagreeing with the union over this issue. The union could make arguments regarding safety hazards at the facility and suggest two alternatives: management can allow cleanup time before the end of the shift or the union can lodge a safety complaint with the Occupational Safety and Health Administration (OSHA). Management negotiators would prefer the first alternative because they know it would not cost the union anything to file the complaint, and an OSHA investigation might uncover other safety problems whose correction would be more expensive.

Some factors can affect both union and management costs and related bargaining power equations. Others might pertain to either the union or the management negotiators.

Factors Potentially Affecting Both Bargaining Power Equations Some factors that may affect union and management bargaining power are *unemployment, goodwill, public image,* and *government intervention.*

Unemployment This factor can affect both bargaining power equations presented in Exhibit 6.7. High unemployment in the area increases the union's cost of disagreeing with management because strikers would find it difficult to find employment at other firms. It reduces management's disagreement costs because high unemployment tends to make it easier to find strike replacements.

Goodwill, Public Image, and Government Intervention One factor that can influence the decision to strike or not, especially in small plants, is goodwill, which pertains mostly to internal relationships. Neither management nor the union wants antagonistic attitudes to develop that linger after the strike. Neither wants plant relations to deteriorate or trust between the parties to decline. Therefore, careful attention must be given to goodwill throughout the process.

Public image, another factor in the strike decision, involves mostly the attitudes and opinions of people external to the strike. Union and company officials certainly do not want their activities labeled irresponsible or heedless of the public interest. Possible government intervention for vital industries must also be considered, especially if management or the union believes government intervention will weaken its bargaining position.

Factors Affecting the Union's Disagreement and Agreement Costs Financial supplements given to union members can lower both the union's disagreement costs and management's bargaining power. Employees might be able to supplement their incomes during a strike through their spouses becoming employed, strike benefits, and public aid.

The strike benefits received by many union members, usually less than $50 per week, often determine whether union members will vote to strike as well as how long they will strike. Although the amount that each union member receives during a strike is minimal, the total amount of annual strike payments can be large. Most unions pay strike benefits when funds are available and the strike has been sanctioned by the national union leadership, but there are often additional stipulations: that the member be in good standing, complete a waiting period, and establish a need for the payments.

When the strike is settled, the strike benefits usually end. Sometimes the benefits stop or the payments are reduced before the strike is over. Some unions set a minimum for their strike fund balance, and payments cease when the minimum is reached.

Other unions will either terminate or reduce the benefits for individual members who work for other employers or do not perform their strike duties.

Public aid (welfare and unemployment compensation, for example) can also reduce union members' disagreement costs by supplementing their incomes when they go on strike. These assistance programs might exist at the federal or state level and are subject to various qualifications. For example, New York has extended the qualifying period for unemployment compensation from 1 week to 8 weeks when employees are off their jobs due to a strike or lockout. In one case involving a strike of 7 months, striking employees began collecting unemployment compensation only after an 8-week waiting period.

Many arguments can be made for and against public aid given to union members on strike. Proponents of public aid might claim

- Strikers are taxpayers when they work, so when they do not work, they should receive aid.
- Tax dollars are used to feed hungry people in other countries and prisoners in this country. Strikers who are needy should receive the same consideration.
- Even though some persons may be against public aid for strikers, they should not be against public aid for the families who are directly affected.
- Eligibility for public support should be based on need as determined by law, not on whether a person is on strike.

Opponents of public support to strikers also make several arguments:

- Legislators never intended to provide public aid to strikers, particularly since strikers have refused bona fide employment by refusing to go back to work.
- Giving public aid to strikers violates a traditional policy of government neutrality in labor-management relations.

Factors Affecting Management's Agreement and Disagreement Costs The individual company's characteristics have considerable effect on the bargaining power equation of Exhibit 6.7. Management's agreement costs (and bargaining power) can be reduced if it can pass on the cost of a negotiated settlement to customers.[19] Electrical utilities may represent examples of this situation. Management's disagreement costs (and union bargaining power) can be increased if any of the following factors occur: low inventories combined with high customer demand, fear of permanent loss of customers during a strike, and fixed costs such as rent, interest on loans, payments for equipment, and salaries of nonunion personnel being incurred without goods or services being produced.

Employer costs may also depend on the durability or perishability of the product or the substitutability of goods or services offered by the company. A strike for a short period at a large automaker having a large stockpile of autos would be only a small inconvenience; in fact, it could even save the automaker money if inventories were excessive. However, a farmworker strike of 2 weeks during harvest season could cause enormous damage, and the cost to the farmer would be prohibitive. A strike by a local bus service that transports only a small percentage of the commuters might be inconsequential, especially if these commuters are able to find alternative means of getting to work. But if the bus service transports a large percentage of commuters, serious and time-consuming traffic problems could develop, leading to poor public relations for both the employer and the union.

Limitations of the Bargaining Power Model

The bargaining power model is a theory that tries to explain real-world situations. The "Labor Relations in Action" concerning the Writers' Guild and the Motion Picture and Television Producers represents one application that illustrates limitations of the bargaining power model, particularly, the model's inability to predict bargaining behavior and related settlements with complete accuracy. Two general and related limitations are uncertainty and dramatic, sudden change.[20]

Many factors contribute to bargaining uncertainty. First, one negotiator cannot always assess the other's behavior and thought processes. In some cases, one negotiator appears irrational from the other's perspective. Some low-cost issues (providing employees with an additional pair of safety gloves each month, for example) assume distorted importance.

Second, it is difficult to determine bargaining costs. Consider, for example, a union's proposal for eliminating a previously agreed-upon contract provision that all employees can be required to perform "minor repairs." It is difficult to determine the cost of removing this provision, although management will probably have to assign more overtime and possibly hire more employees if maintenance employees have to repair items that were formerly repaired by production employees. Even if the cost of this item could be measured in economic terms, this figure might be complicated by political costs – the union negotiator determines that failure to eliminate the "minor repairs" clause will result in political defeat in the next election of union officers. A single item or bargaining proposal can become a matter of moral principle. "Costs" therefore assume economic, political, and moral dimensions; the combination of these varied components results in a confusing sum.

Finally, cost calculations are derived from estimates based on future events. The usual ultimate threat to management is a strike. Management must then estimate both the likelihood and length of a strike. Other uncertain future events might also contribute to the bargaining power model.[21] For example, a recent strike involving hotel employees at the elegant Waldorf- Astoria in New York was "enhanced" by Teamsters union members refusing to pick up trash.

Another limitation of the bargaining power model is that it is subject to rapid and sudden change. Government wage-price controls or guidelines can suddenly be announced, forcing unions to agree to wage settlements comparable to the limits set by the government. Or, management could receive a sudden influx of rush orders from a major customer near the contract expiration date. Management's disagreement costs are then sharply increased, particularly if the customer indicates he or she will take unfinished orders to a competitor.

The limitations of the bargaining power model do not eliminate its usefulness. Union and management officials do assign costs, however crudely, and direct their strategies toward increasing the other party's disagreement costs relative to agreement costs.

Ethical Considerations in Collective Bargaining Behavior

Union and management negotiators' bargaining behavior often involves at least two general ethical dimensions that were first mentioned in Chapter 5. The first ethical dimension, *moral or ideal behavior,* is subject to varying definitions instead of an either/or distinction. However, the following bargaining behaviors and tactics no doubt exemplify the unethical end of this continuum.[22]

- Using gifts, entertainment, or even bribes to get an opponent to soften his or her position.
- Using networks or "spies" to try to learn about an opponent's confidential information and resistance point.
- Undermining an opponent in the eyes of his or her constituency by persuading or even bribing that constituency.
- Using electronic surveillance to "bug" an opponent's office or constituency meetings.
- Theft of an opponent's private files or confidential information.
- Trying to demean or humiliate an opponent by making charges or accusations either publicly or privately.
- Misrepresenting one's own office, credentials, status, or reputation in order to fool the opponent.

Some bargaining behaviors have more general and longer range ethical implications. Consider, for example, the reflections of Lee Iacocca, the prominent automobile industry executive:

> As long as Detroit was making money, it was always easy for us to accept union demands and recoup them later in the form of price increases. The alternative was to take a strike and risk ruining the company.
>
> The executives at GM, Ford, and Chrysler have never been overly interested in long-range planning. They've been too concerned about expediency, improving the profits for the next quarter—and earning a good bonus.
>
> They? I should be saying "we." After all, I was one of the boys. I was part of that system. Gradually, little by little, we gave in to virtually every union demand. We were making so much money that we didn't think twice. We were rarely willing to take a strike, and so we never stood on principle.
>
> I sat there in the midst of it all and I said: "Discretion is the better part of valor. Give them what they want. Because if they strike, we'll lose hundreds of millions of dollars, we'll lose our bonuses, and I'll personally lose half a million dollars in cash."
>
> Our motivation was greed. The instinct was always to settle quickly, to go for the bottom line. In this regard, our critics were right—we were always thinking of the next quarter.
>
> "What's another dollar an hour?" we reasoned. "Let future generations worry about it. We won't be around then."
>
> But the future has arrived, and some of us are still around. Today we're all paying the price for our complacency.[23]

Labor Relations in Action

Bargaining Cost Complexities: Negotiations between the Writers' Guild of America and the Alliance of Motion Picture and Television Producers

Union and management bargaining power depends on the costs of agreement and disagreement. A party having higher disagreement than agreement costs is likely to agree with its opponents. Costs, however, are often difficult to calculate and predict. Indeed, cost estimates may differ within a bargaining team. These uncertainties are reflected in the 1988 negotiations between the Writer's Guild of America (WGA) and the Alliance of Motion Picture and Television Producers (Alliance).

The WGA initiated a strike on March 7, 1988 over the Alliance's proposal for a large reduction in writers' earnings for reruns of 1-hour domestic television shows and a bigger share for writers in the increased foreign market. Before the strike, writers could earn a maximum of $16,000 for a rerun show; producers proposed limiting this maximum to $9,000.

Management (or the Alliance) maintained that the strike would not increase their disagreement costs, at least in the short term. Indeed, three categories of television shows—daytime soap operas, game shows, and late night talk shows—could manage for some time without writers and resulted in little disagreement cost to the Alliance. Some game shows (Wheel of Fortune, for example) do not employ writers; soap operas had approximately 2 weeks of shows previously recorded on tape; and reruns or "best of" shows could replace live late-night shows such as Johnny Carson and David Letterman. News programs' writers were covered by a separate labor agreement settled in 1987. Interestingly, the writers of soap operas and late-night talk shows, who could inflict the highest disagreement costs for the Alliance, were unaffected by the strike's major compensation issue.

The unique characteristics of the WGA membership translated into unexpected disagreement cost calculations. A minority of WGA members support themselves primarily from screen and television writing. Approximately 11 percent of the members contribute 50 percent of the union dues, which are based on writing income. At any given time, only about half of the guild's 9,000 members are employed. Many WGA members are "hyphenates"—persons who hold another job in addition to writing (writer-producer, writer-dentist, or writer-waiter, for example). Those hyphenates making little to no money for their writing skills have low disagreement costs and may have high agreement costs.

George Axelrod, writer-producer of "The Manchurian Candidate," reflected both of these cost considerations when he tried to explain why WGA members voted by a 3 to 1 margin to reject the Alliance's "final offer" more than 3 months after the strike began: "It seems a vote for principle over greed. . . . Either we have an extraordinary group of heroes, or else a large portion of the people don't make their living from writing and are simply playing strike."

Management's offer included a 14.7 percent pay increase, but the rerun issue was left unresolved, and another writer-producer commented, "We are very well paid, but we also create the product. . . . We are first among equals. Without our vision no one else can go to work. I think because we do create the work we should be compensated with residuals." By adhering to this principle, which was not reflected in the Alliance's proposed settlement, the WGA raised its agreement costs, thereby forestalling contract settlement.

Work cessation continued through July, and management reassessed its original disagreement costs. In July, 1988, fewer than 60 percent of television viewers were watching network (ABC, CBS, and NBC) television. Viewers turned to cable stations, Home Box Office (HBO), and Turner Broadcasting System (TBS), who predicted that more viewers would switch because the WGA strike now hindered the networks' traditional fall programming start. One TBS official commented, "We do very well when the networks are out of original programming," and an HBO official agreed, "We think there is going to be a gaping hole on the dial. We will pick up disenchanted viewers in droves."

The Alliance now knew that its disagreement costs had increased because it could not offer new television series to the networks. However, Alliance negotiators also realized that their agreement costs would increase if they gave in to the union's proposal. They felt bargaining concessions to WGA would influence subsequent negotiations with two other unions, the Teamsters and the International Alliance of Theatrical and Stage Employees.

The 22-week strike ended on August 5, 1988, with indefinite bargaining victories compounded by future bargaining cost uncertainties. An unparalleled, thorough account of last-minute negotiations and results was presented in the *Los Angeles Times* ("Hollywood Drama: The Story Behind the Settlement," August 9, 1988, pp. 1, 19). Other accounts in *Newsweek* and *The Wall Street Journal* noted that the writers' 150-day strike did delay the traditional start of the fall television season, and that they received a slightly larger share of the revenue from shows sold abroad. However, the writers also accepted the producers' main demand: a sliding payment schedule for one-hour reruns which will reduce residual payments.

A West Hollywood bank manager assessed the potentially devastating disagreement costs incurred by the writers,

> Many of them will not make it back to their former economic positions. They have used up their savings, borrowed money and charged up their credit cards, and they will never get back the nearly six months they have lost . . . . For those who had no other income during the strike, it will be a few years, literally, before they have the same credit standing they once had. . . . And look what they were fighting for—residuals that they won't get until sometime in the future.

Other future costs may have been incurred for WGA union leaders as well. Some union members expressed deep concern over the direction and eventuality of a bargaining settlement just before the agreement was reached. Also, a group of 21 dissidents, the Writers Coalition, had resisted the strike for months and threatened to leave the WGA in the final days of the labor negotiations. This internal division may weaken WGA officials' future position in the organization.

The partial victory the media assigned to the Alliance and network television purchasers over WGA was further complicated by subsequent operational considerations. On the one hand, the Alliance's demonstration that it could take a long strike might result in more favorable negotiation settlements with other unions. However, management overestimated the number of shows that could be quickly written after the strike. The disrupted fall schedule resulted in the three networks losing 4 million nightly viewers from mid-September to mid-December, 1988. The networks could incur the following costs for 1989.

- $200 million in lost ad revenues.
- $50 million in "make goods," free spots to compensate for low ratings.
- $100 million to produce specials that covered for unwritten shows.

The biggest and most uncertain management cost could be a permanent shift in viewer attitudes—an erosion of TV watchers' habit of automatically turning first to the networks.

Union and management negotiators consider bargaining agreement and disagreement costs and the bargaining power model in their collective bargaining efforts. However, as illustrated by the WGA-Alliance negotiations, these costs are neither precise nor consensually measured, and change over time.

The second ethical dimension, *conforming to professional standards,* is more complicated when applied to negotiators' behaviors. Top union and management bargaining team officials would likely view at least these professional commitments in their bargaining behaviors:

- Obtaining a settlement as close to the optimal bargaining range as possible (upper range for the union negotiator and lower range for the management negotiator).
- Convincing their respective bargaining team members and other constituents that they are effective negotiators.
- Communicating with the other negotiating team in an honest, respectful fashion to enhance the continuing labor relations relationship after the collective bargaining agreement is reached.

All three of these standards are attainable, although maximizing the first two may strain and alter the third. In other words, it is difficult to convince your bargaining constituents that you obtained the best settlement possible if you "tell the truth, the whole truth, and nothing but the truth" to your negotiating opponent.[24] Consider for example the following story of a young executive who had just taken over the helm of a company:

> Imbued with idealism, he wanted to end the bickering he had seen take place during past negotiations with labor. To do this, he was ready to give the workers as much as his company could afford. Consequently he asked some members of his staff to study his firm's own wage structure and decide how it compared with other companies, as well as a host of other related matters. He approached the collective bargaining table with a halo of goodness surrounding him. Asking for the floor, he proceeded to describe what he had done and with a big smile on his face made the offer.
>
> Throughout his entire presentation, the union officials stared at him in amazement. He had offered more than they had expected to secure. But no matter, as soon as he finished, they proceeded to lambaste him, denouncing him for trying to destroy collective bargaining and for attempting to buy off labor. They announced that they would not stand for any such unethical maneuvering, and immediately asked for . . . more than the idealistic executive had offered.[25]

In other words, a completely honest and open negotiator may be exploited by his or her opponent, commit to a position that allows no further concessions, or sacrifice what might have been successfully gained through less candid approaches.[26] Most successful negotiations have featured ritualistic elements such as describing elaborate but irrelevant statistics, using histrionics, or staging false fights or temper tantrums. One management negotiator, for example, noted that his union counterpart approaches him at the start of negotiations and whispers, "We'll get together privately and talk about what we are really going to do to make a deal as soon as this show is over."[27]

Experienced negotiators realize "to be successful, whether it's in negotiations or in anything else dealing with people, you have to live by your words. You have to have integrity."[28] Most negotiators would consider lying ethically wrong and against professional standards, particularly if a lie represents,

> a deliberate false statement which is (i) either intended to deceive others or foreseen to be likely to deceive others, and (ii) either the person who makes the state-

ment has promised to be truthful or those to whom it is directed have a right to know the truth.[29]

There is, however, a fine line between lying and withholding the truth. Negotiators are not going to volunteer items that could damage their bargaining positions. They might also exaggerate and bluff on occasion. Successful negotiators are also skilled in asking the correct questions and interpreting the meaning of omissions from the other party's remarks.

> The principled negotiator doesn't resort to trickery, but that doesn't mean he naively gives away his position. He doesn't have to reveal what his final best offer will be. Not all principled negotiators agree on just how principled you have to be. It's OK to mislead the other side as to your intentions, [one principled negotiator] argues. You can say I'm not going to give in, and then give in five minutes later. But never give the other side misinformation about the facts.[30]

Parties can therefore communicate in a flexible manner while still maintaining their integrity and ethical responsibilities.

The Good Faith Bargaining Requirement

Union and management officials are not completely free to shape or ignore ethical considerations in collective bargaining. The government through the National Labor Relations Act has indicated that both union and management organizations must negotiate in good faith—they must demonstrate a sincere and honest intent to consummate a labor agreement and be reasonable in their bargaining positions, tactics, and activities.

However, *good faith* represents a state of mind difficult to define precisely. For example, this obligation does not specifically require that a party must agree to the other's proposal or make a concession to the other party. Violations of good faith bargaining can come from four sources: the nature of the bargaining issues, specific bargaining actions (called *per se violations*), totality of conduct, and successor employer bargaining obligations.

Nature of Bargaining Issues Over the years, the NLRB and the courts have categorized bargaining issues as illegal, mandatory, or voluntary. *Illegal* subjects are not bargainable, and it is illegal for the parties to insert them into the labor contract even if they are in agreement over the issue. Examples of illegal subjects include a closed shop, a "whites only" employment clause, mandatory retirement at 62, and compensation arrangements that violate the provisions of the Fair Labor Standards Act (for example, not paying bargaining unit employees overtime for work in excess of 40 hours per week).

Mandatory bargaining issues are related to wages, hours, and other conditions of employment. Examples of mandatory subjects are wage systems, bonus plans, pensions, profit sharing, vacations, holidays, plant rules, grievance procedures, and management rights. These subjects must be bargained, and the party advancing these subjects may insist on their inclusion to a point of impasse. However, failure to reach agreement does not automatically constitute a bargaining violation.

Union and management officials can also negotiate *voluntary* (also called *permissive* or *nonmandatory*) subjects like industry promotion plans, strike insurance, an interest arbitration clause, and benefits for retired employees. Unlike mandatory issues, these do not require either party to bargain. In fact, insisting on their bargaining and inclusion in the labor agreement to a point of impasse would be an unfair labor practice.

Specific Bargaining Actions In some cases a specific, single action by an employer constitutes an unfair labor practice in bargaining. For example, management commits a *per se* violation whenever it

- Refuses to meet with the union to negotiate its proposals.
- Insists to a point of impasse on a provision requiring that a secret ballot election be held before a strike can be called.
- Refuses to supply cost and other data relating to a group insurance plan when the union requests this information and management claims inability to pay.
- Announces a wage change without consulting the union.

A union commits a *per se* violation when it

- Insists on a closed shop or discriminatory hiring.
- Refuses to meet with a legal representative of the employer about negotiations.
- Refuses to negotiate a management proposal involving a mandatory subject.

Totality of Conduct Sometimes the NLRB and the courts have determined that one activity alone does not constitute a bargaining violation; however, a combination of activities, *totality of conduct,* might. A prominent and controversial example of this legal consideration involved General Electric's bargaining approach, **Boulwarism,** named after the vice president of General Electric, Lemuel Boulware.

General Electric contended that it simply approached bargaining in a manner similar to its product marketing–by finding out what the employees desired, and, on the basis of employee survey results, formulating a bargaining proposal. General Electric contended that this approach was not capricious, but "fair and firm," as management's bargaining position was based on a careful examination of the "facts" and was capable of being altered if the union presented new and significant information at the bargaining table. This approach, the company maintained, represented a sincere bargaining effort, one that was not aimed at destroying the union, but rather at eliminating a time-consuming and unnecessary ritual from collective bargaining (for instance, initial unrealistic offers that both parties know will not be accepted).

However, General Electric's totality of conduct was found violative of good faith bargaining, primarily because it went directly to the employees rather than working through the employees' exclusive bargaining agent (the union). The NLRB found several bargaining activities that contributed to General Electric's "take it or leave it" bargaining approach. These activities included refusal to supply cost information on an insurance program, vague responses to the union's detailed proposals, a prepared lecture series instead of counteroffers, and a "stiff and unbending patriarchal posture" even after it was apparent that the union would have to concede to the employer's terms.[31] This decision suggests that presenting and holding to your "best bargaining offer," while it appears to be ethically correct, is legally wrong.

Other factors involving employer or union conduct have provided indicators of good and bad faith bargaining. The following factors, while they probably would not individually constitute bad faith bargaining, might be considered so if many of them were committed together.

- *Surface bargaining:* The party is willing to meet at length and confer but merely goes through the motions of bargaining. Surface bargaining includes making proposals that cannot be accepted, taking an inflexible attitude on major issues, and offering no alternative proposals.
- *Concessions:* Although the LMRA does not require the making of concessions, the term *good faith* certainly suggests a willingness to compromise and make a reasonable effort to settle differences.
- *Proposals and demands:* Advancing proposals that open the doors for future discussions indicates good faith, whereas proposals that foreclose future negotiations and are patently unreasonable are reflectors of bad faith.
- *Dilatory tactics:* Unreasonable procrastination in executing the agreement, delay in scheduling meetings, willful avoidance of meetings, evasive tactics, delay in providing data for bargaining, and similar tactics are evidence of bad faith.

- *Imposing conditions:* Attempts to specify conditions on bargaining or the administration of the agreement will be scrutinized closely to determine whether such conditions are onerous or unreasonable (for example, insisting that all grievances be resolved before collective bargaining can start). In addition, the requirement of agreement on a specific item as a prerequisite to negotiating other issues reflects bad faith bargaining.
- *Unilateral changes in conditions:* Such actions as changing the compensation or fringe benefits plan unilaterally during bargaining is a strong indicator of bad faith bargaining. Unilateral changes *per se* may not be illegal, but justification must be reasonable and accurate.
- *Bypassing the representative:* Since the collective bargaining agreement supersedes the individual employee contract, the employer must not refuse to negotiate over mandatory issues. The duty to bargain is essentially equivalent to the duty to recognize the exclusive bargaining representative of the employees. Attempts to bypass this representative are evidence of bad faith.
- *Commission of unfair labor practices:* Committing unfair labor practices (such as promoting withdrawal from the union, reducing working hours, and engaging in discriminatory layoffs) during negotiations is indicative of bad faith.

In addition, the NLRB and court rulings have been consistent in deciding that unions should have sufficient information to understand and intelligently discuss the issues raised in collective bargaining and in subsequent contract administration. Related examples include wage increases given to nonunit employees, work contracted to another employer, wage and employment data, seniority lists, and in some cases (when an employer claims inability to meet a union's financial proposal) production and sales data and other financial information.[32] This information is, however, subject to the following prerequisites.

1. The union must make a good faith demand or request for the information.
2. The information sought must be relevant to the bargaining relationship.
3. The information must be supplied to the union promptly and in a form reasonably useful for negotiation purposes.

As suggested by the General Electric Boulwarism case, determining the totality of conduct can become complicated and controversial. In NLRB's *Milwaukee Spring* decision the company asked the union at one of its locations to forego a wage increase scheduled by the existing labor agreement. The company indicated that it lost business during the previous 4 months and was thinking of transferring its production at Milwaukee Spring to a nonunion facility in order to improve its competitive position on labor costs. The employees voted against the company proposal, and the company in turn transferred its production to the other facility.

The union contended that the employer's unilateral action violated good faith bargaining since it failed to obtain the consent of a union bargaining agent before implementing changes that would modify the terms and conditions contained in an existing collective bargaining agreement. However, the NLRB agreed with management that management did not violate its good faith or modify the terms of the labor agreement since[33]

- There was no explicit work preservation clause (one reserving or guaranteeing work for the employees) in the contract (therefore, no clause could be modified).
- Neither the wage agreement nor the union security clause implied that work would continue at Milwaukee Spring.
- The employer did bargain to a point of impasse over the mandatory (wage) issue that was written in the contract. The NLRB ruled that if no agreement is reached, at impasse the employer may unilaterally implement its bargaining proposal with respect to the matter (relocation) not covered in the labor agreement.

Successor Employer Bargaining Obligations Employer successorship tests and corresponding bargaining obligations have been formulated through several NLRB decisions and subsequent Supreme Court interpretations. The successor employer will probably have to continue a bargaining relationship with the former employer's union if [34]

- There is substantial business operations continuity between the former and present employers. This occurs when the new employer acquires a substantial amount of its predecessor's real property, equipment, and inventory; employs workers to do essentially the same jobs that they performed for the predecessor under the same working conditions; and continues its predecessor's product lines.
- The bargaining unit remains appropriate after the change of employers.
- The predecessor employed a majority of the new employer's workers.

Collective Bargaining under Bankruptcy Proceedings: The *Bildisco* Decision

What happens to the existing bargaining agreement if management files for bankruptcy and contends that it can no longer honor the labor agreement? This question was approached in the Supreme Court's 1984 *Bildisco* decision, which involved a building supply distributor who filed a petition for reorganization under Chapter 11 of the bankruptcy code. After this filing, the company failed to make the wage increases scheduled in the collective bargaining agreement and also failed to give collected union dues to the union. The company also moved to reject the collective bargaining agreement entirely.

The NLRB agreed with the union that this unilateral action violated the good faith bargaining provision in the National Labor Relations Act. However, the Supreme Court disagreed with the NLRB and determined that management's behavior in this situation did not violate the good faith provision.

Bildisco has given management more discretion in its collective bargaining efforts with the union. Yet management cannot simply eliminate the existing labor agreement when it files for bankruptcy. Courts have denied some employers who attempted to eliminate the collective bargaining agreement under this procedure. For example, one apparel manufacturer was denied this option since it had assets twice its liabilities and no pervasive evidence of financial trouble. Further, an employer must show that removal of labor agreement provisions is "necessary" to aid the reorganization and "fair and equitable."[35] Congress passed amendments to the federal bankruptcy code (P. L. 98-353) in June 1984 that made it more difficult for employers to abdicate labor agreement prescriptions:

> In general, the law requires that a company propose contract modifications which are necessary to the reorganization to its union(s) and provide the union(s) with relevant information by which to evaluate the proposal. Only if the union(s) rejects the company's proposal "without good cause" and the "balance of equities . . . clearly favors" termination of the unexpired labor contracts can a bankruptcy court approve the company's modifications. If the court fails to act within 30 days after a hearing is held on the company's request, the company then is free to unilaterally impose new contract terms.[36]

Legal Remedies Associated with Violations of Good Faith Bargaining

In 1987, 43 percent (9,760 of 24,084) of NLRB cases alleging employer violations involved employer refusal to bargain in good faith, and 7.5 percent (716 of 9,495) of NLRB cases alleging union violations involved similar union activities.[37] Although there are many cases to be handled, the NLRB is limited in its remedial powers. As one NLRB member illustrates this situation: "The Board under the act is constituted as the midwife of the bargaining relationship. It oversees the birth of that relationship and attempts to prevent any miscarriage."[38]

Once a violation is found, the board orders the violator to cease and desist bad faith bargaining and to take affirmative action. These actions include bargaining upon request, posting notices pledging to bargain in good faith, and notifying offices of the NLRB of steps being taken to comply with the order.

Union officials have contended that the lack of significant remedies makes correction of good faith bargaining violations a farce. Since NLRB decisions can be appealed to the courts, it might take 3 or more years for a final determination. If the final decision finds the company guilty, affected employees are not entitled to any remedies.

Attempts to expand the NLRB's remedial power have failed. In the *H. K. Porter* case, the NLRB granted the union a contract clause that allowed checkoff of union dues after the employer repeatedly refused to bargain in good faith on the checkoff issue. The Supreme Court concluded that the bargaining obligation "does not compel either party to agree to a proposal or require the making of a concession," and "it is the job of Congress, not the Board or the courts, to decide when and if it is necessary to allow governmental review of proposals for collective bargaining agreement and compulsory submissions to one side's demands."[39] In addition, the NLRB cannot currently order an employer to compensate employees for monetary losses incurred as a result of an employer refusal to bargain until it has obtained a court test of the validity of the bargaining unit's certification.[40]

Summary

Collective bargaining occurs when union and management attempt to resolve conflicting interests by exchanging commitments. Sometimes this activity is centralized and more than one appropriate bargaining unit is included in the negotiation unit (the employees and employers who are subject to the provisions of the labor agreement).

Management and union negotiators are involved in three general prenegotiation activities: selecting the negotiating team; estimating the other negotiator's bargaining behaviors and perspective; and formulating proposals and the bargaining range and costing these proposals. Bargaining behavior during collective negotiations is extremely varied but can be classified into four bargaining situations: distributive bargaining, integrative bargaining, attitudinal structuring, and intra-organizational bargaining. Bargaining tactics are found in each of these situations. Many times these tactics are combined to form a broader strategic approach. Bargaining tactics and strategies are in turn communicated to the opposing side through language analysis, package discussion of proposals, and argumentation.

A resolution framework, the bargaining power model, serves to place the varied collective bargaining behaviors into perspective. In essence, union and management negotiators try to manipulate each other's agreement and disagreement costs on the assumption that if it costs more to disagree than to agree, then agreement will be reached. Bargaining costs are calculated in negotiations, albeit imprecisely as explained in the "Labor Relations in Action" on the Writer's Guild of America strike. Collective bargaining is shaped by ethical and legal considerations, the latter pertaining to good faith bargaining, successor employer bargaining obligations, and bargaining under bankruptcy proceedings.

Key Terms

collective bargaining
pattern bargaining
negotiating unit
centralized bargaining
bargaining ranges
distributive bargaining
integrative bargaining
attitudinal structuring
intra-organizational bargaining
language analysis
bargaining power
mandatory bargaining issues
Boulwarism

Discussion Questions

1. What are some situations in which management or the union would prefer centralized bargaining? In what instances might both prefer centralized bargaining? Discussion should take into account specific legal considerations affecting centralized bargaining.
2. Our discussion of bargaining power touched on only three variables: timing of negotiations, unemployment, and company characteristics. Relate three other

variables (from either Exhibit 1.1 in Chapter 1 or your own experience) to the bargaining power model, indicating how they could affect the equations.

3. Assume that you are a management negotiator and the union presents the following proposal: Any overtime assignment will be guaranteed a minimum of 2 hours at time-and-one-half the base hourly rate for the classification. Previously, employees working overtime received time-and-one-half payment for the hours they worked but no 2-hour guarantee. Indicate in some detail how you would cost out this proposal. Also discuss some arguments the union might use to make it easier to accept this proposal (to reduce your agreement costs).
4. Good and bad faith regulations might be easier to define than implement. Discuss problems management and unions believe they face in attempting to bargain in good faith. (Boulwarism, *Milwaukee Springs, Bildisco,* and legal remedies, for example, are considered problems by management or unions.) What recommendations would you suggest for improving these situations?
5. Fully assess the following statement, qualifying it as appropriate: "Communication plays a very small role in labor-management negotiations since this activity is largely determined by established rituals."
6. Explain how attitudinal structuring can relate to the three other collective bargaining strategies discussed in the text.

References

1. Audrey Freedman and William E. Fulmer, "Last Rites for Pattern Bargaining," *Harvard Business Review* 60 (March–April 1982), p. 31. See also "Recent Shift from Pattern Bargaining Seen Contributing to Lower Labor Costs," *Daily Labor Report,* March 19, 1985, pp. A-1, A-2.
2. Jack Hoover, "The Impact of Law on Relative Bargaining Power," *Employee Relations Law Journal* 10 (January 1984), pp. 78–93.
3. Douglas L. Leslie, "Labor Bargaining Units," *Virginia Law Review* 70 (April 1984), p. 414.
4. See, for example, Frances Bairstow, "The Structure of Bargaining: International Comparisons—A Story of Diversity," *Labor Law Journal* 31 (August 1980), p. 561; James L. Perry and Harold L. Angle, "Bargaining Unit Structure and Organizational Outcomes," *Industrial Relations* 20 (Winter 1981), p. 57; and Wallace E. Hendricks and Lawrence M. Kahn, "The Determinants of Bargaining Structure in U.S. Manufacturing Industries," *Industrial and Labor Relations Review* 35 (January 1982), p. 191.
5. Gavin Kennedy, John Benson, and John McMillan, *Managing Negotiations* (Englewood Cliffs, N.J.: Prentice-Hall, 1982), pp. 35–36.
6. Philip Sperber, *Attorney's Practice Guide to Negotiations* (Wilmette, Ill.: Callaghan, 1985), 351–361.
7. Stephen J. Holoviak, *Costing Labor Contracts and Judging Their Financial Impact* (New York: Praeger Publishers, 1984), p. 38. See also Wayne F. Cascio, *Costing Human Resources,* 2nd ed. (Boston: PWS-Kent Publishing Company, 1987).
8. For a review of several considerations affecting the costing process, see Gordon S. Skinner and E. Edward Herman, "The Importance of Costing Labor Contracts," *Labor Law Journal* 32 (August 1981), pp. 497–507.
9. Walton and McKersie, *A Behavioral Theory,* pp. 4–6. For an empirical study of union and management negotiators that lends some support to the independent nature of these processes, see Richard B. Peterson and Lane Tracy, "Testing a Behavioral Theory Model of Labor Negotiations," *Industrial Relations* 16 (February 1977), pp. 35–50.
10. Robert W. Johnston, "Negotiation Strategies: Different Strokes for Different Folks," *Personnel* 59 (March–April 1982), p. 38.
11. Roy J. Lewicki and Joseph A. Litterer, *Negotiation* (Homewood, Ill.: Richard Irwin, 1985), p. 108.
12. Dean G. Pruitt, *Negotiation Behavior* (New York: Academic Press, 1981), p. 813.
13. John P. Hoerr, *And the Wolf Finally Came* (Pittsburgh: University of Pittsburgh Press, 1988), p. 10.
14. David L. Cole, *The Quest for Industrial Peace* (New York: McGraw Hill, 1963).
15. Albert Blum, "Collective Bargaining: Ritual or Reality?" *Harvard Business Review* 39 (November–December 1961), p. 65.
16. Richard E. Walton and Robert B. McKersie, *A Behavioral Theory of Labor Negotiations* (New York: McGraw Hill, 1965), p. 96.
17. Samuel Bacharach and Edward J. Lawler, *Bargaining Power: Tactics and Outcomes* (San Francisco: Jossey-Bass, 1981), p. x.
18. Neil W. Chamberlain and James W. Kuhn, *Collective Bargaining,* 2nd ed. (New York: McGraw-Hill, 1965), pp. 162–190.
19. Charles Craypo, "The Decline of Union Bargaining Power," in *New Directions in Labor Economics and Industrial Relations,* ed. Michael J. Carter and William H. Leahy (London: University of Notre Dame Press, 1981), p. 109.
20. For a fuller discussion of various considerations affecting bargaining behavior, see Terry L. Leap and David W. Grigsby, "A Conceptualization of Collective Bargaining Power," *Industrial and Labor Relations Review* 39 (January 1986), pp. 202–213.
21. William Earle Klay, "Contending with Uncertainty in Collective Negotiations," *Journal of Collective Negotiations in the Public Sector* 11, no. 3 (1982), pp. 189–200.
22. Lewicki and Litterer, *Negotiation,* p. 326.
23. Lee Iacocca, *Iacocca: An Autobiography* (New York: Bantam Books, 1984), p. 304.

24. Carr, A. Z., "Is Business Bluffing Ethical?" *Harvard Business Review* 46, p. 144.
25. Blum, "Collective Bargaining," p. 64.
26. Lewicki and Litterer, *Negotiation,* pp. 323–324.
27. Meyer S. Ryder, Charles M. Rehmus, and Sanford Cohen, *Management Preparation for Collective Bargaining* (Homewood, Ill.: Dow Jones–Irwin, 1966), p. 61.
28. Fritz Ihrig, "Labor Contract Negotiations: Behind the Scenes," *Personnel Administrator* 31 (April 1986), p. 57.
29. Thomas L. Carson, Richard E. Wokutch, and Kent F. Murrmann, "Bluffing in Labor Negotiations: Legal and Ethical Issues," *Journal of Business Ethics* 1 (1982), p. 17.
30. Jeremy Main, "How to Be a Better Negotiator," *Fortune* 108 (September 19, 1983), p. 143; Roy J. Lewicki and Joseph A. Litterer, *Negotiation* (Homewood, Ill.: Richard D. Irwin, 1985), p. 8.
31. *NLRB* v. *General Electric,* 72 LRRM 2530 (1969); *General Electric* v. *NLRB,* 397 U.S. 965 (1970). See also Thomas P. Brown IV, "Hard Bargaining: The Board Says No, the Courts Say Yes," *Employee Relations Law Journal* 8, no. 1 (Summer 1982), pp. 37–51. For management's position in General Electric's bargaining, see Virgil B. Day, "Bad Faith Bargaining?" *Contemporary Labor Issues,* ed. Walter Fogel and Archie Kleingartner (Belmont, Calif.: Wadsworth Publishing, 1968), pp. 388–392; and Lemuel R. Boulware, *The Truth about Boulwarism* (Washington, D. C.: Bureau of National Affairs, Inc., 1969).
32. Harold C. White and Lynn M. Meyer, "Employer Obligation to Provide Information," *Labor Law Journal* 35 (October 1984), pp. 643–650. See also James A. Craft, "Information Disclosure and the Role of the Accountant in Collective Bargaining," *Accounting Organizations and Society* 6, no. 1 (1981), pp. 97–107; Richard A. Beaumont, "The Risks of Opening the Corporate Books to Unions," *The Wall Street Journal,* October 18, 1982, p. 34; and James T. O'Reilly, *Unions' Rights to Company Information* (Philadelphia: University of Pennsylvania, The Wharton School, 1980).
33. "Decision of District of Columbia Circuit in *United Auto Workers* v. *National Labor Relations Board," Daily Labor Report,* June 20, 1985, pp. D-1–D-6.
34. Robert F. Mace, "The Supreme Court's Labor Law Successorship Doctrine after Fall River," *Labor Law Journal* 39 (February 1988), pp. 102–109. See also Robert H. Bernstein and Richard Cooper, "Labor Law Consequences of the Sale of a Unionized Business," *Labor Law Journal* 36 (June 1985) p. 327.
35. For related considerations see James J. McDonald, Jr., "Bankruptcy ReOrganization: Labor Considerations for the Debtor-Employer," *Employee Relations Law Journal* 11 (Summer 1985), pp. 7–31; and George S. Roukis and Bruce H. Charnoy, "*NLRB* v. *Bildisco* and the Legislative Aftermath: A New Frontier for Arbitrators?" *Arbitration Journal* 41 (no. 2, June 1986), pp. 43–50.
36. Linda LeGrande, "Labor Problems at Eastern Air Lines," Congressional Research Service Updated, February 22, 1989, pp. 2–3. For insights into Congressional adjustment of the *Bildisco* decision see Congress, Senate, Committee on Labor and Human Resources, *Oversight on the Taft-Hartley Act, the Railway Labor Act, and the National Labor Relations Act,* 98th Cong., 2nd sess., September 13 and 18, 1984; Congress, Senate, Committee on Labor and Human Resources and the Committee on the Judiciary, *Oversight of Collective Bargaining Agreement and the Bildisco Decision,* 98th Cong., 2nd sess., April 10, 1984; and Congress, House, Committee on Education and Labor, *Oversight Hearing on Effect of Bankruptcy Actions on the Stability of Labor-Management Relations and the Preservation of Labor Standards,* 98th Cong., 1st sess., October 5, 1983.
37. National Labor Relations Board, *Fifty-Second Annual Report* (Washington, D.C.: Government Printing Office, 1989), p. 19.
38. Peter D. Walther, "The Board's Place at the Bargaining Table," *Labor Law Journal* 28 (March 1977), p. 131.
39. *H. K. Porter,* 73 LRRM 2561 (1970).
40. *Ex-Cello Corp.,* 74 LRRM 1740 (1970).

Resolving Negotiation Impasses and Developing Cooperation

"Labor and management are beginning to perceive each other in a new light. They seek cooperation for mutual survival, despite long-standing and persistent adversarial attitudes.

Management's need to respond to the competitive pressures of the international marketplace forces them to reevaluate labor's role within the corporate structure, and compels them to consider alternative labor policies such as employee involvement in corporate decisionmaking and shared profits.

Labor's concern for preserving jobs has forced them to reevaluate their role in maintaining and strengthening corporate financial well-being. Ensuring jobs for workers forces labor to balance their interests with the long term interests of the employer."

America Works: The Report of the President's Advisory Committee on Mediation and Conciliation, 1988, p. 13.

Labor-management negotiations do not lead to strikes very often; in fact, only 1 of every 5,000 working hours was lost due to strikes in 1988. Media coverage of the small percentage of strikes that do occur may cause one to believe that strikes are common; however, the overwhelming majority of negotiations are settled on time and without strikes.

This chapter begins with a discussion of the ratification of the negotiated labor agreement and explains the impasse resolution procedures involving third parties, such as mediation, varieties of contract arbitration, and fact-finding. It then examines strikes, pickets, and boycotts in terms of their administrative and legal considerations. A concluding section illustrates the potential of various cooperative efforts aimed at avoiding union-management conflicts.

Contract Ratification

Negotiators, after resolving their differences and agreeing on tentative contract language, submit the proposed agreement to the union members for ratification, which usually requires a favorable majority vote.[1] Although a vote by the members is not legally necessary, some affirmation via referendum or delegated authority is normally used in the ratification process. For example, the Steelworkers, Auto Workers, and United Mine Workers have a direct referendum, whereas the Teamsters traditionally have delegated authority for ratification to a bargaining committee. In recent years, union members have shown increasing interest in greater participation, and more ratification elections have been held.

One interesting and controversial contract ratification occurred in 1988 when the Teamsters General Executive Board ratified its master freight agreement (covering 187,000 workers and setting a pattern for another 500,000) even though 64 percent of the membership voted against ratification. The Teamsters constitution authorized the board to ratify the agreement unless two-thirds of the membership vote against ratification. After the ratification, dissident Teamsters filed suit to have the board's decision overturned.

The ratification process determines whether members can live with the proposed agreement, even though they may not be completely satisfied with all of its provisions. Acceptance by the membership gives management some assurance that the employees will comply with the letter and spirit of the agreement. A vote to accept, therefore, is considered a commitment or willingness to be bound by the agreement.[2] When and if union members find the agreement unacceptable, they may vote to reject it, which they do about 10 percent of the time.[3]

Explanation of Voting Behavior

It is overly simplistic to say that union members vote for the contract when they like it and against it when they don't like it. Researchers have attempted to explain why and when union members will vote to accept or reject the tentative agreements. When employees are vulnerable to layoff, the members tend to vote to accept the agreement, especially if they believe ratification will help to save their jobs. In addition, individual workers may have personal reasons for voting for contract acceptance. For example, in the 1984 General Motors–United Auto Workers negotiations in which workers with over 10 years seniority became eligible for the guaranteed income security plan, those workers could be counted on to favor ratification.

A "no" vote in a ratification election confronts workers with potential costs of a loss of income and the uncertainty of when they will begin work again. While the potential for contract rejection may create incentives for the union negotiators to try to get a little extra for the members, such extras come with increased anxiety as the strike deadline approaches.[4]

Reasons for Rejection of Tentative Agreements

The most frequent reason given for rejection of tentative agreements in one study was that employees felt that they were shortchanged in comparison to other agreements in their vicinity. Internal union politics was the second most frequent reason mentioned for contract rejection. Sometimes union leaders are elected by slight majorities, and their rivals will campaign against any labor agreement negotiated by the incumbent leaders.

Other factors contributing to contract rejections include feelings of inequity and lack of upward communication within the union itself. For example, in industrial unions, skilled workers usually represent a minority of the membership, and they might vote to reject the contract when their wages do not compare favorably with those of skilled tradespeople in the building and construction industry.

Other groups (women, racial minorities, and younger workers) may claim intraplant inequities. Although equal employment opportunity laws have been passed, wage differentials continue to exist for racial minorities and women. Moreover, young employees with low seniority view pensions and layoffs, which are usually based on seniority or retirement age, differently from the older employees, causing additional internal friction. Unless people in these subgroups feel that the agreement reflects their own personal needs, they will vote to reject it.[5]

Another study found that a major cause of rejection is union members' economic concerns – rejection percentages generally corresponded to a downturn in economic activity. High employee expectations coupled with reasons for union members to question the employer's wage offer led to rejection of the tentative contract. To confirm their conclusions, the researchers followed up on the agreements that were ultimately accepted and found that 65 percent included an increase in the final wage package above that of the initial tentative settlement.[6]

It may be that the definition of contract rejection in some studies is too broad and overestimates the number of contract rejections and overemphasizes their problematic nature. For example, considerably lower rejection rates are found when the term *contract rejection* is redefined. Less than 3 percent of the tentative agreements were rejected when a majority of the bargaining committee recommended acceptance.[7]

Impasse-Resolution Procedures Involving a Third-Party Neutral

Usually both parties attempt to resolve impasses, which can occur either before or after the contract's expiration date. In some cases, union and management officials need third parties either to facilitate the negotiation process or to resole the bargaining difference with finality. There are five impasse-resolution procedures involving third parties: mediation, conventional contract arbitration, final-offer selection arbitration, mediation-arbitration (med-arb), and fact-finding.

Mediation

Many union-management impasses are resolved with help from neutral third-party mediators, obtained either from the Federal Mediation and Conciliation Service (FMCS), from state agencies, or privately. Mediators perform a number of functions: they assist in scheduling meetings, keeping the parties talking, carrying messages back and forth, and making suggestions. The mediator has no authority to make binding decisions and must rely on persuasion and recommendations; the negotiators make the final decisions.[8] The mediator is the "invited guest" who can be asked to leave. However, acceptance of mediators is an indicator of the effort of one or both of the parties to bargain in good faith.

The FMCS was involved in 24,293 cases in fiscal year 1987.[9] Added to this number should be the activities of separate mediation agencies in some 18 states and Puerto Rico that assist parties in their own jurisdictions.

The mediation process is much more an art than a science. There is no general theory of mediation; rather it has been described as a process that "has been helpful in a haphazard way largely because of the talents of certain individuals who themselves would find it difficult to say why they had been successful."[10]

Several characteristics and practices of labor mediators have been associated with mediator effectiveness. First is mediator tenacity, which means that the mediator does not give up without exhausting himself or herself, the parties, and all reasonable avenues of settlement. A second characteristic is mediator experience, which simply indicates that the more times a mediator is involved in mediating labor disputes, the more effective he or she is likely to be in settling one. Finally, mediators who are active, pressure the parties to reach a settlement, generate their own settlement terms, and play an independent role in the mediation process are more likely to be effective mediators.[11] A judge experienced as a mediator explains the role of the mediator, how mediators do their job, and what it takes to be a good mediator and then offers advice to mediators in the "Labor Relations in Action."

Carl Stevens's study of mediation focusing on the mediator's functions and tactics has identified several causal factors that lead to negotiated settlements—the bottom-line criterion of successful mediation. Timing of the mediator's involvement was identified as one of the most important considerations. The mediator should enter before the parties become too fixed in their positions but not so early as to upset the power balance between the parties, causing them to harden their bargaining positions.

In some instances, the mere entrance of the mediator may be sufficient for dispute settlement. For example, assume that one of the chief negotiators leaves an active negotiation in a temper tantrum, vowing never again to return to the bargaining table. Upon subsequent reflection, the negotiator realizes a mistake was made but feels that calling the opposing negotiator would be embarrassing and perhaps indicate weakness. A common tactic used in such situations would be to call the mediator, who could schedule another meeting. Thus, mediation in this sense represents a very potent face-saving device.[12] In other cases, the parties do not desire any specific help from the mediator, but the availability of that mediator and the very existence of the mediation forum facilitates the bargaining process.[13]

Mediators vary in their roles, behaviors, and styles. Some have been characterized as "deal-makers"; they enter the negotiations at an early stage and attempt to manipulate the content of the negotiations. Others seem to serve as "orchestrators" of the process; they try to improve the structure of the negotiations, facilitate communication between the parties, and gain a deeper understanding of the issues. The role assumed by the mediator frequently depends on the intensity of the dispute; where a strike or lockout is pending, the mediator may become very active.[14]

A successful mediator is frequently an interpreter, who clarifies perceptions of the bargaining climate and possible costs of impasse. For instance, if the parties

Labor Relations in Action

What Is the Role of the Mediator?

It is to get the parties to do what they say they don't want to do; what, indeed, they may even believe they don't want to do, but what deep down in their hearts they really want to do; and in the end, with rare exceptions, what they should and must do.

What do mediators do and what should they do? (As) we taught our children when first crossing the street, (mediators) should "stop, look and listen."

Stop means "Do nothing until you have learned." Don't rush in, sure that you know the answers better than the parties; you'll just prove to them what they may suspect anyway, that you're an idiot.

Look means "Identify the parties and the problems," in hope of understanding how they can be dealt with.

Listen, which is probably the most important of all, means simply what it says: "Listen to what the parties tell you." Equally important, listen to what they don't tell you because, as you know, there are many messages that are given to you in nonverbal terms, and they often are the keys that open the locked doors of the impasse.

How do they do it?

1. You don't allow the parties to bargain over positions.
2. You separate the people from the problem.
3. You focus on interests, not positions.
4. You invent options for mutual gain.
5. You seek, find, and insist upon the use of objective criteria, just another way of saying get the facts—the real facts of the case.
6. You try to make the process nonadversarial—no losers, everybody wins. That's not easy. We're all geared to looking at everything in terms of winning or losing.

What does it take to be a good mediator?

1. The wisdom of Ulysses.
2. The courage of Achilles.
3. The strength of Hercules.
4. The agility of an acrobat.
5. The foresight of an ancient Hebrew prophet.

What advice can you give to mediators?

1. Never say never.
2. Never stop listening.
3. Never stop learning.
4. Never do anything to affect your credibility.
5. Never close a door completely.
6. Never allow anyone to lose face (even when you are alone together).
7. Never back anyone into a corner unless you have arranged an exit for him, in case he needs it.
8. Never lose control of your own emotions, unless contrived for a purpose, and then only with extreme care, and if you're a Laurence Olivier or a Sarah Bernhardt.
9. Never lose your objectivity.
10. Never lose your sense of humor; it may be the only thing that will keep you sane.
11. Never promise what you cannot deliver. ("Have it in your pocket before you offer it" is the jargon of the trade, as you know.)
12. Never forget that when it's over—win or lose—you go home, but the parties must, as a rule, continue to deal with each other one way or another, and make the best of a bad job.
13. Never forget Murphy's first law: "If anything can go wrong it will"; and, of course, Callahan's corollary: "Murphy was an optimist."
14. Never, never give up even when you know it's impossible.

Source: Address by Alan B. Gold, Chief Justice of the Superior Court of Quebec, Canada, before the National Academy of Arbitrators at its Annual Meeting, 1988, *Arbitration 1988;* adapted from Roger Fisher and William Ury, *Getting to Yes* (Boston, Mass.: Houghton Mifflin Company, 1981).

disagree on data about the cost of living, comparative wage rates, and productivity, the mediator could assist in reaching agreement on the statistical data. If a negotiator underestimates the cost of a strike or lockout or overestimates the cost of an agreement, the mediator may be able to provide insights enabling the negotiator to evaluate his or her positions more realistically. Frequently a mediator will hold separate meetings with each group before calling for a joint meeting.

Helping each party to understand the tactics or intentions of the other can also aid the bargaining process. If management bluffs about its willingness to accept a strike or to allow an ongoing strike to continue indefinitely, the mediator may attempt to diagnose management's true intentions and then advise the union. On the other hand, if the union threatens a strike to obtain an excessive bargaining demand, the mediator could attempt to diagnose what the union is "really trying to say" and so inform the company negotiator. It is understood that the mediator can be believed as to the real meaning of the words of each party. By holding private caucuses with each, the mediator is privy to much confidential information. While no mediator would reveal this information to the other party, he or she can determine the magnitude of the real differences and encourage the parties that a settlement may be near if they continue bargaining.

The mediator also may facilitate the bargaining process by proposing solutions to the parties. There can be little effective bargaining without an overlap of at least some of the issues. Therefore, the mediator must create and propose alternate solutions, compromise settlements, and definitions of the respective bargaining positions.[15]

Mediators attempt to build the parties' trust and confidence by clarifying their role, establishing ground rules for the negotiations, demonstrating competence and understanding, and showing that they are neutral. They also try to reduce interpersonal conflict and avoid unrealistic expectations on the part of the negotiators. Mediators apply pressure for settlement by using delays and deadlines, placing responsibility for settlement on the parties, engaging in marathon bargaining, reviewing the costs of a strike or lockout, and making recommendations in a joint conference.[16]

The parties, however, play the dominant role in shaping the mediation process. For example, in cases where experienced negotiators have a clear understanding of their bargaining objectives and strategies, the mediator is primarily the servant of the parties. But where less sophisticated negotiators have not clearly defined their bargaining objectives, the personal qualities and actions of the mediator have their greatest impact. Here, an aggressive mediator may be able to gain the trust of the parties and create the type of negotiating atmosphere that achieves a settlement.[17]

Agreements are more likely to be reached when the disputing parties have had previous bargaining experience. Also, the parties are more likely to reach an agreement when a contract expiration is approaching. In this case, the parties have to consider the possibility of a job action such as a strike or lockout occurring, which may affect hundreds of people.[18]

Because there is no widely adopted code of professional conduct for mediators, and because potentially great danger exists from inept and unscrupulous practitioners, national organizations led by the Society for Professionals in Dispute Resolution (SPIDR) are developing a code of professional conduct to promote ethical behavior by mediators. This code will articulate qualifications for mediators, standards of practice, and ethical behavior. This code will proscribe impermissible actions of mediators, such as holding meetings with one of the parties without prior consent of the other party and revealing to one party what would be considered an acceptable settlement to the other. This code will be patterned after the widely accepted Code of Professional Responsibility for Arbitrators of Labor-Management Disputes, adopted by the National Academy of Arbitrators, American Arbitration Association, and Federal Mediation and Conciliation Service, which has existed since 1951 (revised in 1974).[19]

Interest (or Contract) Arbitration

Interest (or **contract**) **arbitration** involves the selection of a neutral person or panel to hear the bargaining positions of the parties and make a final and binding decision on what should be included in the negotiated agreement. This process differs from grievance arbitration (see Chapter 9), which is concerned mostly with interpreting and applying the terms of the existing labor agreement.

Interest arbitration in the United States dates back to the eighteenth century in the copper mines of Connecticut. It has not been used very frequently in the private sector (approximately 2 percent of the negotiations), with a number of notable exceptions: the Amalgamated Transit Union has arbitrated over 700 cases; over 200 baseball salary disputes have been settled by arbitration; and the law requires that impasses in the postal service are to be resolved by arbitration.[20]

Management and unions in the private sector prefer the arbitrator's decision when it reflects their own final position and avoids a strike. On the other hand, both parties have concerns about the delay created by scheduling an arbitrator and the extra cost involved. In addition, management becomes particularly concerned if the arbitrator fails to take into account the economic effect of the decision or if the award is above the norm for the industry.

Interest arbitration has been criticized because arbitrators may tend to "split the difference," thereby causing the parties to take more extreme position. Yet research reveals that extreme positions may not be significant. Final offers of the two parties do not appear to play the major role in the arbitrator's decision process. Rather, the employees' present wage rates seem to be the most important consideration. Since neutrals may vary in the norms of their decision making, the parties should define the criteria to be used by arbitrators.[21] (A more thorough discussion of interest arbitration in the public sector appears in Chapter 14.)

Final-Offer Selection Arbitration

Final-offer selection (FOS) arbitration is a type of interest arbitration that gives the arbitrator the authority to select one of the proposals made by the parties. In other words, "splitting the difference" is not an alternative to the arbitrator. Procedurally, union and management present their separate final proposals to the arbitrator, who selects only one proposal, making no change in any of the provisions. Since the parties know in advance that the arbitrator cannot make a compromise decision, they will try to present to the arbitrator an acceptable proposal. Theoretically, if both parties attempt to present acceptable proposals, their positions will converge, and they will possibly settle their differences without third-party intervention. (Variations and results of FOS arbitration in the public sector will be discussed in Chapter 14.)

FOS arbitration has some shortcomings, particularly if standards for arbitration decisions are not supplied. More importantly, the labor negotiations usually involve several issues, making FOS arbitration a very complex process. If the parties do not change or compromise their initial positions on some or all of these issues, the offers will not converge. The arbitrator must then select one of the extreme proposals, possibly heightening union-management tensions during the life of the contract and causing future difficulties in negotiating subsequent contracts.[22]

Mediation-Arbitration (Med-Arb)

Mediation-arbitration, or **med-arb,** occurs when the parties agree in advance that contract language, whether reached by mediation or arbitration, will be final and binding. Usually no decisions on the contract language will be sent back to the parties—either the board of directors or the union membership—for ratification. Once the parties agree to med-arb, those issues that cannot be resolved by mediation will be resolved by arbitration. The neutral will wear the mediator's hat at first, but if no agreement is reached by a predetermined date, he or she will become the arbitrator and decide the remaining unresolved issues. Under this procedure, most issues will be resolved by the parties because, in addition to the traditional pressures, there will be the pressure of knowing that the mediator-arbitrator will make a final and binding decision if the parties do not. Med-arb received much acclaim when it was used in the 1978 postal negotiations (see Chapter 14).

Fact-Finding

Somewhere between the extremes of mediation and interest arbitration lies **fact-finding.** This is a semijudicial process in which the major focus is placed on gathering the facts and using some of the principles of mediation and arbitration. The fact-finder's purpose is to assess the facts and to organize and display them publicly in the hopes that the parties will feel an obligation to settle their differences.

Fact-finding may be used in major disputes under the National Labor Relations Act and Railway Labor Act, and fact-finding reports are useful to presidents in determining what actions to take in national emergency disputes, such as when to seek an injunction or recommend legislation. Because of its lack of finality, this process does not have a good record in resolving disputes. Mediation, arbitration, and fact-finding all involve a third party, who either assists or directs union and management officials in resolving a negotiation impasse. As is discussed in the following section, management and union officials might prefer not to use a third party in this situation, but to rely instead on economic tests of strength.

The Strike and Related Activities between Union and Management

Work stoppages include both strikes and lockouts that cause a business to stop production, distribution, and sales of its goods or any organization to cease its operations. Generally a **strike** is a temporary stoppage of work by a group of employees for the purpose of expressing a grievance or enforcing a demand. The counterpart to the strike is the **lockout,** which is an act by an employer of withholding or denying employment during a labor dispute in order to enforce terms of employment on a group of employees.[23]

Within this general framework there are a number of different types of strikes, which are designed to increase management's costs of disagreement and to achieve the union's bargaining goals:

- *Economic strikes* are work stoppages during the negotiation of a contract to gain economic goals such as higher wages, improved pensions, and longer vacations.
- *Wildcat strikes* are strikes that occur in violation of the labor agreement and usually without approval from higher-level union officials.
- *Unfair labor practice strikes* are work stoppages that occur as a reaction to an employer's unfair labor practice. Examples include strikes in response to an employer's refusal to bargain or its discharge of a union member for engaging in union activities. The determination of whether a strike is an unfair labor practice strike is made by the NLRB.
- *Secondary strikes* are work stoppages by employees who have no dispute with their own employer but are striking to support another union.

Usually accompanying the strikes, especially the economic strike, are pickets and boycotts. Picketing refers to the outside patrolling of the employer's premises, usually using placards and handbills to achieve a specific objective. For example, **recognitional picketing** is used to gain recognition of the union as the employees' bargaining representative. Recognitional picketing is limited by law to 30 days, at which time the union must petition for an election. Also, recognitional picketing is illegal where a certified union exists or where an election has been held within the last 12 months.

Informational picketing occurs when the union attempts to inform the public that a labor dispute exists between the workers and their employer. **Product or consumer picketing** attempts to persuade customers to refuse to purchase products from the employer with whom the union has a labor dispute. Often the employees and their supporters also **boycott** the employer, or refuse to purchase products made by the employer with whom they have the dispute.

Reasons for Strikes

Exhibit 7.1 shows that work stoppages in 1989 in terms of numbers of workers involved and days idled were at the highest level since 1983. The years 1983–1988 averaged less in percentage of working time lost and percentage of workers involved than any other time period. As shown in Exhibit 7.1, strike and lockout activity hit a record low in 1988. There were fewer work stoppages, fewer workers involved, and less time lost due to work stoppages; however, 1989 changed the trend with labor disputes in the airline, telephone, and mining industries.

Work stoppages are not caused by one factor alone, but usually by many factors. Even so, there can be little argument that the main issue is wages, followed by plant administrative issues, such as safety issues, promotion policies, and job assignments. The decision to strike depends on the total environment in which bargaining takes place. Interrelated influences include the economic positions of the union and company, characteristics of the production process, the market structure, location of the plants, and occupational and demographic characteristics of the work force.[24]

Exhibit 7.1 **Work Stoppages Involving 1,000 or More, in the United States, 1947–1986**

		Workers Involved	Days Idled	
Years	Number	Number (Thousands)	Number	Percent of Working Time
1947–50	300.3	1824.8	31,414	.29
1951–60	331.5	1508.2	24,902	.19
1961–70	298.8	1390.9	22,833	.14
1971–80	269.4	1320.5	22,818	.11
1981	143	729	16,908	.07
1982	96	656	9,061	.04
1983	81	909	17,461	.08
1984	62	376	8,499	.04
1985	54	324	7,079	.03
1986	69	533	11,861	.05
1987	46	174	4,481	.02
1988	40	118	4,381	.02
1989	51	452	16,996	.07

Source: "U.S. Work Force Shows Record Low Number of Work Stoppages in 1988," *Daily Labor Report,* February 24, 1989, p. B-2; "Major Strikes and Lockouts Last Year Hit Highest Level Since 1983, BLS Say," *Daily Labor Report,* February 20, 1990, p. B-1.

At a single location, strikes may occur not only to enforce a demand, but because of the parties' misconceptions about collective bargaining and their lack of information about the positions of their bargaining counterparts. The nature of the bargaining process causes each party to hold back on its "real" position. Thus, strikes frequently occur when one party misperceives the other's position. Then, when the strike occurs, both parties learn more about what the other party considers unacceptable. Thus, strikes often improve the information exchange between the parties.[25] For example, if the union is asking for a 10 percent increase in wages and the company negotiators believe that the union will accept an 8 percent increase, the union may have to strike in order to show the company that it was serious in its demand of 10 percent.

Although strikes have traditionally been viewed as economic or legal conflicts, the psychological aspects are important. Psychologically, strikes can be categorized as a protest, or a group process for organizational change. Protest strikes include actions by the membership of walking off their jobs without the approval of their leadership (wildcat strikes). These spontaneous protests may be in reaction to a unilateral change by management in introducing production quotas or working conditions, or even in lowering thermostats in winter months.

As a group process, strikes require an issue around which to revolve, as well as the machinery to mobilize the membership and adequate strike resources. The union leadership is critical, as the leaders must instill unity among the membership, control courses of action, respond to the feelings of the group, and maintain communication with management.

Striking employees may picket the struck firm to inform the public of the dispute and to gain recognition for their goal or union.

Source: Courtesy of Wide World Photos.

A strike can be a process for change for the individual as well as the working environment. An individual union member's participation in union actions is motivated by perceived costs and benefits. These costs and benefits can be categorized as three types: (1) costs and benefits related to the goal of the activity, (2) social costs and benefits related to the expected reactions of significant others, and (3) material costs and benefits related to participating in the activity. If the perceived benefits are small and the costs are high, willingness to participate will be low. However, if the benefits are perceived to be high and the costs are low, willingness to participate will be high.[26]

Employees who feel that their pay is inequitable are not very willing to strike for a small wage increase. On the other hand, they may be willing to strike to support the union for a high increase. Thus, it appears that employees use a calculative strategy to help them determine whether and how long they can afford to strike for specific wage increases. Thus, the union must put forth efforts to reduce hardship (by providing strike benefits, for example) in order to gain support for the strike.[27]

An issue such as a wage increase may remain at the center of the dispute; however, other elements that enter the bargaining process may subsequently change. Strikes can have traumatic effects on the parties' attitudes; they can temper the militants with realism and radicalize the conservatives. Strikes may cause the members to question the credibility of their leaders or management. Furthermore, once a strike is over, much rebuilding must occur.[28]

Strategic Purposes of a Strike While the main purpose of the strike is to secure a contract, it also serves other purposes. For example, it may be part of an overall union strategy to help resolve internal problems. It may have a cathartic effect on the union members, removing accumulated tensions and releasing frustrations resulting from monotonous jobs. In fact, strikes under these conditions might improve productivity when the strikers return to work. A strike might also help to unify union members – rallying the diverse pre-strike membership factions to work toward a common goal.

In some cases, the union calls a strike just to show management it can unify the membership over a collective bargaining issue. Over a period of time, threats of a strike lose their effectiveness. If such threats are not carried out, management views the union leader as "the boy who cried wolf." Therefore, union leaders are sometimes forced to carry out a bluff or threat in order to substantiate future threats.

Union leaders might also believe that their members would be more willing to accept a slightly modified offer if they have not received wages during a brief strike. In this sense, strikes are used to "roll the steam" out of employees and their initially unrealistic expectations.[29]

Unions also have to consider the effects of a strike on their institutional security. During the strike, some union members might accept jobs elsewhere and decide not to return after the strike. Sometimes employers hire permanent replacements for union strikers, and the negotiations are never consummated. Possibly rival unions are waiting on the sideline for the legally recognized union to falter. With these considerations, the union must be aware that a concerted decision to strike may be a risk to its own survival.

Some companies include the hiring of striker replacements in their bargaining strategy and begin advertising for permanent replacements before their contracts expire. At the International Paper plant in Jay, Maine, the company started accepting applications at the plant 2 weeks before the contract expired and while the present employees were working. Applicants formed long lines outside of the paper mill in view of the employees inside.[30]

Unions try to deter strike-breaking by including in their constitutions provisions to levy fines on union members who return to work during an authorized strike. In fact, many of these provisions prohibit a union member from resigning from the union during the strike. However, in 1985 the Supreme Court restricted the union's ability to deter resignations and ruled that union members enjoyed an absolute right to resign from membership, regardless of union rules and reputations to the contrary, during a strike or when a strike is imminent. If the union imposes a fine on union members who submit their resignation from the union and then cross the union picket line, it violates the Taft-Hartley Act.[31]

Later in 1985 the NLRB ruled that employees who resign from *full* union membership during a strike to become *financial core* members only (members who pay union fees and dues but who are not subject to any other obligations of union membership) cannot be fined by the union for crossing a picket line.[32]

A strike may serve a strategic purpose for management as well. While management cannot call a strike, it can take actions that it knows are likely to result in a strike. For example, management can demand that the union collect dues rather than have management deduct them from worker paychecks (a procedure called *checkoff*). Unions view this demand as a threat to their security and will often strike in response to it. Management's demand to subcontract at will or to change the wage system will almost certainly lead to a strike. Thus, management may attempt to cause a strike when a strike is to its advantage, such as when inventories are high and customer demand is low. If nonunion workers can produce at a sufficient level to maintain acceptable production, if the union is weak, or if management knows that all employees will not support the strike, it may force an impasse in order to secure a more favorable contract.

Previous Strike Experiences Unions and management must consider their previous strike experiences. Strikes can range from very peaceful conflicts of short duration to outrageous, unlawful conflicts of months, even years. They have no uniform sequence, although strikers are usually most enthusiastic during the early days of the strike. Indeed, the first few days on a picket line often draw a large proportion of union members in an almost carnival-like atmosphere. After several weeks, it may be difficult to recruit members to walk the picket line.

Frustrations, antagonisms, and anxieties usually increase as the strike continues, with increased membership pressure being placed on union leaders to resolve the impasse.[33] The relative peacefulness of a strike is influenced by the attitudes of community citizens, particularly merchants and creditors, toward the dispute. The striker's spouse is perhaps the most influential individual in shaping the striker's behavior and attitudes. It is of course much easier for a striker to sustain a long strike if her or his spouse lends moral and, in some cases, financial support to the cause. On the other hand, tensions created by the strike can create permanent divisions among family members, friends, and other groups in the community as the strike endures and as individuals are asked for their support.[34]

Tensions can be heightened if the company continues to operate the business with either supervisory personnel or strike replacements. Bernard Karsh has described several possible striker responses to this situation in his detailed account of one industrial strike.[35]

- Mill supervisors hung in effigy on lampposts around the mill.
- Bedroom-sized mirrors brought to the picket line to reflect the sun on the nonstriking workers to annoy them while they tried to work.
- Setting up circular saw blades mounted on wooden horses for strikers to pound with automobile axles (the noise is deafening).
- Setting fire to 50-gallon oil drums filled with old tar and tar paper, then placing them in an alley directly in front of a loading dock and shipping entrance so that the odor from the smoke would be drawn into the mill every time the door opened.
- Throwing rocks through windows, tacks on driveways, and eggshells filled with colored paint on cars.

Preparation for a Strike

Both parties must prepare for a possible strike before the contract expiration date, whether a strike is called or a settlement is reached. Union leaders must be certain of the extent to which members will actively participate during a strike and present a unified front against the employer. Division within the ranks causes much difficulty and dilutes the union's bargaining strength. Usually, the strike vote taken before the contract deadline will indicate the strength of the membership's willingness to strike.

As the strike date approaches, union officers must schedule pickets, assure appropriate support for those on the line, and properly prepare the pickets for various situations, such as what to do when strike replacements cross the picket line. The union also has to determine qualified recipients of strike benefits as well as to inform the members of appropriate procedures for obtaining any available public aid, such as unemployment compensation, aid to families with dependent children (AFDC), or medical assistance. Finally, communication channels (telephone hot lines) must be established to inform members of the negotiations' progress.

Management often spends much time in its strike preparations, particularly if it is essential that the employer continue to operate during a strike, as public utilities must do. Management in manufacturing facilities must determine the feasibility of building inventories in advance of the possible strike and its strategy of hiring striker replacements if the strike occurs.

Many organizations have emergency strike manuals that provide specific and detailed plans in the event of a strike. The manual typically has two major components: (1) specific job assignments for nonstriking employees, professional employees, and managers and (2) checklists of appropriate strike activities, such as notifying customers and suppliers, contacting law enforcement officials, and providing food and housing for those staying on the job. In cases where the work is highly automated, such as in the telephone industry, workers' strikes were much less potent and companies found it easier to continue to operate, at least during short strikes. Management might also seek professional assistance from employer colleagues, such as members of the Society for Human Resource Management, which has published a *Strike Preparation Manual.*[36]

Although union and management officials carefully consider the advantages and disadvantages of strikes, lockouts, and pickets, they are not entirely free to implement these activities as they please. Various legal considerations can raise additional problems and prospects.

Legality of Strikes and Related Activities

The Right to Strike The right to strike has long been subject to philosophical debate. Opponents of the right to strike usually cite examples of violence and civil disobedience that have occurred in strike activities. Strikes are, however, basic to the industrial relations system—inseparable from collective bargaining because they cannot be severed without hurting both.[37] Strikes are usually not entered into lightly; both parties realize that the strike can hurt as well as help their respective positions.[38]

The potential or actual occurrence of strikes is an inherent aspect of labor-management relationships where the parties seek to obtain their preferences over their opponent's disagreement.[39] Unions that always agree with management over the years may cease to be effective; similarly, management will reduce its effectiveness if it always agrees with the union. Therefore, conflict is inevitable in collective bargaining, and strikes are sometimes viewed as a necessary alternative for expressing this conflict.

Legal guidelines have been formulated that attempt to balance employee and employer rights during a strike. The *Commonwealth* v. *Hunt* decision of 1842 (discussed in Chapter 3) was the first judicial decision that recognized employees' right to participate in concerted activities for their own economic welfare. Section 7 of the National Labor Relations Act guarantees employee rights to engage in "concerted activities for the purpose of collective bargaining or other mutual aid or protection." Section 13 also states: "Nothing in this Act, except as specifically provided for herein, shall be construed so as to interfere with or impede or diminish in any way the right to strike or to affect the limitations or qualifications on that right."

The right to strike is not absolute; there are restrictions on national emergency strikes, secondary strikes, jurisdictional strikes, and recognition strikes. Yet current legislation implicitly assumes that most strikes occur only after months of intensive negotiations under the rules established by the NLRB and the courts. While both parties are required by law to negotiate in good faith, they do not always reach agreement and strikes do occur, but usually only after authorization from the national union office and a strike vote by the membership.[40]

Many legal questions concerning strikes, pickets, and boycotts involving the employees' immediate, or *primary,* employer have been resolved over the years by statute or judicial decisions. Other activities concerning employers not directly involved in the labor dispute (*secondary* employers) are usually subject to much more complex legal interpretation. While secondary activities often have narrow applications, their significance is especially pertinent to those unions and employers that frequently face these issues.

Strikes and Related Activities Involving the Primary Employer When the union and management fail to reach an agreement upon the expiration of their labor agreement, the union normally calls an economic strike accompanied by picket lines and a boycott of the product. If only the immediate employer and the union are involved, the strike, picket, and boycott are considered primary. The overwhelming majority of strikes, pickets, and boycotts that occur in the United States in any given year are of this type.

Management has the right to continue to operate by hiring temporary or permanent replacements during an economic strike. However, if the strike is determined by the NLRB to be an unfair labor practice strike, that is, if the strike has resulted from an employer unfair labor practice such as a refusal to bargain in good faith with the union, striking workers are entitled to reinstatement.

Any employees unfairly discharged for union activities must be returned to their former positions with back pay. However, if strikers participate in activities classified as unacceptable striker misconduct, they lose their reinstatement rights. Such misconduct includes preventing entry to the plant, jumping in front of moving cars, following nonstrikers by car as they leave work, and throwing rocks, eggs, and tomatoes while on the picket line.[41] Today all strike misconduct is examined in light of the surrounding circumstances, and only conduct that may reasonably tend to coerce or intimidate nonstrikers in the exercise of their rights is unprotected.

In the past, when replacement workers were hired during a strike, those on strike went back to work after a settlement was reached, and the replacements were dismissed. However, now if the replacements are hired as "permanent" employees and are dismissed after a settlement is reached, they may file a civil suit against the company for misrepresentation and breach of contract. It is predicted that economically distressed firms will continue to use replacement workers and declare them as "permanent." However, healthier firms consider the potential costs of court suits and tend not to hire permanent replacements during strikes.[42]

Other practical considerations can also prevent the employer from exercising the legal right to replace strikers. It is usually not easy to replace all of the striking employees, especially if the operations are complicated and employees cannot be trained in a short period of time. Finally, extreme tensions can occur between strikers and striker replacements at the picket line, possibly resulting in violence and community disorder.

Employees on strike may forfeit the right to reinstatement if they commit acts sufficiently harmful to render them unfit for further employment with the employer. Also, if employers discipline a striker for engaging in a protected activity, such as an economic strike, the employee has the right to be reinstated.

Wildcat strikes, as mentioned earlier, include work stoppages that involve the primary employer-employee relationship and that are neither sanctioned nor stimulated by the union, although union officials might be aware of them. They can vary in length and number of affected departments in the facility. They may also take the form of heavy absenteeism for several days, especially under no-strike pledges and contracts.[43]

Wildcat strikes are affected by factors external to the relationship between the parties, such as national economic and political trends. But, in essence, they appear to be the culmination of factors indicative of a poor relationship between workers and management, such as increased production demands and poor safety conditions. When this relationship is poor, workers will use any and all means at their disposal to protest their problems. Thus, to prevent wildcat strikes, labor and management officials should work on the qualitative aspects of the total relationship.[44]

Since most labor agreements provide for arbitration as the final step in the grievance procedure and such agreements to arbitrate are usually accompanied by a no-strike clause, a wildcat strike represents a violation of the labor agreement. Employers can respond to wildcat strikes in several ways: (1) by requesting informally and formally that strikers return to work, (2) by contending that employees have voided their labor agreement, (3) by disciplining or discharging the strikers, and (4) by bringing suit against the union for damages suffered. Two Supreme Court decisions discussed in Chapter 9 (*Boy's Market* and *Buffalo Forge*) suggest that employees can be legally enjoined from continuing a wildcat strike under certain conditions.

Some strikes that have resulted from extremely dangerous and unsafe working conditions, although commonly thought of as wildcat strikes, do not fit the definition, because arbitrators exempt such behavior from the no-strike clause, and Section 502 of the NLRA allows such actions as a protected concerted activity.[45]

Lockouts are related to work stoppages involving the primary employer. The right of single employers to lock out employees is considered the analogue of employees' right to strike. Lockouts can be used legally by employers (1) after an impasse has been reached over a mandatory bargaining issue, (2) to prevent seizure of a plant by a sit-down, (3) to forestall repetitive disruption in plant operations by "quickie strikes," (4) to avoid spoilage of perishable materials, and (5) to preserve unity in a multi-employer bargaining arrangement. Yet the right to lock out employees is qualified, particularly since the NLRB maintains that the employer already has the power to counterbalance the strike by permanently replacing the strikers, stockpiling, subcontracting, maintaining operations with nonstrikers, and unilaterally instituting working conditions once the contract has expired.

The NLRB and courts have been more lenient with employers in situations in which the union attempts to "whipsaw" by striking individual employers in a multi-employer bargaining association one at a time to force a more favorable agreement by putting pressure on the struck firm while the others operate. The NLRB and the courts have allowed temporary lockouts to preserve the association's unity. In addition, nonstruck firms in a multi-employer bargaining association have been allowed to hire temporary replacements during the lockout to preserve the bargaining unit structure and to maintain operations. Because the struck firm can hire permanent replacements in order to continue operations, the courts have reasoned that it would be unfair to require that the nonstruck firms be shut down completely while the struck firm operates.[46]

Because employers may hire temporary replacements during legitimate lockouts, companies have been aggressively taking advantage of lockouts (44 percent increase in lockouts from 1985 to 1986),[47] and the balance in most labor disputes has shifted to the management side. In early 1990, several U.S. Senators and Congressmen cosponsored a bill to prohibit the hiring of replacements during labor disputes, an act that they believed would return to a more favorable balance between management and labor during labor disputes.

Strikes and Related Activities Involving Secondary Employers Secondary parties are those who are not directly bound by the terms of the labor agreement in dispute. They are not at the bargaining table; however, they become affected by the labor dispute when the union attempts to persuade them to influence the primary employer to agree with the union's proposals.

It is not always easy to distinguish between a primary and secondary party to a negotiations impasse, as will be illustrated by the following discussion of activities involving product boycotts and picketing, common situs picketing, the ally doctrine, and hot-cargo agreements.

Product (Consumer) Boycotts and Picketing Activities such as handbilling, carrying placards, and urging customers to refuse to purchase products from a particular retail or wholesale business are involved in boycotts and picketing. As an example of how the primary and secondary roles can be blurred in these activities, consider that the striking employees of a clothing manufacturer might legally boycott and picket a nearby retail clothing store owned by the manufacturer, say, the factory outlet. But if these employees travel a considerable distance to picket a retail clothing store that sells many items, only one of which is bought from the manufacturer, the legal issue becomes more complex.[48] Picketing in front of a retail clothing store in another city (a secondary employer) violates the NLRA if, but only if, the picketers attempt to convince customers to refuse to shop at the store. If instead the picketers make an appeal to the customers to refuse to buy only the struck product (clothing items produced by the primary employer), the picket is legal.

The presence of shopping malls that include a multitude of separate employers has given rise to interesting questions about legalities of union actions. While the Taft-Hartley Act made secondary boycotts illegal, prohibition against certain acts such as picketing and handbilling may be inconsistent with First Amendment rights. The U.S. Supreme Court has upheld the right of unions to peacefully distribute handbills urging customers not to shop at stores located in a mall (the handbill used is shown in Exhibit 7.2) until all construction conducted in the mall was performed by contractors paying "fair" wages. Justice White stated:

> The handbills involved here truthfully revealed the existence of a labor dispute and urged potential customers of the mall to follow a wholly legal course of action, namely, not to patronize the retailers doing business in the mall. The handbilling was peaceful. No picketing or patrolling was involved. On its face, this was expressive activity arguing that substandard wages should be opposed by abstaining from shopping in a mall where such wages were paid.[49]

Another leading case on picketing and handbilling, *Tree Fruits,* involved a strike against some fruit-packing firms that were members of a multi-employer bargaining association and that sold Washington State apples to Safeway, a retail grocery chain. As part of the boycott effort, the union picketed and handbilled 46 Safeway stores, appealing to the customers to refrain from buying Washington State apples. The union carefully avoided making appeals to employees at the stores, instructed the individuals on the picket line not to interfere with employees, and made certain there was not a general appeal to request that potential customers not patronize the store. As a result, the picketing was peaceful, the employees continued to work, no obstructions occurred, and the courts upheld the legality of the picketing activities.[50]

Product boycotts also may involve larger multi-plant operations and subsidiary operations. In one case, the union had a dispute with a wholly owned subsidiary manufacturer of Pet, a diversified, billion-dollar conglomerate with plants and retail stores located throughout the United States. Because of the nature of Pet's operations, in which one facility provides support for others, and because the struck manufacturer produced products sold by Pet, the union's publicity urging a total consumer boycott of Pet's products was protected and legal.[51]

Common Situs Picketing Common situs picketing involves both the primary and neutral secondary employers who share the same physical work location, as is the case at construction sites and shipping docks. The problem arises when the union that is picketing the primary employer also adversely affects the work or business of the neutral employer located at the same site. The union has the right to picket the primary employer with whom it has a labor dispute. Yet the neutral, or second-

Exhibit 7.2 **Handbill Used at Shopping Mall to Influence Shoppers**

PLEASE DON'T SHOP AT EAST LAKE SQUARE PLEASE.

THE FLORIDA GULF COAST BUILDING TRADES COUNCIL, AFL-CIO is requesting that you do not shop at the stores in the East Lake Square Mall because of the Mall ownership's contribution to substandard wages.

The Wilson's Department Store under construction on these premises is being built by contractors who pay substandard wages and fringe benefits. In the past, the Mall's owner, the Edward J. DeBartolo Corporation, has supported labor and our local economy by insuring that the Mall and its stores be built by contractors who pay fair wages and fringe benefits. Now, however, and for no apparent reason, the Mall owners have taken a giant step backwards by permitting our standards to be torn down. The payment of substandard wages not only diminishes the working person's ability to purchase with earned, rather than borrowed, dollars, but it also undercuts the wage standard of the entire company. Since low construction wages at this time of inflation means decreased purchasing power, do the owners of East Lake Mall intend to compensate for the decreased purchasing power of workers of the community by encouraging the stores in East Lake Mall to cut their prices and lower their profits? CUT-RATE WAGES ARE NOT FAIR UNLESS MERCHANDISE PRICES ARE ALSO CUT-RATE.

We ask your support in our protest against substandard wages. Please do not patronize the stores in East Lake Square Mall until the Mall's owner publicly promises that all construction at the Mall will be done using contractors who pay their employees fair wages and fringe benefits.

IF YOU MUST ENTER THE MALL TO DO BUSINESS, please express to the store managers your concern over substandard wages and your support of our efforts.

We are appealing only to the public—the consumer. We are not seeking to induce any person to cease work or to refuse to make deliveries.

Source: Supreme Court decision in *DeBartolo* v. *Florida Gulf Coast Building & Construction Trades Council,* U.S. (1988).

ary, employer has a right to be free from economic pressure from unions with whom it has no bargaining relationship.[52]

Unions argue that the employers who occupy the same work site *(common situs)* are so intertwined that a labor dispute with one employer is a labor dispute with all; therefore, unions allege that there are no neutral employers on the site. Employers argue they are independent operators and should be legally protected from picketing. The Supreme Court ruled on a case involving a general contractor on a construction project who subcontracted some electrical work to a nonunion subcontractor who paid less than the union scale.[53] When the nonunion employees arrived at work, the union set up pickets on the entire work site, and other union employees honored the picket line and refused to work. The Court ruled that general contractors and subcontractors on a building site were separate business entities and should be treated separately with respect to each other's labor controversies.[54] Therefore, unions in a labor dispute with their employer cannot picket neutral employers on the common site.

In another common situs case, the union had a dispute with a restaurant employer that was located on the 46th floor of a 50-story office building. In support of its contract demands, it struck and stationed pickets on public sidewalks at every entrance and distributed leaflets in the foyer of the 46th floor, which was under the exclusive control of the employer. The restaurant employer alleged trespassing by those distributing leaflets, demanded they leave, and threatened them with arrest. Thus, the NLRB had to reconcile protected rights of employees and property rights of employers. The board's decision follows:

> [R]estricting strike-related activity to the public sidewalks would excessively hinder the unions' efforts to communicate a meaningful message to its intended audience (and) . . . the property rights of the neutral employer must yield to the right of the union to publicize its disputes with the primary (employer).[55]

Unions have been limited in their flexibility in applying economic pressure via picketing at work sites by another case in which the company, General Electric, used independent contractors to construct a new building, rearrange operations for a new product, and perform general repair work. In order to minimize contact between General Electric employees and employees of the contractor, a separate gate *(reserve gate)* was set aside for employees of the contractor. The union, which had a labor dispute with General Electric, called a strike and picketed all gates, including the separate gate, and most of the employees of the contractor honored the picket line. The NLRB found that picketing at the separate gate was designed to enmesh employees of a neutral employer in the labor dispute and was therefore illegal. The Supreme Court agreed to sustain the NLRB order unless the NLRB found through further investigation that the separate gate was established for the purpose of entry by employees who performed work that was necessary for the normal operations of the plant—work normally performed by General Electric employees. Once the neutrality of the reserve gate has been breached, such as if the reserve gate is used by the contractor's employees to perform work normally done by employees on strike, the gate loses its neutrality and the union can lawfully picket the gate.[56]

Alliance between Employers (Business Ally Doctrine) If a secondary employer is closely associated with the primary employer and its labor dispute with the union, neutrality is lost, and the secondary employer should be treated as a primary party to the labor dispute. For example, a secondary employer would lose its neutrality by accepting a subcontract to do work that would normally be done by workers on strike.

This work performed by the employees of the secondary employer can be classified as *struck work,* which includes "work that but for the strike would be performed by the employees of the primary employer." Another situation occurs in cases where the business relationship of the primary and secondary employer is so intertwined as to almost create a co-employer relationship.[57] Close business relationships can easily be so intertwined within conglomerated manufacturing or insurance companies that picketing the secondary employer is permissible.

Yet the courts have determined that single employers can be protected when distance between facilities is great and the operations are autonomous. For example, when union members having a labor dispute with the *Miami Herald* went to Detroit to picket the *Detroit Free Press* (both owned by Knight-Ridder), the board found the common ownership alone did not in and of itself create an allied relationship. In fact, more recently the board has concluded that separate divisions of the same corporation may also be able to claim protection from secondary picketing if the dispute exists at only one division.[58]

Hot-cargo Agreements Designed to promote union-made products and support union members on strike, hot-cargo agreements were negotiated in labor agreements to specify that employees may refuse to use or handle products of certain employers, such as nonunion companies and companies experiencing strikes. Before the enactment of the Landrum-Griffin Act in 1959, these clauses were not illegal and were considered loopholes in the provisions of the Labor-Management Relations Act, which dealt with secondary boycotts. While they had the same effect as secondary boycotts, they adversely affected neutral employers. In 1959 they were designated as unfair labor practices;[59] by the 1959 amendments, however, a special exception was provided for the apparel, clothing, and construction industries. In addition, in the construction industry the union is permitted to strike in order to obtain a hot-cargo clause.[60]

Resolution Procedures for National Emergency Disputes When labor disputes develop to a stage where they are regarded as having an adverse effect on the U.S. national interest, they assume a special significance. Certain legal procedures apply to these occasions. Strikes that have an adverse impact on national economic or defense interests are classified as *national emergency strikes,* and the federal government uses three methods in dealing with them: (1) presidential seizure or other intervention, (2) procedures under the Railway Labor Act, and (3) procedures under the Labor Management Relations Act.

Studies have shown that the economic effects of such strikes often have less impact than a casual observer may believe. Furthermore, it has been extremely difficult to estimate all the effects of a particular strike, even after it is over.[61]

Presidential seizures or attempts at seizure occurred 71 times under four presidents – Lincoln, Wilson, Franklin D. Roosevelt, and Truman – in the interests of maintaining production when actual strikes or threatened strikes caused national emergencies, mostly during wars.

The *Railway Labor Act* provides a procedure for resolving national emergency work stoppages in the railroads and airlines that includes the following:

- The National Mediation Board (NMB) attempts to mediate the dispute, and if unsuccessful, recommends voluntary interest arbitration.
- If arbitration is rejected, a 30-day time period is established during which wage rates, working rules, working conditions, and so forth remain the same.
- If the dispute threatens to substantially interrupt interstate commerce in any section of the country and deprive it of an essential transportation service, the president is notified, and an emergency board is appointed.
- The emergency board investigates the dispute and reports, with recommendations, within 30 days. During this time, the status quo is maintained.

Since the act's passage in 1926, its emergency provisions have been invoked about 190 times, an average rate of four times per year, and work stoppages have occurred at the end of the 60-day period at a rate of one per year since 1947.[62] Before 1941 the parties never refused the recommendations of the emergency boards. However, since a 1963 congressional decision regarding firemen on diesels, it is not uncommon for one of the parties to pursue its interest to the fullest extent by relying more on third-party intervention and ad hoc legislation than on its own negotiations. Congress intervened eight more times between 1963 and 1975, then not again until 1982, when it imposed a settlement on the Brotherhood of Locomotive Engineers.

The enactment of the Labor Management Relations Act in 1947 authorized the president to invoke its national emergency provisions, Section 206 through 210, in labor disputes of the national emergency magnitude. These provisions provide a step-by-step procedure to halt the strike for 80 days and provide the parties assistance in resolving their disputes.

Exhibit 7.3 displays the steps in the national emergency procedure of the Labor Management Relations Act. It includes the requirements specified for all parties: the 60-day notice to the other party that a change in the present agreement is desired and the 30-day notice to the Federal Mediation and Conciliation Service and state agencies that the negotiations are in process and a settlement has not been reached.

The first step for the president is the appointment of a board of inquiry when the strike or the threat of a strike is believed to be of sufficient severity to imperil the national health or safety. Because of the urgency of the matter, the board will investigate the issues in dispute, gather relevant facts, and make a report to the president in a very short time—usually in about 1 day.

After the president receives and studies the report, he or she may direct the attorney general to secure an 80-day injunction from an appropriate federal district court to prevent or end the strike. Once the injunction is issued, the board is reconvened, and after the first 60 days of the injunction period, it will be asked to report to the president on the employer's last offer and any other relevant factors. During the interim period, the FMCS continues to assist the parties in reaching a settlement. After the board reports the final employer offer, the NLRB will conduct and certify a secret ballot election (between the 60th and 80th days of the injunction period) to determine whether the employees will accept this offer. If they refuse, the attorney general must ask the federal district court to dissolve the injunction at the end of 80 days, and the union may legally strike. The last step involves a full and comprehensive report by the president to Congress, accompanied by any recommendations that he or she may have.

Although the national emergency strike provisions have been invoked, on the average, less than once per year during the last 30 years, national emergency strikes have involved some of the more interesting personalities of the labor movement—for example, John L. Lewis and David McDonald. In the 1948 coal miners' strike, United Mine Workers President John L. Lewis was found guilty of both criminal and civil contempt of court and was fined $20,000; his union was fined $1,400,000 for criminal violations. Neither fine was ever paid.

The 1959 steel strike, lasting 116 days and involving 12 basic steel producers, also received considerable national attention because it affected other industries—auto, construction, and coal. The negotiations took place at very high levels and involved not only top company and union officials but also the president, vice president, and secretary of labor.

The last time the Taft-Hartley procedure was invoked was during the 1977–78 coal strike. Even then, the strike was settled shortly after the injunction was obtained, but before it was enforced.

Exhibit 7.3 **National Emergency Procedure under LMRA**

The date on which contract expires (zero point in the diagram) may or may not be the first day of the planned strike.

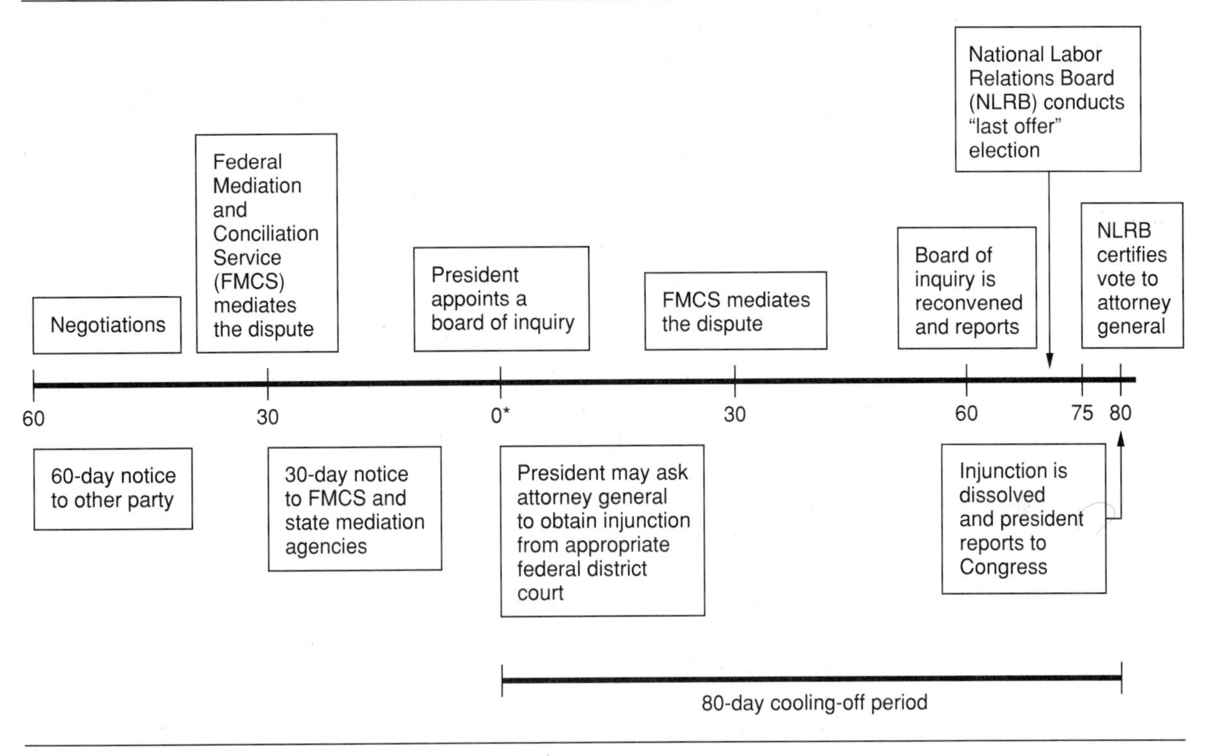

Source: Diagram created by Dr. Roy Moore, Professor, Department of Management, Delta State University, Cleveland, Mississippi.

Throughout the years, every time there has been a major strike, critics have believed the procedures do not adequately resolve national emergency strikes. The strongest criticism has been directed toward the rigidity and predictability of the procedures. When each step is predictable, either party may include the issuance of the injunction as part of its bargaining strategy. Another area of criticism is the secret-ballot election on the employer's last offer, which has often solidified the union position rather than facilitating the bargaining process toward settlement. Lastly, because the presidential boards of inquiry are prohibited from proposing settlements, their effectiveness in securing the necessary public support and pressure to move the parties toward settlement are limited.[63]

Cooperation between Union and Management to Reduce Conflicts

Preceding sections of this chapter have emphasized impasse-resolution procedures and conflict. However, there is growing support for greater union-management cooperation, to avoid the necessity for such resolution procedures. Of course, such cooperation is not always possible. Union-management cooperation requires a stimulus, and some parties do not have the necessary stimulus. Also, effective cooperation requires that each party trust the other and that each offer the other a potential benefit. Where credibility is lacking, or where one party perceives no potential benefit in cooperation, a resolution is unlikely. Cooperation should be viewed as a process that, once begun, can be modified to suit the needs of the particular parties involved.[64]

Exhibit 7.4 lists opportunities created by cooperation for the company in terms of performance, for the employee in terms of positive job-related outcomes, and for both parties in terms of improved relationships. Although many union-management cooperation programs have stemmed from union concessions on wages, employee benefits, work rules, and so on, collective bargaining has proven conducive to discussion of these concessions.[65]

Most business and union leaders strongly favor a more cooperative relationship between labor and management. Reasons given for these opinions include the need for increased productivity and the threats posed by international competition, slower economic growth, and automation.[66] Although there is still support for the belief that we cannot have free collective bargaining without reliance on the strike or lockout, management and labor have learned that many basic common interests outweigh the use of the strike or lockout.[67]

Labor-management cooperation has met some resistance from both sides. Employers fear cooperative efforts might give unions increased prestige and reduce managerial prerogatives. Other employers question the value of the individual worker's contributions toward cooperative efforts.[68] Some union officials are also reluctant to participate in cooperative efforts if they believe these efforts' sole goal is to increase productivity, which can ultimately reduce the size of the work force. Other union leaders believe that these projects might result in a "happier" work force, thereby adversely affecting membership allegiance to the union.[69]

A major influence in delaying cooperative efforts is the absence of signals upward from the rank and file for involvement in these projects. In fact, unions continue to focus their efforts and interests in collective bargaining on the traditional issues—wages, job security, economic supplements, and so on—and overall there has been limited interest in union-management motivational programs via collective bargaining.[70] Only 3.9 percent of 1,550 labor agreements studied by the Bureau of Labor Statistics in 1980 included labor-management study committees that examined such sensitive issues as subcontracting, seniority, and wage incentives and made appropriate recommendations to the negotiators. On the other hand, there were more joint committees that periodically met separately from negotiations to improve safety conditions (these existed in 36.8 percent of the 1,550 agreements).[71]

Within unions there have been various reactions to labor-management cooperation. The Steel Workers at National Steel (jointly owned with Japan's Nippon Kokan) rejected a negotiated agreement patterned after one ratified at Bethlehem Steel three years before that gave workers unprecedented job security and involvement in management decisions. Within the Auto Workers, a group of dissident members under the label of "New Directions" have challenged the union leadership's "cozy" relationships with management. The dissidents' leaders contend that by participating in joint cooperation programs the union is betraying the interests of the union members and contradicting the union's traditional role as an adversary to manage-

Exhibit 7.4

Summary of Opportunities Created by Cooperative Union-Management Programs

Performance Indicators	Employee Outcomes	Relationship Changes
Productivity improvement	Increase job satisfaction	Attitude change among key actors
Reduce labor costs	Job influence and involvement	Union influence on key decisions
Quality improvements	Information about job and company	Reduce likelihood of future strikes
Product design changes	Commitment to company	Reduce grievances
Reduce absenteeism	Improve conditions of work	Better understanding of labor-management issues
Reduce turnover	Improve supervision	Examine outdated contract language
Reduce tardiness	Reduce job frustration	Continuous study of ongoing problems
Reduce accidents	Improve earnings	Facilitate technological change
Improve manpower utilization	Upgrade job characteristics	
	Increase trust	
	Increase job security	

Source: Michael Schuster, "Problems and Opportunities in Implementing Cooperative Union-Management Programs," *Proceedings of the Thirty-fifth Annual Meeting: Industrial Relations Research Association* (Madison, Wis.: Industrial Relations Research Association, 1983), p. 192.

ment. The recent book, *Choosing Sides: Unions and the Team Concept,* alleges that cooperative teamwork is nothing more than a "union-busting" device designed by companies to do away with unions.

Several important legal issues must also be addressed. When union-management cooperation programs thrust employees into higher-level decision making, their involvement and influence may be sufficient to classify them as "managerial employees,"[72] which may exclude them from coverage under the National Labor Relations Act. In addition, Section 9(a) of the NLRB requires a union certified by the NLRB to be the exclusive representative of all the employees in the bargaining unit for purposes of collective bargaining in respect to rates of pay, wages, hours, and other conditions of employment. This "exclusivity" doctrine prohibits employers from bargaining with a union other than the one certified, if one exists, and it prohibits employees from bargaining collectively through any other labor organization. Employers who choose to negotiate with representatives other than the certified union will be circumventing the collective bargaining agent or will be committing an unfair labor practice [Section 8(a)(5)]. If a case arose in which the union challenged an employee committee operating outside union control and directly with the employer, the NLRB and courts would probably rule that the committee violated the union's exclusivity jurisdiction and that the employer was committing an unfair labor practice.[73]

Section 8(a)(2) of the NLRA prohibits an employer from dominating or interfering with the formation or administration of any labor organization or from contributing financial or other support to it. In the past the NLRB has construed Section 8(a)(2) very narrowly so as to preclude many forms of employee interaction with management. However, in 1982 the Sixth Circuit Court of Appeals dismissed case precedent as an "antiquated relic" and emphasized the acceptability of innovations in the workplace with regard to employee involvement; and the NLRB has afforded greater latitude for management to interact with employees ever since.[74] Nevertheless, if union-management cooperation programs continue to grow, the issues of managerial employees, bypassing the union, and employer domination and interference will have to be addressed.[75]

An interesting issue emerges when consideration is given to employee participation programs within the nonunion setting. A legal analysis of NLRB and court decisions concluded that employee participation programs will probably be found permissible under the National Labor Relations Act if the following factors are present: (1) employee terms on the participation committees are rotated frequently and employees are elected by their coworkers, (2) there is no evidence of anti-union bias or employee dissatisfaction with the program, (3) there are no union organizing activities at the time the program is established, (4) participation is voluntary, (5) employees are permitted to join a union, (6) the committee is delegated final and binding decision-making authority, and (7) the subjects are restricted to those not considered bargainable in the collective bargaining arena.[76]

Successful Labor-Management Cooperation Programs

Several successful labor-management cooperation programs have received national attention. These include the major programs of the Federal Mediation and Conciliation Service (FMCS)—Relations by Objectives (RBO) and joint labor-management committees—and the automobile plants in Fremont, California and Spring Hill, Tennessee.

Programs of the FMCS (RBO and Joint Committees)

In 1975 the FMCS introduced a new program, Relations by Objectives (RBO). This program was designed to eliminate factors that cause breakdowns in negotiations and prolong strikes. RBO focuses on intergroup team building, intragroup image clarification and diagnosis, confrontation meetings, coaching, and other developmental approaches. The program consists of four phases:

1. Problem solving and goal setting.
2. Action planning and programming.
3. Implementation of plans and programs.
4. Periodic review and evaluation of progress toward goal accomplishment.

Phases 1 and 4 take place at a neutral, off-site location for 3 intensive days. Ten to fifteen members of the union and management attend sessions with federal mediators. Separate and joint sessions are held until neutral problem and goal statements are clarified, covering such subjects as communication, grievance handling, supervisor and steward training, and attitudes and positions of both the union and management.[77] Since its inception, over 100 RBO programs have been initiated with positive results including improved stability in the parties' relationship, less grievance activity, improved production and plant morale, and smoother contract negotiations after the program.

Joint Labor-Management Committees

Hundreds of joint labor-management committees have been established on the parties' own initiative and with the assistance of the FMCS. These committees provide labor and management with an opportunity to discuss problems without the pressures of the bargaining table.[78]

The committees attempt to resolve problems between contract negotiations and through cooperative efforts develop trust and a spirit that carries over to the bargaining table. Examples of neutral problem solving in the retail food industry include a study of working conditions, such as exposure to hazardous materials, use of protective gloves and aprons, and using knives and other cutting equipment.[79] In the health care industry, joint committees have explored the alternatives to strikes for achieving peaceful settlements, treatment of registered nurses by physicians and hospital administrators, use of temporary employment agencies, work shifts, quality of care, and staffing.[80]

A follow-up study by the FMCS reported that 84 percent of the parties believed that their relationships with the other side had improved as a result of the work of the labor-management committees. These improved relationships were also reflected in better working conditions, reduced grievances, and improved bargaining relationships.[81]

Fremont, California–United Auto Workers, General Motors, and Toyota

One example of joint cooperation is the venture incorporated as New United Motor Manufacturing Inc. (NUMMI) established by General Motors and Toyota. The venture will build a limited number of one model of automobile over 12 years and then cease to exist. With agreement from the United Auto Workers, it has provided about 2,700 jobs in the Fremont, California, plant. In 1982 before the venture began, the plant's absenteeism rate was 20 percent and as high as 40 percent on Mondays and Fridays. There were some 8,000 grievances pending, and work slowdowns occurred at the drop of a hat. The plant was inefficient, had frequent occurrences of violence and drug abuse, and was characterized by overall poor labor-management relationships.[82] With the introduction of Japanese management and manufacturing techniques with American workers and a guarantee of union cooperation, the parties created an environment of trust. Time clocks and reserved parking spaces were eliminated and there is only one cafeteria for all employees and management, and the same benefits for all. The results have been that the plant has become the "most efficient automobile manufacturing facility in North America." There were less than 30 grievances in 1987 and an absenteeism rate of 1 percent.[83]

Statistics show that it takes far less time to produce a car at NUMMI (20 hours versus 28 hours at other GM facilities) largely because of the low proportion of unexcused absences. Likewise, work rules have been modified where there are only three job classifications (two skilled and one unskilled at the facility). The union and company have agreed that there will be no layoffs unless compelled by severe economic conditions that threaten the company's long-term financial viability. Management has agreed to consider other cost saving alternatives, such as salary reductions of managerial employees, eliminating sub-contracting, and seeking voluntary layoffs, before laying off any employees involuntarily. To assure quality of production, hourly employees have the right and obligation to indicate when the assembly line should be stopped to prevent a defective car from continuing down the line.[84]

Saturn Agreement–United Auto Workers and General Motors

General Motors and the United Auto Workers negotiated the Saturn agreement to cover a new plant in Spring Hill, Tennessee that will employ 6,000 workers. The agreement, which was negotiated and agreed on before the plant was opened, included the following key features:

1. *Job security*–Permanent job security to all UAW-GM members hired into the Saturn plant; new employees will gain permanent job security based on seniority; 80 percent of the work force will have permanent job security at all times.
2. *Decision making*–Full participation of the workers and their union, free flow of information, and consensus decision making at all levels of the organization.
3. *Artificial distinctions between workers and management* in methods of pay, options to buy GM products, separate cafeterias, reserved parking spaces, separate entrances, etc., are eliminated.
4. *Employee identification*–All production and skilled tradesmen will be designated as "Saturn" members.
5. *Compensation*–Base rate will be pegged to 80 percent of the other competitive base rate plus a cost of living adjustment (COLA) at UAW-represented domestic auto manufacturers; additional compensation will be related to performance, product quality, and profit sharing.
6. *Job classifications*–There is one production classification and three to five skilled classifications.[85]

Characteristics of Successful Labor-Management Cooperative Efforts

The Saturn agreement incorporates several of the important characteristics of labor-management cooperative efforts in other places, which include:

- Involvement of the organization's CEO, the union as an institution, and supervisory management.
- Mutual trust between the parties.
- Joint problem solving, which in turn relies on the formulation of clear objectives.
- Willingness to experiment and innovate.
- Constant communication between the parties.

The "Labor Relations in Action" displays these characteristics in actual experiences.

Summary

Earlier research led to the conclusion that contract rejection is relatively high; however, more recent research finds a lower rate when contract rejection is redefined as rejection of the bargaining committee's recommended labor agreement.

Third-party procedures to assist the parties in resolving negotiation impasses range from mediation–where the third party attempts to facilitate resolution by keeping the parties bargaining, acting as a go-between, and offering alternatives–to arbitration, a quasi-judicial procedure in which the bargaining positions are presented

Labor Relations in Action

Characteristics and Examples of Labor-Management Cooperation

1. Mutual Trust between Employer and Union: Southern Bell and the Communication Workers of America (CWA) The parties established 416 joint quality-of-work-life (QWL) committees throughout the company. One QWL committee in Florida developed a new work process that eliminated eight jobs—their own. The committee members had enough trust in the system to make the recommendation because they knew that they would be prepared for comparable or better jobs in the organization.

2. Problem-Solving Approach to Bargaining: General Motors and United Auto Workers (UAW) The company and union at the Doraville, Georgia, plant adopted a spirit of cooperation to work together to resolve mutual problems. Outsourcing of work, a problem for the union because it meant job losses for members, had been a focal point of potential strikes. To overcome the negative impact of outsourcing, a joint union-management team was formed to study the feasibility of keeping the work within the company. The team studied the possibility of building seat cushions for mid-sized models and discovered a way to produce the seat cushions within the plant for slightly less than the outside contractors. The company allowed the team to bid on the work and it won the contract, and seat cushions are now built in-house. Also, bids are now accepted from in-house teams not only to counter new outsourcing but to insource (bring back work that has been outsourced) as well.

3. A Willingness to Experiment and Innovate with Joint Activities to Meet Mutual Needs: Pacific Maritime Association and International Longshoremen's and Warehousemen's Union (ILWU) The companies and union committed to joint problem-solving to adjust to technological changes that increase productivity while preserving work opportunities for ILWU members. The result was the Mechanization and Modernization Agreement, which dealt with problems of displacement caused by improvements in technology. Economic security of the existing work force was maintained and no layoffs resulted from lack of work. However, employers were able to reap net gains in productivity due to mechanization.

4. Constant Communication between Parties: General Electric and International Union of Electronic, Electrical, Technical, Salaried and Machine Workers of America (IUE) The company concluded that it would no longer enter negotiations with its own conclusions about what is good for employees, asking the union to tell them what is wrong with the company's approach. Instead, the company encourages sharing of information, explanation of issues, and participative development of solutions. In negotiations, the company typically provides the union with an idea of the overall size of the negotiated package and then the parties jointly shape the individual items in the package. Throughout the years of the agreement, the parties continuously communicate with each other. For example, if an issue arises that may have legal implications for their relationship, they will discuss it before any action is taken. Neither party wants to be surprised, so the key officials talk to each other several times a week.

Source: Donald P. Crane and Michael Jay Jedel, "Mature Collective Bargaining Relationships," in Gladys W. Guenberg, ed., *Arbitration 1988: Emerging Issues for the 1990s* (Washington, D.C.: Bureau of National Affairs Inc., 1989), pp. 346–364.

to the arbitrator, who makes a final and binding decision. Within this range are the med-arb procedure (which attempts mediation first and then arbitration if mediation fails) and fact-finding (in which the parties present their positions to the fact-finder, other facts are collected, and a report, which includes a recommended resolution of the impasse, is written and presented).

Not all bargaining issues are resolved through negotiations; strikes, boycotts, pickets, lockouts, and related activities do occur. However, both parties have to seriously consider their positions and the consequences of their actions before taking any actions. Each hurts the costs, profits, and production of the companies and the income and public image of the union. While both parties may prepare for work stoppages, a high percentage of strikes, boycotts, pickets, and lockouts have taken their toll in terms of costs to both parties.

The right to concerted actions by employees is an intricate part of the labor relations process and is guaranteed by law. On the other hand, possession of a right to strike does not mean that it should be exercised frequently. The data show that strikes occur very infrequently, but those that do occur can be damaging economically and are well publicized by the media.

Most strikes and related activities involve primary employers, but often secondary employers (not directly involved in the employer-employee relationship) are affected. A complex body of law and judicial decisions covers such activities as consumer and product boycotts and picketing, common situs picketing, employer-ally relationships, and hot-cargo agreements.

Strikes and related activities that have an adverse effect on the national interest may be declared national emergency strikes. In this regard, resolution procedures are available in the Railway Labor Act and the Labor Management Relations Act to facilitate their resolutions. While such impasses occur infrequently, they are significant when they do occur.

Efforts by unions and management to organize and develop cooperative efforts to reduce the possibility of conflict are still relatively infrequent. However, several unions and companies have spent much time, money, and effort to minimize conflicts. A number of successful labor-management cooperation programs have received national attention.

Key Terms

interest (or contract) arbitration
final-offer selection (FOS) arbitration
mediation-arbitration or med-arb
fact-finding
strike
lockout
recognitional picketing
informational picketing
product or consumer picketing
wildcat strike

Discussion Questions

1. What are the chief reasons for rejection of tentative agreements by union members?
2. What problems may be caused as a result of contract rejection?
3. Define the major types of third-party interventions. How do they differ, and how do they appear similar?
4. What specific qualities should a mediator possess? Why do these qualities facilitate impasse resolution?
5. Why is interest arbitration used so infrequently in the private sector?
6. Discuss the following statement: "Strikes are an intricate and essential element of the collective bargaining process."
7. Discuss the following: "It appears that the balance in labor-management relations during labor disputes has shifted to management."

8. Define and discuss the various types of secondary activities of unions that may occur during impasses.
9. Explain the alternatives that could be made available for resolving national emergency strikes.
10. List the issues in which management and the union can cooperate to their mutual advantage. Do you know of other cooperative efforts by union and management to reduce conflict? List the strong and weak points of these efforts.

References

1. Clyde W. Summers, "Ratification of Agreements," in *Frontiers of Collective Bargaining,* ed. J. T. Dunlop and N. W. Chamberlain (New York: Harper & Row, 1967), pp. 82–83.
2. Ibid., p. 83.
3. Federal Mediation and Conciliation Service, *Thirty-Fourth Annual Report* (Washington, D. C.: Government Printing Office, 1982), p. 21 (FMCS does not collect these data at this time).
4. Peter Cappelli and W. P. Sterling, "Union Bargaining Decisions and Contract Ratifications: The 1982 and 1984 Auto Agreements," *Industrial and Labor Relations Review* 41 (January 1988), p. 195.
5. William E. Simkin, "Refusal to Ratify Contracts," *Industrial and Labor Relations Review* 21 (July 1968), pp. 528–529.
6. Charles Odewahn and Joseph Krislov, "Contract Rejections: Testing the Explanatory Hypothesis," *Industrial Relations* 12 (October 1973), pp. 289–296.
7. D. R. Burke and Lester Rubin, "Is Contract Rejection a Major Collective Bargaining Problem?" *Industrial and Labor Relations Review* 26 (January 1973), pp. 832–833.
8. William E. Simkin, *Mediation and the Dynamics of Collective Bargaining* (Washington, D.C.: Bureau of National Affairs Inc., 1971), pp. 25–28.
9. Federal Mediation and Conciliation Service, *Fortieth Annual Report* (Washington, D.C.: FMCS, 1988), p. 21.
10. Carl Stevens, "Mediation and the Role of the Neutral," in Dunlop and Chamberlain, *Frontiers of Collective Bargaining,* p. 271.
11. Steven Briggs and Daniel J. Koys, "What Makes Labor Mediators Effective?" *Labor Law Journal* 40 (August 1988), pp. 517-520.
12. Stevens, "Mediation and the Role of the Neutral," pp. 280–284.
13. Joseph Krislov and Amira Ealin, "Comparative Analysis of Attitudes Towards Mediation," *Labor Law Journal* 30 (March 1979), p. 173.
14. Richard B. Peterson and Mark R. Peterson, "Toward A Systematic Understanding of the Labor Mediation Process," in *Advances in Industrial and Labor Relations,* vol. 4, eds. David Lewin, David B. Lipsky, and Donna Sockell (Greenwich, Conn.: JAI Press, Inc., 1987), p. 145.
15. Stevens, "Mediation and the Role of the Neutral," pp. 280–284.
16. Richard B. Peterson and Mark R. Peterson, "Toward a Systematic Understanding," pp. 152–153.
17. Thomas A. Kochan and Todd Jick, "The Public Sector Mediation Process," *Journal of Conflict Resolution* 22 (June 1978), p. 236.
18. Homer C. LaRue, "An Historical Overview of Interest Arbitration in the United States," *The Arbitration Journal* 42 (December 1987), pp. 13–17.
19. Robert A. Baruch Bush, "Efficiency and Protection or Empowerment and Recognition?: The Mediator's Role and Ethical Standards in Mediation," *Florida Law Review* 41 (Spring 1989), pp. 253–286.
20. William H. Ross, Jr., "Situational Factors and Alternative Dispute Resolution," *The Journal of Applied Behavioral Science* 24 (no. 3, 1988), pp. 251–260.
21. Max H. Bazerman, "Norms of Distributive Justice in Interest Arbitration," *Industrial and Labor Relations Review* 38 (July 1985), pp. 568–570.
22. David E. Fuller, "The Impetus to Contract Arbitration in the Private Area," *Twenty-fourth Annual NYU Conference on Labor* (New York: Matthew Bender, 1972), pp. 95–98.
23. U.S. Department of Labor, Bureau of Labor Statistics, *Analysis of Work Stoppages, 1975* (Washington, D.C.: Government Printing Office, 1977), p. 78.
24. Bruce Kaufman, "The Determinants of Strikes Over Time and Across Industries," *Journal of Labor Research* 4 (Spring 1983), pp. 173–174.
25. Martin J. Mauro, "Strikes as a Result of Imperfect Information," *Industrial and Labor Relations Review* 35 (July 1982), pp. 536–538.
26. Bert Klandermans, "Perceived Costs and Benefits of Participation in Union Action," *Personnel Psychology* 39 (Summer 1986), pp. 380–381.
27. James E. Martin, "Predictors of Individual Propensity to Strike," *Industrial and Labor Relations Review* 39 (January 1986), pp. 224–225.
28. N. Nicholson and J. Kelly, "The Psychology of Strikes," *Journal of Occupational Behavior* (October 1981), pp. 275–284.
29. William Serrin, *The Company and the Union* (New York: Knopf, 1973), p. 4.
30. "Testimony of Senator George Mitchell before the Subcommittee on Labor-Management Relations of the Committee on Education and Labor, U.S. House of Representatives," March 30, 1988, *Daily Labor Report,* March 31, 1989, p. F-1-F-3.
31. "Supreme Court Endorses Board Holding That Union Members Can Resign During Strike," *Daily Labor Report,* June 28, 1986, p. AA-1.
32. "NLRB Holds 'Financial Core' Members May Not Be Fined for Crossing Picket Line," *Daily Labor Report,* December 12, 1985, p. A-3.
33. George Getschow, "Strike Woes Pile Up for Leader of Local That Started It All," *The Wall Street Journal,* August 8, 1977, pp. 1, 17.
34. John R. Emshwiller, "Strike is Traumatic for a Quiet Village in Michigan Woods," *The Wall Street Journal,* July 30, 1977, pp. 1, 24.
35. Bernard Karsh, *Diary of a Strike* (Urbana: University of Illinois Press, 1958), pp. 70–73.
36. American Society for Personnel Administration, *Strike Preparation Manual* (Berea, Ohio: American Society for Personnel Administration, 1974). Also see L. C. Scott, "Running a Struck Plant: Some Do's and Don't's," *SAM Advanced Management Journal* 38

(October 1973), pp. 58–62; and John G. Hutchinson, *Management under Strike Conditions* (New York: Holt, Rinehart and Winston, 1966).
37. Theodore W. Kheel, "Is the Strike Outmoded?" *Monthly Labor Review* 96 (September 1973), pp. 35–37.
38. For a discussion of strike costs, see James Stern, "The Declining Utility of a Strike," *Industrial and Labor Relations Review* (October 1964), pp. 60–72.
39. Lloyd G. Reynolds, *Labor Economics and Labor Relations* (Englewood Cliffs, N.J.: Prentice-Hall, 1970), pp. 440–442.
40. Kheel, "Is the Strike Outmoded?" pp. 35–37.
41. John R. Erickson, "Forfeiture of Reinstatement Rights through Strike Misconduct," *Labor Law Journal* 31 (October 1980), pp. 602–616.
42. David B. Stephens and John P. Kohl, "The Replacement Worker Phenomenon in the Southwest: Two years after *Belknap, Inc.* v. *Hale*," *Labor Law Journal* 37 (January 1986), pp. 48–49.
43. K. C. Miller and W. H. Form, Industrial Sociology, 2d ed. (New York: Harper & Row, 1964), pp. 385–388.
44. Dennis M. Byrne and Randall H. King, "Wildcat Strikes in U.S. Manufacturing, 1960–1977," *Journal of Labor Research* 7 (Fall 1986), p. 400.
45. B. A. Brotman, "A Comparative Analysis of Arbitration and National Labor Relations Board Decisions Involving Wildcat Strikes," *Labor Law Journal* 36 (July 1985), p. 440.
46. Walter E. Oberer and Kurt L. Hanslowe, *Labor Law* (St. Paul, Minn.: West Publishing, 1972), pp. 482–483. See *Buffalo Linen Supply Company*, 353 U.S. 85 (1956); and *Brown Food Store et al.* 380 U.S. 278 (1965).
47. Thomas P. Murphy, "Lockouts and Replacements: The NLRB Gives Teeth to an Old Weapon," *Employee Relations Law Journal* 14 (Autumn 1988), pp. 253–261.
48. Ralph M. Dereshinsky, Alan D. Berkowitz, and Philip A. Miscimarra, *The NLRB and Secondary Boycotts*, rev. ed. (Philadelphia: Industrial Research Unit, University of Pennsylvania Press, 1981), pp. 191–195.
49. "Supreme Court Endorses Union Right to Handbill in Support of Consumer Boycott of Shopping Mall," *Daily Labor Report*, April 21, 1989, pp. A-5–A-6.
50. *Tree Fruits*, 377 U.S. 58 (1964).
51. *Forty-Fourth Annual Report of the NLRB* (Washington, D.C.: U.S. Government Printing Office, 1979), pp. 150–151. For thorough discussion, see Robert C. Castle and Richard Pegnetter, "Secondary Picketing: The Supreme Court Limits the *Tree Fruits* Exception," *Labor Law Journal* 33 (January 1982), pp. 3–16.
52. Dereshinsky et al., *NLRB and Secondary Boycotts*, pp. 9– 11.
53. *NLRB* v. *Denver Building Trades Council*, 341 U.S. 675 (1951).
54. Stephen J. Cabot and Robert J. Simmons: "The Future of Common Situs Picketing," *Labor Law Journal* 27 (December 1976), p. 775. A law allowing common situs picketing was passed by Congress but vetoed by President Ford. Another attempt was made in 1977 when President Carter said he would sign the bill; however, the House of Representatives refused to pass the law.
55. *Forty-Fourth Annual Report of NLRB*, p. 147–150.
56. Ibid.
57. Dereshinsky, et al., *NLRB and Secondary Boycotts*, p. 128.
58. Robert J. Deeny, "Secondary Boycotts," in *Strikes, Stoppages, and Boycotts, 1978*, ed. Walter B. Connolly, Jr. (New York: Practicing Law Institute, 1978), pp. 128–135.
59. Dereshinsky, et al., *NLRB and Secondary Boycotts*, pp. 237–239. 237–239.
60. Joshua L. Schwarz and Taryn Shawstad, "Establishing Stability in Labor Law: A Lesson from the Landrum-Griffin Act's Provisions for the Construction Industry," *Labor Law Journal* 38 (December 1987), p. 767.
61. Donald E. Cullen, *National Emergency Strikes* (Ithaca, N.Y.: NYSSILR, Cornell University, 1968), pp. 45–48.
62. U.S. Congress, House, House Document No. 91-266, *Congressional Record* 116, no. 30, 91st Cong., 2d sess., March 2, 1970, p. H1385.
63. Oberer and Hanslowe, *Labor Law*, pp. 901–902.
64. Michael Schuster, "Models of Cooperation and Change in Union Settings," *Industrial Relations* 24 (Fall 1985), pp. 393–394.
65. Mark S. Plovnick and Gary N. Chaison, "Relationship Between Concession Bargaining and Labor-Management Cooperation," *Academy of Management Journal* 28, no. 3 (1985), p. 703.
66. "LTV Corp. Survey on Outlook for Labor-Management Cooperation," *Daily Labor Report*, September 7, 1982, p. E-1–E-2.
67. David L. Cole, "The Search for Industrial Peace," *Monthly Labor Review* 96 (September 1973), p. 37.
68. Sumner H. Slichter, James J. Healy, and E. Robert Livernash, *The Impact of Collective Bargaining on Management* (Washington, D.C.: Brookings Institution, 1960), p. 842.
69. Ted Mills, "Human Resources: Why the Concern?" *Harvard Business Review* 53 (March–April 1975), pp. 127–129.
70. Raymond Katzell et al., *Work Productivity and Job Satisfaction* (Chicago: Psychological Corporation, 1976), p. 95. Also see E. E. Lawler and J. A. Drexler, Jr., "Dynamics of Establishing Cooperative Quality-of-Work-Life Projects," *Monthly Labor Review* 101 (March 1978), pp. 25–27; A. A. Blum, M. L. Moore, and B. P. Fairly, "The Effect of Motivational Programs on Collective Bargaining," *Personnel Journal* 52 (July 1973), pp. 633–641.
71. U.S. Department of Labor, Bureau of Labor Statistics, *Characteristics of Major Collective Bargaining Agreements, July 1, 1980*, Bulletin 2095 (Washington D.C.: Government Printing Office, 1981), p. 32.
72. Kenneth O. Alexander, "Worker Participation and the Law: Two Views and Comment," *Labor Law Journal* 36 (July 1985), p. 433.
73. Donna Sockell, "The Legality of Employee-Participation Programs in Unionized Firms," *Industrial and Labor Relations Review* 37 (July 1984), pp. 541–556.
74. Raymond Hogler, "Employee Involvement Programs and *NLRB* v. *Scott & Fitzer Co.*: The Developing Interpretation of Section 8(a)(2)," *Labor Law Journal* 35 (January 1984), pp. 21–27.
75. Bureau of Labor-Management Relations and Cooperative Programs, *U.S. Labor Law and the Future of Labor-Management Cooperation*, Washington D.C.: U.S. Department of Labor, 1987.
76. Barbara A. Lee, "Collective Bargaining and Employee Participation: An Anomalous Interpretation of the National Labor Relations Act," *Labor Law Journal* 38 (April 1987), pp. 206–219.
77. David A. Gray, Anthony V. Sinicropi, and Paula Ann Hughes, "From Conflict to Cooperation: A Joint Union-Management Goal-Setting and Problem-Solving Program," in *Proceedings of the Thirty-Third Annual Meeting: Industrial Relations Research Association*, ed. B. D. Dennis (Madison, Wis.: Industrial Relations Research Association, 1982), pp. 26–28.
78. *Thirty-Seventh Annual Report, Federal Mediation and Conciliation Service* (Washington, D.C.: U.S. Government Printing Office, 1986), pp. 8–29.
79. Philip E. Ray, "The Retail Food Industry," in *Proceedings of the Thirty-Fourth Annual Meeting: Industrial Relations Research Association*, ed. B. D. Dennis (Madison, Wis.: Industrial Relations Research Association, 1982), pp. 146–149.
80. Laurence P. Corbett, "The Health Care Experience," *Proceed-*

ings of the Thirty-Fourth Annual Meeting: Industrial Relations Research Association, ed. B. D. Dennis (Madison, Wis.: Industrial Relations Research Association, 1982), pp. 156–157.
81. Internal Study by the Federal Mediation and Conciliation Service, June 1, 1987.
82. Douglas Henne, Marvin J. Levine, W. J. Ussery, Jr., and Herbert Fishgold, "A Case Study in Cross-Cultural Mediation: The General Motors–Toyota Joint Venture," *The Arbitration Journal* 41 (September 1986), pp. 14–15; Donald P. Crane and Michael J. Jedel, *Patterns of Industrial Peace,* (forthcoming).
83. "Speakers at Labor Law Conference Stress Theme of Mutual Respect and Cooperation," *Daily Labor Report,* 2-29-88, p. A-1.
84. John Holusha, "No Utopia, But to Workers It's a Job," *The New York Times,* January 29, 1989, pp. 3–10.
85. *New United Motor Manufacturing, Inc., and the United Automobile Workers: Partners in Training* (Washington, D.C.: U.S. Department of Labor, 1987), pp. 1–8.

CHAPTER 8

Contract Administration

"The grievance procedure constitutes the central focus of day-to-day union-management activity."

David A. Peach and E. Robert Livernash, *Grievance Initiation and Resolution: A Study in Basic Steel* (Boston: Harvard University Press, 1974), p. 1.

" 'Voice' refers to the use of direct communication to bring actual and desired conditions closer together. It means talking about problems . . . "

Richard B. Freeman and James L. Medoff, *What Do Unions Do?* (New York: Basic Books, 1984), p. 10.

Labor agreement negotiation is usually the most publicized and dramatic aspect of labor relations. Strike deadlines, negotiators in shirt sleeves working around the clock to avert a possible strike, and the economic settlement of the labor agreement receive attention from the news media. The day-to-day administration of the labor agreement, on the other hand, receives little if any recognition beyond that given by the involved parties.

Yet contract administration is significant as it transforms the negotiated labor agreement. Grievance settlements over a period of time will establish interpretative principles or common laws that supplement or even modify the terms of the agreement. Administration of the negotiated contract gives dynamic meaning to its rather skeletal terms.

During the life of the labor agreement, hundreds (even thousands in a large bargaining unit) of decisions must be made within its confines. Management must decide whom to promote, whom to lay off, whether just cause exists for discipline, and so on. The union monitors these decisions and may file a grievance when they appear inconsistent with the provisions of the agreement.

This chapter first defines employee grievances, then explores their sources and significance. The next section examines the grievance procedure: its typical steps, the relationships among grievance participants, and theoretical as well as practical concerns involved in contract administration. The final section discusses a legal requirement, "fair representation," in the grievance procedure.

Grievances: Definition, Sources, and Significance

An employee **grievance** represents the core of contract administration and is defined as any employee's concern over a perceived violation of the labor agreement that is submitted to the grievance procedure for resolution. A grievance is therefore distinguished from an employee's concern that is unrelated to labor agreement provisions and is not submitted to the grievance procedure. Most grievances are written out, which has several advantages for management and/or union officials:

1. Both union and management representatives need a written record of their daily problem resolutions. This record generates precedents that can guide future actions and save time in deciding similar grievances.
2. Written grievances tend to reduce the emotionalism present in many employee concerns. Verbal confrontation on an emotional issue can produce exaggerated accusations that may irreparably harm the relationship between the parties. Consequently, writing the grievance may be necessary for its rational discussion.
3. Having the concern written out allows management representatives to focus on the employee's original grievance. As will be discussed further, a grievance can proceed through several steps that involve many more individuals than the aggrieved employee. Union officials may alter an employee's initial concern into a broader philosophical issue. (For example, a complaint over the company's unilateral selection of candy bars for the vending machine could conceivably be magnified in subsequent steps to protest the company's arbitrary and capricious actions in other working conditions.) Management always has the option of returning to the concern(s) expressed in the original grievance since it is in written form.
4. Written grievances can benefit management in cases where the employee is apprehensive about signing a written protest. Even though most labor agreements permit a union officer to file a grievance on behalf of the grievant, requiring grievances to be written probably reduces the total number that management representatives must administer.

Our definition of a grievance is extremely broad and hinges on the employee's perception that he or she has a grievance. Assume, for example, that Employee A protests Employee B's "immoral" behavior. This protest could be an oral complaint without reference to the grievance procedure, or the employee could insist the complaint represents a violation of the terms of the labor agreement. The supervisor can attempt to convince the employee that the complaint is unrelated to the terms of the labor agreement.

Yet what happens if the employee insists that the concern is a grievance and should be processed as such? Further, suppose the employee cites a contractual provision in the argument such as an article stressing the "company's obligation to maintain a work environment in as safe a condition as possible." After unsuccessfully discussing the issue with Employee A, the supervisor has two options: (1) to refuse to accept the employee's grievance or (2) to accept the employee's grievance and deny it in the written grievance answer on the basis that there is no contractual violation. Not wishing to risk a time-consuming unfair labor practice charge, the supervisor will probably take the second alternative.

The broad definition of a grievance realizes, then, that there is a difference between accepting an employee's grievance and deciding the merits of an employee's grievance. The broader definition safeguards against unfair labor practice charges and at the same time preserves management's right to deny the grievance in its written answer.

Reasons for Employee Grievances

Some research has focused on differences between employees who do not file grievances and employees who do. One related study found that employees who file grievances are younger, more active in their unions, and less satisfied with their job, supervisor, and union.[1]

In order to better understand the reasons behind employee grievances, the following example is given. A first-line supervisor administers a labor agreement that has the following provisions pertaining to management's rights and the scheduling of work to be performed on a holiday:

Article III: Management Rights

Section 1. The company's right to hire, fire, and direct the working force, transfer or promote is unqualified as long as this right is not used in any conflict with any provision of this contract.

Article IX: Holiday Scheduling

Section 1. When less than a normal crew is required to work on a holiday, the following procedure will apply:

(a) The senior employee working in the classification desired will be given the opportunity to work.

(b) Employees assigned holiday work will be paid a minimum of 8 hours at time and one-half the contract rate of pay.

(c) If an employee works out of classification on the holiday, the senior employee in the appropriate classification will also be paid a minimum of 8 hours at time and one-half his or her contract rate of pay.

With these provisions in mind, consider the following chain of events. A crane operator is needed to work the July 4 holiday. The senior employee in this classification starts work on his shift; however, after he has worked 1/2 hour, the crane breaks down and can no longer be operated. Management believes the maintenance department will be able to repair the crane within 3 hours. All job classifications typically perform some minor housekeeping and cleanup work, such as dusting and picking up debris around the work station; however, there is also a janitor's classification in the labor agreement.

The first-line supervisor has three options. He can send the employee home, although Section 1(b) of the labor agreement compels management to pay that employee 8 hours at one and one-half times the employee's hourly pay rate and the same amount to another employee who is called to work once the crane is repaired. Consequently, the first option is not attractive to management.

The second option would have the employee remain at work and do nothing until the crane is repaired. Since management is already obligated to pay the employee for the entire shift, it does not cost any additional money to have the employee sit in the work shed until crane operations can be renewed. The first-line supervisor is not likely to take this option, particularly if higher-level management officials and other hourly employees see this individual being paid while not performing work.

The third option, having the crane operator perform minor housekeeping chores until the crane is repaired, appears most beneficial to management. Yet there is a good possibility that this action will result in a grievance from the senior employee in the janitorial classification, asking payment for 8 hours at time and a half since Section 1(c) would apparently have been violated. The aggrieved employee could file this grievance for one or more of the following reasons.

1. To Protest a Contractual Violation When labor and management officials negotiate a labor agreement, they are mainly concerned with agreement over the major issues. The negotiations are not concerned with determining the precise meaning of every word in the labor agreement, particularly if there have been few or no previous problems arising from the contract language. Similarly, these officials cannot possibly anticipate all of the unique situations that could potentially distort or add to the negotiated terms of the labor agreement. Consequently, union and management negotiators often gloss over the "unimportant" provisions, leaving potential interpretational problems to those who must live with and administer the labor agreement on a daily basis.

In the crane operator example, local union officials could contend that the crane operator did "work out of classification"—a clear violation of Section 1(c). Management, on the other hand, could contend that the needed holiday work was within the scope of a crane operator's job and point out the impracticality of paying an employee an amount equal to 12 hours pay simply to dust or straighten up the workplace. Another management contention could be that minor housekeeping chores are performed by all employees; therefore, the crane operator did not work out of classification on the day in question. Hence, Article III, "Management Rights," would prevail in this situation.

2. To Draw Attention to a Problem in the Plant Some grievances do not protest violation of the labor agreement; instead, they stress that management has obligations beyond the scope of the labor agreement. Most grievances over alleged safety hazards fall into this category, as few labor agreements specify management's obligation in this area. The employee might realize that there is no contractual violation but still file the grievance to communicate concern to management over a safety issue. In our example, the grievance over holiday scheduling might have been filed, not over receiving payment for the senior janitor in the classification, but in order to give union officers the forum in which to stress the inadequate number of maintenance employees for equipment repair.

Unions quite often draw attention to a problem in the hopes of setting the stage for future labor agreement negotiations. A common union tactic is to file several grievances over a particular issue to buttress and document union demands during negotiation of the subsequent labor agreement.

For example, labor unions adhering to a job-protection philosophy do not want supervisory personnel performing their members' work since these activities could reduce overtime opportunities or even result in employees being laid off. In the course of a workday, supervisors may perform several chores that could be classified as bargaining-unit work. A union wishing to obtain a contractual restriction against supervisors performing bargaining-unit work might encourage employees to file a grievance whenever the supervisor engages in this practice no matter how minor that physical activity may be (for example, changing a light bulb). Armed with several grievances, in formal contract negotiations the union can dramatize its concerns that (1) supervisors performing bargaining-unit work is a widespread problem and (2) a contractual provision restricting supervisors from performing bargaining-unit work would save the company time and money by eliminating related grievances.

3. To Get Something for Nothing Some managers believe that a few employees file grievances to receive pay related to their skill in formulating and writing grievances instead of their work efforts. The janitor in our crane operator example might not have been inclined to file a grievance at the time the work was denied. Indeed, he may have had previously scheduled holiday plans and refused to work if management had made the initial offer. However, assuming the janitor's classification paid $6 an hour, the janitor might have felt that time and one-half for 8 hours ($72) was worth the effort to file a grievance. This payment could be particularly attractive to an individual who did not have to alter holiday plans to obtain it.

Employees filing grievances for this reason find opportunities in the area of overtime administration. A common labor agreement provision requires management to equalize overtime opportunity among qualified bargaining-unit employees desiring overtime. Additionally, management is often contractually required to pay the employee for the overtime worked by another employee if an administrative error was made. For example, assume the following list represents the names of employees in the electrician's classification who signed the daily overtime list, thereby volunteering to work overtime if the assignment occurs after the completion of their normal work shift.

Name of Employee	Number of Overtime Hours Worked and/or Refused Since January 1
A. Jones	89 hours
T. Grant	76 hours
B. Simms	43 hours

The figure to the right of the employee's name represents the number of overtime hours worked by the employee to date and also includes any overtime assignments refused by the employee—if Jones refused to work an 8-hour overtime assignment eventually worked by Grant, both employees are charged the 8 hours. If an overtime assignment for electricians is needed on the day in question, the supervisor checks the overtime list and determines that Simms is lowest in overtime hours.

Consequently, the supervisor would give Simms the first opportunity to accept or refuse the overtime assignment.

Suppose, however, that Simms desires to receive the overtime payment without having to work the overtime assignment. Simms could accomplish this by actively avoiding the supervisor. Confronted with an overtime emergency, the supervisor has to offer the assignment to Grant, the employee next lowest in overtime. The next day, Simms could file a grievance on the "administrative error" and be paid the equivalent of Grant's overtime assignment for no corresponding work effort. Needless to say, this reason for filing a grievance draws management's ire, particularly since some employees appear to make a contest out of acquiring grievance "freebies," or payment for time not worked.

4. To Make the Grievant and Union Feel Important In nonunion settings, the authority of managerial policies and actions often goes unchallenged. However, the grievance procedure permits, and encourages, an employee to protest an alleged wrong committed by management officials. Some employees raise their perceived organizational status by calling their organizational superiors on the carpet to explain their actions. Such grievances are often filed against a supervisor who flaunts authority unnecessarily, to protest the supervisor's personality as well as actions.

Similarly, some union officials wish to emphasize their importance through grievance involvement. Those falling into this category use grievances and contract administration problems to advance to high political office in the union. One research study has found a positive relationship between encouragement of grievances and union rivalry as measured by closeness of vote in the most recent union election. "As incumbent union leaders contend with challenges for member support, they may seek to use the grievance process to extend support for themselves."[2] Grievances in these cases provide a forum where the union steward can demonstrate his or her verbal and intellectual capabilities to other management and union officials. Other union officials might wish to strengthen the union as an institution through the grievance procedure. Here, the importance of the union (not of the union official) is stressed; the union is safeguarding its members from management's arbitrary and capricious actions. A comment of one union steward follows:

> Every so often you'd hear a couple of guys really lambasting the foreman in the washroom—that's where you can really hear the gripes. But when I'd write up the grievance and take it to the fellows, they'd say it was too small. I'd say "the hell with you" and push it anyway.
>
> Soon the company would be coming to me and saying, "Those guys don't have a grievance. They're perfectly satisfied." And I'd say, "The hell they don't. If you don't want to recognize it, I'll take it to the next step." I didn't care if the guys supported me, I went through with it.[3]

There are other reasons employees file grievances. Motives are as varied and complex as the employees' personalities and life experiences. For example, an argument with the employee's family, friends, or work associates might provoke a grievance. Other motives, such as poor employee/job match or a generally poor managerial climate, are perhaps more easily rectified by managerial action. Uncovering the motive behind a grievance may be helpful to management. However, it must be stressed that management must process the grievance even if it feels the employee's motives are illegitimate or improper.

Significance of Employee Grievances

Unresolved employee grievances or concerns can significantly affect both nonunion and union firms. In some cases, unsettled employee grievances or concerns have prompted successful union-organizing drives. In unionized firms, employees often have unique concerns that are neither addressed in collective bargaining nor explicitly covered in the labor agreement. Union officials therefore demonstrate their intent to represent members' particular job interests against conceivable arbitrary managerial actions through the use of the grievance procedure. A union not demonstrating its interest in union members through an effective grievance procedure runs the risk of lawsuits (discussed later in this chapter under "fair representation") or membership dissatisfaction with union leaders.

Employee grievances and the grievance procedure can also serve two important organizational functions: conflict rationalization and communication. The two quotes at the beginning of this chapter reflect the grievance procedure's two major organizational advantages: *conflict institutionalization* and *open upward communication*. Employees at an organization having no grievance procedure who attempt to resolve grievances might create chaos:

> [W]orkers may seek to deal with the management representative they feel has the most clout and thereby undercut the person with the responsibility to act; the management person contacted may pass the buck by stating the problem does not fall within his or her jurisdiction; or workers may seek out the union representative with the most authority to handle their complaint. If settlements are reached, the union may find that they conflict sharply with each other, and as a result, the union may be forced to justify to the membership why one worker received a better grievance settlement than another.[4]

Subsequent employee dissatisfaction with not having a workplace problem resolved might lead to: sabotage (damage of product or equipment), work slowdown, or quitting the job. All of these options are costly to management, particularly when recruiting and training costs of employee replacements are considered.[5]

A grievance procedure, however, institutionalizes conflict. It recognizes that disagreements between employees, management, and the union are inevitable and provides an orderly, consistent approach for resolving differences.

Grievances also represent an open, upward communication channel whereby employees can communicate suggestions to management. Although managers can communicate to employees in a variety of ways, they cannot be assured that employees will in turn generate concerns and suggestions to them. Employee silence does not always equal satisfaction; grievances and the grievance procedure offer the potential for open discussion.

As noted in Chapter 5, nonunion firms might also have grievance procedures to achieve the aforementioned organizational advantages and possibly to preclude a union organizing drive, which will typically stress the benefits of negotiated grievance procedures. However, one related study has found that unionized companies are more likely to have grievance procedures and arbitration (discussed later in this chapter) than their nonunion counterparts.[6]

Steps in the Grievance Procedure

The process for resolving employee grievances is specified in approximately 99 percent of existing labor agreements.[7] However, the procedures are as varied as the labor agreements themselves. Some consist of only one step, whereas others contain as many as nine. While no one grievance procedure is applicable to all labor-management relationships (21 percent of surveyed grievance procedures have two steps, for example), the four-step procedure illustrated in Exhibit 8.1 and discussed here is fairly representative (48 percent of these procedures, according to one survey).

First Step of Grievance Procedure

The first step of the typical grievance procedure consists of two phases. First, the employee (with or without the union steward) discusses the alleged grievance with his or her first-line supervisor. Actually, the employee can file a grievance without any union endorsement. If agreement is not reached, then a written grievance is filed by the grievant or the union steward acting on the grievant's behalf. The supervisor then answers the employee's grievance in writing. Time limits for filing a grievance and managerial response exist in 66 percent and 53 percent of the grievance procedures, respectively.

The purpose of the discussion is to resolve the grievance as early and as informally as possible. However, in some cases, the oral discussion is *pro forma*—the employee initiates this step with a written grievance on the assumption that no amount of discussion will change his or her mind. As is true with the next two steps of the grievance procedure, if the employee accepts management's answer to the written grievance, then the grievance is considered resolved and subsequent steps are unnecessary.

Second Step of Grievance Procedure

In addition to the individuals in the first-step grievance meeting, the union grievance committeeperson and management's industrial relations representative are brought in to discuss the supervisor's first-step grievance answer. Both of these individuals are aware of administrative precedent throughout the entire shop; their main role is to determine whether the grievance should be resolved at this stage on the basis of this precedent.

For example, say Employee A files a grievance protesting management's unilateral action in reducing wash-up time in her work area. The grievance committeeperson might be aware, however, that (1) the contract does not have a provision pertaining to wash-up time and (2) employees in other departments do not receive any time before the end of the shift to clean their hands. Therefore, he or she would probably encourage the grievant to accept the reduction in wash-up time rather than risk losing the privilege entirely in subsequent steps of the grievance procedure.

On another issue—for example, an employee working out of his or her normal work classification and demanding an upgrade in pay for the time worked—the industrial relations representative might reverse the supervisor's first-step answer to avoid sending the grievance to the third step, where it might affect employees with similar work experiences in other departments. The second-step written grievance answer is furnished by the industrial relations representative, and any precedent resulting from this answer usually applies only to the particular work department instead of the entire facility.

Exhibit 8.1 **Example of a Typical Grievance Procedure**

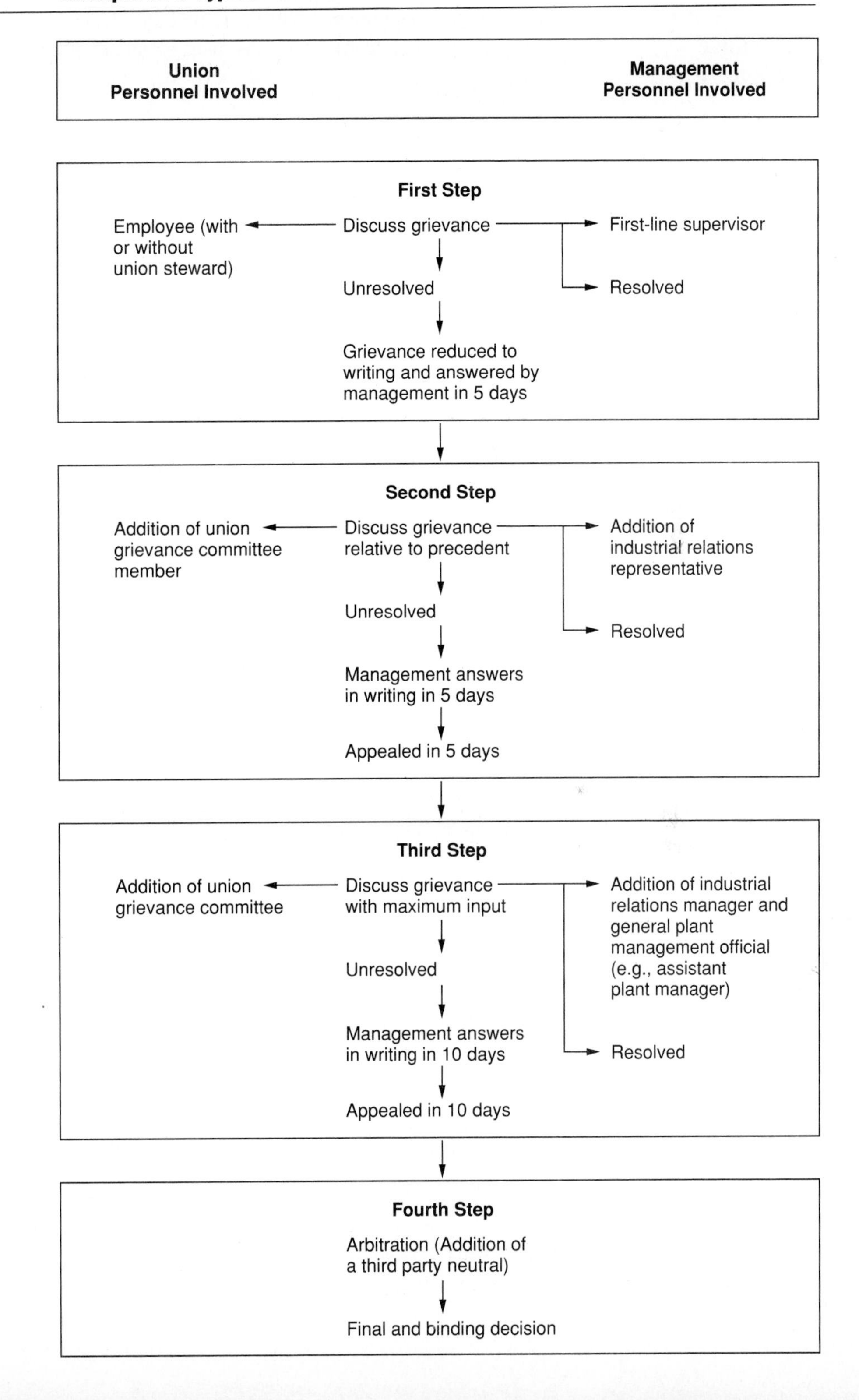

Third Step of Grievance Procedure

The third-step meeting involves the same individuals as the second step but in addition includes the industrial relations manager and another management official (such as a general foreman, superintendent, or assistant plant manager) and members of the union's grievance committee (see Chapter 4). These individuals are added because the grievance answer at this level could affect the entire industrial operation, and both management and union representatives wish to obtain as much input as possible before making the decision.

These additional individuals also serve other purposes, particularly from the union's standpoint. First, the third-step meeting can be used as a training or educational device for relatively new union officers. Since many labor agreements require paid time off for grievance meetings, a new union official can learn the often complex issues and strategies involved in grievance resolution at the company's expense. The union grievance committee can also serve tactical purposes and political functions because the sheer number of individuals on the committee can impress upon the grievant that the union is forcefully representing his or her interests.

Also, the committee can serve as a buck-passing device for the union steward or committeeperson who informs the grievant that he or she did all that was possible to win the grievance but was turned down by other members on the committee. Supervisors can also claim to their managerial counterparts that they were not wrong, merely "sold out" by higher-level management officials.

This step can also serve a therapeutic function for the grievant, who simply wishes to express concern to many levels of management officials. Perhaps the most important function of the third-step meeting is the inclusion of additional union and management officials who are not personally involved in the grievance outcome and can assess its merits with relative objectivity. The third-step grievance answer is usually written by the industrial relations manager because the decision probably will have plantwide implications and applications.

Fourth Step of Grievance Procedure: Arbitration

The final step in the procedure, particularly in the private sector, involves the same individuals as Step 3 and adds a third-party neutral who is selected by both parties, hears the grievance, and makes a final decision resolving the issue. The **arbitration** process is of such significance and complexity that it warrants a more thorough discussion in a separate chapter (see Chapter 9); however, this process terminates the typical grievance procedure.

At first glance, management cannot "win" in arbitration—the best it can expect is for the arbitrator to uphold its original action. Yet management typically exchanges strictures of arbitration for the union's agreement not to strike or stage work disruptions during the term of the labor agreement.

Even though they may vary in terms of steps, time limits for the processing of each step, and participants, all grievance procedures represent a progression of the initial grievance to higher-level management and union officials for consideration. Such procedures written in labor agreements have the drawback of being formal instead of tailored to an individual's personality and concerns. Yet this formality ensures that any bargaining-unit employee can have his or her grievance heard. While many procedures may appear inflexible, they merely serve as the arena for dynamic social relationships and interactions among management and union officials.

Grievance Resolution: Relationships and Flexibility

A wide variety of activities, tactics, and relationships occur between the most frequently involved union and management participants: the union steward and first-line supervisor.[8]

Codified Relationships

Codified relationships stress the rights and privileges of union stewards and first-line supervisors established through the labor agreement and various union and management publications. These publications urge the steward and first-line supervisor to treat each other as "organizational equals" in grievance resolution, and to realize that both benefit from resolving grievances at their level instead of involving higher-level and possibly disinterested officials.

Foremen and union stewards may be aware of normative philosophies and codes but often do not take them into account when interacting. For example, the *AFL-CIO Manual for Shop Stewards* strongly urges union stewards to present their grievances directly to the first-line supervisor in the first step of the grievance procedure.

> It is important to observe the steps in the grievance procedure even if the foreman has limited authority. Leapfrogging to a higher step may have undesirable effects. The lower level of management will resent this and will be more difficult to deal with the next time, or the company may seek to get the grievance thrown out because the proper steps were not followed.[9]

Yet some research has shown that many first-line supervisors believe union stewards violate this aspect of a codified relationship.[10] The supervisors maintain that they are often completely bypassed by the union steward in the grievance process. Indeed, the steward can also bypass the employee involved by filing a grievance in the name of the union. This "bypass capability" given to the union steward is not given to management or to the employee.[11]

Many first-line supervisors do not implement another codified relationship aspect: treating the union stewards as "organizational equals" in the grievance process. It is often difficult for a first-line supervisor, accustomed to giving daily work orders to the union steward, to turn around in a grievance meeting and consider the union steward as a peer. Some first-line supervisors can accept this situation; others have problems:

> This guy, Walker (union steward) here, doesn't realize that the gang is kidding him. They haven't got anything to kick about. All the stuff he is bringing up is old stuff. We've gone over it before with the other representatives. The other representative was sick of the job and gave it up. So the gang decided to elect this squirt because nobody else wanted the job. This fellow doesn't know anything about the department. He's only been there three months. He's only a kid and doesn't know what it's all about. I haven't got time to rehash this all over again. . . . He's not qualified to talk about anything that happens in my department, and I haven't got time to waste with him. He brings up all this stuff and nonsense just so he can be a big shot.[12]

Codified relationships also suggest that first-line supervisors should have authority for resolving grievances at the first step of the procedure in order to give the employee a prompt response. Resolution of grievance at the first step can also help prevent the plantwide precedents that are established in the third step. However, other management officials, who prefer to be kept informed on employee grievances, often instruct the supervisors to inform the industrial relations representative of the situation before taking any action. Indeed, one study found that 27 percent of 800 first-line supervisors believed that higher-level managers sharply curtailed their authority to settle grievances informally or at the first step.[13]

Power Relationships

Conflicting **power relationships** develop in situations where the foremen and union stewards pursue differing interests or goals. This situation has recently characterized shop floor relationships in the steel industry:

> The local unions became highly politicized; any leader who made peaceful overtures to the company was promptly denounced as a "sell-out artist." Union officials and supervisors conducted daily warfare over such matters as discipline, job assignment, and the handling of worker grievances. It was as though each side had to prove to itself, day after day, that it had the capacity to hurt the other.[14]

Power relationships typically begin when both steward and supervisor are encouraged by their superiors to be attentive to problems in the department. The foreman is encouraged to discover problems before they become grievances, whereas the steward is encouraged to talk to the potential grievant before that employee talks to the foreman. Competition for the employee's attention might become particularly intense, as one research study found that stewards and supervisors are equally successful in communicating with employees.[15]

Another type of power relationship results from the union steward's knowing the labor agreement better than the foreman does. Union stewards can concentrate on particular provisions of the labor agreement and their application to the shop. The foreman, on the other hand, has major responsibilities for production scheduling, meeting departmental quality and quantity standards, participating in cost-reduction programs, and so on, which reduce the amount of time available for grievance and labor agreement analyses.

> Most first-line supervisors are screened from both managerial communications networks and meaningful decision making. For example, often they are not informed about the disposition of grievances beyond the first stage. Sometimes union stewards know the results of organizational decisions before the supervisor does.[16]

The steward's relatively superior knowledge of the labor agreement and related grievances is advantageous when he or she discusses the problem one-to-one with the first-line supervisor. One steward emphasizes the results of this practice: "Any steward who knows his stuff can talk rings around a foreman. If he says the foreman's wrong and talks enough, whether he's entirely accurate or not, he's apt to buffalo him."[17]

Intimidation is another power relationship strategy that can be employed by both the union steward and the foreman. In some situations the union steward anticipates that the foreman is vulnerable when he or she receives an excessive number of grievances—the foreman will be concerned with how management officials will react to this apparent inability to resolve labor relations problems. Even though the grievances might not be valid, some management officials might hold the following opinion:

A supervisor who is the subject of grievances creates red flags for us. We expect supervisors to be able to handle most employee relations issues, and if they can't then we question whether or not they have a future with us. I know that grievances are sometimes filed with no justification whatsoever, but on the whole a supervisor who avoids formal grievances looks a lot better to management than a supervisor who's tying up his and our time in grievance hearings.[18]

Consequently, a union steward can use the threat of additional grievances (bogus or real) to persuade the foreman to concede to the grievance in question or to alter the foreman's overall approach to industrial relations. The practice is explained by a union official:

A short time ago we had a lot of trouble with a certain foreman. . . . He was making them toe the line . . . no quitting early, work from whistle to whistle, no sitting down, no horseplay, this and that. I told the committeeman there, "You do the same thing. Every time he does any work, even if he picks up a box, write a grievance. . . ." The first thing you know grievances started mounting–finally had a pile like that.

Things got so bad . . . this foreman was removed from that department. He was moved to our department and it's his last chance. If he doesn't do good in this department, out he goes. So I went to the guy and told him, "It's your last chance here and you know it. You cooperate with us and we'll cooperate with you. If you don't we'll put the screws on you and out you go." Things are working out pretty good so far.[19]

Intimidation tactics are not always one-sided; a clever foreman can make industrial life very difficult for the union steward, probably without incurring an unfair labor practice charge. For example, many job classifications have a wide variety of work assignments, with some of these assignments being less desirable than others. A foreman could assign undesirable work assignments to the union steward, who would have little recourse as long as they were within his or her job classification. The foreman could also undermine the steward's formal position in the union by: (1) restricting the amount of freedom and time for the steward to investigate the grievance and (2) refusing to resolve any grievance in the first step when the union steward is present with the grievant. These tactics are usually successful only if the union steward is inexperienced.

Regardless of the "success" of such actions, a grievance relationship governed by power and intimidation tactics distorts the primary purpose of contract administration, rational decision making.

Sympathetic Relationships

Sympathetic relationships occur between individuals when each is aware of the other's situation and is guided by an understanding appreciation. An example of this appreciation comes from a union steward's comment:

You can't have industrial relations without giving and taking on both sides. You'll always win more cases by getting along with supervision than by being tough. You've got to swap and make trades. . . . Sometimes I have to talk like hell to explain some of the deals I make with them and sometimes I keep what I'm doing to myself if I see a chance to get something good later on. The thing some grievers never get through their heads is that a lot of bosses are on the spot themselves. If you go a little easy on them when they're on the pan, by God–you make friends–they'll stand by you sometime when you're back of the eight ball. Some-

> times when I have a rotten grievance, I'll take the case up to the supe [superintendent] and let him know I won't push it hard.[20]

Sympathetic relationships are aided when the first-line supervisor and the union steward realize that they both occupy marginal positions within their own organizations. For example, one study found that first-line supervisors can have a rather loose identification with upper management. This might be due to several factors, including transient upper and middle management and reconsideration of the supervisor's original decision by other management officials.[21]

Union stewards have also experienced this situation in contract administration. On one hand, constituents expect their union steward to actively press every grievance, reasoning that the union's sole purpose is to represent its members. Consequently, it is difficult for the steward to accept the foreman's first-step rejection of the grievance, even if he or she feels the foreman is correct. On the other hand, union officials receiving the grievance in subsequent steps of the grievance procedure may tend to view the union steward as either ignorant of the labor agreement or gutless.

Flexible Consideration of Employee Grievances

The preceding varieties of interpersonal relationships reveal how individual objectives, strategies, and personalities force the contractual procedure to be more flexible in practice. This real-world consideration negates the theoretical principle that each grievance be considered on its individual merits. The grievant wishes to receive an answer uncolored by any political or tactical concerns, but the union must consider political influence and overall strategy in its determination of which grievances will be filed and pursued. Not all grievances are clear-cut issues; in fact, many involve confusing or opposing interpretations of the labor agreement. In these cases, management has two options—decide the grievance in the employee's favor or appeal the grievance to arbitration. The latter alternative is not always attractive, particularly if management realizes there is little contractual guidance in the issue (as in the example on the holiday scheduling of a crane operator) and insufficient past practice or precedent to support the decision. There are many gray areas in contract administration that are open to interpretation. This uncertainty is compounded when the parties solicit a neutral party to resolve the issue in binding arbitration. Also, the arbitrator's decision might refute management's action in terms that further erode management's discretion in future matters. Unions also tend to use arbitration only as a last resort because arbitration cases can drain the union's treasury.

In these instances, flexibility may be possible with the addition of an informal **third and one-half step** in the grievance procedure. This step is not found in the grievance procedure specified in the labor agreement. It occurs after management's "final" third-step decision but before the arbitrator hears the grievance. During the third and one-half step meetings, management and union representatives meet to discuss and trade grievances, dispatching several cases originally scheduled for arbitration. Usually the grievances involved in the negotiated package are settled "without prejudice to either party's position" in future related issues. This statement preserves management's discretion on these issues and the union's right to file future related grievances.

Opponents of this practice contend that valid employee grievances are bargained away for an expedient settlement. Grievance trading in the third and one-half step can also discourage first-line supervisors from actively trying to resolve grievances if they believe their efforts will be overturned in a mass grievance settlement. For example, the following remarks were made by a foreman who had sent an employee home for repeated tardiness. The employee filed a grievance with the foreman's supervisor, who sent the employee back on the job.

> I went over to O'Brien's (the superintendent's office) to find out why he had overruled me. He handed me a line of salve about "having to do it." Said "it was a small item after all" and that he "might want a big favor from the union sometime in the future." He said, "We have to trade back and forth. Sometimes we give in; sometimes they give in. That's why we never have any big trouble!" Then he said he might have to reverse some of my decisions again sometime, but if he did, not to get sore about it, because he wouldn't mean no offense by it. Well damn that noise! If O'Brien wants to make me look like a fool every time I make a decision, why by God, he can make all the decisions. You know two can play that game. I can give the boys (workers) every damn thing he can give them. Then when they come up with a big one that I know well he can't give them, I'll tell 'em to take it up to him.[22]

As a result of management using the third and one-half step in the grievance procedure, unions might be encouraged to file more grievances in the belief that they can obtain more from a trade involving 50 fabricated grievances than they can from 5 legitimate ones. Furthermore, those settlements "without prejudice" can result in more grievances of the same sort since the issues are not considered jointly resolved by management or union officials.

Advocates state that this process merely represents another legitimate cooperative effort between labor and management officials in efficiently dealing with day-to-day administrative problems. These individuals indicate that the union's and management's organizational self-interests require considerations and possible use of the third and one-half step grievance trading session. Opponents state that the third and one-half step hinders the union's fair representation obligation discussed next.

The Legal "Fair Representation" Obligation in the Grievance Procedure

Thus far we have discussed grievance procedures from the perspectives of the union, management, and employee participants. As is true with most labor relations activities, grievance resolution can be strongly influenced by the fourth participant, the government. As noted in Chapter 5 the union has the right to be the exclusive bargaining agent for all employees in the appropriate bargaining unit. This right has a corresponding *fair representation* legal responsibility to represent all of the bargaining-unit employees, union members and non–union members alike. This section focuses on the extent of the union's obligation, particularly when some of the bargaining-unit employees believe the union has acted in an unsatisfactory manner.[23]

The fair representation issue is one of the most difficult to resolve. On the one hand, there must be some sacrifice of individual freedom if the union wishes to effectively represent its members. However, the individual member's right to dissent must also be protected, and all employees represented must be safe from negligent or corrupt representatives. The Railway Labor Act and the National Labor Relations Act add to this issue's complexity, since they do not contain any explicit provisions obligating the union to represent fairly all bargaining-unit employees.[24]

Fair representation has been subsequently interpreted by the courts. Related decisions have reasoned that the purpose of labor legislation, industrial peace, imposes on the union the duty of fair representation.[25] While unions cannot completely ignore certain bargaining-unit employees, the following question remains: How far must the union go in representing employees whose interests or claims could potentially disrupt union goals and policies? The importance of this question is magnified when we consider that there are many decisions that help some members while hurting others. However, if unions were required to process contradictory claims, nothing would be accomplished.

One such double-edged issue is seniority. Union actions pertaining to this issue (such as merging seniority rosters and calculating seniority credits for employees returning from the armed services) will hurt some bargaining-unit members while helping others. Not surprisingly, two Supreme Court cases involving fair representation concerned the seniority issue.[26] These decisions indicated that the union must consider all employees and make an honest effort to serve the interests of all members without hostility to any. However, the decisions also realized that unions cannot effectively operate if they must press every unit member's concern to the fullest:

> Inevitably, differences arise in the manner and degree to which the terms of any negotiated agreement affect individual employees and classes of employees. The mere existence of such differences does not make them invalid. The complete satisfaction of all who are represented is hardly to be expected. A wide range of reasonableness must be allowed a statutory bargaining representative in serving the unit it represents, subject always to complete good faith and honesty of purpose in the exercise of its discretion.[27]

Thus, the union satisfies its fair representation obligation in collective bargaining and enforcing the labor agreement if it considers the interests of all members and takes its ultimate position honestly, in good faith, and without hostility or arbitrary discrimination.

These rather broad guidelines were also applied in another landmark Supreme Court decision, *Vaca* v. *Sipes,* which considered the union's fair representation obligation in the grievance procedure. A bargaining-unit employee claimed that the union "arbitrarily, capriciously and without just or reasonable reason or cause" refused to take his grievance to arbitration. The employee, a long-term high blood pressure patient, returned to work after a sick leave and was judged by the company's doctor as being unfit for reemployment. The employee's personal physician as well as a second doctor indicated that the employee was fit for work; therefore, the employee asked the union to seek his reinstatement through the grievance procedure. The grievance was processed; however, the union, in attempting to strengthen its case before going to arbitration, sent the employee to a third doctor. The third doctor did not support the employee's position; therefore, the union refused to take the employee's case to arbitration.

The Supreme Court decided that the union, in this case, acted in good faith and was neither arbitrary nor discriminatory. It also indicated (in this and in another case) the following:[28]

- The employee has the burden of proof in establishing that the union breached its fair representation obligation.
- Fair representation does not require the union to take every grievance to arbitration, since this would create an intolerable expense for the union and management, and would destroy the effectiveness of the lower steps in the grievance procedure.

Currently, fair representation poses two difficult questions to the union and employer. First, what are specific types of conduct that constitute violation of the fair representation duty? As previously noted, the Supreme Court has given only broad benchmarks ("arbitrary," "bad faith," "dishonest," and so on). Sometimes these guidelines can be rather easily applied; for example, a union refusing to process grievances of any black, female, or nonunion employees is clearly guilty of violation.[29] Other cases can become more complicated. The union, while not obligated to take every grievance to arbitration, has an obligation to consider the merits of the grievance[30] and effectively use the grievance procedure. In some cases the courts have determined that union "perfunctory conduct" (simply going through the motions) makes the union liable for breach of fair representation.[31] Related actions include

- Providing inadequate defense of the grievant at an arbitration hearing.
- Delaying grievance processing until the time limits in the grievance procedure have expired. This violation can include failing to file a timely request for arbitration,[32] although at least one judicial decision has indicated that a union does not violate fair representation if it does not appeal an arbitrator's award to the courts.[33]
- Failing to inform the grievant that the union accepted a different remedy than that asked for by the grievant.[34]
- Failing to keep members informed about an arbitration award that affects members' seniority rights.[35]

Yet some courts have suggested that negligence or "honest mistakes" alone will not constitute a fair representation violation since union members always have the option of voting in new officers or even a new union to do a better representation job.[36]

A second question concerns employer and union liability if the union does not file a grievance. Employees currently can sue the union and the employer for breach of the labor agreement including fair representation under Section 301 of the National Labor Relations Act. Assume, for example, that an employee is discharged, then later establishes that the union breached its duty of fair representation. Both organizations can be liable according to the Supreme Court in its *Bowen* v. *United States Postal Service* decision.

Bowen, an employee for the Postal Service, was discharged for an altercation with another employee. Bowen sued both the union and the employer in the district court. His evidence at trial indicated that the responsible union officer, at each step of the grievance procedure, had recommended pursuing the grievance but that the national office, for no apparent reason, had refused to take the matter to arbitration. The jury found that the service had discharged Bowen wrongfully and that the union had breached its fair representation obligation.

The Supreme Court eventually found that both the employer and the union contributed to this wrongful discharge. The employer of course made the initially wrong termination decision and therefore owed Bowen reinstatement with some of his back wages. However, the court also agreed that the union also owed Bowen a portion of his lost wages since he could not have proceeded independently of the union but if the union had arbitrated his grievance, he would have been reinstated. It also contended that joint employer-union liability might be in the interest of national labor relations policy.

> In the absence of damages apportionment where the default of both parties contributes to the employee's injury, incentives to comply with the grievance procedure will be diminished. Indeed, imposing total liability solely on the employer could well affect the willingness of employers to agree to arbitration clauses as they are customarily written.[37]

The Bowen case has controversial implications for the labor-management relationship. Managers believe that they should not be held accountable for the union's errors, particularly since management is legally prohibited from dealing in the internal affairs of the union. However, it can easily be argued that the union would not have violated the law in the first place if the company had not wrongly discharged the employee. There is also the possibility that this decision would encourage the union to take many marginal grievances to arbitration to avoid any possible breach of fair representation and related financial liability. This situation, while potentially detrimental to the labor-management relationship, has not yet been verified in research.

This chapter has suggested the variety of reasons for filing employee grievances and of relationships involved, and the organizational and legal significance of grievance procedures. These characteristics have prompted many recent research efforts into employee grievances.[38] "Labor Relations in Action" explores some assumptions inherent in many of these efforts.

Summary

Employee grievances and grievance administration extend collective bargaining by giving dynamic meaning to the negotiated terms of the labor agreement. Grievances are broadly defined as any employee's concern over a perceived violation of the labor agreement that is submitted to the grievance procedure for resolution.

An employee might file a grievance for any of various reasons, such as to protest a contract violation, to draw attention to a problem in the plant, to get something for nothing, or to feel more important. Regardless of motives for filing grievances, management must process them through the grievance procedure specified in the labor agreement.

Although no one grievance procedure applies to all labor-management relationships, two important aspects of a typical grievance procedure are inclusion of higher-level management and union personnel and, particularly in the private sector, binding arbitration by a third-party neutral. Grievance procedures typically of-

Labor Relations in Action

Considerations Affecting Research into Employee Grievances

Richard Peterson has estimated that employees file some 11,000,000 grievances in the United States each year. This figure carries tremendous time and cost implications for management, a situation that should encourage investigation by both practitioners and academics. Seemingly logical research focal points are grievance statistics such as:

- Grievance rates (number of grievances filed per 100 employees, for example).
- Proportion of grievances settled at each step in the grievance procedure.
- Percentage of grievances where management modified its original position.

Grievance statistics cannot be completely dismissed, as they directly summarize related behavior. However, reliance on these figures is presumably based on two assumptions.

Assumption One: The number of grievances can be quantified, since a discrete number of grievances, which are clearly decided in either management's or the union's favor, are filed by specified grievants in an organization or organizational unit. Some studies have either implicitly or explicitly used this assumption when comparing grievants versus nongrievants, analyzing sociodemographic characteristics (age, race, sex, or seniority, for example) of those employees who file grievances, or comparing grievance statistics between departments or organizations. These studies might overlook the following situations, which are allowed in most organizations:

- A grievance can be filed by a union steward or committeeperson on behalf of the affected employees, some of whom might never desire to contest the issue. Grievant differences might therefore refer more to differences among union officers than to differences among employees.
- Grievances typically can be initiated and signed by an unlimited number of employees. Should a grievance signed by 12 employees count 12 times as much as a grievance signed by one employee, particularly if many of the 12 signed the grievance under pressure from coworkers?
- As noted earlier in this chapter, management and union officials might settle grievances on political grounds instead of contractual merits. The aforementioned third and one-half step in the grievance procedure where many grievances are traded and classified as settled further distorts the distinction between "won" and "lost" grievances.

Assumption Two: Differences in grievance statistics can be compared and clearly translated into qualitative aspects of the labor-management relationship since grievances are inherently negative and should be avoided. This assumption might seem plausible at first glance. An issue may be resolved without a grievance being filed, and the absence of a grievance "statistic" apparently reflects a positive relationship between union and management officials.

But there are many instances where a lack of grievances indicates a poor labor-management relationship. In some cases, supervisors might believe that they will be criticized by higher-level managers for having a large number of grievances in their departments. Grievances can of course be precluded by giving the union everything it wants. In other cases a low number of grievances might reflect an incompetent union steward, one who does not know labor agreement provisions, or one who fears managerial retaliation if a grievance is filed.

This assumption also ignores the many different motives behind grievance filing. The union might be filing and processing grievances to press a point for future negotiations or to satisfy its legal fair representation obligations. Employees might file grievances because of factors and motives unrelated to managerial style (problems at home or the desire to "get something for nothing," for example).

Grievance statistics often do not show basic differences between grievance topics and the number of employees who are or could be affected by the grievance's resolution. A grievance protesting the exclusion of a

(continued)

(continued)

candy bar from a vending machine might represent the personal crusade of one or a few employees whereas a grievance protesting subcontracting of a major operation could have great impact on the daily labor-management relationship and subsequent contract negotiations. This potentially wide variation among grievance topics and their merits and significance often curtails a meaningful statistical comparison.

Finally, this assumption considers grievances to be either reflective of or contributing to a bad labor-management relationship. As previously noted in this chapter, grievances, while involving the time of many organizational officials, can offer the advantages of conflict institutionalization and upward communication. A study might therefore have difficulty when it considers grievances to have a uniformly negative impact on the participants in the labor relations process.

Some studies have apparently considered the aforementioned shortcomings of grievance statistics, and have focused instead on one or more of the following related subjects:

- *Union member attitudes toward the grievance procedure.* These attitudes might for example be concerned with the procedure's "fairness." A situation where many see this decision making process as unfair might be subsequently associated with fair representation lawsuits or union decertification. Union members' attitudes toward the grievance procedure's results (whether it strengthens or weakens job security, for example) have also been researched.
- *Post-grievance behavior of participants.* For example, are some participants more likely to leave the organization or have more absenteeism? Another related area could be subsequent election results of union officials who have been relatively inactive or active in grievance filing.
- *Innovative grievance resolution procedures*[39] *that could offer both labor and management officials advantages over the traditional grievance procedure.*

These research areas might still reflect some assumptions inherent in grievance statistics or create additional assumptions that might limit industrial applicability. However, industrial relations research on significant topics such as grievances that attempts to account for its assumptions will benefit academics and practitioners alike.

---

fer an organization two major advantages: conflict institutionalization and open upward communication. However, the grievance procedure as actually carried out involves a variety of behavioral dimensions, including social relationships (codified, power, and sympathetic) enacted among the grievance participants in resolving the grievance according to appropriate contractual provisions. The variety of personalities and motives of the participants suggests a flexible approach in grievance resolution instead of considering each grievance on its individual merits.

Unions have a legal obligation to fairly represent their members in the grievance procedure. While unions do not have to take each grievance to arbitration they must consider and process grievances in an effective, good faith manner. Legal complications can arise when the courts determine whether the union has violated its fair representation obligation and whether the employer should be financially liable for this activity.

There has been a recent surge of research on employee grievances. This topic has great academic and practical potential although, as suggested by the "Labor Relations in Action," extensive reliance on grievance statistics might be counterproductive.

Key Terms

grievance
arbitration
codified relationships
power relationships
sympathetic relationships
third and one-half step

Discussion Questions

1. There is a thin line differentiating employee grievances and employee complaints. Discuss the problems involved in defining a grievance, indicating why a broad definition of employee grievances is both confusing and necessary.
2. Discuss two reasons grievances might be filed, furnishing examples of these reasons other than those found in the text.
3. Why does a typical grievance procedure have so many steps, since the employee is either right or wrong, and a one- or two-step procedure would save time and money? In your answer, discuss the various functions, opportunities, and problems each of the grievance steps can offer.
4. Why is it difficult for union and management officials to resolve each grievance on its own merits?
5. Briefly discuss the broad judicial guidelines concerning unions' fair representation obligations to members. Also discuss the reasoning behind these guidelines, furnishing some appropriate examples.

References

1. Robert E. Allen and Timothy J. Keaveny, "Factors Differentiating Grievants and Nongrievants," *Human Relations* 38 (November 1985), p. 529.
2. Chalmer E. Labig, Jr., and I. B. Helburn, "Union and Management Policy Influences in Grievance Initiation," *Journal of Labor Research* (Summer 1986), pp. 269–284.
3. Leonard R. Sayles and George Strauss, *The Local Union,* rev. ed. (New York: Harcourt, Brace & World, 1967), p. 50.
4. Bob Repas, *Contract Administration* (Washington, D.C.: Bureau of National Affairs Inc., 1984), p. 61.
5. Richard B. Freeman and James L. Medoff, *What Do Unions Do?* (New York: Basic Books, 1984), p. 10.
6. Casey Ichniowski and David Lewin, "Characteristics of Grievance Procedures: Evidence from Nonunion, Union, and Double-Breasted Businesses," *Proceedings of the Fortieth Annual Meeting of the IRRA* (Madison, Wis.: IRRI, 1988), p. 415.
7. Bureau of National Affairs Inc., *Basic Patterns in Union Contracts* (Washington, D.C.: Bureau of National Affairs Inc., 1989), p. 33.
8. See, for example, Ralph Arthur Johnson, "Grievance Negotiation: An Analysis of Factors Popularly Associated with Success," *Labor Studies Journal* 9 (Winter 1985), pp. 271– 279.
9. *AFL-CIO Manual for Shop Stewards* (n.p., n.d.), p. 37.
10. John A. Patton, "The First Line Supervisor: Industry's Number One Problem," *Business Management* 40 (September 1971), p. 38. See also Ken Jennings, "Foremen's Views of Their Involvement with the Union Steward in the Grievance Process," *Labor Law Journal* 25 (September 1974), p. 541.
11. William D. Todor and Dan R. Dalton, "Union Steward: A Little Known Actor with a Very Big Part," *Industrial Management* 25 (September–October 1983), pp. 7–11.
12. Paul Pigors, "The Old Line Foreman," in Austin Grimshaw and John Hennessey, Jr., eds., *Organizational Behavior* (New York: McGraw-Hill, 1960), p. 98.
13. Michael E. Gordon and Roger L. Bowlby, "Propositions about Grievance Settlements: Finally, Consultation with Grievants," *Personnel Psychology* 41 (Spring 1988), p. 120.
14. John P. Hoerr, *And the Wolf Finally Came* (Pittsburgh: The University of Pittsburgh Press, 1988), p. 22
15. P. Christopher Earley, "Supervisors and Stewards as Sources of Contextual Information in Goal Setting: A Comparison of the United States with England," *Journal of Applied Psychology* 71 (February 1986), pp. 111–117. See also Mick Marchington and Roger Armstrong, "Typologies of Union Stewards," *Industrial Relations Journal* (Autumn 1983), p. 44.
16. Steven Kerr, Kenneth D. Hill, and Laurie Broedling, "The First-Line Supervisor: Phasing Out or Here to Stay?" *Academy of Management Review* 11 (1984), p. 106.
17. James W. Kuhn, *Bargaining in Grievance Settlement* (New York: Columbia University Press, 1961), p. 29.
18. David Lewin and Richard B. Peterson, *The Modern Grievance Procedure in the United States* (New York: Quorum Books, 1988), p. 195.
19. Delbert C. Miller and William Form, *Industrial Sociology,* 2nd ed. (New York: Harper & Row, 1964), pp. 401–402.
20. Melville Dalton, "Unofficial Union-Management Relations," *American Sociological Review* 15 (October 1950), p. 613.
21. Marc G. Singer and Peter A. Veglahn, "Correlates of Supervisor-Steward Relations," *Labor Studies Journal* 10 (Spring 1985), pp. 46–55.
22. Melville Dalton, "The Role of Supervision," in Arthur Kornhauser, Robert Dubin, and Arthur Ross, eds., *Industrial Conflict* (New York: McGraw-Hill, 1958), pp. 183–184.
23. For related legal violations (unfair labor practices), see Paul A. Brinker, "Labor Union Coercion: The Misuse of the Grievance Procedure," *Journal of Labor Research* 5 (Winter 1984), pp. 93–102.
24. Edward H. Nakamura, "The Duty of Fair Representation and the Arbitral Process," in Joyce M. Najita, ed., *Labor Arbitration for Union and Management Representatives* (Honolulu: Industrial Relations Center, University of Hawaii, 1976), p. 87.
25. See, for example, *Steele* v. *Louisville and N. R. R.,* 323 U.S. 200; and Harry H. Wellington, *Labor and the Legal Process* (New Haven, Conn.: Yale University Press, 1968), p. 146. For a more detailed account of jurisdictional issues between the NLRB and the courts over fair representation cases, see Benjamin Aaron, "The Duty of Fair Representation: An Overview," in Jean T. McKelvey, ed., *The Duty of Fair Representation* (Ithaca, N.Y.: Cornell University, 1977), pp. 8–16; and Timothy J. Boyce, *Fair Representation: The NLRB and the Courts* (Philadelphia: The University of Pennsylvania, 1978).
26. *Ford Motor Co.* v. *Huffman et al.,* 345 U.S. 320 (1953); and *Humphrey* v. *Moore,* 375 U.S. 335 (1964).

27. Ibid., p. 339.
28. *Vaca* v. *Sipes,* 386 U.S. 191 (1967); and *Amalgamated Association of Street, Electric, Railway and Motor Coach Employees of America* v. *Wilson P. Lockridge,* 403 U.S. 294 (1971).
29. For an example of a relatively straightforward breach of fair representation, see *Hines* v. *Anchor Motor Freight Inc.,* 424 U.S. 554 (1976).
30. Marvin J. Levine and Michael P. Hollander, "The Union's Duty of Fair Representation in Contract Administration," *Employee Relations Law Journal* 7 (Autumn 1981), p. 203.
31. Jeffrey A. Swedo, "*Ruzicka* v. *General Motors Corporation:* Negligence, Exhaustion of Remedies, and Relief in Duty of Fair Representation Cases," *Arbitration Journal* 33 (June 1978), pp. 6–15. For a discussion of varied judicial interpretations of fair representation, see Aaron, "Duty of Fair Representation: Overview," pp. 18–21; and Clyde W. Summers, "The Individual Employee's Rights under the Collective Agreement," in *Duty of Fair Representation,* pp. 60–83.
32. "Union Held Liable for Late Arbitration Request," *Daily Labor Report,* August 2, 1983, p. 2.
33. "Fair Representation Duty Ends with Arbiter's Award," *Daily Labor Report,* November 14, 1984, p. 2.
34. Robert W. Kopp, "The Duty of Fair Representation Revisited," *Employee Relations Law Journal* 5 (Summer 1979), pp. 6–10.
35. "Union Failure to Publicize Award Held Fair Representation Breach," Bureau of National Affairs Inc., *Daily Labor Report,* no. 112 (August 13, 1984), p. 1.
36. "Ineptitude Does Not Breach Duty of Fair Representation," *Daily Labor Report,* June 9, 1983, p. 2. See also *Daily Labor Report,* April 28, 1983, p. 4.
37. *Daily Labor Report,* June 11, 1983, p. D-5. See also T. Charles McKinney, "Fair Representation of Employees in Unionized Firms: A Newer Directive from the Supreme Court," *Labor Law Journal* (November 1984), pp. 693–700.
38. For a fine research framework for grievances, see Michael E. Gordon and Sandra J. Miller, "Grievances: A Review of Research and Practice," *Personnel Psychology* 37 (Spring 1984), pp. 117–146. See also David Lewin, "Empirical Measures of Grievance Procedure Effectiveness," *Labor Law Journal* 35 (September 1984), pp. 491–496; Thomas R. Knight, "Feedback and Grievance Resolution," *The Industrial and Labor Relations Review* 39 (July 1986), pp. 487–501; Richard B. Peterson and David Lewin, "A Model for Research and Analysis for the Grievance Process," in B. D. Dennis, ed., *Proceedings of the Thirty-Fourth Annual Meeting: Industrial Relations Research Association* (Madison, Wis.: Industrial Relations Research Association, 1982), pp. 303–312; Dan R. Dalton and William D. Tudor, "Antecedents of Grievance Filing Behavior: Attitude, Behavioral Consistency and the Union Steward," *Academy of Management Journal* 25 (March 1982), pp. 158–169; Casey Ichniowski, "The Effects of Grievance Activity on Productivity," *Industrial and Labor Relations Review* 39 (October 1986), pp. 75–89; David A. Peach and E. Robert Livernash, *Grievance Initiation and Resolution: A Study in Basic Steel* (Boston: Harvard University Press, 1974); Chalmer A. Labig, Jr., and I. B. Helburn, "Union and Management Policy Influences on Grievance Initiation," *Journal of Labor Research* 7 (Summer 1986), pp. 269–277; Paul F. Clark and Daniel G. Gallagher, "Membership Perceptions of the Value and Effect of Grievance Procedures," *Proceedings of the Fortieth Annual Meeting of the IRRA* (Madison, Wis.: IRRA, 1988), pp. 406–413; Richard B. Peterson, "A Multiple-Measure Test of Grievance Procedure Effectiveness," *Proceedings of the Fortieth Annual Meeting of the IRRA* (Madison, Wis.: IRRA, 1988), pp. 398–405; Michael E. Gordon, "Grievance Systems and Workplace Justice: Tests of Behavioral Propositions about Procedural and Distributive Justice," *Proceedings of the Fortieth Annual Meeting of the IRRA* (Madison, Wis.: IRRA, 1988), pp. 391–397; and Thomas R. Knight, "Correlates of Informal Grievance Resolution Among First-Line Supervisors," *Relations Industriel* 41 (no. 2, 1986), pp. 281–291.
39. For insights into related procedures, see Steven Briggs, "Innovative Approaches to Complaint/Grievance Resolution," *Labor Law Journal* 33 (August 1982), pp. 454–459; Mollie H. Bowers, Ronald L. Seeber, and Lamont E. Stallworth, "Grievance Mediation: A Route to Resolution for the Cost-Conscious 1980s," *Labor Law Journal* 33 (August 1982), pp. 459–466; Gordon A. Gregory and Robert E. Rooney, Jr., "Grievance Mediation: A Trend in the Cost-Conscious Eighties," *Labor Law Journal* 31 (August 1980), pp. 502-508; S. B. Goldberg and J. M. Brett, "An Experiment in the Mediation of Grievances," *Monthly Labor Review* 106 (March 1983), pp. 23–30; and Stephen B. Goldberg, "Grievance Mediation: A Successful Alternative to Labor Arbitration," *Negotiation Journal* 5 (January 1989), pp. 9–16.

CHAPTER 9

Labor Arbitration: A System of Industrial Jurisprudence

The American system of voluntary grievance arbitration is unique among industrialized nations. More importantly, it works. Indeed, it is perhaps the only aspect of our industrial relations system that is widely accepted by labor, management, and the public.

Jack Steiber, "The Future of Grievance Arbitration," *Labor Law Journal,* June 1986, p. 366.

Resolving labor disputes in an arbitral forum is a fascinating process that involves a host of diverse, and often conflicting, dynamics. Each participant enters arbitration with his or her unique pressures and expectations, often with little or no understanding of the perspectives of the other players.

Christine D. Ver Ploeg, "Labor Arbitration: The Participants' Perspective," *Arbitration Journal* 43 (March 1988), p. 36.

The preceding quotations indicate that arbitration is both a significant and an uncertain process. Arbitration might even exert more influence than grievances on labor-management relationships since the arbitrator's decision often establishes a binding precedent for similar issues.

Rights or grievance arbitration is found in almost every labor agreement and is used far more today than interest or collective bargaining arbitration. Labor and management officials have typically had a long, successful tradition of rights arbitration whose scope is narrow (resolving one grievance). Interest arbitration, on the other hand, can have a very broad scope, including many unresolved labor agreement issues. Few parties are willing to place this much responsibility in the hands of a third-party neutral.

This chapter will consider only grievance or "rights" arbitration, which concerns the interpretation and application of provisions of the existing contract; interest arbitration over terms of a new contract is discussed in Chapters 7 and 14. Arbitration is first discussed from a historical perspective; then elements of a typical arbitration proceeding and arbitrator's decision are described. Current jurisdictional issues involving the arbitrator and various government agencies are also discussed, and, finally, the process is appraised.

Development of Labor Arbitration

1865 through World War II

Arbitration was first used in the United States in 1865, but was used rarely before World War II, when it was used by the War Labor Board. In many cases employee grievances were resolved through sheer economic strength. For instance, a union desiring resolution of a particular grievance often needed to mobilize the entire work force in a strike against the employer—a difficult task—before the company would attempt to resolve the grievance. Union and management officials were legally free to ignore the arbitrator's decision if they did not agree with it.

Other factors limiting the early growth of arbitration were the relatively few unionized facilities and the vague language found in labor agreements, which gave little contractual guidance for the arbitrator's decision. Consequently, the early arbitration process combined elements of mediation and humanitarianism in an effort to reach a *consensus decision,* one that would be accepted by both parties to a grievance. The arbitrator under these circumstances had to draw on diplomatic and persuasive abilities to convince the parties the decision should be accepted.

Arbitration's popularity increased during World War II, when President Roosevelt's Executive Order 9017 provided for final resolution of disputes interrupting work that contributed to the war effort. Essential features of this order included a no-strike, no-lockout agreement and a **National War Labor Board** (NWLB) comprised of four management representatives, four union representatives, and four representatives of the public—all presidential appointees. The board was to encourage collective bargaining and, if necessary, resolve disputes over the terms of the agreements.

The advent of World War II encouraged the role of arbitration in several ways. Many union and management officials realized that uninterrupted wartime production was essential and that grievance resolution was more effectively accomplished through arbitration than through strikes.

The NWLB urged labor and management officials to resolve their own disputes and encouraged the parties to carefully define the arbitrator's jurisdiction in the labor agreements. Thus, the board gave any negotiated restrictions full force when deciding cases and denied arbitration where it was reasonably clear that the arbitration clauses meant to exclude a subject from arbitral review. It further defined grievance arbitration as a judicial process, thereby limiting a decision solely to the evidence presented at the hearing.

Results of the NWLB's activities further popularized and enriched the arbitration process, as the board resolved some 20,000 disputes during its tenure.[1] Additionally, these efforts served as a training ground for many arbitrators, who were able to apply their acquired skills to the arbitration process after the war. In fact, some NWLB members are still active.

The Postwar Years and the Steelworkers' Trilogy

Although the use of arbitration increased during World War II, the relationship among arbitrator, management, and union officials was far from resolved.[2] Both parties still remained legally free to ignore the arbitrator's award. In 1957, however, the Supreme Court declared in its *Lincoln Mills* decision that an aggrieved party could legally bring suit against a party that refused to arbitrate a labor dispute for violation of the labor agreement, under Section 301 of the Taft-Hartley Amendments.

Thus, grievance procedures including arbitration could be subjected to judicial review, although much confusion remained over the court's role in these activities.

Either party could refuse to submit the grievance to arbitration if the labor agreement did not cover the issue in question. Some state statutes that made the agreement to arbitrate enforceable resulted in attempts to persuade the court to compel arbitration of various issues. Many courts then became involved in assessing the merits of a particular grievance and whether it should be arbitrated. These actions, of course, contradicted arbitral belief that arbitrators alone should rule on the merits of the grievance. Confusion resulted when labor and management representatives played the courts against the arbitrators in their attempts to obtain favorable decisions.

In 1960 the Supreme Court clarified and strengthened the arbitrator's role with three decisions commonly referred to as the **"Steelworkers' Trilogy."** The first was *United Steelworkers of America* v. *American Manufacturing Company.* In this case, the union brought suit in district court to compel arbitration of a grievance involving an employee who was awarded 25 percent disability pay on a permanent basis. Two weeks after this determination the union filed a grievance charging the employee was eligible according to the seniority provisions of the labor agreement to return to the job. Management contended that the grievant was physically unable to perform the job and that this type of dispute was not arbitrable under their labor agreement. After reviewing the merits of the grievance, both the district court and court of appeals upheld management's action. However, the Supreme Court noted that there were no explicit restrictions placed on arbitration in the labor agreement; therefore, the grievance procedure should be given "full play" in the resolution of the dispute. Accordingly, the Supreme Court reversed the lower courts' decision with the following reasoning:

> The function of the court is very limited when the parties have agreed to submit all questions of contract interpretation to the arbitrator. It is confined to ascertaining whether the party seeking arbitration is making a claim which on its face is governed by the contract. Whether the moving party is right or wrong is a question of contract interpretation for the arbitrator. . . .
>
> The courts, therefore, have no business weighing the merits of the grievance, considering whether there is equity in a particular claim, or determining whether there is particular language in the written instrument which will support the claim. The agreement is to submit all grievances to arbitration, not merely those which the court will deem meritorious. The processing of even frivolous claims may have therapeutic values of which those who are a part of the plant environment may be quite unaware.[3]

In the second case of the Trilogy, *United Steelworkers of America* v. *Warrior and Gulf Navigation Company,* the union filed a grievance over employee layoffs that were in part due to management's contracting out work previously performed by bargaining-unit employees. The collective bargaining agreement did state that "matters which are strictly a function of management shall not be subject to arbitration." Again, both the district court and court of appeals reviewed the merits of the grievance and decided against the union on the reasoning that contracting out was within management's discretion. However, the Supreme Court decision noted that the employment relationship generates a common law born out of the experiences of a particular industrial facility. The experiences and precedents shaping this common law also clarify the often vague terms and conditions expressed in the labor agreement. The reliance on common law suggests that the labor arbitrator is more effective than the courts in interpreting and resolving a dispute over the terms of an existing labor agreement.

> The labor arbitrator's source of law is not confined to the express provisions of the contract, as the industrial common law—the practices of the industry and the shop—is equally a part of the collective bargaining agreement although not expressed in it. The labor arbitrator is usually chosen because of the parties' confidence in his knowledge of the common law of the shop and their trust in his personal judgment to bring to bear considerations which are not expressed in the contract as criteria for judgment. The parties expect that his judgment on a particular grievance will reflect not only what the contract says but, insofar as the collective bargaining agreement permits, such factors as the effect upon productivity of a particular result, its consequence to the morale of the shop, his judgment whether tensions will be heightened or diminished. . . . The ablest judge cannot be expected to bring the same experience and competence to bear upon the determination of a grievance, because he cannot be similarly informed.[4]

In assessing the exclusion from arbitration provisions, the Supreme Court interpreted "strictly a function of management" to mean that in which the contract expressly "gives management complete control and unfettered discretion." This issue would not have been arbitrable had there been an explicit statement excluding contracting out from the arbitration process. Since there was no related contractual language, the Supreme Court believed the arbitrator (not the lower courts) should resolve the contracting out issue.

These two decisions underscored the arbitrator's role in interpreting the labor agreement, particularly in determining whether the grievance should be arbitrated. However, the role of the arbitrator in fashioning an appropriate grievance remedy remained unsettled until the case of *United Steelworkers of America* v. *Enterprise Wheel and Car Corporation.* This decision concerned a grievance over management's dismissal of a group of employees who walked out of the plant to protest the discharge of another employee. Management refused to arbitrate the grievance; however, the district court, considering the union's suit under Section 301, ordered the case arbitrated. Eventually, the arbitrator determined that the employees should be reinstated to their jobs with back pay for all but 10 days (to be considered as a disciplinary suspension). Management, noting that the labor agreement had expired before the arbitrator's decision was rendered, challenged the arbitrator's authority to fashion the reinstatement remedy. While the district court compelled compliance with the remedy, the court of appeals furnished advice as to what would constitute an appropriate remedy. Justice Douglas, in writing the Supreme Court's opinion, drew upon the previous decision and indicated the relatively superior knowledge arbitrators have in resolving industrial disputes:

> A mere ambiguity in the opinion accompanying an award, which permits the inference that the arbitrator may have exceeded his authority, is not a reason for refusing to enforce the award. Arbitrators have no obligation to the court to give their reasons for an award. To require opinions free of ambiguity may lead arbitrators to play it safe by writing no supporting opinions. This would be undesirable for a well reasoned opinion tends to engender confidence in the integrity of the

process and aids in clarifying the underlying agreement. Moreover, we see no reason to assume that this arbitrator has abused the trust the parties confided in him and has not stayed within the areas marked out for his consideration. It is not apparent that he went beyond the submission.[5]

In summary, the Steelworkers' Trilogy greatly enhanced the authority and prestige of the arbitrator in interpreting the terms of the labor agreement and the merits of a particular grievance. It also endorsed the arbitrator as most qualified to fashion a resolution of a grievance if it is based on the essence of the labor agreement. However, the Supreme Court has recently reaffirmed that the courts should determine whether a grievance should be submitted to arbitration when one party refuses, on the basis of its contention that the labor agreement excludes this particular subject from the arbitration procedure.[6] Other related decisions are presented in the next section.

Legal Obligations to Arbitrate and Enforce Arbitration Decisions

The Supreme Court has determined that the obligation to arbitrate a grievance cannot be nullified by a successor employer[7] or by the termination of a labor agreement. Management representatives in this latter situation argued that arbitration is a feature of the contract that ceases to exist when a contract terminates; therefore, a grievance cannot be processed to arbitration if the labor agreement is no longer in effect. Consequently, management representatives felt that the issue of severance pay was not subject to arbitration since the labor agreement had expired and management had decided to permanently close its operations. However, the Supreme Court indicated that arbitration was still appropriate, since the parties continued to express confidence in the arbitrator's expertise and in arbitration as a prompt, inexpensive alternative to lawsuits.[8]

Another issue resolved by the Supreme Court in recent years concerns how far the courts are willing to go in enforcing the role of the arbitrator. More specifically, what happens when one party is willing to arbitrate a grievance while the other party prefers to use the strike or lockout in order to resolve a dispute? As previously mentioned, a strike was a plausible alternative in resolving a grievance in the early years of arbitration. Also, the Trilogy did not specifically consider this alternative in its conclusions.

The award enforceability issue was brought before the courts in 1969 when a union protested a work assignment given to non–bargaining-unit personnel. The union expressed its concern by striking even though the labor agreement contained a provision for arbitrating disputes over the terms of the agreement. In federal district court, management officials stressed that the union should use the contractually specified arbitration procedure and be enjoined or prevented from striking the employer. The Supreme Court agreed in its *Boys Market* decision.[9]

Elements of a Typical Arbitration Proceeding

Selection and Characteristics of Arbitrators

The Supreme Court has encouraged the use of arbitration, contending that this essentially private process is best suited to labor relations issues and to the unique needs of the parties at a particular facility. This means there are no universally applicable rules concerning arbitration hearings. For example, the number of participants (even arbitrators) can vary; also, the location of the hearing might be at the production facility, a hotel room, or a courtroom. There are, however, some considerations and procedures that are common to most, if not all, arbitration hearings.

First, the number of arbitrators needed to resolve a grievance must be determined. Sometimes (in about 15 percent of the related labor agreement provisions) the labor agreement specifies a three-member arbitration board or panel, with management and the union each nominating a member and these two individuals selecting the third member (a single arbitrator). Most decisions are made by the impartial arbitrator since the other two members of the panel are influenced by their respective management and union constituents, although the impartial arbitrator does consult with the other members. The most common method (approximately 75 percent of related provisions), however, is for the impartial arbitrator selected by management and union officials to be solely responsible for the decision, with no help from other individuals in formulating the written decision. In either case, the arbitrator's decision is final and binding unless, in extremely rare circumstances, both management and the union agree to disregard or set aside the arbitrator's award.

About 6 percent of the labor agreements in the United States provide for a **permanent arbitrator** or umpire to resolve all disputes during the life of the labor agreement.[10] Usually, this provision applies to large companies or industries, in which it is anticipated that a large number of grievances will be filed. Presumably, the permanent arbitrator can better allocate and schedule time to meet the grievance load of the union and employer, so that settlements can be reached more promptly. This type of selection arrangement also allows the permanent arbitrator to become more knowledgeable of the complex and unique terms of the parties' labor agreement and industrial operation. Assume, for example, that an arbitrator is hearing a grievance in the railroad industry for the first time. How long would it take for the arbitrator to accurately interpret the meaning of the following witness's testimony?

> At 3 p.m. Mott Haven Yard was a busy place. A crew of gandy dancers tamped methodically on a frong near the switching lead. L.S. 3 was all made up and ready to be doubled over. She had forty-six hog racks on the head end and sixty-five empty reefers on the hind end. Her crew were all new men on the run. Mike Madigan, the hog-head, had just been set up. Bill Blanchard, the fire-boy, was a boomer who had recently hired out. Jack Lewis, the brains of the outfit, had been a no bill since he was fired out of the Snakes for violating Rule "G." Brady Holms, the flagman, used to work the high iron in a monkey suit, and J. B. Wells was a "stu" brakeman, right off the street. Over the hump lead, the yard rats were riding 'em in the clear and typing 'em down. The east side switcher was kicking loaded hoppers around, despite the violent washouts of the yardmixer who had discovered a hot box. Two Malleys were on the plug and three more were at the coal pocket. Our train, Number B.D.5, was all ready to pull out.[11]

A permanent arbitrator saves time and expense since the parties do not have to repeatedly explain the meaning of these terms in the arbitration hearing. Greater consistency can be attained where one individual applies the same decision-making criteria to all of the arbitrated grievances. Consistent decisions aid union and management officials in the day-to-day administration of the labor agreement. They also should enable the parties to better predict the arbitrator's subsequent decisions on similar issues, perhaps decreasing the number of frivolous grievances referred to arbitration as the parties become more certain of the arbitrator's reasoning. On the other hand, a retainer paid to the permanent arbitrator might encourage the parties to increase the grievance case load so that they can "get their money's worth."

Most labor agreements specify an **ad hoc arbitrator,** meaning that the arbitrator will be selected on an *ad hoc,* or case-by-case, basis; union and management representatives choose an arbitrator for a specific grievance, then select other arbitrators for subsequent grievances arising during the life of the labor agreement. Particularly in the case of an established collective bargaining relationship, management and the union often reach an informal agreement regarding the appropriate arbitrator for a particular grievance. However, if they cannot agree, they usually obtain a list of arbitrators' names from either the Federal Mediation and Conciliation Service or the American Arbitration Association. In some cases when the parties cannot agree on an arbitrator from the list provided then they might request that these organizations select an arbitrator.

Clearly, for unions and companies having few grievances, ad hoc arbitrators are less expensive than permanent arbitrators. Regardless of the grievance load, ad hoc arbitration offers the advantage of flexibility. Permanent arbitrators usually are appointed by the parties for a specified period of time; neither side can discontinue the appointment alone if it views the permanent arbitrator's decisions with disfavor. There is no obligation to retain the ad hoc arbitrator in future grievances if one or both sides are displeased with the award.

Since some ad hoc arbitrators specialize in particular categories of grievances, such as job classification or wage incentives, they should be better informed than the permanent arbitrator on such issues. Permanent arbitrators may be more familiar with the parties, but may have seldom encountered a particular issue in their arbitration experience. Since both types of arbitrators have comparative advantages and disadvantages, management and union officials should carefully assess their particular situation before agreeing to either selection method.

Two surveys of arbitrator characteristics have found that arbitrators are likely to be males over 50 years of age with more than 14 years experience as an arbitrator and a law degree or a graduate degree in another discipline.[12] Arbitrators' characteristics can be significant for at least two reasons. First, union and management officials select an arbitrator possessing certain characteristics that might, according to one study, include name recognition, reputation for integrity, and a specific geographic location. Another study found that employers tend to prefer arbitrators with training in economics, while unions prefer arbitrators who have legal training.[13]

Second, there is at least the possibility that certain background characteristics might influence arbitrators' decisions. One study, however, found little correlation between arbitrators' age, experience, and education, and the decision outcome,[14] although another found some evidence to suggest that male arbitrators were more lenient with female than with male grievants in discipline cases.[15]

Prehearing Briefs

Prehearing briefs, which highlight the issues and positions of the parties, can be filed by management and union representatives before the arbitrator arrives at the hearing. These briefs alert the arbitrator to the matters he or she will face at the hearing. These optional briefs, which are uncommon, vary in length from a one-page letter to an extensively footnoted document.

The prehearing brief might backfire for the presenting party, who is subject to challenges on the assumed facts and inconsistencies that may surface in the witnesses' testimonies. On the other hand, prehearing briefs can be viewed as keeping the parties honest—they tend to approach their contentions thoroughly and are forced to adhere to them during the arbitration proceedings.

Perhaps more arbitrators would agree to the value of *prehearing stipulations*—joint union-management statements as to the issues involved and certain applicable grievance "facts." They save time in the arbitration hearing, for neither party feels obligated to repeat what the other has either previously said or agreed to in principle. Additionally, through the process of working together to stipulate the issues and facts, the parties may be able to resolve the disputes without arbitration. If briefs or stipulations are not agreed to prior to the hearing, the parties will have to educate the arbitrator on the background of the case.

The Arbitration Hearing

Held on a date convenient to the arbitrator and parties, the **arbitration hearing** varies in length from half an hour to 10 or more hours. Union and management officials from the grievance site (the local union president and the labor relations manager, for example) will likely be at the hearing, and might present their versions of the arbitration case. However, either party might defer to another presenter, such as an international union representative or corporate manager of industrial relations, at the hearing. Sometimes one or both parties might employ an attorney, who is likely, according to recent research, to discourage pre-arbitrated settlements between union and management and increase the use of pre- and post-hearing briefs.[16]

Variations also occur in the extent to which courtroom procedures and behaviors are used or required during the hearing. Usually, the union and management representatives initiate the proceedings with opening statements that establish their respective issues and contentions on the issues. They attempt to focus the arbitrator's attention on points that they will attempt to prove in the subsequent discussion.

One arbitrator has noted the following paradox: the union and management officials own the arbitration hearing but the arbitrator is in charge of it. Union and management officials wrote the labor agreement and hired the arbitrator. Therefore, the arbitrator should not treat the process as his or hers, act like a judge, be arrogant, or talk too much.

> Let the parties do the talking, work out the problems. You will be surprised how many knotty issues will be resolved during the hearing if you just ask the other side to respond, and then ask the original side to add something, and so on. By the time they have killed off each other's contrariness, the problem has disappeared.
>
> Do not try to take their procedure away from them. Give it back whenever they try to abdicate or place the burden of procedure on you. For example, it is an old ploy for one party or the other to say, Mr. or Ms. Arbitrator, do you want us to put in some evidence on this subject? This can put you into a trap. If your answer is no, then it is your fault when they lose the case because you excluded crucial evidence. If you say yes, then you are implying that the subject is important. Tell them it is up to them. Remind them that this is an adversary proceeding to elicit information and that it is their obligation to select whatever information they think is important.[17]

Yet the arbitrator must obtain sufficient information to fashion a final decision having important implications for the participants.

The *grievance issue* (or submission agreement) to be resolved in the arbitration hearing is often complex, although it may be stated with deceptive simplicity. It is usually a one-sentence question to be answered by the arbitrator's award. Typical examples are

- Did the company violate Section VI, Part 3, of the labor agreement when it transferred S______ S______ from the position of leadman to Welder III?
- Was B______ B______ discharged for just cause? If not, what shall be the remedy?
- Did the duties of Machinist A's job undergo a significant change, thereby allowing the company to change the wage scale?
- Did J______ J______'s off-the-job activities have a sufficiently adverse effect on the company to justify dismissal?

Unfortunately, the issue is not always agreed upon by union and management representatives, and the arbitrator has to frame the issue after hearing the case. The holiday scheduling grievance example in Chapter 8 illustrates the problems surrounding issue information. Assume, for example, that the labor agreement has two provisions pertaining to arbitration:

Article XX: Arbitration Procedures
Section 1. The arbitrator's authority is solely derived from the clear and unequivocal terms of the labor agreement.
Section 2. The arbitrator may not add to, subtract from, or otherwise modify the express terms of the labor agreement.

In this situation, the union would claim that the issue pertains to the senior janitor's entitlement to holiday pay for the time involved due to the violation of Section 1 on the day in question. Management would contend that the issue of arbitrability is at stake, questioning whether the arbitrator has the authority to hear the case.[18] The determination of the specific grievance issue could take a lot of time, but it is important, for the nature of the issue often determines whether the grievance is upheld or denied.

The major part of the hearing is devoted to the presentation of (1) the opening statement by each party's spokesperson, in which the major issues and background of the case are presented to the arbitrator, (2) union and management witnesses for testimony and cross examination, (3) related evidence to support union and management contentions (such as pictures of a job site, warning letters, performance ratings, and so on), and (4) union, management, and joint exhibits (such as the collective bargaining agreement and the employee's written grievance). The hearing is concluded with summaries and closing statements by the union and management representatives that stress why their respective positions should be accepted by the arbitrator. However, closing arguments and summaries are usually not presented when the parties submit posthearing briefs.

One or both parties can file a written *posthearing brief* after the arbitration proceedings have ended. This device can be helpful when the arbitration case is very technical or complicated or includes statistical data that are difficult to explain in an oral argument. In many cases, however, a posthearing brief is unnecessary if the parties have prepared and presented their cases well during the hearing.

This summary of arbitration proceedings does not do justice to the considerable effort and drama in preparing and presenting an arbitration case. "Labor Relations in Action" gives some techniques for preparing for an arbitration hearing.

Mental effort, skill, and tensions are not eliminated once the hearing begins. Assume for example that you are an industrial relations manager charged with proving an employee deserved discharge for smoking marijuana on company premises. Related concerns are

- How do you prove the employee actually smoked the marijuana, since the evidence was destroyed, and it is the employee's word against supervisory observations?
- Will the grievant's testimony be strengthened or broken under cross-examination?
- How long can the supervisor remain calm under union cross-examination, without losing his temper?
- What if the arbitrator gives little weight to the circumstantial evidence presented by the company and a great deal of weight to the grievant's previous long and exemplary work record with the company?
- Will the union introduce a surprise contention or witness not previously discussed in the grievance proceedings (for example, that the grievant's discharge was due to the racial bias of the supervisor)?

Management and union officials often enter arbitration hearings emotionally charged and uncertain. They are usually skillful in establishing their respective positions to the arbitrator's satisfaction, and damaging their opponents' case by exploiting the opponents' weaknesses and uncertainties. The arbitrator must also display many skills in keeping an orderly hearing while at the same time objectively understanding and recording all of the facts presented.

Arbitration and Judicial Proceedings Compared

The arbitration proceedings share some similarities with judicial proceedings, but their differences are profound. Many arbitration hearings differ from courtroom proceedings in that testimony of witnesses is not taken under oath and transcripts of the proceedings are not taken. Except in a few states, arbitrators do not have the power to subpoena witnesses, and arbitrators nearly always have much more latitude than judges in determining admissibility of evidence, including, for example, hearsay testimony. Arbitrators accept evidence under the general guideline proposed by management/union arbitration participants: "For whatever it is worth."

Common Law of the Shop

The most significant difference between arbitration and judicial proceedings is the arbitrator's reliance on **common law of the shop** principles in the resolution of disputes. Arbitrators, unlike judges, are selected by the parties to the dispute, and they are responsible for interpreting contract provisions that were negotiated and written by the parties to cover the specific location. Judges are responsible for interpreting laws that were enacted by state and federal legislatures.

Labor Relations in Action

Preparation Techniques for the Arbitration Hearing

1. Study the original statement of the grievance, and review its history through every step of the grievance machinery.
2. Review the collective bargaining agreement. Often, clauses that at first glance seem to be unrelated to the grievance will be found to have some bearing.
3. Assemble all documents and papers you will need at the hearing. Make photostatic copies for the arbitrator and for the other party. If some of the documents you need are in the possession of the other party, ask that they be brought to the arbitration. The arbitrator [might have] authority to subpoena documents and witnesses if they cannot be made available in any other way.
4. Interview all of your witnesses. Make certain they understand the theory of your case, as well as the importance of their own testimony. Run through the testimony several times. Rehearse the probable cross examination.
5. Make a written summary of the testimony of each witness. This can be useful as a checklist at the hearing to ensure that nothing is overlooked.
6. Study the case from the other side's point of view. Be prepared to deal with opposing evidence and arguments.
7. Discuss your outline of the case with others in your organization. A fresh viewpoint will often disclose weak spots that you may have overlooked.
8. Read published awards on the issues that seem to be involved in your case. While awards by other arbitrators on cases between other parties are not decisive as to your own case, they may be persuasive. The American Arbitration Association has published summaries of thousands of labor arbitration awards in its monthly publications. Use these summaries and their cumulative indexes as a research tool.

Source: Robert Coulson, *Labor Arbitration—What You Need to Know*, 3rd ed. (New York: American Arbitration Association, 1981), pp. 51, 52.

Thus, the arbitrator's major responsibility is to resolve a dispute in a manner that the parties can live with. Unlike judicial decisions in lower courts, the arbitrator's decision is usually final and not subject to further appeals. Consequently, the arbitrator must be concerned with the subsequent effects of his decision on union-management relationships. A judge has no such allegiance to the particular parties, the major responsibility being adherence to the statute in question, to established courtroom and legal procedures, and to precedent resulting from other applicable cases.

The common law of the shop often narrows the scope of arbitral decision making to the labor agreement language, intent of the parties, and past practices of the union and management officials at a particular industrial facility. The arbitrator uses these elements to convey to the union and management participants that their grievance is being resolved in terms of shop floor realities.

The distinction between judicial reasoning and common law of the shop principles can be shown through the following example. Assume that an employee has been discharged at Company A for drinking alcohol on the job. After an arbitral decision upholding the discharge has been reached, an employee at Company B is also discharged for drinking alcohol on the job. Strict adherence to judicial principles would uphold the second employee's discharge for drinking on the job. More specifically, the judicial principle of *stare decisis* (letting the decision at Company A stand in Company B's situation) would probably disregard the differences in work environments of the two companies.

However, the common law of the shop principles governing arbitration could lead the arbitrator to render an opposite decision at Company B than that reached at Company A. For example, supervisors at Company B may have been condoning this behavior and other employees at this company may have been caught drinking on the job without being discharged for the infraction. Consequently, the arbitrator recognizes the two companies are independent with potentially unique circumstances, and therefore deserve mutually exclusive decisions.

Evidence in Arbitration versus Judicial Proceedings

It is also important to note that arbitrators are much more liberal than the courts in the types of evidence permitted at the hearing. For example, lie detector tests (polygraphs) have been allowed by some arbitrators under certain conditions (having the administrator of the polygraph present for cross examination), although their use and weight in the arbitrator's decision remains controversial.[19] Usually, arbitrators give this evidence little weight unless the obtained information is corroborated by supporting evidence. The rationale for liberal admission of evidence is that the parties are seeking a solution to their perceived unique problem. In addition, some arbitrators maintain that arbitration performs a therapeutic function, that the parties are entitled to air their grievances regardless of the eventual decision. Arbitrators may allow aggrieved employees to digress from the pertinent subject or "tell it like it is" in front of higher-level union and management officials in order to serve this function.

Occasionally, new evidence is introduced by one or both parties in the arbitration hearing. The arbitrator may accept or reject this new evidence, depending upon the weight attached to the following sometimes conflicting considerations: (1) the arbitrator's desire to learn all of the pertinent facts surrounding the grievance, (2) the need to protect the integrity of the pre-arbitral grievance machinery, and (3) general concepts of fairness.[20] Since union and management officials and their designated arbitration panels are entitled to receive all evidence presented at the hearing, it may be necessary to allow the opposing party additional time to review and respond to new evidence.

Offers of compromise settlements before the hearing are given no weight by the arbitrator. Management officials, for example, might compromise their third-step discharge decision before arbitration by offering the grievant reinstatement with no back pay. A union could use this evidence to indicate to the arbitrator that management admitted being wrong by revising its original decision. However, arbitrators maintain that the parties should make every effort to resolve their disputes internally instead of going to arbitration. Thus, a compromise settlement between the parties is viewed by the arbitrator as a genuine attempt to accommodate differences, not an admission of guilt.

Other types of evidence are subject to varying arbitral consideration. As previously cited, hearsay testimony is usually admitted; however, it is typically given little or no weight, particularly if it is deduced that the witness has self-serving motives for testifying. Many of the more controversial sources of evidence are presented in discipline cases, which are further discussed in Chapter 10.

The Arbitrator's Decision

Characteristics and Scope

The *arbitrator's decision* is a written document submitted to the management and union officials. Its components are as follows:

1. A statement of the issue(s).
2. A statement of the facts surrounding the grievance.
3. Names of union and management representatives involved in the case, along with others who gave testimony.
4. Pertinent provisions of the labor agreement.
5. A summary of the union and management contentions.
6. A discussion and opinion of the validity and relative weight of the facts and contentions.
7. The arbitrator's award (grievance upheld, grievance denied, or a compromise between union and management contentions).

Few proscriptive guidelines govern the form and content of the arbitrator's decision. However, the arbitrator should demonstrate through the decision a thorough understanding of all the facts and contentions raised in the arbitration hearing. Some arbitrators address the decision to the losing party in the arbitration hearing because the winner does not have to be convinced he is right.

The necessity of the arbitrator's opinion has been subjected to considerable controversy. At least one labor lawyer has suggested that the arbitrator's decision is important, but not the opinion explaining the reasoning behind the decision.

> I turn to the award and find out whether I won or lost. If I won, I really am not concerned with why I won. If I lost, I may read the opinion in order to confirm my conviction created by the award that the arbitrator was, is, and undoubtedly will continue to be as blind as a bat and as ignorant as an ass.[21]

The contrary view maintains that the arbitrator's opinion performs a necessary function for the arbitrator and others who may read his or her decision.

> The parties do not retain counsel, then spend days in preparation and more days in hearing simply to find out whether Jones rather than Smith should have been promoted from the labor pool to machine operator. The parties are interested in principles and guidelines for the future. For their future guidance, they are entitled to the arbitrator's findings of fact, his or her view of the evidence, understanding of the respective contentions of the parties, and finally, the relevant interpretation and application of the parties' agreement.[22]

The decision should tell the parties what will happen to their dispute and why. "Ideally, an opinion convinces the losing party that its arguments were heard, that the system used to decide its case is a fair one, and that the result makes sense."[23] Thus, the arbitrator's decision should *educate* the parties (including other union and management officials, who often select an arbitrator after researching his or her published decisions) within the context of the common law of the shop and established arbitration principles.

One survey found that an overwhelming majority of union and management officials believed that arbitrators should gear their decisions to the presenters responsible for the case and its possible precedents, and not to the grievants, who likely have a very narrow perspective.[24] As noted later in this chapter, the arbitrator also realizes that his or her decision, if appealed by one of the parties, might be reviewed by the courts to determine whether related labor legislation was considered.

In some cases, the arbitrator's opinion can be even more important than the award. Assume, for example, the union grieves management's assignment of work normally performed in Job Classification A, loading trucks on Saturday, to an employee in Job Classification B, a laborer. Further, the union seeks a remedy of 8 hours at overtime rate of pay for the appropriate employee in Job Classification A, the senior employee in the shipping department, on the reasoning that the company's violation of the contract had deprived a Classification A employee from the overtime opportunity. However, the arbitrator denies the grievance and stresses the following in his opinion: "The various job classifications are for pay purposes only and do not restrict management's prerogative to assign work across different job classifications." This statement significantly harms the union in related matters, particularly if the language was not expressly stated in the labor agreement. Now the union will have a difficult time in grieving any work assignment controversy, even though the above decision pertained to one specific situation.

In other situations the arbitrator's gratuitous advice in the opinion may harm one or both of the parties. There is often a thin line between advising management and union practitioners on more effective and humane ways to run the operation and arbitrating the grievance solely on the merits of the case. The latter approach does not advise, but merely determines if management's action was justifiable under the terms of the labor agreement and applicable *past practice* (which will be discussed later in this chapter).

Decision-Making Criteria Used by Arbitrators

There are few consensually defined principles applicable to arbitrators' decisions, as arbitrators do not follow precise or identical methods in making decisions. Nonetheless, generally accepted guidelines have been developed and serve as focal points subject to interpretation, consideration, and application by arbitrators in resolving grievances.

Provisions of the Labor Agreement Obviously, an important criterion will be the provisions of the labor agreement, which reflect the collectively bargained rights of union and management officials. Adherence to common law of the shop principles stresses that the major function of the arbitrator is the interpretation of the labor agreement's provisions. Indeed, many arbitrators adhere at least in part to the **parole evidence rule,** which in its classic form holds that evidence, oral or otherwise, cannot be admitted for the purpose of varying or contradicting written language recorded in the labor agreement. Rationale for this rule is that the parties have spent many hours in negotiating standardized employment conditions; thus, disregarding negotiated terms would damage stable labor-management relationships and communicate to the parties that there is little or no point in reducing contract terms to writing. The *parole evidence* rule is applicable when the parties "intend that the written agreement is the final and complete integration of all the terms of the contract."[25]

A problem remains when the labor agreement language is ambiguous, since it normally cannot prescribe all essential rules or guidelines for day-to-day administration of industrial relations. Also, many labor agreement terms, such as "reasonable," "make every effort," "minor repairs," and "maintain the work environment as safely as possible" might have resolved negotiation impasses but still pose interpretive problems for the arbitrator.

Some contract provisions that appear clear on the surface can cause differences of opinion among union and management officials as well as arbitrators. Consider the following three examples and related questions.[26]

Example 1: "The company will provide required safety equipment." Does the company have to pay for safety equipment or merely make it available for employees to purchase?

Example 2: "An employee must work on the scheduled day before and after the holiday in order to receive holiday pay." What happens when the employee works 3 hours the day before the holiday, goes home because of sickness, and works the full 8 hours the day after the holiday?

Example 3: "Management will distribute overtime as equally as possible." Does a supervisor making overtime request calls to employees' homes stop making such calls until contact is made with an employee whose telephone is busy or goes unanswered?

Arbitrators prefer to approach the ambiguity problem initially in terms of the labor agreement, and ambiguous language or provisions of the labor agreement would be construed so as to be compatible with the language in other provisions of the agreement. Thus, the contract should be viewed as a whole, not in isolated parts, and any interpretation that would nullify another provision of the contract should be avoided. When ambiguity remains, the arbitrator must seek guidance from sources outside the labor agreement.

Intent of the Parties Another guideline, the **intent of the parties,** refers to what union and management officials had in mind when they (1) negotiated the labor agreement or (2) engaged in an action that resulted in a particular grievance. Intent is entirely subjective; however, arbitrators consider observable behavioral manifestations of the intent to determine what a reasonable person would conclude from that behavior. For an example of labor agreement intent, consider the previously cited holiday pay situation. To demonstrate that it intended for holiday pay to be given only to those individuals who worked a full 8 hours the day before and the day after the holiday, management might supply the arbitrator with negotiation notes. The parties will retain copies of their proposals, counterproposals, and compromises to prove what they intended the contract language to mean. Arbitrators are strongly influenced by this evidence of intent since they are reluctant to give in an award what could not be obtained at the bargaining table.

An example of an action's intent might occur when a supervisor believes an employee has stolen some company property. The supervisor approaches the employee stating the following:

> You and I both know you were caught stealing. Therefore, you have two options. You can file a grievance which will be denied in arbitration and the discharge on your record will make it difficult for you to find a job elsewhere. Or you can sign this resignation slip, quit, and we won't tell any other companies about the stealing incident.

The employee hastily signs the slip and leaves the company premises. However, the next day she returns, informing management that she wants to work, since she never really quit. If the company refuses the employee's request and a grievance is filed, the arbitrator would have to determine the grievant's and management's intent. Observable behaviors of an employee intending to quit are cleaning out the locker, saying good-bye to colleagues, and asking management for the wages earned for that week. An employee usually resigns only after giving the decision careful thought and consideration. Since none of these behaviors were operative in this case, the arbitrator might attempt to determine management's intent in this action. Possibly, the supervisor was simply trying to do the employee a favor by letting her off the hook. However, management may have given the employee the alternative of quitting to avoid subsequent arbitration of the discharge and the risk of the discharge decision being overturned. The latter intent is viewed by arbitrators as being *constructive discharge.*

Under this principle, the arbitrator would view the termination of employment as being subject to the employee discipline provisions of the labor agreement. These provisions usually call for union representation and written explanation at the time of the employee's discharge. Since these procedures were not followed, many arbitrators would reinstate the grievant will full back pay. Sometimes, union and management officials attempt to convince the arbitrator of their specific intent by producing written notes of previous discussions so that there will be documentation of their related past behaviors.

Past Practice The guideline of **past practice** demonstrates to the arbitrator how the parties have carried out the labor agreement.

> Much of what is considered a part of the labor agreement is unwritten. As with any working relationship, the parties to a labor agreement do not specify every detail and understanding in their interactions, but rely on implicit acceptance of certain practices that have been developed over the years.[27]

This consideration has been used by both management and the union. Management is usually more concerned about past practice, since it administers the labor agreement through various supervisory directives to the hourly employees. Since established contractual provisions place restrictions on managerial discretion, management attempts to avoid further reductions on supervisory decision making by pressing for a past practices clause to be included in the labor agreement, similar to the following:

> Article XXVIII: Other Agreements
>
> Section 2. The parties do hereby terminate all prior agreements heretofore entered into between representatives of the company and the unions (including all

> past understandings, practices, and arbitration rulings) pertaining to rates of pay, hours of work, and conditions of employment other than those stipulated in this agreement between the parties.[28]

However, this clause does not guarantee that management does not add to its contractual restrictions by repeatedly handling a situation in a similar manner. Thus, a continued managerial practice of unilaterally giving employees a Christmas bonus might become a binding, implied term of the labor agreement. Further, management will likely have to negotiate a labor agreement provision to the contrary (even if the current labor agreement is silent on the subject) if it wishes to discontinue the Christmas bonus in subsequent years.

In addition to interpreting ambiguous language or resolving problems not covered in the agreement, past practices may even alter clear and convincing contractual provisions. At one company, it had been a practice for many years to require clerks to perform cleanup operations at the end of their work day and to pay them no money for up to 10 minutes' work, 15 minutes straight time for 11 to 15 minutes' work, and time and one-half for work of more than 15 minutes in duration. There was clear contractual language specifying that work in excess of 8 hours per day would be computed at time and one-half overtime premium. The union eventually filed a grievance stating that clear contractual language compelled overtime payment for any amount of daily work exceeding 8 hours. However, the arbitrator maintained that past practice was more significant than the express terms of the labor agreement in this case.

> The written contract is, of course, the strongest kind of evidence of what the parties willed, intended or agreed upon. An arbitrator will not ordinarily look beyond its *unambiguous* language. Where, *however,* as here, the parties have unmistakably demonstrated *how they themselves* have read and regarded the meaning and force of the language, and *where the meaning varies* from its normal intendment, the arbitrator *should not,* indeed, *cannot* close his eyes to this demonstration.[29]

Past practice refers to a specific and identical action that has been continually employed over a number of years to the recognition and satisfaction of both parties.[30] Moreover, since there are no uniform standards of time, it is very difficult to determine for certain how long or how frequently an action must be continued before it is considered a binding past practice.

De Minimis A technical but insignificant violation of the labor agreement is referred to as ***de minimis.*** Arbitrators using this principle might deny a grievance because of its trivial, inconsequential nature. In one related situation, the union claimed that a contractual provision prohibiting supervisors from performing bargaining unit work was violated. The supervisor in this instance adjusted the prongs of a fork lift mechanism so that it could pick up an object. The supervisory effort took no more than 2 seconds, as he simply kicked one of the prongs with his foot to make the distance between the prongs wide enough to pick up the object. Therefore, the arbitrator denied the grievance, stating that the union was wrong in pursuing such a small and insignificant issue. To award the union this grievance would be to encourage the filing of more trivial grievances, making a mockery of the labor-management relationship.

As is true with past practice, *de minimis* is not easily defined. This principle would probably be applicable if the supervisor changed one light bulb. The union might have a legitimate grievance, however, if the supervisor changed eight light bulbs (for a time period of 15 minutes), and if the act deprived a union member of a call-out or overtime opportunity.

Previous Arbitration Awards and Arbitration Principles Also used as a guideline are previous arbitration awards when they could bolster either party's position in the arbitration case. Similarly, the arbitrator may cite these awards to refute the parties' contentions or to illustrate the arbitral opinion. However, one study analyzing the role and effectiveness of prior arbitration awards found that arbitrators tend to either ignore or refute them in their decisions.[31] Prior arbitration awards involving other facilities are at best illuminating but they do not override contract language or past practices at the facility in question. However, arbitrators will consider other awards that focus on important principles that can be applied to the immediate case.

The common law of the shop diminishes the weight of prior arbitration awards from other properties, as arbitrators recognize the uniqueness and autonomy of a particular operation. In fact, arbitrators might regard the introduction of prior arbitration awards into a current arbitration hearing negatively:

> Unwillingness to present a case solely on its own merits may come to be interpreted as a sign of weakness. Also it may be considered that citation of prior arbitration awards indicates either a lack of confidence in the judgment of an arbitrator or a belief that he may be swayed by irrelevant considerations. An attempt to induce an arbitrator to follow some alleged precedent may come to be recognized as at least bad etiquette.[32]

Prior arbitration awards presented at the same location carry more weight, particularly if the situation and contractual language are similar. Of course, few prior arbitration awards contain these elements, since the parties would be extremely reluctant to arbitrate the same issue a second time, given the first arbitrator's decision.

Current Issues Affecting Arbitration

Legal Jurisdiction

Although the current role of labor arbitration has been clarified and enhanced through judicial decisions, jurisdictional problems still remain when a case heard by an arbitrator is also covered by legislation. Consider a case in which a black union steward is discharged for insubordination. A grievance is filed and proceeds to arbitration under the terms of the labor agreement. However, the employee claims that the discharge was prompted by racial bias and the fact that he was a union steward as well. Conceivably, the discharge grievance could claim the attention of a number of persons—the arbitrator and representatives from the Equal Employment Opportunity Commission (EEOC), and the National Labor Relations Board (NLRB). The problem involves untangling the various jurisdictional squabbles that could arise over this one grievance.

Arbitration and the Equal Employment Opportunity Commission

The passage of the 1964 Civil Rights Act (amended by the Equal Employment Opportunity Act of 1972) and subsequent judicial decisions have emphasized that management's well-meant intentions are not sufficient to preclude a possible charge of racial discrimination. Indeed, in administering this aspect of public law, the EEOC holds that employers must actively devise and implement employment procedures that remove present as well as possible residual effects of past discrimination. Hiring and promotion procedures may be carefully scrutinized by the EEOC to protect minority employees from arbitrary and discriminatory practices. In a unionized facility, arbitrators also often assume a related decision-making role, particularly in grievances protesting discipline of a minority employee. This situation poses at least two questions:

1. Should management, the union, and the employee turn to the arbitrator, the EEOC, or both in resolving a minority employee's grievance?
2. How do the courts and the EEOC view the arbitrator's decision in terms of Title VII of the 1964 Civil Rights Act?

The first question was answered by a 1974 Supreme Court decision, *Alexander* v. *Gardner-Denver Company.* In this case, a discharged minority employee claimed racial discrimination; however, management's action was upheld by the arbitrator. Following the EEOC's subsequent determination that there was not reasonable ground to believe that a violation of Title VII of the 1964 Civil Rights Act had occurred, the employee sought relief from the alleged discriminatory action in the federal district court. This court (subsequently upheld by the court of appeals) dismissed the employee's action since the petitioner, having voluntarily elected to pursue his grievance under the nondiscrimination clause of the collective bargaining agreement, was bound by the arbitral decision and thereby precluded from suing his employer under Title VII. However, the Supreme Court reversed the previous judicial decisions, finding that Title VII does not expressly permit deferral and that the arbitrator's major concern is to interpret the labor agreement, not federal law. Additionally, the Court found that the intent of Congress was to have the federal courts exercise final responsibility for the enforcement of Title VII, particularly since the arbitrator's expertise (as outlined in the previously discussed Trilogy) pertains to the interpretation of the labor agreement. Further,

> the factfinding process in arbitration usually is not equivalent to judicial fact-finding. The record of the arbitration proceedings is not as complete; the usual rules of evidence do not apply; and rights and procedures common to civil trials, such as discovery, compulsory process, cross-examination, and testimony under oath, are often severely limited or unavailable.[33]

Consequently, a minority employee is almost encouraged to pursue the arbitration process as well as appropriate judicial procedures.

Some predicted that the *Gardner-Denver* decision would create havoc as every discrimination grievance lost in arbitration would be overturned by the appropriate government agency or the courts. Yet research does not support this prediction. One study found that a grievance reviewed by the EEOC or related agencies only stood a 1-in-6 chance of being reversed.[34] Also, the chances of a trial court overturning a discrimination grievance heard by an arbitrator are slim, 6.8 percent according to one study[35] and 10 percent according to another.[36] Apparently, the courts believe that arbitrators are adequately covering the legal considerations of discrimination in their decisions.[37]

Arbitration and the National Labor Relations Board

Perhaps the most frequent supplements to arbitral decisions have come from the National Labor Relations Board, because the grievant could have been discharged for reasons pertaining to provisions of the labor agreement that are similar to laws, such as engaging in union activities on the job or acting overly aggressive in the capacity of a union official. Section 10(a) of the National Labor Relations Act provides that the NLRB "is empowered . . . to prevent any person from engaging in any unfair labor practice (listed in Section 8) affecting commerce. This power shall not be affected by any other means of adjustment or prevention that has been or may be established by agreement, law, or otherwise."

Although it has the power, the NLRB does not ignore arbitration awards covering unfair labor practice issues. In fact, it often withholds its jurisdictional determination and investigation pending the arbitrator's decision. In 1955 the NLRB's deferral to arbitration policy was formulated in the *Spielberg Manufacturing Company* case. In that case, the board honored an arbitration award that denied reinstatement to certain employees guilty of strike misconduct. Resulting deferral guidelines stressed that the arbitration proceedings must be fair and regular, there must be adequate notice and representation, the arbitrator must address the issue of the alleged unfair labor practice, and all parties must agree to be bound by the arbitration award.[38] However, the board will disregard the arbitrator's award if it is ambiguous or if the board obtains pertinent evidence not presented in the arbitration proceeding.

The NLRB's deferral to arbitration policy was enhanced in the *Collyer* case, in which the NLRB trial examiner had found that the company had committed an unfair labor practice when it made certain unilateral changes in wages and working conditions.[39] The company maintained that the issues should be resolved through existing arbitration proceedings instead of the NLRB. The board in essence agreed with the company's position. While reserving the right to investigate the merits of the issue, the board maintained that

1. Related disputes can be better resolved through the special skills and experiences of the arbitrators.
2. The objectives of the National Labor Relations Act, industrial peace and stability, can be significantly realized through adherence to arbitration procedures established in the labor agreement.

Under *Collyer,* the employee was obligated to use the arbitration procedure before the NLRB would review the merits of the case.[40]

The NLRB's subsequent *Olin Corporation* decision (1984) established new guidelines that make it even more likely that the NLRB will defer to arbitration decisions. Under *Olin,* the unfair labor practice does not have to be considered at all in the arbitration hearing. The NLRB will still defer to an arbitrator's award "if the contractual and unfair labor practice issues were factually parallel and the facts relevant to resolving the unfair labor practice were presented generally to the arbitrator."[41]

In summary, the Supreme Court has recognized the ability of arbitrators to interpret the labor agreement provisions and has even encouraged parties to arbitrate the issue before proceeding to the NLRB. However, this encouragement is not given to the same extent in Title VII disputes. Additionally, government agencies such as EEOC and NLRB retain jurisdiction of a related issue and can modify an arbitrator's decision if it conflicts with their conception of public policy.

Arbitration and Public Policy: The *Misco* Decision

Can a court overturn an arbitrator's decision if it perceives this decision runs counter to public policy?[42] The Supreme Court approached this question in its recent *Misco* decision. Misco fired an employee who operated a "slitter-rewinder," which cuts rolling coils of paper, and allegedly smoked marijuana on company property. The grievant was arrested in his car in the company's parking lot. Police found a lit marijuana cigarette in the front ashtray of the car, and a subsequent police search of the car revealed a marijuana residue.

The arbitrator reinstated the grievant because of insufficient evidence that did not establish that the grievant smoked or even possessed marijuana on the company's premises. He noted the grievant had been in the back seat of the car. The arbitrator also refused to consider the police report as evidence, and ruled that the case must be limited to what the employer knew at the time of the firing. (We are fortunate to have the arbitrator's personal reflections on this case in the "Labor Relations in Action").

The lower courts set aside the arbitrator's award as contrary to state law prohibiting the possession and use of marijuana, the employer's rule against bringing drugs onto company property, and using dangerous machinery while under the influence of drugs. This case was eventually heard by the Supreme Court, which reiterated an earlier decision *(W. R. Grace)* that a "court may not enforce a collective bargaining agreement that is contrary to public policy." However, the Supreme Court noted that the public policy must be "explicit," "well defined and dominant," and "ascertained by reference to the laws and legal precedents and not from general considerations of supposed public interests." The Supreme Court upheld the arbitrator because the Court of Appeals made no attempt to review existing laws and legal precedents to demonstrate that a "well defined and dominant policy against the operation of dangerous machinery while under the influence of drugs exists." Further, even if the public policy argument was accepted, the evidence that the grievant violated this policy was "tenuous at best."[43]

Misco therefore reinforces the wide latitude given to arbitrators' decision-making authority by the Trilogy. It will probably reduce the number of instances in which the courts "second-guess" the arbitrator's award on public policy grounds. However, the public policy exception, while made narrow by *Misco,* still exists. An employer does not have to honor an arbitration award that would require a violation of law (reinstating a bus driver who lacks a driver's license, for example).[44]

Appraising Labor Arbitration's Effectiveness

Although the courts have praised the effectiveness of arbitration, some critical assessments have come from the participants—union and management officials and even some arbitrators (see "Labor Relations in Action" on page 280 for some related insights). There appear to be two general areas of criticism: the arbitrator's capability and ethics and the potential procedural problems in the arbitration process.

Labor Relations in Action

Reflections of Arbitrator M. J. Fox, Jr. on the *Misco* Case

The decision of the U.S. Supreme Court in *United Paperworkers International Union* v. *Misco Inc.* (484 U.S. 29) was handed down on December 1, 1987. The case worked its way to the Supreme Court under the guise of a public policy issue. The public policy allegedly violated was a Louisiana law prohibiting the operation of dangerous machinery by an employee under the influence of marijuana. I rendered a decision in favor of the grievant because the company had failed to prove that the grievant had been under the influence of marijuana or had brought marijuana onto company property, both of which were dischargeable offenses under the company's unilaterally promulgated work rules.

The company's concern about marijuana use in the plant arose when two marijuana roaches were found in a restroom several weeks before the grievant was fired. On the night in question, a policeman had the grievant and two other employees under surveillance from the time the three came out of the plant on break until the police arrived from the grievant's house. This officer never saw anyone light or smoke a cigarette, even though the events took place after dark, during the swing swift break (between 6:30 p.m. and 6:50 p.m.). When the police arrested the grievant in the company parking lot for "possession of marijuana" found at his home, his car was searched. One unobserved policeman allegedly found a scales case under the driver's seat that contained gleanings of marijuana. The police evidence was not discovered by the company until a week before the hearing and was presented to the union for the first time at the arbitration hearing. Since this evidence was unknown at the time of the grievant's discharge, I did not admit it.

The grievant was taken to the police station, booked, released on bail, and was back on the job in less than an hour. The grievant was kept on the job for several days before he was discharged. One problem complicating the company's case was that the swing shift supervisor was told that a drug bust was occurring in the company's parking lot and suddenly went to the other end of the plant. This supervisor was no longer a company employee at the time of the hearing, so his testimony was not available.

The company had the police in attendance at the third-step grievance meeting. When the grievant was asked for his side of the incident, the police informed him that anything he said could be used against him in a court of law. The grievant then said nothing.

One problem in this case was that no transcript was made of the hearing by a court reporter. Only I had a tape recording of the hearing and was able to listen repeatedly to the testimony of the various parties and make a detailed analysis of each witness's testimony. The briefs presented to the courts definitely suffered from the lack of a hearing manuscript.

The District Court supported the company's position and overturned the award. The 5th Circuit Court of Appeals upheld the District Court's decision and added its own fact finding and analysis of the activi-

Capability and Ethics of the Arbitrator It has been contended that the arbitrator's decisions are adversely linked with financial dependence on the parties:

> A proportion of arbitration awards, no one knows how large a proportion, are decided not on the basis of the evidence or of the contract or other proper considerations, but in a way which in the arbitrator's opinion makes it likely that he will be hired for other arbitration cases. It makes no difference whether or not a large majority of cases is decided in this way. A system of adjudication in which

ties that had led to the grievant's discharge. The Circuit Court objected to my statement to the parties at the hearing that I am a Creek Indian, unaware that I was following the *Code of Professional Responsibilities for Arbitrators of Labor-Management Disputes,* 2B(4) and (5), by informing the parties that I am a member of a protected minority, as was the grievant. If either party so desired, another arbitrator could have been selected for the case.

The Circuit Court also made a finding of fact regarding the effect of possible passive inhalation of marijuana in a closed automobile. The evidence in this case showed that the grievant was in the closed car about 10 minutes, during which time marijuana may or may not have been smoked by someone in the car. The grievant was standing outside the car when arrested, after which a lit marijuana cigarette was found in the right front ashtray. The grievant had been sitting in the back seat of the two-door car. Considerable research has been published regarding passive inhalation in automobiles, but none of it has resulted in any testable detection of marijuana in a person's body for this short a period of time.

Arguments were presented before the U.S. Supreme Court in October 1987, during which the company attorney, in reply to Justice White's questions, told the court in part that the company knew the grievant was under the influence of marijuana while at work because the grievant had access to marijuana in his home. Justice White pointed out that no one had ever seen the grievant smoking marijuana. Furthermore, Justice White noted that I had not ordered the company to reinstate the grievant as an operator on the dangerous machinery to which he had been assigned at the time of his discharge.

The case is a classic justification of the Supreme Court's position that absent fraud or dishonesty, the courts may not reconsider the merits of an award for errors of fact or alleged contract misinterpretation. In this case, I set forth my reasons for believing that the company had not proven its case against the grievant. Unfortunately, as in most awards, I did not list every single item that led to my conclusion. In making its ruling in favor of the union and upholding my award of reinstatement to the grievant's old job, or an equivalent job, with full back pay, the Supreme Court only touched on the public policy issue. The decision was primarily a reaffirmation of the Steelworkers' Trilogy, in which the arbitrator is the finder of facts, not the courts. The Supreme Court did say that a refusal to enforce an award for contravention of public policy is only justified when such policy is well-defined, denominated, and ascertained by reference to laws and legal precedents rather than general considerations of supposed public interest. The matter of public policy and arbitral awards has not been settled, as shown by S.D. Warren I, II, and III; 845 F. 2d 3 (1st Cir. 1988); and 846 F. 2d (1st Cir. 1988).

Note: For a detailed account of this case, see "Impact of Public Policy on Judicial Review of Arbitral Awards Involving Substance Abuse," Ph.D. dissertation by John Steven Grainger, available from University Micro Film, Inc.

the judge depends for his livelihood, or for a substantial part of his livelihood or even for substantial supplements to his regular income, on whether he pleases those who hire him to judge is per se a thoroughly undesirable system. In no proper system of justice should a judge be submitted to such pressures. . . .

We know that a large proportion of the awards of arbitrators are rendered by incompetents, that another proportion—we do not know how large but are permitted by the circumstances to suspect that it is quite large—is rendered on the basis of what award might be best for the arbitrator's future.[45]

Labor Relations in Action

Things They *Never* Told Me Before I Became an Arbitrator

The difficulty of setting up a hearing date when union and company representatives have such busy schedules.

The ease of reading finished cases and the difficulty of writing one from scratch.

The need to know about admission of evidence and reasons for sustaining and overruling objections at a hearing and making quick decisions about them.

How physically tiring it is to fly or drive to some of the hearing sites.

How unglamorous travel and hotels can be when all airports look alike and you are not even sure where you are.

How mature and conscientious some parties can be in trying to do "what is right" while some parties enter the hearing armed for combat and confrontation.

How much money, time, and effort could be saved if the parties prepared better and attempted to resolve their differences before arbitration.

The role of the cancellation fee in making sure the parties are going forth to arbitration. (If there is no cost of cancelling, one of the parties can abuse the arbitration process by cancelling at a late date.)

How one party will hold out for a compromise settlement until right before the hearing. When no settlement is forthcoming and their case is weak, the party will drop the grievance.

How important the fee is to the parties–it cannot be too low because the parties think you are not good enough; it cannot be too high because you price yourself out of a job.

Source: From an experienced, somewhat weary arbitrator who enjoys relaxing in anonymity.

ETHICS

In some instances, union and management practitioners believe that the arbitrator "owes them one" due to their support (financial and otherwise). One arbitrator, who expressed surprise to officials at being selected to replace another prominent arbitrator, was given the following reason why the previous arbitrator was fired:

> "I'll tell you why we fired him. The last case he had ended here at about 4:00. Mr.________ expressed considerable concern since he had to make a plane for New York and was running late. I assured him that he would have no problem. I carried his bags to his car, drove in excess of all the speed limits, went through back roads, even proceeded through changing traffic lights. After a hectic ride and at considerable risk, I got him to the airport just in time to make the plane. I parked my car in a no parking zone. I even carried his bags to the gate. After all this, you know, that [deleted] ruled against me."[46]

Yet other participants or students of arbitration maintain that the arbitrator's indebtedness to the parties is a necessary ingredient of dispute resolution. They maintain that the arbitrator owes allegiance to both union and management and thus is accountable rather than indebted to the parties: An unsound, hastily conceived decision "will very quickly make the arbitrator responsible unacceptable to companies and unions alike."[47]

The ethics issue has been directly approached by three organizations, the National Academy of Arbitrators, the Federal Mediation and Conciliation Service, and the American Arbitration Association, involved with the selection and monitoring of arbitrators. Some of the professional responsibility provisions of these organizations are as follows:[48]

ETHICS

- An arbitrator, deciding that he or she does not have the technical competence to deal with the issue under consideration, is expected to withdraw from the case. Commonly included in this category are incentive systems, job evaluation plans, and pension and insurance programs.
- An arbitrator is not to make an award public without the consent of the parties.
- Prior to an arbitrator's appointment the parties should be made aware of the arbitrator's fees for the hearing, study time, travel time, postponement or cancellation, office overhead expenses, and any work of paid assistants.
- If either party requests the arbitrator to visit the workplace, the arbitrator should comply.
- An arbitrator should not consider a posthearing brief that has not been given to the other party.
- If the arbitrator knows any of the parties or has any private interest in the organization, he or she must make disclosure of any potential conflict of interest before the hearing.

Other criticisms have focused on the quality of the arbitrator's decision. The arbitrator's written opinion and award dissatisfy the parties if they do not reflect the original expectations and understandings of one or both regarding the nature or scope of the grievance. But many arbitral decision problems may be attributed in large part to the union and management officials instead of the arbitrator. For example, some union and management officials ask the arbitrator to isolate and define the issues from the presentations of the case and then resolve the issues on the basis of that haphazard record. Under this situation, the officials must share the greater burden of blame if the arbitrator's decision does not directly and concisely resolve the particular problem.

Management and union representatives might also obtain poor arbitration awards under the *garbage in–garbage out* theory. Since the arbitrator's decision is based on the merits of the grievance, a sloppy grievance formulation and presentation might result in a relatively lackluster arbitral decision. Sometimes union and management officials present the arbitrator with poorly conceived grievances that should have been resolved before going to arbitration. Such grievances are often prompted by political considerations—the union or management officials take the grievance to arbitration to show support for their union stewards or first-line supervisors even though they know them to be wrong. Arbitration in this sense serves as a buck-passing device; the errant union steward or supervisor is apparently given support but in reality is provided an education through the arbitrator's decision.

One almost inescapable concern arises from the finality of the arbitrator's award. While the Supreme Court has encouraged single-person resolution of an industrial dispute, opponents of this practice suggest that an arbitrator has more authority than a judge, whose decision may be overturned through judicial appeal. Unfortunately, there would be many problems if arbitration awards were subjected to an appeals procedure. Any such procedure would be time-consuming and expensive. If the arbitrator's award were reversed by a second arbitrator in the appeals procedure it would be impossible to determine which arbitrator wrote the "correct" decision. Also, the "arbitrator as judge of last resort" situation might beneficially place pressure on the arbitrator to produce high-quality opinions.

Procedural Problems There are two general categories of procedural problems: time lag and expense of the arbitration proceedings. Two studies found the length of time from request for arbitration to the arbitrator's award averaged 200 and 263 days, respectively.[49] Clearly, this delay affects employees, who rightfully maintain that their complaint should be resolved promptly and efficiently. Similarly, management equates the arbitral decision-making delay in many grievance issues, such as discipline and job reclassification, with unnecessary expense, since adverse awards can also include remedies for back pay retroactive to the date of management's original action.

Many times this delay is due to a limited supply of experienced arbitrators, who hear a large proportion of the cases. However, the causes for this short supply of arbitrators appear mainly attributable to union and management practitioners, many of whom candidly admit that they will wait months for the "old hands" instead of taking their chances with "newcomers."

> [I]t is reassuring and convenient to present one's case before an arbitrator with whom you've worked before, one who knows the ropes, who goes quickly to the heart of the case, and whose evidentiary rulings and written opinions have a track record of acceptability to the parties.[50]

In some cases experienced arbitrators have assumed responsibility for training new arbitrators. In this situation, often called *internship,* the intern progresses from merely observing hearings and discussing cases to drafting awards for the arbitrator's use and sitting as a hearing officer.[51]

Time delay is only one of several expenses associated with arbitration. Other expenses include the arbitrator's daily fee, normally between $400 and $500; the arbitrator's travel and study time, normally paid at the daily rate; the fees for the parties' attorneys, which usually exceed the arbitrator's fee; wage payments to plant personnel who take part in the proceedings; and stenographic transcription costs, if a record of the hearing is desired. While most labor agreements provide for sharing of arbitral expenses, excluding the expenses associated with the parties' attorneys and witnesses, the cost of a 1-day hearing could be several thousand dollars for each of the parties.

Arbitral fees have increased over the years, which is understandable in view of inflation. In many cases, however, management and union officials bring added expenses upon themselves when they insist that the arbitrator review unnecessary materials, such as transcripts, prior arbitration awards, superfluous witnesses, and prehearing and posthearing briefs. They may also insist on expensive frills, such as the renting of a hotel suite for a neutral arbitration site, that do not materially affect the quality of a decision.

Some union and management officials have reduced expenses by using expedited arbitration procedures, such as those used by the ten major steel producers (the Coordinated Steel Companies) and the United Steelworkers of America when they used some 200 relatively inexperienced arbitrators to decide routine (non–precedent-setting) grievances in brief (one- or two-page) decisions within 2 days after the hearings.[52]

Other possibilities exist for streamlining the arbitration process. For example, some grievances solely concern interpretations of the labor agreement. Unlike discipline cases, these grievances do not personally involve employee grievants and thus do not entail related therapeutic or political considerations. Perhaps these grievances could be argued on paper without the necessity of a hearing and related expenses.[53]

The use of experimental approaches illustrates two fundamental issues concerning arbitration:

1. This process, while not perfect, appears to offer great advantages over alternative methods of grievance resolution, such as sudden strike activity.[54]
2. Union and management officials created the arbitration process and are charged with controlling it in accordance with their jointly determined needs. They must monitor the process as well as their related actions and attitudes to ensure a relatively inexpensive, efficient, and objective means of dispute resolution.

Summary

The arbitration process was little used during the period from 1865 to World War II; however, during World War II, the National War Labor Board encouraged its widespread use. While the increased reliance upon arbitration continued after World War II, a major problem of enforcing the arbitrator's decision remained. Either party could refuse to abide by the arbitrator's decision, with uncertain consequences from the courts. This problem was initially approached in the *Lincoln Mills* decision, which provided a judicial avenue for enforcement, and the Steelworkers' Trilogy, three cases that established the superiority of the arbitration process to the courts in resolving industrial grievances. Subsequent Supreme Court decisions have indicated that termination of the labor agreement does not eliminate the possibility of arbitration, and injunctive relief might be granted when one party refuses to arbitrate according to grievance procedures established in the labor agreement.

Before the arbitration hearing, arbitrators must be selected on either an ad hoc or permanent basis. Each of these selection techniques has unique advantages, depending on the particular circumstances. The same can be said of prehearing and posthearing briefs. Other elements of an arbitration hearing include the grievance issue, presentation of witnesses for testimony and cross examination, and presentation of separate and joint exhibits.

The hearing scene is a dramatic one; union and management officials display their skills in attempting to convince the arbitrator their positions are correct. The arbitration hearing shares many similarities with a judicial trial but differs in several ways. Perhaps the most significant difference is the arbitrator's reliance on the common law of the shop.

In determining the common law of the shop, arbitrators give particular weight to the provisions of the labor agreement, the intent of the parties, and past practice. Arbitrators may also consider the *de minimis* principle and, to a much lesser extent, prior arbitration awards in arriving at their decisions. Since arbitration procedures differ in some respects from those used in a courtroom, various jurisdictional disputes can occur regarding interpretations of contract provisions by arbitrators and the legal interpretation of federal policy. For example, a discharge case decided by the arbitrator could be subsequently considered by the Equal Employment Opportunity Commission, and the National Labor Relations Board.

Some criticisms directed toward arbitration pertain to the arbitrator's capability and ethics and potential procedural problems in the arbitration process. Certain arbitral problems such as expense, time lag, and excessive formality may be due to labor and management preferences rather than any characteristics inherent in the arbitration process. Management and union officials have reduced some of these problems by using expedited arbitration and new arbitrators.

Key Terms

National War Labor Board
Steelworkers' Trilogy
permanent arbitrator
ad hoc arbitrator
arbitration hearing
common law of the shop
parole evidence rule
intent of parties
past practice
de minimis

Discussion Questions

1. How did World War II and the National War Labor Board greatly expand the use of arbitration?
2. "The Steelworkers' Trilogy greatly enhanced the arbitrator's authority when compared to previous years, yet did not give the arbitrator final jurisdiction over certain issues." Thoroughly discuss the preceding statement in terms of the specific features of these judicial decisions; also consider current jurisdictional issues arbitrators face in terms of government agencies.
3. Discuss the similarities and differences of arbitration and judicial hearings, with particular emphasis on the common law of the shop, admission of evidence, and the role of the arbitrator versus that of the judge.
4. Why are arbitrators' decisions usually lengthy, since one sentence could indicate who was right and wrong? Your discussion of this question should include the purposes of arbitration and advantages as well as disadvantages of an extensive arbitral decision.
5. Discuss two decision-making criteria used by arbitrators, furnishing specific examples (not mentioned in the text) of how these criteria can come into play.
6. Cite and defend three specific methods you would use to make the typical arbitration procedure more effective. Also indicate the advantages and disadvantages of your suggestions.

References

1. Frank Elkouri and Edna Asper Elkouri, *How Arbitration Works*, 3d ed. (Washington, D.C.: Bureau of National Affairs Inc., 1973), p. 15.
2. For a detailed historical perspective of labor arbitration, see Dennis R. Nolan and Roger I. Abrams, "American Labor Arbitration: The Early Years," *University of Florida Law Review* (Summer 1983), pp. 373–421.
3. *United Steelworkers of America* v. *American Manufacturing Company*, 363 U.S. 566–567 (1960).
4. *United Steelworkers of America* v. *Warrior and Gulf Navigation Company*, 363 U.S. 582 (1960).
5. *United Steelworkers of America* v. *Enterprise Wheel and Car Corporation*, 363 U.S. 598 (1960).
6. *"A T & T Technologies Inc.* v. *Communication Workers of America," The United States Law Week*, April 8, 1986, p. 4341.
7. The case is *John Wiley and Sons* v. *Livingston*, (1964), discussed in Ralph S. Berger, "The Collective Bargaining Agreement in Bankruptcy: Does the Duty to Arbitrate Survive?" *Labor Law Journal* 35 (November 1984), pp. 385–393.
8. *Nolde Brothers Inc.* v. *Local No. 358, Bakery and Confectionary Workers Union AFL-CIO*, 430 U.S. 254 (1977). See also Irving M. Geslewitz, "Case Law Development Since Nolde Brothers:

When Must Post-Contract Disputes be Arbitrated?" *Labor Law Journal* 35 (April 1984), pp. 225–238.
9. *The Boys Market Inc.* v. *Retail Clerk's Union, Local 770,* 398 U.S. 249, 250, 252–253 (1970). It should be noted that injunctive relief applies only when one party refuses to arbitrate issues that are subject to grievance procedures specified in the labor agreement. For additional details, see *Buffalo Forge Company* v. *United Steelworkers of America,* 428 U.S. 397 (1970); and John Hoerr, "Why a Labor Pact Won't End Steel's Problems," *Business Week,* September 26, 1977, p. 56.
10. Bureau of National Affairs Inc., *Basic Patterns in Union Contracts* (Washington, D.C.: Bureau of National Affairs Inc., 1986), p. 38.
11. Delbert C. Miller and William Form, *Industrial Sociology,* 2d ed. (New York: Harper & Row, 1964), p. 264.
12. John Smith Herrick, "Profile of a Labor Arbitrator," *Arbitration Journal* 37 (June 1982), p. 18; and A. Dale Allen, Jr. and Daniel F. Jennings, "Sounding Out the Nation's Arbitrators: An NAA Survey," *Labor Law Journal* 39 (July 1988), pp. 424–425.
13. David E. Bloom and Christopher L. Cavanagh, "An Analysis of the Selection of Arbitrators," *American Economic Review* (June 1986), pp. 408–422.
14. Clarence R. Deitsch and David A. Dilts, "An Analysis of Arbitrator Characteristics and Their Effects on Decision Making in Discharge Cases," *Labor Law Journal* 40 (February 1989), pp. 112–116.
15. Brian Bemmels, "The Effect of Grievants' Gender on Arbitration Decisions," *Industrial and Labor Relations Review* 41, no. 2 (1988), p. 262.
16. Clarence R. Deitsch and David A. Dilts, "Factors Affecting Pre-Arbitral Settlement of Rights Disputes: Predicting the Method of Rights Dispute Resolution," *Journal of Labor Research* 12 (Winter 1986), p. 76.
17. Ronald W. Haughton, "Running the Hearing," in Arnold M. Zack, ed., *Arbitration in Practice* (Ithaca, New York: ILR Press, 1984), p. 37.
18. For a fine conceptualization of arbitrability's dimensions and implications see Mark M. Grossman, *The Question of Arbitrability* (Ithaca, New York: ILR Press, 1984).
19. See, for example, Daniel T. Dennehy, "The Status of Lie Detector Tests in Labor Arbitration," *Labor Law Journal* 31 (July 1980), pp. 430–440. See also James B. Dworkin and Michael M. Harris, "Polygraph Tests: What Labor Arbitrators Need to Know," *The Arbitration Journal* 41 (March 1986), pp. 23–33; Kimberly Janisch-Ramsey, "Polygraphs: The Search for Truth in Arbitration Proceedings," *The Arbitration Journal* 41 (March 1986), pp. 34–41; and Herman A. Theeke and Tina M. Theeke, "The Truth About Arbitrators' Treatment of Polygraph Tests," *Arbitration Journal* 42 (December 1987), pp. 23–32. See also Marvin F. Hill, Jr., and Anthony Sinicropi, *Evidence in Arbitration,* 2nd ed., (Washington, D.C.: Bureau of National Affairs Inc., 1987); and Owen Fairweather, *Practice and Procedure in Labor Arbitration,* 2nd ed., (Washington, D.C.: Bureau of National Affairs Inc., 1984), pp. 357–341.
20. Elkouri and Elkouri, *How Arbitration Works,* p. 302.
21. Stephen C. Vladek, "Comment: The Use and Abuse of Arbitral Power," in Barbara D. Dennis and Gerald G. Somers, eds., *Labor Arbitration at the Quarter-Century Mark* (Washington, D.C.: Bureau of National Affairs Inc., 1973), p. 84.
22. Charles M. Rehmus, "Writing the Opinion," in Zack, *Labor Arbitration,* pp. 209–219.
23. Steven Stark, "Arbitration Decision Writing: Why Arbitrators Err," *Arbitration Journal* 38 (June 1983), pp. 30–33.
24. Donald J. Petersen and Julius Rezler, "Arbitration Decision Writing: Selected Criteria," *Arbitration Journal* 38 (June 1983), p. 18.
25. Marvin Hill, Jr., and Anthony V. Sinicropi, *Evidence in Arbitration* (Washington, D.C.: Bureau of National Affairs Inc., 1980), p. 50.
26. The first two examples are from Allan J. Harrison, *Preparing and Presenting Your Arbitration Case: A Manual for Union and Management Representatives* (Washington, D.C.: Bureau of National Affairs Inc., 1979), pp. 23–24. The third example is suggested by Thomas R. Knight, "Arbitration and Contract Interpretation: Common Law v. Strict Construction," *Labor Law Journal* 34 (November 1983), pp.714–726.
27. C. Ray Gullett and Wayne H. Goff, "The Arbitral Decision-Making Process: A Computerized Simulation," *Personnel Journal* 59 (August 1980), p. 666.
28. This provision on past practice taken from Walter E. Baer, *Practice and Precedent in Labor Relations* (Lexington, Mass.: Lexington Books, 1972), p.8.
29. Ibid., p. 38.
30. Richard Mittenthal, "Past Practice and the Administration of Collective Bargaining Agreements," in Zack, *Arbitration in Practice,* p. 183. For arbitration examples of these dimensions of past practice, see Arthur Dobbelaere, William H. Leahy, and Jack Reardon, "The Effect of Past Practice on the Arbitration of Labor Disputes," *Arbitration Journal* 40 (December 1985), pp. 27–43.
31. Ken Jennings and Cindy Martin, "The Role of Prior Arbitration Awards in Arbitral Decisions," *Labor Law Journal* 29 (February 1978), pp. 95–106.
32. William H. McPherson, "Should Labor Arbitrators Play Follow the Leader?" *Arbitration Journal* 4 (1949), p. 170.
33. *Harrell Alexander, Sr.,* v. *Gardner-Denver Company,* 415 U.S. 60 (1974).
34. Michelle Hoyman and Lamont E. Stallworth, "The Arbitration of Discrimination Grievances in the Aftermath of *Gardner-Denver,*" *Arbitration Journal* 39 (September 1984), p. 55.
35. Ibid., p. 42.
36. Karen Elwell and Peter Feuille, "Arbitration Awards and Gardner-Denver Lawsuits: One Bite or Two?" *Industrial Relations* 23 (Spring 1984), p. 295.
37. Aubrey R. Fowler, Jr., "Arbitration, the Trilogy, and Industrial Rights: Developments Since *Alexander* v. *Gardner-Denver,*" *Labor Law Journal* 36 (March 1985), pp. 173–182. See also Elaine Gale Wrong, "Courts' Review of Arbitration Awards in Discrimination Grievances," *Labor Law Journal* 37 (February 1986), pp. 123–126.
38. *Spielberg Manufacturing Company,* 112 NLRB 1080 (1955).
39. *Collyer Insulated Wire and Local Union 1098, International Brotherhood of Electrical Workers,* 192 NLRB 150 (August 20, 1977).
40. Curtis L. Mack and Ira P. Bernstein, "NLRB Deferral to the Arbitration Process: The Arbitrator's Demanding Role," *Arbitration Journal* 40 (September 1985), pp. 33–43. For a related research effort, see Benjamin W. Wolkinson, "The Impact of the Collyer Policy of Deferral: An Empirical Study," *Industrial and Labor Relations Review* 38 (April 1985), pp. 377–391.
41. Pat Greenfield, "The NLRB's Deferral to Arbitration Before and After *Olin:* An Empirical Analysis," *Industrial and Labor Relations Review* 42 (1) 1988, pp. 34–49.
42. For discussion of several instances where this question has been raised see Bernard D. Meltzer, "After the Labor Arbitration Award: The Public Policy Defense," *Industrial Relations Law Journal* 10, no. 2 (1988), pp. 241–251; and Robert F. Wayland, Elvis C.

Stephens, and Geralyn McClure, "*Misco:* Its Impact on Arbitration Awards," *Labor Law Journal* (December 1988), pp. 813–819.
43. "Decision of Supreme Court in *Paperworkers* v. *Misco, Inc.,*" Bureau of National Affairs Inc., *Daily Labor Report,* no. 230 (December 1, 1987), D-1–D-5.
44. "Practitioners Assess Impact of Court Decision Bolstering Finality of Labor Arbitration Awards," Bureau of National Affairs Inc., *Daily Labor Report,* no. 238 (December 14, 1987), A-1. For additional consideration of public policy intertwined with arbitration decisions in drug testing see Lorynn A. Cone, "Public Policies Against Drug Use: *Paperworkers* v. *Misco Inc.,*" *Labor Law Journal* 40 (April 1989), pp. 243–247.
45. Paul R. Hays, *Labor Arbitration: A Dissenting View* (New Haven, Conn.: Yale University Press), pp. 112–113.
46. Dworkin, "How Arbitrators Decide Cases," p. 203.
47. Burt L. Laskin, "Arbitration and its Critics," in Charles M. Rehmus, ed., *Proceedings of the Twenty-first Annual Meeting, National Academy of Arbitrators* (Washington, D.C.: Bureau of National Affairs Inc., 1968), p. 134. For details concerning legal accountability of arbitrators, see Leslie Alan Glick, "Bias, Fraud, Misconduct, and Partiality of the Arbitrator," *Arbitration Journal* 22 (1967), pp. 161–172.
48. Bob Repas, *Contract Administration* (Washington, D.C.: Bureau of National Affairs Inc., 1984), pp. 218–219.
49. "Labor Arbitration Seen in Need of Improvement," *Daily Labor Report,* May 14, 1983, p.1.
50. Arnold M. Zack, "Who is Responsible for the Development of Arbitrators—the Parties or the Arbitrators?" *Arbitration Journal* 36 (June 1981), p. 12.
51. John Van N. Dorr III, "Labor Arbitrator Training: the Internship," *Arbitration Journal* 36 (June 1981), p. 6.
52. For a discussion of various types of expedited arbitration and related successes, see Marcus H. Sandver, Harry R. Blaine, and Mark N. Woyar, "Time and Cost Savings through Expedited Arbitration Procedures," *Arbitration Journal* 36 (December 1981), pp. 11–21.
53. Dennis R. Nolan and Roger I. Abrams, "The Future of Labor Arbitration," *Labor Law Journal* 37 (July 1986), pp. 441–442.
54. This attitude was generally expressed in the following survey of 239 union officials: Harry E. Graham, Brian P. Heshizer, and David B. Johnson, "Grievance Arbitration, Labor Officials' Attitudes," *Arbitration Journal* 33 (June 1978), pp. 21–24.

Cases for Part 2

CASE

2.1 *Toll Bell Company* v. *Workers of America:* Protected Rights and Company Interference

On August 6, 1985, the collective-bargaining agreement between the company and the union expired. Two days later, the union called a strike at the company's facilities, including those at 3303 Weslaylan, St. Louis, Missouri. The strike ended on August 28 with the signing of a new 3-year agreement. The following day, employees began returning to work. During the strike, a substantial number of bargaining-unit employees at 3303 Weslaylan continued to work behind the union's picket line.

On September 2, the union distributed materials to its stewards for posting on its bulletin boards at the company's facilities, including the following commentary by Jack London:

Definition of a Scab

After God had finished the rattlesnake, the toad, and the vampire, he had some awful substance left with which he made a SCAB. A SCAB is a two-legged animal with a corkscrew soul, a water-logged brain, and a combination backbone of jelly and glue. Where others have hearts, he carries a tumor of rotten principles.

When a SCAB comes down the street men turn their backs and angels weep in Heaven, and the devil shuts the gates of Hell to keep him out. No man has the right to SCAB, so long as there is a pool of water deep enough to drown his body in or a rope long enough to hang his carcass with. Judas Iscariot was a gentleman . . . compared with a SCAB; for betraying his master, he had the character to hang himself—a SCAB hasn't. Esau sold his birthright for a mess of pottage. Judas Iscariot sold his Savior for thirty pieces of silver. Benedict Arnold sold his country for a promise of a commission in the British Army. The modern strikebreaker sells his birthright, his country, his wife, his children, and his fellow man for an unfulfilled promise from his employer, trust or corporation.

Esau was a traitor to himself. Judas Iscariot was a traitor to his God. Benedict Arnold was a traitor to his country. A strikebreaker is a traitor to himself, a traitor to his God, traitor to his country, a traitor to his family and a traitor to his class.

THERE
IS
NOTHING
LOWER
THAN
A
SCAB . . .

Union steward Cora Able immediately posted "Definition of a Scab" along with another article, entitled "From Bessie's Desk," praising the strikers and criticizing those who worked behind the picket line, on a union bulletin board in the computer terminal room, adjacent to Room 1002 at the company's 3303 Weslaylan facility. A chief steward, employee Anita Cain, had left the articles for Able with a note requesting that she post them.

Able has been responsible for posting material on the union bulletin board in the computer terminal room since she became the union job steward in 1982. Able had previously posted campaign literature of candidates for union office, notices of union meetings, and articles from union newsletters on this bulletin board. She had also removed comic strips from the bulletin board. Prior to September 2, no company supervisor had ever told Able what she could or could not post on the union's bulletin board. Nor had any company supervisor ever removed anything from this board prior to September 2.

There were no company rules concerning the posting of literature on the union's bulletin boards on the company's premises. The company's supervisors reflected the absence of any such rules. The collective bargaining agreements in effect since 1980, covering the company's employees, contain no provisions regarding the union's bulletin boards at the company's facilities.

During the afternoon of September 2, company supervisor Joe Bay saw several employees near the bulletin board, apparently reading the posted articles. He removed the "Definition of a Scab" and deposited it in a garbage can. Able noticed the article had been removed and asked Bay where it was. Bay told her he had removed it, balled it up, and thrown it into the garbage can.

Able took the sheet from the can, then got another copy from her desk and hung it on the board. Bay promptly snatched this copy down, telling Able, "This mess [isn't] going to hang up here." He then specifically prohibited her from posting another copy and warned her of disciplinary action if she did so. Able called chief steward Miller, who spoke to Bay and requested that he leave the literature on the bulletin board. Bay told Miller that the "Definition of a Scab" had no business on the board and was causing animosity among the clerks.

A half hour later, supervisor Linda Trevino informed Able that a second-line supervisor, Ralph Coe, wanted to see her. Coe had a copy of "Definition of a Scab" in his hand as he told Able, "We're not going to have this mess hanging in this office." In the presence of Trevino and Bay, Coe also warned Able that Bay could discipline her "for insubordination." Able asked to be excused and upon returning to her desk called Miller again.

Fifteen minutes later, Trevino told Able, "We would like to see you for 5 minutes." Able told Trevino that she did not want to go back to Coe's office. However, she complied upon Trevino's assurance that the return to Coe's office would take only 5 minutes, long enough to receive an apology. Coe then asked Able to tell her side of the incident. Coe apologized, as did Bay, for the way Bay had treated Able in front of the employees. Coe did not retract his support for Bay's action in removing the article and preventing its reposting.

On September 1, union job steward Milton Musk posted a copy of "Definition of a Scab" on a union bulletin board located in a break room next to Rooms 208 and 209, the Switching Control Center at the company's 3303 Weslaylan facility. Musk had been responsible for posting material on this bulletin board from 1980 through November 1983. As a matter of practice, Musk had posted on the board notice of union meetings, listings of job vacancies provided by the union, lists of union officers' names, announcements for an employee charitable organization, and the campaign material of candidates for union office. Occasionally, Musk removed from the board cartoons that had been posted by employees. Prior to September 1, no supervisor had ever told Musk what he could or could not post on the union bulletin board.

"Definition of a Scab" remained on the union bulletin board in the Switching Control Center break room until about 4 p.m., September 1. About that time, company supervisor Wesley Vie directed Musk to remove "Definition of a Scab." Musk said he did not wish to do so. Vie removed it as Musk watched.

The following day, before 7 a.m., "Definition of a Scab" again appeared on the bulletin board. Company supervisor Tom Davis summoned Musk to his office at approximately 8 a.m. and told him to take down the "Definition of a Scab" from the union's bulletin board. Musk protested that he did not put it up and he should not have to take it down. Davis then warned that he would suspend Musk if he persisted in his refusal. Davis asked for Musk's building pass and key, whereupon Musk requested permission to make a telephone call. After consulting a union district steward,

Musk removed the "Definition of a Scab." Musk again told Davis it was unfair that he had to remove the article when he had not posted it. Davis told Musk that he "didn't want trash like that posted."

The union contended that the company violated Section 8(a)(1) of the NLRA by removing "Definition of a Scab" from union bulletin boards and by threatening employees with punishment if they posted or reposted London's commentary to those bulletin boards. The company denied that it violated the NLRA on the ground that the posting of Jack London's pejorative appraisal of nonstriking employees had disrupted the discipline of its employees and thus was beyond the protection of Sections 7 and 8(a)(1) of the act.[1]

[1]Section 7 of the NLRA provides in part, "Employees shall have the right to self-organization, to form, join, or assist labor organizations, to bargain collectively through representatives of their own choosing, and to engage in other concerted activities for the purpose of collective bargaining or other mutual aid or protection."

Section 8(a)(1) of the NLRA provides in pertinent part, "It shall be an unfair labor practice for an employer—to interfere with, restrain, or coerce employees in the exercise of the rights guaranteed in Section 7."

Questions

1. How does a union gain the right to the use of a bulletin board on company premises?
2. Why was the union so insistent on having the "Definition of a Scab" posted on the bulletin board?
3. Since the union already exists and already has an agreement, how does Section (8)(a)(1) apply to this case?
4. Could this case go to arbitration? Why? Why not?
5. You be the NLRB administrative law judge. How should you rule? Why?

References

Container Corporation of America, 244 NLRB 318 (1979).
Nugent Service, Inc., 207 NLRB 158 (1973).
Southwestern Bell Telephone Co., 200 NLRB 667 (1972).
Republic Aviation Corp. v. *NLRB,* 324 US 793 (1945).
Old Dominion Branch No. 496 National Association of Letter Carriers v. *Austin,* 418 US 264 (1974).
Cambria Clay Products Co., 106 NLRB 267 (1953).

CASE 2.2 Unilateral Implementation of Drug/Alcohol and Attendance Incentive Programs

Johnson-Bateman manufactures concrete pipe, and the Machinists represent the production and maintenance employees. The parties have had collective bargaining agreements since 1960 and their current agreement has several provisions relevant to the issues in this case. The provisions are

Section 3: Management's Rights

.1 The management of the plant, direction of the working forces, and work affairs of the Company, including but not limited to the right . . . to discipline or discharge for just cause . . . to issue, enforce and change Company rules [is reserved to the Company] . . . Thus, the Company reserves and retains, solely [sic] and exclusively, all of the rights, privileges and prerogatives which it would have in the absence of this Agreement, except to the extent that such rights, privileges and prerogatives are specifically and clearly abridged by express provision of this Agreement.

Section 8: Wage Rates and Classifications

.1 The rates of pay and classifications set forth in Appendix "A" are agreed upon by the parties and are attached hereto and made a part of this Agreement.

.2 The wage rates as set forth are minimum rates under this Agreement and are not to be construed as preventing the employer from paying or the employee accepting additional pay or benefits.

Section 17: Discrimination

.3 Except as provided herein, this Agreement resolves all the bargainable issues for the term hereof.

Since 1960 the company has unilaterally implemented numerous work rules without objection from the union. For example, in 1962, the company unilaterally implemented work rules prohibiting numerous forms of employee misconduct including immoral conduct, sabotage, insubordination, horseplay, and fighting. In 1982, the company again acting under the management's rights clause unilaterally implemented a set of work rules covering such items as adherence to work hours, use of timecards, excused absences, timely notification of unanticipated absences, and adherence to safety regulations.

Two of the plant work rules relevant to this case are

Perfect Attendance

All employees who have a perfect attendance record in a 12 month calendar year will receive special recognition.

Discharges

The company shall have the right to discharge or discipline any employee for just cause. The term "just cause" shall include . . . drinking or possessing any alcoholic beverages on company premises or on company time or reporting for work while under the influence of alcohol or drugs.

The company has had in effect for some time an extra-contractual policy, to which the Union has not objected, requiring newly hired employees to undergo drug/alcohol testing at the time of their hiring.

The company, which had required all newly hired employees to be tested for drugs and alcohol use at the time of hiring, decided on a new drug/alcohol program for current employees. On December 1, 1986, the company, again without notifying the union or bargaining with the union, unilaterally posted the following notice:

Attention All Employees

As of December 1, 1986, any injuries requiring treatment will now be accompanied by a drug/alcohol test.

Thank you

Management

On December 4, 1986, the union notified the company in writing that the "union is not in agreement with the policy; neither have we been contacted to negotiate such a policy." The union requested that the company not implement the policy and remove the posted notices immediately. The company did not reply to the union's letter and did not grant either of the union's requests. Rather, the company implemented the policy as announced on December 4, 1986.

On March 23, 1987, the company, again without any advance notice to the union or opportunity to bargain, posted a notice announcing a new attendance incentive bonus plan for employees hired after September 1, 1986. Those employees who achieved perfect attendance for a week would receive a wage bonus of $1 per hour for that week. Those employees who achieved perfect attendance for an entire month would receive a total wage bonus of $1.50 per hour for the month. After the program's implementation, several employees qualified and received the attendance bonuses.

The union contended that the drug/alcohol testing program and the attendance bonus program related to wages, hours, and other terms and conditions of employment and were therefore mandatory subjects of bargaining. The union contended the company violated Section 8(a)(5) and (1) of the National Labor Relations Act by unilaterally implementing these programs without giving the union prior notice of them and providing the union an opportunity to bargain with the company about them.

The company contended that it had exercised its rights under the management's rights clause of the agreement, which was negotiated with the union. Moreover, the company had unilaterally implemented work rules in the past under the same provisions.

Questions

1. Do either of or both the drug/alcohol testing program and the attendance incentive program come under the definition of wages, hours, and other terms and conditions of employment? If yes, what is the company's legal obligation?
2. Why would the union protest the implementation of the attendance bonus program, which benefits some of the employees?
3. Has the company established a practice of unilaterally implementing work rules?

4. If the company is in violation of the National Labor Relations Act, what is the appropriate remedy?
5. Explain why the union has accepted unilateral implementation of work rules before and now has challenged them.
6. What should be the decision of the National Labor Relations Board? Explain your answer.

CASE

2.3 Contacting Advertisers to Ask for Help in Negotiations

In May 1985, the Newspaper Workers of America agreed to extend its agreement with the *Metropolis Star* for another year because of the newspaper's financial condition. The union later agreed to forgo a wage increase even though one was included in the extended agreement. In early 1986, the union accepted a wage cut because of the company's financial difficulties.

In March 1986, the parties began negotiating a new agreement to replace the extended contract, but the talks failed to produce a new agreement. In July 1986, the union authorized the bargaining committee to call a strike if necessary, and the company unilaterally implemented a wage cut one month later. A local business weekly published an article a month later criticizing the management of the newspaper and mentioning that rumors were circulating about the paper's impending demise.

The negotiations continued into September and the union bargaining committee became frustrated with the "stalling" tactics of the company. On October 1, the union committee sent a letter on the union's letterhead to 50 of the newspaper's best retail advertisers. This letter highlighted the possibility that only one newspaper would remain in the city in a short period of time. It indicated that the union had been negotiating with the company for 1 1/2 years but could not obtain a fair contract. The letter informed the advertisers that the newspaper's circulation had dropped, good employees had left the newspaper for better jobs, the quality of advertising had suffered, and the newspaper was speeding downhill. It said the employees wanted to get the newspaper back on track and requested help from the advertisers. Phone numbers of the newspaper's president and editor were included and advertisers were urged to call.

On October 7, the president and general manager of the newspaper suspended four employees pending an investigation into the matter. On October 15, these employees were fired for "disloyalty to the company." The termination letter indicated that the union's letter contained half-truths, exaggerations, and blatant misrepresentation that disparaged the newspaper and disrupted its relationship with its advertisers.

Upon the termination of these employees, the union filed an unfair labor practice charge with the National Labor Relations Board.

Questions

1. Are the union committee's actions considered to be protected concerted activity under Section 7 of the National Labor Relations Act?
2. Assess the union committee's strategy in taking such action.
3. Do you believe that there was just cause for discharging these employees, i.e., disloyalty to the company?
4. Has the union committee committed an unfair labor practice by bypassing the company and going directly to the advertisers?
5. How should the National Labor Relations Board rule? Explain your answer.

CASE

2.4 Company Failure to Match Christmas Savings

For 18 years prior to the year in question, the company had maintained a Christmas savings program for its employees, most of whom were members of the carpenters' union. Under the program, participating employees agreed to have 5 percent of their monthly wages withheld and deposited in a separate fund. The company agreed to contribute a matching amount to the fund and distribute the proceeds on December 10 of each year. The agreement provided that if an employee left the company before distribution of the fund "for any reason," he or she would receive only his or her own contribution, not the portion contributed by the company.

In July 1988, the union began an economic strike against the company. Some workers later abandoned the effort and the company permanently replaced the remaining strikers before December 10. Of the workers remaining on strike, 18 refused to withdraw their contributions to the Christmas fund, and when the company would not meet the contribution with matching funds, the union filed an unfair labor practice with the National Labor Relations Board.

The union contended that the company's action violated Section 8(a) of the Taft-Hartley Act, which states that it is an unfair labor practice for an employer "by discrimination in regard to . . . any term or condition of employment to . . . discourage membership in any labor organization." The union argued that the company should disburse matching funds to its members because they were the only employees in the fund's history to have wages on deposit on the distribution date who did not receive matching contributions. Further, such withholding of accrued matching contributions on the apparent basis of a protected strike activity warrants the inference of unlawfully discriminatory conduct.

The company acknowledged that the reason for withholding the benefits was the strike, but argued that it was justified in its action based on past practice and a contract interpretation that the matching funds could be denied to any employee not "actively working" on the disbursement date. Moreover, during the 18 years of the program, those employees who were on leave or layoff status on December 10 were ruled ineligible to receive matching funds because they were neither actively working nor necessarily expected to resume active work. The company claimed that this denial of matching funds did not hinder the union's future bargaining position or the exercise of the union members' rights. The company did not discriminate against these striking union members; they had been replaced by permanent employees.

Questions

1. How important is the fact that the program has been in effect for 18 years?
2. Is the matching contribution considered under the "wages, hours, and other terms and conditions of employment"?
3. Does the agreement provide a justification for the company to refuse to make the matching contribution?
4. Is this a matter of contract interpretation or application of the Taft-Hartley Act?
5. Does it matter whether the economic strikers had been permanently replaced or temporarily replaced?
6. Did the company violate the Taft-Hartley Act? If so, what should be the appropriate remedy?

CASE

2.5 A Work Stoppage by Nonunion Mechanics

In August 1989, six mechanics in a nonunion shop met and reached a group decision to ask for a meeting with the company president to talk about their job-related complaints. These workers gathered around the break area at the start of work on August 29, 1989. They decided that they would not start on their jobs until the president of the company agreed to meet with them. Their supervisor suggested that they put their grievances in writing and he would take the written grievances to the president. Meanwhile, the president heard about their actions and directed the supervisor to tell the six mechanics either to go to work or go home.

Two of the mechanics left the workplace but four remained. At noon, the company president went to their work area and read a brief statement to the remaining employees. He stated that if they did not leave the premises, they would be fired. The employees left the premises, and that afternoon the president placed an advertisement in the local newspaper seeking new mechanics and offering a $500 starting bonus. During the NLRB's investigation, the president was asked whether a meeting would be scheduled with the employees to discuss their grievances and the president refused to answer.

All the mechanics returned to work on September 2 and completed the workday. On September 3, the mechanics learned that their immediate supervisor had been fired, causing them concern because they believed that he had sympathized with their grievances. The six mechanics then left the premises for a nearby restaurant to discuss their options. They returned to work about 2 hours later at 9:30 a.m. Upon arrival they were told that they had been fired. They were allowed to remove their tools from the shop, and they left the premises.

The president then replaced the six mechanics with new recruits who had responded to the newspaper advertisement. The word about being replaced got back to the six mechanics, and they filed charges with the National Labor Relations Board.

Questions

1. Were the six mechanics involved in protected concerted activities under the National Labor Relations Act?
2. Did the employer lawfully replace these mechanics, who were involved in a work stoppage?
3. Did the president recognize these employees as a labor organization by meeting with them?
4. Did the company commit an unfair labor practice when it terminated the employment of these mechanics?
5. Does it matter that these mechanics were not union members?
6. How should the National Labor Relations Board rule? Explain.

The Outcomes of the Labor Relations Process: Collective Bargaining Issues

Part 3 examines the variety of work rules that represent the outcomes of the labor relations process. Employee discipline is a significant factor in establishing work rules as well as the basis for much arbitration. Next, institutional issues pertaining to the rights and responsibilities of unions and management, including their responsibility to minorities and women, are explored. A discussion of many administrative and economic issues that are resolved through collective bargaining concludes this section.

CHAPTER 10

Employee Discipline

"Discharge cases comprise a large percentage of arbitration cases, and it is obvious that the arbitral process in such cases serves to protect the individual employee from an unfair or abusive decision to terminate this employment. But, at the same time, arbitration also serves to protect the employer's right to be intolerant of abuses from an employee who may be dishonest, excessively absent, insubordinate, or a sloppy, substandard worker. These are both important protections, and the arbitrator's task is not an easy one as he sorts through the differing evidence, the advocates' arguments, and his own biases."

John E. Drotning and Bruce Fortado, "The Science of Discharge Arbitration," *Labor Law Journal* 35 (September 1984), p. 505.

We devote an entire chapter to employee discipline because this important union-management issue is

- The most frequently heard grievance in arbitration (35 percent of total arbitrated grievances according to one study).[1]
- The best generator of common principles shared by arbitrators.[2]
- The most likely to involve the reader, who is likely to discipline an employee in his or her career in unionized or nonunionized settings and have that action challenged by the union, government agencies such as the Equal Employment Opportunity Commission, or the courts.

This chapter approaches employee discipline by discussing its changing significance over time and its elements and how they affect labor-management relations.

The Changing Significance of Industrial Discipline

Employee discipline represents both organization conditions and actions. Organization conditions can lead employees to form a disciplined work group that is largely self-regulated and willingly accepts management's directions and behavioral standards. Managerial actions are taken against an employee who has violated organizational rules. This dimension has changed over time.

Historical Overview of Employer Disciplinary Policies

During the eighteenth and nineteenth centuries, the employer exercised "uncontrolled discretion" in directing the work crew. Discipline during this time was sometimes harsh. Employees who were verbally insolent to employers could have their tongues burned with a hot iron or be subjected to public humiliation (a public whipping in the town square, for example).[3]

By 1935, management's total discretion to discipline employees was challenged on pragmatic and legal grounds. Frederick Taylor's *scientific management,* popular by 1920, stressed the financial waste that occurred when employees were discharged in an arbitrary or capricious manner. According to Taylor, management had an obligation to determine and obtain desired employee work behavior, and to correct, rather than discharge, the employee who deviated from managerial standards.

The Wagner Act of 1935 legally shaped management's disciplinary policies. A primary feature of this legislation was the prohibition of discriminatory discipline of employees because of their union activities or membership. An independent agency, the National Labor Relations Board (NLRB), was created, in part, for enforcement purposes. Management often had to defend disciplinary actions against charges filed with this agency, with a potential remedy being reinstatement with back pay. This was the first time that management could be legally held accountable for employee discipline, a situation that encouraged further development of corrective disciplinary principles and policies.[4] The NLRB also affected organizational discipline procedures indirectly when it ruled that discipline and grievance procedures were mandatory issues subject to collective bargaining. As a result of this NLRB decision, nearly all existing collective bargaining agreements now have both a provision regulating discipline and a grievance procedure that makes possible the submission of discipline issues to arbitration.

From the 1940s to the present, managerial policies regarding employee discipline were greatly influenced by the growth and development of labor arbitration. Currently, arbitrators have three broad powers regarding discipline:

1. To determine what constitutes "just cause" for discipline.
2. To establish "standards of proof and evidence."
3. To review and modify or eliminate the penalty imposed by management when warranted.

Restrictions on Discipline in the Nonunion Firm: Challenges to "Employment at Will"

This chapter's introduction noted that many readers must understand principles of employee discipline even if they are managers in a nonunion firm. For example, many states allow court challenges if an employee is discharged, even if the employee is not represented by a union or covered by a labor agreement. These states no longer strictly adhere to the *"employment at will"* concept, whereby both employee and employer are free to sever the employment relationship at any time, if there is no contractual provision to the contrary.

Employees in nonunion situations have had their discharges overturned under two general exceptions to employment at will:

- *Implied contract* (applicable in courts in 34 states) relies on oral or written evidence (statements made in employment interviews, employee handbooks, and so forth) indicating that the company will make every effort to develop the employee and treat the individual fairly in personnel decisions.
- *Public policy* (applicable in courts in 39 states) prohibits management from discharging an employee who refused to commit perjury on the employer's behalf, reported illegal company activities, filed a legal worker's compensation claim, and so forth.

Currently, more than 25,000 challenges to employment at will filed by managers and hourly employees alike in nonunion firms ("wrongful discharge" cases) are pending in state and federal courts.[5] Most if not all of these cases will employ disciplinary considerations found in unionized firms and related labor agreements.

Present-Day Significance of Discipline

Management and union officials as well as employees at unionized firms are strongly affected by disciplinary actions and arbitrators' decisions concerning disciplinary actions. (See the "Labor Relations in Action" for a management official's perception of this situation.) An arbitrator has two general options regarding the discharged employee. He or she can (1) uphold management's discharge decision or (2) reinstate the employee to work either with or without back pay for wages lost due to the employee's forced absence.

The second alternative modifies management's decision and in one study of 1,724 discharge cases occurred 57 percent of the time.[6] From a statistical perspective, management generally loses in arbitration of discipline grievances, and its loss is advertised when the reinstated employee is brought back to the shop floor. Reinstatement of the employee with back pay represents a financial loss to management, and supervisory authority may also be lost, for it is a rare supervisor who, upon experiencing the return of one disciplined employee to his work group with a large back pay check, will pursue subsequent disciplinary action with as much vigor and initiative.[7]

There is also no guarantee that the reinstated employee will perform well when returned to the job. According to one study, managers believed that reinstated employees (who were still employed by the company) had made "normal progress" in 28 out of the 47 cases. However, only 23 of these individuals had no subsequent disciplinary problems—8 employees repeated the same offense and 16 employees engaged in different disciplinary offenses.[8] Another study found that the seniority of the discharged employee was insignificant in predicting the employee's performance after reinstatement.[9]

Arbitral reversal of management decisions can also create tensions between different levels of management officials. As noted in Chapter 1, management participants in the labor relations process do not constitute a unified group. The first-line supervisor is often most involved in employee discipline: he or she has typically trained the employee, created past practices in the department that might influence the arbitrator's decision, and witnessed, reported, and in some cases participated in the events resulting in discipline. The supervisor also directly administers discipline to employees.

Labor Relations in Action

Discipline from a Managerial Perspective

The following interview is with Wayne Lauten, who has 20 years of experience with unions and discipline in both the private and public sectors. Mr. Lauten is Director of Labor Relations at the Naval Air Station, Jacksonville, Florida, which has 7,000 employees and 23 separate bargaining units. His responses suggest some additional considerations in regard to discipline.

In discipline cases, are strong unions easier to deal with than weak unions?

No doubt about it. A strong, well-organized union such as the Teamsters does not want to waste a lot of its time representing an employee that is known to be a problem employee. The union is an economic institution as well as management. It therefore does not want to waste the time of the business agents or national representatives, plus have the cost of arbitration on a poor case.

Discipline is supposed to be employee-specific in that it corrects a specific person's behavior. Yet, do discipline situations ever have much impact on the organization?

Disciplinary situations have a tendency to polarize an organization. Take the example of the poor performer. Other poor performers will relate to this disciplined employee because there is unity in numbers. Employees who are good performers will not take this individual's side because they are resentful that he or she does not do a fair share of the work.

Straight, forceful discipline is a good morale factor. Management has the obligation to provide a proper work environment, provide reasonable pay, and inform the employee of its expectations. If management fulfills these obligations and the employee fails to live up to expectations, then a disciplinary situation arises.

How significant are the first-line supervisor and union steward in administering employee discipline?

The first-line supervisor is the key, as he or she is the final link of communication of company expectations. [These supervisors are] the last ones that pass down the rule to the employees. They are also the enforcers of discipline. Supervisors need to properly posture the discipline. Do they have the facts? Are they aware of which rule or regulation was broken? Is it a fair rule or regulation? Then, very specifically, exactly what did the employee do that was wrong? What evidence do you have to support this infraction?

The supervisor's testimony is crucial in arbitration; therefore, you need to obtain the supervisor's written statement immediately at the time of the disciplinary action. When you finally enter arbitration, memories are vague and testimony is not as exact. The written statement helps the supervisor recall all the details leading to the action taken.

Many supervisors are reluctant to discharge the employee because they know it will cost the employee wages. Other times the supervisor says, "Why should I discipline the employee? Management will not support me anyway." Sometimes the labor relations representative has to "coerce" the supervisor into taking appropriate disciplinary action, but this tactic can backfire. The supervisor can become a hostile witness in the arbitration hearing. And God forbid you end up losing the arbitration case, because the supervisor sits back and says, "See, I told you we should not have done it!"

The union steward has to play just as significant a role as the supervisor. The steward is the primary challenger of the supervisor's authority, and it is important that the supervisor keeps the steward fully informed about the disciplinary situation. If management informs the steward early in a potential disciplinary problem, the steward can help correct the situation. Management can improve the working relationship with all union officials by keeping them well informed as to the actions of management. An employee often asks the steward if he or she knows what management is doing. If the steward can't answer the question, management will not have the stewards on their side.

What are the two or three most common reasons arbitrators reinstate discharged employees?

The usual reason is that the arbitrator misinterpreted the facts of the case. Second, arbitrators in many cases have tried to split the fine line and have decided that they owe one for the union instead of management. For example, we attempted to discharge an employee leaving work with the tools in the trunk of his car. The arbitrator overturned our decision, contending the employee was not really trying to steal the tools. Obviously, the arbitrator had a different value judgment of why an employee places his non-personal tools in the trunk of his car. The arbitrator did not place much importance on the fact that work tools are not even supposed to be removed from the work site.

How do you select an arbitrator for discharge cases?

My main concern is that the arbitrator has the ability to interpret the reams of federal sector rules and regulations that must be applied in the specific case. Age can also be significant. For example, older arbitrators usually view theft and insubordination cases more seriously. When we are discharging an employee in a technical classification—engineer, for example—I'd prefer an arbitrator with an engineering background. Because a professional individual expects professionalism of the people in their trade or profession.

What advice would you give management officials to increase the odds that the arbitrator will uphold the discharge decision?

Management must thoroughly prepare its case even before it makes its initial disciplinary action. You cannot prepare enough, as the arbitrator will often reach for something in testimony that was not anticipated. That's where the supervisor often crosses you up. You think you have prepared them completely, asking them for every significant detail that [you] can possibly anticipate. And lo and behold, when they get on the witness stand, they'll surprise you. For example, one supervisor kept a detailed written record on a disciplined employee, but he could not fully explain his various notations under cross examination. However, the next day he recalled them clearly.

What proportion of discharged employees reinstated by the arbitrator are successful (remaining with the organization for a long time and exhibiting corrective behavior)?

I wish I could think of a case, but I can't. It seems ultimately that they will commit another infraction. In fact, I think sometimes they think that they enjoy a certain degree of immunity as a result of being sustained in their appeal.

This interview was abstracted from research conducted by Ken Jennings and Steven Williamson, University of North Florida.

Other management officials such as industrial relations representatives monitor these activities to make sure that supervisory actions are consistent with company policy, reversing them if they are not to avoid adverse arbitration. This reversal can cause tensions, as indicated in the following remarks of a first-line supervisor:

> I had this one troublemaker. He was a solid goldbricker. He couldn't cut the buck on any job. I tried everything, but he was lazy and he was a loud-mouth. I caught him in the toilet after being away from his machine for over an hour. I told him he was through and to go upstairs and pick up his check. And [deleted]. Do you know what those college boys in personnel did? He gives them some bull about being sick and weakly and the next day he is sitting on a bench in the department next to mine. He says to me, "Well wise guy, you don't count for nothin' around here. Every time I see you, I'm going to call you Mr. Nothin'."[10]

What management loses in arbitration hearings appears to be the union's gain. Most if not all union members believe the union should be responsive to problems arising from their day-to-day working conditions that remain after the formal labor agreement has been negotiated. There is no more dramatic example of union concern for its members than "saving" an employee's job. Almost every union newspaper contains at least one article per issue that describes (along with appropriate pictures of union representatives, the grievant, and the back pay check) how the union successfully defended an employee against an unjust act of management. A representative article from one union newspaper proclaimed in bold headlines, "Worker Wins $5,895 in Back Pay When Fired for Opening Beer Can."[11]

Perhaps a disciplinary action carries the most significance for the affected employee. Discharge, the ultimate disciplinary act, has been viewed by many arbitrators as *economic capital punishment,* for it deprives the employee of presently earning a livelihood and at the same time (with the discharge on his or her work record) makes it difficult to find future employment elsewhere.

Discharge can also have powerful psychological consequences for the employee.

> When you are fired, you have no place to go. You have . . . no function. You reach out for friends, but find that they are busy and have no time for you. Suddenly, you know you are a failure. Unemployment shatters the worker's self-image as a valuable, productive person.[12]

At the least, any form of discipline represents an embarrassment to individuals who do not like being told they are wrong and, in some instances, have to explain a disciplinary layoff or discharge to their friends and family.

Principles and Elements of Discipline

Discipline for Just Cause

Most labor agreements contain a statement indicating that management retains the right to discipline employees for **just cause** or simply *cause;* for example, one survey found 86 percent of 400 separate labor agreements contained this provision.[13] Arbitrators consider this concept in any discipline grievance, their rationale being that just cause is an implicit, necessary prerequisite for the collective bargaining relationship.

Unfortunately, the arbitrator receives little help from the union and management representatives in defining just cause.

> For more than a half century, labor arbitrators have been asked to review discharges based on the just-cause standard. Over this long history, no mechanical formula has evolved for determining whether that standard has been met. An arbitrator cannot do his or her job simply by programming a computer and punching in "RUN." There is judgment to be exercised in resolving a discharge case. But that judgment cannot be based on the subjective values of an individual neutral. The needs and interests of the parties and their legitimate expectations must control.[14]

There is no uniform, precise definition of just cause that applies to all companies or even all circumstances within one company. However, arbitrators tend to accept three broad principles of just cause in guiding their consideration of the individual case:[15]

1. There is clear and convincing evidence that a disciplinary offense was committed by the grievant.
2. The disciplinary action taken by management was appropriate for the offense committed.
3. The discipline cannot be arbitrary or discriminatory; instead, it must be applied equally to employees given similar circumstances.

These just cause principles will likely prevent management from successfully disciplining a group of employees for actions such as horseplay, sabotage, wildcat strikes, and defective performance where it cannot establish the extent of each employee's awareness of possible disciplinary consequences and/or individual guilt. Indeed, all employees might be reinstated when management imposes blanket discipline, with arbitrators reasoning,

- "Justice is not done when an innocent man is punished simply because a guilty man refuses to confess his guilt."
- "Since neither the company nor the arbitrator has been able to single out the guilty employees, then the entire group must go unpunished."[16]

Arbitrators apply several tests or guidelines to establish just cause. Exhibit 10.1 represents a schematic diagram indicating the approximate progression of these considerations. Each consideration will be discussed in terms of its significance for employee discipline.[17]

Legitimate Purposes of Employee Discipline

Arbitrators have long held that management has the right to direct the work force and manage its operations efficiently. Indeed, inefficient operations harm both the employer and employees since subsequent reduced profits can result in employee layoffs. Discipline can improve efficiency through the following interrelated purposes:

- *Set an example of appropriate behavior.* For example, management impresses upon its employees the seriousness of being tardy by giving one tardy employee a 5-day suspension.
- *Transmit rules of the organization.* As illustrated in the preceding purpose, management has transmitted a rule of the organization—lateness will not be accepted.

Exhibit 10.1 **Schematic Diagram Indicating Elements of Discipline**

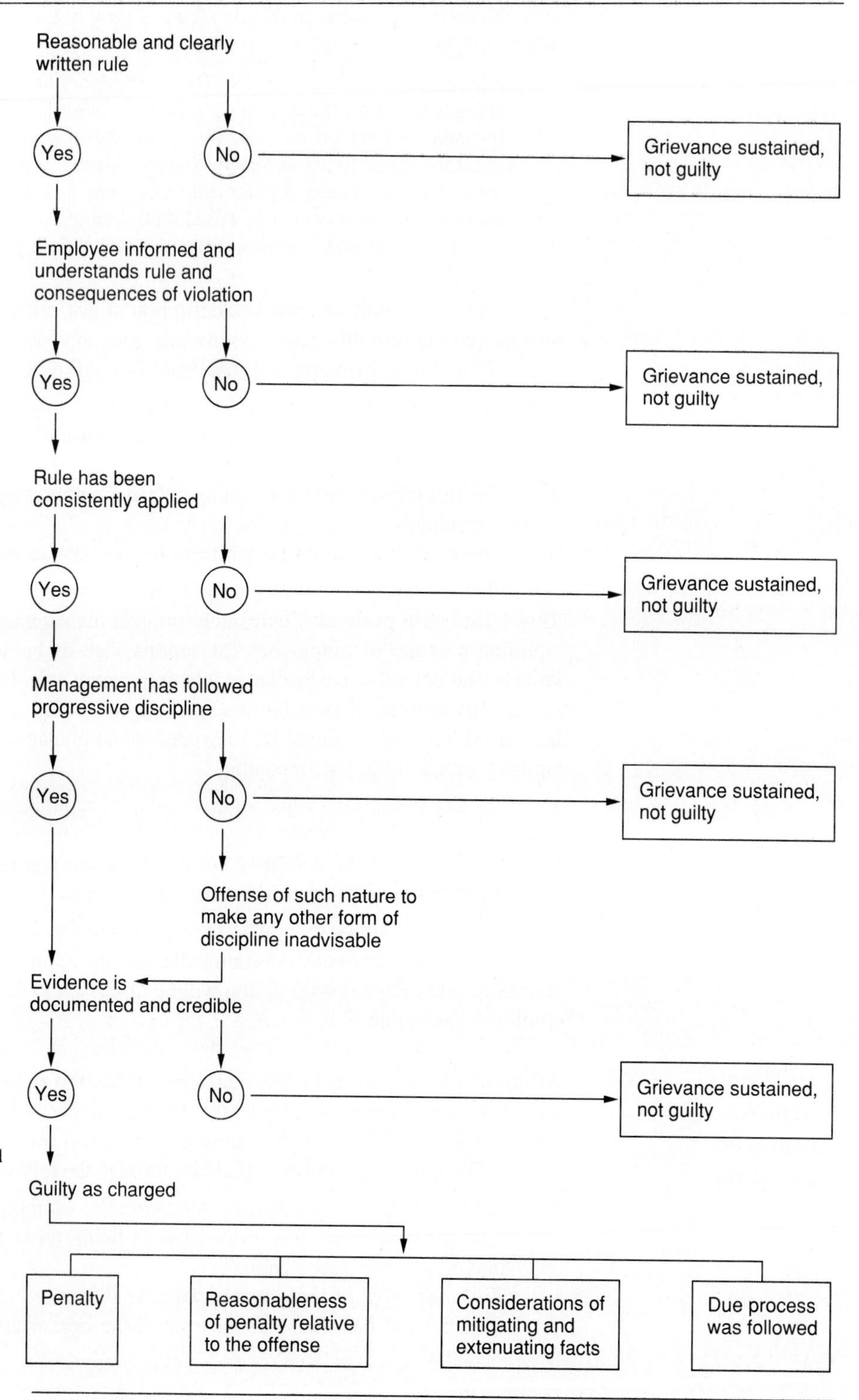

Sources: Modified from Floyd S. Brandt and Carroll R. Daugherty, *Instructor's Manual for Conflict Cooperation Cases in Labor-Management Behavior* (Homewood, Ill.: Richard D. Irwin, 1967), p. 6.

- *Promote efficient production.* Discipline those employees who either cannot or will not meet production standards.
- *Maintain respect for the supervisor.* In a sense, discipline show the employee who is the boss. A supervisor who does not discipline poor employees weakens managerial authority.
- *Correct an employee's behavior.* Indicate what is expected, how he or she can improve, and what negative consequences might result in the future if the behavior does not change. The assumption here is that most employees have good intentions and will improve if management will simply show them the error of their ways.

Discipline can accomplish all these purposes, but labor arbitrators primarily recognize the last purpose, *correction,* as the legitimate disciplinary objective. Arbitrators usually view discipline as corrective rather than punitive in purpose; their corrective emphasis influences the following dimensions of just cause.

Effect of Work Rules on Discipline

Management's right to establish (even without initially advising the union) and administer work rules is generally acknowledged as fundamental to efficient plant operations. Yet managerial administration of work rules also assumes some fundamental responsibilities and obligations that, if not followed, may affect management's disciplinary efforts.

A first question that arises is, what happens if management has no rule governing the alleged offense committed by the employee? And such an event is not uncommon since employers cannot possibly anticipate the endless variety of employee misbehaviors. Arbitrators, for example, have upheld the discharges of employees who

- Watched a fire develop and destroy a portion of a company over a lengthy period of time without notifying the company.[18]
- Called management officials in the early morning hours to belch over the telephone.[19]
- Urinated on the floor of a delivery truck even though there were restroom facilities nearby.
- Threw a pie at a management consultant.
- "Streaked" (ran naked) through a portion of the airport.[20]

Needless to say, management had no previously established work rules covering these subjects. Arbitrators have also upheld management's right to discipline employees for those offenses that are commonly regarded as unwritten laws—prohibitions against stealing or striking a supervisor, for example.

However, in most disciplinary situations, particularly those cases that are somewhat common in industry (poor performance, absenteeism, insubordination, and so forth) management is on weak ground with the arbitrator when it does not have established work rules. Further, written work rules must have several characteristics if they are to be effective. A written rule must be reasonable, clear, and state the possible consequences of its violation.

Reasonable rules are related to the orderly, efficient, and safe operation of the employer's business, and the performance that the employer might properly expect of the employee. Unions will contend a rule is unreasonable if it is unrelated to business operations or outweighed by the employee's personal rights on and off the job.

For example, in one grievance the union protested management's attempt to prevent an employee from bringing a small television to work and watching soap operas at her desk during a lunch break. Management contended her actions disturbed other employees and hurt the company's image if potential customers observed her. However, the arbitrator agreed that the rule was unreasonable since no related employee complaints were registered. He further maintained that watching television was not likely to create a worse customer impression than card playing—a lunch break activity that the employer accepted.[21]

The reasonableness of an industrial work rule can vary according to industrial or company differences. A unilateral ban on moonlighting (working a second shift with another employer) is regarded as reasonable in the utility industry, which often needs emergency work performed during off shifts. Other industries not having emergency-related concerns might have a difficult time in establishing the appropriateness of this rule.[22] Rule reasonableness can also vary within an industrial production facility. For example, an employer might reasonably require a long-haired employee working in the cafeteria to wear a hair net (for sanitary reasons); it would be unreasonable to request the same compliance if he worked in the shipping department.

As noted in Chapter 1, work rules reflect changing workplace conditions that are sometimes influenced by public opinion and societal values. Therefore, the reasonableness of these rules can also change. Not too long ago a unilateral no-smoking rule would have been declared unreasonable. Today this is not the case.[23]

Employees can also be reasonably discharged for off-job conduct if their actions hurt the company's productivity or public image.[24] However, related rules and actions have to balance business necessity with employee rights. For example, a pipe fitter who pleaded guilty to possession of cocaine was fined $500 and placed on probation. The company discharged the employee because he violated the following rule: "an employee convicted of a felony or any crime of violence may be summarily discharged." The arbitrator recognized the employers' "legitimate concern for the safety and welfare of the workforce and its given stake in the community." However, he reinstated the grievant because the company failed to establish a sufficient relationship between the conviction and the grievant's work performance at the refinery during the time until he was terminated.[25]

The clarity of a work rule is also an important issue in corrective discipline, the rationale being that employees cannot adequately perform or correct behavior if they do not know what is expected. Work rules can only serve as guidelines and cannot be applied to every problem. Management officials can, however, create a problem when they discipline employees for infractions of a vague or confusing work rule. For illustration, consider the following work rules:

- Horseplay can inflict serious physical harm on other employees and therefore will not be tolerated in any form by the company.
- Any individual found guilty of gambling on company premises will be subject to immediate discharge.

These rules may, at first glance, appear clear and conclusive; however, their vagueness becomes very apparent to the first-time supervisor who tries to enforce them. Horseplay can take place without physical touching. Suppose a group of employees puts a dead fish in a "lazy" inspector's testing pan, giving her equipment a lasting smell before she actually performs inspection duties. A question arises whether this is actually a form of horseplay. A fine distinction between relatively harmless practical jokes and horseplay may haunt management if it discharges the employees on the rationale that such behavior was indeed horseplay.

A problem also arises with the term *gambling,* particularly if management discharges employees caught at a card game while at the same time a management representative is sponsoring a World Series pool with hourly employee participants. Also, does gambling occur when employees are playing cards during their lunch break for matches or a numerical score that management (perhaps correctly) assumes will be converted into cash payments once the employees are off the company premises?

The existence of work rules carries the implicit if not explicit obligation for management to inform its employees of the rules as well as the consequences of their violation. In some instances, an employee disciplined for violating a rule contends that he or she was unaware of the directive. In these cases, management usually has to prove that the employee was indeed informed of the rule, a difficult task. Some arbitrators have even suggested that a card signed by an employee indicating he or she has read the rules is insufficient since it is signed in haste as part of the employee's orientation, and the signed card does not indicate that management has actively and patiently explained each rule to the employee, allowing time for questions.

Little has been written on the managerial obligation to inform the employee of the consequences of rule violation, although many arbitrators appear to give this item serious weight in their decisions. The training, or corrective, element in discipline should include a discussion of which rules are most important; a related feature of employee orientation would be informing the employee what type of penalty could be expected for violation of a particular work rule. Returning to the work rule examples, it can easily be seen that the admonition "will not be tolerated in any form" fails to inform the employee of the punishment for engaging in horseplay. The employee could interpret the vague penalty to mean a stern oral reprimand, which he or she would accept in view of successfully completing a practical joke. Knowing in advance that the activity would likely result in a suspension or discharge, the employee would probably think twice before committing the offense.

Management's statement that rule-breakers are "subject to discharge" is qualified. This qualification is necessary in order that the unique mitigating circumstances of each offense be given consideration, thereby avoiding arbitrary disciplinary measures. Yet management should be advised that arbitrators regard the phrase "subject to discharge" as carrying explicit potential for disciplinary measures other than discharge; the burden of proof is on management to establish why it chose discharge as opposed to the lesser penalty options.

Finally, management must administer the rules consistently for those employees violating the rules under similar circumstances. In assessing the degree of consistency, arbitrators place particular emphasis on past practice, which refers to the "customary way of dealing with given classes of rule violations and covers both methods of handling and the relationship of penalties to offenses."

Some companies seek to impose consistent discipline by including a **price list** in the labor agreement; it cites specific rules and furnishes uniform penalties for single or repeated violations (see Exhibit 10.2). This form of rule making has advantages: (1) the employee is clearly informed of the specific rules and consequences of violations, (2) the standardized penalties suggest consistent disciplinary action is implemented, and (3) if agreed to by the union, the price list assumes more legitimacy than a unilateral work rule posted by management. However, some individuals contend that the price list represents a mechanical imposition of discipline that runs counter to the corrective philosophy, since it does not consider each case on its individual merits. Say, for example, management finds two employees fighting—one a short-term, the other a long-term employee with a fine work record. According to the price list approach, management is obligated to discharge both employees; yet it is likely that the arbitrator will reinstate the senior employee, who, because of his past record, will typically respond to corrective measures in order to retain job seniority investments.

Progressive Discipline

Progressive discipline refers to increasingly severe penalties corresponding with repeated identical offenses committed by an employee. It relates to correction in at least two ways: (1) by impressing upon the employee the seriousness of repeated rule infractions and (2) by furnishing the employee additional chances to correct his or her behavior before applying the ultimate penalty of discharge. Management typically has to give an oral warning, a written warning, and at least one suspension before it can discharge an employee for repeatedly committing a similar offense, such as failure to wear safety equipment, poor attendance, or ineffective performance.

An **oral warning** represents an informal effort to correct and improve the employee's work performance. The informality of this reprimand is for corrective training purposes; however, the oral warning can be prejudicial to the employee if it is entered as evidence in arbitration hearings. This disciplinary action, however, is subject to the following employee defenses: (1) the employee might have thought the supervisor's remarks were instructional and been unaware of the disciplinary aspects or consequences of the warning and (2) an oral warning given in private can lead to conflicting testimony—the employee can state that the supervisor never gave him or her an oral warning. However, because of its relative harmlessness, the union seldom contests this form of discipline.

A **written warning** is a much more serious matter because it summarizes previous oral attempts to correct the employee's behavior and is entered in the employee's work record file. More official than an oral reprimand, it brings disciplinary actions into focus by warning the employee of future consequences of rule violation.

Suspensions are disciplinary layoffs without pay given by management to impress upon the employee the seriousness of the offense. Oral and written reprimands might also achieve this purpose, but they do not involve a financial sacrifice on the part of the employee. A suspension serves as an example of the economic consequences associated with discharge and at the same time indicates that management

Exhibit 10.2 **Example of a Disciplinary Price List**

Type of Offense	First Offense	Second Offense	Third Offense	Fourth Offense	Fifth Offense
1. Abusive Language toward a Supervisor	3-day Suspension	Discharge			
2. Failure to Punch In and Out on Time Clock	Oral Warning	Written Warning	3-day Suspension	5-day Suspension	Discharge
3. Failure to Report an Absence	Oral Warning	Written Warning	3-day Suspension	5-day Suspension	Discharge
4. Stealing Company Property	Discharge				
5. Sleeping on the Job	Written Warning	3-day Suspension	5-day Suspension	Discharge	
6. Damage of Company Equipment or Property	Written Warning	5-day Suspension	Discharge		
7. Gambling or Engaging in a Lottery on Company Premises	5-day Suspension	Discharge			
8. Striking a Supervisor	Discharge				

is willing to retain the employee who will comply with directives and change errant ways. Management initially imposes a mild (1- to 3-day) suspension and will seldom impose a suspension greater than 10 days for a repeated offense. Under these circumstances, arbitrators are reluctant to reduce the suspensions, unless it can be shown that other employees were given lesser penalties for identical offenses under similar circumstances.

Discharge, unlike suspension or warnings, is not a corrective measure, since it means the employee is permanently released from the company. As mentioned earlier, arbitrators have attached tremendous significance to the effects of discharge upon the employee, regarding it as a last resort to be used when all other corrective attempts have failed and the employee's usefulness to the firm is totally lacking. An exception to this procedure occurs when the nature of the offense is so heinous (stealing, striking a supervisor, setting fire to company property, sexual assault of another employee) as to make other forms of corrective discipline inappropriate.

Progressive discipline also implies a *statute of limitations*. For example, it would be difficult to discharge an employee who has previously received two suspensions for failing to report his or her absence to management if the worker has worked for a fairly long period of time (say, 3 to 5 years) before committing a similar present offense. Management is usually not obligated to return to the first step, that is, an oral warning; however, discharge is not warranted—the employee's offense-free period indicates that corrective measures did have some effect and should be tried again before separating the employee from the firm.

How long a period of offense-free employment should justify an alteration of the progressive discipline procedure? One company has explicitly answered this question with the following labor agreement provision:

> With regard to discipline imposed for any cause other than those set forth above, the company will not refer to any disciplinary notices received by an employee more than five years prior to the current situation for which the employee is being disciplined.[26]

This provision is advantageous to management since it furnishes the arbitrator specific guidelines to be applied in progressive discipline. Furthermore, the 5-year statute of limitations is longer than that imposed by most arbitrators. One possible disadvantage of this strategy is that its specific inclusion in the labor agreement subjects the time period to collective bargaining—the union will be encouraged to negotiate a reduced statute of limitations, perhaps a time period shorter than most arbitrators would regard as being appropriate.

Finally, it should be noted that a discipline price list does not take the statute of limitations into account—its penalties are for repeated infractions regardless of the intervening time period. In these circumstances, should management negate its own price list by returning to a suspension even though discharge is the next step in the procedure? Or should it proceed with the discharge, knowing that many arbitrators, employing a statute of limitations, would reinstate the employee because of the period of time between his or her previous and recent offenses? Both courses of action have risks: In the first case, management might establish precedent that can adversely affect other cases; in the second, management might appear arbitrary in its discipline administration.

Degree of Proof in Disciplinary Cases: Nature of the Evidence and Witness Credibility

The burden of proof for all disciplinary actions rests with management; however, the degree of proof necessary varies among arbitrators. There are two schools of thought regarding the degree to which a person should be proven deserving of discipline. One arbitral attitude is that an employee must be shown guilty beyond reasonable doubt. This high degree of proof is used more often in discharge cases for criminal offenses (stealing or assault) rather than in discharge cases for noncriminal offenses (absenteeism, sleeping on the job, and so on), because it would be much more difficult for the employee to obtain employment with a work history that includes a discharge for criminal offenses.[27]

The second approach, used by a majority of arbitrators, is that the preponderance of the evidence must establish the employee's guilt. The testimony and evidence must be adequate to overcome opposing presumptions and evidence; the grievance decision is influenced by who presents the best case instead of an absolute standard. A common problem facing management and union representatives is that neither party knows for sure how much evidence the arbitrator will require to uphold the disciplinary penalty.

Another problem can occur when management uncovers the evidence while using search and seizure techniques. Few arbitrators deny the employer's right to impose, as a condition of employment, an inspection of the employee's clothes and packages on entering and leaving the plant; however, a problem arises when company officials search an employee's locker or, in some cases, home, with or without the employee's permission. Many arbitrators (and the Supreme Court in *Dennis M.*

O'Conner v. *Mango Ortega*) permit evidence obtained without the employee's knowledge if it is from company property, even if the property (such as a locker or tool chest) is momentarily under the control of the employee. On the other hand, few, if any, arbitrators believe evidence should be accepted if management obtained the evidence by forcibly breaking into the employee's personal property, even if the property is located on company premises.

Arbitrators must also consider the credibility of witnesses in discipline cases. This is particularly crucial in cases where there is direct contradictory testimony.

> Arbitrators know there are three sets of "facts" that radiate from each dispute: there are "the honest-to-God facts" (what actually did happen), "the perceptual facts" (the trier's evolving and changing views of the matter as it unfolds during and after the hearing), and "the facts as found" (final reconstruction may or may not coincide with the first set).[28]

Arbitrators may rely on several criteria in assessing witness credibility. Yet, one arbitrator notes,

> it is simply impossible to tell by observation if someone is lying under oath. You cannot tell by looking at and listening to the person. A trial judge in Chicago once compiled a list of tests to see if a witness is telling the truth: does he perspire; lick his lips; fidget in his seat; is he shifty-eyed? From my experience as an arbitrator, I can tell you that shifty-eyed people often tell the truth, while most honest-looking people will lead you by the nose right down the primrose path.[29]

Because of these difficulties some arbitrators attempt to avoid the credibility issue whenever possible. For example, in one case a union steward was discharged for allegedly shouting an obscenity at a supervisor during a grievance meeting. Much debate occurred over whether the steward had actually uttered the obscenity; however, the arbitrator did not particularly care about credibility because the action if true would still not warrant dismissal.[30]

Sometimes credibility is determined by applying the "who stands the most to gain by lying" or the "self-interest" principle. A supervisor might color his testimony to avoid embarrassment if the arbitrator reinstates the employee. However, an employee stands to gain more by lying, namely, his or her job. Thus, arbitrators using this principle will reduce the employee's credibility and usually decide the credibility issue in management's favor.

Many management officials have used the disciplinary elements of Exhibit 10.1 to establish the grievant's "guilt" of a disciplinary offense. Yet additional elements need to be considered if an arbitrator is to regard employee discipline, particularly discharge, as appropriate.

Nature of the Penalty Involved in Discipline

In some instances, management establishes that the employee was guilty of the offense but not that the penalty was appropriate. Arbitrators consider the reasonableness of the penalty relative to the offense, particularly if the employee was discharged. Few offenses merit discharge for their single commission, even if management regards the offense as being exceptionally serious. For example, termination might be too severe a penalty for an employee who loses $500 of company money. Arbitrators, while reluctant to modify suspensions, have no reservations about reducing a discharge penalty to a suspension. They reason that arbitrary or capricious discharge is a total waste to the employee as well as the firm, which incurs employment costs in hiring a replacement.

> Some cases make one wonder why management wanted to enforce a rule in such a silly way . . . ten electricians at a nuclear construction project had been dismissed by the . . . Company for refusing to remove American flag decals from their hard hats. The reason? They were accused of defacing company property, a violation of the published work rules. One worker said, "I'm so proud of being fired for this that I'd do it again tomorrow." Another proclaimed, "The flag's a symbol of our country. We've been promoting patriotism on the job and thought it would help boost morale . . . The decals don't damage or deface the hat, interfere with the quality of our work or slow down production." If you were chief executive of that company, how would you regard the judgment of your project manager?[31]

In determining whether the penalty is appropriate, arbitrators look to previous practices in the company or, in some instances, when management has never encountered the particular disciplinary situation, to their attitudes concerning an employer's ethical obligations toward its employees. Some arbitrators, for example, will contend that an employee with a previous good work record should first be offered some attempts at rehabilitation before being discharged for an alcohol problem, even if the labor agreement or other company policies do not specify or mandate these efforts.[32] Many managers contend that arbitrators exceed their authority under the labor agreement when they include these ethical considerations.

ETHICS

> Published arbitration opinions reveal an ever-increasing trend among arbitrators to invade the priesthood. Indeed, in divining the judgment to be meted out in discipline cases they have assumed the role not only of clergymen, but trial judges and psychiatrists. . . . In far too many cases the arbitrators' opinions demonstrate that the touchstone for evaluating the appropriateness of disciplinary penalties is simply the subjective views and personal prejudices of the arbitrators.[33]

Arbitrators also scrutinize the disciplinary proceedings to see whether mitigating circumstances were involved and due process was followed.

Mitigating Circumstances in Disciplinary Cases

If certain mitigating circumstances have influenced the offense, then arbitrators will tend to reduce a disciplinary penalty under one of two assumptions:

1. Management contributed to a problem and must therefore assume part of the responsibility for the wrongdoing.
2. The circumstances of the case were so unusual as to give great doubt that it will occur again, particularly if management uses corrective techniques instead of discharge.

An example of mitigating circumstances under the first arbitral assumption occurs when management has provided the employee with faulty tools and equipment and subsequently disciplines the employee for low production output.

A more common example of mitigating circumstances occurs when a management representative provokes the employee into committing physical or verbal abuse. In a representative discharge grievance, a fellow employee made vulgar and apparently misguided remarks about the fidelity of the grievant's wife. Later in the shift, another employee reported to the grievant that the foreman was asking other employees about the grievant's wife. The grievant thereupon confronted the foreman, who responded by treating the situation as a joke. The arbitrator reinstated the grievant on the basis that the foreman's poor judgment contributed to the grievant's subsequent physical attack on the supervisor.[34] In essence, arbitrators maintain that management must make every effort to avoid continuing an argument with the employee in order that the argument will not turn into a serious breach of industrial discipline.

Management might also contribute to a disciplinary infraction by condoning, either openly or tacitly, offenses committed in the shop. This situation is illustrated in a brief summary of an arbitration case from *The Wall Street Journal:*

> Humiliating the boss isn't grounds for dismissal, an arbitrator rules.
>
> On the night before his wedding day, a plant supervisor for International Harvester Co. was seized on the factory floor by six male workers. They removed some of his clothes and held him while a female worker put grease on his body. The company fired all seven employees, charging that the pre-wedding prank amounted to "physical abuse of the most degrading and humiliating form."
>
> The union agreed the prank was wrong, but argued that dismissal was an overly severe penalty. Agreeing with the union, arbitrator Louis Crane ordered the workers rehired, reducing the penalty to an unpaid suspension. He reasoned that the workers' "crude joke" wasn't physically harmful and was tacitly condoned by other supervisors who saw it happen.[35]

In some cases the foreman might encourage employees to break rules. Sometimes this encouragement is unintentional—a supervisor who doesn't wear specified safety equipment might encourage his or her employees to do likewise. In some instances the foreman might actually encourage the employee to violate the rules in order to maintain or increase productivity. Perhaps the most vivid documented example of this situation occurred at an airplane manufacturing facility. One of the most serious offenses (resulting in automatic discharge) is the use of a tap to rethread unaligned bolt holes. The use of a tap is strictly prohibited by Air Force regulations; however, the alternative is disassembling and reassembling previous installations to make sure the holes line up for bolt insertion.

In most instances, the supervisor cannot afford to have a large amount of down time recorded for the department. Therefore, many supervisors condoned and encouraged serious rule infractions in the name of efficiency, and the following remarks made to their employees were not uncommon:

> Now fellas, there's a big drive on taps. The Air Force just received a special memo. For God's sake, don't use a tap when I'm around. If somebody sees it while I'm in the area, it'll be my [deleted]. Look around first. Make sure I'm gone.[36]

A thorough discussion of the numerous mitigating circumstances suggested by the second arbitral assumption is beyond the scope of this chapter, but the following example is illustrative: An employee has been repeatedly warned and suspended for failure to report his absence to management when he is unable to work a production shift; the last suspension informed the grievant that another infraction would result in discharge. One month after suspension, the employee again fails to report his absence to management and is discharged when he reports to work the following morning. The employee contends (and adds evidence in the form of a doctor's slip) that his wife became suddenly and seriously ill and that his concern for his wife, coupled with no telephone in the apartment, resulted in his failure to report his absence to management. Here, management has followed all the principles of progressive discipline; however, the employee's discharge might be set aside if the arbitrator maintains the circumstances were so unusual as to give management no reason to think it will happen again in the future.

Arbitrators often consider the mitigating effects of the grievant's role as a union officer. Compared to other employees, union officials usually have special rights and privileges, particularly when conducting union business. Many arbitrators regard the union steward and foreman as organizational equals in discussion of union matters. Arbitrators therefore give the union steward leeway if harsh words are exchanged in these meetings, while other employees might be successfully charged with insubordination for identical actions.[37]

Union officers can also have greater responsibilities that correspond to their rights. For example, arbitrators and the National Labor Relations Board have upheld more serious disciplinary action for union officers who failed to prevent a wildcat strike than for employees who actually participated in the strike. This differential penalty implies that union stewards should be more knowledgeable about contractual prohibition against a wildcat strike and thus should uphold their contractual obligation to maintain uninterrupted production during the term of the labor agreement.

Perhaps the most commonly considered mitigating circumstance in discharge cases is the employee's work record. An arbitrator will likely consider reinstating a discharged employee who violated a work rule (one that prohibits insubordination, for example) if that employee has a long and good work record with the company. The arbitrator in this situation realizes the potential of the employee returning to previous work habits, so he or she might reinstate the employee with no back pay, which would represent a suspension. One study has shown that discharges of grievants with little seniority (less than 2 years' service with the organization) are more likely to be upheld than discharges of grievants having more than 11 years of seniority.[38] Indeed, a long, good work record might mitigate even a serious offense. The following situation involved an employee found guilty of sexual harassment. Yet, the arbitrator reinstated the grievant with no back pay (in effect, a 7-month suspension) with the following contention:

> Indeed, the Grievant's acts were clearly disgraceful. . . . On the other hand, the Arbitrator also has a duty to consider the effects of the penalty on the individual and to weigh any mitigating circumstances. Here the Grievant has given twenty-eight years of his life to the Company. There was no evidence that his work was in any way deficient or that he had past discipline problems involving sexual misconduct or any other kind of difficulties. Further, the Arbitrator notes that Ms. I______ did not complain to the Company about the incident but felt that she could handle it herself. Additionally, discharge would be particularly severe in light of the present economic recession and the dim prospects of reemployability of someone of the Grievant's skills at his age. Thus, the Grievant's length of service and his work record tips the balance just slightly against discharge.[39]

Due Process and the Weingarten Decision

Due process has both substantive and procedural aspects. Substantive due process focuses on the purpose or rationale of the work rules to ensure that an employee has not been arbitrarily disciplined or discharged.[40] This aspect is reflected in the previously discussed purposes and elements of discipline. Procedural aspects of due process are usually covered in labor agreements and include the following:[41]

1. The discipline process will follow certain time limits specified in the labor agreement.
2. The employee will be entitled to union representation when discipline is being administered and be given an opportunity to respond (defend himself or herself).
3. The employee will be notified of the specific offense in writing.

The due process procedure of union representation has been influenced by NLRB decisions and by the Supreme Court in its *Weingarten* decision. This decision will be discussed in detail because it illustrates the model of the labor relations process presented in Chapter 1 (Exhibit 1.1), and because it illustrates the impact of the fourth participant, the government, on labor-management relations.

The *Weingarten* decision pertained to an employee who was believed to have paid only a fraction of the price of food she took out of the store. During the interview with management representatives she repeatedly asked for a union representative to be present but was denied. Management subsequently found her version of the incident to be supported, but in her emotional state she admitted that over a period of time she had taken free lunches (totaling approximately $160) from the store, something a management official and other employees had also done. She was not disciplined for her actions; however, she informed her union representatives of the events, and an unfair labor practice was filed. The NLRB decided that management did commit an unfair labor practice, violating Section 8(a)(1) of the National Labor Relations Act (mentioned in Chapter 3), by denying the employee union representation.

Union representation must be given to the employee at the employee's request when the employee reasonably believes an investigation will result in disciplinary action. Employers, however, have no legal requirement to bargain with any union representative who attends the interview.

The NLRB's *Weingarten* decision was appealed through the courts, and eventually upheld by the Supreme Court. Rationale for this decision was in part based on the union official's potential contribution to the disciplinary investigation:

> A single employee confronted by an employer investigating whether certain conduct deserves discipline may be too fearful or inarticulate to relate accurately the incident being investigated, or too ignorant to raise extenuating factors. A knowledgeable union representative could assist the employer by eliciting favorable facts, and save the employer production time by getting to the bottom of the incident occasioning the interview. Certainly his presence need not transform the interview into an adversary contest.[42]

The NLRB has unanimously agreed, however, that *Weingarten* does not extend to employees who are not represented by a union.[43]

This decision also refuted the company's contention that union representation is only necessary after the company has made its discipline decision. The Supreme Court contended that this practice would diminish the value of union representation, thereby making it increasingly difficult for the employee to vindicate himself or herself in the subsequent grievance proceedings. There have been many judicial decisions interpreting procedural issues of *Weingarten.* For example, does an employee waive his or her right to representation if he or she is silent in the meeting? The answer to this question along with other legal implications are illustrated in "Labor Relations in Action."

Labor Relations in Action

Conditions Affecting Union Representation under *Weingarten* Decision

I. Representation must be requested.
   - A. Silence can be an effective waiver.
   - B. There is no voluntary waiver of the right when the employee is threatened with a harsher penalty if the matter goes to a higher level.
   - C. The employee does not have to remain adamant in his request for union representation.
   - D. The employee may not leave the interview and seek out a union representative in violation of his supervisor's orders and established company policy.
   - E. A specific union representative need not be provided if he is unavailable due to personal or other reasons for which the employer is not responsible.

II. The employee must reasonably believe that the investigation will result in disciplinary action.

III. The exercise of the right may not interfere with legitimate employer prerogatives.
   - A. The employee cannot delay the meeting by calling for a representative who is not available.
   - B. The union cannot urge employees to interfere with the management's investigative process by instructing its members not to cooperate with management.
   - C. The employer does not have to postpone the interview because a particular representative is unavailable, nor does it have to secure or suggest an alternate.
   - D. The employee may not refuse an order to report to a supervisor's office.

IV. The employer is not required to bargain with the union representative at the meeting.
   - A. The union representative has the right to participate in the interview.
   - B. The employee may consult with his representative prior to the investigatory meeting.
   - C. The employee has a right to a general statement of the charge before his consultation with the union representative.
   - D. The employer is free to hear the employee's explanation first and delay until conclusion of the interview the union representative's additions and clarifications.

V. At present, the right to representation at investigatory interviews does not apply to nonunionized employees.

Source: Michael Procopio, "A Weingarten Update." Modified from the June 1986 issue of *Labor Law Journal*, Vol. 37, p. 340, published and copyrighted by Commerce Clearing House, Inc., 4025 W. Peterson Avenue, Chicago, Illinois 60646.

The written notice element of due process has caused some problems for management and is a major reason for the involvement of industrial relations representatives in the discipline process. Say an employee gets into a heated argument with the supervisor, refuses to work the assignment, and shouts an obscenity at the supervisor. The foreman could discipline the employee for "directing obscene and profane language toward a management representative." Once the charges are in writing, management must convince the arbitrator that this charge warrants discipline, a task that is not easy given the usual arbitral recognition that obscene language is regarded as common shop talk in an industrial facility. In this instance, management would have been wiser to have disciplined the employee for a more serious offense: "Insubordination: refusal to follow supervisory orders." However, management can seldom change the offense once it is in writing and handed to the grievant.

Consequently, a member of the industrial relations department is usually present for consultation (or in some cases direction) before the charges are reduced to writing.

Another related element of due process is *double jeopardy*—assigning an employee a more severe penalty than the one originally given. The rationale against double jeopardy is that management is held to any decision that purports to be final; therefore, it is important that it acts only after ascertaining all relevant facts and determining the magnitude of the offense. Management can avoid the problem of double jeopardy if it makes clear to the grievant that the action taken in the first instance is tentative, pending further investigation by higher company officials. Usually, this takes the form of an indefinite suspension that, pending a subsequent investigation, can be converted to discharge without arbitral disapproval. A final element of due process is the keeping of secret records on the employee, which most arbitrators maintain are worse than no records at all.

One arbitrator notes three alternative positions that the arbitrator can take regarding procedural or due process irregularities:

> (1) [T]hat unless there is strict compliance with the procedural requirements, the whole action will be nullified; (2) that the requirements are of significance only where the employee can show that he has been prejudiced by failure to comply therewith; or (3) that the requirements are important, and that any failure to comply will be penalized, but that the action taken is not thereby rendered null and void.[44]

Arbitrators tend to favor the third alternative, reasoning that management should suffer the consequences of its errors, but not to the point of exonerating an employee who is guilty of a serious offense (particularly if it has not prejudiced the employee's case). Currently, the NLRB, in its *Taracorp* decision, indicates that an employee who is discharged for cause will not be reinstated simply because his or her *Weingarten* rights were violated.[45]

Summary

In many respects, employee discipline represents the most significant day-to-day issue in administering the labor agreement. For the union and management organizations, administration of discipline is a key factor related to control and production; the supervisor and the affected employee are even more directly and personally affected.

Management had a unilateral right to discharge or discipline employees until the 1930s, although psychological reform and efficiency movements in the early 1900s urged management to critically examine its disciplinary policies. Some managers realized that an employee represented an investment that could be unnecessarily lost due to whimsical disciplinary actions. These individuals realized that they had an obligation to provide employees with clear work rules and proper training, which would minimize the number of discipline problems and lead to increased productivity. The establishment of the NLRB further refined employers' disciplinary policies, as employees discharged for their union activities could be reinstated to their jobs with back pay.

Discipline in unionized settings must be for just cause, a concept consisting of several dimensions. While discipline can accomplish several purposes for the organization, management may have to prove that its actions were taken to correct an employee's behavior. Correction suggests that an employee must be aware of work rules that are clear in their content as well as consequences for their infraction. The work rules must also be reasonable—that is, related to the job—and consistently applied to all employees under similar circumstances.

Discipline's corrective emphasis also suggests progressive or more severe penalties be given to an employee for repeating a similar offense. Progressive discipline impresses upon the employee the seriousness of repeated rule infractions while giving the employee additional chances to correct work behavior. Usually, management has to give an employee an oral warning for the first offense, then a written warning and suspension for subsequent, similar offenses. Discharge is a last resort, used only when all other attempts at correction have failed or the nature of the offense is so unacceptable as to make corrective efforts inappropriate.

Arbitration of discipline grievances places the burden of proof on management to establish that the employee committed the offense. Arbitrators may require the company to prove the employee guilty beyond a reasonable doubt or by establishing a preponderance of the evidence. Additional dimensions of evidence can occur when the company attempts to enter the employee's work record into the hearing or uses search and seizure techniques, or when contradictory testimony is entered into the hearing. Management must also establish that the penalty fits the crime and that it considered all possible mitigating circumstances before imposing discipline.

Management must also provide the employee with due process in the disciplinary procedure; that it, it must ensure that the appropriate contractual provisions are upheld. The employee usually has the right to union representation and the right to be notified of the offense in writing.

Key Terms

just cause
price list
progressive discipline
oral warning
written warning
suspensions

Discussion Questions

1. Why is discipline a most significant issue for the union and management organizations? Describe how this significance has shifted over time.
2. One union newspaper indicated how it saved an employee's job. The employee was in the mechanic's classification and was discharged for refusing to comply with management's sudden, unilateral rule that mechanics must perform janitorial duties. Given this sketchy situation, discuss the many possible reasons for the disciplinary action, indicating why the arbitrator might not have been convinced that management's discipline was for a legitimate purpose. (You are free to make assumptions in your answer.)
3. Explain in some detail the difficulties management would have in administering the following work rule in accordance with the disciplinary principles established in the chapter: "Any employee reporting to work under the influence of alcohol will be subject to discharge."
4. Indicate the comparative advantages and disadvantages of a checklist of disciplinary prerogatives in the labor agreement and a one-sentence contractual provision indicating "management has the right to discipline or discharge an employee for cause."

5. While not subject to judicial scrutiny, evidence in an arbitration hearing still has its complexities. Discuss the complexities that could be involved in an arbitration hearing involving an employee who was discharged for smoking marijuana on the job.
6. Assume you are in charge of establishing a training program for supervisors in administering discipline. Based on the supervisor's potential role in the disciplinary process, formulate and discuss three major principles you would stress in this session.

References

1. Robert E. Meade, "AAA Labor-Management Arbitration Case Analysis," *The American Arbitration Association,* May 1986, p. 1.
2. Clyde W. Summers, "Protecting All Employees against Unjust Dismissal," *Harvard Business Review* 58 (January–February 1980), p. 106.
3. Lawrence Stessin, *Employee Discipline* (Washington, D.C.: Bureau of National Affairs Inc., 1960), pp. 2–3.
4. For an example of how the NLRB can alter an organization's discipline policies, see Marcia A. Graham, "Obscenity and Profanity at Work," *Employee Relations Law Journal 11* (Spring 1986), pp. 662–677.
5. Milo Geyelin, "Fired Managers Winning More Lawsuits," *The Wall Street Journal,* September 7, 1989, B-1. See also, William H. Holley, Jr. and Roger S. Wolters, "An Employment-at-Will Vulnerability Audit," *Personnel Journal* 66 (April 1987), pp. 130–138; William H. Holley, Jr. and Roger S. Wolters, *Labor Relations: An Experiential and Case Approach* (Hinsdale, Ill.: The Dryden Press, 1988), pp. 33–35.
6. Kenneth M. Jennings, Barbara Sheffield, and Roger S. Wolters, "The Arbitration of Discharge Cases: A Forty Year Perspective," *Labor Law Journal* 38 (January 1987), p. 35. See also, Ahmad Karim and Thomas H. Stone, "An Empirical Examination of Arbitrator Decisions in Reversal and Reduction Discharge Hearings," *Labor Studies Journal* 13 (no. 2, Spring 1988), p. 47.
7. See, for example, Thomas R. Knight, "The Impact of Arbitration on the Administration of Disciplinary Policies," *Arbitration Journal* 39 (March 1984), pp. 43–56.
8. Arthur Anthony Malinowski, "An Empirical Analysis of Discharge Cases and the Work History of Employees Reinstated by Labor Arbitrators," *Arbitration Journal* 36 (March 1981), p. 39.
9. Chalmer E. Labig, Jr., I. B. Helburn, and Robert C. Rodgers, "Discipline, History, Seniority, and Reason for Discharge as Predictors of Post-Reinstatement Job Performance," *The Arbitration Journal* 40 (September 1985), p. 49. For additional considerations of this relationship, see Robert C. Rodgers, I. B. Helburn, and John E. Hunter, "The Relationship of Seniority to Job Performance Following Reinstatement," *Academy of Management Journal* 29 (March 1986), pp. 101–114.
10. D. C. Miller, "Supervisor: Evolution of a Forgotten Role," in *Supervisory Leadership and Productivity,* eds. Floyd Mann, George Homans, and Delbert Miller (San Francisco: Chandler, 1965), p. 113.
11. "Oil, Chemical, and Atomic," *Union News,* July 1970, p. 9.
12. Robert Coulson, *The Termination Handbook* (New York: The Free Press, 1981), p. 7. See also John Herrick, "Labor Arbitration as Viewed by Labor Arbitrators," *Arbitration Journal* 38 (March 1983), p. 42.
13. Bureau of National Affairs Inc., *Basic Patterns in Union Contracts* (Washington, D.C.: Bureau of National Affairs Inc., 1989), p. 7.
14. *Knauf Fiberglass,* 81 LA 336 (R. Abrams, 1983).
15. *Hoosier Panel Co., Inc.,* 61 LA 983 (M. Volz, 1973).
16. Marvin Hill Jr. and Diana Beck, "Some Thoughts on Just Cause and Group Discipline," *Arbitration Journal* 41 (June 1986), pp. 60–62.
17. For more thorough explanations of this Exhibit, see Donald S. McPherson, "The Evolving Concept of Just Cause: Carroll R. Daugherty and the Requirement of Disciplinary Due Process," *Labor Law Journal* (July 1987), pp. 387–403; and Adolph M. Koven and Susan L. Smith, *Just Cause: The Seven Tests* (San Francisco: Kendall/Hurst, 1985).
18. *Buick Youngstown Company,* 41 LA 570–573 (H. Dworkin, 1963).
19. *A. B. Chance Company,* 57 LA 725–731 (P. Florey, 1971).
20. Terry L. Leap and Michael D. Crino, "How to Deal with Bizarre Behavior," *Harvard Business Review* (May–June 1986), pp. 18–25. This article also furnishes eight criteria for management in determining if discharge for previously unconsidered disciplinary infractions is justified.
21. Koven and Smith, *Just Cause,* pp. 86–87.
22. For additional consideration of the "moonlighting" employee see Muhammad Jamal, "Moonlighting Myths," *The Personnel Journal* 67 (May 1988), pp. 48–53.
23. See, for example, Douglas Massengill and Donald J. Petersen, "Smokers vs. Nonsmokers in the Work Place: Clearing the Air," *Employee Relations Law Review* 10 (Winter 1984–1985), pp. 546–548.
24. Marvin Hill, Jr., and Donald Dawson, "Discharge for Off-Duty Misconduct in the Private and Public Sectors," *Arbitration Journal* 40 (June 1985), pp. 24–37.
25. "Cocaine Conviction Is Insufficient Cause for Discharge, Arbitrator Rules," Bureau of National Affairs Inc., *Daily Labor Report,* no. 171 (September 2, 1988), pp. A-1, A-2.
26. *Inmot Corporation,* 58 LA 18 (J. Sembower, 1972).
27. It should be noted, however, that one research study of discharge for theft cases found many arbitrators using a lesser degree of proof than "beyond a reasonable doubt." Larry D. Farley and Joseph A. Allotta, "Standards of Proof in Discharge Arbitration: A Practitioner's View," *Labor Law Journal* 35 (July 1984), p. 425.
28. *Gindy Manufacturing Company,* 58 LA 1038–1040 (M. Handsaker, 1972).
29. Edgar A. Jones, Jr. "Selected Problems of Procedure and Evidence," in *Arbitration in Practice,* ed. Arnold M. Zack (Ithaca, N.Y.: ILR Press, 1984), p. 62.

30. *Ibid,* p. 63. For further insights into this area see Ann Gosline, "Witnesses in Labor Arbitration: Spotters, Informers, and the Code of Silence," *The Arbitration Journal* 43 (March 1988), pp. 44–54.
31. Coulson, *The Termination Handbook,* p. 91.
32. Michael Marmo, "Arbitrators View Alcoholic Employees: Discipline or Rehabilitation?" *Arbitration Journal* 37 (March 1982), p. 24.
33. William M. Saxton, "Discipline and Discharge Cases," Address before the National Academy of Arbitrators, Dearborn, Michigan, *Daily Labor Report* (Washington, D.C.: Bureau of National Affairs Inc., 1979), cited in Malinowski, "An Empirical Analysis." For a subsequent "debate" of this quotation, see John R. Phillips, "Their Own Brand of Industrial Justice: Arbitrators' Excesses in Discharge Cases," *Employee Relations Law Journal* 10 (Summer 1984); and Robert Coulson, "The Arbitrator's Role in Discharge Cases: Another Viewpoint," *Employee Relations Law Journal* 10 (Summer 1984), pp. 61-63.
34. *Gindy Manufacturing Company,* 58 LA 1038–1040 (M. Handsaker, 1972).
35. "Labor Letter," *The Wall Street Journal,* August 30, 1977, p. 1. Reprinted by permission of *The Wall Street Journal,* © Dow Jones & Company, Inc., 1977. All rights reserved.
36. Joseph Bensman and Israel Gerver, "Crime and Punishment in the Factory: The Function of Deviancy in Maintaining the Social System," *American Sociological Review* (August 1963), p. 593. For positive aspects of the supervisor's role in discipline see R. Dirk Van Horne, "Discipline: Purpose and Effect," *Personnel Journal* 48 (September 1969), pp. 728-731.
37. See, for example, *H. P. Smith Paper Company,* 81 LA 896 (I. Lieberman, 1983).
38. Jennings, Sheffield, and Wolters, *The Arbitration of Discharge Cases,* p. 43.
39. *Dayton Power and Light,* 80 LA 21–22 (T. Heinsz, 1982).
40. John D. Aram and Paul F. Salipante Jr., "An Evaluation of Organizational Due Process in the Resolution of Employee/Employer Conflict," *Academy of Management Review* 6 (1981), p. 200. See also Raymond L. Hogler, "Industrial Due Process and Judicial Review of Arbitration Awards," *Labor Law Journal* 31 (September 1980), pp. 570–576.
41. In some cases, arbitrators and the courts have contended that due process procedures, such as the rights of employees to be heard before management's discharge decision is reduced to writing, are implied from the "just cause" provision. An employer might therefore be responsible for due process procedures even though they are not specified in the labor agreement. John S. Irving and Carl L. Taylor, "Pre-Disciplinary Hearings: An Unbargained Procedural Trap in Arbitration," *Employee Relations Law Journal* 6 (1980–1981), pp. 195–206.
42. *NLRB* v. *J. Weingarten, Inc.,* 420 U.S. 262, 1974. For a discussion of subsequent NLRB cases that appear to expand the principles expressed in *Weingarten,* see Bruce Stickler, "Investigating Employee Misconduct: Must the Union Be There?" *Employee Relations Law Journal* 3 (Autumn 1977), pp. 255–265; Lewis H. Silverman and Michael J. Soltis, "*Weingarten:* An Old Trumpet Plays the Labor Circuit," *Labor Law Journal* 32 (November 1981), pp. 725–736; Paul N. Erickson Jr. and Clifford E. Smith, "The Right of Union Representation During Investigatory Interviews," *Arbitration Journal* 33 (June 1978), pp. 29–36. See also M. J. Fox, Louis V. Baldovin, Jr., and Thomas R. Fox, "The Weingarten Doctrine," *The Arbitration Journal* 40 (June 1985), pp. 45–54. The Weingarten decision has also been held by an appeals court to be applicable in at least some federal sector situations. "Court Permits Union Representation at Meetings with DOD Investigators," Bureau of National Affairs Inc., *Daily Labor Report,* no. 173 (September 7, 1988), A-1.
43. "NLRB Limits Weingarten Rights to Union-Represented Employees," Bureau of National Affairs Inc., *Daily Labor Report,* no. 132 (July 11, 1988), p. 2.
44. R. W. Fleming, *The Labor Arbitration Process* (Champaign: University of Illinois Press, 1965), p. 139.
45. Raymond L. Hogler, "*Taracorp* and Remedies for Weingarten Violations: The Evolution of Industrial Due Process," *Labor Law Journal* 37 (July 1986).

CHAPTER 11

Institutional Issues: Managerial Rights, Union Security, and the Rights of Minority and Female Employees

"Unions continue to have a powerful impact on the decision-making process in our economy. We must not lose sight of the role that unions continue to play in protecting workers against injustice in the work place and in the decisions regarding the distribution of shares in production. The fact that many managements are following aggressive strategies in dealing with unions demonstrates that the unions have not become impotent."

Comments by Paul Yager in *Unions Today: New Tactics to Tackle Tough Times* (Washington, D.C.: Bureau of National Affairs Inc., 1985), p. 139.

A major collective bargaining issue pertains to the rights and obligations of labor and management organizations. Management's major institutional issue concerns its rights to manage. The union has a corresponding institutional concern of union security, or its ability to preserve its organization—mainly by enrolling and retaining employee members. These two concerns are discussed in this chapter, as is the relationship between organized labor and minority and female employees.

Managerial Rights

Background and Extent of Managerial Rights

Before the passage of the National Labor Relations Act in 1935, management rights and discretion in operating facilities were seldom questioned, and managers were virtually free to run their operations as they saw fit. In many cases unions were considered intruders into managerial prerogatives, since there were few laws regulating managers' actions toward employees. Consider, for example, the following managerial quotation, which could have been widely applicable in the early 1900s but is out of date today due to employment laws:

> Who but a miserable, craven-hearted man would permit himself to be subjected to such rules, extending even to the number of apprentices he may employ, and the manner in which they shall be bound to him; to the kind of work which will be performed in his own office, at particular hours of the day, and to the sex of the persons employed. . . . For ourselves, we never employed a female as compositor, and have no great opinion of apprentices; but sooner than be restricted on these points, or any other, by a self-constituted tribunal outside of the office, we would go back to the employment of our boyhood and dig potatoes. . . . It is marvelous to us how any employer having a soul of a man within him can submit to such degradation.[1]

Although unions have become more accepted today, managers remain concerned over the gradual erosion of their rights in the labor relations process. Two related questions are

1. Does management have inherent rights regarding its employees?
2. To what extent does the union desire to assume managerial discretion?

Under common law, management officials were relatively free to manage their businesses and their employees. In unilaterally running the operation, the employer drew from the concepts of property rights and the laws of agency as well as the legal and social acceptance of "private enterprise," "ingenuity," and the "profit motive." Hence, management assumed the right to manage derived from the property rights of the owners or stockholders. The authority of these owners is delegated to management, which in turn directs the employees in achieving the goals of the company. Following this line of reasoning, management contends it cannot share its prerogatives with employees or any other group, as that would represent a dereliction of legal responsibility to the stockholders.

There is no question that management can organize, arrange, and direct the machinery, materials, and money of the enterprise; however, at least one author contends that managers have no comparable right to direct the employees. Property rights carry no duty on the part of others to be managed—they can quit or be discharged without regard to the employer's property rights. Thus, management's property rights have never extended over the employees. "What has happened is that, through the union, the employee has acquired sufficient power to exercise the legal right that he has always possessed."[2]

Most unions in the United States, unlike their European counterparts (see Chapter 15), are typically reluctant to become "partners with management"—directly involved in managerial rights pertaining to layout of equipment, financial policies, sources of materials, and so forth. Union officers realize that many union members

second-guess or challenge management decisions instead of supporting or echoing them.

Yet the union's reluctance to avoid the management rights issue is not absolute. Management rights are implemented to achieve significant managerial goals of organizational flexibility and efficiency. These goals are often challenged and limited by a union organization that is concerned about arbitrary or inconsistent managerial actions and job security protections for its members.[3] Some research has found that craft and industrial unions have become more interested in joint determination of traditional management issues (products to be manufactured, services to be performed, and customer relations, for example) over the past 20 years. This new emphasis is largely attributed to competitive pressures, which have influenced union officials to evaluate a broader range of managerial decisions that could reduce union members' job opportunities.[4]

Reserved Rights and the Collective Bargaining Agreement

Management does not have any inherent rights over employees, and employees can sometimes alter working conditions through collective bargaining and the negotiated labor agreement. Yet problems sometimes occur when management claims it has full discretion to administer issues that are not covered in the labor agreement. There is a **reserved rights doctrine** that indicates management has full authority and discretion regarding all matters that are not covered in the labor agreement. For example, if the labor agreement is silent on overtime administration then under the reserved rights doctrine management can assign overtime to whomever it sees fit. Yet the reserved rights doctrine is qualified or diluted by the following three factors:[5]

- *Legal obligations* placed on management to negotiate "mandatory" collective bargaining issues with the union.
- *Arbitrators' decisions,* which often interpret labor agreement provisions differently from management (consider the implications of "just cause" for discharge in Chapter 10, for example). Arbitrators also consider past practices, which can add to the terms of the labor agreement. (See Chapter 9.)
- *Attitudes and related actions of some arbitrators, management, and union officials* that the labor agreement is a "living document" reflecting the dynamics of labor-management relationships. Holders of this attitude tend to view the labor agreement in flexible terms. Management, for example, might wish to establish "mid-contract bargaining" with the union, particularly when the firm is unstable due to changes in the economy or when there is a need for productivity improvements.

Thus, management cannot rely too strongly on the reserved rights doctrine. In fact, management officials usually negotiate either a long or short form *management prerogatives* or *management rights* provision in the labor agreement. The following management rights provision illustrates the short form:

> Employer retains all rights to manage, direct, and control its business in all particulars, except as such rights are expressly and specifically modified by the terms of this agreement or any subsequent agreement.

Some managers prefer this all-encompassing provision on the assumption that it guarantees management complete discretion in those matters not cited in the labor agreement. Originally, managers felt this provision could justify their refusal to go to arbitration over an issue not specifically stated in the labor agreement. However, as discussed in Chapter 9, the Supreme Court (*United Steelworkers* v. *Warrior and Gulf Navigation Company*) stated that the arbitrator should determine whether an issue is a managerial prerogative if it is not specifically included in the labor agreement.

Many management officials responded to this decision by adopting the long form of the management rights provision—indicating several specific areas where management rights are unqualified (see Exhibit 11.1). Presumably, arbitrators, upon seeing these prerogatives clearly stated in the labor agreement, would rule in management's favor on whether the grievance is subject to arbitration. However, the long-form management rights clause has its problems:

1. It is difficult to list items that clearly specify management's unilateral discretion.
2. Management rights is a mandatory subject for negotiation. For management to obtain a strong management rights provision, it may have to trade elsewhere; for example, it may have to allow the union a strong union security clause (a "dues checkoff" and/or "union shop" clause, discussed later in this chapter, for example).
3. Management may overlook an item and fail to include it in the labor agreement. Arbitrators view a detailed management rights provision as expressing managerial intent to define all its prerogatives. Although it is impossible for management to express all of its felt prerogatives, most arbitrators would conclude that management should not view an omitted issue as being within its exclusive domain.

Both long and short forms of management rights clauses can cause additional problems. Most of the items cited in these provisions are subject to union involvement. Items in the short form are usually qualified by the terms of the agreement, whereas items in the long form can eventually become collective bargaining topics. By insisting on including the management rights clause in the labor agreement, management runs the risk of stirring up ideological differences with the union. The items in the management rights provision might also influence the union's bargaining goals in subsequent negotiations.

Management apparently believes the advantages of the management rights clause offset potential risks. Approximately 79 percent of labor agreements contain management rights clauses that help remind arbitrators, union officials, and other managers (particularly first-line supervisors) that management never gives up its administrative initiative to establish the status quo.[6] The union likewise seeks contractual language to strengthen its security. This issue is discussed in the following section.

Union Security

A **union security clause** in the labor agreement makes it easier for the union to enroll and retain members. Unions are essentially guaranteed only a 1-year existence upon NLRB union certification under the National Labor Relations Act. They therefore can be challenged by a rival union or by a decertification election after 12 months or at the end of the negotiated labor agreement (not to exceed 3 years'

Exhibit 11.1

Example of a Long-Form Management Rights Clause

Except as otherwise specifically provided in this Agreement, the Employer has the sole and exclusive right to exercise all the rights or functions of management, and the exercise of any such rights or functions shall not be subject to the grievance or arbitration provisions of this Agreement.

Without limiting the generality of the foregoing, as used herein, the term "Rights of Management" includes:

a. the right to manage the plant;
b. the right to schedule working hours;
c. the right to establish, modify or change work schedules or standards;
d. the right to direct the working forces, including the right to hire, promote, or transfer any employee;
e. the location of the business, including the establishment of new plants or departments, divisions or subdivisions thereof, and the relocation or closing of plants, departments, divisions or subdivisions thereof;
f. the determination of products to be manufactured or sold or service to be rendered or supplied;
g. the determination of the layout and the machinery, equipment or materials to be used in the business;
h. the determination of processes, techniques, methods, and means of manufacture, maintenance or distribution, including any changes or adjustments of any machinery or equipment;
i. the determination of the size and character of inventories;
j. the determination of financial policy, including accounting procedures, prices of goods or services rendered or supplied, and customer relations;
k. the determination of the organization of each production, service maintenance or distribution department, division or subdivision or any other production maintenance, service or distribution unit deemed appropriate by the Employer;
l. the selection, promotion, or transfer of employees to supervisory or other managerial positions or to positions outside of the bargaining unit;
m. the determination of the size of the working force;
n. the allocation and assignment of work to employees;
o. the determination of policy affecting the selection or training of new employees;
p. the establishment of quality and quantity standards and the judgment of the quality and quantity of workmanship required;
q. the control and use of the plant property, material, machinery, or equipment;
r. the scheduling of operations and the determination of the number and duration of shifts;
s. the determination of safety, health, and property protection measures for the plant;
t. the establishment, modification and enforcement of plant rules or regulations, which are not in direct conflict with any of the provisions of this Agreement;
u. the transfer of work from one job to another or from one plant, department, division or other plant unit to another;
v. introduction of new, improved or different production, maintenance, service or distribution methods or facilities or a change in existing methods or facilities;
w. the placing of production, service, maintenance or distribution work with outside contractors or subcontractors;
x. the determination of the amount of supervision necessary;
y. the right to terminate, merge or sell the business or any part thereof; and
z. the transfer of employees from one job to another or from one plant, department, division or other plant unit to another.

It is agreed that the enumeration of management prerogatives above shall not be deemed to exclude other management prerogatives not specifically enumerated above.

Source: Reprinted by permission of the publisher from Walter E. Baer, *Practice and Precedent in Labor Relations* (Lexington, Mass.: D. C. Heath and Company, Copyright 1972 by D. C. Heath and Company).

duration). A union security provision does not eliminate this possibility but can make it easier for the current union to enroll members, which is an initial step in winning their loyalty.

Union security provisions also tend to strengthen the union's financial resources by increasing the number of dues-paying members. Unions would like to recoup their initial time and money investments spent on organizing employees at an industrial facility by subsequently obtaining dues from the eligible members. Union leaders also feel they are morally justified in asking employees to pay for services provided by the union, since it is legally obligated to represent all bargaining-unit employees regardless of their union membership.

Union security provisions are therefore sought to strengthen the union, which can offer benefits to the employer as well as the union. Many might contend that employers prefer dealing with a weak instead of a strong union. Weak unions might aid the employer who wishes to terminate the union-management relationship, but they frustrate an employer who earnestly tries to resolve working condition disputes through an established union-management relationship. It is commonly the union, not the employer, who sells the collective bargaining agreement to the membership. A union has difficulty in accomplishing this objective when there are non–union member factions that vocalize their dissent.

Union officials contend that union security provisions also offer other advantages to the employer. They contend that less time will be spent in recruiting new members and collecting dues of existing members during the workday. However, management officials counter that this time saving will not result in more production, since union officials might use the extra time to police the labor agreement and formulate additional grievances. Unions also maintain that morale would be improved if all employees were union members. Tensions arise when some people do not pay for the services shared by all. However, a counterargument could be made that tensions are not reduced by union security, merely redirected. The possible anger of union members working with nonunion employees is replaced by the anger of forced members who feel they have to pay for unwanted services.

Union Security Provisions

In view of their potential advantages and disadvantages, union security provisions have taken one or more of the following forms.

Closed Shop In order for an employee to obtain a job in a **closed shop,** he or she must first become a member of a union. The closed shop was made unlawful by the Taft-Hartley Act of 1947.

Union Hiring Hall According to the **union hiring hall** provision, employers must hire employees referred by the union if the union can supply a sufficient number of qualified applications. This provision is usually found in the construction trades, where a union provides the employer with qualified employees for a relatively short-term project. This provision has been supported by the Supreme Court, with the provision that the union hiring hall does not discriminate between union and non-union applicants.

Union Shop Under a **union shop** contract provision, the employee does not have to be a union member in order to be hired by the company. However, he or she must become a union member after a probationary period of not less than 30 days in order to remain employed by the company. Under a union shop provision, the company does not always have to discharge an employee who is not a union member if (1) the employer believes union membership was not offered the employee on the same terms as other employees or (2) membership was denied for reasons other than the failure to tender dues.[7] The union shop provision does not give the union the right to reject certain employees for membership and then seek their discharge for not being union members.

Agency Shop An employee is not required to join the union by an **agency shop** provision; however, in order to remain employed by the company, the employee must pay to the union a sum equal to membership dues. This provision assumes that employees should not be forced to join a union but nonetheless should help defray the bargaining and grievance costs. The Supreme Court has upheld the validity of the agency shop in both the private and public sectors.[8]

The Supreme Court (*Communication Workers* vs. *Beck*) has limited the amount of fees that a union can collect under an agency shop arrangement. Now unions cannot exact fees beyond those necessary to finance collective bargaining (contract negotiation and grievance handling) whenever a nonmember objects to the use of his or her dues payments for political or other purposes. The agency fee payer must notify the union of his or her objection to this use of the funds. However, the union must set up accounting practices to anticipate the agency fee payer who raises this objection. The impact of *Beck* on the number of employee charges to seek dues returns is uncertain, although one observer anticipates that many agency shop members will raise objections to get some of their dues payments back, since he estimates the union's collective bargaining costs to be only 20 percent of the dues they collect.[9]

Maintenance of Membership This provision does not require all employees to become members of a union as a condition of employment. However, an employee who joins the union must remain a member for a specified period of time, such as the duration of the labor agreement. Maintenance of membership provisions also contain an escape period (usually 15 days) after the subsequent labor agreement becomes effective. Employees who do not leave the union during the escape period must remain members until the next escape period.

"Quasi-Union Shop" It is illegal to require the union shop provision in right-to-work states. However, these legal restrictions are sometimes avoided through **quasi-union shop** provisions in the labor agreement. Usually, the first page of the agreement states that employees will have to join the union as a condition of employment—a union shop provision. The union steward shows the new employee this provision, which usually results in that employee joining the union. A second provision, usually buried in a footnote elsewhere in the labor agreement, states, "Any provision found in this agreement that conflicts with local, state, or federal law is considered null and void." These provisions have the same effect as a union shop (because the new employee will seldom research the labor agreement when confronted by the union steward) and at the same time comply with anti–union shop legislation.

Contingency Union Shop Some labor agreements in right-to-work states (where union membership is not a condition of employment) have a **contingency union shop** provision stating that the union security provision presently in force will automatically convert to a union shop provision if the state's right-to-work laws are changed. This clause, unlike the quasi-union shop, does not try to dupe new employees into joining the union; instead, it mandates a labor agreement clause change if state legislation permits.

Preferential Treatment Clause A negotiated labor agreement provision that indicates union members will be given employment preference over non–union members when a new facility is opened is called the **preferential treatment clause.** This arrangement was negotiated between the United Auto Workers and General Motors for the new Saturn manufacturing plant located in Spring Hill, Tennessee and was upheld by the National Labor Relations Board.

Dues Checkoff A provision that can be used in connection with any of the previously cited union security provisions or can stand alone in the labor agreement is the **dues checkoff** clause. It is not a union security clause in the strict sense of the word, as it does not guarantee that some or all employees will become union members. However, dues checkoff allows the union members to have their dues automatically taken out of their payroll checks (as for any other payroll deduction) and transferred to the union. This provision is most important to the union; indeed, most unions given an either/or choice would prefer dues checkoff over any other union security provision, because it assures the union of an uninterrupted flow of income. Without a systematic dues deduction, union officers would have to spend a great deal of time with recalcitrant members who kept delaying their dues payments. In many cases, the employer automatically agrees to this provision in the first contract negotiation on the assumption that every other labor agreement contains it. Often an administrative fee is charged the union for the collection of dues and other paperwork. In negotiations, astute management officials usually bargain for something in return for this provision, such as flexibility in making work assignments, subcontracting, and writing job descriptions.

Union security provisions were found in 98 percent of the labor agreements reviewed in a recent survey. Union shop provisions were by far the most common (62 percent of the surveyed agreements) followed by agency shop (11 percent) and maintenance of membership provisions (4 percent). Likewise, over 90 percent of the agreements provided for checkoff procedures for dues, assessments, and initiation fees.[10] In many cases, however, the parties are not free to negotiate a particular union security provision. Right-to-work laws that restrict this discretion are discussed in the next two sections.

Right-to-Work Laws: Controversy and Effects

Employers, some employees, and the courts have long been concerned with union security provisions.[11] The Taft-Hartley Act in 1947 gave federal permission to states to enact right-to-work laws. More specifically, Section 14(b) of the act remains in force today and states:

> Nothing in this Act shall be construed as authorizing the execution or application of agreements requiring membership in a labor organization as a condition of employment in any State or Territory in which such execution or application is prohibited by State or Territorial law.

Under this provision, states may initiate legislation prohibiting union membership as a condition of employment. However, continuing lobbying efforts must be made by individuals or organizations to pass such a state law, a difficult task since there are corresponding attempts by others to oppose right-to-work legislation. Current efforts are mainly conducted by the National Right to Work Committee, founded in 1955. Both employees and individuals have joined this committee, whose stated purpose is to protect the employee's right to determine whether to join a union. The committee does not regard itself as being against unions, merely union security provisions that compel employees to become members. However, it has been alleged that the committee's "pro-union, anti–union security" stance has been modified to a flat "antiunion" approach in recent years. A related but separate organization, the National Right to Work Legal Defense Foundation, provides legal representation in right-to-work cases.

Exhibit 11.2 shows the votes in 40 years of elections concerning the right-to-work issue in various states. In terms of vote totals in these elections, more voters in various state elections have voted against right-to-work laws. The South is the only geographic region in the United States where voters have clearly and repeatedly supported right-to-work laws. Controversy occurs over right-to-work laws' meaning, morality, and impact on the union organization.

Meaning and Morality of Right to Work Supporters of **right-to-work laws** contend the underlying definition affirms the right of every U.S. citizen to work for a living, whether or not he or she belongs to a union. In their view, compulsory unionism in any form (union shop, agency shop) contradicts a fundamental human right—freedom to join or not to join a union. Even Samuel Gompers, at least on occasion, stressed the necessity for "voluntarism" in labor unions:

> The workers of America adhere to voluntary institutions in preference to compulsory systems which are held to be not only impractical but a menace to their rights, welfare, and their liberty.[12]

Exhibit 11.2 **Aggregate Totals in Right-to-Work Elections, 1944–1986**

Region	Yes	No	Percent Ratio
East	566,060	1,416,595	29/71
South	1,484,753	1,129,302	57/43
Midwest	2,598,680	3,492,567	43/57
West	4,708,018	7,000,251	40/60
National Totals	9,357,511	13,038,715	42/58

Source: Gilbert J. Gall, "Right-to-Work Referendum Voting: Observations on the Aggregate Historical Statistics," *Labor Law Journal* 39 (December 1988), p. 810.

They further contend that nobody should be required to join a private organization, particularly if that organization uses the individual's dues to support causes that the individual believes are morally unjust or contrary to his or her religious beliefs. This attitude has been reinforced by an amendment to the National Labor Relations Act and actions by the Supreme Court that have in effect stated that employees may refuse to pay union dues because of religious objections.[13]

Opponents of right-to-work laws contend the term "right-to-work" represents a gimmicky public relations slogan designed to restrict union security and related bargaining power.[14] They argue that unions do not deny anyone the fundamental freedom to seek work. Union security represents one of many negotiated working conditions such as work schedules, type of work performed, or wages. If an employee does not like a particular working condition, he or she is free to seek employment elsewhere. This argument can also be supported by a quotation from Samuel Gompers:

> [T]he union shop, in agreement with employers, mutually entered into for the advantage of both employees and unions and the maintenance of industrial peace . . .is to the economic, social and moral advancement of all our people.[15]

They further believe that union security provisions requiring some union attachment are moral because a person is a member of society with responsibility for contributing to the common good. Industrial society's common good might demand that individuals conform to norms (for example, a union security provision) for the good of all.

Impact of Right-to-Work Laws on the Union Organization Currently, 21 states have right-to-work laws.[16] Some believe that right-to-work laws have had little if any influence on unions' activities and bargaining power. For example, one study found that unfair labor practice charges against employers are not higher in right-to-work states.[17]

Additional research has found that the average resident of a right-to-work state cannot be consistently influenced by this legislation (vote for or against a union or refuse to become a union member, for example) because he or she is misinformed or uninformed about related legal rights.[18] Yet, another research effort found that in the first 10 years of passage of right-to-work laws, union organizing is reduced 32 to 38 percent.[19]

The right-to-work laws' impact on employees' economic and democratic welfare are subject to controversial speculation. Advocates of right-to-work laws contend employees benefit economically in states where these laws are established. They contend that right-to-work states attract new firms and jobs. However, opponents of right-to-work laws counter that firms relocate because of the low wages found in right-to-work states.

Right-to-work advocates also claim that voluntary union membership increases union democracy by making leaders more responsive to members. With compulsory union membership, the members cannot express their dissent by withdrawing from the union. They must remain "captive passengers" of the union if they wish to keep their jobs. Union leaders can become indifferent or even corrupt, since members have no economic way of voicing their displeasure. Union leaders should have to earn their dues through their responsive, diligent actions. "Good unions don't need compulsory unionism—and bad unions don't deserve it."[20]

Opponents stress that under the National Labor Relations Act, unions are responsible for representing all bargaining-unit employees. Also, unions may be sued for lack of fair representation by bargaining-unit employees who are nonmembers. Those individuals who do not join the union are regarded by union members as being free riders—they never go near the kitchen but always show up for dinner.[21] Unions believe that all employees represented should pay their fair share, just as citizens pay taxes for public services.

Right-to-work laws can also affect the composition of a particular union, which in turn can affect membership attitudes and behaviors. Since union security clauses are prohibited in right-to-work states, employees in bargaining units can determine whether or not to become union members. One research effort examined union members at a police organization in a right-to-work state. Dues-paying members were more likely to be male, married with more financial dependents, and have longer organizational tenure.[22] These and other sociodemographic characteristics are sometimes associated with attitudes toward unions and participation in union activities.[23]

Thus far, we have discussed institutional issues that affect the union and management organizations in their relationships with each other. However, intra-institutional issues also exist, such as the relationships between labor unions and black and female employees, which are discussed in the next section.

Unions and Minority Groups

Unions and Black Employees

Historical Overview There is tremendous variation both historically and currently in union response toward black employees. Trade union policies regarding black employees have varied from outright exclusion to full acceptance with all privileges of membership. Most of the generalizations in this section focus on the extent to which the union movement has discriminated against black employees. Such discrimination has had two general dimensions: exclusion (through constitutional provisions, initiation rituals, or tacit agreements) and segregation (in either separate locals or separate job classifications).

The Knights of Labor (KOL) actively recruited black members and attempted to treat them in an equalitarian manner. Much of the KOL's enthusiasm was due to its social reform philosophy (discussed in Chapter 2). However, pragmatic reasons also prompted this organization's recruiting efforts, because employers during the late 1800s and early 1900s often used black employees as strikebreakers to put pressure on white strikers to resolve their differences.

A typical handbill distributed by strikebreaker recruiting agents during an 1896 to 1897 strike read as follows:

> WANTED! COLORED coal miners for Weir City, Kan., district, the paradise for colored people. Ninety-seven cents per ton, September 1 to March 1; 87½ cents per ton, March 1 to September 1 for screened coal over seven-eights opening. Special train will leave Birmingham on the 13th. Transportation advanced. Get ready and go to the land of promise.[24]

The presence of black employees working while white employees were on strike increased tension and thwarted the KOL's goals of social betterment. One way perceived to stop this disruption was to bring black employees into the union membership.

The American Federation of Labor (AFL) assumed the KOL's equalitarian racial attitude almost from its inception. The AFL's president, Samuel Gompers, proclaimed a firm antidiscrimination policy regarding black employees. He initially effected this policy by refusing to grant an AFL charter to national unions whose constitutions formally excluded blacks from membership. One such membership qualification clause was found in the Order of Sleeping Car Conductors' Constitution: "The applicant for membership shall be a white male, sober and industrious, and must join of his own free will. He must be sound in mind and body."[25]

Gompers quickly found out that stating a policy is much easier than enforcing it. His first departure from his anti-exclusionary stance indicated that unions would be refused to charter only if they had an explicit racial exclusion clause in their constitution. In essence, the AFL was unconcerned if national unions resorted to less explicit practices in denying membership to black employees.[26] For example, the International Association of Machinists dropped its constitutional provision prohibiting black members and was granted an AFL charter in 1895. However, the union excluded blacks from its initiation ritual—in effect, excluding them from membership—until 1948.[27] Indeed, 11 unions affiliated with the AFL had formal race bars as late as the 1930s.[28]

Gompers rationalized accepting unions that discriminated against black employees on the basis that the AFL would have no power to effect change if the unions were outside its jurisdiction. Presumably, once in the AFL, national union leaders would see the error of their ways and accept black members. This belief was not supported by facts, as a 1902 study found that (1) forty-three international unions did not have any black members and (2) there were only 40,000 black members in the AFL unions, with half of this total belonging to one union, the United Mine Workers.[29] A second strategy to increase black membership while not offending national unions was the AFL's granting of charters to segregated black locals, a policy that continued until 1939.

As early as 1905, the AFL's policy became less enthusiastic and aggressive. Gompers, obviously recalling black strikebreaking activities, expressed only qualified support for racial membership integration:

> Tis true that some men have been angered at the introduction of black strike breakers. I have stood as champion of the colored man and have sacrificed self and much of the labor movement that the colored man should get a chance. But the caucasians are not going to let their standard of living be destroyed by Negroes, Chinamen, Japs, or any others.[30]

In essence, Gompers informed black employees that they had to earn consideration by the AFL by not engaging in efforts that could hurt their potential union brothers and by obtaining requisite job skills.[31] This self-help emphasis for black employees continued for several decades. In 1941 William Green, Gompers' successor, and two other AFL officials expressed their attitudes toward black membership along the following general lines: "[1] discrimination existed before the AFL was born and human nature cannot be altered . . . [2] the AFL, per se, does not discriminate because it gladly accepts Negro workers into its directly affiliated federal locals . . . and [3] . . . Negroes should be grateful for what the AFL has done for them."[32]

At least two forces have influenced a more progressive union stance for black employees: a prominent black labor leader, A. Philip Randolph, and the emergence of the Congress of Industrial Organizations (CIO). Randolph, president of the Brotherhood of Sleeping Car Porters, became involved in the AFL's racial betterment activities when his union received a national charter from the federation in 1936; his 35,000 members comprised one-half of the total black AFL membership at the time. In 1941 his threat to lead 50,000 blacks in a Washington, D.C., protest march resulted in President Roosevelt's executive order that created the first federal Fair Employment Practices Committee.[33] He also clashed with AFL leadership on civil rights issues.

In 1961 Randolph was censured by the AFL's Executive Committee for getting close to "militant groups," thereby creating a "gap between organized labor and the Negro community."[34] It is difficult to measure the precise success of Randolph's efforts; however, at the least, he continually ensured that the AFL's leadership could not forget the black employee.

The independent CIO also pressured the rival AFL to enroll black employees. Unlike the AFL craft unions, the CIO's unions had no control over employment. Therefore, they had to organize all existing employees, black and white, at a facility if they were to be successful.[35] The CIO also needed broad-based support in pressing its legislative goals of minimum wages, unemployment insurance, and social security. The AFL, on the other hand, usually having higher wage earners as members, could not see similarities between their craft jobs and lower wage classifications that were populated largely by black employees.

Current Relationships between Unions and Black Employees Many union leaders at the local, state, and Federation levels maintain that their organizations' democratic characteristics hinder racial integration. Leaders feel obliged to respond to white majority members who often feel economically threatened by black employees, with whom they compete for jobs, promotions, and job security. White member concerns might also be attributed to racism.[36]

Union leaders therefore tend to stress racial equality solutions that are outside their organizations. Efforts are directed toward seeking equal employment opportunity legislation, other government policies that create more jobs for all employees, and employer fair employment practices in employee recruiting, training, and promotion.

However, there have been recent developments within some union organizations that are likely to further racial progress. Today, black employees are more unionized than the work force as a whole.[37]

In some cases, all-black organizations have been formed within the local or national union to monitor or change the union's policies toward minority members. Coordinated efforts across national unions have been made through the Coalition of Black Trade Unionists (CBTU), which was formed in 1972 and insists "that black union officials become full partners in the leadership and decision making of the American labor movement."[38]

Blacks have held leadership positions in some unions (the United Auto Workers, United Steelworkers, National Union of Hospital and Health Care Employees, and Associated Actors and Artists of America, for example). Only recently have blacks held leadership posts that have affected all union members nationwide. In 1989, two blacks were elected to the 35-member AFL-CIO Executive Council. Four current examples of black leadership in national unions include John N. Sturdivant, president of the 156,000-member American Federation of Government Employees; Mary Futrell, president of the 2.0 million-member National Education Association; Gene Upshaw, president of the National Football League Players' Association; and William Lucy, the secretary-treasurer of the 1 million-member American Federation of State, County and Municipal Employees.

Lucy suggests that the ascendancy of black union influence was reflected when the AFL-CIO leaders urged their member unions not to endorse a presidential candidate before the party conventions in 1988. He attributes this action to the AFL-CIO recognition that most black union members strongly backed Jesse Jackson and might have taken issue with the endorsement of another candidate.[39]

Recently, black union members' influence has been complemented by government agencies and the courts. In Chapter 9 we noted that under the *Gardner-Denver* decision minority employees can file a grievance over alleged discriminatory action while also filing charges with the Equal Employment Opportunity Commission. Unions can also be legally liable for discrimination if they do not fairly represent minority and female employees (discussed in Chapter 8), or if they actively discriminate (or cause employers to discriminate) against an employee.[40]

Minority employees can also seek legal recourse if they believe that a union seeking and winning the representation election discriminates racially. A 1973 court of appeals decision (*NLRB* v. *Mansion House Center*) upheld the National Labor Relations Board's contention that unions engaging in racial discrimination or sexism should be denied initial certification and that employers could invoke the discriminatory practices of a union as a reason for refusing to bargain with that union.

However, minorities cannot protest alleged racial discrimination by using "self-help" techniques. A related Supreme Court decision (*Emporium Capwell*) concerned several black employees who believed the grievance procedure in the labor agreement was an inadequate forum to resolve racial discrimination issues. Over the objections of their union officers, these employees picketed the allegedly discriminatory employer instead of processing a grievance and were eventually discharged for their picketing activities. The Supreme Court addressed itself to the following question: Are such attempts to engage in separate bargaining protected by the National Labor Relations Act? The Supreme Court concluded that the employees' actions were not protected by the act; employees can be discharged for engaging in these unprotected activities. The Court further reasoned as follows:

> The potential for conflict between the minority and other employees in this situation is manifest. With each group able to enforce its conflicting demands—the incumbent employees by resort to contractual processes and the minority employees by economic coercion—the possibility of strife and deadlock is high; the likelihood of making headway against discriminatory practices would be minimized.[41]

Minority employees' rights in promotion and layoffs have also occupied the time of union and management officials and the courts. These issues are discussed in Chapter 12 since they are typically intertwined with seniority systems.

Unions and Female Employees

Many of the issues confronting female employees are similar to those black employees face. This is especially true of legal remedies, since both groups are covered by the Equal Employment Opportunity Act. Yet some differences in relationships of women and unions emerge when the history of female union workers is considered.

Historical Overview One difference is that female employees, unlike their black counterparts, were involved in collective action including strike activities in the early 1800s. The first major strike conducted by females occurred in 1828. The dispute was not over wages; rather, it protested paternalistic work rules prohibiting gambling, drinking, or other "debaucheries" and requiring church attendance.[42] A woman who became known as Mother Jones was one of the more fiery and energetic figures of the U.S. labor movement from the 1880s through the 1920s. Her role in mine workers' strikes and in helping to form the IWW reached legendary proportions. However, female unions during the 1800s were usually short-lived—the organizations were formed prior to a strike and lasted only for its duration.

From its formation until World War I, the AFL felt that the woman's place was in the home—allowing women to work would be contrary to its public principles supporting motherhood and the family. In addition to the lack of support from the AFL, union leaders faced many difficulties in organizing female employees into permanent union organizations, such as

- Low wages of female employees made it difficult for them to pay union dues.
- Many female employees' belief that they would only be working for a short period of time.
- Strong employer opposition to unions.
- Lack of female union organizers.

The AFL increased its attention toward female workers when it appeared likely that the United States would enter World War I. Gompers was initially concerned about women's ability to do work traditionally performed by men. However, he was also concerned that women who might be employed during the war could pose a threat to the unionized male employees returning from the war. Trained, experienced female employees who would work for lower wages could place higher-salaried male union members at a competitive disadvantage. Hence, the AFL—perhaps out of organizational necessity rather than ideological commitment—became interested in the prospects of enrolling female union members.

The AFL's encouragement of female unionization continued through World War II, although some maintained the AFL was long on words and short on action. The number of female union members increased from 800,000 at the time of Pearl Harbor to 3,000,000 in 1945; however, only one out of five working women belonged to a union. Many male union leaders and members contended that female union members were basically unenthusiastic, even hostile to union principles and efforts, following World War II. Some of this hostility was due to the fact that many of the female employees working in the factories during the war were summarily sent home following Armistice Day.[43]

Current Relationships between Organized Labor and Female Employees Union growth now may well depend on the ability to organize female employees. During the past 20 years the rate of female participation in the labor force has nearly doubled to almost 50 million employees, a figure that represents 44 percent of the labor force. Only 12.6 percent of female employees are union members, a challenging situation for unions, especially since one survey found that unorganized women have a greater interest in joining unions than do unorganized men.[44]

Some unions have converted these statistics and attitudes into successful representation elections. For example, the Service Employees International Union (SEIU) has won 93 percent of its representation elections involving clerical workers since 1980.[45] To help promote the organization of office workers, for example, the SEIU and Working Womens' National Association of Workers created District 925, named after a recent movie *(9 to 5)*. Another union, the International Union of Electrical Workers (IUE), has told women employees in representation elections, "If you don't organize in 1983, maybe in 1993 your daughter will be making the minimum wage because you didn't do anything to prevent it."[46]

Unions will represent large groups of female employees if they address the following issues:

- *Child care,* a popular issue, since nearly 48 percent of women with children under 1 year old are in the work force today.[47] This issue includes facilities or subsidies for child care, parental leave, extended pregnancy disability benefits, and flexible and/or reduced work hours and shifts. Recent AFL-CIO lobbying efforts for parental leave legislation typically argue,

  > The growth of two wage earner families and the rapid rise in the number of single parents are making it more and more difficult for parents to have the kind of interaction with their young children so important to good child development. Child care experts contend that the first months after birth are the most important to the future growth and development of a child. The bonding that takes place during this time is crucial to both child and parent. Yet, too often, parents are denied the option of spending this important time with their children because to do so will endanger their employment.[48]

- *Pay equity,* or equivalent pay for different jobs having similar skills and responsibilities. One union, AFSCME, has been particularly successful in obtaining pay adjustments for female-dominated job classifications (secretaries and nurses, for example) under the "comparable worth" rationale (discussed more in Chapter 13).
- *Safety problems* such as chronic back or eye problems and potential reproductive difficulties associated with video display terminals. Other safety problems particularly affecting female employees arise from jobs having repetitive motion and a variety of chemicals used in copying machines.
- *Career development* with specific job progressions for many entry-level positions.

- *Sexual harassment* or undesired and illegal (under the Equal Employment Opportunity Act of 1973) verbal, physical, and mental behavior directed toward female employees.

However, addressing a particular issue is often easier said than done, particularly since some issues can complicate the traditional labor relations process. Consider, for example, the sexual harassment issue, which, in one form or another, affects many female employees. Some unions have proposed specific actions:[49]

1. Educate members as to the reality and dimensions of the issue.
2. Determine the extent of sexual harassment at the workplace, possibly through questionnaires sent to employees.
3. Indicate how union members should conduct themselves when they are sexually harassed.

Unions might also attempt to negotiate a labor agreement provision pertaining to sexual harassment (see Exhibit 11.3). This provision has several implications for the union. For example, the union might be subjected to rather vague legal liabilities (fair representation, as discussed in Chapter 8, and sexual discrimination) if a female union member unsuccessfully presents her sexual harassment claim directly to management officials.

There is also a possibility that sexual harassment can be initiated by either managers or union members. One study found that "leering and pornography are most often directed against female employees by coworkers, while touching and proposition complaints arise most often from the behavior of supervisors."[50] The question becomes: Does a sexual harassment provision in the labor agreement apply when this activity is committed by fellow union members? If so, who is the grievance filed against? Obviously, this situation can cause internal problems within the union.

Another indicator of female potential in the labor movement is the degree of influence that women can exert in labor organizations. There has been a recent, large increase in female leadership at the local and regional levels. For example, one AFSCME publication indicated that about half of its officers in 3,000 local unions across the country were female.[51]

Exhibit 11.3 **Sample Labor Agreement Provision Concerning Sexual Harassment**

Article ________
Sexual Harassment

The employer recognizes that no employee shall be subject to sexual harassment. In this spirit a statement of commitment to this principle will be posted in all work areas. Reference to sexual harassment includes any sexual attention that is unwanted. In the case of such harassment, an employee may pursue the grievance procedure for redress. Grievances under this Article will be processed in an expedited manner. If, after the grievance is settled, the employee feels unable to return to his/her job, the employee shall be entitled to transfer to an equivalent position at the same salary and grade as soon as a vacancy exists for which he/she is qualified.

Source: *Sexual Harassment* (Washington, D.C.: American Federation of State, County and Municipal Employees, n.d.), pp. 25–26.

However, equal representation for women at the national level is far from a reality. Exhibit 11.4 indicates that for several unions the percentage of female officers at the national level is far lower than the percentage of female union members. There are several possible reasons for this situation. One reason is that

> . . . many women have two jobs, one paid and the other at home. Also, although the number of women with careers interrupted by childbearing is declining, women are more likely than men to have interrupted careers. The time when women leave the labor force is also the time when people interested in union office generally take their first positions. Women are also less likely than men to be in the high-status, visible positions from which union officers are generally selected . . .[52]

Another reason is that many male union members do not perceive women as being capable of leading unions, but this perception may be changing, if the following remarks of one male union member are representative.

> For too long we have looked cynically at the problems of women in industry, only wanting to send them home in order to solve the unemployment problem. But now we realize we can't replace women, and we might as well accept that.[53]

Some progress occurred in 1980 when the AFL-CIO Executive Council elected Joyce Miller, Vice President of Amalgamated Clothing and Textile Workers Union, as its first woman member. Miller's appointment required some political negotiations as the council's 34 members eased unwritten rules that an affiliated union couldn't hold more than one seat and that all union delegates must be president of their union. Lane Kirkland, president of the AFL-CIO, said that Miller's election "is symbolic of our interest and concern for the problems of women workers. . . . We are anxious to enlist them in the trade union movement."[54] Two subsequent female additions to the AFL-CIO Executive Council were Barbara Hutchinson of the American

Exhibit 11.4

Percentage of Female Union Members and Female Union Officers for Selected Unions

Union	Percent of Female Members 1985	Percent of Female Officers 1985
ACTWU	65	9
AFGE	31	10
AFSCME	45	14
AFT	60	32
CWA	52	6
HERE	50	8
IAM	15	0
IBEW	30	0
IBT	26	0
ILGWU	85	13
IUE	40	8
SEIU	50	18
UAW	13	4

Source: Naomi Baden, "Developing an Agenda: Expanding the Role of Women in Unions," *Labor Studies Journal* 10 (Winter 1986), p. 238.

Federation of Government Employees and Lenore Miller, President of the Retail, Wholesale, and Department Store Union.

Influence of female union members can also cut across local and national unions. For example, the Coalition of Labor Union Women (CLUW), formed in 1974, is largely staffed by female officers from AFL-CIO affiliated unions. There are an estimated 8,000 members, slightly more than 1 percent of eligible female union members.[55] The CLUW works with other women's organizations in carrying out its four major goals: seeking affirmative action in the workplace, strengthening the role and participation of women in their unions, encouraging legislative and political activity among union women, and organizing unorganized women.

Summary

Management and union officials want to maintain and strengthen their respective organizations through the collective bargaining process. Management has been long concerned about maintaining its rights to run the organization. While union officials do not appear to be particularly concerned about management's property rights pertaining to the machinery, materials, and money of the enterprise, management's prerogatives regarding its employees have been weakened or eroded through decisions by arbitrators, the NLRB, and the courts, as well as collective bargaining. Management rights are usually specified in the labor agreement in either the long or short form.

Unions are also concerned about their organizations when they attempt to negotiate a union security provision (such as union shop, union hiring hall, or agency shop) into the labor agreement. However, certain union security provisions cannot be negotiated in states having right-to-work laws, permitted under Section 14(b) of the Labor-Management Relations Act. Controversy occurs over right-to-work laws' meaning, morality, and impact on the union organization.

A variety of relationships occur between unions and minority employees. Although there have been exceptions, historically blacks have not been well received by organized labor. At least three forces have influenced a more progressive union stance for black employees: a prominent labor leader, the emergence of the CIO, and civil rights legislation. Although female employees became active in labor relations earlier than blacks, women have not been as well integrated into the labor-management relationship in terms of the percentage of unionized female employees. Unions have recently attempted to correct this situation by addressing relevant issues, organizing occupations that are dominated by women, and developing female organizations within the AFL-CIO.

Key Terms

reserved rights doctrine
union security clause
closed shop
union hiring hall
union shop
agency shop
quasi-union shop
contingency union shop
preferential treatment clause
dues checkoff
right-to-work laws

Discussion Questions

1. What are the comparative advantages of the long and short forms of management rights clauses?
2. Discuss how management rights can be eroded, even though most unions have no desire to "run the business."
3. Formulate a one- or two-sentence argument for or against the right-to-work philosophy. Fully defend your statement from arguments that could be made against your position.
4. Discuss the similarities and differences between black and female employees' experiences with unions.

References

1. George A. Stevens, *New York Typographical Union No. 6, Annual Report of the Bureau of Labor Statistics* (New York: State Department of Labor, 1911), part 1, pp. 240–241; cited in Neil W. Chamberlain, "The Union Challenge to Management Control," *Industrial and Labor Relations Review* 16 (January 1963), pp. 185–186.
2. Stanley Young, "The Question of Managerial Prerogatives," *Industrial and Labor Relations Review* 16 (January 1963), p. 243.
3. Marvin Hill Jr. and Anthony V. Sinicropi, *Management Rights* (Washington, D.C.: Bureau of National Affairs Inc., 1986), p. 6.
4. Martin M. Perline and David J. Poynter, "Union Orientation and the Perception of Managerial Prerogatives," *Labor Law Journal* 40 (December 1989), pp. 781–788.
5. We are grateful to Paul Gerhart for suggestions in formulating these factors.
6. Bureau of National Affairs Inc., *Basic Patterns in Union Contracts* (Washington, D.C.: Bureau of National Affairs Inc., 1989), p. 79.
7. Billie Ann Brotman and Thomas J. McDonagh, "Union Security Clauses as Viewed by the National Labor Relations Board," *Labor Law Journal* 37 (February 1986), pp. 104–115.
8. *Retail Clerks International Association Local 1625 AFL-CIO* v. *Schermerhorn et al.*, 373 U.S. 746 (1963); and, *D. Louis Abood et al.* v. *Detroit Board of Education*, 431 U.S. 209 (1977). See also Charles M. Rehmus, "The Agency Shop after *Abood.* No Free Ride, but What's the Fare?" *Industrial and Labor Relations Review* 34 (October 1980), pp. 92 -100.
9. Bureau of National Affairs Inc., *Daily Labor Report,* no. 131, (July 8, 1988), pp. A-1–A-2. For subsequent NLRB administrative implications and interpretation of this decision see Bureau of National Affairs Inc., *Daily Labor Report* no. 255, (November 22, 1988), p. D-1. See also Jan W. Henkel and Norman J. Wood, "Limitations on the Uses of Union Shop Funds after Ellis: What Activities are Germane to Collective Bargaining?" *Labor Law Journal* 35 (December 1984), pp. 736–746; and "Supreme Court Sets Standards for Collection of Agency Fees," *Daily Labor Report,* March 5, 1986, p. AA-1.
10. Bureau of National Affairs Inc., *Basic Patterns,* pp. 99–100.
11. For further historical insights into the right-to-work issue see Gilbert J. Gall, *The Politics of Right to Work* (New York: Greenwood Press, 1988).
12. "The Voluntarism of Samuel Gompers," National Right to Work Committee (Fairfax, Va.: n.d.), p. 1. For a fine discussion of many of these controversial dimensions, see *Journal of Labor Research* 1 (Fall 1980), p. 285–415.
13. See, for example, "Supreme Court Revives Objection to Agency Fee," *Daily Labor Report,* May 3, 1982, pp. 2, 3. Amendments to the NLRA put restrictions on religious reasons and can require a donation to a charity (other than the religion) equivalent to a fair share of union costs.
14. Norman Hill, "The Double Speak of Right-to-Work," *American Federationist* 87 (October 1980), p. 13.
15. *The Truth About 'Right-to-Work' Laws* (Washington, D.C.: American Federation of Labor and Congress of Industrial Organizations, January 1977), p. i.
16. These states include Alabama, Arizona, Arkansas, Florida, Georgia, Idaho, Iowa, Kansas, Louisiana, Mississippi, Nebraska, Nevada, North Carolina, North Dakota, South Carolina, South Dakota, Tennessee, Texas, Utah, Virginia, and Wyoming. This citation applies to private sector employees. The list would be greater if states having similar legislation for the public sector were considered.
17. Ralph D. Elliott and James R. Huffman, "The Impact of Right-to-Work Laws on Employer Unfair Labor Practice Charges," *Journal of Labor Research* 5 (Spring 1984), pp. 165–176; and Robert Swidinsky, "Bargaining Power under Compulsory Unionism," *Industrial Relations* 21 (Winter 1982), pp. 62–72. For additional articles on the impact of right-to-work laws on union existence and collective bargaining, see William J. Moore and Robert J. Newman, "The Effects of Right-to-Work Laws: A Review of the Literature," *Industrial and Labor Relations Review* 38 (July 1985), pp. 571–575; and Walter J. Wessels, "Economic Effects of Right-to-Work Laws," *Journal of Labor Research* 2 (Spring 1981), pp. 55–75.
18. Marc G. Singer, "Comprehension of Right-to-Work Laws among Residents of the Right-to-Work States," *Journal of Collective Negotiations in the Public Sector* 16 (1987), pp. 311–326.
19. David T. Ellwood and Glenn Fine, "The Impact of Right-to-Work Laws on Union Organizing," *Journal of Political Economy* 95 (April 1987), pp. 250–274.
20. Reed E. Larson, "Are Right-to-Work Laws Desirable? Yes," in *Contemporary Labor Issues,* ed. Walter Fogel and Archie Kleingartner (Belmont, Calif.: Wadsworth Publishing, 1968), p. 272.
21. Mike LaVelle, "Half a Loaf Better Than Right-To-Work," *Chicago Tribune,* July 27, 1976, Section 2, p. 4.
22. John M. Jermier, Cynthia Fryer Cohen, Kathleen J. Powers, and Jeannie Gaines, "Paying Dues: Police Unionism in a Right-to-Work Environment," *Industrial Relations* 25 (Fall 1986), pp. 265–276.
23. See, for example, Michele M. Hoyman and Lamont Stallworth, "Participation in Local Unions: A Comparison of Black and White Members," *Industrial and Labor Relations Review* 40 (April 1987), pp. 323-335; and Jack Fioritio and Charles R. Greer, "Gender Differences in Union Membership, Preferences, and Beliefs," *Journal of Labor Research* 7 (Spring 1986), pp. 144–148.

24. Herbert G. Gutman, "The Negro and the United Mine Workers of America," in *The Negro and the American Labor Movement,* ed. Julius Jacobson (Garden City, N.Y.: Doubleday, 1968), p. 99.
25. Herbert Hill, *Black Labor and the American Legal System,* vol. 1 (Washington, D.C.: Bureau of National Affairs Inc., 1977), p. 20.
26. Marc Karson and Ronald Radosh, "The American Federation of Labor and the Negro Worker: 1894-1949," in *The Negro and the American Labor Movement,* ed. Julius Jacobson (Garden City, N.Y.: Doubleday, 1968), p. 155-156.
27. Ray Marshall, *The Negro and Organized Labor* (New York: John Wiley, 1965), p. 16.
28. Derek C. Bok and John Dunlop, *Labor and the American Community* (New York: Simon and Schuster, 1970), p. 119.
29. Karson and Radosh, "AFL and the Negro Worker," p. 156. For more details of the role of blacks in the United Mine Workers, see Herbert Gutman, *Work, Culture, and Society in Industrializing America* (New York: Alfred A. Knopf, 1976), pp. 121-208.
30. Samuel Gompers, "Talks on Labor," *American Federationist* 12 (September 1905), p. 636.
31. For a more detailed account of this shift in philosophy, see Bernard Mandel, "Samuel Gompers and the Negro Workers: 1866-1914," *Journal of Negro History* 40 (January 1955), pp. 34-60.
32. Herbert R. Northrup, *Organized Labor and the Negro* (New York: Harper & Bros., 1944), p. 13.
33. For more details concerning this march see Herbert Garfinkel, *When Negroes March* (New York: Antheneum, 1959).
34. Herbert Hill, "The Racial Practices of Organized Labor: The Contemporary Record," in *The Negro and the American Labor Movement,* ed. Julius Jacobson (Garden City, N.Y.: Doubleday, 1968), p. 288. For additional details concerning Mr. Randolph and his union, see William H. Harris, *The Harder We Run: Black Workers Since the Civil War* (New York: Oxford University Press, 1982), pp. 77-94.
35. Summer M. Rosen, "The C.I.O. Era: 1935-1955," in *The Negro and the American Labor Movement,* ed. Julius Jacobson (Garden City, N.Y.: Doubleday, 1968), p. 202. For a detailed account of the CIO's efforts to mobilize black employees' support in organizing the steel industry, see Horace R. Cayton and George S. Mitchell, *Black Workers and the New Unions* (1939; reprint ed. Westport, Conn.: Negro Universities Press, 1970), pp. 190-224. For a provocative, well-researched discussion of the negative impact of the AFL-CIO merger on black employees, see Herbert Hill, "The AFL-CIO and the Black Worker: Twenty-Five Years after the Merger," *The Journal of Intergroup Relations* X (Spring 1982), pp. 1-78.
36. For an example of racist attitudes of some union members, see Scott Greer, *Last Man In: Racial Access to Union Power* (Glencoe, Ill.: The Free Press, 1959), pp. 149-150.
37. Norman Hill, "Forging a Partnership Between Blacks and Unions," *Monthly Labor Review,* August 1987, p. 38.
38. Hill, "The AFL-CIO and the Black Worker," p. 9.
39. Kenneth B. Noble, "The Black Ascent in Union Politics," *New York Times,* January 1, 1989, p. 4E. It should also be noted that the late Elizabeth Duncan Koontz was the first black president of the National Education Association and Director of the Women's Bureau in President Nixon's Department of Labor.
40. Barbara N. McLennan, "Sex Discrimination in Employment and Possible Liabilities of Labor Unions: Implications of *County of Washington* v. *Gunther," Labor Law Journal* 33 (January 1982), p. 30. See also Peter Feuille and David Lewin, "Equal Employment Opportunity Bargaining," *Industrial Relations* 20 (Fall 1981), pp. 322-334; and Russell K. Schutt, "Craft Unions and Minorities: Determinants of Change in Admission Practice," *Social Problems* 14 (October 1987), pp. 388-401.
41. *Emporium Capwell Co.* v. *Western Addition Community Org.,* 420 U.S. 68-69 (1975). For additional details regarding the rights of minority employees when they picket over an alleged racial injustice, see Kenneth M. Schwartz and Martin Simone, "Civil Rights Picketing," in *Strikes, Stoppages and Boycotts: 1978* (New York: Practising Law Institute, 1978), ed. Walter B. Connolly, Jr., pp. 397-419. The potential for racial discrimination issues being resolved through arbitration is discussed in Lawrence R. Jauch, "The Arbitration of Racial Discrimination Cases as a Result of Employment Practices," *Labor Law Journal* 24 (June 1973), pp. 367-375.
42. John B. Andrews and W.D.P. Bliss, *History of Women in Trade Unions* (New York: Arno Press, 1974), p. 24.
43. For additional historical insights, see Ruth Milkman, ed., *Women, Work, and Protest* (Boston: Routledge and Kegan Paul, 1985).
44. *Statistical Abstract of the United States* (Washington, D.C.: U.S. Department of Commerce, 1989), p. 416; and Thomas A. Kochan, "How American Workers View Labor Unions," *Monthly Labor Review* 102 (1979), p. 29.
45. "Pink Collar Workers: The Next Rank and File?" *Business Week,* February 24, 1986, pp. 118-119.
46. Martin F. Payson, "Wooing The Pink Collar Work Force," *Personnel Journal* 63 (January 1984), p. 51. For further insights into this situation, see Roberta Goldberg, *Organizing Women Office Workers* (New York: Praeger, 1983).
47. "AFSCME on the Move for Working Women" (Washington, D.C.: n.d.), p. 9.
48. "AFL-CIO Strongly Backs Parental Leave Measure," Bureau of National Affairs Inc., *Daily Labor Report,* no 78 (April 23, 1986), p. D-1. See also, Cathy Trost, "More Family Issues Surface at Bargaining Tables as Women Show Increasing Interest in Unions," *The Wall Street Journal,* December 2, 1986, p. 70.
49. Modified from material in American Federation of State, County and Municipal Employees, *Sexual Harassment* (Washington, D.C.: n.d.), pp. 9-10.
50. *Sexual Harassment and Labor Relations* (Washington, D.C.: Bureau of National Affairs Inc., 1981), p. 32. See also Carol Hymowitz, "In the Pits: Women Coal Miners Fight for Their Rights to Lift, Shovel, Lug," *The Wall Street Journal,* September 10, 1981, pp. 1, 20.
51. "AFSCME on the Job for Working Women" (Washington, D.C.: n.d.), p. 9.
52. Karen S. Koziara and David A. Pierson, "The Lack of Female Union Leaders," *Monthly Labor Review* 104 (May 1981), pp. 30 and 31. See also Daniel J. Brass, "Men's and Women's Networks: A Study of Interaction Patterns and Influence in an Organization," *Academy of Management Journal* 28 (June 1985), pp. 327-343.
53. Lucretia M. Dewey, "Women in Labor Unions," *Monthly Labor Review* 94 (February 1971), p. 48. For a more recent account of this realization after sexist activities of male union members at one location, see Stan Gray, "Sharing the Shop Floor," *Radical America* (September-October 1984), pp. 69-88.
54. Joan S. Lublin, "AFL-CIO Council Elects Female Activist to a Spot Previously Filled by Seafarers," *The Wall Street Journal,* August 22, 1980, p. 4.
55. Mim Keller, "AFL-CIO for Men Only?" *The Nation* 228-229 (November 17, 1979), pp. 490-492.

CHAPTER 12

Administrative Issues

"We recommend that the adoption of new workplace technologies be accompanied by employment policies that strengthen employment security; such policies include retraining of affected workers for other jobs and a reliance on attrition rather than on permanent layoffs wherever possible. At the same time, workers and unions must recognize their stake in a more productive workplace and consider modifications of work rules and job classifications in exchange for such employment security polices."

Richard M. Cyert and David C. Mowery, eds., *Technology and Employment: Innovation and Growth in the U.S. Economy* (Washington, D.C.: National Academy Press, 1987), p. 15.

Several important administrative issues can cost as much as or more than negotiated wage increases. This chapter focuses on four broad administrative issues: (1) technological change and its impact on labor relations; (2) personnel changes and their relationship to subcontracting, work assignments and jurisdiction, work scheduling, and the role of seniority; (3) employee development and job restructuring; and (4) safety and health.

Most of these issues involve conflicting priorities. Management wishes to have complete discretion in arranging its work content and schedules in order to maximize efficiency. Unions seek to protect employees' jobs and job rights in cases of new job assignments. The attempts of management and labor to achieve their respective priorities are discussed throughout this chapter.

Technological Change and Job Protection

Technological change refers to changes in the production processes that result from the introduction of labor-saving machinery and changes in material handling and work flow. **Automation,** a type of technological change, goes one step further in that machines perform tasks formerly performed by humans, and the human operator is replaced by automatic controls.[1]

Technological change and its impact on the work force have been the focus of much attention in the United States and around the world. Innovations include advanced communication systems, industrial robots, flexible manufacturing systems, computer-assisted design (CAD), and computer-assisted manufacturing (CAM). These modern technologies incorporate microelectronic devices that increase productivity while reducing effort in production tasks. A Department of Labor study of 35 industries made the following findings:

- The pace of introduction of new technology appears to be increasing as industries modernize their facilities to reduce costs and compete more effectively in domestic and overseas markets.
- Generally, relatively few employees have been laid off because of these technological changes.
- Industries that have led the way in the introduction of new technology have been those with above-average rates of productivity.
- New technologies are changing the structure of occupations: there is more demand for professional and technical workers, computer system analysts, and programmers, less demand for operatives and laborers, and less need for certain worker characteristics such as manual dexterity and physical strength.
- Measures are being taken to facilitate the orderly introduction of new technology, including advance notice to affected workers, coordination between the labor adjustment and technical planning, provisions for training of new skills, and provisions for job security.[2]

Successful implementation of new technology often requires considerable change in the tasks performed and the skills required. If employees are to exercise greater control over the pace and character of the work, the duties and responsibilities of supervisors and middle managers will be modified. First, successful adoption of new technology at the workplace requires strong assurance of job security, extensive retraining for managers and workers, and probably modification of job classifications, seniority, and pay structures. It will also require advance notification of the change, reorganization of the production process, and an increase in employee responsibility for product quality and production rates. In addition, worker involvement in planning the adoption of the new technology and worker input into the design and purchase of the equipment will be necessary.

Unions and management have a long history of bargaining over the effects of technological change. In fact, 25 percent of agreements now have provisions that address the introduction of new technology. Only 15 percent provide for discussion with or notification to the union prior to the introduction of new technology and only 6 percent require retraining of displaced workers. There are, however, important agreements containing these requirements covering large numbers of employees.

Some companies will involve employees and union representatives in the early stages of selecting new technology. Employees and union representatives accompany engineers on trips to vendors, assess the new technology, and render opinions on what types of equipment to purchase. They are consulted on how to operate the equipment and how to organize the work after the new technology is introduced. This approach has shown that when the union is consulted early in the technological development process, it is more likely to become an advocate for the new technology and is more able to assure its members that the technology will secure more jobs than it threatens.

At Boeing, union representatives attend an annual technology briefing to learn about robotics, material-handling projects, and CAD/CAM projects in process within the company to keep abreast of new technology.[3] The General Motors–United Auto Workers agreement provides for advance notice, special committees to deal with technology-related layoffs, and guaranteed employment with full pay as long as the displaced employee is willing to be retrained. The agreements between the Communication Workers of America and American Telephone and Telegraph Corporation and regional telephone companies have similar provisions, but comparable guarantees do not exist in some other industries.[4]

Southern Bell and the Communication Workers of America have included a "responsible union-company relationship" clause in their labor agreement and have set up joint committees to help introduce new equipment. See the "Labor Relations in Action." General Electric and Westinghouse negotiated provisions with the International Union of Electrical Workers that require advance notification of technological change, joint technology committees, retraining, and safety measures for people who work with robots.[5]

Ford Motors has agreed to a lifetime pay guarantee program covering workers with 15 years or more service. If these employees are laid off, they will continue to receive pay until they reach retirement age or 62 years of age. With such guarantees of employment or income, employees will more likely accept technological change, and employers will be motivated to make training available so employees can adjust to new technology.

While more manufacturing companies are adopting some or all of these elements, many firms have not. It is believed that the reasons for the failures extend beyond information available, to the traditional adversarial relations between the parties. Many times, the union and management must address mistrust before adopting new technology. This may require continuous joint problem-solving sessions and labor-management committees to deal with work life quality or workplace safety. The need for consultation with the work force may be viewed as a loss of authority by supervisors and middle managers, who may resist transferring their power to workers. Upper management and union leaders will have to communicate their commitment to cooperation so that innovative work practices can be effective.[6]

Labor unions respond to technology introduction in several ways. Obviously, they would prefer to increase the number of jobs and the compensation of the jobholders. If this is not possible, they will seek a realistic tradeoff between more jobs at the same compensation or the same number of jobs at increased compensation. In the short term, unions try to protect the members by attempting to include the following issues in the labor agreement:

Labor Relations in Action

Responsible Union-Company Relationship

The company and the union recognize that it is in the best interests of both parties, employees and the public that all dealings with them continue to be characterized by mutual responsibility and respect. To insure that this relationship continues and improves, the company and the union and their respective representatives at all levels will apply the terms of this contract fairly in accord with its intent and meaning and consistent with the union's status as exclusive bargaining representative of all employees in the unit.

Each party shall bring to the attention of all employees in the unit, including new hires, their purpose to conduct themselves in a spirit of responsibility and respect and of the measures they have agreed upon to insure adherence to this purpose.

Joint committees the parties have organized include the following:

- The *Joint Technological Study Committee* functions to keep everyone informed of technological change and how it will impact on employees.
- *Joint Steering Committees* operate in each state to administer joint programs. They provide overall guidance for the Quality of Work Life effort.
- *Quality of Work Life (QWL) Committees* operate in each state and at lower levels throughout the Company to explore and recommend improvements in technology and work methods, cost savings ideas, and so on. Members of these committees define their own issues and perform substantial research and analysis in preparing their recommendations.
- *Common Interest Forum,* comprised of top people from both union and management, meets on a regular basis to discuss future common interest plans.

Source: Donald P. Crane and Michael J. Jedel, *Patterns of Industrial Peace* (forthcoming) prepared under a grant from the U.S. Department of Labor.

seniority rules	"bumping" clause
advance notice to union	layoff recall rights
layoff prohibitions	severance pay
joint committees	preferential hiring
income guarantees	other job guarantees

At the same time, unions may take the long-term, future-oriented perspective and negotiate such issues as training, transfers to replacement facilities, and moving allowances.[7]

In general, technological progress in the United States has resulted in higher productivity, the elimination of many menial and dangerous jobs, higher wages, shorter hours, and a higher standard of living.[8] Technological advances have brought about numerous positive effects: more wealth is produced with less effort; machinery that performs tasks that humans cannot or performs with more reliability and efficiency has lowered the costs of production and allowed products to be sold at lower prices; better working conditions prevail; back-breaking work assignments are minimized; and skill levels of workers have increased, with consequent increases in pay.

While technological advancement has brought about much positive change for the employee, it has also increased the sophistication of methods of monitoring employees at the workplace. This monitoring includes supervisors listening to telephone conversations, computerized tracking systems of phone use, and computer monitoring where video display terminals (VDTs) keep track of employee productivity and activity including counting keystrokes, error rates, time taken to complete tasks, and time away from the terminal. Printouts are provided to supervisors who may use the data to determine production standards and pay rates, monitor speed and accuracy, evaluate performance, and discipline for failure to perform in a satisfactory manner.[9]

ETHICS

Opponents of employee monitoring question the ethics of these practices. They contend that it creates harmful stress, robs the workers of dignity, and invades the employees' privacy, and regard it as "Big Brother" at the workplace. Supporters argue that supervision of quantity and quality of work is a tradition, that ensuring accuracy and productivity is an absolute requirement of business survival, and that using the computer software capacity of VDT systems is the most objective basis possible for making fair evaluation of employee performance. Moreover, employees are protected from unfair production standards or arbitrary treatment by grievance and arbitration procedures.

The introduction of work monitoring is considered by management to be a managerial prerogative, and information gathered as evidence in employee disciplinary action will be considered by arbitrators. Unions may negotiate provisions to regulate supervisory monitoring of employees. For example, monitoring may be used only for training and assignment purposes, not for discipline. Other provisions may include advance notice when the employee is being monitored and employee access to all records generated by monitoring.[10]

Job Security and Personnel Changes

A primary concern of unions is ensuring that members' jobs are protected from elimination due to technological change or managerial decision making. Unions have been able to protect jobs by negotiating clauses about job security, subcontracting, work assignments and jurisdiction, work scheduling, and use of seniority in personnel changes.

During the early 1980s, some unions were successful in attaining greater job security for their members by postponing plant closing and stopping *outsourcing* (purchasing parts and services from outside firms) in exchange for wage concessions or postponement of contractual wage increases and changes in work rules.[11] Some unions, mostly at the local level, have changed long-standing work rules to increase productivity and profits in order to help their ailing employers:

- Truck drivers have agreed to eliminate costly rehandling of certain freight.
- Aluminum workers have agreed to a reduction in their craft groups from 18 to 12 and expanded the types of jobs each worker does.

Job-Security Work Rules

Job-security work rules are provisions that attempt to make jobs more secure, such as spreading the workload by placing limits on the load that can be carried, restricting the duties of employees, limiting the number of machines one operator can tend, prohibiting modern tools or equipment, and requiring standby crews.[12] Such practices carried to an extreme are known as **featherbedding,** which exhibits "unreasonable limits to the amount of work employees may do in a given period, . . . payment for unneeded workers, unnecessary tasks, work not performed, or jobs duplicating those already done."[13] This practice is viewed negatively by the public as a waste of resources.

Work load restrictions lie at the foundation of many labor relations conflicts. From an overall (macro) viewpoint, union leaders agree that change is necessary for economic progress, but from an individual (micro) view, where significant adjustment would be necessary, change is resisted.[14] Congress attempted to help reduce featherbedding practices when it amended the National Labor Relations Act in 1947 and included Section 8(b)(6), which prohibits a labor union from causing or "attempting to cause an employer to pay or deliver or agree to pay or deliver any money or other thing of value, in the nature of an exaction, for services which are not performed or not to be performed."

After two Supreme Court decisions involving newspapers, Section 8(b)(6) lost much of its potential for restricting featherbedding practices. In one case, the Supreme Court agreed with the NLRB that some of the work practices at issue were wasteful, but that the work was actually performed and that employees had been hired by the employer to perform this work, although some of it was not necessary.[15] Thus, the courts have given fairly specific direction to unions and management to resolve these featherbedding practices in collective bargaining. Recognizing that there may be some value to this approach rather than a purely legalistic one, the NLRB and the courts have set ground rules for these issues. The same means by which unions seek to improve wages, hours, and working conditions are available to maintain or establish job security provisions. Employers can resist these union demands, but they may also have to give up or trade something in return.

This tradeoff is the essence of collective bargaining. Resolving such employment security issues through collective bargaining enables the parties themselves to deal with the problem in a manner suited to their specific needs and situation (see Chapter 13 on productivity bargaining). Such issues include the following:

- *Job assignment:* Reducing crew size, adding duties, or eliminating unneeded jobs.
- *Job content:* Combining jobs such as millwright, welder, rigger, and boilermaker, allowing journeymen to perform helpers' tasks.
- *Hours:* Providing no relief or wash-up time, more flexibility in schedules, or more hours for the same pay.
- *Seniority:* Restricting the use of seniority in filling vacancies, bumping, and scheduling shifts.
- *Wages:* Permitting pay for knowledge, not function.[16]

Unions would attempt to minimize any adverse effect on the members. Abolishing featherbedding and make-work practices in one stroke by legislative decree would abruptly increase the burden of unemployment, with serious economic and social consequences.[17]

Work rules negotiated between the longshoremen and shipping companies that prevent truckers and warehousemen from unloading cargo from containers within

50 miles of the pier were upheld by the Supreme Court. These work rules were designed to preserve a portion of the traditional longshore work that is dwindling because of use of containers.[18]

International Harvester and the UAW negotiated a Job Content Preservation Program aimed to protect jobs from company decisions to outsource, use overtime, and introduce technological change. The agreement commits the company to a minimum guarantee of straight-time hours.[19]

The commitment to employment security has several advantages: it induces employees to support change, encourages employers to invest in training employees, helps all employees to concentrate on a common goal, reduces costs associated with turnover, retains skills, avoids costs and turmoil associated with "bumping," and maintains employee morale.[20]

Recently, unions have shown their willingness to assist management in remaining competitive by adjusting long-standing work rules. General Motors placed a high priority on work rule concessions in recent negotiations. In fact, it reported that changes in the following work rules had the potential of increasing productivity by as much as 25 percent:[21]

- Reduction of relief time (46 minutes).
- Alteration or elimination of production quotas in nonassembly plants.
- Broadening job classifications so that employees perform a wider variety of tasks.
- Penalizing employees whose "controllable absences" exceed 20 percent of the available work hours during a 6-month period by reducing their vacation pay and supplemental unemployment benefits.

Plant Closure

In 1983 to 1984 about 7,800 employers either shut down or initiated layoffs affecting over 1 million employees. Eighteen percent of the employers gave at least 3 months notice to their employees, 42 percent gave less than 14 days, and 13 percent gave no notice at all. These data show why legislation was needed to require advance notice of plant closings.[22] In 1985, only 26 percent of agreements had plant shutdown or relocation provisions. Almost half of these provided transfer rights for displaced employees, but less than 20 percent required the company to pay relocation expenses. Only 13 percent of the agreements required advance notice to the union or discussion with the union prior to closing or relocating a plant.[23]

The Supreme Court ruled that a company may close a plant without bargaining with its union, provided that the shutdown is partial (one of several plants) and the reason is "purely economic," as opposed to any antiunion reasons.[24] However, the employer is required to bargain over the effects; that is, layoffs, transfers to other jobs, severance pay, and so on.

In 1988 Congress passed the Worker Adjustment and Retraining Notification Act (WARN). This law *requires* employers with 100 or more employees to give 60-day advance notice to employees (excluding those employed less than 20 hours per week), unions, and state and local governments of a plant closing or major layoff. WARN also *allows* negotiation of a clause requiring more than 60 days advance notice. (See Chapter 3.)

Subcontracting, Outsourcing, and Work Transfer

Subcontracting (also called "contracting work out") usually occurs when a firm determines that it cannot perform all the tasks that are necessary to operate its business successfully or that another firm can perform the needed tasks (janitorial and cafeteria services, equipment repair, parts production, and so on) better and/or at a lower cost. **Outsourcing,** a similar process, is a cost-cutting strategy of shifting work away from one's own plant to lower-cost producers—sometimes nonunion producers—and purchasing parts needed in production from these producers. For example, Ford Motor now gets 58 percent of its parts from outside its company.[25] In either case, the firm may contract with others to assume responsibility for certain work requirements.

In some cases, the parties attempt to reverse the outsourcing activities. For example, at the General Motors plant in Doraville, Georgia the UAW and the company organized a joint union-management team to study the feasibility of keeping outsourced work. The committee found a way to produce seat cushions for one of GM's midsized models in-plant for less than the vendor charged. The team bid on the work and won the contract; now the cushions are produced at the Doraville plant. Since that time, the corporate office has decided to assign the assembly of GM-10 cars to that plant rather than shutting it down.[26]

The subcontracting process, apparently a normal economic practice, is a volatile and complicated collective bargaining issue. From management's view, subcontracting raises issues of managerial flexibility, the firm's ability to progress economically, and its right to pursue its economic goals free from union interference. From the union's perspective, subcontracting raises problems of job security, challenges from competing groups of workers, and undermining of contract standards.[27]

Unions have increasingly attempted to influence management's decisions to subcontract. These decisions usually are motivated by the company's need to reduce production costs. Unions generally try to limit management's freedom to subcontract in order to protect and maximize work and economic opportunities for their members and to protect the members' jobs against competition from nonunion firms. The example of a subcontracting clause in Exhibit 12.1 shows how employers' actions can be limited.

Subcontracting is a mandatory issue of collective bargaining. However, in 1986 the NLRB ruled that a company does not violate the Taft-Hartley Act when it fails to grant the union a chance to bargain about management's decision to subcontract bargaining unit work as long as the decision to subcontract does not turn on labor costs but on a significant change in the nature and direction of the business.[28]

Unions have made significant inroads on this issue in collective bargaining. It is now limited or prohibited in 54 percent of the labor agreements, and inclusion of these clauses has increased significantly in the last 10 years. Labor agreements seldom strictly prohibit subcontracting but often limit it in one or more of the following ways: they require advance consultation with the union, prohibit subcontracting if layoffs would result, allow subcontracting only if the necessary skills and equipment are not available, or require use of skilled workers for maintenance and construction jobs within the bargaining unit.[29] AT&T Information Systems, for example, employs 50,000 people who are represented by the Communication Workers of America and has agreed to make monthly disclosures of the amount of subcontracting being done and quarterly projections of future subcontracting as well.[30]

Exhibit 12.1 **Example of Subcontracting Clause**

The Company agrees that it will not contract normal routine maintenance work, excluding dryer, coagulation, recovery unit cleaning and the cleaning of any other equipment which has normally been contracted or requires special cleaning equipment, so long as it has the necessary manpower and equipment to timely and properly perform such work. On occasions when it is necessary to contract such work, such contracting shall not result in the displacement of bargaining unit employees. Before such work is contracted, the Union will be given advance notice. Such contract is to be for specific work of a definite duration and shall not be for the purpose of performing any such work on a full-time basis for the sole purpose of eliminating work from the bargaining unit. If it should become necessary to contract such work under this condition, the Company will determine whether such a job will be contracted to an outside contractor, to the Company's Roving Crew, or through another source and the Union will be so notified. (Phillips Chemical Company and Oil Workers)

Source: *Collective Bargaining Negotiations and Contracts* (Washington, D.C.: Bureau of National Affairs Inc., 1982), p. 65:183.

Arbitration likewise has played an increasingly important role in the subcontracting issue. This role has usually involved such aspects as determining whether subcontracting is an arbitrable issue without explicit contractual language on the subject. Arbitrators are commonly asked to interpret the recognition clause and any accompanying bargaining-unit work and appraise commonly specified criteria, such as "good faith," proof of "sound business practices," and "no harm to members of the bargaining unit."[31]

AT&T and Communication Workers of America had negotiated an agreement in which the company retained the right to subcontract work as long as doing so did not lead to layoffs. After the agreement, 109 grievances were filed from employees who alleged their jobs were downgraded or they had been laid off in violation of the agreement. In the first case, the arbitrator ruled in favor of the union, and this decision led to a settlement of the remaining grievances that amounted to $6 million paid to 1,000 Pennsylvania Bell employees.[32] Bell South, one of the former subsidiaries of AT&T, negotiated a memorandum of agreement to protect jobs. (See "Labor Relations in Action.")

Subcontracting is frequently arbitrated under the management rights clause of the agreement (see Chapter 11). When agreements do not explicitly provide management the right to subcontract, the unions seek to bargain over the subject. When and if management refuses, the union will frequently petition the NLRB, alleging that the employer has committed an unfair labor practice by refusing to bargain in good faith. Where a management rights clause is written in generalities, not specifically alluding to subcontracting, the union challenge will more likely be decided in arbitration.

Work transfer is similar to subcontracting and outsourcing. An employer who unilaterally transfers work from a union subsidiary to another subsidiary during the life of a labor agreement in order to cut labor costs violates the National Labor Relations Act when the labor agreement contains a work preservation clause such as the following:

> It is the intent of the parties to this Agreement to protect the work performed by employees in the bargaining unit.

Labor Relations in Action

Memorandum of Agreement

The parties recognize that in the post-divestiture environment, special competitive and operational problems must be addressed if the Advanced Systems Division of the two operating companies are to capture and maintain an appropriate share of the terminal equipment market; and that a successful ASD is in the long range best interests of both the companies, its employees, and the Union. It is also recognized that the nature and variety of work which must be performed by or on behalf of the ASD in establishing itself successfully in the new environment is still evolving.

One of these special problems is the extent to which the ASD will need to utilize employees of other firms to perform work which exceeds the capacity of its employees—particularly during the early stages of its development when, in order to establish itself as a force in the marketplace, it is seeking business in a variety of locations and is offering equipment manufactured by a wide range of vendors. This need is even more critical as the result of the FCC requirement that the regulated telephone operating companies cannot perform intrasystem wiring work. While the parties differ as to the extent to which the labor contract permits the use of employees of other firms under the circumstances faced by the ASD, they agree that an ASD which establishes itself early as a quick-response, competitive, and reliable vendor is the best hope for overcoming the head-start other vendors have enjoyed and therefore the best hope for realizing substantially greater and more stable levels of employment of represented employees as the organization matures.

In recognition of the unusual manpower needs associated with such a small growth organization with a widely fluctuating load, and in a spirit of cooperation and in keeping with what it feels will on balance best serve its membership but without prejudice or change to its long standing positions on contracting out; CWA agrees, for the life of the current working agreement, not to challenge the use of non-company employees to perform work in those exchanges where ASD has no employees. The Company will not contract out job functions normally performed by the populated titles in those exchanges where resident ASD forces are assigned, except in those situations where the work demand is greater than that which can reasonably be performed by the resident ASD forces

---

The Employer recognizes that it is important and desirable to utilize its own equipment and drivers to the greatest extent possible prior to using sub-haulers and/or non-Company trucks.

The Union recognizes that under certain conditions, such as those dictated by customer demands, equipment requirements, daily dispatch determinations, materials to be hauled and similar factors, that sub-haulers and/or non-Company trucks are necessary and have been so utilized throughout the industry for many years.

The Employer, in accordance with the above, must, however, determine the number, type and location of its working equipment in conformity with its business requirements. The Employer further must be able to determine, in keeping with sound business practices, the extent to which it will replace equipment which is too costly to operate, obsolete or damaged.

(for example, several large projects to be accomplished concurrently).

The Company also agrees that during the life of the current contract, the ASD will not surplus any regular employee as result of contracting out any kind of work.

The Company further agrees, semiannually during the life of the current contract, to provide the Union at the bargaining (executive) level with a report on the dollar amounts of I&M work contracted out, the approximate number of man hours involved, and the kinds of work functions involved; and will meet with the Union's representatives at the bargaining level to review and discuss any and all aspects of the report on request.

Grievances in which the Union contends that the performance of work by non-employees violates the intent of this agreement, shall be filed initially at the bargaining (executive) level.

The Company and CWA are jointly concerned over the present status of surplus and laid off employees. The Company agrees that, to the extent permitted by the terms of the Southern Bell and South Central Bell working agreement, the "Amended Memorandum of Agreement" (new entities agreement) or the Plan of Reorganization, such employees will be given special consideration for filling vacancies in the ASD Installation and Maintenance forces, provided such employees are qualified to perform the work.

This agreement shall not serve to prejudice the position either party may take with respect to the contracting out of work when this agreement has expired.

AGREED:

____

Communication Workers of America

____

Southern Bell Telephone and Telegraph Company

Date: ______________________________

Source: Donald P. Crane and Michael J. Jedel, *Patterns of Industrial Peace* (forthcoming). Prepared under a grant from the U.S. Department of Labor.

Under these conditions, the Employer agrees the sub-haulers and/or non-Company trucks will not be utilized as a subterfuge to defeat the protection of the bargaining unit work.

In keeping with the above, the Union recognizes that the Employer will utilize such sub-haulers and/or non-Company trucks as required by location and classification only after all the available Company trucks at such locations and in similar classifications have been initially dispatched.[33]

However, the NLRB has ruled that an employer is free to transfer bargaining-unit work during the life of a labor agreement after bargaining to an impasse with the union when there is no work preservation clause in the agreement.[34] (See the *Milwaukee Springs* decision in Chapter 6.)

The company has no bargaining requirements if it plans to completely abandon a particular product line or service or to close a business. Determining whether the employer must bargain over transferring bargaining unit work depends on whether the transfer is based on a change in the nature or direction of the business or on labor costs. Bargaining with the union is required only if the decision is based on labor costs. On the other hand, bargaining on the *effects* of the decision to transfer work is a mandatory bargaining requirement.

Practically speaking, there is usually good reason for the company to bargain about this decision as well as its effects. The union may offer helpful suggestions or offer concessions that make the relocation less practical. More importantly, if the company acts unilaterally and its acts are later determined to be unlawful, it risks large back pay awards and in isolated cases a costly order to reopen a closed operation.[35]

Work Assignments and Jurisdiction

In an organizational setting, management can assign individual duties and tasks to employees on the job more easily than it can assign employees to jobs that have permanent job classifications.[36]

Yet these assignments often give rise to union-management confrontations, especially where changes in operations, job descriptions, and technology occur and where more than one union represents employees. While the National Labor Relations Act prohibits unions from engaging in or inducing strike action to force an employer to assign work to a particular union or craft, disputes do occur.[37] Such disputes occur usually under three types of circumstances:

1. When two or more unions claim jurisdiction over specific work assignments.
2. When bargaining-unit employees believe their work is being assigned to other employees outside the bargaining unit, such as supervisors.
3. When disagreement occurs within a union over particular work assignments.

These disputes over work assignments are called *jurisdictional disputes,* and they are costly and frustrating to employers if not settled rapidly. Under the Taft-Hartley Act, there is a special NLRB procedure for deciding these cases within 10 days of filing an unfair labor practice charge. Factors considered by the NLRB in resolving these types of disputes are skills and work involved, the union certifications already awarded by the NLRB, industry and local practice, awards of arbitrators, the employer's desires, and economy and efficiency of operations.[38] The Building and Construction Trades Department and several national contractors' associations have attempted to avoid the NLRB by establishing a national joint board to consider and decide cases of jurisdictional disputes in the building and construction industry.[39]

Some labor agreements require that bargaining-unit work be performed only by bargaining-unit employees except in instructional, experimental, or emergency situations. In instructional situations, there must be a clear, direct, and immediate connection between work done by members of management and instructions given to bargaining-unit employees. Experimental work includes the introduction of a new technique, method, or procedure, and emergency conditions occur as the result of unforeseen circumstances, such as a tornado, fire, or power outage, that call for immediate action.[40] However, it is generally recognized that bargaining-unit work may be performed by supervisors in *de minimus* situations even though not addressed in the labor agreement. Although most companies do not resist these clauses, several interesting issues regarding this matter must be addressed:

- Is a clear division between hourly employees and management in the best interest of effective labor relations?
- With more college graduates becoming first-line supervisors, how can they realistically get a feel for their subordinates' jobs if they are precluded from working on these jobs?
- If challenged over a production standard or promotion, how can management prove that the jobs can be done a certain way and within a certain time?

Intra-union work assignment problems, although not as critical and dramatic as other issues, often are very sensitive matters for local union leaders. Conflicts between members of the same union over work assignments can cause problems, especially in industrial unions having both craft and semiskilled employees as members. Whenever production processes are automated, reassignment of work from skilled employees to semiskilled production workers causes emotional conflicts within the union. For example, having pipefitters do welding tasks when welding is not included in their job description gives rise to disputes.

To resolve these conflicts, unions favor specific, written job descriptions and would like to refuse to perform work outside their jurisdictions. However, companies prefer general job descriptions that include phrases such as "perform related duties" and "make minor repairs" in order to provide flexibility in making work assignments.[41] Whether detailed or vague, the particular duties included in a job description often result in disagreements between management and union officials.

Work Scheduling

Collective bargaining agreements frequently deal with **work scheduling,** such as regulating shifts and fixing the workday or work week. Management also has the right to schedule work unless restricted by the agreement. For example, it usually has the right to suspend operations temporarily, reduce the number of shifts, and change the number of days to be worked. Moreover, it can usually make unscheduled emergency changes in the work schedule if such changes are made in good faith and for reasonable cause, such as extreme weather conditions, bomb threats, and civil disturbances.[42]

Unions and management continue to negotiate the workday and work week issues. While the 5-day, 40-hour work week has been standard since 1938, when the Fair Labor Standards Act was passed, unions have continued their attempts to reduce the hours of work.

Individual unions continue to attempt to adjust the work week. The United Auto Workers inched closer to the 4-day work week with its "paid personal holiday," which allowed auto workers with one year's seniority seven personal holidays per year. However, these were essentially eliminated by the concessions made in the 1982 negotiations.

Unions in the United States and elsewhere have shown increasing interest in *flexitime programs,* which allow an employee to start and finish work at his or her discretion, as long as the specified total number of hours per week or per day are worked and the employee is present at work during the core-hour period (for example, 9:00 a.m. to 11:00 a.m. and 1:30 p.m. to 3:30 p.m.). These programs are designed to fit together job requirements and personal needs to individual employees. While flexitime has much potential for meeting employee needs, some operations require all workers to be on the job at the same time, and in these cases work schedules cannot be altered unless the entire group accepts the alternative schedule.[43]

The Role of Seniority in Personnel Changes

Employers usually have a free hand in selecting employees who best fit the needs of their organizations and who best meet the prescribed job requirements. However, once any employee has been selected and placed on a job within the bargaining unit, the employer must abide by provisions of the labor agreement regarding personnel decisions such as promotions, transfers, and layoffs. This section highlights issues involving administrative determination and presents the concept of **seniority** (an almost sacred consideration to the union), which is usually measured by the length of an employee's continuous service.

> [Seniority is] an integral part of the institutionalized web of rules that affect the administration of human resources in the internal labor market. Specifically, seniority has come to represent an enforceable priority under a collective bargaining agreement which qualifies an employee for benefits from the employer and provides a common basis for employees to estimate their relative status in terms of job security and opportunities for advancement.[44]

Seniority has played a key role in labor relations since the 1920s, when foremen's discretion (often abused) in personnel decisions was replaced by seniority-based decisions such as compensation or reward structures and promotion, transfer, layoff, and recall systems.[45]

Seniority can be divided into two categories of employee rights:[46]

1. *Job rights* (also called *competitive rights*) apply in decisions on promotion, layoff and recall, transfers, work assignments, shift preference, selection of days off, overtime, and vacation date selection. The most senior employee usually will be given preferential treatment – will be laid off last, recalled first, and offered a shift preference and overtime first.
2. *Benefits rights* concern eligibility for certain employee benefits, such as vacations, pensions, severance pay, sick leave, and insurance. These rights are not competitive with those of other employees and begin to accumulate immediately upon employment with the organization.

Seniority provisions, found in 91 percent of all labor agreements,[47] show how seniority accrues over an employee's continuous service and, in some cases, how it can be lost for a variety of reasons (layoff, failure to respond to recall, unauthorized absences, or taking a job elsewhere during leave of absence).

Job seniority may be measured in a number of ways: total length of time with an employer (employment, mill, or plant seniority), length of service in a line of progression (progression line seniority), and length of service in a job classification (job seniority). While the particulars of the seniority system may vary greatly, some type of preference is usually accorded the more senior workers.

Seniority is considered "sacred" by most union members, yet it is doubtful that any other concept of labor relations has been as troublesome in collective bargaining. Management seldom objects to providing some sense of security to long-service employees, and unions and management generally agree that senior employees should be entitled to greater security and superior benefits as a matter of equity and fairness. However, for other reasons, seniority has played an increasingly important role in the labor relations environment. For example, it serves as an important objective measure for making personnel decisions—the concept dictates that length of service, not managerial discretion, determines who will be promoted or laid off. In addition, the number and types of employee benefits tied to seniority have increased dramatically.[48]

Seniority can be very costly to the company as well as to union members. For example, Lockheed has claimed that it lost $15 million in 2 years as a result of its complicated seniority system, which allows layoff-threatened employees with more than 6 years' service to take junior employees' jobs. A study of Lockheed's seniority system, which had been in effect for 15 years, showed that each layoff caused an average of 5 job changes—which caused serious problems with employee training.[49] It is difficult to compute the specific costs of other problems caused by seniority systems, such as an aging work force, the possibility of lessening ambition and motivation in younger workers, and the loss of key personnel low in seniority.

Union and management representatives carefully negotiate the seniority provisions of their agreements in anticipation of future negotiation issues and in accordance with rules of clarity, equity, and simplicity. Seniority provisions usually include such items as the *seniority unit* (company, plant, department, job), *how it is used* (promotion, transfer, layoff, recall), and *how it accumulates* (effects of interruptions of service such as military leave or layoff); *rules on loss of seniority* (voluntary quit, discharge for cause, failure to report from layoff, unexcused absence, and misuse of leave of absence); *administration of the seniority list* (posting requirements, supplying lists to the union, and keeping lists up to date); *special arrangements* (mergers, acquisition of firms, and succession); and *special exemption of certain employees.* In some cases, unions and management include a seniority provision called *superseniority,* which provides that highly skilled technical employees and union officials will be the last ones laid off. This provision allows the company to retain essential skills and at the same time promote stable labor relations.

Promotions and Transfers Personnel changes within an organization that advance the employee to a position of more responsibility, usually accompanied by a wage increase, are **promotions.** Appearing in 74 percent of collective bargaining agreements,[50] promotion provisions usually state that seniority and ability are the deciding factors. While seniority can be easily measured, determination of ability is more complex.[51] **Transfer** provisions, appearing in nearly 60 percent of agreements, cover personnel changes from one position to another with relatively equal authority, responsibility, and compensation. Seniority and ability are also usually the determining factors used in making the transfer decision.[52]

Four basic types of seniority clauses are used in promotion and transfer decisions:

1. Seniority as the sole factor.
2. Seniority used after minimum ability to perform the job is demonstrated.
3. Seniority and ability as two determining factors.
4. Relative ability used before seniority.

Straight seniority (the first type of clause) is the easiest to administer for determining eligibility for promotions and transfers. However, there is a possibility that the eligible senior employee is unfamiliar with the new job and will need extensive training.

Seniority with minimum ability (the second type of clause) simply means that the more senior employee gets the job if minimum qualifications can be demonstrated. Such a provision requires that the employer promote or transfer not the most competent candidate, but the most senior employee among the qualified candidates.

In the third type of clause, seniority and ability are given equal weight as determining factors. Arbitrators have concluded that this clause means that when seniority is relatively close, it is reasonable to use relative ability, but when seniority differs extensively, ability must be substantially greater to justify equal consideration.[53] The fourth type of clause prescribes the use of relative ability before seniority and uses seniority as the determining factor only if management determines that all the candidates for a vacancy have approximately the same qualifications for the job.[54]

Ability, the measure usually accompanying seniority, includes "some combination of skill, knowledge, attitudes, behavior, performance, pace, and production and perhaps talent."[55] While the employer has the right to establish any criteria for assessing ability, it must comply with the standards negotiated and written in the collective bargaining agreement. The employer may be required to meet the "Uniform Guidelines on Employment Selection Procedures" covering race, sex, national origin, and religious discrimination. These guidelines, used by the Equal Employment Opportunity Commission, Office of Personnel Management, and Departments of Labor and Justice, specify requirements covering employment defined broadly as tests and other selection procedures that serve as a basis for any employment decision including hiring, promotion, demotion, selection for training, or transfer. Moreover, the provisions of the labor agreement itself must not be discriminatory or perpetuate past discriminatory practices.

Even though promotion and transfer procedures differ, job vacancies must be posted for a specified period of time in 72 percent of contracts. Then, these jobs are bid for by employees interested in being considered. Usually, employees are given only a specific period of time to complete the bidding process.[56]

A study of 276 managerial decision-making processes on promotion decisions revealed that seniority is a major consideration of promotion in both union and nonunion settings. When jobs are posted, the more senior employees have the first opportunity to apply. If they do apply, managers usually favor them over more junior employees. Some managers believe that because seniority is objective, it is the fairest basis for advancement.[57]

Employers may design selection techniques to determine employees' qualifications for promotions and transfers. Techniques most commonly used are tests, experience, education, production records, performance ratings, personality traits, and absence, tardiness, and discipline records.[58] Because each of these criteria may be limited in its specific relationship to the needs of particular jobs, the determination of employee qualifications is usually based on several criteria. Where superior qualifications are identified, the determination may be clear-cut. However, where the criteria produce conflicting results, the burden is on the employer to assure accurate determination.

Transfer procedures are basically the same as those for promotion, except that employee requests are used more frequently. An employee dissatisfied in his or her present job and requesting transfer to more pleasant working conditions or a preferred work group, or to a more favorable line of progression, is generally granted the transfer if the employee qualifies and a vacancy occurs.

Other related labor agreement provisions are included to prevent possible administrative problems. For example, agreements should prescribe whether an employee carries his or her seniority to a new position or whether seniority will be retained only after a predetermined period of time. Other provisions should specify whether an employee who transfers out of the bargaining unit or is promoted to supervision will be allowed to retain seniority or will lose it.[59]

Layoffs and Recall Layoff provisions included in most contracts consider seniority first in retaining employees during layoffs. Increasingly, seniority has become the sole factor in layoff determination; however, some contracts still consider seniority as the determining factor only if employees are qualified for available jobs. In others, seniority is given consideration only when ability is equal.

Of course, there are exceptions to these general rules. For example, union stewards and local union officers may have *superseniority* and will be the last ones laid off in their respective departments. Unions sometimes desire this provision to encourage members to run for the many positions available in the union. In some cases, superseniority can be a strong incentive, if not the only one, to become a union steward. To protect the organization from having unqualified employees, some contracts stipulate that the union representatives must be qualified for the jobs available if they are to be exempt from layoff.

Advance notice of impending layoffs to the employees and the union is required in 49 percent of agreements, such as 1 to 4 days' notice. Frequently, employees scheduled for layoffs are permitted to displace or "bump" less senior employees, although they usually must qualify for the jobs in order to do so. While companywide or plantwide bumping is allowed in some agreements, it is confined to the employee's own classification or work group in a majority of cases. Most agreements provide for recall of employees after layoff. These provisions usually specify that employees be rehired in reverse order of layoff, but only if they are qualified for the open position.[60]

Over 80 percent of the senior employees in private, nonconstruction jobs enjoy substantial protection against losing their jobs. These employees are covered by plans that specify that no senior employee will be involuntarily terminated before a junior employee. Only about 40 percent of the nonunion employees are equally protected.

Although nonunion employers, like the unionized companies, are not required to provide any form of job security, there are several reasons that they do. It retains their investment in training employees, maintains morale of the work force, and preserves the firm's reputation as a fair employer.[61]

Alternatives to layoffs include pay freezes, pay cuts, productivity improvement through changed work rules, new products, attrition and hiring freezes, voluntary leave, early retirement, buffer production demands, hours reduction, rotating layoffs, moving work, and work sharing.[62]

Work sharing is provided for in 18 percent of agreements. These labor provisions specify that work sharing will be implemented for a limited time or that the company must consult with the union before work sharing may be implemented. Work sharing enables the employer to retain the skill mix of a full work force and consequently to retain its investment in employee training, keeps the employer's unemployment compensation tax contribution rates from increasing, and is considered by many employers as more equitable than retaining some employees and laying off others. Unions have shown a preference for the use of seniority in layoffs, rather than work sharing. Moreover, employers have no right to institute work sharing arrangements without first bargaining to an impasse unless such action is permitted in the labor agreement, such as in the management rights clause.[63]

Legal Issues Involving Seniority in Administrative Determinations Job rights guaranteed by the labor agreement may conflict with employee rights guaranteed by the U.S. Constitution, Civil Rights Act of 1964, and Equal Employment Opportunity Act of 1972. Use of seniority in administrative determinations such as promotions and layoffs has been the focus of much legal attention. In some cases it has been shown that minorities have been locked in departments or jobs with unfavorable lines of progression, and these practices tend to perpetuate past employment discrimination.

The Supreme Court has encouraged unions and management to engage in voluntary affirmative action programs for the hiring and promotion of minorities to rectify past discrimination. In some cases adjustments might need to be made for those minorities who were improperly denied previous employment opportunities.

While the Supreme Court encourages voluntary affirmative action plans, in 1989 the high court upheld the right of white employees to challenge promotions made under a court-approved affirmative action plan when the white employees did not participate in the negotiation of the plan. The white employees sued their employer, claiming racial discrimination, and alleged that they had been denied promotions under the affirmative action plan, which had been given to less-qualified black employees.[64] Two years before, the Supreme Court had upheld an employer's promotion of a female who had made two points lower on an interview score than a male in order to rectify employment disparities between males and females, as long as rights of other workers are not "unnecessarily untrammeled."

Another Supreme Court decision involved a white male employee who was denied entrance into an apprenticeship program even though he had more seniority (days employed with the organization) than some minority employees who were accepted into the program. This affirmative action arrangement between the employer and the union was found to be appropriate as the plan was temporary (limited to a short time) and did not greatly harm the interests of nonminority employees. Thus, a certain number of promotions in various job classifications can be reserved for minority employees even though these individuals have less seniority than qualified nonminority employees and have not been specifically identified as being a victim of past discrimination.[65]

The Supreme Court has tended to view affirmative action in employee layoffs in a different perspective, contending that layoffs represent a potentially permanent loss of income, thereby placing great harm on employees. Also, layoffs represent the loss of something one already has, whereas promotions represent something one wants. In one decision the Supreme Court indicated that a court cannot award "competitive" seniority to black employees (more days of service than they have actually worked) if black employees who are given this extra credit were not specifically identified victims of past discrimination.[66]

The Supreme Court has also limited layoff procedures favoring minority employees even if the procedures are specified in the labor agreement. One such situation occurred between a Board of Education and a teacher's union. The labor agreement provided that in the event of a layoff, those with the most seniority would be retained, except that at no time would there be a greater percentage of minority personnel laid off than the current percentage of minority personnel employed at the time of the layoff.

During layoffs, nonminority teachers were laid off while minority teachers with less seniority were retained. The court recognized that the labor agreement provision represented an affirmative action attempt. However, it stated that this provision could not be implemented because[67]

- Affirmative action for racial classifications must be justified by a compelling stated purpose. The rationale that minority teachers needed to be retained to provide "role models" for minority students was not found to be compelling.
- Societal discrimination alone is not sufficient to justify racial classifications in layoff situations. There must also be convincing evidence that remedial action is needed in the specific workplace.

Employers as well as unions face difficult dilemmas. Assuming that employers have been hiring minorities recently at a greater rate than in the past, the company seniority list would consist of white males toward the top and minorities toward the bottom. At times when product demand is low the employer may face the probability of laying off the newly hired minority employees in accordance with the last-hired, first-fired provision in the labor agreement.[68] In those cases where plant, department, or job seniority is used, the layoffs would erase much of the employer's progress in its affirmative action plan and affect minority employment disproportionately.

Minority groups have attacked these seniority and layoff practices on the basis of two theories:[69]

1. The last-hired, first-fired layoff practice perpetuates past discrimination, since it takes the minority ratio of the work force back to the days when employment discrimination was practiced.
2. As an employment criterion having a disparate effect on minority employees, the last-hired, first-fired layoff rule can be justified only on the grounds of its "business necessity" or as a "bona fide occupational qualification," conditions that minority groups feel are not present.

In 1989, the Supreme Court also sharply curtailed the use of discriminatory claims under seniority systems when it ruled that a lawsuit challenging an allegedly discriminatory feature of the seniority system must be filed within 300 days of the change in the seniority rights. If the seniority rights are included in the collective bargaining agreement, the date of signing the agreement would be the date of record. For example, if the company and union negotiate a change in the seniority system from plantwide seniority to departmental or job seniority, those minority employees who are harmed would have 300 days from the signing of the agreement to challenge the loss of their seniority rights, not from the date an adverse decision has been made. Otherwise, the minority employees would have to pursue their alleged mistreatment through the grievance procedure.[70] (The Civil Rights Act of 1990 was proposed in early 1990; the proposed law would modify many Supreme Court decisions in equal employment opportunity.)

The Supreme Court also recognizes that the Equal Employment Opportunity Act affords broad immunity and latitude to seniority systems, particularly those that are *bona fide:* established before 1964, were adopted in a good faith (nondiscriminatory) fashion, and do not exhibit any intent to discriminate in the layoff activity. Indeed, the Supreme Court has stated that layoffs based on this type of seniority will be upheld even if a disproportionate number of minorities are adversely affected.

Employee Training and Work Restructuring

Apprenticeship and Training Programs

Many employees receive training after employment by the company. Unions tend to become much more involved in a particular form of training, **apprenticeship programs.** Apprenticeships are formal, supervised programs of training and experience, often supplemented by off-the-job instruction. They combine about 144 hours of classroom training and 2,000 hours of on-the-job (OJT) for up to 6 years depending on the skill. OJT teaches the apprentice how to work in a trade; classroom instruction teaches why things are performed as they are. In the construction industry 86 percent of apprentices are enrolled in joint union-management programs, whereas in non-construction industries only 48 percent are enrolled in joint programs.[71]

About 46 percent of labor agreements have provisions governing apprenticeship programs, although certain industries have considerably more (printing and publishing, 85 percent; rubber and plastics, 91 percent; primary metals, 88 percent; fabricated metals, 64 percent; transportation equipment, 85 percent; construction, 67 percent).[72]

Labor and management officials became more deeply involved in the administration of apprenticeship programs than in other types of training. Apprenticeship is of particular interest to craft unions. Over 40 international unions deal with apprenticeship programs in their constitutions and bylaws. For example, the constitution may set the ratio of apprenticeships to journeymen, length of the apprenticeship, and requirements for admission, completion, and admission to journeyman status.

Labor agreements often control apprenticeship programs in five ways:

- Determine conditions of entry, such as age, education, and test score.
- Establish joint apprenticeship committees composed of an equal number of union and employer representatives.
- Determine the number of apprentices per journeyman and the duration of the apprenticeship program (average 4 to 5 years).
- Set standards for training, which is divided between on-the-job and classroom work.
- Establish employment rules, such as wages, probationary period, supervision by journeymen, and certification.

Craft unions have a particular interest in apprenticeship programs because these programs allow their members to maintain high wages while protecting members' jobs from being taken by nonapprentices. They also combine with union hiring halls to preserve the union's power to provide services to employers. Employers have union help in training apprentices, as well as placement services through the union hiring halls.

Industrial unions also have an interest in apprenticeship training, but because they do not operate union hiring halls, and the employers do their own recruiting, selection, and placement, their interest is not as strong. Industrial unions deal with apprenticeship programs through collective bargaining and joint company-union administered training programs funded by employers and/or government. Such provisions of the labor agreement include the following:[73]

- Protecting the wage standards of journeymen.
- Providing rights to training for incumbents as a way to minimize wage and job loss caused by technological change, mergers, relocation, and shifts in demand.
- Providing training opportunities in the form of wage supplements or fringe benefits to support the employee on outside job-related training.

Enrollment in registered apprenticeship programs was 303,000 in 1988, less than 1 percent of the civilian labor force, and 100,440 of this number were new apprentice registrations.[74] While this number may appear high, if the proportion of apprentices in the United States equaled that of Austria, Germany, or Switzerland, there would be 7 million American apprentices.[75]

Because craft unions have played a vital role in training and have greatly influenced the labor supply, their *nepotism* (practice of hiring relatives) and discriminatory practices that have prevented minorities from entering skilled occupations have made them prime targets of civil rights suits. Since labor unions are now covered under the Equal Employment Opportunity Act, they too must be conscious of EEOC regulations. Through union hiring halls and apprenticeship programs, craft unions have an important role in selecting apprentices and assigning union members to jobs. Therefore, the EEOC agencies have been very interested in their operations.

The EEOC and the courts have significantly affected the internal affairs of craft unions through affirmative action plans, conciliation, consent decrees, and court cases. The following policies are the result of EEOC regulations and interventions:[76]

1. Acceptance for apprenticeship training based on valid testing and licensing procedures, legitimate experience requirements, and standard initiation fees.
2. Union advertising of vacancies with the time and place for tests.
3. Policies abolishing nepotism (long a tradition with craft unions).
4. First-in, first-out referral procedures continued, but master referral registers, which include names, addresses, sign-in books, and availability sheets, maintained and operated in a nondiscriminatory fashion.
5. Craft unions and construction companies agreeing to an affirmative action plan, including goals, timetables, and specific actions that will increase minority employment in the specific crafts.

Unions and employers have developed some new collective bargaining responses to the need to train employees. General Motors, Ford, and Chrysler with the United Auto Workers, and American Telephone and Telegraph with the Communication Workers of America have launched new concepts in the areas of training programs arising from collective bargaining. These programs are directed to employees' personal career needs and meeting the new challenges of increased competition.

For example, the UAW-Ford Employee Development and Training Program (EDTP) uses a national training center, financed by the company and jointly managed by a board of union and company representatives. The company continues its traditional programs such as apprenticeship training, routine job changes and promotions, and health and safety training as separate entities. The EDTP funds such programs as career services and reemployment assistance, which includes professional career counseling, job placement assistance, tuition assistance, and relocation seminars for displaced employees.

The AT&T-CWA program is called Alliance for Employee Growth and Development. As in the auto industry, job-specific training programs continue, but the Alliance has taken on new directions in light of the divestiture and continued technological changes in the industry. The Alliance provides career assessment and planning that includes access to information about anticipated job changes and opportunities within the company. It encourages joint training committees to survey present and future employment opportunities and to develop proposals to help qualify bargaining-unit employees for the company's future job needs. In addition, local committees are designed to assist displaced workers with counseling on resumé writing, job-search assistance, and relocation assistance. In addition, vocational training assistance is made available for employees who apply within 6 months of layoff.[77]

Work Restructuring

Unions and companies are changing the nature of the work performed by employees. While these work restructuring programs come under many different labels, such as employee involvement, worker participation, labor-management jointness, or self-managed work teams, they all involve major departures from the traditional way of assigning specific tasks to each employee. For example, a work team may include 5 to 12 multi-skilled workers who rotate jobs and produce an entire product with a minimal amount of supervision. The team approach wipes out tiers of managers and tears down bureaucratic barriers between departments. It requires employees to improve their technical and behavioral skills. Some work teams not only gain a more direct voice in shop-floor operations, but also take over some managerial duties, such as scheduling work and vacations, hiring new members, and ordering materials. These programs have unleashed enormous energy and creativity in employees and increased their feelings of dignity and self-worth, and have enjoyed successes in such companies as General Electric, General Motors, Champion International, and Ford. A newly created subsidiary of AT&T Credit Corp. reported productivity increases of 100 percent after restructuring employees' jobs and organizing the team concept.

These new ventures have their disbelievers as well. Some union leaders believe these programs are similar to the old "speed-up" campaigns by companies. Others complain that they are "union-busting" techniques to do away with the union. Within the United Auto Workers, a minority of members have challenged the international leadership for becoming "too cozy" with management. There are disbelievers within management as well. Some managers don't want to give up authority to team members. They feel threatened by the team concept and believe that their usefulness and value to the company has been reduced and that they will be replaced.

Interestingly, while unions proposed "industrial democracy" early in the 20th century, many managers today are pushing it. At the same time, other managers are fighting it. The future will tell the directions that will be taken.[78]

Safety and Health: The Occupational Safety and Health Act

Occupational safety and health clauses are found in 86 percent of labor agreements. The topics covered range from a general statement of responsibility for the safety and health of employees to details about such issues as safety equipment (43 percent), first aid (22 percent), physical examinations (33 percent), investigation of accidents (18 percent), employee obligations (40 percent), hazardous work (26 percent), and joint union-management safety committees (48 percent).[79] Many of these provisions have resulted from legislation, namely, the Occupational Safety and Health Act (OSHA), passed in 1970 in an attempt to improve industrial safety statistics.[80]

The employer's overriding duty under OSHA is to furnish each employee with conditions free from recognized hazards that may cause illness, injury, or death and to comply with all occupational safety and health standards adopted by the Department of Labor. Employers must permit inspectors to enter their establishments and conduct inspections, and must post notices, provide equipment, and maintain records.

Thus far, OSHA has been found to have had at most a minor impact on lowering occupational injury rates. Support for this conclusion is suggested by the following:

- The agency has inspected few establishments (4 percent each year), with low penalties given for serious violations.
- Lost work days due to job related accidents increased.[81]
- 6.4 million occupational injuries and illnesses were reported in 1988; 300,000 more than in 1987 and 700,000 more than in 1986.
- 8.6 accidents and injuries per 100 full-time workers were reported in 1988 as compared to 8.3 in 1987 and 7.9 per 100 workers in 1986.[82]

Yet, a 1986 study reported that OSHA did a better job than previously reported.[83] The agency has made some headway in establishing regulations concerning possible cancer causing agents,[84] other hazardous chemicals, and chemicals that could possibly cause fetal damage. In addition, OSHA indicated that employees removed from their jobs because of excessive lead levels in the body would be protected against loss of pay, seniority, and other job rights.

Under the Reagan administration, OSHA attempted to cooperate with employers having good safety records and joint collaboration with unions. These firms received exemptions from routine safety inspections. The Reagan administration claimed that this program produced lower injury rates.

However, Congress and unions were some of the more outspoken critics of OSHA. Congressional hearings revealed that OSHA had excessively lenient policies that exempted some employers from full-scale inspections, had made generously lenient settlements of citations and fines, had bureaucratically restricted procedures for responding to worker complaints, and was understaffed and underfunded for its field enforcement.[85]

In 1987, OSHA began more vigorous enforcement of the regulations and found several companies in serious violation. Major fines were levied: IBP, a meat-packing subsidiary of Occidental Petroleum, was fined $2.6 million for altering accident and illness records; General Dynamics was fined $615,000 for record-keeping violations; Union Carbide settled a $1.4 million fine for bookkeeping violations by agreeing to pay $408,500 and to make significant health and safety improvements; and Chrysler Corp. agreed to pay $1.6 million to settle charges against it for safety violations.[86]

Contemporary OSHA Issues

Occupational safety and health regulations have raised other issues. One issue is the right of employees to refuse to perform hazardous work. While none of the provisions of the Occupational Safety and Health Act explicitly protect employees who refuse to perform work for safety and health reasons, employees are protected from discipline under certain circumstances. For example, when two employees refused to remove debris from an overhead wire mesh screen one week after an employee fell to his death through the screen, the employer sent them home with a loss of wages for 6 hours. The Secretary of Labor, on behalf of the employees, contended that the suspension was a discriminatory act under the OSHA, and on appeal, the Supreme Court agreed.[87] However, the Court placed two cautions on employees who refused work:

> The employees have no power under the regulation to order their employer to correct the hazardous condition or to clear the dangerous workplace of others. Moreover, any employee who acts in reliance on the regulations runs the risk of discharge or reprimand in the event a court subsequently finds that he acted unreasonably or in bad faith.[88]

In a related matter, employees who walk off their jobs in an expression of concern over unsafe working conditions are protected by the National Labor Relations Act. Under the NLRA, when employees act as a group, they are protected for their concerted activities, if they believe in good faith that they are exposed to a safety risk. In such cases, they may protest exposure to the dangerous condition without being subjected to subsequent discipline or discrimination by the employer.[89]

A second issue is the controversial OSHA rule that allows employees, their designated representatives, and OSHA inspectors the right to examine on-the-job medical records as well as company records of exposure to hazardous conditions. Employers are not required to measure exposure to toxic substances or to conduct medical surveillance of employees. However, if an employer does conduct these activities and records the results, this information must be accessible to employees, their representatives, and OSHA inspectors. Refusal by the employer or occupational physician to provide such information is allowed only when the information would be detrimental to the employee's mental health, such as information about the employee's psychiatric state or a diagnosis of terminal illness.[90] The union as well as the NLRB may become involved. Recently, a federal appeals court upheld a NLRB order that a company honor a union's request for information about industrial chemicals and medical conditions of employees exposed to potentially hazardous substances.[91]

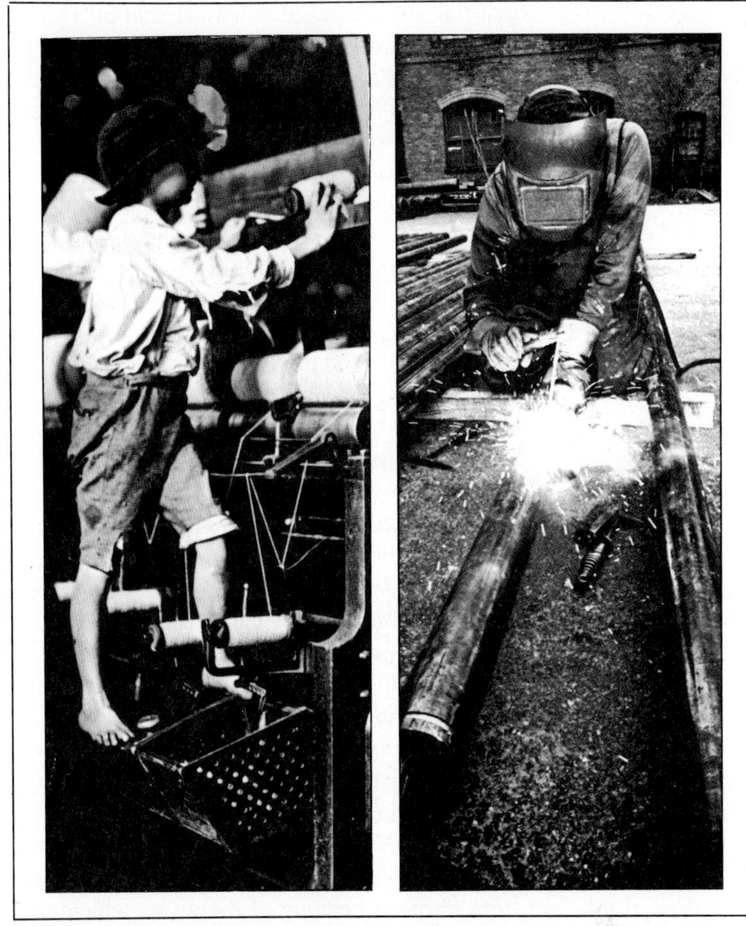

Many safety and health hazards, commonplace in the past, have been eliminated through the use of safety equipment. Yet safety remains an issue in current collective bargaining.

Sources: Photo above left reproduced from the collection of the Library of Congress. Photo above right by Bohdan Hrynewyvch, Stock/Boston.

A third issue is the controversy over the employees' right to know the toxic substances to which they are exposed on the job. OSHA estimates that 32 million workers are potentially exposed to one or more chemical hazards and estimates that there are 575,000 chemical products. Chemical exposure may cause or contribute to many serious health effects, such as heart ailments, kidney and lung damage, sterility, cancer, burns, and rashes. Because of the seriousness of the potential problems and because many employers and employees know little about them, OSHA issued a rule called the Hazard Communication Standard. This rule's basic goal is to assure that employers and employees will know about work hazards and how to protect themselves. Employers must identify and list the hazardous chemicals in their workplace, place labels on each container of hazardous chemicals, and conduct formal training programs to ensure that all employees are informed of the presence of the chemicals and steps to take in an emergency.[92]

OSHA estimated that the first-year compliance cost for the new standard would be $687 million and that the total compliance costs over the first 40 years would be $1.57 billion. However, OSHA predicts that the new standard will prevent 148,000 cancer cases, 119,000 chronic illness cases, and 74,800 deaths—yielding benefits of $6.7 billion over the next 40 years.[93]

Other serious health and safety-related issues involve acquired immune deficiency syndrome (AIDS), repetitive motion injuries, smoking at the workplace, and substance abuse, which must be dealt with by employers, unions, the government, and the public alike. AIDS is transmitted by sexual contact, sharing of contaminated needles, and blood transfusions. The disease had infected 30,000 persons by 1987 and 54 percent of them had died from the disease. It is projected that as many as 270,000 Americans will have contracted AIDS by 1991, with 179,000 deaths resulting from the disease. To show how staggering these numbers are, 292,000 Americans were killed in World War II.

The AIDS issue is complicated by co-employee fear that the disease is contagious even though medical research has indicated that the virus cannot be transmitted by casual contact such as working alongside another employee. Also, whether AIDS is covered under the Rehabilitation Act of 1973 is still debated. Under the labor agreement, the union must defend both AIDS victims who may be discriminated against and co-employees who may be disciplined for refusing to work with someone who may have AIDS.[94]

Repetitive motion injuries, called cumulative trauma disorder or carpal tunnel syndrome by doctors and "the VDT disease" by employees, had increased to 73,000 in 1987, making these injuries the fastest-growing occupational injury in the United States. The National Institute for Occupational Safety and Health estimates that 5 million people, or 4 percent of the work force, are affected. These injuries result from frequent bending of the wrist, which causes tendons and tissues to swell in the tunnel formed by the carpal bones and ligaments, pinching and incapacitating the median nerve, which gives feeling to the hand. Meat cutters, food processors, assembly workers, office workers who work at VDTs, and others are likely to be affected.[95]

In 1987, the state of New York announced a VDT policy for state workers that requires state agencies to address such issues as lighting, design of work stations, noise, and work breaks. Suffolk County in New York passed a county law that requires employers to provide ergonomically designed work stations and safety training in private businesses having 20 or more VDTs where operators spend at least 26 hours a week on the terminals. The U.S. House of Representatives held a hearing wherein one member predicted that repetitive motion injuries will be the "number one occupational hazard of the 1990s."[96]

This prediction is reinforced by the estimate by the International Labor Organization that North America in 1990 will have 40 million VDTs in use at workplaces, 25 million in homes, and 7 to 8 million more portable units that will accompany employees at home and work.[97] A related safety and health concern has been the radiation emitted from VDT units; health professionals suspect that these emissions are linked to cataracts, miscarriages, and abnormal pregnancies. Research is continuing to determine the degree of the linkage.[98]

Smoking, since the 1964 U.S. Surgeon General's report on its health consequences, has gradually moved to the labor relations area. In 1986, the Surgeon General's Report on the Health Consequences of Involuntary Smoking disclosed that sidestream smoke may expose the involuntary smoker to greater amounts of carcinogens than those to which the smoker is exposed, which raised the level of concern at the workplace. As a result, employers began considering "no smoking" rules, "smoke free" workplaces, and/or designated places for smoking. Emerging issues will be the rule-making procedures (unilateral and negotiated) and union action to protect bargaining unit employees who may be disciplined for rule violation.[99]

Substance abuse (covered in Chapters 1 and 10) has emerged as a major health and safety problem in today's workplace. While many still have a stereotyped view of substance abusers as unemployed drifters, one authority accurately gives the following description:

> The modern substance abuser is a gourmet who frequents a veritable delicatessen of drugs, licit and illicit, some of them ingeniously created just for his pleasure. The shelves are lined not only with contraband, such as cocaine and marijuana, but also with widely used prescription drugs, like tranquilizers and amphetamines. He may reach for the "designer drugs," imitations of standard substances whose molecules have been rearranged to maximize effects and minimize detectability. Many abused substances can be lawfully purchased without a prescription; according to medical experts, much of the population comes to work each morning under the lingering influence of over-the-counter preparations, such as diet pills, sleep aids, and cold remedies.[100]

Summary

The four general categories of administrative issues—technological changes, personnel changes, employee and job development, and safety and health—have many important facets that may be negotiated and often end up in labor agreements.

Technological change, an essential ingredient of a dynamic economic system, is broadly defined to include such activities as introduction of labor-saving machines, power-driven tools, and automatic loading equipment. While unions generally accept these changes as inevitable, they attempt to negotiate provisions in labor agreements to protect members' present jobs and establish the means for assuring future protection. Collective bargaining has provided avenues for working together to resolve complicated problems emanating from technological changes; significant examples have occurred in the auto, communication, and meat-packing industries.

Two interrelated issues, job security and personnel changes, raise questions about employee protection. Often, unions will seek to protect their members by negotiating work load restrictions, limiting management's rights to subcontract, demanding specific work assignments and jurisdiction, and structuring jobs and scheduling work to the advantage of the employees. When personnel changes are made, seniority becomes a key issue. Likewise, where firms are growing and opportunities for advancement are present, seniority and merit are key considerations.

Employers and unions must consider EEOC regulations and court rulings in addition to labor agreement factors in deciding courses of action on personnel adjustment.

Employee and job development incorporate employee training, emphasis on apprenticeship, and work restructuring programs. Unions and employers alike place great emphasis on and expend much effort in apprenticeship programs. Work restructuring efforts are often initiated by management, but union cooperation is essential to complete success of such programs. While some unions are reluctant to become involved with them, major breakthroughs have been identified in selected unions, such as the United Auto Workers.

Safety and health issues have become important since the passage of the Occupational Safety and Health Act of 1970. Criticism of the act's administration has led to reevaluation, elimination of nit-picking rules, and a focus on major problems. Some progress has been made in its administration, but vital issues remain: clarification of operations, rules concerning regulation of chemicals that may cause cancer, and emerging problems such as AIDS, repetitive motion injuries, and smoking in the workplace. On the positive side, considerable progress has been made by employers and unions toward cooperative programs and toward meeting the objectives of the act.

New directions of OSHA include focusing on high-hazard industries, reducing legalism, and developing greater cooperation. Employee rights have been established that include the right to refuse hazardous job assignments, to examine records, and to know about exposure to toxic substances.

Key Terms

technological change
automation
job-security work rules
featherbedding
subcontracting
outsourcing
work scheduling
seniority
promotions
transfer
ability
apprenticeship programs

Discussion Questions

1. Why do unions' reactions to technological change vary in accordance with their industry affiliation?
2. Think of an industry or company with which you are familiar, and assume that you are the local union president. What types of clauses regarding technological issues would you attempt to negotiate with your employer?
3. Explain why unions place priority on seniority in personnel decisions, while employers seek to identify other determining factors.
4. Assess the 1989 Supreme Court decisions in terms of their fairness to minority groups.
5. Compare the legal restrictions that apply in selecting applicants for apprenticeship programs and promoting employees in the bargaining unit.
6. Why are many unions critical of OSHA, whose purpose is to protect the physical well-being of their members?
7. Evaluate potential reaction of employees to AIDS, VDTs, smoking on the job, and substance abuse by other employees.

References

1. Julius Rezler, *Automation and Industrial Labor* (New York: Random House, 1969), pp. 5–6.
2. Jerome A. Mark, "Technological Change and Employment: Some Results from BLS Research," *Monthly Labor Review* 110 (April 1987), pp. 26–29.
3. Richard E. Walton and Robert B. McKersie, "Managing New Technology and Labor Relations: An Opportunity for Mutual Influence," *The Challenge of New Technology to Labor-Management Relations* (Washington, D.C.: U.S. Government Printing Office, 1989), p. 41.
4. Richard M. Cyert and David C. Mowery, eds., *Technology and Employment: Innovations and Growth in the U.S. Economy* (Washington, D.C.: National Academy Press, 1987), p. 129–133.
5. "Changing 45 Million Jobs," *Business Week,* August 3, 1981, pp. 66–67.
6. Richard M. Cyert and David C. Mowery, eds., *Technology and Employment: Innovation and Growth in the U.S. Economy* (Washington, D.C.: National Academy Press, 1987), p. 133.
7. Janet S. Solomon, "Union Responses to Technological Change: Protecting the Past or Looking to the Future?" *Labor Studies Journal* 12 (Fall 1987), p. 51.
8. Richard W. Riche, "Impact of New Electronic Technology," *Monthly Labor Review* 105 (March 1982), p. 37.
9. Marcia L. Greenbaum, "Employee Privacy, Monitoring, and New Technology," in *Arbitration 1988: Emerging Issues for the 1990s,* ed. Gladys W. Gruenberg (Washington, D.C.: Bureau of National Affairs Inc., 1989), pp. 163–166.
10. Alan F. Westin, "Monitoring and New Office Systems," in *Arbitration 1988: Emerging Issues for the 1990s,* ed. Gladys W. Gruenberg (Washington, D.C.: Bureau of National Affairs Inc., 1989), p. 168–175.
11. George Ruben, "Collective Bargaining in 1982: Results Dictated by Economy," *Monthly Labor Review* 106 (January 1983), p. 29.
12. Sumner H. Slichter, James J. Healy, and E. Robert Livernash, *The Impact of Collective Bargaining on Management* (Washington, D.C.: Brookings Institute, 1960), pp. 317–335.
13. Robert D. Leiter, *Featherbedding and Job Security* (New York: Twayne Publishers, 1964), pp. 32–33.
14. William Gomberg, "The Work Rules and Work Practices," *Labor Law Journal* 12 (July 1961), pp. 643–653.
15. Benjamin Aaron, "Government Restraint on Featherbedding," *Stanford Law Review* 5 (July 1953), pp. 687–721.
16. "A Work Resolution in U.S. Industry," *Business Week,* May 16, 1983, pp. 100–103.
17. Kirsh, *Automation and Collective Bargaining,* pp. 16–17.
18. "Supreme Court Upholds Container Rules on Lawful Work Preservation Measures," *Daily Labor Report,* June 28, 1985, p. A-12.
19. Sheldon Friedman, "Negotiated Approaches to Job Security," *Labor Law Journal* (August 1985), pp. 556–557.
20. "Study Attacks Notion That Employment Security Plans Are Too Expensive, Otherwise Impractical," *Daily Labor Report,* October 17, 1984, p. A-3.
21. "The Work Rule Changes GM is Counting On," *Business Week,* April 5, 1982, pp. 30–31.
22. "Plant Closings or Mass Layoffs Affected One Million Workers in 1983–84, GAO Funds," *Daily Labor Report,* May 1, 1986, p. A-12.
23. William D. Torrence, "Plant Closing and Advance Notice: Another Look at the Numbers," *Labor Law Journal* (August 1985), pp. 463–465.
24. Bennett Harrison, "Plant Closures: Efforts to Cushion the Blow," *Monthly Labor Review* 107 (June 1984), p. 41.
25. John Bussey and Bridgett Davis, "Ford Cost-Cutting Move Is Issue in Strike," *The Wall Street Journal,* August 8, 1986, p. 6.
26. Donald P. Crane and Michael Jay Jedel, "Mature Collective Bargaining Relationships," *Arbitration 1988: Emerging Issues for the 1990s,* ed. Gladys W. Gruenberg (Washington, D.C.: Bureau of National Affairs Inc., 1989), p. 358.
27. Slichter, Healy, and Livernash, *Collective Bargaining,* pp. 280–285.
28. "NLRB Holds Subcontracting Decisions Not Subject to Mandatory Bargaining," *Daily Labor Report,* March 26, 1986, p. A-1.
29. Collective Bargaining Negotiations and Contracts, *Basic Patterns* (Washington, D.C.: Bureau of National Affairs Inc., 1989), p. 65:2.
30. "CWA Strike against AT&T Information Systems Averted with Agreement on Subcontracting," *Daily Labor Report,* October 31, 1985, p. A-9.
31. Slichter, Healy, and Livernash, *Collective Bargaining,* pp. 309–312.
32. "AT&T, Union Reach $6 Million Settlement over Subcontracting," *The Wall Street Journal,* January 12, 1987, p. 10.
33. "Board Holds Mid-Term Transfer of Bargaining Unit Work Unlawful," *Daily Labor Report,* March 18, 1986, p. A-4.
34. *Milwaukee Spring II,* 115 LRRM 1065 (1984).
35. Leonard E. Cohen, "The Duty to Bargain over Plant Relocations and Other Corporate Changes: *Otis Elevator* v. *NLRB,*" *The Labor Lawyer* 1 (Summer 1985), p. 525–532.
36. Frank Elkouri and Edna A. Elkouri, *How Arbitration Works,* 3d ed. (Washington, D.C.: Bureau of National Affairs Inc., 1973), p. 458.
37. NLRB, *42nd Annual Report of the National Labor Relations Board* (Washington, D.C.: Government Printing Office, 1977), p. 133.
38. James K. McCollum and Edward A. Schroeder IV, "NLRB Decisions in Jurisdictional Disputes: The Success of the 10(k) Process," *Employee Relations Law Journal* 13 (Spring 1988), pp. 649–652.
39. NLRB, *42nd Annual Report,* p. 113. This board uses two procedural rules that are worthy of note: 1. A request for a decision in a specific case does not have to wait until the dispute occurs. Once the contractor makes the initial work assignments, a request for a decision can be made. Thus, time is saved by facilitating the dispute resolution process. 2. Decisions of the board are not precedent-setting. This does not mean that similar decisions within an area are not based on patterns; it means that conditions vary from region to region, union to union, even agreement to agreement. Therefore, the board is not bound completely by precedent, but past practice is also a factor. Custom in the industry and skills, training, and job content are important elements that are considered.
40. Elvis C. Stephens, "A Supervisor Performs Bargaining Unit Work: Is the Contract Violated?" *Labor Law Journal* 31 (November 1980), pp. 683–688.
41. Slichter, Healy, and Livernash, *Collective Bargaining,* pp. 266–276.
42. Elkouri and Elkouri, *How Arbitration Works,* pp. 469–487.
43. Jeffrey M. Miller, *Innovations in Working Patterns* (Washington, D.C.: Communication Workers of America and German Marshall Fund of the United States, 1978); and W. H. Holley, A. A. Armenakis, and H. S. Feild, "Employee Reactions to a Flexitime Program: A Longitudinal Study," *Human Resource Management* 15 (Winter 1976), pp. 21–23.

44. James A. Craft, "Equal Opportunity and Seniority: Trends and Manpower Implications," *Labor Law Journal* 26 (December 1975), p. 750.
45. Katherine G. Abraham and Henry S. Farber, "Returns to Seniority in Union and Nonunion Jobs: A New Look at the Evidence," *Industrial and Labor Relations Review* 42 (October 1988), pp. 3–19.
46. Roger I. Abrams and Dennis R. Nolan, "Seniority Rights Under the Collective Agreement," *The Labor Lawyer* 2 (Winter 1986), pp. 99–110.
47. Editors of Collective Bargaining Negotiations and Contracts, *Basic Patterns,* 1989, p. 75:1.
48. Slichter, Healy, and Livernash, *Collective Bargaining,* pp. 104–105.
49. "Lockheed's Strike," p. 31.
50. Editors of Collective Bargaining Negotiations and Contracts, *Basic Patterns,* p. 68:1.
51. Elaine F. Gruenfeld, *Promotion: Practices , Policies, and Affirmative Action* (Ithaca, N.Y.: New York State School of Industrial and Labor Relations, Cornell University, 1975), p. 12.
52. Editors of Collective Bargaining Negotiations and Contracts, *Basic Patterns,* p. 68:241.
53. Thomas J. McDermott, "Types of Seniority Provisions and the Measurement of Ability," *Arbitration Journal* 25 (1970), pp. 101–105. Also see W. E. Howard, "The Interpretation of Ability by Labor-Management Arbitrators," *Arbitration Journal* 14 (1959), pp. 122–123.
54. McDermott, "Seniority Provisions," p. 106.
55. Gruenfeld, *Promotion,* p. 12.
56. Editors of Collective Bargaining Negotiations and Contracts, *Basic Patterns,* p. 75:3.
57. D. Quinn Mills, "Seniority versus Ability in Promotion Decisions," *Industrial and Labor Relations Review* 38 (April 1985), pp. 424–425.
58. William H. Holley, Jr., "Performance Ratings in Arbitration," *Arbitration Journal* 32 (March 1977), pp. 8–25.
59. U.S. Department of Labor, Bureau of Labor Statistics, *Seniority in Promotion and Transfer Provisions* (Washington, D.C.: Government Printing Office, 1970), pp. 15–21, 42.
60. Editors of Collective Bargaining Negotiations and Contracts, *Basic Patterns,* pp. 60:1–60:4.
61. Katherine G. Abraham and James L. Medoff, "Length of Service and Layoffs in Union and Nonunion Work Groups," *Industrial and Labor Relations Review* 38 (October 1984), pp. 96–97.
62. Gary Hansen, *Preventing Layoffs* (Washington, D.C.: U.S. Department of Labor, 1986), pp. 2–4.
63. Steven Briggs, "Allocating Available Work in a Union Environment: Layoffs vs. Work Sharing," *Labor Law Journal* 38 (October 1987), pp. 650–657.
64. *Martin* v. *Wilks, Daily Labor Report,* June 13, 1989, D-1–D-11.
65. "Decision of Supreme Court in *Firefighters Local 93* v. *City of Cleveland,*" *Daily Labor Report,* July 3, 1986, p. E-2.
66. "Decision of Supreme Court in *Fire Fighters Local 1784* v. *Stotts,*" *Daily Labor Report,* June 13, 1984, p. D-1.
67. *"Wendy Wygant* v. *Jackson Board of Education," Supreme Court Reporter* 106 (June 1986), pp. 1842–1843.
68. William H. Holley, Jr., and Hubert S. Feild, "Equal Employment Opportunity and Its Implications for Personnel Practices," *Labor Law Journal* 27 (May 1976), p. 285.
69. Barbara Linderman Schlei and Paul Grossman, *Employment Discrimination Law* (Washington, D.C.: Bureau of National Affairs Inc., 1976), pp. 458–459.
70. *Lorance* v. *AT&T Technologies, Daily Labor Report,* June 13, 1989, p. E-1–E-6.
71. "Statements on Apprenticeship Training Before House Labor Subcommittee on Employment Opportunities," *Daily Labor Report,* November 17, 1983, pp. E-1–E-8.
72. Bureau of Labor Statistics, *Major Characteristics of Collective Bargaining Agreements, January 1, 1980* (Washington, D.C.: U.S. Government Printing Office, 1981), p. 105.
73. Jack Barbash, "Union Interests in Apprenticeships and Other Training Forms," in *Essays on Apprenticeship,* ed. Norman F. Duffy (Madison, Wis.: University of Wisconsin, 1967), p. 36.
74. Anthony P. Carnevale and Leila J. Gainer, *The Learning Experience* (Washington, D.C.: U.S. Department of Labor, 1989), p. 13.
75. Vernon M. Briggs, Jr., "Conference Summary and Critique," in *Apprenticeship Research,* ed. Vernon M. Briggs, Jr., and Felician F. Foltman (Ithaca, N.Y.: Cornell University, 1981), p. 218.
76. Bureau of National Affairs Inc., *EEOC Compliance Manual* (Washington, D.C.: Bureau of National Affairs Inc., August 1977), p. 660:0001.
77. Everett M. Kassalow, "Employee Training and Development: A Joint Union-Management Response to Structural and Technological Change," *Proceedings of the 40th Annual Meeting of the Industrial Research Association* (Madison, Wis.: Industrial Relations Research Association, 1988), pp. 107–117; Steven Deutsch, "Successful Worker Training Programs Help Ease Impact of Technology," *Monthly Labor Review* 110 (November 1987), pp. 14–20.
78. John Hoerr, "The Payoff from Teamwork," *Business Week,* July 10, 1989, pp. 56–62.
79. Collective Bargaining: Negotiations and Contracts, 95:1 to 95:5.
80. The year that OSHA of 1970 was passed, the following statistics were presented to Congress: 14,500 killed–average of 55 per workweek; 2.2 million injured; 390,000 disabling occupational diseases (lung cancer, asbestos, and so on); 250 million man-days lost, ten times that lost from strikes; $1.5 million in lost wages; $8 billion lost to GNP. Benjamin L. Brown, "A Law Is Made: The Legislative Process in the Occupational Safety and Health Act of 1970," *Labor Law Journal* 25 (October 1974), p. 597.
81. Evan E. Anderson, Rogene A. Buckholz, and Mohamed N. Allan, "Regulation of Worker Safety Through Standard-Setting: Effectiveness, Insights, and Alternatives," *Labor Law Journal* 37 (October 1986), p. 732.
82. "BLS Annual Survey Shows Increase in Workplace Injuries, Illnesses in 1988," *Daily Labor Report,* Washington, D.C.: Bureau of National Affairs Inc., November 16, 1989, p. B-7.
83. Robert S. Smith, "Greasing the Squeaky Wheel: The Relative Productivity of OSHA Complaint Inspections," *Industrial and Labor Relations Review* 40 (October 1986), pp. 47–48.
84. Leon Bornstein, "Industrial Relations in 1978: Some Bargaining Highlights," *Monthly Labor Review* 102 (January 1979), pp. 63–64.
85. "Administration Influence Weakens OSHA, Hearing Witnesses Tell Senate Committee," *Daily Labor Report,* April, 20, 1988, p. A-3.
86. "OSHA Awakens from Its Six-Year Slumber," *Business Week,* August 10, 1987, p. 27; Jeanne Sadler, "OSHA's Crackdown on Records Draws Praise, but Some Question Focus on Data," *The Wall Street Journal,* July 27, 1987, p. 8; George R. Salem, "Develop-

ments in the Law at the U.S. Department of Labor," *Labor Law Journal* 39 (September 1988), pp. 578–590.
87. *Whirlpool Corp.* v. *Marshall,* Secretary of Labor, Slip Opinion, Supreme Court of the United States, No. 78–1870, February 26, 1980.
88. Ibid.
89. "Taft-Hartley Act Held to Protect Workers Who Protest Unsafe Conditions," *Daily Labor Report,* November 26, 1982, p. A-5–A-6.
90. Mary Hayes, "OSHA Final Rule Gives Employees the Right to See Their Exposure and Medical Records," *Personnel Administrator* 27 (March 1982), pp. 71–75.
91. "Court Upholds NLRB Ruling on Disclosure of Safety and Health Data to Unions," *Daily Labor Report,* July 5, 1983, p. A-6.
92. U.S. Department of Labor, Occupational Safety and Health Administration, *Chemical Hazard Communication* (Washington, D.C.: U.S. Government Printing Office, 1989), p. 1–5.
93. Willis J. Goldsmith, "Current Developments in OSHA," *Employee Relations Law Journal* 13 (Spring 1988), pp. 695–697.
94. Michael R. Brown, "AIDS Discrimination in the Workplace: The Legal Dilemma," *Case and Comment* 92 (May–June, 1987), p. 3.
95. "An Invisible Workplace Hazard Gets Harder to Ignore," *Business Week,* January 30, 1989, p. 92.
96. "Lantos Questions OSHA's Ability to Address Ergonomic Problems in 1990s," *Daily Labor Report,* June 7, 1989, p. A–6.
97. "Growth in VDT Use Outstripping Knowledge about Possible Health Problems, Report Finds," *Daily Labor Report,* Washington, D.C.: Bureau of National Affairs Inc., August 18, 1989, p. A-1.
98. Staff of the Bureau of National Affairs Inc., *VDTs in the Workplace: A Study of the Effects on Employment* (Washington, D.C.: Bureau of National Affairs Inc., 1985), p. 8.
99. Elizabeth M. Crocker, "Controlling Smoking in the Workplace," *Labor Law Journal* 38 (December 1987), pp. 739–746.
100. Tia Schneider Denenberg, "Substance Abuse: The Challenge to Industrial Relations," *Proceedings of the 40th Annual Meeting of the Industrial Relations Research Association* (Madison, Wis.: Industrial Relations Research Association, 1988), pp. 303– 304.

CHAPTER 13

Economic Issues

"[T]he new pay arrangements as well as other productivity improvement projects are revolutionizing the traditional attitudes of employers and unions. But we should not assume too much. Change always comes very slowly, and several of the new techniques may not survive if economic conditions change. Nevertheless, the new, more cooperative approach may be reordering labor-management priorities. Unions have clearly become much more directly involved in the financial health of the companies with whom they are negotiating than ever before. And it is clear that workers who own stock or who participate in profit sharing arrangements can be expected in the future to have a very different attitude about the companies for whom they work.

We live in exciting times. We should not fear change. Instead, we should work to understand what we can learn from the present about what is likely to happen in the future. Only by adequate preparation can we ensure a prosperous employment future that is enjoyed by all worker groups in this country."

"Remarks of BLS Commissioner Janet Norwood on Future of Employment," *Daily Labor Report,* October 20, 1986, p. D-4.

Wages and other economic benefits represent income to the employee, cost to the organization, and a basis for taxes to the government. In addition, wages serve as a factor in the allocation of resources; they influence the individual's selection of an occupation and movement from one firm, industry, or location to another; they influence decisions on plant location and investments in machinery and capital equipment; and they affect employment and unemployment. More importantly, if wages become exorbitant, employees may be priced out of particular labor markets. Thus, wages are both economic indicators and determinants.[1]

Unions and management are required by the NLRA to bargain in good faith with respect to wages. As a result of NLRB and court decisions, wage-related topics such as pensions, overtime, shift differentials, job evaluation, and incentive systems must be bargained over if either party presents such topics during negotiations.

Union and management negotiators spend many hours annually bargaining over wages and wage-related issues.[2] This chapter focuses on the methods of wage determination and factors used by negotiators in determining the wage package—wages and other economic benefits.

Wage Determination

Union and management officials have to agree on what the term *wages* means before they can successfully bargain over this issue. For instance, wages may mean the basic wage rate, average gross hourly earnings, average weekly earnings, or incentive pay (payment per product completed). Basic wage rates for each job class are usually listed in the labor agreement; however, other wage payments (overtime, incentive pay, shift differentials, and other compensation earned in the regular work week) may have to be computed in accordance with provisions in the labor agreement.[3]

After agreeing on the language for the basis of wage negotiations, the parties determine those wage rates and related terms of employment.[4] In this process, the parties will consider various factors and will determine numerous wage rates, job classes, and wage ranges. As most readers have already experienced, jobs with varying duties and responsibilities are assigned different wage rates. Besides these occupational differentials within a firm, there are regional, industry, and shift differences that cause an employer to pay different combinations of wage rates. Textile workers in the South generally earn less than those in the North; electricians and laborers in the building trades generally have higher wage rates than electricians and laborers in factories.

Wage differentials among individuals, jobs, industries, or regions can be explained in a variety of ways. However, any explanation must consider the interrelationships between labor and capital as factors of production and as contributors to productivity. An example follows:

> It is sometimes said that if productivity rises by "x" percent and the workers receive an "x" percent increase in compensation, then the workers are getting all of the productivity increase, leaving nothing for others. This is incorrect. If productivity rises, say 10 percent, and output increases commensurately, then each factor of production—labor, management, capital—can receive a 10 percent increase. If output does not rise commensurately . . . then total compensation of input factors and rates of return to those factors will depend on the difference between the output increase and the productivity increase, the size of the hourly compensation increase, and the cost of new capital investment.[5]

Industrial Wage Differentials

Industrial wage differentials may be explained in terms of three interrelated factors: (1) the degree of competition or monopoly in the product market, (2) the value added by workers in a particular industry, and (3) the percentage of total costs that labor costs represent.

Competition in the Product Market First, if a firm has a monopoly or near monopoly (the product is essential, with no available substitute), then increased labor cost can easily be passed on to the consumer. In such cases, the employer will resist higher wages less rigidly in negotiation. For example, if a private or public utility agrees to a 12 percent increase with cost-of-living adjustments, it then can add the increased cost to its customers' bills (unless the utility is heavily regulated). Consumers in this situation frequently have little choice but to pay the higher prices. Thus, in those industries where the firm controls the pricing without competitive threats, wages tend to be proportionately higher.

Value Added by Employees The term *value added* refers to the contribution of factors of production to the value of the final product. Comparing labor's contribution for different industries helps to explain industrial wage differentials. For example, the value added by labor in sawmills, cotton weaving, clothes manufacturing, and the mobile home industry is significantly lower than corresponding figures in the steel, petrochemical, and tire industries. However, because employees must use machines, which represent capital investments, and because there is such a close interrelationship between labor and capital investments in machinery and equipment, exact determination of labor's contributions has become a complicated process. In unionized settings, negotiations between union and management representatives determine labor's share in the amount of value added.

Labor Costs as Percentage of Total Costs The relationship between labor costs and total costs must also be considered in determining the industrial wage rate. Highly interdependent with capital investment per worker and the product market, this relationship is important in wage negotiations. For example, labor-intensive organizations, such as health care facilities, textile firms, and government, have high labor costs in relation to total costs. On the other hand, petroleum and chemical firms and electricity-generating plants have relatively low labor costs as a percentage of total costs.

Usually, firms with a high ratio of labor costs to total costs are more likely to resist wage increases. For example, if a hospital where labor costs are 60 percent of total costs grants a 10 percent wage increase, it must raise prices about 6 percent. A petroleum-processing plant where labor cost is 5 percent of total cost would have to raise its price about 0.5 percent to cover a 10 percent increase in wages. We would therefore expect to find workers in the same job classifications receiving higher wages in chemical and petroleum companies than in hospitals or textile firms. Of course, there are many qualifications to this conclusion in specific incidents—for example, consumers may not accept a higher price and a company may choose to cover the wage increase out of its profits. Nonetheless, the relation of labor cost to total cost can be an important factor in industrial wage differentials.

Occupational Wage Differentials and the Role of Job Evaluation and Wage Surveys

Within a company or industry, maintaining proper and rational wage relationships among various jobs is important. The relationships are often maintained under job-evaluation programs but in other cases are determined by individual or collective bargaining.[6] The process of determining the relative importance of each job to the organization helps in understanding occupational wage differentials; therefore, the following steps in a job evaluation program are presented.[7]

How Jobs are Evaluated within the Organization Before conducting a **job evaluation** program, an organization analysis[8] that appraises and examines the organization's objectives, structure, and authority and responsibility relationships should be done. The findings from this analysis help ensure that the job content is up to date.

Then the organization should select and measure the job factors that are found at least to some extent in all of the organization's job classifications. Job factors vary substantially depending on the organization, but skill (education and training), effort, responsibility (for people and equipment), and working conditions (hazards, surroundings) are typically selected. Management must consider the minimum amount of each job factor or qualification necessary to adequately perform the particular job. For example, it may be nice to employ a typist who can edit, interpret, and make complex economic subjects understandable, but few organizations can find or are willing to pay wages needed to attract such a qualified person.

Next, an appropriate job evaluation system for appraising jobs according to the established job factors is selected from four job evaluation methods: ranking, classification, factor comparison, and point system. The *ranking* and *factor-comparison* methods compare jobs nonquantitatively in terms of one or more job factors; the *classification* and *point system* methods compare jobs to predetermined numerical rating scales designed to measure one or more job factors about each job. Firms' job evaluation systems may use 10 to 15 different job factors, with these factors often divided into subfactors. For example, effort may be divided into physical and mental effort.[9]

The foundation of job evaluation is *job analysis,* which is a process of systematically securing information and facts about the jobs to be evaluated. Throughout the job evaluation process, it is the jobs, not employees in the job classifications, that are being analyzed. The job classifications resulting from job analysis will receive the same rating whether the employee holding the job has a master's degree or high school diploma, is lazy or ambitious, or is a high or low performer.

Job analysts use observation, interviews, and questionnaires to gather data about the jobs that are used to formulate *job descriptions* and *job specifications.* Job descriptions include written summations of the duties and responsibilities; job specifications include the personal characteristics a worker must possess to qualify for the job. Both are used in the job evaluation process. As firms try to relate wages to various degrees of duties and responsibilities, they must also pay more to employ workers who have high qualifications in education, training, and skills.

Management often prefers to conduct its job evaluation independent of the union. Management may prefer not to share its weightings of the job factors, particularly when it believes certain factors (such as training, skill, and responsibility for equipment) should receive more compensation than others. By withholding the weightings, management may avoid confrontations with the union, but the union will probably not accept being totally excluded from the job evaluation process.

Union leaders generally view job evaluation with disfavor, because it tends to limit bargaining and freeze the wage structure.[10] Three surveys of union officials over a 10-year period revealed that unions prefer to establish wage scales through collective bargaining, although their resistance to job evaluation has declined. While unions reserve the right to file grievances to resist or express dissatisfaction with job evaluation, they seldom show strong opposition unless firms attempt to use job evaluation as the sole criterion for wage determination or try to substitute it for collective bargaining.[11] In fact, some unions regard job evaluation techniques not only as useful guides in negotiating wages but as a means by which they can more effectively explain the negotiated wage settlements to their members.[12]

Regardless of the job evaluation method, the objective is to develop a wage structure that prices jobs with less skill, effort, and responsibility at lower wage rates and jobs with greater skill, effort, and responsibility at higher wage rates. Exhibit 13.1 presents an example of a wage structure for a firm that includes job titles,

Exhibit 13.1 **Typical Wage Structure for a Manufacturing Firm**

Job Titles	Labor Grade	Points	Starting Hourly Wage Rates
Janitor	I	200–249	$ 7.00
Material Handler	II	250–299	8.30
Shipper	III	300–349	8.75
Tool Room Keeper	IV	350–399	9.15
Machine Operator B	V	400–449	9.60
Machine Operator A	VI	450–499	10.00
Maintenance B	VII	500–549	10.40
Tool Grinder B	VIII	550–599	10.80
Maintenance A	IX	600–649	11.30
Tool Grinder A	X	650–699	11.70
Electrician A	XI	700–749	12.05
Tool and Die Maker A	XII	750–800	12.60

Source: Adapted (adjusted by current CPI) from U.S. Department of Labor, Bureau of Labor Statistics, *Major Collective Bargaining Agreements: Wage Administration Provisions* (Washington, D.C.: Government Printing Office, 1978), p. 2.

labor grades, point ranges, and starting wage rates for each labor grade. Since a numerical score should indicate the relative value of the job, the greater the score, the higher the labor grade and the hourly wage rate.

Surveys to Compare Firms' Wage Structures *Wage surveys* are conducted to assure that external labor market considerations, such as comparable wages, are included in the wage structure. While firms attempt to rationalize their wage structure internally through job evaluation, they must also maintain competitive wages externally to ensure that the firm can recruit qualified employees and retain productive ones. Usually a wage analyst either visits, sends questionnaires to, or conducts telephone interviews with the wage analysts of similar organizations or comparable firms. The one conducting the survey provides the responding firms with titles, descriptions, and specifications of the jobs in the wage survey. Participating firms will supply the starting wage rate and the economic benefits paid individuals in these job classifications (see Exhibit 13.2). After the wage survey is complete, the firm must determine how the data will be used. For example, does it want to lead the industry, compete with Firm C, or pay the industry average?

These wage surveys may be conducted by the firm or the union, or obtained from trade groups, employer associations, or the Bureau of Labor Statistics, which periodically publishes industry, area, occupational, and national wage survey data.[13] From such abundant data, union and management officials sometimes have difficulty determining which are most appropriate for their particular situation. (This problem is further discussed in the section on wage comparability.)

The wage plan concludes with a certain number of job classes, wages for each job class, wage ranges (from starting to top wages) for each class, policies and procedures for wage adjustments (seniority, merit, and so on), procedures for job changes

Exhibit 13.2 **Typical Results from a Wage Survey**

	Firms						
Job Title	A	B	C	D	E	F	Average
Janitor	6.98	7.11	7.76	6.46	6.98	7.11	7.07
Assembler	7.24	7.63	7.89	8.80	8.02	8.15	8.05
Shop Clerk	8.93	8.80	9.71	8.93	8.80	8.67	9.00
Welder	10.10	10.23	10.75	10.10	10.10	10.10	10.23
Machinist I	9.45	9.32	10.10	9.45	9.58	9.45	9.55
Machinist II	9.97	9.84	10.62	10.10	9.97	10.10	10.10
Machinist III	10.62	10.75	11.40	10.75	10.49	10.75	10.79
Electrician	12.18	12.05	12.96	11.92	12.05	12.18	12.25
Tool and Die Maker	12.70	13.02	14.39	12.18	12.96	13.35	13.10

to a different class, including temporary job changes, procedures for dealing with jobs that pay above or below their wage range, and policy on union involvement.

After the wage plan and policies are established, individual wage adjustments are made on the basis of merit and seniority. A study of 400 labor agreements by the Bureau of National Affairs revealed that 77 percent provided for wage increases during the life of the labor agreement.[14]

Production Standards and Wage Incentives

Unions and management sometimes negotiate provisions in the labor agreement that cover wage-related issues such as production standards, time studies, and wage-incentive payments. Production standards refer to the expected employee output that is consistent with workmanship quality, operational efficiency, and reasonable working capacities of normal operators. These standards are often determined by time studies that involve analyses of time and motions of workers on the job, and the resulting standards are used to assess performance and determine the wage incentives for individual workers or groups of workers.[15]

Where incentive plans are negotiated, the structure and design are included in the contract, although specific details may not be included. The role of the union in setting and protesting production standards and rate changes and its right to be consulted on related issues are also usually included. Some contracts include provisions about time studies and the involvement of unions. A small number permit a union observer during the time study, and a few go as far as to provide special training for the union time study representative. Other provisions include procedures used for timing a worker, specification of the meaning of *normal employee,* advance notice to the employee holding the job being studied, and specification for fatigue and personal allowances in setting production standards.[16]

While wage-incentive plans vary in structure and specific content, their goals are essentially the same: (1) to increase employee productivity, (2) to attract prospective employees to the company, and (3) to reward employees monetarily for their increased productivity. A typical individual wage-incentive plan is one in which workers are paid for the number of pieces or jobs completed. Others pay bonuses or premiums to employees for production above the standard. Many varieties of incentive plans exist, but all are similar in concept.

Until recently, when many companies and unions began to investigate gain-sharing plans, interest in wage-incentive plans as a way to stimulate worker productivity had declined. In fact, the great majority (82 percent) of production workers continue to be paid time rates. The major reasons for time-based compensation plans are that plant jobs are usually machine-paced, so employees have little control over their pace of work. In only six industries—men's and children's hosiery, women's hosiery, leather footwear, men's and boys' suits and coats, men's and boys' shirts, and basic steel and iron—are a majority of the workers paid by incentive plans. In these six industries, machines are controlled by the operators, workers exercise considerable discretion over the pace of work, and output is identifiable and measurable.[17]

Increased interest in incentive plans has resulted from intense competition, foreign and domestic, increased interest in labor-management cooperation, and employer efforts to obtain wage concessions from unions. A Conference Board survey of 504 mostly large companies showed that 121 had profit-sharing, gain-sharing, or bonus plans for nonunion employees, 56 also had them for union employees, and 22 had plans covering union employees only.[18]

Union experience with incentive programs dates back to the nineteenth century. In fact, the AFL, the CIO, and the AFL-CIO have never opposed profit-sharing and other incentive systems, and only a few individual unions have ever taken a position opposing these plans. The Steelworkers had a number of profit-sharing plans in the 1930s and the Auto Workers had profit-sharing as a bargaining goal in the 1958 national bargaining. By the late 1960s, the Auto Workers had 21 agreements with profit-sharing plans, the Steelworkers had 22, and the Machinists had 28.[19]

Profit-sharing plans that provided for cash bonuses based on the company's profit to partially or totally take the place of wage increases have been negotiated with several major companies, including Ford, General Motors, Pan Am, Uniroyal, International Harvester, and the New York *Daily News.* By 1989, Ford Motors had paid $12,200 to employees who qualified under a profit-sharing plan negotiated with the UAW in 1984; in 1987, with record earnings, 160,000 eligible Ford employees received $3,700.[20] So that executives would not receive bonuses when employees do not, the agreement negotiated between Chrysler and the UAW in 1988 prevents top company executives from receiving cash and stock bonuses during years when there is no profit sharing for the UAW-represented hourly workers.[21]

The concept of profit sharing was introduced 35 years ago by Walter Reuther, then president of the United Auto Workers, but the auto industry denounced it as "socialistic." Although interest in profit sharing may last only as long as a recession, experts have concluded that for profit sharing to work, employees, their unions, and management must develop a "common fate" or "we are all in this together for good or for ill" attitude, and management must be willing to provide job security, job training, and a structure for genuine worker participation.[22]

Profit-sharing has been criticized in several ways. First, there is concern that unions will wind up having a key voice in major management decisions other than wages. Second, it is feared that a costly profit-sharing plan will drain company funds that would otherwise be used for capital improvements and research and development. Third, there is concern that the union will use the profit sharing to "beef up" benefits in subsequent negotiations.[23]

In *group incentive plans,* companies make monetary payments to a specific group or groups of employees for producing more than expected. Incentives include group bonuses, group piece rates, profit sharing, production sharing, and cost sharing. In some cases, the plans are limited to a few employees, to specific departments, or to other organizational divisions; in others, the entire company work force is covered. While group incentives aim to increase production and reduce costs, they are also designed to increase teamwork, provide greater job security, and achieve greater acceptance of new technology.

There are a variety of group gain-sharing plans. One of the most popular is the *Scanlon Plan,* a plan for sharing labor cost savings that was developed by former union leader Joseph Scanlon in the late 1930s. It provides bonus payments based on a computed ratio of total labor costs (TLC) to total production values (TPV), which typically equal monthly sales, plus or minus inventory adjustments. A reduction in the ratio would be a labor cost savings. For example, if the workers were to reduce costs by working harder, producing more efficiently, and saving on wastes and the TLC/TPV ratio declined from 50 to 40 percent, the 10 percent labor savings would be shared with the workers in relation to their basic wages.[24]

The *Rucker Plan* is based on a change in the ratio between dollar payroll and dollar value added. The value added equals sales less purchased materials. Under this plan, if employees lower the ratio between payroll costs and dollar value added, the productivity gains are shared.

The term *improshare* is derived from "improved productivity through sharing." Improshare productivity measurements use traditional work measurement standards for a selected base period. Productivity gains are divided evenly between employees and company. A study of Improshare programs in 34 unionized companies showed an average productivity gain of 26.9 percent after the first year, whereas the average gain for 38 nonunion plants was 21.5 percent.[25]

Unions vary in their positions on gain-sharing and other incentive plans. A few, such as the Communication Workers of America, advocate these programs; most take the position of decentralized neutrality (letting the local union decide); others, like the Machinists, generally oppose them.

There are several frequently-given reasons for union opposition to gain-sharing:

- Management may try to substitute gain-sharing for wages.
- Management cannot be trusted.
- Bonus calculations are not understood or trusted.
- Union influence is undermined.
- Increased productivity may reduce need for jobs.
- Grievances may go unprocessed.
- Gain-sharing is incompatible with union goals.

There are also several benefits to employees that serve as good reason for unions to favor gain-sharing:

- Increased recognition.
- Better job security.
- Increased involvement in job activities.
- Increased feeling of achievement and of contributing to the organization.
- Greater contribution to nation's productivity.
- Compatibility with union goals.

A final issue is the question of how unions as organizations can benefit from gain-sharing plans. First, the most productive firms will grow and offer more employment and therefore provide the union with more dues-paying members. Second, successful programs raise the union's visibility among the 80 percent of the work force who are not affiliated with a union. Third, the programs provide more knowledge of the business to the union, making unions better-informed bargainers. Last, these plans provide extra pay when they are successful.[26] Unions in the future may show an increased interest in these plans because of these benefits.

Arguments Used by Management and Union Officials in Wage Determination

Unions and management have recognized that there is no single causal influence on wage determination; however, both parties will use any identifiable influence to support their arguments for or against wage increases. The most common influences are differential features of the work (usually determined by job evaluation), wage comparability, ability to pay (financial condition of the organization), productivity, cost of living, and legal requirements.[27] Union and management officials do not always accept the same criteria. Moreover, each might emphasize different criteria at different times. During prosperous times unions tend to emphasize the ability to pay; during recessions management presents its poor financial position. Similarly, during periods of rapid inflation, unions emphasize cost-of-living adjustments; when prices are stable, management places much weight on the lack of necessity for cost-of-living adjustments.

In the first half of the 1980s pressure from domestic and international competition resulted in management's inability to pass increased labor costs to the customer and caused businesses to emphasize efficiency, cost-cutting measures, and productivity. During this period of relatively high unemployment, the unions' ability to affect wage levels within their industries declined, and companies became less influenced by industry patterns. Instead, companies emphasized their individual labor costs, expected profits, and local wage rates over those prevailing in the industry. Exhibit 13.3 shows the shifts in emphasis between 1978 and 1983 for a number of companies in which productivity or labor cost trends replaced industry patterns as the most important factor used in setting company wage objectives.[28]

Arguments used by management and unions over wages cannot be entered into a computer to yield a precise solution to the wage determination, but they do provide a framework within which the parties attempt to resolve their differences over wage issues through collective bargaining.[29]

Exhibit 13.3 **Relative Importance of Factors Used in Setting Company Wage Objectives**

1983		1978	
Productivity or labor cost trends in company	3.1	2.4	Industry patterns
Expected profits of this company			Local labor market conditions and wage rates
Local labor market conditions and wage rates			Expected profits of this company
Industry patterns			Productivity or labor cost trends in this company
Consumer price index increases			Consumer price index increases
Internal (company) wage patterns (historical)			Influence of this settlement on other wage settlements and/or nonunion wage levels
Influence of this settlement on other wage settlements and/or nonunion wage levels			Potential losses from a strike
Internal (company) benefit patterns (historical)			Internal (company) wage patterns (historical)
Potential losses from a strike			Internal (company) benefit patterns (historical)
National labor market conditions and wage rates			Major union settlements in other industries
Major union settlements in other industries	5.4	5.0	National labor market conditions and wage rates

Note: All companies answering the question used the same bargaining unit for both years (N = 197).

Rankings weighted as follows: If company ranked factor 1 to 3, it was weighted accordingly; if item was checked "not a consideration," it was weighted 8; if neither ranked 1 to 3 nor checked "not a consideration," item was weighted 4.

Source: Audrey Freedman, *The New Look in Wage Policy and Employee Relations* (New York: The Conference Board, 1985), p. 8.

Differential Features of the Work: Job Evaluation and the Wage Spread

The job evaluation process described in the preceding section can influence the wages assigned to various job classifications in an organization. The relative influence of job evaluation can be seen in the wage spread, which represents the internal distribution of the proposed or negotiated wage increase to the bargaining-unit employees (see Exhibit 13.4).

At first glance, the wage spread appears to be a formality, determined after the average hourly rate increase per employee is resolved. Yet the particular wage spread can determine whether the parties ever reach an agreement. For example, the union might refuse the first and second wage spreads and accept the third wage with no spread (see Exhibit 13.4 again) even though the total wage costs of the three spreads are nearly identical.

The six employee job classifications in Exhibit 13.4 range in skill and pay from classification A (highest) to classification F (lowest), which conform to management's job evaluation procedure. Consequently management prefers the second wage spread, since it gives higher-skilled employees higher wages that could maintain or increase their wage differential over unskilled employees. This wage differential is important to management for two reasons:

1. It ensures that present skilled employees do not leave because of higher wages offered by other firms.
2. It offers some motivation to employees in lower-paid classifications to train for higher-level classifications in the company.

Unions are not always concerned with job evaluation as a wage determination factor. The union officers' main concern is to ensure that the negotiated wage spread will result in sufficient votes to ratify the agreement. Satisfied union members will also be likely to vote for reelection of union officers. Assume, for example, that classification C represents a politically influential group of employees. The union officers would not prefer the second wage spread (44.0 cents per hour increase for

Exhibit 13.4 **Three Examples of Internal Wage Spreads**

Examples	Number of Employees	Employee Classification	Total of Plant's Employees (In Percent)	Increase (In Cents per Hour)
1	184	A	16	57.0
	197	B	18	50.0
	165	C	15	48.0
	237	D	21	46.0
	149	E	13	44.0
	193	F	17	42.0
	1,125			
2	381	A&B	34	60.0
	402	C&D	36	44.0
	342	E&F	30	34.0
	1,125			
3	1,125	A,B,C,D,E,&F	100	47.2

classification C employees). Instead, they would prefer the first (48.0 cents per hour increase) or third (47.2 cents per hour increase) wage spread shown in the exhibit. The union might even propose a different wage spread that would give the employees in classification C a much higher wage increase.

Management is also concerned that employees ratify the agreement. Consequently, it might agree to an across-the-board increase to all employees regardless of their job classifications. This wage spread might generate enough votes to ratify the collective bargaining agreement, but it will narrow the wage differential between skilled and unskilled employees. Over a longer period of time, management cannot continually grant this type of increase if it wishes to attract and retain skilled employees.

One of the principal goals of unions has been to reduce dispersion of wages. Their goal is to obtain "equal pay for equal work" across establishments and to reduce differentials based on personal characteristics rather than specific job tasks. Unions seek this goal by negotiating a single rate of pay for each occupational group and a seniority-based progression of rates up to a maximum level. Single rates (one pay level for all workers in a given job category) eliminate wage dispersion and seniority plans control overall wage rates by requiring similar treatment to workers who have the same seniority. Because of the "spillover" effect of union wage practices, even nonunion companies experience less wage dispersion than one might expect.[30]

Wage provisions that specify that newly hired employees will be paid less than other workers are referred to as *two-tier pay plans.* They may be permanent or temporary. The permanent ones pay new hires at a lower rate for the life of the agreement; temporary ones permit new employees to progress from the lower entry-level rates to the rates received by other employees over a specified period of time. In 1988, only 5 percent of agreements had the two-tier wage structure.[31] For reasons for the rise and fall of two-tier pay plans, see "Labor Relations in Action." For an example of a two-tier pay schedule, see Exhibit 13.5.

Because the union may negotiate a wage differential based on skill, type of work, and seniority, it appears to have ample latitude to negotiate two-tier wage levels if they have a purpose in "good faith and honesty." However, there may be a subsequent cost in terms of labor solidarity with potential friction between the newly hired employees and the more senior employees.[32] Or, if the low-tiered employees view the pay situation as inequitable, they may vote to remove the union leaders or support union decertification. Likewise, they may feel less commitment to their employer, be less productive, and cause higher relative labor costs to the company.[33]

The following quote may explain the new employees' view of two-tier wage plans because they are pleased at the beginning to obtain a job, then the reality of the daily comparisons of "equal work for unequal pay" with the upper-tiered employees set in: "When you're starving, you eat anything you can, human nature being what it is. But when you're not starving any more, you start looking around at what other people are eating."[34]

Wage Comparability

A common argument in wage negotiations is that wage rates in one bargaining unit should be equal to or related to the wage rates in comparable bargaining units.[35] Wage comparisons are given considerable weight in wage determination, although

Exhibit 13.5 **Examples of Two-Tier Pay Scales**

Brackets and Hourly Rates for Employees on Payroll Prior to March 1, 1983

Bracket	Wage Rate
0	$8.50
1	8.55
2	8.60
3	8.65
4	8.70
5	8.75
6	8.80
7	8.85

All Employees hired by an individual Employer after March 1, 1983 shall be considered new hires and . . . shall be paid according to the [following] bracket rate:

Brackets and Hourly Rates for Hires in Slaughter and Cooler—Those Hired After March 1, 1983

Bracket	Wage Rate
0	$5.00
1	5.05
2	5.10
3	5.15
4	5.20
5	5.25
6	5.30
7	5.35

(Meat Packing Group and Food and Commercial Workers; exp. 4/89)

Source: *Collective Bargaining Negotiations and Contracts* (Washington, D.C.: Bureau of National Affairs Inc., 1988), p. 93:140.

these comparisons can become quite complicated. Wage surveys can be helpful, but they do not measure how the job content, method of payment, regularity of employment, supplemental unemployment benefits, vacations, pensions, and holidays vary from company to company. Fundamental considerations such as the size of the appropriate labor market and occupational and geographic differentials must be recognized. At first glance, it appears that bus drivers in Miami would have duties identical with those of bus drivers in Chicago. However, many differences in these similar jobs can exist: weather conditions, number of scheduled stops, location of scheduled stops, number of passengers, and so on. Further, a major difference could arise in situations where the bus drivers are required to make change. In such cases, the union would claim that this job responsibility creates a safety hazard by increasing the likelihood of robberies and would seek adequate compensation for this additional risk.

The relative importance of wages to total costs is also an important factor in wage comparability. For example, if a modern, highly automated textile mill pays wages that account for 30 percent of total costs, a 10 percent increase in wages would

Labor Relations in Action

The Rise and Fall of Two-Tier Wage Plans

Two-tier wage plans were highly touted in the early 1980s as a solution to the dilemma of reducing labor costs without losing or angering senior, experienced employees. These plans were negotiated in 5 percent of the labor agreements in 1983, 8 percent in 1984, and 11 percent in 1985. Then there was a gradual decline: 10 percent in 1986, 9 percent in 1987, and 5 percent in 1988. Although scholars differ in their predictions about the future of these plans, there are trends toward "hidden" two-tier plans via low-cost subcontracting, temporary employees, part-time workers, leased employees, home-work employment, and so on.

Some reasons for the rise and decline of two-tier wage plans follow:

Reasons for the Rise in Two-Tier Wage Plans

- They deal with high labor costs, especially during recessionary times.
- They retain experienced employees without lowering their wage scales.
- They increase the wage differential between new employees and the longer-service employees, thereby reducing the wage compression problem.
- They increase the percentage of employees in the lower wage class in those companies having high turnover.

Reasons for the Decline in Two-Tier Wage Plans

- They cause dissatisfaction within the union among new employees, which creates an interest in decertifying the union (often a hidden agenda).
- They cause conflict between the longer-service employees and the new employees and consequently reduce union solidarity.
- They result in lower morale and frequently cause poor workmanship or reduced customer service.
- They raise a question of whether the union is fairly representing the new employees and/or subject the union and company to employment discrimination claims if minorities are disproportionately among the lower-tiered.
- They cause high turnover among the lower-tiered and reduce the ability of the company to recruit qualified employees.
- They violate the principle of "equal pay for equal work" when the lower-tiered employees perform the same job as the upper-tiered ones but receive less pay.

Sources: Ken Jennings and Earle Traynham, "The Wages of Two-Tiered Plans," *Personnel Journal* 67 (March 1988), pp. 56–63; Marvin J. Levine, "The Evolution of Two-Tiered Wage Agreements: Bane or Panacea in Labor-Intensive Industries," *Labor Law Journal* 40 (January 1989), pp. 12–20; Mollie Bowers and Roger Roderick, "Two Tier Pay Systems: The Good, the Bad and the Debatable," *Personnel Administrator* 32 (June 1987), pp. 102–106; James E. Martin and Melanie M. Peterson, "Two-Tiered Wage Structures: Implications for Equity Theory," *Academy of Management Journal* 30 (June 1987), p. 297–315.

equal a 3 percent change in the sales price. But in an old textile mill with out-of-date machinery, where wages account for 65 percent of total costs, a 10 percent increase in wages would equal a 6.5 percent change in sales price. Even though wage data are often largely fragmented or deficient,[36] negotiators still have to rely on wage comparability in arguing for or against certain levels of wages. Therefore, both parties continue to look for commonalities with other companies, local firms, or similar jobs that can provide a base from which to present their proposals.

Ability to Pay

The ability to pay, or the financial condition of the organization, is a commonly used standard for wage determination. Given much weight by unions during periods of high profitability, it is advanced more frequently by management as the "inability to pay."[37]

Ability to pay has limited usefulness in the wage determination process, for a number of reasons:

1. Wages based solely on ability to pay would create a chaotic wage structure and would cause a change in the wage-costs-price-profit relationships that have evolved over time.
2. Unions would not want to apply this criterion uniformly and consistently. To be applicable, it must work both ways, leading to wage reductions when profits are nonexistent or inadequate. Such an approach would be generally unacceptable to unions.
3. It is extremely difficult to determine what part of profits should be used for wage increases. If the profit is distributed to employees in terms of higher wages and none of the profit is shared with stockholders, there will be no incentive for investment, and growth and expansion will be limited.
4. Wages supposedly are paid to workers in accordance with their relative value to the firm, their contribution to its goals, and the relative importance of their services. If ability to pay is the major factor, the relationships between actual pay and actual value could become disproportionate.
5. Wages are negotiated for future application, and there is no necessary relationship between profits of the past and ability to pay in the future. Profits are the result after past costs have been deducted from past sales; they fluctuate greatly in both good and bad times. If wages are dependent upon profits, they too will fluctuate erratically.[38]

Poor economic conditions in the early 1980s resulted in many companies claiming their inability to pay and unions agreeing to wage concessions or "give-backs" in order to preserve employment. However, nearly all of these wage concessions had been restored by the end of the 1980s when the overall economic situation had improved.

Productivity

While no argument has been advanced with more conviction or sophistication than that wages should vary with changes in productivity, the principle has grave difficulties when applied to specific negotiations. For example, the rate of change in productivity varies widely from industry to industry, firm to firm, even plant to plant. Not only is productivity itself difficult to measure accurately, but any change in productivity (usually measured in output per employee-hour) results from many causes, only one of which is labor.[39]

Those who study productivity have generally agreed that new capital investment and mechanization have been the primary causes for greater productivity, but there are still important issues to reconcile: Who shall share the results from increased productivity? The workers, stockbrokers, consumers? What are the relative advantages of higher wages, increased dividends, and lower prices? What is the proper balance among the contributing factors of production—labor and capital investments? Any use of the productivity criterion must be handled carefully because the available data are only approximate. Output per employee-hour often overstates gains attributed to labor, and hourly earnings data fail to account for the relative contributions of advanced technology, improved methods, better machines, and so on.

To be competitive, companies and employees must be more productive. Greater productivity may allow higher wages, but it usually results in a smaller work force.

In 1960 the Longshoremen's Union allowed mechanization of the waterfronts, increasing productivity by 140 percent. Now, wages for top-rated longshoremen average $50,356 plus benefits. But the number of jobs has declined from 16,400 in 1960 to 9,600 in 1986. The same principle applies to other industries; high productivity is the only way to warrant high wages. However, as witnessed in the steel, auto, and other industries, greater productivity and higher wages do not lead to more jobs.[40]

Productivity Sharing Some union and management officials have undertaken cooperative efforts to bring productivity issues directly into collective bargaining. Labeled as *productivity sharing,* this endeavor is meant to enable greater productivity while providing employees a comparable share of the resulting savings in the form of higher wages. Traditionally, labor agreements have provided protection to workers who are subject to loss of employment (in such forms as advance notice, use of attrition in work reduction, early retirement, guaranteed wages, and severance pay), and unions have often resisted speed-up efforts of productivity improvement campaigns.

The General Accounting Office identified about 1,000 productivity sharing programs. Its researchers obtained financial data from 24 firms and found that plans over 5 years old experienced a 29 percent labor savings in the last 5-year period and plans less than 5 years old averaged savings of 8.5 percent. Nonmonetary benefits were also reported: 80.6 percent reported improved labor-management relations; 47.2 percent, fewer grievances; 36.1 percent, less absenteeism; and 36.1 percent, reduced turnover.[41]

Productivity has become a national concern. Although the United States still leads the industrial world in productivity in absolute numbers, it now lags behind all other industrialized countries in productivity growth. Congress has indicated its concern about low productivity in the United States and a White House Conference on productivity designed to bring together individuals who are experts on productivity, labor relations, and management has been held.

Problems with Productivity Sharing Although productivity sharing offers an innovative approach for mutual gain-sharing and cooperative activity, it, too, has its problems. Foremost is the measurement of productivity, because there are many possible measures. Some jobs do not lend themselves to precise measurement of output. It is much easier to measure bricks laid than letters taken by dictation and typed since letters vary in complexity and length. In jobs that are not routine or repetitious, exact measures are impossible.

Another problem is locating and organizing productivity data in such a manner that it may be useful to a firm. Serious arguments over the contribution of specific factors to increased productivity can inhibit the success of any productivity bargaining. What is the chief contributor to productivity gains? Is it the skill, efforts, or attitudes of the employees? Or is it the advanced technology of the machinery and equipment, efficiency of the operations, or scale of operations? Or is it the interaction between these sets of factors?[42] Since productivity gains will be shared under the productivity bargaining concept, they will certainly give rise to rigorous and complicated negotiations, particularly when bargaining-unit employees are accustomed to receiving comparable wages.

Examples of bargaining for productivity improvement have occurred in the construction industry. Negotiations there have resulted in agreements to reduce work stoppages, and provisions covering jurisdictional disputes, inefficient work rules, illegal featherbedding, and nonworking stewards have also been negotiated. Interestingly, the stimulus for productivity bargaining in the construction industry was the loss of work that increasingly went to nonunion and open-shop contractors, along with the desire of union members to protect or expand their employment opportunities, particularly during unfavorable economic conditions.[43]

Joint advisory committees in the steel industry have been formed in plants to deal with productivity problems. The retail food industry has established a joint labor-management committee that aids collective bargaining settlements and technological change. The shipping industry has been involved in joint programs to promote productivity in exchange for improving wages and benefits for longshoremen and their unions. These agreements basically have involved the buy-out of restrictive provisions and practices, which allowed a reduction in the "work gang" size and increased flexibility in manpower use. To obtain these agreements, attractive early retirement provisions and guaranteed work have been included in the labor agreements.[44]

Effect of Unions on Productivity Recently, there has been considerable debate and research about the effect of unions on productivity. On the positive side, William Winpisinger, president of the International Association of Machinists, has identified several ways that collective bargaining has contributed to greater productivity:[45]

1. Unions' continuing pressure for higher wages and benefits makes union workers expensive, so management must seek better methods, such as technological improvements, to maintain lower unit labor costs.
2. Unions' success in reducing the average number of hours worked per week has actually increased worker productivity because the effort is greater in the fewer hours.
3. An orderly and equitable procedure for settling grievances helps resolve employee problems and therefore improves productivity.
4. Collective bargaining involves negotiating subjects related to industrial accidents and diseases. Accident prevention saves time and consequently increases productivity.
5. Union apprenticeship programs help train employees in critical skills and allow them to produce more.

Some labor economists concur that unions can have a positive effect on worker productivity because they influence training, morale, turnover, and interaction between workers and management. Unions also may increase labor productivity by providing an efficient collective voice for workers to negotiate improvements in workplace characteristics and to establish grievance procedures—as well as by energizing management to reduce existing inefficiency. On the other hand, it may be argued that unions decrease productivity by reducing managerial flexibility, limiting the use of merit-based compensation,[46] imposing work rule restrictions such as limits on work loads, restrictions on tasks performed, and requirements for unneeded standby crews or crews of excessive size, and interfering with the introduction of technological change.[47]

In some settings, unions have resulted in higher productivity because of greater capital intensity, higher labor quality, and the presence of institutional grievance procedures. This is most likely to occur where management uses the collective bargaining process to learn about ways to improve the operations of the workplace and the production processes. However, if management reacts negatively to collective bargaining, or if unions try to prevent the reorganization of the workplace, the effect of unions on organizational performance will be negative.[48]

Critics of unions' effect on productivity claim that unions are not the reason that productivity in unionized plants is higher. In fact, these critics contend that higher wages in unionized settings encourage managers to substitute capital (technology) for labor, and it is this technology advancement that increases the productivity per worker, not the union. Also, higher wages in unionized plants motivate the employers to seek out the "better quality" employees; likewise, the "better quality" employees of nonunion plants tend to look for work in the higher-paying unionized plants. In other words, productivity in unionized plants may be higher; however, this higher productivity may not be caused by unions but by several other factors.[49] One analysis of unions' effects on productivity follows.

> [O]ne cannot conclude from the evidence (far less than theory) that unions are good for productivity. Moreover, productivity as measured is not the same as efficiency. We do not observe unit cost reductions in unionized settings![50]

In fact, one study revealed that the presence of the United Auto Workers resulted in a 33 percent increase in compensation with no offsetting productivity increase.[51]

Cost of Living

During periods of rising prices, unions support their wage demands by referring to the cost of living. Union negotiators advance the argument that a rise in the cost of living without a commensurate wage increase is equivalent to a cut in real wages or a drop in purchasing power. Thus, the proposition that wages be raised at least in proportion to the rise in living costs seems quite fair and reasonable. But the complete reliance on this criterion needs careful appraisal.

Unions and management must come to an agreement on the meaning of cost of living. Cost of living usually refers to the Consumer Price Index (CPI) as determined by the Bureau of Labor Statistics; its computation includes such items as housing, food, and automobiles, which may not be purchased regularly by employees in a specific plant or community. The parties must also negotiate the base period, the starting date, and the CPI most appropriate for use (the Bureau of Labor Statistics publishes an all-cities CPI plus CPIs for most major cities).

Automatic increases in general wages present problems in their effect on the cost-price-profit mechanism. In other words, costs of labor that are automatically increased throughout the economy can increase total costs and sales prices unless there is a commensurate productivity increase. The increases in wages are passed on to the consumer; large firms, having some monopolistic control, simply raise their prices. Thus, the market economy is restricted and does not function effectively as a determiner of prices and an allocator of resources—two of its most important functions.

Perhaps management's greatest concern over cost of living is that it receives nothing in return for this wage increase, granted on the basis of factors over which it has no control. The cost-of-living argument seldom if ever considers employees' productivity at a particular facility. Additional considerations of cost of living are discussed in the section on wage adjustments.

Comparable Worth

With female and minority employees' wages at less than 70 percent of white male employees', the comparable worth issue often emerges in wage considerations. As pointed out in Chapter 3, the Equal Pay Act, Civil Rights Act, and Age Discrimination in Employment Act protect against wage discrimination. These laws prohibit paying male employees more than female employees unless the wage difference is justified on the basis of skill, effort, responsibility, working conditions, seniority, or performance.

Proponents of the comparable worth issue state that women earn less pay because they are disproportionately represented in lower-valued, and therefore lower-paying, jobs and that the value placed on these jobs has been arbitrarily established by companies and negotiated with the unions.

Unions are also becoming involved in the comparable worth issue. The Communication Workers of America and the International Brotherhood of Electrical Workers have entered into a joint job evaluation study to resolve the conflict of having mostly female operators, traffic, billing, and office personnel, while line and installation work is performed primarily by higher-paid males.[52]

Some unions, such as the International Union of Electrical Workers (IUE), have sued employers, in this case, Westinghouse. The company had properly evaluated the jobs of men and women; however, the rate for women's jobs thereafter was less than men's of equal value in the job-evaluation plan. This resulted in most females being placed three to four pay grades below the janitor and other unskilled common laborers.

In San Jose, the American Federation of State, County, and Municipal Employees (AFSCME) and the city engaged in a joint job-evaluation study that showed that salaries of jobs held predominantly by females averaged 15 percent less than salaries of male jobs, although the value by points was the same. This caused the study team to ask the following questions:

1. Why do librarians receive less pay than men with jobs requiring less than an eighth grade education?
2. Why do female M.A.'s and Ph.D.'s who supervise as many as 25 people earn less than street sweepers and gardeners?
3. Why do nurses earn less than tree trimmers, painters, and parking lot attendants?
4. Why do male toll collectors earn more than medical stenographers?

The city and the union met for over a year and were not able to resolve their differences. A 9-day strike—supported by both male and female employees—occurred before a settlement was reached.[53]

After suffering setbacks in 1984, backers of the comparable worth concept of pay equity, supported by the unions, primarily the American Federation of State, County, and Municipal Employees, made remarkable progress in 1985. The settlement in the state of Washington called for a $46.5 million adjustment by 1986, and $10 million in allocations until 1992, an overall cost of $106.5 million. Other pay equity settlements include the following:[54]

- 5 percent adjustment for 3,500 employees in 79 predominantly female job classifications in Chicago.
- $12 million for 4,000 clerks and librarians in Los Angeles.
- $20 million for 6,000 employees in the Iowa state government.
- $40 million for 9,000 employees in the state of Minnesota.
- $9.1 million for 10,000 employees in the state of Wisconsin.
- $5.6 million for 9,000 employees in the state of Connecticut.
- $36 million for thousands of employees in the state of New York.

Wage Adjustments during the Life of the Labor Agreement

In addition to wage determination during negotiations, labor and management will likely agree to provisions that will allow adjustment of wages during the life of the contract–usually **cost-of-living adjustments** (or **COLA,** also called *escalator clauses*), deferred wage increases (also called *annual improvement adjustments*), and **wage reopeners** that allow for wages to be negotiated at a predetermined date. Annual wage improvements are specified in 77 percent of contracts, COLA provisions are included in 35 percent, and reopener clauses are written in 9 percent.[55]

COLA, or escalator, clauses, first appeared after World War I in the printing and clothing industries, but they were eliminated during the late 1920s. Immediately after World War II they were renewed, as employees tried to keep up with rapid inflation.[56] These clauses imposed "a contractual obligation upon an employer to change rates of pay in accordance with a formula embodied in a collective bargaining agreement."[57] About 40 percent of employees are covered by these clauses, as shown in Exhibit 13.6. They usually coincide with the long-term contracts that were pioneered by the United Auto Workers and General Motors in 1948. Since then, the average length of contracts has been lengthened.[58] However, GM stopped COLA payments to 110,000 nonunion employees in 1986. This elimination probably means that GM management will be pressuring the union to make concessions regarding its COLA clause.[59]

Coverage by COLA clauses is concentrated in various industries. Nearly 90 percent of the employees in communications, primary metals, rubber, electrical machinery, and transportation industries have COLA provisions.[60] The majority of the workers under COLA provisions are affiliated with the United Auto Workers, Teamsters, Steelworkers, Communication Workers of America, Retail Clerks, and Machinists.[61]

When negotiating COLA provisions, union and management representatives usually consider the following matters:[62]

Exhibit 13.6 **Proportion of Workers Covered by COLAs in Labor Agreements**

Year	Proportion of Workers Covered by COLAs
1971	28%
1972	41
1973	39
1974	39
1975	51
1976	59
1977	61
1978	60
1979	59
1980	58
1981	58
1982	57
1983	60
1984	57
1985	56
1986	48
1987	40
1988	38
1989	40

Source: COLA coverage is from *Monthly Labor Review,* vol. 112 (January 1989), p. 14, and previous January issues.

1. Selection of the particular price index and base point. In 89 percent of the agreements, the all-cities CPI (Consumer Price Index) is selected and the beginning date of the contract is specified.
2. Frequency and timing of the wage adjustment. Seventy percent of the agreements in manufacturing call for adjustments every quarter; but 74 percent in nonmanufacturing businesses call for annual adjustments.
3. Formula for adjustment The most common is a cents-per-hour increase for each point increase in the CPI; the remainder require a percentage change in wages in accordance with a percentage change in the CPI. The most common arrangement is to have wages adjusted 1¢ for each 0.3-point rise in the CPI. (See Exhibit 13.7 for a cost-of-living schedule.)
4. Effect of COLA on other elements of the compensation package. There is little uniformity in this matter. Some agreements adjust the gross hourly earnings after incentives; others adjust only the base wage rate. Still other payments, such as overtime, call-in pay, night work, and differentials, must be considered.
5. Limitations on the adjustment. About one-fourth have formulas with CAPS (limits on the amounts that may be received from cost-of-living provisions within a given period). On the other hand, some agreements specify that wages will not be reduced in the event of a CPI decline.

Exhibit 13.7 **Cost-of-Living Schedule**

—Quarterly adjustments of 1-cent for each 0.3 CPI change, reduced by sum of prior adjustments, plus a 26-cent COLA Earlier Withheld

"Cost-of-Living Adjustment" is calculated as below, and will be payable for the three-month period commencing with the Adjustment Date.

Effective on each Adjustment Date, a Cost-of-Living Adjustment equal to one (1) cent per hour for each full .3 of a point change in the Consumer Price Index shall become payable for all hours actually worked and for any reporting allowance credited before the next Adjustment Date. However, such Adjustment shall be reduced by an amount equal to the sum of all prior Adjustments if any, plus $0.26 cents per hour not paid on August 31, 1980; which shall have been included in the Job Class Guaranteed Hourly Rates for hourly rated jobs and in the Hourly Additives for incentive and tonnage rated jobs. (Atlantic Steel Company and Steelworkers; exp. 9/89)

—Quarterly adjustments of 1-cent for each 0.3 CPI change exceeding 40-cent per hour prepaid COLA.

In addition to the base rate of pay for each employee effective November 22, 1986, a wage payment of forty cents ($.40) per hour shall be paid to each employee. Such wage payment shall be made as a Prepaid COL Adjustment. . . .

Cost-Of-Living Adjustments other than the Prepaid COL Adjustment, shall be paid to employees only in the event and to the extent that the cumulative quarterly adjustments for the Adjustment Period exceed forty cents ($.40) per hour. In the event that COL Adjustments are paid, the payment will only be that amount of the cumulative quarterly adjustments for the Adjustment Period that exceed forty cents ($.40) per hour.

Effective the payroll period commencing on January 3, 1987, the Cost-of-Living Adjustment factor shall be determined in accordance with the following table:

Three-Month Average BLS Consumer Price Index	COL Adjustment Factor
323.3 and below	0
323.4–323.6	.01 per hour
323.7–323.9	.02 per hour
324.0–324.2	.03 per hour
324.3–324.5	.04 per hour
324.6–324.8	.05 per hour
324.9–325.1	.06 per hour
325.2–325.4	.07 per hour
325.5–325.7	.08 per hour
325.8–326.0	.09 per hour
326.1–326.3	.10 per hour
326.4–326.6	.11 per hour
326.7–326.9	.12 per hour
327.0–327.2	.13 per hour
327.3–327.5	.14 per hour

And so forth with $.01 for 0.3 point change in the Average Index for the appropriate date set forth. . . . (Lockhead Corporation, Lockheed-Georgia Company Div. and Machinists; exp. 9/89)

Source: Editors of Collective Bargaining Negotiations and Contracts, *Collective Bargaining Negotiations and Contracts* (Washington, D.C.: Bureau of National Affairs Inc., 1987), p. 93:73.

COLA provisions are becoming more common not only in labor agreements but also outside the collective bargaining arena. For example, 31 million social security recipients and 2.5 million military and civil service retirees are now covered. It has been estimated that over 50 million U.S. citizens now have their incomes adjusted by some automatic cost-of-living adjustment.[63]

Wage reopener clauses are usually written in such a way that wages may be renegotiated at a specified time during the length of the agreement or when the CPI has risen by a specified amount. Some of the agreements allow only wages to be renegotiated, whereas others allow nonwage items or do not specify the items. Deferred wage increases, annual improvement factors, and productivity increases have a broad acceptance in most contracts, and many of these are included with cost-of-living adjustments as well as contract reopeners.

Yet cost-of-living adjustments and wage reopeners have their problems. Cost-of-living adjustments are very difficult to negotiate out of a contract, because union officers and members assume the COLA will continue in subsequent contracts. This situation makes it difficult for either union or management to receive credit for the COLA. Assume, for example, that management anticipates that COLA will cost 60¢ per employee per hour. If the negotiated wage settlement costs 70¢ per employee, then employees will receive only a 10¢-an-hour increase plus continuation of the COLA. The union officer will have a difficult time selling the labor agreement to the members, because they probably take the established COLA clause for granted. It might be easier to sell the labor agreement if there were not any COLA and the wage package were publicized as an annual increase of 70¢ an hour.

Wage reopeners are subject to problems when the union wishes to extend negotiated items to noneconomic items. While this is not allowable in theory, the distinction between economic and noneconomic discussion becomes blurred in practice. Some practitioners have suggested that a wage reopener is similar to an entirely new contract negotiation as the parties bring noneconomic items into the discussion.

Lump Sum Pay Adjustment—Bonuses

The number of **lump-sum pay adjustments** (also referred to as bonuses) has risen to 36 percent of the agreements negotiated in 1989. The most common payment was a flat amount—an average of $848 in the first year, $566 in the second, and $542 in the third.[64] These adjustments are popular with management because they do not apply to employee benefits and do not change the permanent wage structure. Therefore, they appear to be more than an equal wage increase. For example, a $1,000 lump-sum payment to a $20,000-per-year employee is much less than a 5 percent increase, because his or her wage the following year remains at $20,000, and the base of that employee's benefits has not been increased.

A 3-year agreement containing a 3 percent annual wage improvement each year produces a wage rate 9 percent above the initial base in the third year, but a lump-sum payment each year does not raise the base rate at all. Also, new employees hired after the settlement do not receive this payment but do not have the tension caused by the two-tier pay scale because the base pay is the same.

Employee Benefits

In 1987 U.S. employers paid an average of $10,708 per employee in benefits, or 39.0 percent of payroll costs, up from 19.2 percent in 1953. These benefits included insurance costs, pension payments, payments for time not worked (such as vacations, sick leave, and holidays), legally required payments for unemployment and workers' compensation, paid rest and lunch breaks, and profit-sharing and bonuses.

The following sections present major areas of employee benefits, relying largely on studies of 400 agreements by the Bureau of National Affairs.[65]

Insurance

Insurance provisions have been substantially expanded: 99 percent of the contracts provide life insurance, and 63 percent include coverage for basic hospitalization benefits, major medical expenses (57 percent), surgery (61 percent), maternity care, doctor's visits, accidental death and dismemberment (74 percent), and dental insurance (83 percent). Most contracts continue coverage to employees after retirement but reduce the amount of coverage. Hospitalization and surgical insurance for dependents of employees are covered in nearly all of the contracts, and premiums are paid by the company in the majority of cases. There are also increasing numbers of medical-related plans covering new areas: prescription drugs (41 percent), optical care (47 percent), supplements to Medicare (62 percent), and alcohol and drug abuse (49 percent). It is expected that these areas of coverage will continue to grow.

Health-Care Cost Containment

With health-care costs rising so dramatically over the last few years, employers have attempted either to reduce the costs of health-care coverage or to shift part of the cost to employees. At the same time, unions and workers are more inclined than ever to protect their health-care benefits. As a result, widespread work stoppages by the Communication Workers of America and International Brotherhood of Electrical Workers have occurred over these conflicting interests with Bell Atlantic, NYNEX, and Pacific Telesis. In 1989, health-care benefit costs were given as the major issue in work stoppages, involving 78 percent of the workers; in 1986, only 18 percent were involved.[66]

Unions and companies have negotiated contract provisions to lower health-care costs. Such provisions appeared in 72 percent of the agreements in 1989, a steep climb from 55 percent in 1986. Health-care cost containment clauses included surgical fees for procedures performed on an outpatient basis in 74 percent of the agreements; a second surgical opinion was required in 73 percent. The length of hospital stays was reduced by covering home health care in 61 percent of the agreements, and 57 percent of the agreements required non-emergency tests be performed on an outpatient basis before hospital admission. In addition, there has been an increase from 19 percent in 1986 to 28 percent in 1989 in provisions requiring workers to share in premium costs for comprehensive medical coverage.

Income Maintenance

Income-maintenance provisions that provide income protection for employees are now found in 52 percent of the labor agreements. Such provisions usually involve work or pay guarantees, severance pay (separation or termination pay), and supplemental unemployment benefit (SUB) plans. Thirteen percent of the agreements contain work or pay guarantees, with the majority of those providing a weekly guarantee of 40 hours of work.

Severance-pay plans providing for lump-sum payments upon termination are included in 40 percent of the agreements. In most cases, severance pay is extended only to workers whose jobs have been terminated as a result of permanent shutdown, to those whose layoffs continue beyond a minimum length of time, or to those who have no prospect for recall. The amount of severance pay varies with the length of service—each year of service allows for increased benefits. Severance payments are usually restricted to a particular time period (up to one year) or until the worker is reemployed.

Supplemental unemployment benefit plans (SUB), included in 14 percent of the agreements, are usually classified as pooled fund systems (benefits are allowed only in the event of lack of work). A few SUB plans provide individual accounts in which the employee has a vested right and from which he or she may withdraw money for reasons other than lack of work. The most common method provides payment of an amount equal to a percentage of the employee's take-home pay. Plans involving the United Auto Workers are the most lucrative for the workers, with SUB payments and unemployment compensation equaling 95 percent of take-home pay minus $7.50 in work-related expenses. Other plans range from a $10 per week minimum to 90 percent of take-home pay. Other considerations, such as duration of benefits, length of service requirements, and employer financial requirements, must also be included in the composition of the plan.

SUB payments can be extremely expensive for a company, especially in a declining industry. For example, U.S. Steel spent over $284 million on income security in 1984. Its SUB plan (including unemployment compensation) replaces 74 percent of an average steelworker's pay for up to 2 years depending on seniority and the financial position of the SUB fund.[67]

Premium Pay—Overtime and Other Supplements

Most labor agreements specify daily or weekly work schedules, and 97 percent provide premium pay for hours worked beyond the normal hours. Most agreements call for 8-hour days and work weeks of 40 hours—Monday through Friday. Overtime premiums are usually paid for work over 8 hours per day at a time-and-a-half rate, which is more beneficial to the worker than the Fair Labor Standards Act requirement of time-and-a-half payments for work in excess of 40 hours in a week. (Workers on a 4-day, 40-hour work week would receive 8 hours of overtime pay.) A few agreements provide sixth-day and seventh-day premiums, but the majority of agreements prohibit pyramiding of overtime (combining a number of different premium payments, allowing overtime duplication).

Many labor agreements also contain provisions for overtime administration. For example, overtime assignments may be restricted to employees within a job classification or a given department, to a particular shift, to qualified employees, and so on. In some cases, where management has had difficulty getting employees to work overtime, provisions that make overtime mandatory have been negotiated.

Some agreements that provide for equalization of overtime hours count the hours offered when an employee is offered overtime and refuses to accept it. For example, if an employee is offered 4 hours of Saturday morning overtime and he or she turns it down, those 4 hours of overtime offered are the same as 4 hours of overtime worked, as it applies to the equalization of overtime process. Likewise, unions have sought provisions in the labor agreement that would enable their members to better plan their off-the-job activities: advance notice, relief from mandatory overtime if not notified by a certain time, and others.

Various forms of premium pay are included in most contracts. For instance, shift differentials (premium payments for working the night shift, for example) are provided in most of the agreements. Other forms, such as reporting pay (pay for employees who report for scheduled work but find no work) and call-back pay (pay for employees who are called back to work at hours other than normal) are also usually included. Reporting pay guarantees pay for from 1 to 8 hours, except with some maritime firms that provide 1 full week. Call-back or call-in pay guarantees are most frequently for 4 hours. Other supplements include pay for temporary transfer, hazardous work, travel, work clothes, tools, and bonuses other than production.

Payments for Nonwork–Holidays, Vacations, and Rest Periods

While many agreements provide for such nonwork activities as rest periods, cleanup time, time lost to job-related injury, waiting time, standby time, travel time, and voting time, the payments for nonwork involving the most money are holidays and vacations. The median number of holidays provided is 11; the range is from 5 to 17. Nearly all agreements provide holidays for Labor Day, Independence Day, Thanksgiving, Christmas, New Year's Day, and Memorial Day. Good Friday, Christmas Eve, and the day after Thanksgiving appear in about 50 percent of the agreements. Most agreements have eligibility requirements, for example, specified length of service (usually 4 weeks) before being given a paid holiday, or working the day before and after the holiday. More complicated provisions involve issues such as holidays falling on Saturday, Sunday, or a day off or during vacation, and premium pay for work on holidays.

Nearly all agreements provide for vacations for covered employees; there have been sharp increases in agreements allowing 5- and 6-week vacations and slight reductions in amount of service to qualify for nearly all types of vacations. Somewhat surprisingly, vacations for 1 week only are now less frequent than 2-, 3-, and 4-week vacations; however, the amount of vacation is linked to length of service. For example, in most cases, to qualify for a 5-week vacation, an employee must have 20 years of service.

Nearly all agreements have provisions that pertain to the administration of vacations. The majority contain specific work requirements, such as a minimum number of hours, days, weeks, or years necessary to qualify for various lengths of vacation. Vacation scheduling provisions appear in 87 percent of all agreements; they cover such items as annual plant shutdowns and consideration of employee seniority and employee preference. These provisions are essential in organizations employing large numbers of employees, not only to reduce friction between employees but to allow management to properly plan its production schedules.

Pensions

Unions greatly increase pension coverage and alter the provisions of pension plans in ways that benefit the senior workers and equalize pensions among workers.[68] Union members receive larger benefits than nonunion workers at the time they retire and also receive larger increases in their benefits in the years following their retirement. They retire at an earlier age than nonunion workers, too. The overall wealth of the pension funds to union member beneficiaries is 50 to 109 percent greater than that of nonunion workers.[69]

Nearly all labor agreements make some reference to pension plans, whether in the form of a general statement mentioning the plan or a fully detailed provision. Items usually mentioned include age for retirement (normal and early), disability retirement, benefits available and requirements for qualifying, vesting provisions, administration procedures, and financial arrangements.

In 1987, the Age Discrimination in Employment Act was amended to outlaw any mandatory retirement; prior to that amendment, the allowable mandatory retirement age was 70. Although this amendment helped the senior employee, the Supreme Court's controversial *Betts* decision in 1989 hurt. The high court ruled that virtually all employee benefit programs are exempt from challenge under the Age Discrimination in Employment Act *unless* the employee can prove "intentional discrimination" on the part of the employer.[70]

Most plans guarantee the retired employee a flat monthly dollar amount for each year of service ($18.63 is the median; the amounts range from $2.55 to $54.54) or a percentage of earnings times years of service. Special provisions are usually included for employees forced to retire due to total or permanent disability. In addition, voluntary early retirement is allowed in 96 percent of the plans.

Frequently, early retirement plans offer several options to the employee. For example, agreements provide such options as retirement at age 60 after 10 years of service; retirement at age 55 but only when the combined age and service years equal 85; and retirement after 30 years of service, without regard to age. The financial arrangements in 95 percent of the agreements show that the employer finances the pension plan entirely (that is, it is noncontributory); where plans are contributory, labor agreements include very specific provisions about the amounts that the employer and the employees contribute.

Although nearly all of the contracts contain **vesting** provisions stating that an employee whose service is terminated continues to be entitled to earned benefits, the Employer Retirement Income Security Act of 1974 (also known as ERISA or the Pension Reform Act) has very specific regulations governing vesting requirements of pension plans. Although management and labor may negotiate provisions covering pensions that are more favorable than the law requires, most agreements for the time being will no doubt closely correspond to the legal minimum. Under any of these options, an employee must be at least 50 percent vested after 10 years of service and 100 percent vested after 15 years of service, regardless of age.

Prepaid Legal Services

Twenty years ago, prepaid legal services did not exist. In fact, any attorney who contracted with a group to provide legal services for a predetermined fee would have been disbarred.[71] Now legal assistance is available to organized group members who have pooled prepaid amounts. Moreover, prepaid legal plans are growing at an explosive rate; these plans cover 13 million people, up from 1.5 million in 1978. Prepaid legal service plans include the 1.4 million workers under the UAW-General Motors agreement, 400,000 under the UAW-Ford agreement, and 200,000 under the UAW-Chrysler agreement as well as 300,000 members of the New York City Municipal Employees Union.[72]

For a typical plan that costs less than $100 per year, those covered may make unlimited phone calls for consultation and have attorneys make calls or write letters on their behalf. On more complicated issues, clients are referred to outside attorneys who charge a fee from $50.00 to $70.00 per hour.[73]

By 1986, about 5 million union members were covered by employer-paid legal plans in their labor agreements. These plans vary in terms of whether the parties will set up open panels (the client chooses the attorney) or closed panels (legal services are provided by a law firm retained under the plan or by an attorney staff).[74] Some plans offer a full array of services, ranging from counsel for criminal offenses to routine matters such as wills, divorces, house closings, and landlord-tenant problems. Most believe prepaid legal services will become more common; these projections are supported by an American Bar Association study that predicted that prepaid legal service plans would become as common as medical insurance is today.

Family Care Benefits

In 1989, the Communication Workers of America and the International Brotherhood of Electrical Workers negotiated an agreement with AT&T that included a $5 million fund to increase the number of professional organizations to meet child-care and elder-care needs of employees, doubling the length of unpaid child-care leaves (for birth or adoption of a child) to 1 year, a $2,000 payment to employees adopting children under 18, creation of accounts for employees to set aside tax-free funds for payment of dependent care, up to 12 months of unpaid time off over a two-year period to care for seriously ill family members, and flexible time to handle family emergencies. The American Federation of State, County, and Municipal Employees and the regional Bell companies have negotiated similar provisions. Although in 1989 only 10 percent of the 44,000 employers with over 100 employees provided child-care assistance, this figure is likely to increase. With the unions attempting to accommodate the needs of female and service workers, national attention to these provisions will be a bonus to unionizing these workers, especially to two-career families.[75]

Union Effects on Wages and Benefits

The degree to which unions influence wage and benefit levels is a frequently debated subject among labor economists. In a 1963 classic, *Unionism and Relative Wages in the United States,*[76] Greg Lewis concluded that union wages ranged between 10 and 15 percent higher than nonunion wages. Further analysis reveals a greater impact on wages of blue-collar workers, younger workers, and less educated workers. The data in Exhibit 13.8 show that union employees earn $122 more per week than nonunion employees. A difference is present in every occupation and industry listed.

Unions have an even greater effect on fringe benefits. Blue-collar employees covered by labor agreements receive fringe benefits that average 28 to 36 percent higher than those of blue-collar employees in nonunion settings. The union presence positively influences the likelihood that a pension plan will be offered, although they apparently do not raise employer expenditures for pensions once the plans are established.[77]

Unions also contribute to wage equalization by decreasing the differential between unionized blue-collar workers and nonunion white-collar workers, as well as reducing wage dispersion (covered earlier in this chapter). This union contribution frequently results in less turnover, because seniority-based wage increases, promotion possibilities, and other benefits cause employees to stay with their employers longer.[78]

Some studies have shown that the wage differences between union and nonunion workers are the products of other interrelated influences, such as higher occupational skills, fewer females, lower quit rates, larger organizations, and greater capital intensity of production in unionized industries.[79] Other studies have even contended the union-nonunion wage differential is an illusion, because the higher-paid

Exhibit 13.8

Median Weekly Earnings of Full-time Wage and Salary Employees: Union, Nonunion, and Difference, 1989

	Represented by Union	Not Represented by Union	Difference Union over Nonunion
Total (16 years and older)	$494	$372	+$122
Sex			
Men	524	430	+94
Women	417	312	+105
Race			
White	503	384	+119
Black	423	290	+133
Hispanic	420	276	+144
Occupation			
Technical sales and administrative support	431	346	+85
Service	406	226	+180
Precision production, craft, and repair	568	405	+163
Operators, fabricators, and laborers	448	287	+161
Farming, forestry, and fishing	379	239	+140
Industry			
Agricultural wage and salary workers	NA	246	
Private nonagricultural wage and salary workers	485	368	+117
Mining	517	561	−44
Construction	634	393	+241
Manufacturing	458	400	+58
Transportation and public utilities	561	458	+103
Wholesale and retail trade	402	298	+103
Finance, insurance, and real estate	399	407	−8
Services	402	352	+50
Government workers	506	419	+87

Source: "News," Washington, D.C.: Bureau of Labor Statistics, 1990, p. 7.

workers tend to unionize in order to obtain union services.[80] In other words, workers who share a beneficial wage and benefit differential will form unions to protect their advantageous positions.

Unions also have an effect on wages and benefits in nonunion companies. Union wage and benefit changes "spill over" into nonunion companies because nonunion employees who want to maintain their nonunion status will respond to union wage increases by raising wages of their workers. Such increases are provided not only to reduce the threat of unions, but to provide equity and maintain morale and productivity.[81]

Although there have been cases where unions respond to nonunion wages in order to remain competitive, craft unions, which have recently been heavily damaged by job losses, have not reduced their wage premium over the nonunion craft employers. Thus far, these unions have apparently been willing to tolerate even higher unemployment to avoid lowering their wage demands.[82]

Employee Stock Ownership Plans

An **employee stock ownership plan (ESOP)** provides employees an opportunity to become shareholders in the company that employs them. Of course, employees can always buy stock in the stock market; but ESOPs create additional incentives by providing discount prices on shares or by matching employees' payments for stock. These plans provide a method, not necessarily related to profits, for employee participation in ownership.

After much initial opposition to employee ownership, unions are looking at ESOPs more favorably as means to save jobs and rescue failing companies. At first, unions were skeptical and even hostile, even though ESOPs have received favorable tax treatment for years. Unions had expressed three objections to ESOPs: (1) buyouts have the potential for draining union funds; large up-front funds are usually required to purchase the company and repay loans; (2) ownership of the firm is considered incompatible with the union's traditional adversarial role with management, thereby diminishing union solidarity and power and causing the rank and file to lose benefits it might otherwise gain; and (3) ESOPs are a risky use of pension funds because they are based on corporate stock performance. Even with these objections, the unions have recognized that the possible loss of jobs and decline in membership makes employee ownership frequently the only alternative.[83]

With companies such as Procter & Gamble, J. C. Penney, Polaroid, Texaco, and Anheuser-Busch now having ESOPs, it is estimated that about 10,000 companies employing about 10 million workers, about one-fourth of all corporate employees, offer ESOPs. In approximately 1,500 ESOPs, employees own the majority of the stock.[84]

Concession bargaining of trading stock for wages in companies employing more than 1,000 workers has been common in the airline, steel, and trucking industries. Airlines now account for over 11 percent of employee ownership in large firms; in steel, it is estimated that 25 percent of employees were involved in concession-bargaining-based employee ownership in 1985; in trucking, over 20 firms have either used concession-bargaining-based employee ownership or organized their firms with substantial amounts of employee ownership. In many firms in these industries ESOPs played a major role in preventing disaster until the firms could get their businesses under control.[85]

While often called "tax dodges," "socialistic schemes," and "people's capitalism," ESOPs offer several advantages:

1. Tax breaks that include interest payments on the debt, dividends paid on the ESOP shares, and principal on the debt.
2. Defense against corporate raiders and help in leveraged buyouts.
3. Reduction in pension payments because stock is contributed.
4. Productivity increases and better quality due to higher morale and employee effort. Examples of success stories are highlighted in the "Labor Relations in Action."

On the other hand, there are some uncertainties. For example, productivity gains are not likely unless management is willing to give workers a strong and genuine voice in the operations. In fact, managers who alienate the employee-owners may be voted out of their jobs in favor of a corporate raider. Likewise, the govern-

Labor Relations in Action

The United Steelworkers of America Leads the Way in ESOPs

The USWA has had much experience with ESOPs in the last several years. Through this experience USWA now insists on the following conditions in ESOPs in which it is involved:

- ESOP members should be immediately vested in stock held in their names by the ESOP.
- Members should have full voting rights for their shares.
- ESOPs should not replace fully funded pension plans.

Oregon Steel Company (Portland, Oregon) Near collapse in 1983 from foreign competition, a slump in steel prices, and a bitter strike, nearly all the company was sold to an ESOP for $22.8 million. Since then Oregon Steel has experienced huge productivity increases due largely to plant modernization, the elimination of the "us-and-them" attitude, and reduction in labor strife. In 1983, it took 9.3 man-hours to produce and ship a ton of product; in 1988, it took 3.4 man-hours. With plans to grow, the company went public and sold 2.1 million new shares and 1.2 million shares to worker-shareholders. The company's market value in 1988 was $135.8 million, more than 6 times the 1983 value. While Oregon Steel employees are not millionaires, many have stock valued over one-half million dollars.

McLouth Steel Products Corp. (Trenton, Michigan) In 1987, USWA members agreed to a new 5-year contract that sacrificed 10 percent of the wages and benefits and 10 percent of the employment force. Now, the ESOP owns 85 percent of the company. Creditors are owed $130 million, have received preferred stock, and share board control with the ESOP. One month after the purchase, the company reported a profit for the first time in years. Nine months later, the company was still posting monthly profits.

Republic Storage Company (Canton, Ohio) In 1984 when LTV merged with Republic Steel, Republic Storage was put up for sale. The local union decided to seize the opportunity to buy the plant and successfully competed with seven other companies to do so. The local union was afraid the new buyers might do what other buyers had done—transfer work, sell assets, and break off profitable units. The ESOP borrowed $17 million and obtained another $5.7 million line of credit to purchase the company. The employees took $1.75-per-hour wage cuts in exchange for company stock. In the first 3 years, over 20 percent of the loan had been paid and it was anticipated that the entire loan would be paid in 5 years. Then, all of the company's shares would be owned by the ESOP.

E. W. Bliss (Salem, Ohio) In 1985, E. W. Bliss had changed owners, was suffering from the steel industry collapse, and had reduced employment to 35 workers. A shutdown appeared imminent. In 1986, an ESOP was organized and borrowed about $8 million to purchase the company. The workers gave up $6 in wages and benefits, including $2.20 in wages, in exchange for 80 percent ownership of the new ESOP (20 percent is held by management personnel). Today, union members and management sit together on a new Joint Strategic Decision Board, and five problem-solving teams meet once or twice a month to identify and deal with problems. Once each month, the company president and other managers report to the union on the company's financial condition and progress. The work force is now 190 employees, and the company is breaking even and projects its sales to increase next year from $14 million to $20 million.

Sources: James P. Miller, "Some Workers Set Up LBOs of Their Own and Benefit Greatly," *The Wall Street Journal,* December 12, 1988, p. A-1; "A Hardheaded Takeover by McLouth's Hardhats," *Business Week,* June 6, 1988, pp. 90–92; *Steel Labor* 53 (July 1988), pp. 7–13.

ment, a key participant in these programs, provides some uncertainty. The U.S. Department of Labor closely monitors the ESOPs for abuses in the administration of the program and Congress may change the rules of the game at any time. Perhaps the biggest uncertainty to the employee-owner is that each employee stakes his or her future retirement income on the value of the company's stock.[86]

Companies with ESOPs face continuous challenges just like other companies. In 1984, an independent steelworkers union representing 6,670 of Weirton's employees purchased the company and became almost an immediate success. Since 1984, the company has outperformed its competitors and is now the eighth largest steel company in the United States.

In 1984, workers accepted a 20 percent wage cut and a 6-year wage freeze to save the plant and preserve a way of life in the West Virginia mill town. Now, the company is faced with increased competition and a need to modernize its facilities. It needs to raise $585 million for some long-delayed plant modernization and is searching for alternatives. One possibility is to reduce the profit-sharing payments to employees from 50 percent of annual earnings to about 33 percent. Another option is to sell 20 percent of the company's stock to outsiders, which would reduce the employee-owners' control. Still another possibility is the issuance of stock for public sale; however, this sale would also reduce the employee-owners' control. The decision will be made at a stockholders' meeting where many employee-owners will face the realities of business decision-making. Thus, even though the employees may be the majority stockholders, they face the same business decisions other companies do.[87]

All ESOPs have not been successful. In fact, Dan River, Inc. has yet to prove itself. In 1983, workers gave up their pension plan in return for 70 percent of company stock in order to fend off corporate raider Carl Icahn. However, they got no voice in the management of the company. Today, workers complain that the management gets "colder and more distant," and the company has operated at a loss in the last 3 years. The value of the employees' stock has declined from $22.50 to $16.00, thereby causing the employees' retirement benefits to shrink by 29 percent.

On the other hand, the value of the shares owned by Dan River's management has soared. They had purchased a separate class of stock for a 30 percent interest in the company, and this class of stock has doubled in value since 1983. These differences have created much resentment among employees, and some workers have expressed interest in having Icahn return.[88]

Although research on the effects of ESOPs on labor-management relations is tentative at this time because of the lack of widespread or long-term experience, a few preliminary conclusions may be reported:

1. Labor-management cooperation does not emerge automatically when publicly traded companies move into employee ownership.
2. Employee ownership leads to greater identification of the employees with the company and employees receive more information about the company, supervisor-employee relations become more cooperative, and employees and managers express positive attitudes about employee ownership and the organizational climate.

3. There is no evidence that the employees want to take over the companies and run them democratically from top to bottom.
4. Employee ownership does not have an automatic effect on employees' motivation, work effort, absenteeism, or job satisfaction. However, greater integration of the employee into the organization and participation in decisions have positive results.
5. Generally, the role of the union does not change except in cases where the union made an early and ongoing effort to become involved in the whole process in detail, and unions initiate little change in labor-management relations.
6. Companies with an active employee ownership philosophy that try to translate it into concrete cooperative efforts have the strongest effect on positive employee attitudes.
7. The presence of an ESOP does not make a firm more productive, efficient, or profitable; however, most studies show that employee-owned firms performed successfully on a number of financial variables, such as profits, stock appreciation, sales, and employment growth. One study showed that where all employees could participate in an ESOP their firm performed less favorably than the non-ESOP companies on all the measures,[89] although isolating single causes for performance is extremely difficult.

Summary

Economic issues include wages and the variety of economic benefits that make up what is commonly called the wage package. Wage differentials result from several industrial, occupational, and regional factors. Job evaluation begins with an organizational analysis and concludes with a wage structure that includes job classes, wage rates, and wage ranges.

In addition to the basic wage structure, some firms provide either individual or group wage incentives. Negotiators use certain wage-determining criteria in arriving at an acceptable wage structure; commonly accepted criteria include differential features of jobs, comparable wages, ability to pay, productivity, and cost of living.

Since labor agreements usually are negotiated for periods greater than 1 year, provisions are commonly negotiated to adjust wages during the life of the contract. A common form of wage adjustment is the cost-of-living adjustment (COLA), or escalator clause, which adjusts wages in accordance with the Consumer Price Index. Another form of wage adjustment less frequently included in agreements is the wage reopener clause, providing that wages be renegotiated at a predetermined time during the life of the agreement.

Employee benefits have now increased to consume 39.0 percent of the company's total payroll. Numerous types of benefits exist. The major ones include insurance, income maintenance, premium pay, payments for nonwork, and pensions. New benefits, prepaid legal services and family care, have recently come into existence and are likely to increase in popularity.

The chapter concludes with a discussion of employee stock ownership plans (ESOPs) and the roles that unions have played in these plans. Numerous examples were presented, and the advantages and disadvantages of the various plans were discussed. While there are numerous successful plans, other plans were identified as failures for employees.

Key Terms

job evaluation
cost-of-living adjustments (COLA)
wage reopeners
lump-sum pay adjustments
supplemental unemployment benefit plans (SUB)
vesting
employee stock ownership plan (ESOP)

Discussion Questions

1. List the main factors that help explain the wage differentials for five jobs in an organization with which you are familiar.
2. Explain why job evaluation plans must take into consideration external as well as internal factors if they are to be successful.
3. Assume that labor and management are negotiating a labor agreement and the wage spread becomes an issue of disagreement – management wants a wider wage spread, and the union wants a smaller wage spread. Why should management be cautious about the union's proposal, even though the total costs may be the same?
4. For each of the wage criteria given in the chapter, state the union's expected arguments and management's expected counterarguments, given the following conditions:
   a. High profits, a growing firm, a healthy economy, and the cost of living rising at 8 percent per year.
   b. Low profit, no anticipation of growth, questionable economic conditions, and the cost of living rising but by wide variations each month.
5. Assuming that a firm's costs of employee benefits are 39.0 percent of payroll, why doesn't the firm just let the union determine the manner in which the amounts are apportioned to the variety of benefits, such as insurance, holidays, and vacations, without negotiating each specific clause, especially since the overall costs probably would be the same?
6. Evaluate family care benefits as a union organizing instrument.
7. What must be included in the composition of an ESOP for you as an employee to participate?

References

1. Jules Bachman, *Wage Determination: An Analysis of Wage Criteria* (Princeton, N.J.: D. Van Nostrand, 1959), pp. 1–7.
2. Ibid., p. 14.
3. Ibid., pp. 20–21.
4. George W. Taylor, "Wage Determination Process," in *New Concepts in Wage Determination,* ed. George W. Taylor and Frank C. Person (New York: McGraw-Hill, 1957), p. 84.
5. Leon Greenberg, "Definitions and Concepts," in *Collective Bargaining and Productivity,* ed. Gerald Somers (Madison, Wis.: Industrial Relations Research Association, 1975), p. 12.
6. Bachman, *Wage Determination,* p. 58.
7. For further reference, see David W. Belcher, *Compensation Administration* (Englewood Cliffs, N.J.: Prentice-Hall, 1974); J. D. Dunn and F. M. Rachel, *Wage and Salary Administration: Total Compensation Systems* (New York: McGraw-Hill, 1971); Richard Henderson, *Compensation Management* (Reston, Va.: Reston Publishing, 1976); Allan N. Nash and Stephen J. Carroll, Jr., *The Management of Compensation* (Monterey, Calif.: Brocks/Cole Publishing, 1975); M. L. Rock, *Handbook of Wage and Salary Administration* (New York: McGraw-Hill, 1972); Robert E. Sibson, *Compensation* (New York: American Management Association, AMACOM, 1975); T. A. Mahoney, *Compensation and Reward Perspectives* (Homewood, Ill.: Richard D. Irwin, 1979).
8. Approach developed and advocated by L. T. Hawley and H. D. Janes.
9. David W. Belcher, "Wage and Salary Administration," in *Moti-*

vation and Commitment, ed. Dale Yoder and H. G. Heneman, Jr. (Washington, D.C.: Bureau of National Affairs Inc., 1975), pp. 6-95.
10. Harold D. Janes, "Issues in Job Evaluation: The Union View," *Personnel Journal* 51 (September 1972), p. 675; also see Research Department, International Association of Machinists, *What's Wrong with Job Evaluation?* (Washington, D.C.: International Association of Machinists, 1954).
11. Harold D. Janes, "Comparative Issues in Job Evaluation: The Union View, 1971-1978," *Personnel Journal* 58 (February 1979), pp. 80-85.
12. Sibson, *Compensation,* p. 120.
13. Belcher, *Compensation Administration,* pp. 6-98-6-103. Also see footnote 7.
14. Editors of Collective Bargaining Negotiations and Contracts, *Basic Patterns* (Washington, D.C.: Bureau of National Affairs Inc., 1989), p. 93:2.
15. Ibid.
16. Herbert G. Zollitsch, "Productivity, Time Studies, and Incentive-Pay Plans," in *Motivation and Commitment,* ed. Dale Yoder and H. G. Heneman, Jr. (Washington, D.C.: Bureau of National Affairs Inc., 1975), pp. 6-61.
17. Norma W. Carlson, "Time Rates Tighten Their Grip on Manufacturing Industries," *Monthly Labor Review* 105 (May 1982), pp. 15-16.
18. "Incentive Pay Schemes as a Result of Economic Employee Relations Changes," *Daily Labor Report,* October 9, 1984, p. CC-1.
19. John Zalusky, "Labor's Collective Bargaining Experience with Gainsharing and Profit-Sharing," *Proceedings of the 39th Annual Meeting of the Industrial Relations Research Association* (Madison, Wis.: Industrial Relations Research Institute, 1987), pp. 177-178.
20. "Ford Motor Company Profit Sharing Will Average $2,800 Per Employee," *Daily Labor Report,* February 23, 1989, p. A-1.
21. "Chrysler, UAW Reach Tentative Settlement Barring Executives Bonuses Unless Workers Share," *Daily Labor Report,* May 6, 1988, p. A-8.
22. John Hoerr, "Why Labor and Management Are Both Buying Profit Sharing," *Business Week,* January 13, 1983, p. 84.
23. "Potential Dangers in Expansion of Current Auto Profit-Sharing Plans Cited by Attorney," *Daily Labor Report,* March 24, 1982, p. C-1.
24. Zollitsch, "Productivity," pp. 6-66. Also see J. Kenneth White, "The Scanlon Plan: Causes and Correlates of Success," *Academy of Management Journal* 22 (June 1979), pp. 292-312.
25. Mitchell Fein, "Improved Productivity through Workers Involvement," *Hearings before the Subcommittee on General Oversight of the Committee on Small Business* (Washington, D.C.: U.S. Government Printing Office, 1982), pp. 118-123.
26. Timothy L. Ross, Larry L. Hatcher, and Dan B. Adams, "How Unions View Gainsharing," *Business Horizons* 28 (July-August 1985), pp. 15-22.
27. Irving Bernstein, *Arbitration of Wages* (Berkeley: University of California, 1954), pp. 26-27; Craig Overton, "Criteria in Grievance and Interest Arbitration in the Public Sector," *Arbitration Journal* 28 (1973), pp. 159-166; Howard S. Block, "Criteria in Public Sector Interest Disputes" in *Arbitration and the Public Interest,* ed. G. G. Somers and B. D. Dennis (Washington, D.C.: Bureau of National Affairs Inc., 1971), pp. 161-193.
28. Audrey Freedman, *The New Look in Wage Policy and Employee Relations* (New York: Conference Board, 1985), pp. 1-10.
29. Bachman, *Wage Determination,* pp. 14-15.
30. Richard B. Freeman, "Union Wage Practices and Wage Dispersions Within Establishments," *Industrial and Labor Relations Review* 36 (October 1982), pp. 3-21.
31. "Two-Tier Pay Systems," *Collective Bargaining Negotiations and Contracts* (Washington, D.C.: Bureau of National Affairs Inc., 1984), p. 93:121.
32. "IRRA Panelists Address the Two-Tier Implications for Fair Representation and Equal Opportunity," *Daily Labor Report,* January 10, 1985, pp. A-5-A-7.
33. James E. Martin and Melanie M. Peterson, "Two-Tier Wage Structures and Attitude Differences" in *Proceedings of the Thirty-eighth Annual Meeting: Industrial Relations Research Association,* ed. B. D. Dennis (Madison, Wis.: Industrial Relations Research Association, 1986), pp. 78-79.
34. "Two-Tier Wage Plans," *Collective Bargaining Negotiations and Contracts* (Washington, D.C.: Bureau of National Affairs Inc., 1988), p. 16:993.
35. John Dunlop, "The Economics of Wage-Dispute Settlements," *Law and Contemporary Problems* 12 (Spring 1947), p. 282; and Bernstein, *Arbitration of Wages,* pp. 26-27.
36. J. Fred Holly and Gary A. Hall, "Dispelling the Myths of Wage Arbitration," *Labor Law Journal* 28 (June 1977), p. 346.
37. Sumner Slichter, *Basic Criteria Used in Wage Negotiation* (Chicago: Chicago Association of Commerce and Industry, January 30, 1947), p. 25.
38. Bachman, *Wage Determination,* pp. 251-258.
39. Dunlop, "Wage-Dispute Settlements," pp. 286-289.
40. Aaron Bernstein, "Productivity—Not Pay Cuts—Will Keep Union Members Working," *Business Week,* August 25, 1986, p. 32.
41. General Accounting Office, *Productivity Sharing Programs: Can They Contribute to Productivity Improvement?* (Washington, D.C.: U.S. Government Printing Office, 1981).
42. Jerome Rosow, "Productivity and the Blue-Collar Blues," *Personnel* 48 (March-April 1971), pp. 8-10.
43. William F. Maloney, "Productivity Bargaining in Contract Construction," *Proceedings of the 1977 Annual Spring Meeting: Industrial Relations Research Association* (Madison, Wis.: Industrial Relations Research Association, 1977), pp. 533-534.
44. Joseph P. Goldberg, "Bargaining and Productivity in the Private Sector" in *Collective Bargaining and Productivity,* ed. Gerald Somers et al. (Madison, Wis.: Industrial Relations Research Association, 1975), p. 28-42.
45. William W. Winpisinger, "Output: Collective Bargaining and Productivity," in F. J. Havelich, ed., *Collective Bargaining: New Dimensions in Labor Relations* (Boulder, Colo.: Westview Press, 1979), pp. 25-28.
46. Ronald S. Warren, Jr., "The Effect of Unionization on Labor Productivity: Some Time-Series Evidence," *Journal of Labor Research* 6 (Spring 1985), p. 199.
47. Charles Brown and James Medoff, "Trade Unions in the Production Process," *Journal of Political Economy* 86 (June 1980), pp. 355-359.
48. Richard B. Freeman and James L. Medoff, "The Two Faces of Unionism," *Public Interest* 57 (Fall 1979), pp. 69-93.
49. J. T. Addison and A. H. Barnett, "The Impact of Unions on Productivity," *British Journal of Industrial Relations* 20 (July 1982), pp. 145-149.
50. John T. Addison, "Are Unions Good for Productivity?" *Journal of Labor Research* 3 (Spring 1982), p. 137.
51. Robert S. Kaufman and Roger T. Kaufman, "Union Effects on Productivity, Personnel Practices, and Survival in the Automotive Parts Industry," *Journal of Labor Research* 8 (Fall 1987), p. 332-349.
52. Alice H. Cook, "Comparable Worth, Background, and Current

Issues," *Reports* (Honolulu, Hawaii: University of Hawaii, Industrial Relations Center, 1982), pp. 5–6. For an examination of the Chairman of the EEOC's view of the comparable worth issue, see Clarence Thomas, "Pay Equity and Comparable Worth," *Labor Law Journal* 34 (January 1983), pp. 3–12.
53. Winn Newman, "Pay Equity: An Emerging Labor Issue" in *Proceedings of the Thirty-fourth Annual Meeting: Industrial Relations Research Association,* ed. James L. Stern and B. D. Dennis (Madison, Wis.: Industrial Relations Research Association, 1982), pp. 167–170.
54. George Ruben, "Comparable Worth Settlements," *Monthly Labor Review* 109 (March 1986), p. 43.
55. Editors of Collective Bargaining Negotiations and Contracts, *Basic Patterns* (Washington, D.C.: Bureau of National Affairs Inc., 1987), pp. 93.2–93.3.
56. John Zalusky, "Cost of Living Clauses: Inflation Fighters," *American Federationist* 83 (March 1976), p. 1.
57. H. L. Douty, "Escalator Clauses and Inflation," *Collective Bargaining Negotiations and Contracts* (Washington, D.C.: Bureau of National Affairs Inc., December 1975), p. 16:1.
58. The average length increased from 26 months in 1972 to 32.5 months in 1977. Those with COLA averaged 36.1 months, without COLA, 27.4 months. Janice D. Murphy, "Wage Developments during 1977," *Monthly Labor Review* 101 (April 1978), p. 5.
59. Doyle D. Buss, "GM Will Scrap Cost-of-Living Payments in '86," *The Wall Street Journal,* November 6, 1986, p. 6.
60. William M. Davis, "Collective Bargaining 1983: A Crowded Agenda," *Monthly Labor Review* 106 (January 1983), p. 10.
61. LeRoy, "Scheduled Wage Increases," pp. 5–6.
62. Audrey Freedman, "Cost-of-Living Clauses in Collective Bargaining," *Compensation Review* 6 (third quarter 1974), pp. 11–19; Robert H. Ferguson, *Cost-of-Living Adjustments in Union Management Agreements* (Ithaca, N.Y.: Cornell University, 1976), pp. 15–27; and LeRoy, "Scheduled Wage Increases," pp. 7–8.
63. Robert J. Thornton, "A Problem with the COLA Craze," *Compensation Review* 9 (second quarter 1977), pp. 42–44.
64. "Incidence of Lump-Sum Payments Increased Slightly during 1988, BNA Survey Indicates," *Daily Labor Report,* March 13, 1989, p. B-20.
65. Editors of Collective Bargaining Negotiations and Contracts, *Basic Patterns,* 1989.
66. "Disputes Over Health Care Costs Root of Many Strikes, Report Finds," *Daily Labor Report,* February 21, 1990, p. A-6.
67. "Steel Income Security Costly to Employers But Cushions Impact of Worker Displacement," *Daily Labor Report,* May 16, 1986, p. A-11.
68. Richard B. Freeman, "Unions, Pensions, and Union Pension Funds," *Working Paper Series* (Cambridge, Mass.: National Bureau of Economic Research Inc., 1983), p. 50.
69. Steven G. Allen and Robert L. Clark, "Unions, Pension Wealth, and Age-Compensation Profits," *Working Paper Series* (Cambridge, Mass.: National Bureau of Economic Research Inc., 1985), pp. 33–35.
70. "Supreme Court's *Betts* Ruling Expected to Have Major Impact on EEOC," *Daily Labor Report,* July 10, 1989, p. C-1.
71. Sandy DeMent, "A New Bargaining Focus on Legal Services," *American Federationist* 85 (May 1978), pp. 7–10.
72. "Legal Service Plans," *Collective Bargaining Negotiations and Contracts* (Washington, D.C.: Bureau of National Affairs Inc., 1986), p. 16:945.
73. Peter Waldman, "Pre-paid Legal Plans Offer Consultations, Follow-up Calls and Referrals at Low Cost," *The Wall Street Journal,* February 24, 1986, p. 37.
74. "Legal Service Plans," op. cit.
75. Amanda Bennett and Cathy Trost, "Benefit Package Set by AT&T, Unions Shows Power of Families in Workplace," *The Wall Street Journal,* May 31, 1989, p. A-6.
76. Greg Lewis, *Unionism and Relative Wages in the United States* (Chicago: University of Chicago Press, 1963); Richard B. Freeman and James L. Medoff, "The Impact of Collective Bargaining: Illusion or Reality?" in *U.S. Industrial Relations 1950–1980: A Critical Assessment,* ed. Jack Stieber, et al. (Madison, Wis.: Industrial Relations Research Association, 1981), pp. 53–54.
77. Augustin K. Fosu, "Impact of Unionism on Pension Fringes," *Industrial Relations* 22 (Fall 1983), p. 419.
78. Jacob Mincer, "Union Effects: Wages, Turnover, and Job Training," *Working Paper Series* (Cambridge, Mass.: National Bureau of Economic Research Inc., 1985), p. 42.
79. Daniel J. B. Mitchell, "Collective Bargaining and the Economy" in *U.S. Industrial Relations 1950–1980: A Critical Assessment,* ed. Jack Stieber, et al. (Madison, Wis.: Industrial Relations Research Association, 1981), pp. 1–44.
80. Robert J. Flanagan and Daniel J. B. Mitchell, "Wage Determination and Public Policy" in *Industrial Relations Research in the 1970s: A Review and Appraisal,* ed. T. A. Kochan, et al. (Madison, Wis.: Industrial Relations Research Association, 1982), p. 74.
81. Susan Vroman, "The Direction of Wage Spillovers in Manufacturing," *Industrial and Labor Relations Review* 36 (October 1982), pp. 102–103.
82. George Ruben, "Collective Bargaining in 1982: Results Dictated by Economy," *Monthly Labor Review* 106 (January 1983), pp. 28–37.
83. "Unions Warm to Employee Ownership as Option to Save Members' Jobs," *Daily Labor Report,* July 16, 1985, pp. C-1–C-2.
84. "ESOPs: Are They Good For You?" *Business Week,* May 15, 1989, p. 116.
85. Joseph R. Blasi, *Employee Ownership Through ESOPs: Implication for the Public Corporation* (New York: Pergamon Press, 1987), pp. 29–30.
86. "ESOPs: Are They Good For You?" *Business Week,* May 15, 1989, p. 116.
87. "Has Weirton's ESOP Worked Too Well?" *Business Week,* January 23, 1989, p. 66.
88. "How Dan River's ESOP Missed the Boat," *Business Week,* October 26, 1987, p. 34.
89. Joseph R. Blasi, *Employee Ownership Through ESOPs: Implication for the Public Corporation* (New York: Pergamon Press, 1987), pp. 40–44.

Cases for Part 3

CASE

3.1 Racing Cars on Leave of Absence

Background

The Electronic Workers Union (EWU) is the bargaining representative for the production and maintenance employees of Hooper, Inc. in Beauregard, Alabama. During the term of their collective bargaining agreement dated May 5, 1989, the parties were unable to resolve a grievance involving the termination of Bubba Jones, a member of the bargaining unit. Under the provisions of the agreement's grievance procedure, the matter was appealed to arbitration.

The grievance was filed by Bubba Jones and his union representative, Jimmy Short, on August 15, 1990. It states:

> I, Bubba Jones, was terminated on August 5, 1990 from Hooper for engaging in employment while on a leave of absence. I race stock cars Class C at Beauregard Motor Speedway in my spare time for a hobby. I was hurt pretty bad in a car wreck one weekend racing. I then had to go on a leave of absence. While on leave of absence, my name was put in the newspaper for taking a first one time, first and second the second time weeks later. The Company then found out about the articles and terminated me for engaging in employment while on a leave of absence. Now none of these races pays any money at all, just trophies. Also, most of the time I have had someone in my pit crew driving the car for me till I had recovered from injuries back on June 22, 1990. Larry Tate, Jim Grimes, and Billy Jack Jones have alternated driving the car most of the time. If this is employment, where is my paycheck? I wish to be reinstated with all seniority, back pay, and all benefits.

The parties stipulated that Bubba Jones's winnings while he was on leave totaled $65, including $10 won on July 2, $40 on July 9, $5 on July 16, and $10 on July 23. They agreed that he was on a leave of absence at the time he received these prizes and that the injury sustained by the grievant in his June 22 accident was a lumbar strain–injuries to his neck and back.

Bubba Jones testified that he was 29 years old, and had been hired by Hooper in June, 1978. His last day of work was June 21, 1990. He reported off on personal leave on June 22. That night he was injured in a car wreck at the Beauregard Motor Speedway when he was hit from behind and his car went into the wall. He sustained injuries to his neck and back. He reported off on sick leave for 6 or 7 days and then applied for a leave of absence. It was approved. His doctor indicated he would be able to return to work on September 12. During the period following his injury he went to a physician for treatment three or four times per week.

Source: The authors express their appreciation to Dr. Paul Gerhart, Case Western Reserve University, for providing this case.

Mr. Jones testified that at no time during his leave did anyone from the company contact him to tell him he should return to work because he was driving a race car. He said he was not employed by anyone at any time during his leave of absence. He denied receiving any compensation for working while on leave.

Mr. Jones stated that 1990 was his first year of racing. Prior to his injury he had won some prize money but had not won any races. He said there were three classes of racing at the Speedway. Class A is professional or semiprofessional and the drivers receive compensation but he was not aware whether the Speedway owners paid them. They receive prize money for all races. Class B is one step up from amateur and they also receive prize money for all races. Class C is amateur, and only the "feature race" in Class C pays prize money: $50 for first, $40 for second, $30 for third, and $20 for fourth and fifth place. In the feature race, anyone who starts and finishes gets $10; anyone who starts and does not finish gets $5. In addition to the feature race, there are three other Class C races for which only trophies are awarded to winners.

Bubba Jones stated that the owner of the Speedway is Bill Gates. Gates paid him nothing other than the prize money for driving in the races. The grievant's brother introduced him to racing, but before the 5 weeks prior to his accident, he had never raced. He never considered racing as a possible occupation, but only as a hobby.

Mr. Jones stated that while he was on leave, he received sick leave pay of $198 per week. He said he was injured on a Wednesday. He did not race until about 2 weeks after that. At that time, since his car had been demolished in his accident, he drove one of his brother's cars. He said there are four or five people in the pit crew, who receive no compensation.

After August 5, the date of his termination, Mr. Jones said he continued to race and won additional prize money. He said that all the prize money he received was given to his brother to pay for repairs to the car he drove. Mr. Jones did not pay his brother anything in addition to that. His brother did not pay him and Mr. Gates did not consider Bubba Jones to be his brother's employee. Mr. Jones said he finished out the summer and fall races using his brother's car. He said he has not been employed by his brother at any time after his termination.

After his termination, Mr. Jones got a job at Briarwood in landscaping. After he was laid off from Briarwood at the end of the season, he received unemployment compensation and has been unemployed since then.

Mr. Jones said he was never told by anyone at the Hooper Company that racing his car violated the agreement. No one from the company ever called him to say that what he was doing was wrong and that he should stop. He said there was no withholding for taxes or social security from his winnings. His understanding with his brother was that he could keep the trophies, but his brother got the prize money.

Mr. Jones explained that the newspaper articles upon which the company based its decision to fire him reported only "trophy" races in which he had won no money. He explained that that was the reason why his grievance stated there was no money associated with his racing. He said his name was not listed in any newspaper reports of feature races in which he actually did win money, although there was one "championship" race at the end of the year that paid more than $50 in Class C.

Mr. Jones said that when he wrote his grievance he had the newspaper articles about his races and knew they referred only to the trophy races he had won. When he filed the grievance he based what he said on what he knew was in the news articles. No one specifically had told him the company had terminated him for the articles in the newspaper; he figured that was the reason.

Mr. Jones testified that there was a mid-season race in addition to the championship race at the end of the season that paid more than $50 for first place. He did not win that race, but did win $50 in it. That was on June 18, before his injury.

Billy Jack Jones, brother of the grievant, testified that he was employed by Faust Auto Parts, Inc. as a mechanic and that he races stock cars as a hobby in Class C. He also testified that his brother had raced one of his cars in 1990. He said he had not paid his brother anything for driving the car and that he did not consider him his employee. They did have an understanding that any winnings would be put back into the car to keep it going. His brother was entitled to keep any trophies he won. Billy Jack testified that his pit crew members were also not paid; they performed their service as a hobby.

Jim Grimes, president and business manager for the local union, testified he had held that position since 1981 and prior to that had been chief steward. He said in his experience, he was unaware that the company had any practice of monitoring amateur sports activities of employees who were on leave. He stated that there had never been a company directive that employees could not receive prize money while competing in amateur sports. It was the union's understanding that amateur sport activities are not considered employment. If the company had any question about an employee's ability to perform his or her job based on outside activities, the company would have the right to cancel that employee's leave of absence and tell him or her to report to work.

Mr. Grimes recalled only one employee who was terminated for working while on a leave of absence. That employee owned a body shop and was receiving direct compensation for working on cars while on leave. He was self-employed.

Issue

Did Bubba Jones violate Section XII, Leaves of Absence, (G) Working While on Leave of Absence? If not, what is the appropriate remedy?

Relevant Contractual Provisions
Section XII
Leave of Absence
(G) Working While on Leave of Absence

No employee may engage in other employment while on an approved leave of absence unless he first secures written permission from the Manager of Labor Relations. Failure to obtain such permission will result in termination.

Positions of Parties

Position of the Company

In 1983, the company stated that it had terminated under the same language an employee on a medical leave of absence who worked for himself at a body shop and garage during the time he was on leave. This grievant had no intention of deceiving the company and was in fact ignorant of the provisions of the agreement. The provisions of the agreement were clear and unambiguous and the parties have agreed on the penalty for engaging in employment while on leave—termination.

In that case as in this, the grievant was earning money from an activity that he had engaged in before his leave of absence and continued to be engaged in during the leave. In both cases, the grievant did not ask permission from the company to continue to engage in such employment.

The company argued that the applicable language in the case mandates that all other employment must cease while on a medical leave of absence, regardless of whether carried on before the leave, unless written permission is obtained from the company. This mandate is particularly significant where the grievant is unable to perform his duties at the company, but continues to engage in the same activity for profit that he was engaged in when he suffered his injury, thereby depriving the employer of his services.

The company contended that the fact that the grievant earned only $65 while on leave is not at all relevant to this case. If he had advanced to Class A or B, he might have earned as much as a fully employed person in many industries. It is also irrelevant that the grievant gave his brother his earnings. Once the grievant won the prizes, he could do whatever he wished with his prize money. The principle is not the amount earned or the time during which he was employed as a race driver. The principle is that the grievant violated the contractual rule; the penalty is termination.

The company responded to the union contention that this is a recreation or hobby, not employment, by asking, what is the result of that argument had the grievant been so proficient as a driver that during the period of his leave he had raced at tracks all around the Southeast? The point is that he was engaged in this employment for profit while on medical leave without asking permission and that it was the same employment in which he initially injured himself.

The company pointed out that the *American Heritage Dictionary* defines employment as follows:

1. a. The act of employing. b. The state of being em-

ployed. 2. The work in which one is engaged; business. 3. An activity to which one devotes time.

Under these definitions, the grievant was clearly engaged in an activity to which he devoted time, and moreover, from which he received financial remuneration, irrespective of the amount.

The company claimed that if the arbitrator were to allow this grievance, it would be a change in the words of provisions of the agreement, an action prohibited by the agreement.

Position of the Union

The union stated that Bubba Jones's activity was not employment. The majority of cases in which an employer attempts to enforce a provision similar to the one in the instant case involves an employee who is "moonlighting" by holding a second job during off hours. It is usually clear in these cases that the employee has engaged in other employment. Arbitrator Volz, in *Alcan Aluminum Corp.*, 90 L.A 16 (1987), held that the company must meet its burden of proof by showing that the grievant engaged in other employment within the meaning of the applicable provision. He cited *Ballentine's Law Dictionary:*

> Work. Noun: Employment. Any form of physical or mental exertion, or both combined, for the attainment of some object other than recreation or amusement. . . . Physical or mental exertion, whether burdensome or not, controlled or required by an employer.

In *Standard Brands, Inc.*, 52 L.A. 918, 919 (1969), the grievant, while on a leave, frequently waited on customers and closed a friend's tavern at night, but was not paid. Arbitrator Trotta determined that this was not employment.

The company discharged Jones for engaging in employment while on leave of absence. Clearly amateur stock car racing does not fall under the definition of the word "work." Jones raced stock cars purely for recreational purposes. He did not consider himself an employee and no taxes were withheld from his prize money, which he gave to his brother for maintenance for his brother's car. Therefore, Jones was not self-employed, nor did he work for another employer. Jones himself stated this best in his grievance, "If this is employment, where is my paycheck?" The fact that Jones won a little money and two trophies does not turn a recreation into a job or employment.

The union claimed that the company had not published a rule that certain recreation would be considered employment. For discharge to be just, the employee must reasonably know his actions might lead to discharge. An employee could not have known that stock car racing would result in discharge. To give such an interpretation to Section XII, (G) would be unfair to Jones. While stock car racing may not have been the wisest thing to do while on a leave of absence, it certainly is not employment and no different from any other form of recreation.

Jones considered a later job to be employment. After his separation and after he was released for work in September, Jones worked for a landscaping business. This was a job: it was work considered by him to be employment.

The previous arbitration's matter is distinguishable. The employee had established an auto repair and body shop business in 1976. While on a leave in 1982, he was working in his repair shop. The company discharged him for working while on leave. The arbitrator upheld the discharge because he concluded the employee was engaged in self-employment that was supported by a stipulation of the parties that he was "working" during his leave. Unlike that case, Jones was not working while on a leave of absence but was only engaged in recreation.

The union concluded that the company has failed to meet its burden of proof by showing that Jones was engaged in other employment within the meaning of the provision. Therefore, the grievance of Bubba Jones should be sustained and he should be reinstated to his employment with full back pay and without loss of seniority and benefits, less any interim earnings from employment.

Questions

1. Evaluate the use of dictionary definitions in terms of their value in the arbitration proceedings.
2. Of what value is the use of previous arbitration cases and decisions of other arbitrators?
3. Does the arbitrator have any leeway in making a decision based on the language of Section XII?
4. Did Bubba Jones violate the agreement? Explain. If not, what should be the remedy?

CASE 3.2 Lost Income from Free-Lance Work Issues

1. Is the grievance arbitrable?
2. If so, did the company violate Article VIII, Section 3 when it did not approve free-lance work for news department on-air employees? If so, what shall be the remedy?

The grievance is between Professional News Reporters Association (PNRA) and Channel 4, WXYZ in Denver, Colorado. The initial contract between the parties is entitled "Staff News Agreement" and contains 3/8/88 as the date the contract was signed even though 2/19/88 is printed in the contract as the signing date.

On October 19, 1988 Rod Landers, an on-air reporter, submitted a request to the company for permission to write a story on the alleged "murder/assassination" of Rog Weel for possible publication. The company denied the request by letter dated December 9, 1988. On January 8, 1989, Landers (a union steward) wrote a letter that stated in part, "This is to refer to the Joint Standing Committee (JSC) a grievance concerning your letter of December 9th, denying me permission to free-lance an article on the 1984 murder of Rog Weel." On January 23, 1989 the executive secretary of the union wrote the company requesting a meeting of the JSC regarding Landers's denied request. This letter stated

> I am requesting a meeting of the Joint Standing Committee, as provided for in Article III of the PNRA Contract.
>
> The matter in controversy is the refusal of management to grant Rod Landers permission to submit for publication a free-lance article on the 1984 murder/assassination of Rog Weel. PNRA takes the position that the request was reasonable and should have been granted. We intend to seek compensation as a portion of the remedy in this matter.
>
> Please contact me as soon as possible to establish a meeting date and time.

On April 7, 1989, Landers submitted four complaint items to the company member of the JSC, only one of which involved the Landers article denial. On April 11, 1989, Landers, as steward and JSC member, wrote the company's JSC member, stating in part that "violations of Articles IV and V are now added to the 4 complaints listed in the letter of April 7."

Positions of the Parties

Union

The union contended that the company has approached requests for approval of free-lance work in an unreasonable manner. Employees have not been treated like responsible employees or adults; the company's approach is more like a parent who will not let his child leave the house or go to a dance for fear that something bad would happen. This was not the company's approach before the union's adoption of the contract that included Article VIII, Section 3. As adopted, according to the company at the bargaining table, Article VIII, Section 3 was only intended to codify existing practice.

The union argued that this case involves a crucial and fundamental issue to the union and its membership—it involves free-lance speech, career success, image, and income. In this industry, where the employees pit their career success (not to mention their financial achievement) against a marketplace where employees advance through public exposure, it is clear that the policy adopted by the company is a major setback to all employees within this bargaining unit. Such a setback could not have reasonably been anticipated under the plain language of Article VIII, Section 3, much less from the reasonable explanations and ex-

Source: The authors express their appreciation to Dr. Milden J. Fox, Jr., Texas A&M University, for providing this case.

amples offered by company spokesmen at the bargaining table.

The union submitted that the company had violated Article VIII, Section 3, by converting it into a "blanket no" provision as to paid free-lance work and by unreasonably denying or delaying a response to employee requests to do free-lance work. While Article VIII, Section 3 requires on-air personnel to obtain prior written approval before doing free-lance work, the company must make its decisions on a case-by-case basis. The company must exercise its rights in good faith and must not unreasonably deny approval in instances where the free-lance work would not adversely affect the image of the company or interfere with the employee's time requirements as to his or her company job. By definition, a failure to respond to a request for free-lance work is an unreasonable action by management and a violation of Article VIII, Section 3.

There can be no real doubt that the company's violation of Article VIII, Section 3, has impeded the career advancement and free speech of employees. This violation has chilled employees' efforts to seek out and do free-lance work on a paid and unpaid basis; therefore, monetary damages are difficult to assess on these matters. On the other hand, the record contains a clear basis for monetary awards to Landers and four others. Although Landers was the most persistent in seeking paid free-lance work opportunities and has documented his losses, the four other employees presented clear and unrebutted testimony of lost free-lance opportunities for which they would have been paid.

During cross-examination of Landers, the company suggested that there was no real proof that Landers would have sold articles he intended to write, since he had not written them and sold them. This same argument would apply to the efforts of the four others, to do free-lance work for which they had been sought, including industrial free-lance tapes and films, interviewing, and voice-over work. All testified they would have sought permission to do paid free-lance work, but for the known futility of seeking permission in light of the company's responses to earlier requests. Each also believed he or she would have been entitled to compensation.

The union claimed that the company is well aware that it violated the contract by making known a "blanket no" policy concerning paid free-lance work. This decision is cutting into the income of its employees who would otherwise supplement their income through free-lance work. The company was well aware that prior to negotiating this contract, the free-lance policy had been liberal and reasonable and that its post-contract actions have cost employees money that can be restored through the grievance procedure. Where the union has adhered to the policy of "comply now – grieve later," it would be a substantial abuse to deny a monetary remedy for this grievance. Accordingly, the union requested that the arbitrator fashion a damage remedy for each of the affected employees from the evidence in this case.

Company

The company's position was that this case was simply not arbitrable and might be summarily disposed of on that ground. A reading of Article VIII in its entirety clearly demonstrates that the news department on-air employees have agreed to devote their entire time and attention, best talents and abilities, to their jobs at the company. They have absolutely no contractual right to engage in free-lance activities; the union bargained away that right in hard-fought negotiations. In particular, Section 3 of Article VIII, by its very terms, is a blanket denial of any type of free-lance activity. A minor exception is provided for employees who obtain the *prior* written approval of the vice president and general manager of the company. Whether to grant such permission is a determination entirely within the discretion of the vice president and general manager. In this case, no permission was obtained.

Regarding the merits of the case, the union's arguments about the company denying employees the "opportunity for advancement" and "restricting free speech" are simply nonsense. In fact, the arguments emphasize the important business considerations underlying the company's insistence on Article VIII. Reporters work for the company because they chose that, and that alone, to be their job. The company does not consider its newscast a stepping-stone to the greater glory of industrial videos, voice-overs, or commercial endorsements. If the Great American Novel is trapped within a reporter's soul, he or she should by all means give up broadcast journalism and write it. Ernest Hemingway did not dash off *The Old Man and the Sea* during his lunch break at the *Morning Globe*.

The company argued that it was committed to bringing serious, responsible journalism to its viewers. Fundamental to that undertaking is the necessity to avoid even the appearance of conflicting interests or the impression that its reporters are "for sale." The company has given its reporters the opportunity to work in the field they have trained for and, presumably, chosen as their life's work. In exchange, those reporters and their union have agreed to give their jobs their entire and exclusive time and attention, their best talents and abilities. The company concluded that no contract provision had been violated and the grievance should be denied.

Pertinent Provisions of Agreement

Article IV: Non-Discrimination

The Company and the Union agree not to discriminate against any person because of race, sex, color, creed, age, ethnic group, religion, or national origin, or because of his/her membership in or affiliation with, or non-membership in or non-affiliation with, the Union, each party fully recognizing that each employee has individual rights under existing state and federal laws.

Article V: Management Functions

Section 1. It is expressly agreed that all rights which ordinarily vest in and are exercised by employers who have no collective bargaining agreement with their employees, except those which are clearly relinquished herein by the Company, shall continue to vest exclusively in and be exercised exclusively by the Company. It is agreed that the parties have fully bargained about the rights of management by the Company and that, except as otherwise expressly limited by this Agreement and by law, the Company retains the full and exclusive right to fully manage and conduct its business affairs, which rights include specifically, but are not limited to the following: to hire, train, demote, transfer, suspend, discipline or discharge for just cause, to assign and allocate work to and direct the working force; to relieve employees from duty because of lack of work, or for other legitimate reasons; to establish and change work schedules; to establish and enforce reasonable rules and regulations for the conduct of its employees; to adopt any technological changes or processes; to determine the number of employees to be employed; to determine the type and location of all facilities, all types of services to be rendered, all kinds and amounts of equipment, machinery, apparatus, et cetera, all technological processes to be used to determine all methods and schedules of operation; to subcontract work; and to manage the Company's business and affairs.

Section 2. The Company will exercise all of the aforesaid rights in good faith. Insofar as this Article is concerned, none of the aforesaid exclusive management rights are subject to arbitration procedure, provided, however, if the Union claims that an act of management pursuant to this section violates any other provision of this Agreement, such claim of a violation, but not this Article, shall be subject to the grievance and arbitration procedures of this Agreement.

Article VIII: On-Air Personnel

Section 3. News Department on-air employees are to devote their entire and exclusive time and attention to the performance of the services herein provided for and shall not devote any of their time or render any services of any kind or nature whatsoever for any radio or television station, network or community antenna television system or for any other person, firm, association, entity, corporation or business whatsoever, without the prior written approval of the Vice President and General Manager of WXYZ.

Questions

1. In determining whether the grievance is arbitral, review the Supreme Court's decisions in the first part of Chapter 9. Is the grievance arbitral? Why? Why not?
2. Review the criteria used by arbitrators in making decisions in Chapter 9. Which principles should be used in this case?
3. Weigh the contract language and the positions of the parties. How should the arbitrator rule? What are your reasons?

CASE 3.3 Discharge of the Two-Last-Name Employee

Issue: Was Marcia Kaye discharged for just cause? If not, what is the appropriate remedy?

Aegean, the employer, operates a plant in St. Paul, Minnesota where room air conditioning units are manufactured. The Allied Workers, the union, is the exclusive bargaining agent for all production and unexcluded nonproduction employees.

On March 3, 1988, Marcia Kaye, the grievant, completed a form entitled, "Aegean Employment Application," an employment form that provides an employer with information concerning a prospective employee's work history, educational background, and related data. This information allows the employer to make a decision on whether or not to hire the applicant. The form also contains a signature line for an applicant to sign to attest to the truth of the information provided. The line is immediately preceded by the following language: "I authorize the investigation of all statements contained in this application. I understand that misrepresentation or omission of facts called for is cause for dismissal."

Ms. Kaye signed and dated the signature line. Also included on the employment application was the question, "Have you ever been employed by this company or an affiliated company?" After this question Ms. Kaye checked the "No" box. After interviewing Ms. Kaye and examining the information contained on the employment application, Aegean hired her on March 9, 1988.

From the date Ms. Kaye was hired on March 9, 1988, until the date of her discharge on March 24, 1989, she had what the employer characterized as an extremely poor attendance record, including 25 full days of absences and 11 days where she either left early or was tardy. These absences do not include the 29 days Ms. Kaye was out in early 1989 for a work-related injury, for which she received worker's compensation. Nor do these absences include the 4 weeks of work Ms. Kaye missed in August 1988 when she was laid off. Ms. Kaye's poor attendance record and the numerous occasions on which she was tardy or left work early resulted in her receiving three written warnings in her short period of employment. However, Ms. Kaye was not terminated in 1989 because of her attendance. Ms. Kaye's severe attendance problem brought her to management's attention and the realization she had worked for the company previously.

In March, 1989, Aegean's personnel director discovered that Ms. Kaye had worked for Aegean on prior occasions under a different last name. An investigation disclosed that she had worked for Aegean on two prior occasions; once from October 2, 1967 until she quit on February 29, 1969, and again from September 10, 1973 until July 25, 1974. Ms. Kaye was technically on the payroll until May 17, 1976, but was laid off from July 25, 1974 until May 1976, when she voluntarily quit after being recalled. During these periods of employment, Ms. Kaye had worked under the name Marcia Smith. During her second term of employment with Aegean from September 1973, until July 1974, she had a serious attendance and tardiness problem, and received a written warning that further discipline would be taken if her record did not improve. A report by one of her supervisors during her second term of employment referred to her poor attendance record. This report also gave her a "below average" performance rating as an employee, noting that she was not dependable, and concluded with the recommendation that she not be rehired by Aegean if that possibility ever occurred.

After discovering that Ms. Kaye had worked for Aegean on two prior occasions under the name of Marcia Smith, the personnel director requested that the Personnel Department search for prior applications of the grievant under the name Marcia Jones. This search

Source: The authors express their appreciation to Dr. James P. O'Grady, Jr., St. Louis Community College, for providing this case.

resulted in finding that Marcia Jones had applied for employment on three prior occasions, twice in 1980 and again in 1981. Although only one application form was used, the date on the application was changed each time she resubmitted it or inquired about the status of the application. On the application filed in 1980 and 1981, Marcia Jones had indicated that she had been employed by Aegean on prior occasion, unlike the answer given on the application she filed in 1988. Although the grievant applied in 1980 and 1981 and the employer hired or recalled a substantial number of employees, she was not hired because of the poor attendance and work record she had when she was employed under the name Marcia Smith. Additionally, the fact that one of Marcia Smith's supervisors did not recommend that she be rehired was influential in the decision not to hire the grievant in 1980 and 1981.

The employer claimed that the grievant's identity might have been discovered earlier, except that none of the supervisors she had had during her prior employment were still employed by Aegean at the time she was hired in 1988. Additionally, no one in the Personnel Department—the department responsible for hiring and reviewing applications—had been employed in that department when the grievant last worked for the company. When it did become apparent that Marcia Kaye had lied on her employment application in 1988, the employer took action and discharged the grievant. The employer stated that it had acted in a similar manner on other occasions when employees had falsified their employment applications.

On March 28, 1989, the grievant filed a grievance. The grievance was processed in accordance with the terms of the labor agreement without resolution. The parties asserted that the matter was properly before the arbitrator for a final and binding decision.

Pertinent Provisions of the Agreement

Article 21: Prerogatives of Management

21.1 Management Rights and Functions The Union agrees that the function of Management belongs solely to the Company, and that it will not interfere with the Company's free exercise of this function.

21.1 Management's Functions Defined The functions of Management include, among others: to select and hire new employees; to direct the working force; to formulate and enforce the plant rules; and to discipline, suspend or discharge for cause; to transfer or relieve employees from duty because of lack of work or other reasons consistent with efficient operation; to assign work to employees; to decide the number and location of its facilities; to determine the items to be manufactured; including the means, place, and processes of manufacturing; to determine the methods of work measurements and to establish standards of performance; and to introduce new or improved production methods or facilities.

Relevant Provisions from the Employee Handbook

Attendance

Employees must be at their appointed work places ready to work at the scheduled starting time, and shall remain at such work places and at work until the scheduled cleanup or quitting time.

If you should become ill while at work, report immediately to your Supervisor, or the First Aid nurse on duty, or to the Personnel office. Absence from work for any reason, except where permission has been granted previously, must be reported as soon as possible, but, in any case, no later than the beginning of your shift on the third day of absence. Failure to report in the allotted time constitutes a voluntary quit. If your absence continues more than a period of one week, it will be necessary for you to apply through the Personnel Department for a written "Leave of Absence" in order to retain your employment status. All "Leaves of Absence" will be granted in accordance with the provisions outlined in the Employee Agreement.

Failure to report back to work after a "Lunch Break," unless excused by your Foreman, will be considered a voluntary quit and services will be terminated.

* * *

How We Live Together

* * *

Unless there are extenuating circumstances, the Management considers the following violations, and similar infractions sufficient reason for imposing a penalty ranging from minor disciplinary action up to and including discharge.

* * *

16. Falsifying any reports or records, including personnel, absence, sickness, production records, work tickets and time cards.

Employer Position

The employer argued that the grievant's falsification of her employment application was willful and purposeful. Moreover, the false information was material to the employer's decision to hire her. The employer maintained that the agreement states that the right to select and hire new employees belongs solely to the employer. By falsifying her application, Marcia Kaye had effectively obliterated that right. Therefore, Aegean held that the discharge of Marcia Kaye was for just cause and asked that the grievance be denied.

Union Position

The union first argued that the mere falsification of an employment application in itself was not sufficient to discharge Marcia Kaye unless the falsification materially affected or could affect the employee's ability to perform her assigned tasks. Moreover, the application is not a record as defined in Rule No. 16. In other cases, where the employer had discharged other employees, the false information given by the applicant involved a prior injury suffered by the employee. Further, Marcia Kaye's absenteeism record is not listed as a basis for her discharge, and therefore, absenteeism should not be considered. Ms. Kaye is simply being adversely affected because her last name changed; there is no law against that. As a result of these arguments, the union requested that Marcia Kaye be reinstated with full back pay.

Questions

1. Was the rule governing the information on application forms job-related?
2. Does the change in the last name of the grievant mean that the information on the application form was not falsified?
3. In what way, if any, should the arbitrator consider the grievant's absenteeism and tardiness records?
4. Is it appropriate to use false information on an application form to discharge an employee after the employee has been hired?
5. Is it reasonable for a job applicant to withhold certain information if he or she knows that the inclusion of that information will cause the employer to refuse him or her employment?
6. Weigh the evidence and the arguments. You be the arbitrator. How should you rule? Why?

CASE 3.4 Discharge for Possession

Issue: Was the discharge of grievant Ron Gates for just cause? If not, what is the appropriate remedy?

Statement of Grievance

"Protest termination. The Union demands that the Company cease and desist from violating the Labor Agreement, that the incident(s) be rectified, that proper compensation, including benefits and overtime, at the applicable rate of pay, be paid for all losses; and further that those affected be made whole in every respect."

Source: The authors express their appreciation to Dr. A. Dale Allen, Jr., Baylor University, for providing this case.

Provisions of the Company's Information Booklet

Drug or alcohol use will not be tolerated at our place of work, not only from the standpoint of an employee's personal safety, but the safety of fellow employees, the community, and the safety and protection of the Company's operations. Everyone should be aware of our policies on drug and alcohol abuse which are:

> The abuse of any drug (including a prescription drug) and use, possession, sale, or transportation of any illegal drug on Company premises is cause for discipli-

nary action up to and including discharge and possible referral to law enforcement agencies.

Being in a partially or completely intoxicated state, resulting from the consumption of alcoholic beverages, or introducing, possessing, or using alcoholic beverages while on Company premises is cause for disciplinary action up to and including discharge. An exception is that alcoholic beverages may be kept (but not consumed) inside a vehicle in the parking lots outside the primary gates.

Position of the Company

The Company noted that at the time of his discharge in April 1988, grievant Ron Gates was a Refinery Process Operator in the Alkylation/Thermal Cracking Department. He was hired in June 1984. As a Process Operator, he was responsible for controlling the operating conditions of his unit including maintaining correct pressures, temperatures, and flows through the columns, furnaces, and compressors. These process units must be continuously operated safely. To do otherwise presents a hazard to life and property within the complex and the neighboring community.

The Company has repeatedly emphasized over the years the incompatibility of drugs and the Company's business. Nevertheless, drug-related problems continued to surface. Back on December 28, 1982, employees were advised by a bulletin board posting that searches of employee-operated vehicles may occur "on all Company property including Company property outside the primary Refinery and Chemical work areas, such as the parking lots, entry roads, cafeterias, etc." Search efforts that followed resulted in the discharge of two employees who refused to allow a search after suspected contraband was observed in cars parked in employee parking lots.

On July 3, 1984, the month following the grievant's employment, the complex manager sent another letter to all employees, this time noting that "we need to continue to work together to achieve a *drug-free environment* at the Complex *for the safety and welfare of everyone.*" Employees were told that in keeping with this goal, "Each employee is responsible for assuring that no illicit drugs are in his or her possession when on Company property. Also, each employee is considered responsible for the contents in his or her vehicle while on Company property. Therefore, each employee should take measures to ensure his or her vehicle is drug free before entering the Complex." All employees, through the issuance in 1985 of the updated *Employee Information Booklet* (Handbook), were further warned that "the abuse of any drug (including a prescription drug) and use, possession, sale, or transportation of any illegal drug on Company premises is cause for disciplinary action up to and including discharge." As the abuse of drugs continued, the Company strengthened its policy to include drug testing by urinalysis.

The likelihood that contraband was present in the grievant's car first came to light on the morning of April 20, 1988. The grievant was working the graveyard shift when Officer Grace Jackson, a protection guard, on a routine patrol of the refinery's employee parking lot, approached and looked into the window of the grievant's car. Jackson observed a small plastic bag and a package of cigarette papers in the partially open dash ashtray. Since marijuana is commonly kept in plastic bags and cigarette papers are often used to make marijuana cigarettes, Jackson immediately informed her sergeant of the discovery. Company Security Inspector Dave Smythe went to the grievant's car. He, too, noticed the contents from outside the car, but he ordered no search because he could not see what was in the plastic bag, nor did he see any marijuana.

The next night, April 21, 1988, at 12:30 a.m., Security Inspector Smythe checked Gates's vehicle again and observed what appeared to be a marijuana roach (the butt of a marijuana cigarette) in the right rear portion of the vehicle. Smythe said: "There was an ashtray attached to the door panel there and the roach was lying on a portion of the ashtray."

Employees have access to the parking lot during their shifts. Two hours before Inspector Smythe's April 21 visit to Gates's car, the grievant exited the refinery from his graveyard shift assignment and entered his vehicle. Gates explained that he went there to retrieve a picture and took it back to his process unit.

Once the marijuana roach was observed on April 21, the car was searched in accordance with Company policy. Permission to search the vehicle was received from Gates and keys supplied by him were used to open the car. Gates was shown the marijuana roach lying in the ashtray prior to the beginning of the search.

As Gates watched, a plastic bag containing marijuana, cigarette papers, and a second roach were retrieved by Smythe from the dash ashtray. They initially observed a marijuana roach was also retrieved from the back ashtray. Smythe testified there were numerous marijuana seeds and stems in the carpet and on the seats. Smythe stated "I picked up a few of them, but there were so many you couldn't pick them all up."

Gates told Smythe that the vehicle belonged to his mother-in-law and pointed out he very seldom drove it. In the presence of Gates, a narcotics identification kit was used by Inspector Smythe to test the substances for the presence of THC, the active ingredient in marijuana. The test was positive. The plastic bag, the two marijuana roaches, and some of the seeds were photographed by Smythe. Then Gates was suspended pending further investigation.

An investigatory meeting was held with Gates at 3:00 p.m. on April 21, 1988. Department Manager Bill Colt, who conducted the meeting, testified, "Gates started out his summary by giving us a little bit of background. He mentioned that when he was in high school, he hung around with several folks that were on the football team and that particular crowd while in high school smoked marijuana. Gates himself admitted he had smoked marijuana in high school."

At the meeting, Gates further told the Company officials that the car he was driving was his mother-in-law's and he normally drove it to work. This was contrary to what he had told Inspector Smythe at the time of the search. Gates stated he had loaned his car to a friend and the marijuana belonged to the friend, a parolee named Keith Zeeland. Gates commented that he normally checked his car for marijuana and other things because he knew that this friend used marijuana and that it could affect his job if found there. Gates admitted that he very clearly understood that drugs were not acceptable on Company property.

The next day, April 22, 1988, Department Manager Colt and Employee Relations Representative Liz Rope held a telephone conversation with someone who claimed to be Keith Zeeland. Colt said Zeeland stated he had been using Gates's car, but he denied ownership of the marijuana, stating it belonged to two other individuals who happened to be with him each time he used the car that week. Zeeland further stated they smoked marijuana every day they used the car and would usually drink a six-pack of beer. Zeeland would check to make sure the beer cans and other alcoholic beverages were out of the car, but didn't check for marijuana.

Gates called Colt at home on the night of April 26. Gates knew that termination was in order, as Colt explained: "Gates wanted to tell me that he hoped that I could find it in my heart not to terminate him as a result of this particular incident."

In making their decision, the Company officials considered the above facts, Gates's work record, and his short service. In addition, the Company applied the standard set forth by a previous arbitration decision, as it had in other cases. In that case the arbitrator dealt with the Company's prohibition against possession of drugs and concluded the rule was violated when an employee brought an automobile containing marijuana on Company property when the employee knew or had reason to know the marijuana was present. Gates was informed of the Company's decision to terminate him on April 27, 1988.

Gates stated that he took a drug test on Friday, April 22. Yet, the results of that urinalysis showed an admission date of April 28. When pressed on this discrepancy, the grievant said that he had taken two drug tests, one on April 22 at McGregor Clinic and one on April 28 at Ben Taub Hospital. No document was presented showing the first drug test had ever occurred.

The union, in hopes of saving the grievant's job, argued disparate treatment. In this connection, the union emphasized the cases of three individuals, Fury, Matthews, and Provorse, who were found to have marijuana in their personal vehicles while at work but were not discharged. The union explained that there was another case in which the employee was discharged. Like discrimination, disparate treatment is an affirmative defense and the burden of proof is on the claimant.

In 1984, hourly employee Fury indicated a friend might have left behind the marijuana found in his car in 1984. At that time, the lack of clarity in Company policy as to an employee's responsibility for marijuana present in his or her car parked in an employee lot led the Company to the conclusion that something less than termination was appropriate.

In the 1987 Matthews case, a single marijuana roach was found on the floorboard in an otherwise clean vehicle. When employee Matthews was questioned, he denied any knowledge of it. There was an implication that perhaps the marijuana had been "planted" in the vehicle. Matthews further pointed out that his power door locks did not work properly. The search procedure at the time did not include showing the individual the item that caused the search to be requested. As a result, the Company changed procedures, requiring the alleged contraband to be pointed out to the person prior to the opening of the vehicle.

In the Provorse case that arose in June 1987, Ms. Provorse parked her van in an unauthorized parking space. The guards looked in the window of the vehicle in order to determine ownership. In so doing, they saw a marijuana roach in an ashtray in the console between the seats. In that case, again, the employee stated she did not know where the marijuana came from. She said she had loaned her van to her brother to move furniture and was subsequently able to establish his responsibility for the marijuana. There was no proof that Provorse had reason to know that her brother used marijuana or that marijuana would be in her car. These facts, along with her cooperation, led the Company to conclude she had not breached Company rules.

In another case arising after the Matthews and Provorse cases but also in 1987, hourly employee Windsor was discharged for possession of marijuana on Company premises. A single marijuana roach was found in the front seat of his vehicle in the Company parking lot. In that case, Windsor's claim that the marijuana belonged to someone else turned out not to be credible. The standard outlined by the earlier arbitration case was applied and Windsor was discharged. That case was dropped by the union prior to arbitration.

Gates suggested that he was discharged because of racial discrimination. However, neither Gates nor the union made this allegation during the investigation prior to his discharge. Additionally, Gates did not file a grievance or an EEOC charge as a result of the alleged discrimination. Evidence regarding the race of other employees who were found with marijuana in their vehicles was presented. Matthews (black) and Provorse (white) were not terminated. Windsor is white and was terminated.

A letter was written by a Keith Zeeland, but he did not appear at any hearing. In his letter, he claimed to be involved with marijuana and stated that he was Gates's friend.

The Company argued that there were serious policy considerations in this case. Marijuana in an employee's car on the premises of a petrochemical complex is a recognized hazard. This is particularly so when employees can only reach a refinery parking lot by driving for almost a mile along a Company road surrounded by process units and storage tanks. When employees, as here, have access to their cars throughout their shifts, the Company is properly alarmed with these findings. If one can be exonerated by just saying "it belongs to my friend," what is to stop employees from smoking marijuana in their cars? The Company requested that this grievance be denied.

Position of the Union

Grievant Ron Gates was hired by the Company in June 1984. In April 1988, he was a No. 1 Operator for the Company and had no active discipline in his record. Very early in the morning on April 21, 1988, during a routine check of vehicles in the Company parking lot, a security guard for the Company spotted what looked like a marijuana roach in the back ashtray of the vehicle driven to work by Gates. Gates was asked if he would allow the Company to search the vehicle. He had no objection, willingly provided the keys, and the vehicle was searched in his presence.

During this search, a substance was noticed in the back ashtray. It was identified as a small marijuana roach. In addition, some seeds were found among the worn and dirty carpet and seats of the vehicle; another small roach and a plastic bag with a small quantity of marijuana were discovered in the partially closed front ashtray of the vehicle. The Company then searched the grievant's locker, but no drugs or drug paraphernalia were discovered therein.

Gates was unaware of the presence of any illegal substance in his car, and stated initially that he did not know how they could have gotten there. When asked who the vehicle belonged to, he said that it was registered in his mother-in-law's name. The company checked on the registration of the vehicle and found that it was registered in the name of Irma Lee Sadie.

The grievant was suspended pending investigation that same morning. He then called his friend, Keith Zeeland, to whom he had loaned the car on 4 of the

5 previous days, to ask if he knew anything about the marijuana in the car. Zeeland initially denied it, but then admitted that some friends had smoked marijuana with him in the vehicle during this time, and that it must belong to them. Gates then notified the Company that the marijuana was there because he had loaned the vehicle to his friend, and gave the Company Zeeland's name and work telephone number. On April 22, at 10:00 a.m., the Company called Zeeland to confirm this.

During a meeting later on the same day, the grievant told the Company that he smoked marijuana when he was in high school, about 10 years earlier, but that he quit once he got into the military service. The Company had absolutely no reason to believe that Gates was a user of marijuana. The union stated that no impairment was ever observed with Gates. He had a good work record, a good safety record, and no prior discipline that remained in his record. Even the Company admitted that Gates was a "good operator," and had been told by several supervisors that he was "one of the best operators in his section." Still, the Company fired him on April 27, 1988, for possession of marijuana, on the grounds that he should not have loaned his car to a known drug user.

Gates did not know that his friend had ever used drugs in his car and there is no work rule that would prevent an employee from doing what he wants with his personal vehicle while he is off duty, or that would prevent him from associating with anyone he chooses during his off-duty hours. The union argued that the charge of possession of an illegal substance requires that the employee have either actual knowledge or, at a minimum, a solid reason to know that an illegal substance might be contained in a vehicle that is brought onto Company property. Gates had stated that he had no actual knowledge that the drugs were in his vehicle, and that he had no reason to suspect that there would be any drugs in his vehicle. Although he knew that Zeeland smoked marijuana, Gates had loaned his vehicle to this friend before and had never seen any drugs left in it afterwards. At the time of this incident, Gates had been working double shifts for 4 of the past 5 days. Therefore, he understandably would have been tired and would not have had an opportunity to check his vehicle thoroughly during the time period in question.

Gates, who does smoke cigarettes, stated that he only smoked one or two cigarettes a week in his vehicle. Therefore, it is not surprising that he would not have used the front ashtray during the time that the plastic bag and roach were left in it, so he would not have been aware of their presence. It was inconceivable that Gates would have noticed them and still driven the vehicle onto Company property because he was well aware of the Company rule prohibiting bringing illegal drugs onto Company premises.

The union acknowledged that Gates's car was "not in mint condition." There was a lot of dirt in the vehicle; the carpeting looked as if it had "never been vacuumed, or not in recent history"; and the upholstery was in a bad state. Even the security guards, who carried powerful flashlights, said that they could not see any marijuana or any other illegal substance in the car on the evening of April 19 or the early morning hours of April 20 when they allegedly first saw a portion of a plastic bag and some cigarette papers protruding from the partially closed front ashtray.

The union agreed that the Company has had a policy prohibiting the possession of illegal drugs on Company property for a number of years. During this time period, several employees have had illegal drugs found in their vehicle. However, Gates was only the third such employee to be terminated. The first terminated employee, James Wilson, took his grievance case to arbitration and was reinstated with full back pay. The second terminated employee, Danny Windsor, got another job in the interim, and elected not to pursue his grievance to arbitration. Therefore, Gates was the *only* employee terminated by the Company for possession who had not been reinstated and who desired to pursue his grievance.

The first Company employee disciplined for possession, Tony Fury, received only a 15-day suspension from the Company. Other employees, whose circumstances were more comparable to those of Gates, received only a written reprimand from the Company. One of these employees was Terry Provorse. The Company observed a marijuana roach in the front ashtray of her vehicle in 1987. She initially testified that she did not know where it came from, but then she said that her brother, to whom she had loaned the vehicle, must have left it there. She admitted in the investigation meetings that she knew that her brother smoked marijuana. At this time, she was already on a written reprimand, a serious stage of discipline, for attendance. However, she was not terminated for this incident; instead, she merely received an additional written reprimand.

Another employee, Brent Matthews, in 1987 drove a vehicle on Company premises in which a roach was discovered. He denied knowledge of how the drug came to be in his vehicle, and claimed that there was a problem with locking the doors on his vehicle. Matthews was not terminated; he received only a written reprimand.

The Company cited three decisions that it believed were applicable to this case. First, Tony Wright was asked for permission to inspect his vehicle, in which two roaches had been observed. Wright adamantly refused to allow the company to search his vehicle, and became loud, belligerent, and profane. He repeated this refusal in spite of warnings that doing so would constitute insubordination that would result in serious disciplinary action, including termination. An arbitrator found that Wright's actions created a suspicion that the roaches, which were observed from outside the vehicle, were only the "tip of the iceberg" and that a thorough search would have revealed additional drugs that Wright was trying to conceal. Consequently, the arbitrator discredited Wright's testimony that the roaches belonged to a friend and denied the grievance. He found that Wright should have disposed of the roaches regardless of who they belonged to, rather than risk discharge.

The union argued that Gates's case differed in two important respects. First, Wright never claimed that he did not know the roaches were present at the time he drove the vehicle on Company property. Second, Wright repeatedly refused to allow an inspection of his vehicle, and was thus terminated for insubordination. Gates, on the other hand, acquiesced to the search and fully cooperated with it in every respect. He stated at every stage of the investigatory meetings and grievance proceedings that he had no prior knowledge that his vehicle contained any illegal drugs.

A second decision cited by the Company was a 1986 case regarding grievant James Wilson. In that case, the grievant was reinstated with full back pay, because the arbitrator found that the employee did not know the marijuana was present in his vehicle and had no reason to know that it might be there. Wilson provided keys and fully cooperated with the search of his vehicle, as did Gates. However, when Wilson was asked to take a urinalysis test, he refused to do so, although he had initially stated that he had not used marijuana for some years. He later admitted that he had smoked part of a marijuana cigarette while he was on vacation in California in the 2 weeks before the search occurred. In addition, he could not explain the presence of the roach found in the back of his vehicle. He originally thought it might have been left there by his girlfriend, but she denied it.

In contrast to the Wilson case, Gates voluntarily took two urinalysis tests that showed negative results. Gates was also able to adequately explain the presence of the marijuana found in his mother-in-law's car, and this explanation was fully confirmed by Zeeland. Thus Gates's defense was even more compelling than that of Wilson, who was reinstated with full back pay.

A third decision cited by the Company was one involving Nathaniel Mims who had attendance problems resulting from his drug and alcohol dependency. He had been arrested twice, had lied to the Company about certain absences, and had obtained and cashed a second pay check for a single pay period. The union found it difficult to see what analogy the company could draw from this distinctly different scenario, which did not involve the unintentional bringing of a minuscule quantity of drugs onto the Company's parking lot.

In the present case, Gates did not know the drugs were present in his mother-in-law's vehicle. The Company had no reason to believe that he had ever been impaired on the job, and had never requested that he take a drug test. Gates's friend, Zeeland, admitted that he was responsible for the drugs in the vehicle. Thus, this case was much more similar to that of Terry Provorse. However, the Company chose to terminate Gates, a black male, whereas Provorse, a white female, received only a written reprimand.

The union argued that in view of Gates's excellent prior work history and the absence of any prior disciplinary record, his complete cooperation during the search of his vehicle and locker, the minor nature of the infraction, the lack of evidence that he ever came to work under the influence of marijuana or suspected that marijuana might be present in his vehicle, and the fact that putting Gates back to work would pose no risk to the Company, to Company property, or to other employees, the grievance should be sustained. Therefore, the union requested that the arbitrator sustain the grievance, reinstate the grievant, and make him whole, with full back pay and all other benefits, including overtime and interest.

Questions

1. Was the Company rule reasonable? Was it communicated effectively?
2. Of what value are the previous incidents presented by both parties?
3. Of what value are the previous arbitrators' decisions presented by the parties?
4. Evaluate the argument that discrimination was involved in the Company's decision.
5. What are the Company's best arguments? The union's best arguments?
6. Since the Company has the burden of proof in this case, should the arbitrator sustain the grievance? Explain.

CASE 3.5 Failure to Pay Laid-Off Employees for Holidays

Newtown Manufacturers operates a furniture plant in Newtown, South Carolina. The employees in the bargaining unit are represented by the Furniture Employees of America. The agreement negotiated by the company and the union became effective on July 1, 1988, and was to remain in effect for two years. The immediate grievance resulted from the company's decision not to pay 48 laid-off production workers, who were members of the bargaining unit, for Memorial Day, May 28, 1989.

The Chief Steward, Claude Castle, filed a timely grievance on June 16, 1989, on behalf of all employees. The grievance follows:

> In violation of but not limited to Act VIII, 5(c), the union grieves that employees' rights have been violated; the employees were on lay-off. There was a written request presented to the company that attendance requirements be waived and the people be paid holiday pay. The company did not pay the employees. The union asks that the employees be paid holiday pay for Memorial Day.

The company's reply came from Roy Nabb, plant manager, in a letter dated June 19, 1989, which follows.

> I have considered the union's request for holiday pay. First, so far as I can tell, the situation was unfortunate and was handled exactly as stipulated in the labor contract. If it is implied that the company contrived the lay-off to avoid paying holiday pay, it is simply not true. The one and only reason for the lay-off was that we had no orders.
>
> We are again rapidly getting in the same fix, especially at Newtown, and I have instructed supervisors to try to let everybody work through July 4 so that they will qualify to get holiday pay.

The union appealed the company's decision for arbitration. A hearing was held, in which both parties were given full opportunity to present their positions, examine and cross-examine witnesses, and write post-hearing briefs. The company provided no witnesses; it presented written statements from David Hunt, the company's president. Both parties submitted written briefs and reply briefs.

Issue

Did the company violate the contract by failing to pay laid-off employees for Memorial Day?

Pertinent Contract Provisions

Article VIII: Holidays

Section 1. The following are recognized as paid holidays:

New Year's Day
Good Friday
Memorial Day
July 4th
Labor Day
Thanksgiving Day
Day after Thanksgiving
Christmas Day

Section 2. In the event a recognized holiday falls on a Saturday, the previous Friday shall be observed as the holiday. In the event a recognized holiday falls on Sunday, the following Monday shall be observed as the holiday. In the event a recognized holiday falls within an employee's vacation, the vacation period shall be extended by one paid day for the purposes of observing such holiday, or the company will pay the employee for the holiday, in which case the company will give the employee at least a one (1) week's notice prior to the vacation shutdown.

Section 3. The amount of holiday pay will be eight (8) times an employee's regular hourly rate at the time of the holiday.

Section 4. In the event that a holiday is worked, the employee shall receive time and one-half (1-1/2) times his regular rate for all hours worked, in addition to holiday pay. Holidays not worked shall count for the purpose of computing overtime. Any employee laid off in the week in which a recognized holiday falls shall be paid for that holiday.

Section 5. An employee shall receive holiday pay provided he meets the following requirements:

(a) An employee must have worked the full scheduled workday before and the full scheduled workday after such paid holiday.

(b) The employee must have performed work for the company within twenty (20) workdays preceding such holiday, in addition to the full scheduled workday before the holiday.

(c) Should an employee fail to meet the foregoing requirements because of an absence from work, for a period not to exceed ten (10) consecutive days, because of illness, injury, jury duty, or other reason beyond his control, the company may, upon request in writing from the employee, grant permission for the absence and waive the attendance requirements for holiday pay.

(d) During the period of probation, new employees are not eligible for holiday pay.

Positions of the Parties

Union Position

The union's positions were presented in oral arguments by Claude Castle; testimony of Joe Horton, a member of the negotiating committee; and a written brief. First, the union argued that the grievance is covered by the provisions of the agreement and is "not limited to Article VIII, 5(c)." The union contended that the words "not limited to" mean that the grievance pertains to contract violations of more than the specific interpretation of one narrow provision.

Following this argument, the union presented the testimony of its only witness, Joe Horton, and its post-hearing brief. Horton, a member of the negotiation committee, testified that Section 4 applied to limited situations in which the company schedules workers, such as maintenance employees, to work during a vacation week shutdown. These employees actually work for the first part of the week but are laid off during the week. According to Section 4, these workers would be entitled to holiday pay.

The union further argued that Section 5 lists the requirements employees must meet to be eligible for holiday pay. The union had proposed a longer period than 20 days in which an employee could be laid off and still receive holiday pay, but it accepted the 20-day period because layoffs usually do not last longer than a month. Thus, even though the company had argued that Section 5 does not apply to layoff situations, Section 5 clearly covers a period of layoff that does not exceed the time limit.

The union contended that all 48 employees had met the requirements of Article VIII, 5(a), "by working the scheduled day before and scheduled day after the holiday." The union concluded the following:

> There is no dispute that the grievants worked their scheduled workday before the holiday and their scheduled workday after the holiday. There is also no dispute that the grievants performed work for the company within 20 workdays preceding the holiday, in addition to working the scheduled workday before the

holiday. All of the grievants had completed their probationary period.

The union's position is that the requirements an employee must meet in order to receive holiday pay have been met in this case. We do not see the last sentence of Section 4 adding to or taking away from the requirements as listed in Section 5.

Because of all the reasons stated above, it is the position of the union that the company violated the language and intent of the contract. The union respectfully requests that its grievance be granted.

Company Position

The company argued its case by presenting a copy of papers handwritten by company president David Hunt, its brief, and its reply brief (also written by Hunt). Hunt spelled out the company's major arguments in his written submissions:

> The facts and occurrences of the case are not in dispute. The disagreement concerns the applicability and interpretation of certain provisions of the contract.
>
> The company holds that the contract clause which governs the situation here involved is Article VIII, Section 4. The last sentence in that section reads: "Any employee laid off in the week in which a recognized holiday falls shall be paid for that holiday." This sentence specifically addresses the situation in dispute.
>
> The union grievance was filed based on Article VIII, 5(c). The company maintains that it did not violate Article VIII, 5(c) of the contract. Section 5(c) was designed to permit the company to give consideration to an individual employee who lost time from work because of extenuating circumstances—some unusual event which prevented that employee from reporting for work.
>
> Section 5 of Article VIII was not intended as a layoff provision for a large portion of the plant employees. Section 5 (with the exception of paragraph (d), which is a blanket exclusion of probationary employees) refers to the individual employee with an individual problem. Section 5(a), (b), and (c) deal with an individual employee, not a large group of employees ("an employee shall . . .," "an employee must . . .," "the employee must . . .," "should an employee fail . . .").
>
> Moreover, the company is not compelled to act in a prescribed way. Article VIII, 5(c) states that the company may act in a certain manner, but it need not. The paragraph does not state that the company must or shall or will grant the requested relief. The paragraph simply states that the company has the sole choice of action. It may or may not waive the attendance requirements. There is no obligation. There is no precedent set. This is entirely an option invested in the company, and it was not intended otherwise.
>
> Should the aim of the grievance be shifted from Article VIII, 5(c), as stated in the grievance, to Article VIII, 5(b), it would be interpreting the 20-workday provision of this paragraph out of context. That is, it implies that it is an unqualified requirement of the company to provide holiday pay in certain cases of layoff, rather than just one of several requirements the individual employee must meet to qualify for vacation pay.
>
> If the following should further be contended, Section 5(b) could be interpreted so as always to prevail in any case in which either was considered, and the contract would operate as if the holiday pay layoff provision of Section 4 did not exist.
>
> (1) If an employee is working and is laid off, then the last day he worked was his last scheduled workday, regardless of how many days, weeks, or months ago the layoff occurred.
>
> (2) Therefore, the employee may be said to have worked the last full, scheduled workday before the holiday, possibly, in this case, satisfying Section 5(b).
>
> It must be strongly stressed that this misuse of Section 5 to indirectly cover a layoff situation specifically addressed and provided for in Section 4 would result in the complete subversion of the holiday pay layoff provision of Section 4 and render it to be of no effect in the contract. This destruction of the layoff provision of Section 4 was clearly not the intention of the parties who included it in the contract for good purpose.

Because Hunt, a member of the company's negotiation team, was not present at the arbitration hearing (due to laryngitis), it was agreed that he could respond to the union's brief in writing. His response follows.

> It is the contention of the company that Section 4, with its specific reference to holiday pay under conditions of layoff, prevails in this case. The provision that "Any employee laid off in the week in which a recognized holiday falls shall be paid for that holiday" was observed, and not violated, no matter what the interpretation of "week," as the most recent preceding layoff was on May 18, and the holiday was observed on May 28.

Section 5(a), (b), and (c) address the situation in which work is available to the individual employee but the employee cannot or chooses not to attend. The language of Section 5, in its entirety, was submitted by the company and accepted verbatim by the union. Without any aim of preempting the findings of this arbitration, and realizing that most language is subject to more than one interpretation, the company feels it has a reasonable understanding of its own submission.

The "within 20 workdays preceding" provision of 5(b) should be taken in context with the "full scheduled workday before and full scheduled workday after" provision of 5(a). The "within 20 workdays preceding" was included only as a safeguard for the company to ensure that the employee had performed recent work for the company, other than just on the day before and the day after the holiday in question.

This safeguard is necessitated by the various provisions of Article VI (i.e., leaves of absence for various reasons such as sickness, union business, personal matters, military service), which allow an individual to remain an employee of the company with full rights as such under the contract, unless otherwise contravened, even though he may not have performed work for the company for an extended period of time. It was felt to be unfair that, after a leave of absence of more than a work month (20 workdays), such employee should become entitled to holiday pay merely by working the full day before and the full day after that holiday. Absent paragraph 5(b), an employee could receive holiday pay even though he may have worked but two (2) days in an extended period of workdays available to him. The intent of 5(b) is to avoid such abuse and, when so interpreted, 5(b) has a validity and purpose in the contract, without contravening or compromising the effect of the holiday pay layoff provision of Section 4. Any interpretation of 5(b) extending it to cover situations of general layoff would make totally irrelevant and render to no effect a straightforward, specific provision dealing with layoff and holiday pay; that is, dealing with the exact circumstances of the dispute.

Then Hunt challenged Horton's testimony at the hearing by stating the following:

The testimony of Mr. Joe Horton in reference to the layoff provision of Section 4 is not in accord with my recollection of the events of negotiation, nor can I find any reference to such argument in my notes. Furthermore, there is ample and specific protection elsewhere in Section 4 that assures the employee who performs work during a holiday or vacation of receiving not just full, but premium pay for the time worked, in addition to his holiday or vacation pay, whether subsequently laid off or not.

The testimony of Mr. Horton in reference to Section 5 is also at odds with my recollection of the negotiations. At no time were any provisions of Section 5 ever related, during negotiations, to layoffs in the language of Section 5.

It follows that the merit of the Company's position need not rest on who has the better memory. Mr. Horton's imputation to Section 5 of the intent of the layoff provision of Section 4, and his imputation to the layoff provision of Section 4 the intent specifically covered elsewhere in Section 4 leaves the union in the position of calling Section 4 "probably necessary," possibly included because this was the first contract and "there had been situations prior to the contract where employees did not receive holiday pay." Yet, under the argument set forth by the union, employees would receive no benefit whatsoever from the layoff provision of Section 4 not conferred in greater measure elsewhere in the contract.

Furthermore, it is of interest to note that the union suggests here that it had the layoff provision of Section 4 included for the protection of its members from abuse by the company. In fact, it was the company that proposed the provision (during the negotiating session of 6/25/88), and the provision was subsequently accepted by the union. A photocopy of the original company proposal, with the union's notation in the upper-left corner, is attached.

The company then concluded that to dismiss as "probably unnecessary" the only specific reference in the contract to the layoff holiday pay situation seemed an exercise in selective reasoning, as the reference is "unnecessary" only if the contract were interpreted as the union said it should be interpreted.

Under the interpretation of the contract offered by the company, Sections 4 and 5 of Article VIII are both meaningful and necessary to carry out the intent of that contract; each section covers different aspects of holiday pay. It is not unreasonable to hold that the various provisions of a negotiated contract are included for good purpose. Any interpretation that arrogates to itself the conclusion that a provision is without purpose suggests a distortion of the intent of the parties to the contract.

Therefore, because:

(1) The company has explained the presence of all the disputed provisions of the contract;
(2) The comments of Mr. Horton are not, in the opinion of the company, in accordance with the events of the negotiation, and are, in respect to Section 4, compromised by the union's own statements; and
(3) The argument advanced by the union, far from explaining the presence of the contested provisions, denies any meaning to one of the provisions of the contract to which it is a party;
the company maintains that Article VIII, Section 4, governs the issue in dispute and that therefore the contract has not been violated, and the grievance with respect to 1989 Memorial Day holiday pay should not be upheld.

Questions

1. How should the arbitrator evaluate the absence of David Hunt, company president, at the hearing?
2. How should the arbitrator evaluate Hunt's written submissions?
3. Since Hunt could not be present at the hearing, did the company make an error in proceeding with the hearing? Explain your answer.
4. How should the arbitrator evaluate the testimony of Joe Horton, a member of the union negotiating committee?
5. Consider the criteria used by arbitrators (see Chapter 9) in making decisions. Weigh the evidence presented by the parties, make the arbitrator's decision, and justify your decision.

Applying the Labor Relations Process to Different Work Arrangements

Part Four presents the opportunity to apply the previous chapters' discussions of the labor relations process to various labor relations situations. Collective bargaining in the public sector at all government levels is discussed, and a discussion of foreign labor relations processes is presented for comparative purposes. A concluding chapter describes labor relations activities in the professional sports, health care, and agricultural industries.

CHAPTER 14

Labor Relations in the Public Sector

"After decades in which collective bargaining with the government was considered virtually 'impossible' in America, unionization achieved in the 1970s and 1980s greater strength in the public sector than in the private sector. In 1986 over a third of public sector workers were organized into unions, and over 40 percent were covered by collective agreements. . . .

Given the greater success of collective bargaining in the public sector than in the private sector in the 1970s and 1980s, the time would seem to have come for researchers and practitioners to begin to ask what the private sector might learn from the public sector experience rather than the converse."

Richard B. Freeman and Casey Ichniowski, "Introduction: The Public Sector Look of American Unionism," *When Public Sector Workers Unionize,* eds. Richard B. Freeman and Casey Ichniowski (Chicago: The University of Chicago Press, 1988), pp. 1, 13.

The public sector has grown to become an important factor in the U.S. labor scene. As the number of public employees has increased, so has the number of these employees joining unions. This chapter presents an overview of labor relations in the public sector and provides a brief summary of the similarities and differences in public- and private-sector labor relations. It also examines public-sector bargaining at the local, state, and federal levels and concludes with a discussion of several affected groups.

Significance of Public-Sector Labor Relations

The field of public-sector labor relations has developed from a time when public employees were required to lobby their respective legislators for favorable employment terms to one in which bona fide collective bargaining occurs. It has moved from a generation characterized by rapid union growth, management's inability to react to collective bargaining, and a fear of strikes to a generation characterized by slow union growth, few states passing enabling public-sector legislation, and a willingness to take strikes.[1] With many state legislatures and the U.S. Congress interested in legislation to cut taxes, many public employees have become more concerned about their job security and welfare. Therefore, union leaders are showing increased attention to public-sector employees, hoping that gains in membership in this area will offset the lack of membership gains in the private sector.

Government employment has grown to 17.6 million employees, with most of the growth occurring at the state and local levels. The AFL-CIO has recognized this growth and the importance of the public sector as a vibrant component of its membership by creating the Public Employee Department to focus attention on issues facing public employees. By 1989, public employees accounted for about one-fourth of the AFL-CIO membership, up from 15 percent in 1976.[2] During the last 15 years, the United Steelworkers, United Mine Workers, and United Auto Workers have lost over 30 percent of their members; however, during this same period the American Federation of State, County, and Municipal Employees (AFSCME) has increased its membership by 68 percent, or 443,000 members.[3] AFSCME now is one of the largest unions within the AFL-CIO, representing over 1.0 million.[4]

In the federal sector, the American Federation of Government Employees (AFGE) represents 675,465 federal government employees. (See Exhibits 14.1 and 14.2 for membership data of public employee unions.) In the public sector, like the private sector, unions are required by law to represent all bargaining unit employees even though they are not dues-paying members (as discussed in Chapter 11). For example, the AFGE represents 675,465 federal government employees in negotiations, contract administration, and grievance arbitration; however, the AFL-CIO reports that only 156,000 are dues-paying members.

Overall, unions represented 7,611,000 or 43.6 percent of all government employees in 1989. The percentage of union representation was higher at the local level than at the state and county levels. In terms of government function, unions represented a majority of teachers, firefighters, and police.[5]

More than two-thirds of federal government employees, including 1,250,000 non-postal employees and 644,000 (or 89.9 percent) postal employees, are represented by labor organizations. In the federal sector, three sets of labor relations policies and programs have emerged. One set applies to the executive branch; another to the postal service; and the third to 19 other organizations (including, for example, the Tennessee Valley Authority with 50,352 employees) whose policies have evolved over a long period of time.[6]

Patterns of union membership in the public sector closely resemble those of the private sector. While non-whites and males are more likely to be union members than are whites and females, the differential is relatively small. Right-to-work laws and part-time employment are negatively associated with the number of union

Exhibit 14.1 **Exclusive Recognition by National Unions**

Federal Employee Unions	Recognition Units	Employees Represented
American Federation of Government Employees (AFGE)	977	675,465
National Federation of Federal Employees (NFFE)	379	148,390
National Treasury Employees Union (NTEU)	47	137,591
National Association of Government Employees (NAGE)	203	69,804
Metal Trades Council (MTC)	44	65,491
International Association of Machinists and Aerospace Workers (IAM) (federal employees only)	82	28,381

Source: Office of Personnel Management, "Union Recognition in the Federal Service," *FLMERC* 89-17 (September 1, 1989), p. 3,

members. Positive influences are mandatory bargaining provisions, strong union security provisions, compulsory agency shop, compulsory checkoff, compulsory arbitration, and the right to strike.[7]

Favorable public sector labor laws appear to be a sufficient condition for union growth in public sector labor relations. Favorable legislation increases the probability that a municipal department will be governed by a collective agreement, and the presence of a comprehensive labor law sharply increases in the percentage of departments that bargain with unions within a state.[8] In states having comprehensive collective bargaining laws, 71 percent of the public employees are represented for bargaining purposes. On the other side, in states without such laws, only 14 percent of the public employees are represented by unions.[9] (See Exhibit 14.3.)

Labor Legislation in the Public Sector

In the public sector, labor relations at the state, county, and municipal levels are governed by policies, statutes, executive orders, and ordinances. At the federal level, most labor relations activities are governed by the Civil Service Reform Act, and postal labor relations are governed by the Postal Reorganization Act of 1970.

An analysis of the existing laws and policies suggests that favorable legislation is concentrated in the states located in the Northeast, North, Midwest, West Coast, Alaska, and Hawaii. The so-called sun-belt states, located in the lower Atlantic Coast, Southeast (except the state of Florida), Southwest, and lower Rocky Mountains, generally do not have labor relations legislation that comprehensively covers the public sector, that is, covering administrative agency, bargaining rights, scope of bargaining, impasse provisions, unfair labor practices, and strike provisions.[10] (See Exhibit 14.3.)

Thirty-eight states and the District of Columbia have statutes or executive orders that provide for collective bargaining for at least one group of employees. However, de facto bargaining occurs in other states or cities.[11] Most states prescribe

Exhibit 14.2 **State and Local Union Membership, 1989**

Name of Union	Number of Members
National Education Association (NEA)	2,000,000
American Federation of State, County, and Municipal Employees (AFSCME)	1,090,000
American Federation of Teachers (AFT)	544,000
Service Employees' International Union (SEIU)	762,000
Fraternal Order of Police (FOP)	170,000
International Association of Fire Fighters (IAFF)	157,000
Teamsters (public sector members only)	150,000
Laborers' International Union of North America (public sector members only)	85,000
Communication Workers of America (CWA) (public sector members only)	85,000
American Association of University Professors (AAUP)	45,000

Sources: "AFL-CIO Membership Hit 14.1 Million in October Due to Union Affiliations," *Daily Labor Report,* December 8, 1989, p. E-1; Sar A. Levitan and Frank Gallo, "Can Employee Associations Negotiate New Growth?" *Monthly Labor Review* 112 (July 1989), pp. 59–61; John Burton, Jr. and Terry Thomason, "The Extent of Collective Bargaining in the Public Sector," *Public-Sector Bargaining,* 2d ed., ed. Benjamin Aaron, Joyce M. Najita, and James L. Stern (Washington, D.C.: Bureau of National Affairs Inc., 1988), p. 54.

bargaining over wages, hours, terms of employment, and working conditions for some or all public employees. However, a majority of the states have statutory limitations on the scope of collective bargaining, such as limitations guaranteeing management rights.[12]

Another important element of labor legislation is unfair labor practices. Although these vary somewhat from state to state, most states (35) have legislation defining unfair labor practices for some or all public employees. The existing legislation typically prohibits strikes. Exceptions to outright prohibition are twofold: either they are not mentioned in the statute, or the states allow strikes only under specific circumstances.

In eight states, Delaware, Georgia, Indiana, Maryland, Minnesota, New York, Oklahoma, and Virginia, mandatory penalties are levied against striking government employees.[13] For example, New York's Taylor Law prohibits work stoppages and provides penalties against both the strikers—loss of 2 days pay for each day on strike, loss of tenure and job security protections—and the union—suspension of dues checkoff.[14]

Many states have sanctions varying from injunctions to dismissals, jail sentences, substantial fines, and loss of union recognition when a strike occurs. An investigation of teacher strikes revealed that increasing the level of sanctions against strikers reduces strike activity up to a point, but beyond that point, more strikes, not fewer, occur. The reason for this occurrence seems to be that severe sanctions are seldom enforced, but more moderate ones are. Thus, it seems that strikes can be reduced if moderate, enforceable sanctions are provided.[15]

Thirteen states have affirmatively sanctioned public sector strikes by some groups of public employees. Nine have done so by statute (Alaska, Hawaii, Illinois,

Exhibit 14.3

States Having Comprehensive Laws Covering Most State and Local Employees (Duty to Bargain, Unfair Labor Practices, Administrative Agencies, and Impasse Procedures)

Alaska	Maryland	Oregon
California	Massachusetts	Pennsylvania
Connecticut	Michigan	Rhode Island
Delaware[a]	Minnesota	South Dakota
Florida	Montana	Vermont
Hawaii	New Hampshire	Washington
Illinois	New Jersey	Wisconsin
Iowa	New York	
Maine	Ohio	

Note: District of Columbia has comprehensive legislation.

[a]No unfair labor practices listed.

Source: Karl O. Magnusen and Patricia A. Renovitch, "Dispute Resolution in Florida's Public Sector: Insight into Impasse," *Journal of Collective Negotiations in the Public Sector* 18 (no. 3, 1989), p. 241.

Minnesota, Ohio, Oregon, Pennsylvania, Vermont, and Wisconsin). In three states (Colorado, Idaho, and Montana), either courts or administrative agencies have interpreted pertinent legislation to confer a limited right to strike to certain public employees. In California, a state court upheld public employees' right to strike without enabling legislation.[16] Thirty-eight states have laws that prohibit strikes by all or some employees in the public sector. Twenty-two states have litigated the strike issues and the courts have found that no right to strike exists unless there is legislation permitting such right.[17]

In states allowing a limited right to strike, certain employees, such as police, firefighters, hospital employees, and correctional employees, are usually named as not being allowed to strike under any circumstances. Services of these employees are deemed to be critical to the health and safety of the citizens. Therefore, a ban of the right to strike is considered justified. Some states prohibit a strike during the negotiations period and some permit a strike only after efforts at mediation and fact-finding have been exhausted and a cooling-off period has elapsed.[18]

Municipal and county policies tend to have similar provisions and coverage. The bargaining obligation is enforced by an administrative agency and includes the duty either to bargain or to meet and confer over such topics as wages, hours, and terms of employment. Strikes are usually prohibited, and procedures have been established in the event an impasse occurs.

Without legislation enabling collective bargaining, unions have difficulty maintaining their membership, collecting dues, and entering into agreements with public officials. Some unions have survived adverse court decisions and the lack of favorable enabling legislation by representing their members in grievance procedures and becoming involved in political activities.[19] The absence of a clear, easily applied recognition procedure frequently leads to much unproductive and unnecessary bickering among the parties. Unfortunately, this bickering spills over into other areas, causing high absences and distrust between parties when bargaining finally occurs.[20]

Provisions in Collective Bargaining Agreements—State, County, and Municipal Employees

Unions representing state, county, and municipal employees generally negotiate collective bargaining agreements similar to those negotiated in the private sector. These agreements in the public sector fall into two categories: (1) contractual agreements and (2) memoranda of understanding. The last Census Bureau study reported 29,759 agreements in effect between state and local governments and their respective employee organizations and 7,124 memoranda of understanding.[21] Although specific bargaining items, such as merit system subjects, are often excluded by statute, most issues are quite similar to those negotiated in the private sector.[22]

Many bargaining issues cut across public employee job classifications. Wages, for example, are a concern of state, local, and county employees regardless of their particular job duties. However, as indicated in Chapter 1, the technological features of the work place can generate certain unique work rules and concerns. For example, firefighters and police are often more concerned than other public employees about safety provisions.[23] Labor and management officials have explored safety-related issues (improved fire hose nozzles, fire coats, chemicals, and so on); however, many of these improvements require rather large expenditures. For example, one company has introduced "Rapid Water," a chemical additive that reduces friction in the fire hoses, resulting in 50 percent more flow with the same pump pressure. Yet only a few of the nation's approximately 25,000 fire departments spent funds to obtain this system.[24]

Police are also concerned about safety problems; a recent demand by a Washington, D.C., police officers' union sought two related proposals: (1) better marksmanship training and (2) deadlier, "all-lead semi-wadcutter" bullets, which are used in other cities.[25] In some cases, safety issues can involve broader issues of management's right to schedule and direct the work force. One of the more emotional issues in police negotiations concerns one-person versus two-person squad cars. Management wants the freedom to assign one-person cars on the basis of crime data reported for various areas and shifts. The unions want two-person cars to maximize patrol officer safety under unsafe street conditions.[26] Police are also concerned about other job-related issues, for example, the benefit of "false-arrest" insurance.[27]

Federal Sector Labor Relations Legislation

Federal sector labor relations are governed by the Civil Service Reform Act (CSRA), which was passed in 1978. While the CSRA retained many provisions of previous executive orders, the following discussion centers on the provisions of the CSRA as they currently exist. The act's ramifications extend beyond the labor relations function—it deals with other functions, such as merit system principles, civil service functions, performance appraisal, adverse actions, staffing, merit pay, and senior executive service. Its Title VII, "Federal Service Labor-Management Relations," is the primary focus here.

The CSRA establishes a new **Federal Labor Relations Authority (FLRA)**,[28] an independent, neutral agency that administers the federal labor relations program and investigates unfair labor practices. The FLRA oversees the creation of bargaining units, supervises elections, and assists federal agencies in dealing with labor relations issues. It is headed by a chairperson and two members, appointed on a bipartisan basis for 5-year terms. Its structure provides for a General Counsel that prosecutes unfair labor practices and incorporates the existing Federal Service Impasse Panel (FSIP), which provides assistance in resolving negotiation impasses.[29]

The FLRA's leadership responsibilities include determining appropriate bargaining units, supervising and conducting elections, prescribing criteria for determining national consultation rights, conducting hearings and resolving complaints on unfair labor practices, and resolving exceptions to arbitrator awards. The General Counsel investigates any alleged unfair labor practices, prosecutes complaints under the act, and exercises such powers as the FLRA may prescribe.

The **Federal Service Impasse Panel (FSIP)** within the FLRA structure consists of at least six president-appointed members and one chairperson. It investigates any negotiation impasse presented to it and is authorized to take any action that it considers necessary to settle the dispute. Although the Federal Mediation and Conciliation Service (FMCS), the federal agency established in 1947 by the Taft-Hartley Act, is required to assist the parties in resolving negotiation impasses, either party may request that the FSIP consider the matter or pursue binding arbitration. The panel must investigate the impasse and recommend a procedure for resolution or assist the parties through whatever means are necessary, including fact-finding and recommendations. If these actions fail, it may conduct a formal hearing and take whatever action is necessary and legal to settle the dispute.

Appropriate Bargaining Units and Union Recognition in the Federal Sector The appropriate bargaining units for exclusive recognition may be established on an agency, plant, installation, function, or other basis in order to assure a clear and identifiable community of interests among employees and to promote effective dealings with efficiency of the agency operations. The criteria used for determining community of interests are similar to those that have been used by the National Labor Relations Board in the private sector. These include common duties and skills, similar working conditions, and common supervision and work site. Similarly, certain positions are generally excluded from the bargaining unit, such as confidential employees, management and supervisory personnel, personnel employees, and professionals unless they vote in favor of inclusion.

Under CSRA, federal agencies may give either exclusive recognition or national consultation rights to unions that meet the appropriate requirements. The granting of **national consultation rights** indicates that the union is the representative of a substantial number (10 percent, or 5,000) of the civilian employees in the specified federal agency. This recognition allows the union to be notified of proposed substantive changes in conditions of employment and provides a reasonable opportunity for the union to present its views and recommendations on any proposed changes.

A federal agency accords **exclusive recognition** to a labor union if the union has been selected as the employee representative in a secret-ballot election by a majority of the employees in the appropriate unit who cast valid ballots. However, there may be a gap between actual members and those represented. The AFGE reports that only one-third pay dues.[30]

Negotiable Subjects in the Federal Sector As in the private sector, the federal agency and the exclusively recognized union must meet at reasonable times and confer in good faith with respect to *mandatory* subjects of collective bargaining, such as certain personnel policies and practices and working conditions, to the extent that appropriate laws and regulations allow such negotiations. The parties are allowed to bargain over subjects that are *permissible,* but the CSRA does not require negotiation over permissible subjects—one party can legally refuse to negotiate these issues. Permissible subjects include numbers, types, and grades of positions assigned to any organizational unit, work project, or tour of duty; technology of the workplace; and methods and means of performing the work. Subjects *prohibited* from negotiations include wages and various management rights and the following:

- To determine the mission, budget, organization, number of employees, and internal security practices.
- To hire, assign, direct, layoff, and retain employees in accordance with applicable law.
- To suspend, remove, reduce in grade or pay, or take other disciplinary action.
- To assign work, subcontract, and select employees for promotion from properly ranked and certified candidates and other appropriate sources.
- To take whatever actions may be necessary to carry out the agency mission during emergencies.

Although the CSRA limits the negotiable subjects, the parties have ample opportunity to negotiate many issues, as illustrated in Exhibit 14.4. However, it should be noted that federal unions and management representatives do not have a totally free hand in negotiating these items, and either party may run the risk of committing an unfair labor practice by refusing to negotiate their mutual working conditions concerns in good faith. The fact that management and the union are required to bargain in good faith means that the parties must intend to reach an agreement.

Unfair Labor Practices in the Federal Sector The Civil Service Reform Act specified unfair labor practices in order to protect the rights of individual employees, labor organizations, and federal agencies. The General Counsel investigates charges of unfair labor practices and prosecutes them before the three-member FLRA. Employee grievances over matters concerning adverse action, position classification, and equal employment opportunity are issues covered by other laws, statutes, or agency rules, and cannot be raised in the forum of an unfair labor practice hearing.

Unfair labor practices under the act are very similar to those covered under previous executive orders, the National Labor Relations Act, and the Labor Management Relations Act. For example, prohibited management activities include restraining and coercing employees in the exercise of their rights; encouraging or discouraging union membership; sponsoring, controlling, or assisting the labor organization; disciplining union members who file complaints; and refusing to recognize or negotiate with a designated labor organization. The labor organization is prohibited from interfering with, restraining, or coercing employees in the exercise of their rights; attempting to induce agency management to coerce employees; impeding or hindering an employee's work performance; calling for or engaging in job action; and discriminating against employees or refusing to consult, confer, or negotiate with the appropriate federal agency. In such cases, the FLRA can issue cease and desist orders and/or require reinstatement with back pay.

The CSRA makes it an unfair labor practice to refuse or fail to cooperate in impasse procedures and decisions. Moreover, an agency cannot enforce regulations

Exhibit 14.4 **Potential Negotiation Issues in the Federal Sector**

Procedures and standards to determine which employee(s) from a group of employees will be selected to perform work.
Merit promotion procedures and union participation on promotional panels.
Reduction-in-force procedures and management's obligation to notify employees and the union.
Procedures on job assignments.
Dues withholding.
Union rights regarding office services and space.
Safety considerations, including inspection, equipment, clothing, and union representation.
Discipline procedures.
Union participation in wage surveys.
Overtime distribution.
Meal and rest periods.
Excused time, including training and sick leave.
Travel time and transportation.

Source: A survey of 2,418 labor agreements by the Office of Personnel Management, published in *The Federal Labor-Management Consultant* (Washington, D.C.: Office of Personnel Management, July 31, 1981), p. 3. For analysis of FLRA cases, see H. H. Robinson, *Negotiability in the Federal Sector* (Ithaca, N.Y.: Cornell University, 1982); and Douglas McCabe, "Labor Relations, Collective Bargaining, and Performance Appraisal in the Federal Government Under the Civil Service Reform Act of 1978," *Public Personnel Management Journal* 13 (Summer 1984), pp. 133–135.

that conflict with a negotiated agreement, and the union cannot picket if it interferes with the agency's operation.

The FLRA has authority to revoke recognition of a union that commits an unfair labor practice or encourages a strike or slowdown. (See "Labor Relations in Action" on the rise and fall of PATCO.) It can also require the parties to renegotiate a labor agreement in accordance with an FLRA decision and seek temporary restraining orders in unfair labor practice cases.

The CSRA requires that all negotiated agreements in the federal sector include a grievance procedure with binding arbitration as its final step. A grievance is broadly defined to include any complaint by any employee or labor organization relating to employment with an agency and any claimed violation, misinterpretation, or misapplication of any law, rule, or regulation affecting conditions of employment. Certain issues are exempt from the grievance procedure, such as employee appointment, certification, job classification, removal for national security reasons or political activities, issues concerning retirement, and life and health insurance. However, the scope of grievance procedure coverage has been extended considerably. In fact, all matters within the allowable limits of the CSRA are within the scope of any grievance procedure negotiated by the parties, unless the parties have specifically agreed to exclude certain matters from coverage. Thus, in departing from previous practices and private-sector practices, the parties will not be negotiating matters into coverage; they will, however, be negotiating them out of coverage.

Negotiated grievance procedures now serve as the exclusive forum for bargaining-unit employees in most cases; however in cases of adverse action and

Labor Relations in Action

The Rise and Fall of PATCO and the Emergence of NATCA

During the Carter administration, the Professional Air Traffic Controllers' Organization (PATCO) had been unsuccessful in bringing about change in the air traffic control system. When Carter sought re-election, PATCO was one of the few unions that supported Ronald Reagan. Soon after Reagan was inaugurated, PATCO president Robert Poli and other union officials met with Reagan to discuss air traffic controller concerns. Shortly thereafter when Reagan froze federal hiring, he exempted air traffic controllers from the freeze.

In 1981, when PATCO and the Federal Aviation Administration (FAA) began negotiating their labor agreement, PATCO sought a boost in annual salaries from $30,000 to $73,420, a 4-day, 32-hour work week, and a more liberal pension plan. On June 22, 1981, a tentative agreement was reached that included a $38,000 annual salary, 42 hours of pay for 40 hours of work, income differentials for night and overtime, and 14 weeks of salary for controllers who were retired for medical reasons. The following week, 90 percent of the PATCO members rejected the tentative agreement. Poli announced that he would return to the bargaining table, but if an agreement was not reached by 7:00 a.m. on Monday, August 3, a national walkout would occur. No agreement was reached and 12,000 PATCO members struck. With a wholesale disruption of the air transportation system and now personally involved, President Reagan warned the strikers to return within 48 hours or they would be fired. When the strikers did not return, President Reagan fired them.

As the strike began, Poli insisted on an agreement before calling off the strike. The government would not negotiate until the strikers announced plans to end the strike. With both sides maintaining fixed positions, there was no room for compromise.

Afterward, the FAA announced that it would take 2 years to recover from the massive firings; 21 airports operated at 50 percent of their normal level; nonstrikers, supervisors, and military air traffic controllers worked 10 to 12 hours per day, 6 days per week. The Federal Labor Relations Authority ordered PATCO to be decertified as the representative of the air traffic controllers for violating the no-strike provision of the Civil Service Reform Act.

By late 1982, one report indicated that relations between air traffic controllers and their supervisors were reverting to the open hostility evidenced before the strike. Examples of complaints included working 25 to 30 planes at once (the average was up to 12 to 15 before the strike), 48-hour work weeks, working 4

removals and demotions for poor performance, the employee may choose either the negotiated procedure or the statutory procedure, but not both. Moreover, in discrimination cases, the grievant may proceed to arbitration and then appeal to the EEOC or the Merit System Protection Board, an independent agency established to hear federal employee grievances under CSRA.

Postal Reorganization Act of 1970

The Postal Reorganization Act (PRA), signed by President Nixon on August 12, 1970, fulfilled the desires of the postal unions to have their labor-management relations programs established by statute. Under Kennedy's executive orders, the Post Office Department never fully accepted collective bargaining, even though it was

straight hours without a break, and outspoken controllers being sent for medical and psychiatric examinations.

A 1984 report by the General Accounting Office revealed that management was not interested in human relations, did not care whether employees were satisfied with their jobs, did not give employees a fair opportunity for promotions, and did not inform employees about what was taking place with the organization. A 1985 House subcommittee reported excessive incidences of high blood pressure, alcohol abuse, and chronic depression among the controllers.

In June 1987, with over 84 percent of the 12,800 eligible air traffic controllers voting, a new union, the National Air Traffic Controllers Association (NATCA) was certified as the bargaining agent by more than a 2 to 1 margin.

On May 1, 1989, NATCA members ratified a 3-year contract that included the following provisions:

- Management agreement not to take any personnel action against employees in reprisal for their whistle-blowing disclosures of fraud, waste, or substantial, specific danger to public health and safety.
- Prenatal or infant care leave without pay for both male and female employees for up to 12 months.
- With union input, management establishment of a policy for operational errors which limits the circumstances under which discipline will be imposed.
- Establishment of a procedure for investigating and reporting operational errors or deviations.
- Establishment of a review board composed of half union and half management members for investigating systems errors.
- Participation of NATCA representatives in National Transportation Safety Board investigation of accidents in which controllers are involved.

During the same month, May 1989, the General Accounting Office released a follow-up report that revealed concerns over staff shortages, controllers handling too many aircraft at once, overtime, quality of training, and morale. Steve Bell, president of NATCA, said that the air traffic controllers were a "tired and demoralized work force that is fed up with the empty promises that have been served up for the past eight years."

Acting FAA administrator Robert Whittington stated that the agency was making progress in hiring more controllers, acquiring more sophisticated equipment, improving procedures, and reducing overtime. He noted that morale had improved, job satisfaction of controllers was higher, and controllers had a larger voice in agency operations.

Source: "Air Traffic Controllers and FAA Reach Final Agreement on Contract," *FLMERC,* May 12, 1989, p. 1; "Air Traffic Controllers Continue to Complain about Work Conditions," *Daily Labor Report,* May 31, 1989, p. A-1.

the largest single employer in the United States and had the largest proportion of employees belonging to unions.

The act created the U.S. Postal Service (USPS) as an independent establishment within the executive branch of the federal government. The office of postmaster general, previously a position in the cabinet, was made independent of Congress and the president. The postmaster general was to be selected by an 11-member board of governors. Further, under the PRA many new policies of vital importance to the postal unions, such as an 8 percent retroactive pay increase, attainment of the highest wage rate in job classifications in 8 years instead of 21, acceptance of the concept of federal-civilian pay comparability, and establishment of a self-supporting postal service by 1984, were adopted.

Under the PRA, the national labor rules that have evolved over the years under the National Labor Relations Act apply to the USPS. Wages, hours, benefits, and terms and conditions of employment are to be determined through collective bargaining. Grievance, adverse action, and arbitration procedures are subject to negotiation. The NLRB supervises representation elections and prosecutes unfair labor practices. Although the right to strike was prohibited, a fact-finding and arbitration procedure was made available if a bargaining impasse persisted longer than 180 days after bargaining began.

Since the PRA was passed, contracts have been negotiated without major disruptions of postal services. Each negotiation, however, has been accompanied by serious threats of work stoppages by urban postal employees, who believed that their wages did not compare with other urban wage earners of similar skills and responsibilities.[31]

Over the 20 years since the passage of the Postal Reorganization Act, there were two occasions when the agreements were reached via three-party arbitration. In 1978, the parties relied on med-arb for a settlement. Then in 1984, the agreement was decided by an arbitration panel. The panel agreed with the management position that wages were higher than comparable jobs, but decided that this discrepancy should be corrected over time rather than all at once. The panel identified wage compression problems that resulted from previous uniform wage increases, and it made appropriate corrections. It awarded a 19 percent average increase, but new employees would start at 25 percent of the current scale. In addition, the union was awarded as a tenth holiday the birthday of Martin Luther King, Jr., and the uniform/work clothes allowance was increased.

The 1987 negotiations were not as dramatic as previous ones. The issue of greatest disagreement was management's proposal to create a new category of part-time workers and to increase the use of "casuals" (workers who do essentially the same job and receive $5.25 per hour with no health, leave, or retirement benefits). The new 40-month contract called for a 7 percent increase in wages and seven cost-of-living increases to be paid over each 6 months of the agreement. Other features included a no-layoff clause for employees with 6 or more years of service, a child-care task force, and purging from employees' files of warning letters that are over 6 months old. Management's proposal for use of more "casuals" and part-time employees was dropped; however, the jurisdiction problems over the introduction of new technology and assignment of new jobs emerged as issues of disagreement that may cause difficulties.[32]

Differences between Private-Sector and Public-Sector Bargaining

Nature of the Public Sector

One difference between the public and private sectors can be explained in terms of the economic system and the market economy. Unlike the private sector, many of the services in the public sector (such as public education and police and fire protection) are supplied to the citizens at little or no additional cost (beyond taxes). The market economy therefore does not operate in the public sector and cannot act as a constraint on the labor union and management negotiators.

Moreover, monopolistic conditions often exist in the public sector, and public organizations often control the services rendered or the products offered. For example, the police and fire departments are the primary organizations that provide certain types of security protection. Public education has very little real competition from the private sector, and even that is usually among only the more affluent families. Thus, products and services provided by the government cannot be readily substituted if they become more costly.[33]

The lack of substitute goods or services distinguishes public-sector collective bargaining from related activities in the private sector and adds to the critical nature of public services. For example, citizens usually take garbage-collection services for granted; yet a strike by city garbage collectors would be regarded by the public as a crisis, since there is no immediate alternative means for garbage disposal. The lack of substitute services also eliminates one of management's strike costs: loss of business to a competitor. In fact, some union leaders contend that municipal leaders use a strike to their advantage—the payroll savings during a strike are transferred to other government budgetary accounts.

Finally, the relatively vague aspects of the particular public service institutions make productivity bargaining difficult. Clear and precise productivity measures are a necessary first step in productivity bargaining (although many private-sector companies have these figures and do not engage in productivity bargaining). Most public-sector bargaining parties do not have specific productivity measures at their disposal and could not engage in productivity bargaining even if they desired this approach. Many public services are provided regardless of customer use. Police officers and bus drivers can legitimately contend that they should not be financially punished for nonuse of their services; their salaries should not be a direct function of the number of crimes detected or riders served, respectively, if the service is available to all. Hence, much of the public-sector wage determination process is based on comparison with similar jobs in the public and private sectors rather than on employee performance records.[34] Because the market does not act as a moderator in the public sector, budgetary limitations, public attitudes, and administrative discretion must operate to successfully maintain order, equity, and balance in collective bargaining relationships.[35]

Relationship between the Budget and Public-Sector Bargaining Processes

The budget usually tends to have a more conspicuous if not significant role in public-sector collective bargaining than in private-sector bargaining. Most municipal budgets are posted in advance before public hearings and subsequent adoption. Although many citizens ignore public hearings, key taxpayers such as local companies give close attention to the budget in terms of its implication for increased property taxes. The anticipated salaries for public employees are recorded as separate line items on the budget, something not done in the private sector. Thus, the opportunity exists for concerned taxpayers to pressure city officials in the hopes of keeping the budget and subsequent taxes at a minimum.

The specific influence of the budget on the public-sector collective bargaining process remains uncertain. Some suggest that there is a great deal of flexibility in the budget-bargaining relationship in terms of budget padding, transfer of funds among line items, and supplemental or amended budgets that can often be filed after the final approval date.[36] In these cases, the government officer in charge of labor relations may have little concern with the agency's financial activities. The following related comments were expressed by a former director of the budget for New York City:

> The director of the budget is less a part of a unified management team than a part of the problem, an adversary not unlike the union leaders themselves. . . .Underlying the situation is the belief held by most labor negotiators that they know "what it takes" to effect a settlement and that, in the large complex public body, alleged or actual limits on available resources have no effect upon the ultimate settlement. And they are, in fact, largely correct.[37]

Similarly, as illustrated by one union official's comment, public-sector unions seldom allow the budget to influence their collective bargaining strategies and settlements:

> The budget does not mean too much to me—if we based our bargaining demands on the budget, we would never get any money. The union is never cognizant as to the amount [in the budget] because there never is enough money. We are aware of the dire need for money and campaign politically [to obtain additional funds], but when we go into negotiations we don't discuss the budgetary problems.[38]

Their major concern pertains to securing benefits for their members; it is up to management to find sufficient funds for an equitably negotiated settlement. Thus, there is little union-management agreement over the budget's significance in contract negotiations; few if any public-sector collective bargaining agreements have provisions specifying the role the budget will assume in the collective bargaining process.

This situation poses a dilemma. On the one hand, if the budget were a controlling factor in contract negotiations, unilateral managerial decision making would render collective bargaining a farce. On the other hand, if collective bargaining were entirely removed from budgetary constraints, fiscal responsibilities would be abated at taxpayer expense. Some degree of union involvement in the budget-making process might be needed in instances of severe fiscal constraints. A hopeful note is reflected in the observations of a New York City Emergency Financial Control Board member: "I have found the municipal labor unions to be the most practical people in this [financial] crisis. They understood the problem more quickly than the city administration."[39]

Collective Bargaining Structures and Decision-Making Processes

It is more difficult to define the appropriate bargaining unit in the public sector than in the private sector.[40] Private-sector legislation and related administrative enforcement agencies provide direction for determining the appropriate bargaining unit. For example, plant guards in the private sector are required to be in separate bargaining units, and supervisors are not eligible for membership in the bargaining unit. The public sector, especially at the state and local levels, experiences many different combinations of appropriate bargaining units. Depending on the particular applicable state law or administrative determination, public-sector supervisors can be prohibited from joining unions, they can be in the same bargaining units as other employees, or they can join unions in separate bargaining units.[41]

In Louisiana, no employee is excluded from appropriate bargaining units. However, managerial employees and confidential employees are excluded in 20 other states, elected and appointed officials in 11 states, and supervisory employees in 9 states. Supervisors are included in the same unit as others in 3 states, but in 10 states, separate units are established for supervisory employees.[42]

Another organizational difference applies to the chief negotiator in the public sector, who often lacks authority to reach a final and binding agreement with the union on behalf of the public organization. The *sovereignty doctrine* makes it difficult to delegate decision-making authority to specific administrative officials. Many elected officials still refuse to give up their legislative authority to make final decisions on matters that they believe are important to effective government operations, since they feel responsible directly to the electorate. They do not want appointed negotiators to bind them to wage settlements and other provisions of collective bargaining agreements that they believe are unworkable.[43] For example, unionized schoolteachers might encounter a variety of managers in collective negotiations—the school principal, the superintendent of schools, the school board, and possibly state education officials. The problem of determining "who is management?" can negatively affect the negotiations process in two ways:

1. Management can pass the buck to other management officials in the bargaining process. Union officers are often shuffled off to a variety of government officials in collective bargaining on the premise that another individual has specific authority for a particular issue or a portion of available funds. Often, political rivalries prompt certain government officials to either intervene or pass the buck in the hopes of looking good at another official's expense.[44] This situation can result in a more confusing collective bargaining relationship than is typically found in the private sector. In some cases, it can almost entirely prevent serious collective bargaining efforts between management and the union.[45]
2. The unwillingness of some government agencies to delegate sufficient authority to a labor relations representative can result in a lack of labor relations understanding on management's side of the negotiation table. In some cases, taxpayers are affected if unions take advantage of the inexperienced management negotiators. Perhaps in other cases a public strike could have been avoided if the parties had had a more realistic understanding of the collective bargaining process.

Negotiable Issues and Bargaining Tactics

Exemption by statute of many of the traditional collective bargaining subjects from negotiations is another difference between private- and public-sector labor relations. Under the Civil Service Reform Act of 1978, wages and position classifications of federal employees cannot be negotiated. (The postal service is covered under another law.) In many states operating under merit system rules and regulations, related subjects such as promotion, pension plans, and layoff procedures cannot be negotiated.[46]

A problem arises if public-sector negotiation topics are restricted to those already found in the labor agreement. One study found that some public-sector labor agreement provisions are not actually negotiated between the parties, while other decisions are jointly determined but not included in the formal labor agreement.[47] Thus, relatively few generalizations can be made regarding collectively bargained items in the public sector.

Sometimes the public-sector bargaining tactics differ from those in the private sector. Certain bargaining practices allowed in the public sector would probably be considered unfair labor practices in the private sector. When maneuvers such as not making genuine proposals are employed, they usually intensify hostilities and create barriers to future negotiations. On the other hand, a union frustrated by management's intransigence at the bargaining table may believe that there is no alternative available.[48]

Negotiations in the private sector stem from a bilateral relationship—management and union representatives negotiate the terms of the labor agreement with little involvement from outside groups. Public-sector bargaining, particularly at the state and local levels, is multilateral, involving various groups of community citizens and government officials as well as the formally designated negotiators. Thus, it often becomes an exercise in politics—who one knows and what one can do to help or hurt a government official's political career can play a decisive role. Public-sector unions therefore often have opportunities to **end-run** the negotiations before, during, or after their occurrence; that is, they make a direct appeal to the legislative body that will make final decisions on the agreement. For example, one mayor made concessions to the police association in return for its endorsement in the gubernatorial primary. He changed the regular police work schedule from 5 days on and 2 off to 4 days on and 2 off (increasing the annual days off by 17), guaranteed two patrol officers in all cars, and agreed that 50 percent plus one of the patrol cars in each police district would be on the street during night hours.[49] Because public labor unions in many settings are politically potent, elected officials are generally more receptive to this end-run process than a corporation president, members of the board of directors, or majority stockholders of a corporation would ever be in the private sector.[50] In fact, such attempts by the union to bypass the management negotiators of a private-sector organization would probably result in an NLRB determination of refusal to bargain in good faith.

Occasionally, the media aid the end-run tactic—management and the union present their positions to the press rather than to the other party at the bargaining table. Public-sector bargaining is usually given more press coverage than similar activities in the private sector since more related information is typically furnished to the press and the eventual settlement will have a more direct impact on the government's constituents. The end-run to the news media can harm the collective bargaining approach, as evidenced by a union leader's account of one-contract negotiations between New York City and the uniformed forces:

> All of this [bargaining issues] should have been brought to the bargaining table. It would have given both labor and management a chance to work out of these very difficult trouble spots. . . . But, almost nothing was done at the table; instead both sides took to the television, advertising, and the loud and dramatic press releases. . . .
>
> Experts . . . know the best way to insure trouble is to bring collective bargaining into the public arena. Instead of labor and management representatives talking to each other, they will talk to the public and to their principals only. Invariably, the wrong things will be said.
>
> Management will talk of the "irresponsibly high demands" of the workers, and about how services will have to be cut back or taxes raised. . . .

> The labor leader now has to talk tough. The strike threat becomes almost obligatory, because he is now put in an impossible squeeze. When the union leader goes public he first must talk to the people he represents, and retain their confidence. Understandably, the public responds not to the facts of the situation but to the militant rhetoric. Everybody loses in the process, a process that has little or nothing to do with collective bargaining.[51]

The media play an important role in determining the priority issues, in providing information about the issues, and in helping the public formulate their attitudes toward the parties in negotiations. The local press is highly influential because many times it is the only channel of information for the general public. Since voters cannot directly observe union and management interactions, they rely on the media, which itself has biases. These biases include personal beliefs, ideologies, and prejudices, budgetary and technological constraints, and dealing with problems stereotypically.

During negotiations both parties try to manipulate the media, because frequently the negotiations are dependent more on the people's perceptions than on the soundness of the position. In fact, sometimes the parties jointly manipulate the media to their own advantage. The union blames the city official for its members receiving less than the wage increase they demanded; the city official blames the union for a tax increase needed to pay for the wage increase that was given.[52]

Accompanying the upsurge of collective bargaining in the public sector have been efforts to open negotiations to citizen observation and participation through the **sunshine laws.** The rationale for this approach is that citizens can provide more input into how tax dollars are spent by their involvement, and openness reduces public distrust. While every state has some form of sunshine law, 25 states require labor negotiations to be conducted in the open, and 12 states even require that the strategy sessions in preparation for labor negotiations be open.[53]

The open approach to public-sector bargaining differs widely from the private sector, as a private enterprise's owners (stockholders) are excluded from collective bargaining sessions. Also, flexibility and honesty are necessary prerequisites of successful labor-management relationships, and these qualities are often lost if union and management negotiators have to posture their efforts before a public audience.

The Right-to-Strike Controversy

The right to strike, considered by many a vital instrument for successful collective bargaining, is usually prohibited by statute in the public sector. The federal government and most state governments prohibit strikes. The basic argument given for legislative prohibition of strikes is that the services provided by public organizations are essential to the general welfare of the citizens, and work stoppages or refusals to work would adversely affect the delivery of these vital services and create disorder in the community. As is true with many industrial relations concepts, the words "essential services" are subject to many diverse interpretations. Some maintain that all public services are essential, while others suggest that many public employee classifications (such as clerks, mechanics, and motor pool personnel) are no more essential than their counterparts in private industry. Police and firefighters are almost always viewed as crucial for public safety; however, at least one police strike saw no increase in the area's crime rate. One police official, believing that criminals fear irate citizens more than they fear the police, commented, "Hoods have no rights without police protection. Shop owners will use their shotguns."[54]

The right to strike in the public sector has other debatable dimensions. Some would prohibit public-sector strikes because they would place too much power in the hands of the unions relative to the taxpayers. Also, unions would unnecessarily benefit at the expense of other groups that are dependent on government revenues but that do not strike or participate in power ploys with public officials.[55]

George Taylor further elaborates on the effect of the right to strike on political processes:

> It is ultimately the legislative and the political processes which have to balance the interests of public employees with the rest of the community. The balancing involves considering the relation of the compensation of public employees to tax rates, an appraisal of the extent and quality of public service desired by the taxpayer, and an evaluation of the efficiency of the performance of public employees. . . . Methods of persuasion and political activity, rather than the strike, comply with our traditions and with the forms of representative government to which we are dedicated as the appropriate means for resolving conflicts of interests in this area. . . . Strikes are not the answer, new procedures are.[56]

One research project found that successful bargaining gains in the public sector occur when unions either use the threat of a strike despite its illegality or intertwine themselves closely with their employers by exchanging patronage for political support. If this assessment is correct, prohibiting strikes leads to changes in patterns of political decision making that subvert the "normal" political processes.[57]

Some contend that prohibiting public-sector strikes distorts the collective bargaining process:

> The conclusion is inescapable that collective bargaining cannot exist if employees may not withdraw their services or employers discontinue them. This is not a statement of preference, but a statement of fact. But it is now also evident that collective bargaining is the best way of composing differences between workers and their employers in a democratic society even though there is much room for improvement in the process. So, if we believe public employees should have bargaining rights, we must accept the possibility of a strike and consider how best to guard against it. If we believe the case against strikes by public employees is so overwhelming that all such strikes must be prohibited, let us then say frankly that public employees cannot be given bargaining rights and that the use of such euphemisms as collective negotiations cannot alter the basic structural differences the strike ban entails.[58]

Yet others believe that the right to strike in the public sector is not essential to collective bargaining, since public-sector unions are already influential interest groups and effectively use their lobbying and political support techniques to obtain collective bargaining goals.[59]

Regardless of the arguments for or against the right to strike or statutory penalties assigned to strikers, significant strikes have occurred in the public sector. The largest number of strikes occurred in education; and seven states, California, Illinois, Michigan, New Jersey, New York, Ohio, and Pennsylvania, accounted for 90 percent of the idle days.[60] Moreover, strikes are often prolonged until all strikers or discharged employees have been granted amnesty or reinstatement to former positions.

Thus, laws have not prevented strikes; they have not been invoked against all employees who have participated in strikes, and, when invoked, the law has not been applied with like effect to all strikers. Some believe that laws prohibiting strikes may have deterred some strikes and injunctions may have had a sobering effect on some strikers, but prohibiting strikes by passing a law has not realized a great degree of success.[61] Some statistics suggest that such laws make no difference at all. There have been strikes in strike-permissive Oregon, Ohio, and Illinois, and there have been strikes in New Jersey where strikes are prohibited.[62]. However, well-enforced penalties against illegal strikes and threats of firing have reduced strikes in the public sector. Poorly enforced prohibitions and legalization of strikes have increased the frequency of strikes.[63]

Employee Rights and Obligations

Another way that public employment differs from private employment is that public employees have some legal rights and obligations that private employees do not. Numerous laws and executive orders pertain only to public employees. Political activities, personal appearance, place of residence, and off-the-job behavior have been regulated more closely. For example, public employees in particularly sensitive jobs and those whose misdeeds are most susceptible to adverse publicity, such as teachers, police officers, and firefighters, are held to higher standards than most other employees.[64] Because citizens pay the taxes that pay public employees' salaries, employers have to be careful of the image employees project.

While freedom of speech and association are constitutional rights, there are limits to their exercise by public employees. The Supreme Court has identified several reasons for which these rights may be limited, including the need to maintain discipline and harmony in the work force, the need for confidentiality, and the need to ensure that the proper performance of duties is not impeded.[65] However, in 1987, the Court ruled that public employers cannot give priority to efficient work operation over an employee's First Amendment right to expression over a matter of public concern.

Generally, the courts have not attempted to substitute their judgment for that of executive branch officials on whether an individual public employee should be dismissed. Rather, they have sought to establish guidelines for the constitutional treatment of public employees in adverse action cases such as a discharge. Procedural due process requires the right of notice of the proposed government action, the reasons for the action, the opportunity to respond, the right to a hearing before an impartial official, and the rights to counsel, to confront accusers, and to cross-examine and subpoena witnesses.

In *Board of Regents* v. *Roth,* the Supreme Court delineated the following grounds upon which a public employee whose employment has been terminated could assert the right to procedural **due process:**

- Where an employee had a property right to the job.
- Where the termination harmed the individual's reputation and/or adversely affected his or her future employability.
- Where termination was in retaliation for an exercise of a protected constitutional activity, such as the freedom of speech or freedom of assembly.

The legislature can confer a property interest upon public employees by statutorily limiting the grounds for the employee's removal. Then the procedure by which dismissals can take place is controlled by the Constitution.[66]

In 1985, in the case of *Cleveland Board of Education* v. *Loudermill*, the Supreme Court held that before tenured public employees can be fired, they must be informed of the charges against them and given an opportunity to respond. Their due process rights under the U.S. Constitution include written or oral notice of the charges against them, an explanation of the employer's evidence, and an opportunity to rebut the evidence.[67]

Differences in Approaches to Labor Relations

Public sector unions have had an effect in ways that range beyond collective bargaining, such as through lobbying and political campaigning that influence the citizen's view of public service. Since public managers are beholden to an electorate that includes public sector workers and politically active unions, they tend to take a less adversarial approach to labor relations than do private employers, who are responsible to stockholders. As one result, labor unions represent twice the proportion of public employees as private sector employees. In the public sector, public unions can be an important ally in convincing the electorate, the legislature, and other government bodies of the need for an increased budget. Another reason for the less conflict-ridden atmosphere is that the right to strike has been limited and has been replaced by other impasse resolution procedures such as arbitration.[68]

Similarities between Private-Sector and Public-Sector Bargaining

While there are differences between private- and public-sector labor relations, there are also similarities. First, many of the participants in public-sector bargaining are trained and gain their experience in the private sector. They tend to mold the emerging institutions in the public sector in a familiar image, using NLRB criteria for appropriate bargaining units, subjects for collective bargaining, use of labor injunctions, and standards for arbitration. Also, some of the unions, such as the Service Employees International Union and the Teamsters, have much experience in the private sector. Other unions, such as the National Education Association, the American Federation of Teachers, the AFSCME, and civil service employee groups, hired their professional staffs from the private sector.[69]

One major similarity shared by public- and private-sector negotiations is that the collective bargaining settlement will often be influenced by the personalities of the negotiators and their abilities to increase their bargaining power relative to the other party (the bargaining power model has been discussed in Chapter 6). To reiterate briefly, each party increases bargaining power over the opponent by either increasing the cost to the opponent of disagreeing or reducing the cost to the opponent of agreeing. Public opinion represents a most significant cost item in public-sector labor relations—both union and government officials often structure their tactics in a manner that gains public support for their position, which places pressure on their opponents to concede negotiation items.

However, public opinion and political support can be a double-edged sword in the bargaining power model. Public unions can use at least three general strategies to increase management's cost of disagreeing with the union's position.[70] The first technique is a union threat to "blow the whistle" on a questionable practice unless the government agency agrees with the desired settlement. Examples include threatening to release information on the unpublicized practice of dumping raw sewage in a river or on the dollar amount of government officials' liquor bills, which are paid by the taxpayers. Of course, the union is hoping that government officials will capitulate rather than risk vote loss in subsequent elections due to the public revelation of an incident. Management's cost of disagreeing can be more directly increased by the union's threat of withdrawing political support.[71] The success of this tactic depends on the number of union members and the ability of the union to mobilize a cohesive voting bloc.

The union can also use various job action techniques to raise management's cost of disagreeing. Strikes by public employees have occurred frequently in spite of legal sanctions. Perhaps these actions are taken under the assumption that most public-sector strikes have eventually been resolved without fines or other sanctions, even though they are illegal. Some other job actions that have been used are also outside the law or proscribed by the job requirements (for example, government employees in New York raising the toll bridges at rush hour when walking off the job), while others are marginally outside the law or job requirements (for example, all public employees calling in to say they are too sick to work).[72]

From the union standpoint, a most promising job action is working within the law while at the same time placing pressure on management to resolve the dispute. Job slowdowns fall into this category marginally, since most public-sector labor agreements give management the right to discipline employees for poor production performance. Yet there is a thin line between a job slowdown and malicious obedience (also called *work-to-rule*), by which the employees follow the agency's rules to the letter. For example, a fingerprint technician is charged with verifying an individual's address during his criminal booking. This can be done by simply telephoning the individual's purported residence. However, fingerprint technicians desiring to follow the malicious-obedience technique might personally visit the individual's residence for a more accurate verification. Needless to say, this approach creates an assignment backlog. Other public employees can also use bureaucratic rules to their advantage. For example, toll booth employees could check paper currency serial numbers against a list of counterfeited bills, and postal workers could check each item to ensure a proper zip code. Malicious obedience has the tactical advantage of cutting back services. More importantly, employees continued to receive wages under this tactic while being relatively immune from disciplinary actions.

The variety of job action techniques depends on the creativity and resourcefulness of the union leaders. New York City's police and firefighters announced that off-duty personnel would distribute a pamphlet at the city's airports, railroad stations, bus terminals, and hotels. The cover of the pamphlet featured a human skull in a shroud with the caption, "WELCOME TO FEAR CITY." Union officials contended that this pamphlet represented an educational "survival guide" for tourists, since the city was contemplating police and firefighter layoffs. Included in the pamphlet were the following helpful hints:

- Stay off the streets after 6 p.m.
- Avoid public transportation.
- Do not walk.
- Beware of fire hazards.

Job actions of this nature, although not initially illegal, run the risk of an eventual restraining order. This occurred in the New York City pamphlet example when the New York Supreme Court at least in part accepted the city's contention that such conduct endangers the citizens' lives and threatens the economic well-being of the city.

Public-sector unions can also reduce management's cost of agreeing with the union by campaigning for referendums to fund the negotiated labor settlement or eliminating some of their initial proposals. They can also push for certain issues that contribute significantly to their economic well-being at little cost to the political incumbents. Employee pensions usually fall into this category since they can be increased without immediate cost implications; the bulk of pension costs will be incurred by some unhappy politician in the distant future.

Management can reduce its political cost of agreeing on wages by publicizing a rather low across-the-board settlement along with general improvements in the pay step plan. This plan usually gives progressive salary increases to each job classification. For example, an employee in a particular classification might receive a 5 percent wage increase after 3 years' service in that classification. Management can improve the employee's situation by either raising the percentage increase or reducing the number of service years needed for a step wage increase. However, it is difficult to determine and report the precise cost of these changes. Most new media presentations are limited to specific reports on the average wage gain of public employees and ignore the more detailed cost implications of the modified pay plan.

Private- and Public-Sector Labor Relations Compared

In summary, public-sector collective bargaining is generally similar to that found in the private sector. In both situations, the parties are trying to increase their bargaining power relative to their opponent's by increasing the cost to the opponent of disagreeing with the party's position or by reducing the cost to the opponent of agreeing with the party's position. There are several differences between public- and private-sector bargaining processes; however, once these differences are acknowledged and understood, one can better appreciate the public sector as it fits into the overall framework of labor-management relations in the United States. Moreover, skills learned in private sector labor relations are easily transferred to the public sector.

Impasse Resolution Procedures in the Public Sector

Since legislation usually prohibits public employees from striking or requires participation in impasse resolution procedures before striking, these procedures play an important role in labor relations in the public sector. Also, since the laws establish many different impasse resolution procedures, much experimentation is occurring in the public sector. These procedures normally involve a third party, who assists the parties in reaching an agreement without interrupting services or endangering the public interest.

Public-sector impasse procedures are controversial and have received considerable attention; they have been instituted in 38 states. The most popular impasse procedure combines mediation, fact-finding, and arbitration (available in 20 states). A variety of other forms also exist: arbitration only (8 states), fact-finding only (7 states), and mediation and fact-finding (9 states).[73]

These impasse resolution techniques are covered in Chapter 7; therefore, they will only be briefly discussed here. Similarities between public and private sector impasse procedures and unique public sector implications will be mentioned.

Mediation Mediation involves a third-party neutral who has no binding authority but assists the parties in reaching an agreement. Mediators often have to rely more on their intense mediation behavior (when disputes are difficult, for example)[74] and personal qualities when the parties are inexperienced.[75] Experienced negotiators tend to use the mediator less.[76] Mediation tends to be more successful when the parties are unsure of themselves or have personality conflicts. It is less effective when it is followed by another impasse resolution procedure,[77] although mediation works better when it is followed by arbitration instead of fact-finding.[78]

Fact-Finding and Arbitration Fact-finding and arbitration are separate impasse resolution procedures; however, they are discussed and assessed jointly because of their many similarities. Both involve a third-party neutral who, through a quasi-judicial hearing, assesses union's and management's collective bargaining positions.[79] Fact-finders interpret data and information that have been presented to them (rather than gathering facts themselves) and recommend settlement positions to the parties.[80] However, this recommendation is not binding. The final decision is generally left to the elected legislative body.

Arbitration entails a binding decision by a third-party neutral that settles the negotiation impasse. A variation of this technique is final offer selection (FOS) arbitration where the arbitrator either selects the best package settlement presented by the union or management or resolves the impasse on an issue-by-issue basis. In both cases, the arbitrator can only select one party's final offer; there is no compromise or splitting the difference.

Fact-finding and arbitration can be successful in resolving impasses because these techniques provide deadlines for the parties to resolve their differences, fresh knowledgeable perspectives, and political advantages since negotiators can blame the neutral for the eventual settlement. Also, the mere possibility of these procedures might pressure the negotiators to resolve their differences for fear that the neutral would not understand their positions.[81]

These techniques can also carry some disadvantages. For example, the fact-finder's recommendation and arbitrator's decision might not resolve genuine union-management differences. Moreover, these techniques might cause the negotiators to cement their respective positions because the parties believe they can get a better deal from the arbitrator or more favorable recommendations from the fact-finder. Instead of earnestly attempting to resolve their differences in the final negotiations, the representatives focus their time and thoughts on preparing for the fact-finder or arbitrator. Also, politicians tend to challenge these individuals as "outsiders" or "limousine liberals," who have no accountability—they make the decisions and then leave town.[82]

Variation in Procedures In the public sector few jurisdictions have the same arbitration scheme. Within the FOS approach there are several variations. In some cases, the parties are permitted to submit several final offers. Another variation specifies the number of steps that may be used. For example, the state of Iowa mandates the intermediary step of fact-finding between mediation and FOS arbitration. Where mediation and fact-finding fail, the dispute proceeds to FOS arbitration at either party's request. Further, the FOS arbitrator may select the fact-finder's recommendation or one of the final offers from union or management.[83] Other variations include use of a single arbitrator or a panel, selection on an ad hoc or permanent basis, different criteria to be used by arbitrators and fact-finders, and the range of issues subject to arbitration.[84]

Effectiveness of Fact-Finding and Arbitration There are many variables that influence the bargaining process and outcomes.[85] However, one general measure of effectiveness has been proposed:

> An effective impasse procedure raises the cost to at least one of the parties of continuing to disagree and, perhaps, at the same time, lowers the cost to the other party of agreeing voluntarily.[86]

Union and management officials are likely to push disputes to the last step of an impasse procedure when one or both parties

- Are uncertain of future costs of continued collective bargaining (a situation that particularly applies to inexperienced negotiators).[87]
- Expect to receive a better settlement through the impasse procedure.
- Need to pass the blame for an "unfavorable" settlement to a third-party neutral instead of accepting personal responsibility for the results.[88]

Assessing fact-finding is particularly difficult. Its effectiveness does not hinge on the fact-finder's ability; this individual is presented facts by the parties in hopes that he or she will agree with their respective positions. The success of such a procedure is based on the assumption that the fact-finder's report will structure public opinion, which will in turn place pressure on the parties to resolve their differences in accord with published recommendations. Thus far, there is no concrete evidence to show that public pressure has noticeably affected public sector management and union officials.[89] (See "Labor Relations in Action.")

Indeed, studies of fact-finding in New York, Wisconsin,[90] and Florida[91] have found a high rejection rate of the factfinder's recommendations. However, in Florida, a closer analysis of the data has discovered that when the unresolved issues are considered "issue by issue," a majority of that factfinder's recommendations are actually adopted by the parties.[92]

Overall, interest arbitration in the public sector seems to have passed the test, at least in the short run; most of the participants as well as the analysts have been satisfied with the process. Its availability has not substantially lessened serious negotiations. Also the number of strikes has been reduced substantially in cases where employees have been covered by compulsory arbitration legislation. Even though

Labor Relations in Action

The Facts about Fact-Finding

There is virtually no consensus about fact-finding. How it is spelled is not even clear. "Fact-finding," "factfinding" or "fact finding" have all found their way into statute or state agency documents. Most dictionaries spell the word with the hyphen.

Just what facts is a fact-finder to find? Naturally the parties have their preferences and *most* of the time they are at odds. In one notable case involving the firefighters of Iowa City, perhaps the clearest analogy ever of the fact-finder's role was presented. There were 5 hours of testimony with respect to the city's ability to pay. The city, of course, noted how various budget lines had been reduced for lack of funds. The firefighters followed, pointing out the growth of other lines, some of which werre labeled "miscellaneous" and all of which, the firefighters asserted, were the new "hiding places" for money in the city's "overflowing coffers."

Finally, the time for closing arguments came. The firefighter spokesman reached under the table for a used brown lunch bag and hauled out three walnut shells and a pea. After refreshing the fact-finder's memory about "the old shell game," he proceeded to demonstrate how, at least in an *honest* shell game, the pea was always present. It was only a matter of finding it. The fact-finder was left with the clear inference that unless he could find a "pea" in Iowa City of sufficient size to fund the firefighters' request, the "game" could not possibly be honest. In the spokesman's opinion, the "facts" the fact-finder was supposed to find were green, but they weren't peas!

Another unsettled question about fact-finding is exactly what role fact-finding should play. One pundit even raised the question, "Should a fact-finder be concerned with whether his report will be rejected?" Given that fact-finding is part of a dispute resolution process, it seems obvious to most of us that he should. In one well-known teacher dispute, the fact-finder was convinced that the teachers' position was correct and, moreover, he was told by the board's negotiator that the superintendent "wants a strike." Foolishly, he recommended the full eight percent increase sought by the teachers even though he believed the teachers would settle for less. The strike lasted 10 weeks.

Most state statutes contain a list of criteria fact-finders shall consider in making their recommendations. Among them is always one that opens Pandora's box, e.g., ". . . and such other factors that are customarily considered in making recommendations in labor disputes." One of the "facts" must be what recommendation will most likely be accepted by the parties. Especially when fact-finding is followed by the right to strike, a failure to recognize the relative power of parties is foolhardy.

Some might argue that the role of the fact-finder is to persuade the union membership and public body's constituency of the righteousness of the fact-finder's recommendations. But most fact finders are not even second-rate prophets, let alone God (though some pretense along these lines does appear to be a prerequisite for the profession). Their recommendations are no closer to what is "right" than are the positions of either party. Besides there is serious doubt about whether a union member or voter ever read a fact-finding report. The bottom line *recommendation* is what gets read, and if it is close enough to what constituents will tolerate, it will be accepted.

A better analogy for a fact-finder is a general, all-purpose maintenance worker with a big, old, rusty station wagon filled with tools and spare parts. No two calls are alike—the parties, the issues, the propensity to want a settlement, and many other factors all differ. Moreover, the fact-finder won't know what is needed until after the process is well along. Even then it is often difficult to diagnose. With experience and good fortune, maybe the "maintenance man" will keep things running smoothly. If he guesses wrong, the boiler may blow up. But the question of who was "right" is irrelevant!

Source: A neutral who wishes to remain anonymous.

some management officials feared arbitration, arbitrators have not stripped them of their rights and authority. The settlements have not been significantly greater than the parties would have reached themselves in similar circumstances, and the public in general has not openly indicated displeasure with the process. Most significantly, arbitration has been increasingly adopted as an impasse-resolution procedure in the public sector, and the parties have expressed satisfaction with their experience.[93]

One of the biggest concerns about public-sector interest arbitration is its so-called **chilling effect** on the parties incentives to reach an agreement. If either believed that it could get a better settlement from an arbitrator than from negotiation, there would be an incentive to maintain excessive demands in hopes that the arbitrator would "split the difference" and make a favorable award. When one side acts in such a manner, the other side has no realistic choice but to respond similarly, widening the gap between the parties.[94]

Research into this aspect of arbitration has produced mixed results. An analysis of arbitral decisions regarding police impasses found that some management officials are reluctant to negotiate their best offer before arbitration on the assumption that the arbitrators will use management's final offer as a starting point in their decisions.[95] Yet this concern is somewhat dampened by a study of several arbitration awards in firefighter interest disputes, which revealed that a large majority of the arbitrators took an intermediate or compromise stance on a few negotiation issues, such as wages and clothing allowances, but did not compromise the other issues; they supported either management's or the union's final position. It seems that there is no guarantee that arbitrators will compromise on any or all of the issues presented for their decisions.[96]

Another concern about public sector interest arbitration is that the mere existence of impasse procedures could create a so-called **narcotic effect.** That is, once the parties start using the procedures, they become increasingly reliant on them in subsequent negotiations. However, this frequently expressed concern is not warranted.[97]

In a study of impasse procedures in Minnesota, researchers found evidence that the types of employees may make a difference in the degree to which there is a chilling effect on the negotiations. When the employees are "essential" and therefore not allowed to strike, and unresolved issues are decided in arbitration, 30 percent of the cases end up in arbitration. This is in sharp contrast to the cases involving "nonessential" employees who are allowed to strike, where only 9 percent go to arbitration. Thus, the strike possibility appears to present a greater incentive to reach an agreement in negotiations.[98]

Strike-potential bargainers spend more time in negotiations, while bargainers in cases resolved in arbitration spend more time in strictly procedural delay. Thus, it seems clear that the greater threat associated with the strike encourages hard bargaining, and the use of arbitration reduces the incentive for hard bargaining and therefore has a chilling effect on negotiations.[99]

Final-offer arbitration has been used in several states (Iowa, Massachusetts, Minnesota, and Wisconsin) and has been found to perform a reasonably good job of protecting the parties' incentives to negotiate[100] when the arbitrators do not "flip-flop" their awards (awarding the decision to one party the first time and to the other party the next time) so they will be rehired in the future.[101] Other studies found that final-offer arbitration could be more effective if it did not follow fact-finding in the impasse procedure[102] and gave the arbitrator more flexibility to determine the particular issues to be decided in this fashion.[103]

Flexibility, however, is relative as some arbitrators believe that there should be some guidelines for wage determination.[104] Some issues, such as the type of union security clause, do not lend themselves to final-offer arbitration.[105]

Arbitrators in interest disputes tend to rely, at least initially, on internal wage comparisons and to consider the unique and historical circumstances of the particular community and the desirability of maintaining such circumstances. The criterion of ability to pay plays a secondary role behind comparable wages and cost of living unless well-supported arguments against this are presented. In addition, interest arbitrators view their role in the arbitral process as continuing the existing nature of the parties' relationship that has stemmed from the bilateral process of negotiations. Arbitrators believe that any major deviations from this relationship must come from the parties, not the arbitrator.[106]

In a study of 302 police interest arbitration awards, arbitrators favored the union position in 47 percent of the cases and the employer position 40 percent. Arbitrators were likely to favor unions in salary decisions and employers in nonsalary decisions. Arbitrators usually based their decisions on comparisons with other police departments and ability-to-pay evidence.[107]

Referendum Another impasse-resolution procedure places the unresolved issues on a taxpayer referendum, or vote. The following item, for example, might be placed on a ballot: "Do you approve of granting a wage increase of 'X' cents per hour to our police officers at an estimated additional annual cost to property taxpayers of 'Y' million dollars?"[108]

This procedure would avoid the problems of an outsider (fact-finder or arbitrator) determining the cost of a negotiated settlement. Citizens could not complain if the union's settlement was achieved in a democratic manner. Similarly, the union's integrity would be at stake if it refused to abide by the "will of the public." Yet, this procedure could turn collective bargaining into a public relations campaign directed at a body of individuals (citizens) largely unfamiliar with labor relations' complexities. Further, the procedure has no precedent in private-sector labor relations, since no company submits labor agreement proposals to stockholders or consumers.

Referenda, or direct submission to the electorate for final and binding settlement of labor-related issues, have been used in several Texas cities for over 30 years. Employees have won over two-thirds of the elections involving civil service and bonus issues, but lost 56.6 percent where the issue was pay parity.[109]

Use of the referendum has two potential advantages:[110]

1. It ensures that the negotiations will be conducted in a pragmatic, realistic environment where the parties have an incentive to reach an agreement and costs are too high to fail to reach an agreement.
2. It motivates citizens to take an active interest in the matter of public employment.

However, in cities where this method has been used, assessment of this approach has not been favorable. First, the electorate has little understanding of the law and the issues, and it is highly susceptible to propaganda campaigns by both parties. Second, the referendum appears to help make the strong stronger and the weak weaker without regard for what is equitable or reasonable for all the parties involved.[111]

There are many varieties and combinations of public impasse-resolution procedures, yet the objectives remain the same: to avoid strikes, to minimize dependence on outsiders, to maximize good faith bargaining between parties, to protect the public interest, and to build a commitment to accountability and mutual problem solving.[112]

Labor Relations Activities among Various Groups in the Public Sector

The following section highlights labor relations in some of the major employee groups in the public sector. Included are elementary and secondary teachers, college professors, police, firefighters, and federal government employees.

Elementary and Secondary Teachers

More than 80 percent of public elementary and secondary teachers belong to the American Federation of Teachers (AFT) or the National Education Association (NEA), and more than 60 percent are covered under a formal collective bargaining agreement. Teacher unions have successfully used a dual strategy of collective bargaining and political action that has significantly improved their salaries and working conditions.

By the 1980s, a majority of teacher bargaining units had negotiated contract provisions that regulated the school day, allowed teacher response to administrator evaluations of teaching performance, permitted teachers to exclude disruptive students from their classrooms, and provided a detailed procedure for reducing the size of the teacher force. However, less than a third had attained contract provisions that limited class size, curbed requirements of teaching outside of one's field, or established an instructional policy at each school.[113]

Where elementary and secondary teachers have chosen to be represented by unions, they have made significant inroads into educational issues, including curriculum, student placement, teacher placement, grading policies, transfer rights, class size, school calendar, length of school day and/or year, textbook use, promotion and tenure, and use of substitutes.[114]

Higher Education

In higher education, 226,875 faculty members are represented by unions on 1,027 campuses. The American Federation of Teachers represents 76,234 faculty members on 309 campuses, and the National Education Association represents 60,982 on 417 campuses. Separate bargaining units of graduate teaching assistants or fellows are included on the campuses of the University of Michigan, University of Oregon, University of Massachusetts, and University of Wisconsin.[115]

Initially, faculty unions considered monetary compensation the primary reason for unionization and unions proved to have a positive effect on faculty salaries.

In the mid-1970s, the emphasis shifted to issues involving personnel matters such as job security, tenure, faculty appointment, dismissal, seniority, promotion, and grievance administration, and the faculty's role in setting institutional policy. Faculty members wanted to strengthen their job security and gain greater access to policy-making power and autonomy. In recent years, faculty unions have made inroads into academic areas related to class size, the academic calendar, work load, and class scheduling.[116]

Police

By the 1970s police officers had become one of the most highly unionized segments of the public sector. Twenty-five states and the District of Columbia now have duty-to-bargain laws and three states have meet-and-confer laws. The scope of bargaining varies greatly, but most agreements focus on salary and fringe benefits, pay supplements, equity, union security, working conditions, and individual security. Police unions have successfully pushed salary levels above those prevailing in nonunion locations (however, this differential is smaller than the 10 to 30 percent reported in the private sector), and the favorable bargaining climate created in 16 states having compulsory arbitration of unresolved disputes has increased police salaries even more.

No state allows police the right to strike, but strikes do occur, usually in the form of the "blue flu" (police calling in sick on the same day). Collective bargaining is extremely decentralized and membership in a police union is almost always limited to police department personnel. It is extremely rare for employees in different cities to join together for bargaining purposes. While there is no single dominant police union, the largest is the Fraternal Order of Police with about 170,000 members. A local union may be affiliated with a national organization, but the focus of police bargaining remains primarily local with no intervention from the national union.

Police unionism has increased the costs of delivering police services; however, it has also given police officers considerable protection from arbitrary, inconsistent, and inequitable managerial actions. Unionized police officers are not required to work extra hours for no pay, they have due process in internal investigations, and their agreements have a grievance procedure for appealing managerial decisions that are perceived as unfair.[117]

Firefighters

The International Association of Fire Fighters had its origin in the nineteenth century as a fraternal organization that addressed work-related problems encountered by firemen. The American Federation of Labor recognized the IAFF as a trade union in 1901 and the union has grown to a membership of 157,000, with 1,658 local unions throughout the United States.[118] Unions represent 66.5 percent of state and local employees in fire protection.[119]

Federal Government Employees under the CSRA

Labor relations in the federal sector under the Civil Service Reform Act (CSRA) of 1978 have been struggling since the act's inception. A 1988 congressional hearing presented an analysis of the CSRA that revealed the following problems:

- Over 400 labor-management disputes were pending in various appellate courts.
- Over 1,000 cases were pending with the General Counsel of the Federal Labor Relations Authority (FLRA).

- Over 2,000 cases that could have been resolved through the labor-management procedures had been submitted to the Merit Systems Protection Board where each case was waiting for review.
- 5,600 unfair labor practices were filed in 1987 and 5,900 in 1988.
- During the worst period of case handling by the FLRA, questions of negotiability of issues took 621 days to decide in 1985, 863 days in 1984, and 662 days in 1983.
- At the Louisville, Kentucky Naval Ordnance Station, there were 304 pending arbitration cases, and 91 negotiability appeals, 19 unfair labor practices complaints, and 469 grievances were filed in a bargaining unit of only 2,000 employees.[120]

It is widely recognized that negotiators on both sides in the federal sector are more often novices in labor relations than trained, experienced professionals. Because management traditionally dominates its employees and federal employee unions lack the authority to strike, management is prone to "dally at the bargaining table because it sees little advantage in pressing for a contract."[121] The unions have complained about the lack of real penalties for failure to bargain. National Treasury Employees Union President Robert Tobias says, "Management thinks: Why should I bargain if all I have to do is post a notice and bargain 2 years later?"[122]

Federal labor relations are further complicated by rules and regulations from the Office of Personnel Management, the nonnegotiability of wages and fringe benefits, active lobbying in Congress, and decisions by the comptroller general affecting employment. Identifiable problems include the following:[123]

- The parties reach negotiation impasses, refer the issues to the FLRA or FSIP to gain time in avoiding a disliked settlement, and then place the decision in the hands of the FLRA or FSIP.
- The parties waste time and effort dealing with numerous small bargaining units.
- Management negotiators continue to claim issues are nonnegotiable in hopes that the union will withdraw them or to avoid bargaining.
- There is no pressure on the parties to come to an agreement principally because there is no threat of a strike.
- Management negotiators often lack the authority to make decisions; negotiators appear to be errand boys running between the bargaining table and those in command.
- There appears to be a lack of sophistication in bargaining due to lack of training and the absence of mature bargainers.

The federal employee unions have concluded that the real bargaining occurs on Capitol Hill; thus, they focus their efforts on political lobbying. Further, grievances are brought to arbitration and appealed to the courts at an "alarming and unthinkable rate" when compared to the private sector.

The labor relations goals of the Office of Personnel Management in the Reagan administration were (1) to play down the need for collective bargaining and adversarial dealings and to push toward "constructive consultation" with employees directly, (2) to promote the Merit System Protection Board (each member appointed by the president) as the favored appeal body and to deemphasize the negotiated grievance and arbitration procedure, and (3) to continue to take an aggressive position toward federal employee unions.[124] The Bush administration appears to be more willing to cooperate with federal employee unions; however, it is too early to draw any definite conclusions.

A recent analysis provides some promise of optimism for the administration of the CSRA for the following reasons:

- All of the parties have gained experience in processing a large number of cases.
- Operational case handling methods and procedures have improved.
- Over a decade of experience, substantive case law has developed on which to base future similar cases.
- There has been a growing stability in federal sector labor relations.[125]

Summary

Public employee unions have struggled against unfavorable public opinion and publicity and adverse state legislation, but with permissive legislation, favorable judicial interpretations of constitutional rights, and an increasing interest among public employees, many public employees have joined unions. Union efforts culminated in organizational representation for a majority of employees in education, police protection, and fire protection in state and local governments.

Permissive state labor relations legislation or policy generally developed according to geography. Alaska and Hawaii passed favorable legislation, as did states located on the West Coast and in the Northeast, North, and Midwest. Most of the lower Atlantic Coast, Southeast (except Florida), Southwest, and lower Rocky Mountain states have no comprehensive legislation. In states having laws, the legislation typically specifies the administrative set-up, bargaining rights, impasse procedures, unfair labor practices, and strike provisions. Within this framework, the parties attempt to negotiate labor agreements covering permissible subjects.

In the federal sector, legislation and executive permission to allow federal employee unions was absent for many years. However, unions still developed, even under adverse conditions. Executive Order 10988 did not offer many substantive benefits to federal employee unions but provided the framework for a labor relations system in the federal government and gave tremendous impetus to union organization and growth. Each subsequent executive order added new features, and federal employees were eventually given many rights similar to those of employees under many state statutes and the National Labor Relations Act.

The administrative agencies under the Civil Service Reform Act (CSRA) of 1978 include the Federal Labor Relations Authority, the General Counsel, and the Federal Service Impasse Panel. Also available for assistance are the Federal Mediation and Conciliation Service, labor arbitrators, and fact-finders, who provide important services for the negotiating parties. The direction and interpretations of the CSRA in various types of cases are not yet fully manifest.

Public- and private-sector labor relations differ in several ways: (1) in its very nature, public service differs from private-sector services economically and in its demand characteristics; (2) the effect of the budget on bargaining processes differs; (3) the bargaining structure differs, affecting decision-making processes; (4) negotiable issues and bargaining tactics tend to be less predictable; (5) the right to strike is usually prohibited by law; and (6) effects on and approaches to labor relations differ.

Public- and private-sector similarities include the role of personalities and skills of negotiators and the interplay of bargaining power model variables such as public opinion, political support, and various forms of job actions.

The impasse procedures often established to substitute for the strike alternative include mediation, fact-finding, arbitration, and various combinations of these; the latter seem to be most popular. Such terms as *splitting the difference, chilling effect,* and *narcotic effect* have become common in assessing the effectiveness of these procedures. Definitive conclusions about impasse procedures have not been made, and further research into their effectiveness is needed. However, some promising results, such as serious negotiations and low incidence of strikes, have been identified in many states. In some states, chilling effects and narcotic effects have been identified.

The chapter concluded with highlights of labor relations in several public employee groups that include elementary and secondary teachers, college professors, police, firefighters, postal service employees, and federal employees under the Civil Service Reform Act.

Key Terms

Federal Service Impasse Panel (FSIP)
national consultation rights
exclusive recognition
end-run bargaining
sunshine laws
due process
chilling effect
narcotic effect

Discussion Questions

1. Think of a public organization with which you are familiar. Explain how it differs from a private company in terms of the following:
   a. nature of its service
   b. relationship between its budget and collective bargaining processes
   c. bargaining structure and decision-making processes
   d. negotiable issues and bargaining tactics
   e. its right to strike
2. Using the same public organization as in Question 1, discuss the similarities between collective bargaining in this organization and a typical negotiation between a private company and its union.
3. Give reasons why unions developed later in the public sector than in the private sector.
4. Public-sector labor relations legislation differs on a geographic basis. Explain why this might have occurred.
5. Describe the different types of impasse procedures used in the public sector, and discuss the relative effectiveness of each.
6. Compare the chilling effect and the narcotic effect as they pertain to negotiations and impasse procedures in the public sector.
7. Considering the multitude of subjects that are bargainable in the federal sector, list some of the more important ones that are not.
8. Compare and contrast the negotiated grievance procedures under the CSRA with those found in the private sector.

References

1. David Lewin, Peter Feuille, and Thomas Kochan, *Public Sector Labor Relations: An Analysis and Readings,* 2d ed. (Glen Ridge, N.J.: Thomas Horton & Daughters, 1988), pp. 1-5. The reader may wish to refer to a position essay against public employee collective bargaining in R. S. Summers, *Collective Bargaining and Public Benefit Conferral* (Ithaca, N.Y.: Cornell University, 1976).
2. Michael A. Pollack and Jonathan Tasini, "The Public Sector is Labor's Success Story," *Business Week,* September 22, 1986, pp. 28–29.
3. Mark de Bernando, "Public Sector Sees Organized Labor Boom," *The Wall Street Journal,* December 18, 1986, p. 26.
4. "AFSCME President McEntee Reviews Unions' Progress in Last Five Years," *Daily Labor Report,* December 17, 1986, p. A-6.
5. U.S. Department of Commerce, Bureau of the Census, *Labor-Management Relations in State and Local Governments, 1980* (Washington, D.C.: Government Printing Office, 1983), p. v–vi.
6. Charles J. Coleman, "Federal Sector Labor Relations: A Reevaluation of the Policies," *Journal of Collective Negotiations in the Public Sector* 16 (no. 1, 1989), pp. 37- 40.
7. Greg Hundley, "Who Joins Unions in the Public Sector? The Effect of Individual Characteristics and the Law," *Journal of Labor Research* 9 (Fall 1988), pp. 301–306.
8. Richard B. Freeman and Casey Ichniowski, "Introduction: The Public Sector Look of American Unionism," in *When Public Sector Workers Unionize,* eds. Richard B. Freeman and Casey Ichniowski (Chicago: The University of Chicago Press, 1988), p. 3.
9. "40 percent of State and Local Employees Have No Bargaining Rights, AFL-CIO Finds," *Daily Labor Report,* March 30, 1987, p. A-2.
10. Raymond L. Hogler, *Public Sector Strikes: Employee Rights, Union Responsibilities, and Employer Prerogatives* (Alexandria, Va.: International Personnel Management Association, 1988).
11. Roger E. Dahl, "Public Sector Bargaining Issues in the 1980's: A Management View," *Proceedings of New York University Thirty-Third Annual National Conference on Labor* (New York: Matthew Bender, 1981), p. 288.
12. Schneider, "Public-Sector Labor Legislation," pp. 192–212.
13. Michael Grace, "The Chaos in Public Sector Bargaining," *AFL-CIO American Federationist* 88 (July 1981), pp. 9–12.
14. Joel M. Douglas, "Injunctions under New York's Taylor Law: An Occupational Analysis," *Journal of Collective Negotiations in the Public Sector* 10, no. 3 (1981), p. 249.
15. Alan Balfour and Alexander B. Holmes, "The Effectiveness of No Strike Laws for Public School Teachers," *Journal of Collective Negotiations in the Public Sector* 10, no. 2 (1981), pp. 133–143.
16. Raymond L. Hogler, *Public Sector Strikes: Employee Rights, Union Responsibilities, and Employer Prerogatives* (Alexandria, Va.: International Personnel Management Association, 1988), pp. 5–6.
17. B. V. H. Schneider, "Conferring Strike Rights by Statute: Experience Outside California," *Government Union Review* 9 (Fall 1988), pp. 40–46.
18. Powers McGuire, "A Comparison of the Right of Public Employees to Strike in the United States and Canada," *Labor Law Journal* 38 (June 1989), pp. 304–309.
19. James K. McCollum, "Decertification of the Northern Virginia Public Sector Local Unions: A Study of Its Effect," *Journal of Collective Negotiations in the Public Sector* 10, no. 4 (1981), pp. 345-353; James K. McCollum, "Politics and Labor Relations in Virginia: The Defeat of Public Sector Unionism," *Employee Relations Law Journal* 7, no. 3 (1981), pp. 414–431.
20. Alan Balfour and Sandra Jennings, "Chaos in Union Recognition Procedures: A Case History of Oklahoma's School Teacher Bargaining Law," *Journal of Collective Negotiations in the Public Sector* 11, no. 1 (1982), pp. 82–83.
21. U.S. Department of Commerce, Bureau of the Census, *Labor-Management Relations,* p. vi.
22. U.S. Department of Labor, Bureau of Labor Statistics, *Municipal Collective Bargaining Agreements in Large Cities* (Washington, D.C.: Government Printing Office, 1972); and U.S. Department of Labor, Bureau of Labor Statistics, *Collective Bargaining Agreements for State or County Government Employees* (Washington, D.C.: Government Printing Office, 1976).
23. "Labor Letter," *The Wall Street Journal,* December 7, 1976, p. 1.
24. Jeffrey A. Tannenbaum, "Frustrated Firemen: Fire Fighting Gear Improves, but Cities Can't Afford to Buy It," *The Wall Street Journal,* January 30, 1975, pp. 1, 21.
25. "Labor Letter," *The Wall Street Journal,* April 8, 1975, p. 1.
26. Hervey A. Juris and Peter Feuille, *Police Unionism* (Lexington, Mass.: Lexington Books, 1973).
27. Thomas J. Hilligan, "Police Employee Organization: Past Developments and Present Problems," *Labor Law Journal* 24 (May 1973), p. 298.
28. This agency assumes many of the responsibilities of the Federal Labor Council and Assistant Secretary of Labor for Labor Management Relations.
29. U.S. Civil Service Commission, Office of Labor-Management Relations, *Introducing the Civil Service Reform Act* (Washington, D.C.: Government Printing Office, 1978), pp. 1–4.
30. Gregory Giebel, "Recent Development in Federal/Postal Service: Collective Bargaining 1987," *Labor Law Journal* 38 (August 1988), pp. 509–512.
31. Nesbitt, *Labor Relations in the Government,* pp. 316–347.
32. Gregory Giebel, "Recent Developments in Federal/Postal Service: Collective Bargaining 1987," *Labor Law Journal* 38 (August 1988), p. 510.
33. Harry H. Wellington and Ralph K. Winter, Jr., *The Unions and the Cities* (Washington, D.C.: Brookings Institution, 1971), pp. 10–17.
34. Walter Fogel and David Lewin, "Wage Determination in the Public Sector," *Industrial and Labor Relations Review* 27 (April 1974), pp. 410–431. Productivity bargaining has been approached in some public-sector collective bargaining situations. For a discussion, see Rudy Oswald, "Public Productivity Tied to Bargaining," *American Federationist* 85 (March 1976), pp. 20–21; Walter L. Balk, "Why Don't Public Administrators Take Productivity More Seriously?" *Public Personnel Management* 3 (July–August 1974), pp. 318–324; Paul D. Staudohar, "An Experiment in Increasing Productivity of Police Service Employees," *Public Administration Review* 35 (September–October 1975), pp. 518–522; and Marvin Friedman, *The Use of Economic Data in Collective Bargaining* (Washington, D.C.: Government Printing Office, 1978), pp. 53–56.
35. Michael Moskow, J. J. Loewenberg, and E. C. Koziara, *Collective Bargaining in Public Employment* (New York: Random House, 1970), pp. 14–18; and H. H. Wellington and R. K. Winter, Jr., "Structuring Collective Bargaining in Public Employment," *Yale Law Journal* 79 (April 1970), pp. 806–822.
36. Milton Derber et al., "Bargaining and Budget-Making in Illinois Public Institutions," *Industrial and Labor Relations Review* 27 (October 1973), pp. 49–62; and Kenneth M. Jennings, J. A. Smith, and Earle C. Traynham, Jr., "Budgetary Influences on Bargaining in Mass

Transit," *Journal of Collective Negotiations in the Public Sector* 6, no. 4 (1977), pp. 333–339.
37. Frederick O'R. Hayes, "Collective Bargaining and the Budget Director" in *Public Workers and Public Unions,* ed. Sam Zagoria (Englewood Cliffs, N.J.: Prentice-Hall, 1972), p. 91.
38. Derber et al., "Bargaining and Budget-Making," p. 58.
39. Arvid Anderson, "Local Government-Bargaining and the Fiscal Crisis: Money, Unions, Politics, and the Public Interest" in *Proceedings of the 1976 Annual Spring Meeting: Industrial Relations Research Association,* ed. James L. Stern and Barbara Dennis (Madison, Wis.: Industrial Relations Research Association, 1977), p. 518.
40. William H. Holley, Jr., "Unique Complexities of Public Sector Labor Relations," *Personnel Journal* 55 (February 1976), p. 75.
41. Stephen L. Hayford, "An Empirical Investigation of the Public Sector Supervisory Bargaining Rights Issue," *Labor Law Journal* 26 (October 1975), pp. 641–652; Alan Balfour, "Rights of Collective Representation for Public Sector Supervisors," *Journal of Collective Negotiations in the Public Sector* 4, no. 3 (1975), pp. 257–265; and William H. Holley, Jr., J. Boyd Scebra, and William Rector, "Perceptions of the Role of the Principal in Professional Negotiations," *Journal of Collective Negotiations in the Public Sector* 5, no. 4 (1976), pp. 361– 369.
42. Helen S. Tanimoto and Gail F. Inaba, "State Employee Bargaining: Policy and Organization," *Monthly Labor Review* 108 (April 1985), pp. 51–55.
43. George Hildebrand, "The Public Sector" in *Frontiers in Collective Bargaining,* ed. John T. Dunlop and Neil Chamberlain (New York: Harper & Row, 1967), pp. 126–127; Louis V. Imundo, Jr., "The Federal Government Sovereignty and Its Effect on Labor-Management Relations," *Labor Law Journal* 26 (March 1975), pp. 145–152; Louis V. Imundo, Jr., "Some Comparisons between Public Sector and Private Sector Collective Bargaining," *Labor Law Journal* 24 (December 1973), pp. 810–817. For an excellent discussion on the issue of "who is management?" in the public sector, see Milton Derber, "Management Organization for Collective Bargaining in the Public Sector," in Aaron, Grodin, and Stern, *Public Sector Bargaining,* pp. 80–117.
44. For a vivid example of political considerations affecting collective bargaining, see A. H. Raskin, "Politics Up-ends the Bargaining Table," In Zagoria, *Public Workers,* pp. 122–146; and A. H. Raskin, "Mayor and Governor: Knee-Deep in Trouble" in *Collective Negotiation for Public and Professional Employees,* ed. Robert T. Woodworth and Richard B. Peterson (Glenview, Ill.: Scott, Foresman, 1969), pp. 288–292.
45. For a case study example of this situation, see Arnold R. Weber, "Paradise Lost: Or Whatever Happened to the Chicago Social Workers?" *Industrial and Labor Relations Review* 22 (April 1969), pp. 323–338.
46. I. B. Helburn and N. B. Bennett, "Public Employee Bargaining and the Merit Principle," *Labor Law Journal* 23 (October 1972), p. 619; and I. B. Helburn, "The Scope of Bargaining in Public Sector Negotiations: Sovereignty Reviewed," *Journal of Collective Negotiations in the Public Sector* 3 (Spring 1974), pp. 147–166.
47. Paul F. Gerhart, "The Scope of Bargaining in Local Government Negotiations," *Labor Law Journal* 20 (August 1969), pp. 545–552.
48. W. Gary Vause, "Impasse Resolution in the Public Sector—Observations on the First Decade of Law and Practice Under the Florida PERA," *University of Florida Law Review* 37 (1985), pp. 105–188.
49. Peter Feuille, "Police Labor Relations and Multilateralism," *Journal of Collective Negotiations in the Public Sector* 3 (Summer 1974), p. 216.
50. Lee C. Shaw and R. Theodore Clark, Jr., "The Practical Difference between Public and Private Sector Collective Bargaining," *UCLA Law Review* 19 (August 1972), p. 885.
51. Victor Gotbaum, "Collective Bargaining and the Union Leader," in Zagoria, *Public Workers,* pp. 83–84.
52. Michael Marmo, "Public Employee Collective Bargaining: A Mass-Mediated Process," *Journal of Collective Negotiation in the Public Sector* 13, no. 4 (1984), pp. 291–307.
53. "Characteristics of 'Sunshine' Laws in the 50 States," *The Chronicle of Higher Education,* October 10, 1984, p. 18.
54. "Crime Rate is Same Despite Police Strike," *Miami Herald,* July 20, 1975, p. 15-A.
55. Wellington and Winter, "Structuring Collective Bargaining," pp. 822–851; Paul D. Staudohar, "Reappraisal of the Right to Strike in California," *Journal of Collective Negotiations in the Public Sector* 15, no 2 (1986), p. 91.
56. George W. Taylor, "Public Employment: Strikes or Procedures?" *Industrial and Labor Relations Review* 20 (July 1967), p. 636.
57. John F. Burton and Charles Krider, "The Role and Consequences of Strikes by Public Employees," *Yale Law Journal* 79 (January 1970), pp. 418–440.
58. Theodore Kheel, "Resolving Deadlocks without Banning Strikes," *Monthly Labor Review* 91 (July 1969), pp. 62–63.
59. Wellington and Winter, "Structuring Collective Bargaining," pp. 822–825.
60. "Work Stoppages in Government," *Government Employee Relations Report,* 1986, p. 29.
61. Bonnie G. Cebulski, "Analysis of Twenty-Two Illegal Strikes and California Law," *California Public Employee Relations* 18 (August 1973), pp. 2–17.
62. Robert E. Doherty, "Trends in Strikes and Interest Arbitration in the Public Sector," *Labor Law Journal* 37 (August 1986), pp. 473–475.
63. Craig Olson, "Strikes, Strike Penalties, and Arbitration in Six States," *Industrial and Labor Relations Review* 39 (July 1986), p. 539.
64. Michael Marmo, "Public Employees: On-the-Job Discipline for Off-the-Job Behavior," *The Arbitration Journal* 40 (June 1985), p. 23; Marvin Hill, Jr., and Donald Dawson, "Discharge for Off-Duty Misconduct in the Private and Public Sectors," *Arbitration Journal* 40 (June 1985), pp. 24–33.
65. David H. Rosenbloom, "Public Personnel Administration and the Constitution: An Emergent Approach," *Public Administration Review* 35 (February 1975), pp. 52–59.
66. Deborah D. Goldman, "Due Process and Public Personnel Management," *Review of Public Personnel Administration* 2 (Fall 1981), pp. 19–22.
67. "Public Employees Entitled to Respond to Dismissals," *Monthly Labor Review* 108 (May 1985), p. 46.
68. Richard B. Freeman and Casey Ichniowski, "Introduction: The Public Sector Look of American Unionism," *When Public Sector Workers Unionize,* eds. Richard B. Freeman and Casey Ichniowski (Chicago: The University of Chicago Press, 1988), pp. 1–13.
69. Tim Bornstein, "Legacies of Local Government Collective Bargaining in the 1970s," *Labor Law Journal* 31 (March 1980).
70. These techniques were formulated in various discussions with Paul Gerhart of Case Western Reserve University.
71. See, for example, Raymond D. Horton, *Municipal Labor Relations in New York City: Lessons of the Lindsay-Wagner Years* (New York: Praeger Publishers, 1973), p. 134; Michael Marmo, "Public Employee Unions: The Political Imperative," *Journal of Collective*

Negotiations in the Public Sector 4, no 4 (1975), p. 371; and Jay F. Atwood, "Collective Bargaining's Challenge: Five Imperatives for Public Managers," *Public Personnel Management* 5 (January–February 1976), p. 29.
72. For a discussion of the variety and legal interpretations of these strikes, see Paul D. Staudohar, "Quasi-Strikes by Public Employees," *Journal of Collective Negotiations in the Public Sector* 3 (Fall 1974), pp. 363–371.
73. U.S. Department of Labor, Labor-Management Services Administration, *Summary of Public Sector Labor Relations Policies, 1976* (Washington, D.C.: Government Printing Office, 1976), pp. 1–126. Totals are greater than 38 because some states have different impasse procedures for different types of employees; for example, Connecticut has mediation, fact-finding, and arbitration for state employees; fact-finding and arbitration for municipal employees; and mediation and fact-finding for teachers.
74. Paul F. Gerhart and John E. Drotning, "Dispute Settlement and the Intensity of Mediation," *Industrial Relations* 19 (Fall 1980), pp. 352–358.
75. Thomas A. Kochan and Todd Jick, "The Public Sector Mediation Process," *Journal of Conflict Resolution* 22 (June 1978), p. 236.
76. James L. Stern, "Public Sector Bargaining and Strike Rights: What Lies Ahead?" *IRC Reports* (Manoa, Hawaii: University of Hawaii, 1984), p. 3.
77. Thomas P. Gilroy and Anthony Sinicropi, "Impasse Resolution in Public Employment: A Current Assessment," *Industrial and Labor Relations Review* 25 (July 1972), pp. 500–501.
78. James L. Stern et al., *Final Offer Arbitration* (Lexington, Mass.: D. C. Heath, 1975), p. 175.
79. Robert E. Doherty, "Fact-Finding: A One-Eyed Man Lost among the Eagles," *Public Personnel Management* 5 (September–October 1976), p. 366.
80. Kenneth M. Jennings, Steve K. Paulson, and Steven A. Williamson, "Fact-finding in Perspective," *Government Union Review* 8 (Summer 1987), pp. 54–70.
81. Zack, *Understanding Fact-Finding and Arbitration,* p. 4–5.
82. For a further discussion of related concerns and remedial alternatives see Joseph R. Grodin, "Political Aspects of Public Sector Interest Arbitration," *California Law Review* 64 (May 1976), pp. 678–701; John Delaney, Peter Feuille, and Wallace Hendricks, "The Regulation of Bargaining Disputes" in *Advances in Industrial and Labor Relations,* ed. David B. Lipsky and David Lewin (Greenwich, Conn.: JAI Press, Inc., 1986), pp. 83, 113–115.
83. Daniel B. Gallagher and M. D. Chaubey, "Impasse Behavior and Tri-Offer Arbitration in Iowa," *Industrial Relations* 21 (Spring 1982), p. 129.
84. John C. Anderson, "The Impact of Arbitration: A Methodological Assessment," *Industrial Relations* 20 (Spring 1981), p. 129–130.
85. Lewin, Feuille, and Kochan, *Public Sector Labor Relations,* p. 223.
86. Paul F. Gerhart and John E. Drotning, "Do Uncertain Cost/Benefit Estimates Prolong Public-Sector Disputes?" *Monthly Labor Review* 103 (Sept. 1980), pp. 26–30.
87. David E. Bloom, "Is Arbitration *Really* Compatible with Bargaining?" *Industrial Relations* 20 (Fall 1980), pp. 233– 244.
88. Henry S. Farber, "Role of Arbitration in Dispute Settlement," *Monthly Labor Review* 104 (May 1981), p. 34.
89. Doherty, "Fact-Finding," p. 367.
90. William R. Word, "Fact-Finding in Public Employee Negotiations," *Monthly Labor Review* 95 (February 1972), pp. 60–64. Also see James L. Stern, "The Wisconsin Public Employee Fact-Finding Procedure," *Industrial and Labor Relations Review* 19 (July 1966), p. 8.
91. William McHugh, Seminar for Special Masters, Tallahassee, Florida, Spring 1978. James P. Smith, Jr., "Florida's Public Sector Impasse Resolution Process: An Analysis of the Tendencies of Legislative Bodies to Act Consistently with Special Masters' Recommendations," *Journal of Collective Negotiations in the Public Sector* 15, no. 2 (1986), p. 191.
92. Karl O. Magnusen and Patricia A. Renovitch, "Dispute Resolution in Florida's Public Sector: Insight into Impasse," *Journal of Collective Negotiations in the Public Sector* 18 (no. 3, 1989), pp. 241–252.
93. J. Joseph Loewenberg, "Compulsory Arbitration in the United States" in *Compulsory Arbitration,* ed. J. J. Loewenberg et al. (Lexington, Mass.: D.C. Heath, 1976), p. 166. Also see Hoyt N. Wheeler, "An Analysis of Fire Fighter Strikes," *Labor Law Journal* 26 (January 1975), pp. 17–20; and Charles M. Rehmus, "Legislated Interest Arbitration," *Proceedings of the Annual Meeting: Industrial Relations Research Association, 1974* (Madison, Wis.: Industrial Relations Research Association, 1975), pp. 307–312.
94. Lewin, Feuille, and Kochan, *Public Sector Labor Relations,* p. 229; and Charles M. Rehmus, "Public Employees: A Survey of Some Critical Problems on the Frontier of Collective Bargaining," *Labor Law Journal* 27 (September 1976), pp. 588–599.
95. Craig E. Overton and Max S. Wortman, "Compulsory Arbitration: A Strike Alternative for Police?" *Arbitration Journal* 28 (March 1974), p. 40.
96. Hoyt N. Wheeler, "Is Compromise the Rule in Fire Fighter Arbitration?" *Arbitration Journal* 29 (September 1974), pp. 176–185.
97. Marian M. Extejt and James R. Chelius, "The Behavioral Impact of Impasse Resolution Procedures," *Review of Public Personnel Administration* 5 (Spring 1985), pp. 46–47.
98. Frederic Champlin and Mario F. Bognanno, " 'Chilling' Under Arbitration and Mixed Strike-Arbitration Regimes," *Journal of Labor Research* 6 (Fall 1985), pp. 375–386.
99. Frederic C. Champlin and Mario F. Bognanno, "Time Spent Processing Interest Arbitration Cases: The Minnesota Experience," *Journal of Collective Negotiations in the Public Sector* 14, no. 1 (1985), pp. 53–64.
100. Peter Feuille, "Final-Offer Arbitration and Negotiating Incentives," *Arbitration Journal* 32 (September 1977), pp. 203, 220.
101. Kruger and Jones, "Compulsory Interest Arbitration," p. 359.
102. Gallagher and Chaubey, "Impasse Behavior and Tri-Offer Arbitration," p. 146; also see Daniel Gallagher and Richard Pegnetter, "Impasse Resolution Procedure under the Iowa Multistep Procedure," *Industrial and Labor Relations Review* 32 (April 1979), pp. 327–328.
103. Fred Witney, "Final-Offer Arbitration: The Indianapolis Experience," *Monthly Labor Review* 96 (Mary 1973), pp. 20–25.
104. Theodore W. Kheel, "Strikes and Public Employment," *Michigan Law Review* 67 (March 1969), pp. 939–940. Vague guidelines, such as "public interest," have often plagued at least one fact-finder; see Doherty, "Fact-Finding," p. 366.
105. Gary Long and Peter Feuille, "Final-Offer Arbitration: Sudden Death in Eugene," *Industrial and Labor Relations Review* 27 (January 1974), p. 203.
106. Gregory G. Dell'omo, "Wage Disputes in Interest Arbitration: Arbitrators Weigh the Criteria," *The Arbitration Journal* 44 (June 1989), pp. 4–8.
107. Peter Feuille and Susan Schwochau, "The Decisions of Interest Arbitrators," *The Arbitration Journal* 43 (March 1988), pp. 28–35.
108. J. H. Foegen, "Public Sector Strike-Prevention: Let the Tax-

payer Decide," *Journal of Collective Negotiations in the Public Sector* 3 (Summer 1974), p. 223.
109. I. B. Helburn and J. L. Matthews, "The Referendum as an Alternative to Bargaining," *Journal of Collective Negotiations in the Public Sector* 9, no. 2 (1980), pp. 93–105.
110. Raymond L. Hogler and Curt Kriksciun, "Impasse Resolution in Public Sector Collective Negotiations: A Proposed Procedure," *Industrial Relations Law Journal* 6, no. 4 (1984), pp. 481-510.
111. Donald T. Barnum and I. B. Helburn, "Influence the Electorate Experience with Referenda on Public Employee Bargaining," *Industrial and Labor Relations Review* 35 (April 1982), pp. 330-342.
112. Thomas Kochan, "Dynamics of Dispute Resolution in the Public Sector," in *Public-Sector Bargaining,* pp. 155–189.
113. Steven M. Goldschmidt and Leland E. Stuart, "The Extent and Impact of Educational Policy Bargaining," *Industrial and Labor Relations Review* 39 (April 1986), pp. 350–356; Timothy Loney, "Public Sector Labor Relations Research: The First Generation," *Public Personnel Management* 18 (Summer 1989), pp. 162–175.
114. Lorraine M. McDonnell and Anthony Pascal, *Teacher Unions and Educational Reform* (Santa Monica, Calif.: RAND, 1988), pp. 1-3.
115. "Faculty and Campuses Represented by Certified Bargaining Agents," *Chronicle of Higher Education,* July 12, 1989, p. A16.
116. Gwen B. Williams and Perry A. Zirkel, "Shift in Collective Bargaining Issues in Higher Education: A Review of the Literature," *Journal of Collective Negotiations in the Public Sector* 18 (no. 1, 1989), pp. 73–86; Daniel J. Julius and Margaret K. Chandler, "Academic Bargaining Agents in Higher Education: Do Their Achievements Differ?" *Journal of Collective Negotiations in the Public Sector* 18 (no. 1, 1989), pp. 9–58.
117. John T. Delaney and Peter Feuille, "Police," in *Collective Bargaining in American Industry,* ed. David B. Lipsky and Clifford B. Donn (Lexington, Mass.: Lexington Books, 1987), pp. 263–303.
118. Gary Fink, ed., *Labor Unions* (Westport, Conn.: Greenwood Press, 1977), p. 103.
119. Leo Troy, "The Proposed Fire Fighters' Labor Act of 1987: An Analysis and Critique," *Government Union Review* 8 (Summer 1987), pp. 4–6.
120. *Title VII of Civil Service Reform Act of 1978.*
121. Douglas M. McCabe, "Problems in Federal Sector Labor-Management Relations under Title VII of the Civil Service Reform Act of 1978," *Labor Law Journal* 33 (August 1982), p. 561.
122. "Conflict Abounds in Federal Labor Relations on Civil Service Reform Act's 10th Anniversary," *Daily Labor Report,* February 16, 1988, p. C-1.
123. Douglas A. McCabe, "Problems," pp. 561–563.
124. George T. Sulzner, "Federal Labor-Management Relations: The Reagan Impact," *Journal of Collective Negotiations in the Public Sector* 15 (no. 3, 1986), pp. 202–209.
125. George W. Bohlander, "The Federal Labor Relations Authority: A Review and Evaluation," *Journal of Collective Negotiations in the Public Sector* 18 (no. 4, 1989), pp. 273–288.

Labor Relations in Multinational Corporations and in Other Countries

"Since the end of World War II, the U.S. share of global manufacturing has fallen from 29 percent to 14 percent. Other nations have become increasingly competitive by essentially replicating the proven techniques of scientific management pioneered in the United States almost a century ago. By dividing work into small fractionalized tasks, a well educated or highly skilled labor force is not required. This system can be exported by telephone through the transfer of capital and technology. More than $23 trillion in capital is transferred across national boundaries annually. Wages in . . . some third world nations are only one-tenth of ours, and the gap is widening. . . .

[Korea is now] a major producer and exporter of automobiles. You have already seen the advertisements for what purports to be a well designed and reliable Korean import. [T]o compete with the Koreans, we would need to remove an additional $10 to $11 from U.S. labor costs. And some are suggesting that there is a sleeping giant just to the west of Korea, namely China, where hourly labor costs may be less than one dollar per hour."

John R. Stepp, "New Directions in Labor-Management Relations," *Proceedings of Industrial Relations Research Association Spring Meeting* (Madison, Wis.: Industrial Relations Research Association, 1986), p. 455.

With the development of a global economy, movement in Eastern Europe toward greater political democracy and market-oriented economies, and the elimination of trade and travel restrictions within the western European countries, the study of labor relations within multinational corporations (MNCs) and foreign countries becomes imperative to today's student. This chapter begins with a general discussion of the operations of multinational corporations in a global economy and unions' approaches and problems in dealing with MNCs. Then, principal characteristics of the labor relations systems of the major trading parties of the United States are presented.

Multinational Corporations and Transnational Collective Bargaining

The growing interdependency among nations and the activities of **multinational corporations (MNCs)** have become important facets of economic life. Although multinational corporations have existed for more than 150 years, their numbers and share of world output have expanded their importance and visibility in recent years. To appreciate the enormity of the MNCs, consider the following example. Mitsui, a Japanese firm, had sales of $117 billion in 1988; General Motors, a U.S. company, had sales of $110 billion. The sales of each of these companies exceeded the value of the total gross domestic products of such countries as Denmark, Finland, Greece, Ireland, Norway, Portugal, Turkey, and New Zealand.[1]

MNCs are now producing as well as marketing their products in several countries, instead of producing only at the home base and selling abroad, and they are doing so with increasing impact. For example, U.S. firms invested $48.1 billion in foreign production facilities in 1989, an increase of 24 percent over 1988,[2] and sales by U.S. MNCs have reached over $3.7 trillion.[3] Interestingly, foreign direct investment in the United States reached $328.9 billion in 1989, an increase of over $57 billion over 1987.[4]

Japan has now surpassed the United Kingdom and Canada with the largest direct investment in the United States. Japan's total U.S. assets have increased to over $200 billion, of which $15 billion was acquired in 1988. U.S. companies, in turn, invested $2.3 billion in Japan in 1988, more than double the 1985 amount. In 1988, total U.S. assets of affiliates of foreign companies were $926 billion, and their net income was about $10 billion.[5]

Exchange rates have a great deal to do with the trade between countries and production within a specific country. For example, U.S. firms' competitive position was improved in 1987 as a result of the change in value of the U.S. dollar. In 1987, U.S. firms experienced a 1.5 percent decline in unit labor cost while Japan's unit labor cost rose by 0.5 percent. After the adjustment in the exchange rates, unit labor cost in Japan rose by 13 percent. The change in the exchange rates with European countries ranged from 13 percent with the United Kingdom to 25 percent with Denmark. Thereby, U.S. manufactured goods become comparatively more attractive in the international marketplace and the job market within the United States reflected this increased demand.[6]

The importance of fluctuating exchange rates is reflected in Exhibit 15.1, which shows the indexes of hourly compensation costs for production workers in manufacturing for 30 countries during four time periods from 1975 to 1987. In 1987, hourly compensation costs for manufacturing production workers in Germany, Norway, and Switzerland were 25 to 31 percent higher than those in the United States, and the hourly costs in Belgium, Denmark, the Netherlands, and Sweden were 8 to 12 percent higher. On the other side, costs rose to more than 90 percent of the United States figure in France, Italy, Austria, and Finland, 84 percent in Japan, 90 percent in Canada, 60 percent in the United Kingdom, Australia, and Spain, 20 to 50 percent in Hong Kong, Korea, Taiwan, and Brazil, and less than 10 percent in Mexico.

Because the value of the U.S. dollar has fallen in value in relation to the currencies of most other countries, the relative hourly compensation costs of these coun-

Exhibit 15.1

Indexes of Hourly Compensation Costs for Production Workers in Manufacturing for 30 Countries or Areas, 1975 to 1987

[United States = 100]

Country or area	1975	1980	1985	1987
United States	100	100	100	100
Canada	92	86	84	89
Brazil	14	14	9	11
Mexico	31	30	16	10
Australia	84	82	61	64
Hong Kong	12	15	14	16
Israel	35	39	31	–
Japan	48	57	50	84
Korea	5	10	10	13
New Zealand	50	54	34	–
Singapore	13	15	19	18
Sri Lanka	4	2	2	–
Taiwan	6	10	11	17
Austria	68	87	56	95
Belgium	101	134	69	112
Denmark	99	111	63	108
Finland	72	84	62	97
France	71	91	58	92
Germany	100	125	74	125
Greece	27	38	28	–
Ireland	47	60	45	–
Italy	73	81	57	92
Luxembourg	100	122	59	–
Netherlands	103	123	67	112
Norway	107	119	82	131
Portugal	25	21	12	–
Spain	41	61	37	58
Sweden	113	127	75	112
Switzerland	96	113	75	127
United Kingdom	52	76	48	67

Note: Dash indicates data not available.

Source: Patricia Capdevielle, "International Differences in Employers' Compensation Costs," *Monthly Labor Review* 111 (May 1988), p. 44.

tries have increased. For example, in 1985 Japan's hourly cost was 50 percent of that of the United States; however, it had increased to 84 percent by 1987. In Germany, in 1985 the cost was 74 percent of that of the United States; it had risen to 125 percent by 1987.[7]

Operating in different countries creates opportunities for MNCs to bypass protective tariffs by making parts in one country and assembling the final product in another. For example, the European Community accused Ricoh, a maker of photocopiers, of making 90 percent of its parts in Japan, doing the assembly work in the United States, and shipping products from the United States as U.S. exports. Such situations create other possibilities in the auto industry because England limits the Japanese share of its auto market to 11 percent, France to 3 percent, and Italy allows only 3,300 cars per year. With Japanese automakers locating in the United States, such issues will provide challenges in trade between countries.[8]

MNCs have the capacity to force concessions from unions by threatening to shift production to another country and essentially pit one group of workers against another. One automaker that operates a plant in Ohio sought to introduce new technology; the union resisted because the membership would lose jobs. The company then took a number of the union leaders to a new plant in Juarez, Mexico—just across the border from El Paso—showed them the technologies used in the plant, and said: "It is your choice. Either you concede what we are asking in terms of bargaining or the work that you do in Ohio will be transferred to Juarez. If you think this is an idle threat, this is the plant. This is the production process."[9] See "Labor Relations in Action" for an explanation of how MNCs may deal with workers in different countries to achieve their goals. Although such practices are not illegal, one could easily argue that the practices are not ethical.

Organized labor has been critical of the U.S. MNC's effect on employment and labor relations for the following reasons:

- MNCs' foreign investments deplete capital resources needed for domestic investment and undermine economic growth and new job creation at home.
- MNCs export U.S. technology to exploit low-cost foreign labor, depriving American workers of their rightful share of the rewards of technology.
- MNCs substitute imports from their affiliates in low-wage countries for American-made goods, thereby undermining the American wage standard, depressing economic conditions at home, and decreasing employment and payrolls.
- MNCs displace U.S. exports with foreign-produced goods from their foreign affiliates, thereby adversely affecting our trade balance.[10]

Foreign-based MNCs have grown rapidly in the United States and now employ 1.4 million Americans in manufacturing plants. Unions have often viewed MNCs with suspicion, but the management and employment practices tend to be more similar to those of home-based firms than dissimilar. The labor relations activities and decisions tend to be locally determined and highly decentralized. Unions have found that organizing foreign-based MNCs has been just as difficult as organizing a home-based company. In addition, the management of the various plants use essentially the same tactics to keep unions out of the plant. These tactics include use of lawyers and management consultants, positive human resources management, consultation with workers on decisions, delays allowed under National Labor Relations Board procedures, and local politicians making statements to support the company. Unions essentially use the same organizing tactics, with the addition of negative publicity directed toward the foreign owners and appeals to American patriotism. With these counteractive tactics, the results of elections have not been significantly different—fewer than 50 percent wins for the unions. Whenever U.S.-based unions have con-

Labor Relations in Action

Dealing with an MNC – A Scenario

When the 500 employees of a forklift factory in Irvine, Scotland, reported to work, they were instructed to attend a plant meeting in the company cafeteria. At 9:00 a.m. the plant manager and senior staff announced that the company was willing to invest $60 million in the present plant, close two production lines at its Dutch factory, and increase employment at the Irvine plant by 1,000. In return, the company wanted the workers to take a 14 percent pay cut; and they had 48 hours to decide whether or not to accept this proposal.

The next day each employee received a letter from the company president, who was located in Portland, Oregon, stating that he did not know whether Irvine was the best alternative. He indicated that he was trying to make up his mind whether the Irvine plant should be the lead plant in Europe. At the bottom of the letter, each employee could vote "yes" or "no."

Only 11 employees voted no. While the plant industrial relations manager stated that if the employees had refused the proposal, the work would have been done elsewhere. The union president made no bones about his bitterness; he called it "industrial rape – do it or else." Thus, while the workers in Irvine considered their destiny, at corporate headquarters the staff calculated the alternatives in the far corners of the world through the screen of a desktop personal computer.

The corporate management could have taken the following approach: The Irvine workers could have been told that the work was going to the Dutch plant if the 14 percent pay cut was not approved. Then the Dutch workers could have been told that the Irvine employees were willing to go as far as a 14 percent cut and could have been asked for a proposal. Next, the Portland workers could have been told that the European employees were more cooperative and that unless there were fewer grievances, arbitrations, and conflicts, work would be transferred from Portland for economic reasons.

Because employees and their unions do not have a systematic communication mechanism, rarely exchange vital information, and do in fact compete with each other for jobs, MNCs have the opportunity to take advantage of the situation in the manner just described.

In this case, 2 days after the employees voted "yes" or "no," the votes were tallied, the pay cut was accepted, and the company president telexed the Dutch plant manager and told him that the work normally done in Holland would be moving to Scotland. The end result was the termination of a number of Dutch workers and the early retirement of the plant manager.

Since Dutch law requires advance consultation about plant closures, the union took the company to court. The judge ordered the company to discuss its strategy with members of the factory work councils and reveal the corporate plan. The union did not like the plan and went to court again.

After a long legal battle, the company struck a deal – the employees would drop the suit, and the company would not transfer production for 3 years. As a result, the Scottish workers were held in limbo during the interim period.

During all this time, the director of European operations continued his concern about increasing shares of the market gained by Japanese producers.

Source: Barry Newman, "Single-Country Unions of Europe Try to Cope with Multinationals," *The Wall Street Journal*, November 30, 1983, pp. 1, 24.

tact with foreign-based unions, these contacts are generally of an information-sharing nature.[11]

In some cases, MNCs transplant their management practices into their foreign affiliates. In recent years, Japanese MNCs have been successful in making this transfer in unionized plants. In Fremont, California, New United Motor Manufacturing, Inc., the joint venture between General Motors and Toyota, was successful; successes have also been noted by Bridgestone Tire, which purchased the Firestone plant in LaVergne, Tennessee, and by Sumitomo Rubber, which purchased the Dunlop tire plant in Birmingham, England. The Freemont plant had one of the worst labor relations records in the United States in 1982, but its performance became one of the best in the industry by 1988.

Japanese practices that have been introduced include elimination of executive perks, such as reserved parking places and separate cafeterias, work teams of six to eight members who rotate jobs, emphasis placed on trust between managers and employees, managers spending more time on the shop floor with the workers, regular meetings to inform workers about production and financial results of the company, wearing of "team" jackets by managers and workers, flexibility in job assignments, and holding each employee responsible for the quality of products produced.

Not all results of management transfer are positive, however, especially when sales decline, the foreign manager does not speak the local language, or employees resist imposition of a new way of doing things. In Forrest City, Arkansas, for example, the Sanyo Company, maker of televisions and microwave ovens, had only one Japanese manager who spoke English, so that every meeting required an interpreter. In 1985, when sales lagged, the company demanded medical insurance cuts, changes in the seniority system, and the right to shift workers from job to job. The union reacted by striking for 3 weeks, and there were incidents of stone-throwing, tire-slashing, and charges of an attempted fire-bombing, resulting in 39 persons arrested.[12]

Unions particularly have difficulty dealing with MNCs for the reasons discussed below.

*1. **If there is a strike*** in the parent company country, the union does not shut down the flow of financial resources to the corporation. Operations in other countries continue to function and generate profits, which may relieve management of much pressure in negotiations and reduce the costs of the strike.

2. MNCs have an internal source of products from facilities in several countries and use this position as leverage to bargain down wages, benefits, and other conditions of employment (called **whipsawing** the union). If there is a strike at one facility, the MNCs increase production at other units, destroying the potency of the strike.[13] Many specific examples of whipsawing can be identified. General Motors was able to expand the work week from 37.5 to 40 hours by convincing the union in West Germany that they must increase hours to retain competitiveness. General Motors has considered increasing its auto production in Brazil and Mexico as part of its wage concession demands, and when Canadian unions resisted wage concessions, GM considered shifting production back to the United States.[14] While there are specific examples of using production shifts in bargaining, it does not appear that firms locate production facilities overseas for the primary purpose of discouraging strikes in their home country.[15]

3. MNCs with complex tiers of management do not delegate authority to make labor relations decisions to local management, thereby complicating the negotiation process because unions do not know who is in charge.[16] Empirical evidence indicates that most unions have not encountered different behavior between domestic and foreign-owned MNCs, but there seems to be a wider variation in behavior among the MNCs than among single-nation corporations in terms of grievance settlement prior to arbitration, amount of local autonomy in negotiations, and difficulty in negotiating the first agreement.[17] However, because budget and investment decisions are made at the home office, local negotiations are certainly affected.

4. MNCs shift profits to different facilities, manipulate prices on internal transactions, and change marketing emphasis, confusing the unions in negotiations when they seek the facts necessary to address and resolve collective bargaining issues.

Because U.S. unions are accustomed to bargaining on ability to pay and are entitled to wage and financial information that allows them to conduct informed negotiations, they are frustrated when MNCs furnish only information that is required by law. Such information about MNCs' locating plants in foreign facilities and operating data on these plants may be refused by the MNCs with the approval of the NLRB.[18]

Union Approaches to Multinational Bargaining and Employer Reactions

A primary motivator for unions to seek transnational bargaining and to standardize labor conditions among the MNCs is to lessen competition from lower wage areas and to protect their own standards—in other words, to take wages out of competition. To combat the power of the MNCs and to seek objectives that are mutually beneficial to the unions and their members, union leaders have tried two main approaches: (1) collective bargaining and (2) legislative enactment. Through collective bargaining, unions have either attempted to bargain directly with the MNCs or coordinate their bargaining activities with unions in other countries by sharing information and supporting each other's activities.

The unions have become frustrated with attempts to achieve any degree of transnational bargaining, so they have concentrated on the adoption of codes of conduct to regulate MNC behavior. The International Labor Organization, a tripartite organization with governments, employers, and unions from 150 countries represented, established labor codes that state the MNCs should give priority to human rights, employment, safety, occupational development, social justice, and promotion and advancement of local nationals and should provide stable employment and pay comparable wages.

The Organization for Economic Cooperation and Development, an international organization headquartered in Paris, has also established "Guidelines for MNCs" concerning conduct in labor-management relations.[19] These guidelines include certain rights: the rights to organize and bargain collectively, to have access to data for negotiations, to be trained as a member of the work force, and to be given advance notice of changes in operations. Further, subsidiaries of MNCs are expected to observe employment standards comparable to those in the host countries; MNCs are expected not to threaten to shift production to other countries to influence negotiations or to prevent unionization, and local management representatives should be authorized to negotiate on behalf of the MNCs.[20]

Unions, as well as some governments, have asserted that collective bargaining on a national basis has considerable limitations in facing MNCs. This assertion is based on the belief that MNCs have adopted global strategies, so a union acting alone within one nation cannot effectively respond. Likewise, some governments are uneasy about the fact that MNCs cannot easily be made accountable to any one country's economic and social policies. Moreover, there has been persistent fear that if a union or government in one country acted without the support of unions or governments in other countries, it would risk transfer of operations by the MNC to a more hospitable nation.[21]

Although some form of transnational industrial relations seems to be inevitable, most MNCs generally consider it a distant prospect and one that will not be lightly entertained by management.[22] Part of management's opposition stems from the unions' potential for shutting down production internationally. Further, transnational bargaining would introduce a tri-level structure of bargaining that would include multinational negotiations, followed by national ones, then local. This additional level would increase the complexity of negotiations as well as companies' vulnerability to strikes at the international level without a comparable reduction in vulnerability at the national and local levels.[23]

In some cases, countries themselves are not encouraging investments by MNCs; taxation policies, building limitations, requirements for local partners, the possibility of nationalization and expropriation of facilities, and the risks of political uncertainties are factors deterring MNC investment.[24] Less developed countries seek additional investments by MNCs for economic stimulus to the countries' development, income, employment programs, and so on, and MNCs find these countries attractive because of the low wage structures, tax incentives, and political guarantees. Such advantages are particularly appealing to the MNC that must operate in a very competitive product market.[25] But when unions press via transnational bargaining for improved wages, benefits, and working conditions—all socially desirable goals for the populace—they become a force running counter to the short-run national economic goals of the country.[26] The economic boost MNCs can give a developing nation will not occur if firms fail to locate there; MNCs might well decide to avoid countries with the high wages and benefits that transnational bargaining has instituted.

Obstacles for Unions in Bargaining with Multinational Corporations

Unions face formidable tasks in their efforts to arrange transnational bargaining because they must be successful in mediating and balancing the conflicting interests of different groups encompassed by the MNC's employees, labor leaders, companies, and governments.[27] In fact, unions themselves provide some of the more important obstacles to transnational bargaining; however, these obstacles are not insurmountable. Only when these obstacles are overcome can their attention be turned to external factors.

Differences in Labor Relations Laws There is wide variation in the legal systems for industrial relations among countries. There are different methods for determining union representation, different union jurisdictions and structure, and differences in the scope of bargaining.[28]

Absence of a Central Authority Unions lack a strong, centralized decision-making authority regarding transnational affairs, and most national union leaders are reluctant to allow an international body to make decisions that affect their unions and members.

Cultural Differences Another complicating factor is the differences in ideological and religious beliefs among, for example, free trade unions and socialist- or communist-linked unions. Such differences have made joint undertakings between unions in the free world and elsewhere almost impossible.[29]

Lack of Coordination of Activities Unions have not been very successful in coordinating their international bargaining, boycott, and strike activities. An excellent example occurred in the last major rubber strike of Goodyear, Uniroyal, B. F. Goodrich, and Firestone. (Each has extensive overseas operations; for example, Goodyear has 30 and Firestone 25 non-U.S. operations.) Support for the U.S. strikes was to come from the International Federation of Chemical, Energy, and General Workers Unions (ICEF), which has affiliates in Europe, North America, and Japan. The ICEF Rubber Division approved a ban on overtime by employees of non-strike companies and a system of monitoring and preventing shipments to the United States. At the end of the strike—the longest rubber strike in U.S. history—the ICEF claimed that its efforts had had a significant effect on the bargaining outcome; however, the facts seemed to contradict this claim. A study by Northrup and Rowan of the U.S. rubber workers' strike did not reveal a single instance of interference with tire shipments from Europe, Japan, or North America; in fact, they found that imports jumped substantially in anticipation of the strike and never fell below the pre-strike level. Furthermore, even Canadian imports were significantly increased during the strike, reversing what had occurred several years before, when U.S. rubber workers refused to support a strike by Canadian rubber workers.[30]

Differing National Priorities The economic, social, legal, and political differences among countries serve as yet another obstacle to transnational bargaining. Few if any countries would subvert their national needs in the interest of developing an international system of industrial relations.

Employer Resistance Employer resistance is less obvious than other obstacles at this time, mostly because of the inability of the unions to overcome the other hurdles that they face.[31] Once the initial hurdles are overcome, employers' opinions and attitudes concerning transnational collective bargaining will no doubt emerge, but in the meantime MNCs may sit idly by until the unions get their own houses in order.

Activities of Multinational Unions

Although much of what unions have accomplished in achieving international cooperation and coordination is considered by some a "public relations coup,"[32] there have been some tangible activities among unions. The International Confederation of Free Trade Unions and International Trade Secretariats have proposed that the United Nations adopt charters for MNCs, specifying their obligation to recognize trade unions, observe fair labor standards, observe prevailing wage rates, attempt betterment of social conditions, reinvest profits made from less developed countries in those countries, establish works councils worldwide, and use labor-intensive technology when possible. In Western Europe, unions have backed the European Community statutes that require worker participation and works councils' agreement on such issues as rules for recruitment, career advancement, dismissal, training, health and safety, welfare and social programs, pay methods, and holidays.

In addition, four multinational labor organizations have been quite active in international activities: International Federation of Chemical, Energy, and General Workers Unions (ICEF), International Metalworkers Federation (IMF), International Federation of Petroleum and Chemical Workers (IFPCW), and International Federation of Air Line Pilots Associations (IFALPA). Their activities thus far have essentially included gathering information about MNCs, providing education programs, and coordinating collective bargaining activities (although the federations themselves do no actual collective bargaining).[33] Each of these organizations believes that it must establish a firm foundation upon which to develop more penetrating actions in the future.

Effects of Unions on Multinational Corporations

Research conducted mostly in European countries has indicated that unions have had little direct effect on investment and production allocation policies of MNCs. However, they have had considerable indirect effect because union relations with employers help shape the investment climate of a country.

Thus far, MNCs rarely have been able to afford to switch production to other countries as a bargaining or union intimidation tactic because of the costs involved. They no doubt would shift production to another country in cases where a labor dispute stops production and the move is economically and practically possible. However, such decisions are considerably limited because companies must have the necessary excess production capacity available and management must expect the labor dispute to last sufficiently long to justify any shift in production before it would be feasible.

Overall, there is little evidence of substantial negative effects of MNCs on industrial relations in countries in which they operate. They usually offer prevailing or superior wage standards and provide comparable working conditions for several reasons. The strengths of unions in the respective countries, the highly integrated and institutionalized nature of industrial relations systems, and the socioeconomic and political climates of the countries have clearly constrained the potential for direct adverse effect.[34]

Conclusions and Predictions on Transnational Bargaining

Systematic investigations of transnational collective bargaining reveal that it does not yet exist in any realistic form and is not likely to occur in the near future. MNCs are generally opposed to it, and trade unions are not of a single mind regarding its desirability. While there have been several cases of information exchange between multinational unions and MNCs and a few instances of union-management consultation, only one trade union secretariat—the International Transport Workers Federation (ITF)—has actually negotiated an agreement with shipping companies. Further, only in the unique U.S.-Canadian environment does much transnational bargaining occur.[35]

There has been no identifiable trend toward transnational collective bargaining by companies and unions in the United States, Europe, or Japan.[36] Some believe that there will be no effective transnational collective bargaining in the near future.[37] However, others believe that such collective bargaining is inevitable.[38] It will probably develop first in either the European community, North America, or Central America and deal initially with general topics, such as employment protection, investment policies, and codes of fair practices, before broadening into other bargaining topics.

Unions in Other Countries

With the growing interdependency among nations, major improvements in communication and travel between countries, and the increasing role of multinational corporations (MNCs), there is an imperative need to learn more about labor relations systems in other parts of the world. Books have been written about many of the specific topics in this chapter, and no attempt will be made to present detailed descriptions or analyses of labor relations systems in the countries mentioned. This section presents unique and interesting features of a variety of countries with the hope of encouraging the readers to pursue more thorough investigations. Its coverage ranges from the developing countries of Latin and South America to the countries nearest our borders—Mexico and Canada—to the major trading partners of the United States such as Japan and the Western European countries. The extent of discussion of each country's labor relations system is determined by its proximity to the United States; its trade, economic, and political relationships with the United States; and its uniqueness among the world's labor relations systems. From these discussions, specific attention is directed toward multinational corporations and transnational collective bargaining.

Many U.S. residents tend to view the rest of the world in terms of their own patterns of living. The fact is that virtually no country has a labor relations system like ours; even the most similar country, Canada, has several major departures from typical U.S. labor relations practices. Unions of Eastern and Western Europe have much closer ties to political parties; Japanese unions are organized on the enterprise level; Latin American unions are split along ideological lines. By contrast, the U.S. labor relations system is based on majority rule, exclusive representation for bargaining agents, and political independence. Exhibit 15.2 presents an overview of distinguishing features of foreign labor relations systems; the following discussion briefly explains these systems.

Another distinguishing feature between labor relations in the United States and that of other countries of the world is the percentage of employees who are union members. Exhibit 15.3 shows that the United States is classified among the least unionized countries such as Colombia, Egypt, France, Mexico, Portugal, and Spain. Finland and Sweden are the most unionized countries, with 80 to 90 percent of the work force being unionized.

Exhibit 15.2 **Overview of Distinguishing Features of U.S. and Foreign Labor Relations Systems**

United States

Exclusive bargaining representation
Majority rule
Political independence

Canada

Influence by unions and companies from U.S.
Two major linguistic and cultural groups
Decentralized and fragmented collective bargaining
Legal influence within provinces

Latin and South America

Wide variation in the degree of sophistication in labor relations systems
Close connection between trade unions and political parties
Voluminous labor codes and government regulations that cover wages and terms of employment
Predominantly negotiations at plant level only

Western Europe

Exclusive bargaining representation nonexistent
Much negotiation between employer association and union confederation with individual bargaining under the resulting agreement
Many fringe benefits established by law
Worker participation mandated in many countries

Japan

Labor-management consultation
Lifetime employment in large firms
Enterprise unions
Wage system with much weight on seniority

Australia

Arbitration tribunals
Wage boards
Compulsory arbitration

Eastern Europe

Government-controlled unions
Lack of collective bargaining
No labor agreements

Canada

Canada's labor relations system is affected by a number of variables: foreign influences, climate, natural resources, and two major linguistic and cultural groups. Its economy is subject to cyclical fluctuations resulting from harsh winters, seasonality of its industries, and foreign influences (mostly the United States). In addition, Canada's geographical spread and regional concentration of resources and production have led to decentralized and fragmented collective bargaining. The penetration of U.S. corporations into Canada has had a significant effect on Canadian labor relations due to the fact that many major decisions still are made in the United States. The French- and English-speaking division of Canada has produced two distinct labor movements; further, relationships between management, which is primarily unilingually English-speaking, and the predominantly French-speaking work force have not been ideal[39]

Collective bargaining in Canada remains highly localized with the predominant bargaining unit being the single-establishment union. This bargaining arrangement prevails in over 60 percent of the contracts covering 500 employees or more, and covers over 50 percent of Canada's union members. Corporatewide bargaining occurs in railways, communications, airlines, and broadcasting due to the highly integrated technology in these industries.[40]

Exhibit 15.3 **Trade Union Membership as a Percentage of Economically Active Population**

Percent of Unionization	Countries
80–90	Finland, Sweden
70–80	Belgium, Denmark, Israel
60–70	Austria, Luxembourg, New Zealand, Norway
50–60	Australia
40–50	Algeria, England, Ireland, West Germany
30–40	Argentina, Canada, Ethiopia, Greece, Japan, Switzerland, Venezuela
20–30	Korea, Netherlands, Taiwan
10–20	Colombia, Costa Rica, Dominican Republic, Egypt, France, Honduras, Italy, Mexico, Portugal, Spain, United States
0–10	Chile, Guatemala, Indonesia, Pakistan, Philippines

Source: *World Labor Report* 2 (Geneva: International Labor Office, 1985), pp. 9, 11; updated from *Foreign Labor Trends* (Washington, D.C.: U.S. Department of Labor, 1989).

In sharp contrast to the United States, union membership is 37.6 percent of the nonagricultural work force. The international portion of the union membership has dropped from over half in 1975 to about one-third in 1988, largely through large increases in union membership in the public sector and secession of the Canadian Auto Workers from the United States–based United Auto Workers (UAW). Nearly 90 percent of the workers are covered by labor relations law within the provinces (similar to states in the United States).

There are significant differences in public policy toward collective bargaining in Canada when compared to the United States. The distinction between mandatory and voluntary subjects for collective bargaining has never been adopted in Canada. There is no such thing as a right-to-work law in Canada; in fact, the provinces of Quebec, Manitoba, and British Columbia impose the agency shop as a minimum requirement. British Columbia and Manitoba require the collective bargaining agreements to include "just cause" provisions, although Manitoba excludes probationary employees from coverage.[41]

Unlike the United States, Canadian law does not allow employers to conduct lengthy election campaigns against unions; most provinces allow unions to be certified without any secret ballot election. Unions are required only to obtain 60 percent of the workers' signatures on authorization cards before the union will be certified. In addition, several of the Canadian provinces—British Columbia, Quebec, Manitoba, and Ontario—have assisted new unions in obtaining the first contract with an employer by requiring interest arbitration when negotiations and mediation efforts fail.[42]

In case of strikes, employers in the province of Quebec are forbidden from hiring strike breakers, and in Ontario and Manitoba, firms that provide strike-breaking services are outlawed. Canadian legislation is more favorable to public sector bargaining; the federal government and all of the provinces have extended the right to bargain to the vast majority of public employees. In addition, fewer restrictions are placed on negotiable issues in Canada, and bargaining is practiced more extensively in Canada than in the U.S. public sector.[43]

With free trade between the United States and Canada to be phased in over the next 10 years, the question remains whether the Canadian labor relations system will become more like that of the United States or the U.S. labor relations system will become more like Canada's.[44]

Central and South America

Collective bargaining in Central and South America is far less extensive and sophisticated than corresponding activities in the United States; however, the number of agreements has been increasing. While the percentage of workers covered by labor agreements is greater in Mexico, Venezuela, and Argentina than in the United States, this amount reflects more a government extension of contract terms than actual industrywide bargaining patterns. The extent of development of collective bargaining may be illustrated in three categories:[45]

1. The advanced group, as exemplified in parts of Mexico and Argentina.
2. A much larger middle group in which bargaining ranges from advanced collective bargaining with larger firms to very simple or no bargaining in smaller firms, as in Chile and Brazil.
3. A large third group in which collective bargaining is not widespread, as in Costa Rica, Ecuador, and Nicaragua.

In some countries, such as Mexico, some unions have much clout. For example, the Oil Workers Union, with 100,000 members–mostly employed by the state-run oil company, PEMEX–has the right to award 40 percent of the company's maintenance and service work to subcontractors (subject to PEMEX review) and to receive 2 percent of the value of all drilling contracts, and its leaders receive fees for directing these contracts (which usually go to friends and relatives).[46] PEMEX pays all active and retired workers $16 per month that can be spent only in union-owned shops. The PEMEX labor agreement provides for the union to decide on appointments to most jobs, and the right to terminate workers rests with the union.[47]

In 1965, the U.S. government established the "maquiladora" program. This allows U.S. companies to locate processing plants on the Mexican border, send parts to the Mexican plants from the United States, and assemble the final product in Mexico to be shipped elsewhere, mostly back to the United States. The arrangement requires employers to pay taxes only on the value added to the finished product, which was related to the low employee wage of $0.88 in 1988, compared with the overall wage rate for manufacturing employees in Mexico of $1.57. In 1988 alone, the maquiladora industry grew by 20 percent and now includes about 1,500 foreign-owned plants with over 350,000 employees.[48]

The AFL-CIO and its counterpart in Mexico, the Confederation of Mexican Workers (CTM), have joined forces to combat the challenges of the Mexican maquiladora industries that are locating just south of the U.S. border. The AFL-CIO is concerned about the loss of American jobs, and the CTM is concerned about the low wages of the nonunion workers in these industries.[49]

In early 1990, the Confederacion de Trabajadores de Mexico, a labor union composed of 35,000 members in the city of Matamoros, Mexico, threatened a strike of some 65 plants, which were mostly U.S.-owned. The employers association, the Maquiladora Association of Matamoros, averted the strike by agreeing to increase employees' pay and benefits to $2.22 per hour. Whether this agreement will be carried over to the other locations along the 2,000-mile border with the United States remains to be seen.[50]

In Central and South America, negotiations between unions and employers take place primarily at the plant level. Only Argentina, Venezuela, and Mexico have widespread industrywide bargaining. The principal reason for this arrangement is that legislation in the various countries typically does not require employers to bargain except on a plant-level basis.

An interesting departure from most of the rest of the world is the important role of collective bargaining between employers and nonunion workers. In fact, over 25 percent of the labor agreements in Colombia and Venezuela are negotiated without trade unions. Obviously, the unions look with disfavor on this arrangement because employers use the nonunion groups as a means to bypass trade unions.[51]

In the more industrialized countries of the world, people interpret labor-management relations to mean the wide range of relationships between employers and employees. However, people of Latin American countries tend to define labor relations in terms of the voluminous labor codes and government regulations.[52]

Labor relations vary widely among the countries in Latin America, but they have one common feature: a close connection between trade unions and political parties. For example, in Mexico unions constitute a large section of the ruling political party and therefore are assigned a quota of candidates on the party's ticket for office. Thus, unions have some assurance of having a voice in the party's program and on its council.[53] Some unions have been very effective in gaining relatively high wages for members. For example, the electrical workers in Mexico earn two to three times more than the urban working class.[54] Likewise, unions have been criticized because they have made gains for their own members while neglecting the interests of the great mass of people, including the peasants, who are terribly poor.[55]

Labor agreements vary in content both within countries and among countries. In Argentina, labor agreements include provisions that set forth in some detail the employment conditions and establish a highly developed shop steward system to administer grievances and assure that employers abide by the agreements. In Chile, labor agreements are more general, but they do establish certain minimum rules and include a grievance machinery to enforce the agreement. In Brazil, where unions have struggled since 1945 to have a greater say in determining employment rules and conditions for their members, they have achieved more through labor legislation than by engaging in collective bargaining.

In Latin American countries, political parties maintain close ties with unions for their support, votes, and influence. Likewise, trade unions depend on the politicians for laws to protect their members, to legalize their organizations, and to regulate their relations with employers.[56] On the other hand, political parties have appealed to organized labor to favor their own policies, and in some cases, they have accommodated organized labor in hopes that they will remain satisfied and continue to support the existing economic and political system.[57]

Western Europe

Unionization in Western Europe is significantly greater than in the United States, with the exception of France and Spain. The range is from 42 percent in Germany to over 80 percent in Finland and Sweden. Unions have been able to use this membership strength to accumulate political influence at the national level. Further, they have been able to coordinate their efforts with large, well-established labor parties in government to achieve their goals.

But, as in the United States, unions in Western Europe are declining. Nationwide and industrywide bargaining is less frequent, and employers are winning more concessions for efficient work rules and wages. Also, as in the United States, unions are trying to sign up new members in growing industries, such as leisure and finance, where technological change has fueled worries about job security.[58] Unions have achieved significantly greater worker participation in the operation of the firm—many times through legislative mandate, and sometimes through management reaction to wildcat strikes and worker dissatisfaction.[59] In addition, public opinion in these countries strongly supports the idea that worker participation enhances production, fosters harmony, and enriches the workers personally.[60]

The labor relations system in Western Europe can be contrasted with that of the United States in a number of ways:[61]

1. In the United States, unions are selected by the majority of the appropriate bargaining unit, whereas in Western Europe exclusive representation is not a common concept.
2. In the United States, the exclusive bargaining representative has a monopoly over all employee bargaining, and the employer is required to bargain only with the legally certified union. In Western Europe, the employer often bargains with a number of unions in addition to councils elected by the workers.
3. In Western Europe, negotiations take place between representatives of employer associations and those representing a confederation of unions; in the United States, this bargaining arrangement is adopted only in a few industries.
4. The number of fringe benefits established by law is greater in Europe; therefore, trade unions have found that they can obtain benefits more quickly through the political arena and have tied themselves more closely with political parties.

European Community (EC)

By 1992 the economies in 12 countries in Western Europe will be joined together as the European Community (EC). The EC will introduce deregulation, reduce government, and eliminate trade and travel barriers between these countries, thereby creating a single market for 320 million people. While the final outcome is uncertain, there is no doubt that the EC will have an effect on labor relations, possibly bringing trade unions in the 12 countries closer together.

Of the nations making up the EC, 11 of 12 heads of state endorsed a social charter of worker rights in late 1989 (Britain's Margaret Thatcher voted against). These statements of principles called for certain rights to be guaranteed all workers within the EC, including the right to organize, to participate in company decisions, to work in a safe environment, to be paid equitable wages, to have access to vocational training, to have equal employment opportunities for women, and for children, the elderly, and the disabled to be protected. Because adoption as an EC policy requires unanimous approval, the social charter will be recognized only by the 11 countries that have endorsed it. Such adoption gives some indication of the growing together of similar labor relations principles and policies among the various countries of Western Europe.[62]

Companies are already considering the effects of the EC. Tentatively, they believe there will be increased mobility of employees between operations in the various countries, more recruiting from overseas, more active monitoring of pay and benefits developments in other countries, and increased language training, as well as a premium placed on language skills. These areas and others will provide much opportunity for trade unions to be involved at the bargaining table.[63]

Great Britain

The traditional system in Great Britain is characterized by voluntary collective bargaining, implemented without legal compulsion through unenforceable labor agreements that have been negotiated by a large number of multi-union–multi-employer negotiating committees.[64] There are nearly 600 labor unions in the United Kingdom, over three times the number in the United States, and a manufacturing firm typically negotiates with about seven unions. Over the years there has been little labor relations law; thus, a wide diversity in the collective bargaining arrangements developed. One of the most important negotiations involved the Engineering Employers' Federation, representing 5,000 companies, and the Confederation of Shipbuilding and Engineering Unions, representing 34 unions and over 2 million employees. This agreement sets forth general guidelines that establish the floor for additional bargaining at the plants. Labor agreements are administered at the plant level; however, they are not enforceable by law, and grievances are not subject to private arbitration.

Shop stewards are volunteers serving without pay, unlike their U.S. counterparts, but they cannot be removed by union executives. Often they accumulate much authority and influence at the plant and have more control over local union affairs than any national union official. Steward councils composed of union stewards from various unions and works councils representing members of the various departments are important in the labor relations system.

Labor agreements at the plant level are often negotiated by representatives of the national union, steward councils, and works councils. These agreements usually have no fixed term and include letters of understanding, minutes of meetings, and oral understandings. While there is no legal obligation to negotiate, unions have gained extensive power and control over jobs, refusing to work with any employer whom they find in bad standing and maintaining strict membership discipline.[65]

British unions tend to be closely integrated with the Labor Party. They support state pensions and nationalized health service. Consequently, fringe benefits have not been a major bargaining topic. The law plays a minor part in Great Britain's labor relations system because laws historically have worked against unions, causing much distrust.

Unlike the United States, where strikes result primarily from bargaining disputes, wildcat strikes during the contract term predominate in Great Britain. Grievance arbitration has basically been rejected as a method for resolving disputes during the terms of contracts.[66]

British union membership has declined over 20 percent under three successive Conservative governments, the most recent one led by Prime Minister Margaret Thatcher since 1979. During this time union membership has declined from

54 percent of workers in 1979 to 42 percent in 1987, although it is still 70 percent in manufacturing. While some of this decline has resulted from increases in unemployment, mostly among workers in industries that are heavily unionized, such as manufacturing, a major contributing influence has been a series of labor laws that have had an adverse effect on trade unions. Under the 1984 Trade Union Act, industrial actions such as strikes require secret ballot election before the planned action is to be held. Picketing is restricted to six persons at each entrance and "sympathy" picketing is limited. In 1988, the Employment Act restricted trade unions from taking disciplinary actions against members who do not participate in a strike or other industrial action. Also, employers may now selectively dismiss all employees engaged in an industrial action at one plant even if they retain employees engaged in the same action at another plant.[67]

Other unfavorable legislation to unions include restriction on the right to strike, changes in legal liabilities of unions during strikes, restrictions on union shop agreements, and required balloting procedures for union internal government.[68]

Co-determination Policies in Various Countries (West Germany)

One unique feature of Western European labor relations is the interest in and wide implementation of **co-determination** policies. These policies include the concepts of shared authority on personnel matters, protected employee rights, guarantees of worker participation, and appeal of alleged unfair personnel decisions. West Germany has moved further in co-determination than other European countries, but Denmark, the Netherlands, Luxembourg, France, Austria, Norway, and Sweden all have some sort of legal requirements for worker representation on company boards. Other countries (for example, Belgium, England, Italy, and Switzerland) have no laws requiring worker participation on boards, but forms of worker participation are present in various stages of development, and are frequently discussed.[69]

Industrial relations in West Germany occur within a framework of two subsystems: co-determination and works councils at the plant levels and collective bargaining at the industry level. The co-determination structure establishes three levels of representation: works councils, labor directorates, and worker-elected members of boards of directors. Works councils (required by law in all plants having five or more employees) have equal say with management in job evaluation, overtime, breaks, holiday schedules, recruitment, selection, dismissal, training, and safety.

The industrial relations director, a member of management, is responsible for day-to-day operations and for personnel policies and practices in the company. The worker-elected members of the board make up half of the board's membership; the remainder represent the shareholders. The board elects a chairperson who can vote twice in case of a tie. If the board cannot elect a chairperson, the majority of the shareholders prevail.

While unions are fairly strong at the national level, they are comparatively weak at the plant level. In fact, unions usually defer to the works councils at the plant level. As a result, the West German workers have come to perceive the works councils as more valuable and effective than unions at the plant level. In recent times, the West German unions have responded to this erosion of support by bargaining more aggressively and antagonistically.[70]

West German unions are mainly occupationally based with strong ideological affiliations. The most important federation is the German Trade Union Federation—

Deutscher Gewerkschaftbund (DGW)—with 17 affiliates and 7,745,000 members. The DGW attempts not only to safeguard and improve workers' rights at the workplace and the enterprise levels, but in wider society as well. Industrial relations is highly bureaucratic and legalistic. West Germany has an extensive framework of labor laws that cover rights of employers and employees, hours of work, safety and health, social security, unemployment, and other issues.

Collective bargaining is conducted at the industry and regional levels between employer associations and union federations. The Federation of German Employers Associations represents 46 branch federations that comprise about 90 percent of all enterprises. While the Federation and DGW do not participate directly in the negotiations, they coordinate them and provide information. The real power rests with member organizations at the industry level. Government interference occurs very infrequently and there is no government mediation. If mediation is needed, the parties themselves must arrange for it. No collective bargaining occurs between unions and employers at the plant level. Works councils and employers negotiate within the statutory regulations at this level. The major negotiations occur between employer associations and union federations.[71]

With the inevitable reunification of Germany, it is anticipated that East Germany will be merged into West Germany. Just 44 years after World War II, with its country in ruin and economy in collapse, Germany has gained a position of economic dominance in Europe.[72]

Japan

Japan's labor relations system has four distinguishing characteristics: labor-management consultation, lifetime employment, a wage system based on seniority, and the enterprise or company union. There is considerably more communication between management and workers in Japan than in most other countries. Ninety percent of all Japanese companies have some sort of labor-management consultation. The flow of information is extensive. As examples, management reports to workers on the company's financial status, its problems, and its expectations and plans, and on contemplated technological innovations before they occur. All aspects of employment, training, discipline, working conditions, and employee benefits are open for examination. Joint consultation includes subjects that the U.S. manager would classify as management prerogatives.

Lifetime employment applies to regular employees of large employers (500 or more employees), which make up about one-third of the nonagriculture work force. These "regular employees" are hired after completing high school or college, with the expectation that they will be retained by the company until they reach the mandatory retirement age of 60. There are no legal, written contracts; however, unacceptable behavior may lead to a suggested voluntary resignation or a "hidden discharge." The result of this lifetime employment is the eagerness of employers to invest in training these long-time employees, and responsiveness of employees not only to participate in training but to accept willingly innovation and technological advancement, knowing that they will not be adversely affected by a layoff.[73]

The **wage system** in Japan has several distinguishing characteristics:

1. Salaries are paid monthly, even if the employee has been absent (with justification) from work.

2. Wage differentials are small between regular line employees and staff personnel, all of whom are members of the same union.
3. Wage distinctions exist between amounts earned for one's work (for example, efficiency output) and amounts earned for just being an employee (such as allowances for housing, transportation, and dependents).
4. Wages are accepted as permanent and lasting for the employee's entire career, including a minimum annual increase and a lump sum at retirement.[74]

Length of service and age are more highly correlated with wages in Japan than in other industrially developed countries. For example, between the ages of 40 and 50 the Japanese workers' wages are 67 percent greater than those of 21- to 24-year-old employees, whereas in the United States, the older employees' wages average only 23 percent more than those of younger workers. Peak earnings in Japan are 243 percent greater than entry-level earnings; in the United States, there is a 110 percent differential.[75]

The **enterprise union** is composed of employees working for a single employer at a single location. These unions comprise nearly 90 percent of all union organizations in Japan and include all categories of skills among employees of a company. The development of the enterprise union has been aided substantially by the system of lifetime employment and a heavy reliance on seniority. Thus, the individual employee identifies more closely with the company than does the typical employee in many Western countries.

The enterprise union has led to greater consultation and information sharing between unions and management. For example, management shares financial and operations plans, personnel plans, and managerial philosophy with the union and solicits union input. These exchanges have enabled greater worker participation and a "humanization" of production processes.

The enterprise unions are affiliated at the national level and have national organizations in the textile, electricity, shipbuilding, automobile, steel, appliance, and chemical industries. They hold conferences to discuss industrial policies; however, they do not discuss such topics as wages, working conditions, and other employment policies. These topics are discussed within the enterprise union. At the national level, industrial problems are discussed in a more general context, and issues such as economic growth, employment forecasts, retirement ages, and improved communications are addressed.[76]

Labor unions have declined in numbers and have received low wage increases in the last several years, and are becoming more adversarial. In 1987, the first step toward bringing all Japanese workers into one organization was taken when two federations and part of another formed a new national organization known as "Zenminroren" or "Rengo" with 5.5 million members. Other unions planned to join in the following years and the political clout of labor unions in Japan will be dramatically increased.[77]

With Japan's strong trade balance (exports exceeding imports) and the subsequent appreciation of the yen, products made in Japan and shipped elsewhere have become more expensive and pressures have mounted to reduce production and labor costs or to shift more production of these products to countries where wages are lower, such as Korea, Taiwan, Singapore, or Hong Kong.

There is some evidence that the young Japanese workers do not have the same work ethic that their parents have and are not as interested in working hard. With the increase in life expectancy, lifetime employment (guaranteed employment to age 55) is being re-evaluated by some firms and more employees are changing jobs than ever before.

While the work days lost due to strikes in Japan average less than in Canada, Australia, and the United States, work day losses are greater than those of Sweden, Norway, West Germany, Austria, and the Netherlands, where works councils systems prevail.[78]

In Japan, the spring of each year brings on the annual labor offensive or *shunto*. The unions participate in nationwide demonstrations, singing labor songs, wearing red armbands, and refusing to work for short periods. While these demonstrations may be mistaken by an outsider as an indication of deteriorating labor-management relations, it actually is a time for labor to voice its views and to allow workers to let off steam. In 1988 the major labor demand was bigger pay raises, but the unions settled for 3 percent, among the lowest in 30 years.

In the final analysis, Japanese employers and unions eventually will have to face a number of critical issues that may cause a break with the traditional system: early retirement, higher unemployment, elimination of automatic pay increases and promotions, introduction of labor-saving devices, union emphasis on job security rather than wage hikes, decline of worker loyalty to the firm, and declining competitiveness with rapidly developing countries such as Brazil, China, South Korea, Singapore, and Taiwan.[79]

South Korea

Labor relations in South Korea has dramatically changed since 1987 with the election of President Roh Tae Woo, whose election campaign was based on new freedoms in all aspects of life. During the previous four decades of autocratic and suppressive government, the institution of collective bargaining and the right to strike existed only on paper. Collective bargaining was never open to workers as a viable mechanism to address industrial justice, distribution of income, or oppressive working conditions. Consequently, in the late 1980s when collective bargaining was allowed, the parties lacked basic expertise in bilateral decision making. As a result, 1987 experienced ten times the number of strikes of any previous year. The number of strikes in 1988 was down about 50 percent from the 1987 amount.

South Korea has been considered a developing country for the past several decades; however, this characterization is not proper given the rapid economic development over the past few years. Each year in the late 1980s, South Korea experienced double-digit growth in gross national product; its per capita income exceeds $4,000 per year; its unemployment rate is less than 3 percent. Its work force can be characterized as young, well-educated, and highly motivated.[80]

There are 6,124 labor unions in South Korea with some 1.71 million members. This comprises 22 percent of the total work force, several percentage points higher than the United States. There are 20 industrial federations, and each federation is the exclusive, industrywide union to represent workers within the industrial jurisdiction specified by the federation's charter. Most of the 20 federations and national unions are affiliated with the Federation of Korean Trade Unions (FKTU); however, the FKTU has been criticized for its close ties with the national government. The Trade Union Law, the major piece of legislation governing labor relations, allows organizing and negotiating rights for unions, provides for third-party impasse resolution procedures, and has a defined procedure for unions to follow prior to strikes. The law allows local unions to entrust their negotiations to the industrial federations, and the trend is in this direction.

While wage increases in the last few years have been high, Korean employees work 54 hours per week, more hours than any other country reported by the Industrial Labor Organization. Working conditions are frequently unfavorable; many employees work in small, cramped, and often dangerous sweatshops. There is substantial employment discrimination against women. For example, the average wage of females is 46 percent that of males. Child labor is restricted; however, written approval from parents or guardian allows children to work. As a result, females and children are the majority work force in textile, apparel, footwear, and electronics factories.

Australia

Australian unions are organized more on a craft or occupational basis than on an industrial or enterprise basis. Unions typically include members from more than one industry, and an employer with 500 or more employees must deal with an average of 12 different unions.

The Australian labor force is 55 percent unionized. The majority of union members in Australia are white-collar or service workers. Over half of the employees in government, finance and insurance, transport and storage, and metal products are union members. Australia has over 300 unions, some of which are very small. Most of the unions are organized on a craft or occupational basis, and many are organized within one state only.

Strikes in Australia are among the most frequent and shortest in the world. Unlike strikes in the United States, which are designed to win a favorable negotiation settlement, strikes in Australia are designed to warn the employer and demonstrate that the workers are not to be ignored. Strikes are usually combined with other forms of employee actions to express dissatisfaction or resentment to employer or government actions. These nonstrike actions include refusal to work overtime, work-to-rule campaigns, refusal of police to give tickets, refusal of transit employees to collect fares, and refusal by telephone installers to document installation of phones.

One of the key components of the Australian labor relations system is its system of conciliation and arbitration at the federal and state levels. Arbitrators (often called judges) are appointed by the government and hold office until retirement. The Australian system encourages collective bargaining, but an arbitrator serves as a third-party neutral who may attempt to mediate before arbitrating labor disputes (similar to med-arb in the United States).

Labor relations activities occur at four levels. At the national level, a national wage case is decided every 3 to 9 months by the federal Conciliation and Arbitration Commission. The Commission's action determines the overall wage level for some 85 percent of the unionized work force. At the industry or occupational level, various state tribunals decide cases wherein unions attempt to justify a separate wage increase above the level decided at the national level. Usually, such wage increases are justified on the basis of increased productivity in a particular industry. If the employer and the union reach an agreement without going before the state tribunal, they must register the agreement as a "consent award"; however, the tribunal has authority to reject the award if the award is excessive in relation to national policy. At the company and divisional level, the unions may present their arguments to specific companies for "over-award" pay, that is, a pay increase beyond that granted by the award. While these increases are usually rejected, they are typically granted during times of tight labor markets.

At the shop floor level, labor-management relationships are informal. Issues include working conditions, work rules, employee discipline, work loads, and personnel matters. No multi-step grievance procedures similar to those in the United States exist. If the parties are not successful in resolving their differences, strikes may occur. The concepts of layoffs by seniority and discipline for just cause, which are important to U.S. unions, are not well developed in Australia. Employers are free to lay off employees at will, although unions resist all layoffs. Although laid-off employees have no re-employment rights, unemployment benefits are quite liberal. Since most jobs are located in central cities, employees who have been laid off can obtain employment with another firm without relocating.[81]

Eastern Europe—Soviet Bloc Countries

In Eastern Europe, trade unions have two major functions:

1. Production promotion, which includes promoting the state plan, strengthening work discipline, and raising productivity.
2. Political indoctrination, which includes fostering the political consciousness, dedication to the public interest, and education of trade unionists on party matters.

Other proclaimed functions include defending the workers' interests, complying with labor legislation, administering social insurance, and promoting opportunities for physical training, sport, and recreation. To accomplish these functions, workers have been granted rights ranging from the right to make suggestions to the right to make decisions. These include the right to consummate a collective bargaining agreement that enumerates the rights and obligations of employees. But the agreements are not the result of collective bargaining as in the United States; their content is more the result of legal and political directives. Therefore, the labor agreements differ greatly in content, character, and role from those in the West even though they may be labeled identically.[82]

In 1988, Mikhail Gorbachev took steps to ease political repression and allow freer speech in the Soviet Union *(glasnost)* and developed initiatives and innovations needed to carry out economic reforms *(perestroika)* to revive a stagnant economy.

Perestroika has six features:

1. Enterprises are totally self-financing and funds for wages and social purposes are provided by profits remaining after taxes and repayment of bank loans.
2. Annual and 5-year plans are drawn up by enterprises in light of contractual arrangements and state guidelines, instead of directives from a central government.

3. State contracts assure a supply of important goods, transportation, and technological innovations. These contracts are temporary and will be phased out as the market mechanism develops.
4. The labor force in each enterprise will elect a director. A plan and collective agreement will be developed and approved at a general meeting of all employees. Decisions at the general meeting will be binding on the superior governing bodies as well as for the workers and management.
5. Each enterprise is obligated to pursue an active social program, such as providing adequate housing and social services to employees. These activities are to be paid from the profits set aside as a social development fund.
6. A new manpower tax designed to discourage wasteful use of labor and compensating the state for training expenses and for providing cultural, social, and municipal services.

Because perestroika is such a break with the past, immediate adjustments have been difficult. These adjustments include independence from the central government in production planning and distribution of profits, rights of workers to elect competent managers when higher levels of government attempt to pressure the workers to select their candidate, reluctance to abandon the outworn bureaucratic patterns of management, adjusting to paying workers as a result of their work and contribution without a ceiling.[83]

With the newly gained freedoms and decreased reluctance to take actions, major strikes by coal miners in the Soviet Union have occurred. Strikers sought better pay, more vacations, higher pensions, greater local autonomy for managing their mines, higher prices for the coal, and retention of a greater share of the profits from their coal. Miners reported that they were issued only one bar of soap every 2 months to bathe after spending 6 hours each day in the mines. In addition, they complained about the inadequate supplies of food and consumer goods.[84]

Worker actions and changes in political and economic freedom in the Soviet Union have influenced workers in other communist countries. In Hungary, free, democratic unions are taking form. These unions are being led by white-collar workers and professionals, among the worst-paid workers in the country. While the independent unions are rapidly growing, the communist-controlled unions have lost as many as 300,000 members.[85]

Because of the dismal economic performance from 1986 to 1988 in Yugoslavia, a country long known for its self-managed factories, employees in some plants have relinquished more authority to managers, who are responsible for production performance. While collective bargaining as known in the West does not occur, strikes for union recognition, political action, and economic benefits do occur. In 1988, 400,000 workers were involved in 1,700 strikes that lasted an average of less than 1 day. In November 1988, Yugoslavia became the first communist country to enshrine the right to strike in its constitution. Strikes have occurred over the years but they have not been legitimized because strikes in communist countries are essentially considered strikes by workers against themselves.[86]

In an unbelievable chain of events, Solidarity, a labor union that was outlawed in 1981, and its leader, Lech Walesa, placed under house arrest until 1983, is now the leading political party in Poland. These events occurred as the result of the first free election in Poland in the last 40 years. For the first time since World War II, there is a noncommunist government in Eastern Europe. Solidarity as a free trade union movement became a pivotal force in the changes that spread throughout Eastern Europe. These events occurred with the approval of Soviet President Mikhail Gorbachev, who urged the Polish Communist party to cooperate with its one-time enemy, the union-based Solidarity, which was illegal until the spring of 1989. With the formation of a coalition majority between Solidarity and two small parties, President Wojciech Jaruzelski, who previously had outlawed Solidarity, was persuaded to remain as president in the new government and to name as prime minister Tadeusz Mazowiecki, a former leader of Solidarity and editor of the Solidarity newsletter, *Gazeta Wyborcza.* (See the "Labor Relations in Action.")

With high expectations of more and better food and consumer goods, the new government faces an enormous challenge. Because Solidarity has no experience in governing a country, the new prime minister has mounted a worldwide call for expatriate Poles to return and serve in the government and has sought foreign advisers and assistance. Poland will now try to balance its need for financial aid and assistance from Western countries, remain a member of the Soviet-led Warsaw Pact, and achieve economic development and democracy at home. While Solidarity officials have few illusions about how difficult it will be to firmly plant a democratic form of government and a market economy on Polish soil, a short while ago they would not have imagined that they would have such an opportunity so soon.[87]

As the Western world debated over whether to help the first noncommunist government in Poland in 40 years with an alarming $39 billion foreign debt, a *Business Week* editorial of September 4, 1989 may have said it best: "The West Can't Afford Not to Help Poland." In the words of Lech Walesa before the AFL-CIO convention:

> You helped us survive the most difficult days, the moments of despair and hopelessness. The help provided by you and some other friends enabled us to continue our struggle for the right to set up legal, free trade unions. . . . No one knows how much time we have left to reform our economy, but we all realize it is not much. If we fail to convince people that although things are changing slowly they are nevertheless changing for the better, than this breeze of freedom I spoke of will soon disappear, leaving behind only a sense of bitterness accompanying unaccomplished dreams.

Key Terms

multinational corporation (MNC)
whipsawing
co-determination
wage system
enterprise union

Discussion Questions

1. While we share a common border with Canada, its labor relations system is affected by a number of variables that do not greatly affect the United States. Enumerate and explain these variables.
2. Explain why labor unions in many Latin American countries have developed more slowly than those in the United States.
3. Western Europe seems to be uniquely involved with various forms of worker participation. What are some reasons that these worker participation systems have developed so fully there instead of elsewhere?

Labor Relations in Action

Ascendancy of Solidarity

August 14, 1980 Workers at the Lenin Shipyards in Gdansk launch a sit-in strike that triggered strikes elsewhere in Poland.

August 31, 1980 Polish government signs the Gdansk Accord providing for freedom of association and guaranteeing independence and self-government of the new trade union.

September 24, 1980 Solidarity files for official registration with Lech Walesa as chairman.

October 24, 1980 Warsaw judge is willing to approve registration only after altering Solidarity's constitution to make Solidarity subordinate to the Polish United Workers' Party, an organization controlled by the Communist Party.

November 10, 1980 Solidarity refuses to change constitution and threatens a nationwide strike. Solidarity is registered by the Polish Supreme Court without altering its constitution.

September and October 1981 Solidarity holds national congress. Lane Kirkland, President of the AFL-CIO, plans to attend to show continued support to Solidarity but is denied a visa by Polish government.

December 13, 1981 Polish Prime Minister General Wojciech Jaruzelski imposes a state of war (martial law). Solidarity's leaders, including Walesa, are arrested, and Solidarity's offices are shut down.

October 8, 1982 Polish Parliament formally delegalizes Solidarity.

1983 Lech Walesa awarded the Nobel Peace Prize. The Polish government does not allow him to leave the country because he continues to be under arrest; his wife accepts award on his behalf.

November 1984 Polish government establishes a national organization of officially sponsored unions; Solidarity, now an underground labor union, rejects this organization.

April to August 1988 Two major strike waves cause government to agree to hold roundtable talks with Solidarity.

April 5, 1989 Polish government and Solidarity sign agreement to restore union's legal status and to hold elections for a new parliament.

April 17, 1989 Warsaw court restores Solidarity's legal status.

June 1989 Solidarity-endorsed slate of candidates wins all but 1 of 261 parliamentary seats it was allowed to contest and becomes the major political party in Poland.

November 1989 Lech Walesa visits the United States, attends the AFL-CIO convention to receive the George Meany Human Rights Award, which was granted to him by the AFL-CIO in 1981, and the Medal of Freedom from President Bush.

Sources: Robert A. Senser, "How Poland's Solidarity Won Freedom of Association," *Monthly Labor Review* 112 (September 1989), pp. 34–38; "AFL-CIO Convention Welcomes Walesa; Polish Leader Appeals for U.S. Aid," *Daily Labor Report,* November 15, 1989, pp. A-11 to A-13.

4. What are the four special features of the Japanese system? Why haven't they been adopted in the United States?
5. While multinational corporations seem to be growing in size and influence, what must occur before transnational collective bargaining can be effectively carried out?

6. How does the Polish government's position on Solidarity compare with the U.S. government's position on the PATCO strike?
7. Compare the development of Solidarity with the development of free trade unions in the United States.
8. Which features of Canada's labor relations would you transfer to the United States?

References

1. Rudy Oswald, Director of Economic Research, AFL-CIO, "Multinationals Dominate World Trade," *AFL-CIO News,* August 19, 1989, p. 10.
2. Alicia M. Quijano, "Capital Expenditures by Majority-Owned Foreign Affiliates of U.S. Companies, 1989," *Survey of Current Business* 69 (March 1989), p. 20.
3. Obie G. Whichard, "U.S. Multinational Companies: Operations in 1987," *Survey of Current Business* 69 (June 1989), p. 35.
4. Russell B. Scholl, "The International Investment Position of the United States in 1988," *Survey of Current Business* 69 (June 1989), p. 47.
5. "Japan Took Lead in Foreign Investment in 1987; U.S. Jobs Up 8 Percent to 3.1 Million, Commerce Says," *Daily Labor Report,* June 29, 1989, p. A-13; "Slowly But Surely, the U.S. Is Buying into Japan," *Business Week,* December 19, 1988, p. 44.
6. "Five Other Nations Outpace U.S. Gain in Manufacturing Productivity for 1987," *Daily Labor Report,* July 7, 1988, p. B-1.
7. Patricia Capdevielle, "International Differences in Employers' Compensation Costs," *Monthly Labor Review* 111 (May 1988), pp. 44–45.
8. Thane Peterson, "Is Japan Using the U.S. as a Back Door to Europe?" *Business Week,* November 14, 1988, p. 57.
9. Harley Shaiken, "Globalization and the Worldwide Division of Labor," *Monthly Labor Review* 110 (August 1987), p. 47.
10. Marvin J. Levine, "Labor Movements and the Multinational Corporation: A Future for Collective Bargaining?" *Employee Relations Law Journal* 13 (Winter 1987–88), pp. 382–398.
11. Rajib N. Sanyal, "Unionizing Foreign-Owned Firms: Perceptions of American Union Officials," *Labor Studies Journal* 14 (Winter 1989), p. 66.
12. "Hands Across the Workplace," *Time,* December 26, 1988, pp. 15–18; "Working for the Japanese," *Time,* September 14, 1987; Paul Hemp, "Britain's 'Intransigent' Rubber Workers Bow to Japanese Management Practices," *The Wall Street Journal,* March 29, 1988, p. 26.
13. "Canada's UAW Thumbs Its Nose at Concessions," *Business Week,* July 26, 1982, p. 23.
14. Charles R. Greer and John Shearer, "Do Foreign-owned U.S. Firms Practice Unconventional Labor Relations?" *Monthly Labor Review* 104 (January 1981), pp. 45–47.
15. Duane Kujawa, "Collective Bargaining and Labor Relations in Multinational Enterprise: A U.S. Public Policy Perspective" in *Research in International Business and Finance,* ed. Robert G. Hawkins (Greenwich, Conn.: JAI Press, Inc. 1979), p. 37.
16. Greer and Shearer, "Do Foreign-owned U.S. Firms Practice Unconventional Labor Relations?" p. 47.
17. Kujawa, "Collective Bargaining and Labor Relations," pp. 37–38.
18. Robert F. Banks and Jack Stieber, "Introduction," *Multinationals, Unions, and Labor Relations in Industrial Countries* (Ithaca: New York State School of Industrial and Labor Relations, 1977), p. 1.
19. Roy B. Helfgott, "American Unions and Multinational Companies: A Case of Misplaced Emphasis," *Columbia Journal of World Business* 18 (Summer 1983), p. 81.
20. See Richard L. Rowan, Herbert R. Northrup, and Rae Ann O'Brien, *Multinational Union Organizations in the Manufacturing Industries* (Philadelphia, Penn.: University of Pennsylvania, 1980).
21. Geoffrey W. Latta and Janice R. Bellace, "Making the Corporation Transparent: Prelude to Multinational Bargaining," *Columbia Journal of World Business* 18 (Summer 1983), p. 73.
22. Northrup and Rowan, "Multinational Bargaining Approaches in the Western European Flat Grass Industry," *Industrial and Labor Relations Review* 30 (October 1976), pp. 32–46.
23. George B. McCulloch, "Transnational Bargaining–Problems and Prospects," *Monthly Labor Review* 101 (March 1978), pp. 33–34.
24. Arnold R. Weber, "Bargaining without Boundaries: Industrial Relations and the Multinational Firm" in *Bargaining without Boundaries,* eds. Robert J. Flanagan and Arnold R. Weber (Chicago: University of Chicago Press), pp. 233–249.
25. McCulloch, "Transnational Bargaining–Problems and Prospects," p. 33.
26. Weber, "Bargaining without Boundaries," pp. 233–249.
27. Banks and Stieber, *Multinationals, Unions, and Labor Relations,* pp. 11–12.
28. Levine, "Labor Movements and the Multinational Corporation," pp. 392–398.
29. Herbert R. Northrup and Richard L. Rowan, "Multinational Union Activity in the 1976 U.S. Rubber Tire Strike," *Sloan Management Review* 18 (Spring 1977), pp. 17–28.
30. G. B. J. Bomers, *Multinational Corporations and Industrial Relations* (Amsterdam, The Netherlands: Van Gorcum, Assen, 1976), pp. 179–195.
31. Richard L. Rowan and Herbert R. Northrup, "Multinational Bargaining in Metals and Electrical Industries: Approaches and Prospects," *Journal of Industrial Relations* 17 (March 1975), pp. 1–29.
32. David C. Hershfield, *Multinational Union Challenges Multinational Company* (New York: Conference Board, 1975), pp. 4–5.
33. Banks and Stieber, *Multinationals, Unions, and Labor Relations,* pp. 15–16; and Bomers, *Multinational Corporations and Industrial Relations,* pp. 179–185.
34. Herbert R. Northrup, "Why Multinationals Bargaining Neither Exists Nor Is Desirable," *Labor Law Journal* 29 (June 1978), pp. 330–331.
35. Owen Fairweather, "Trends in International Collective Bargaining with Multinationals and the Respective Strategies," *Proceedings of the Twenty-sixth Annual Winter Meeting: Industrial Relations Research Association* (Madison, Wis.: Industrial Relations Research Association, 1973), pp. 145–154.
36. McCulloch, "Transnational Bargaining–Problems and Prospects," p. 34.

37. Paul A. Heise, "The Multinational Corporation and Industrial Relations," *Labor Law Journal* 24 (August 1973), pp. 480–483; Betty S. Murphy, "Multinational Corporations and Free Coordinated Transnational Bargaining: An Alternative to Protectionism?" *Labor Law Journal* 28 (October 1977), pp. 619–632.
38. Hershfield, *Multinational Union Challenges Multinational Company,* pp. 4–5.
39. "Report of the Task Force of Labour Relations," *Canadian Industrial Relations* (Ottawa: Information Canada, 1968), pp. 14–16.
40. Kevin Quinn, "Canadian Labor Seeks Greater Autonomy from Unions Dominated by U.S. Workers," *The Wall Street Journal,* April 29, 1982, p. 56; Mark Thompson, "Canada" in *International Handbook of Industrial Relations,* ed. Albert A. Blum (Westport, Conn.: Greenwood Press, 1980), p. 86.
41. Thomas R. Knight and Donna Sockell, "Public Policy and the Scope of Collective Bargaining in Canada and the United States," in *Proceedings of the 41st Annual Meeting of the Industrial Relations Research Association,* ed. Barbard D. Dennis (Madison, Wis.: Industrial Relations Research Association, 1989), pp. 283–286.
42. Richard S. Belous, "The Impact of the U.S.-Canadian Free Trade Agreement on Labor-Management Relations: Facing New Pressures," unpublished paper presented at the University of Laval, September 20, 1988, pp. 1–6.
43. Roy J. Adams, "North American Industrial Relations: Divergent Trends in Canada and the United States," *International Labour Review* 128 (no. 1, 1989), p. 59.
44. James O. Morris, "Latin American Collective Bargaining Agreement: An Illustration" in *Workers and Managers in Latin America,* ed. Stanley M. Davis and Louis W. Goodman (Lexington, Mass.: D. C. Heath, 1972), p. 209.
45. "A Powerful Union Resists the Renovation of PEMEX," *Business Week,* October 17, 1983, pp. 196–198.
46. Roger Cohen, "Mexican Labor Leader Wields Power to Test President-Elect Salinas," *The Wall Street Journal,* September 27, 1989, p. 22.
47. Stephen Baker and Todd Vogel, "Will the New Maquiladoras Build a Better Mañana?" *Business Week,* November 14, 1989, p. 102.
48. U.S. Department of Labor, *Mexico* (Washington, D.C.: Superintendent of Documents, 1988), pp. 3–8.
49. "Maquiladora Employers in Matamoros Reach Tentative Settlement with Union," *Daily Labor Report,* February 2, 1990, p. A-3.
50. Arturo S. Bronstein, "Collective Bargaining in Latin America: Problems and Trends," *International Labour Review* 117 (September–October 1978), pp. 590–593.
51. International Labour Office, "Labor Legislation and Collective Bargaining" in *Workers and Managers in Latin America,* pp. 217–229.
52. Everett M. Kassalow, *Trade Unions and Industrial Relations: An International Comparison* (New York: Random House, 1969), pp. 302–303.
53. Howard Handelson, "Oligarchy and Democracy in Two Mexican Labor Unions: A Test of Representation Theory," *Industrial and Labor Relations Review* 30 (January 1977), pp. 205–218.
54. Kassalow, *Trade Unions,* p. 303. For a current discussion, see James L. Schlagheck and Nancy R. Johnson, *The Political, Economic, and Labor Climate in Mexico* (Philadelphia: Industrial Research Unit, University of Pennsylvania, 1977).
55. Robert J. Alexander, *Labor Relations in Argentina, Brazil, and Chile* (New York: McGraw-Hill, 1962), pp. 11–13. For a specific discussion of Brazilian labor relations, see James L. Schlagheck, *The Political, Economic, and Labor Relations Climate in Brazil* (Philadelphia: Industrial Research Unit, University of Pennsylvania, 1977).
56. Hobart A. Spaulding, Jr., *Organized Labor in Latin America* (New York: Harper & Row, 1977), p. x. For excellent discussions on Peru and Venezuela, see Nancy R. Johnson, *The Political, Economic, and Labor Climate in Peru* (Philadelphia: Industrial Research Unit, University of Pennsylvania, 1978); and Cecilia M. Valente, *The Political, Economic, and Labor Climate in Venezuela* (Philadelphia: Industrial Research Unit, University of Pennsylvania, 1979).
57. "Europe's Unions Are Losing Their Grip," *Business Week,* November 26, 1986, pp. 80–84.
58. Everett M. Kassalow, "Conflict and Cooperation in Europe's Industrial Relations," *Industrial Relations* 13 (May 1974), pp. 156–163.
59. Milton Derber, "Cross Currents in Workers' Participation," *Industrial Relations* 9 (February 1970), p. 123.
60. Owen Fairweather, "Western European Labor Movements and Collective Bargaining: An Industrial Framework" in *Western European Labor and the American Corporation,* ed. Alfred Kanan (Washington, D.C.: Bureau of National Affairs Inc., 1970), pp. 69–72.
61. "Eleven European Leaders Endorse EC Worker Rights Code, Thatcher Objects," *Daily Labor Report,* December 12, 1989, p. A-3; "Social Charter: Action Programme Released," *European Industrial Relations Report,* no. 112, January 1990, pp. 11–14.
62. "1992—Evidence of UK Companies Responding," *European Industrial Relations Review,* May 1989, pp. 22–27.
63. John F. B. Goodman, "Great Britain: Toward the Social Contract" in *Worker Militancy and Its Consequences, 1967–75,* ed. Solomon Balkin (New York: Praeger Publishers, 1975), pp. 39–81.
64. Fairweather, "Western European Labor Movements," pp. 71–74. Also see "Britain's Renegade Stewards," *Business Week,* February 19, 1979, pp. 92–95.
65. "Differences in Managing Labor Relation in U.K., U.S. Noted by Ford-U.K. Manager," *Daily Labor Report,* September 15, 1983, p. C-1.
66. Brian Towers, "Running the Gauntlet: British Trade Unions Under Thatcher, 1979–1988," *Industrial and Labor Relations Review* 42 (January 1989), pp. 163–186.
67. William Brown, "The Effect of Recent Changes in the World Economy on British Industrial Relations" in *Industrial Relations in a Decade of Economic Change,* ed. Hervey Juris, Mark Thompson, and Wilbur Daniels (Madison, Wis.: Industrial Relations Research Association, 1985).
68. Robert Ball, "The Hard Hats in Europe's Boardrooms," *Fortune* 93 (June 1976), p. 189; and Robert J. Kuhne, "Co-determination: A Statutory Restructuring of the Organization," *Columbia Journal of World Business* 11 (March–April, 1976), pp. 17–25.
69. James B. Dworkin, Charles J. Hobson, Ekkehart Frieling, and David M. Oakes, "How German Workers View Their Jobs," *Columbia Journal of World Business* 18 (Summer 1983), pp. 48–54.
70. Friedrich Fuerstenberg, "Industrial Relations in the Federal Republic of Germany," *International and Comparative Industrial Relations,* eds. Greg J. Bamber and Russell D. Lansbury (London: Allen & Unwin, 1987), pp. 166–172.
71. Arthur Schlesinger, Jr., "Germany's Fate Will Determine Europe's," *The Wall Street Journal,* December 21, 1989, p. A-18.
72. Joseph Krislov, "How Does the Japanese Industrial Relations System Differ?" *Labor Law Journal* 40 (June 1989), pp. 338–344.
73. Katsumi Yakabe, *Labor Relations in Japan* (Tokyo: International Society for Educational Information, 1974), pp. 1–14; Hisashi

Kawada and Ryuji Komatsu, "Post-War Labor Movements in Japan" in *The International Labor Movement in Transition,* ed. Adolph Strumthal and James G. Scoville (Urbana: University of Illinois Press, 1973), pp. 122–148; and Tadashi A. Hanami, "The Multinational Corporation and Japanese Industrial Relations" in *International Labor and Multinational Enterprise,* ed. Duane Kujawa (New York: Praeger Publishers, 1975), pp. 183–185.
74. Krislov, "How Does the Japanese System Differ?" p. 340.
75. Koji Taira and Solomon B. Levine, "Japan's Industrial Relations: A Social Compact Emerges," in *Industrial Relations in a Decade of Economic Change,* pp. 283–286.
76. Glenn Halm and Clinton R. Shiels, "Damage Control: Yen Appreciation and the Japanese Labor Market," *Monthly Labor Review* 111 (November 1988), pp. 3–5.
77. Krislov, "How Does the Japanese System Differ?" p. 342.
78. "An Aging Work Force Strains Japan's Traditions," *Business Week,* April 20, 1981, pp. 72–85.
79. Mario F. Bognanno, *Korea's Industrial Relations at the Turning Point* (Seoul: Korea Development Institute, 1988), pp. 4–90; Bureau of International Labor Affairs, *Foreign Labor Trends: Korea* (Washington, D.C.: U.S. Government Printing Office, 1989), pp. 3–9.
80. George Strauss, "Australian Labor Relations through American Eyes," *Industrial Relations* 27 (Spring 1988), pp. 131–147.
81. Vladimir Bukovsky, "We Have Looked with Hope at the West," *American Federationist* 84 (March 1977), pp. 20–21.
82. "Perestroika and the Worker," *ILO Information,* undated, p. 6.
83. "Revolution Down Below," *Time,* July 31, 1989, p. 22.
84. "Free, Democratic Union Emerges in Hungary," *AFL-CIO News,* January 11, 1989, p. 9.
85. U.S. Department of Labor, *Yugoslavia* (Washington, D.C.: U.S. Government Printing Office, 1989), pp. 1–9.
86. Gail E. Schares and John Templeman, "Solidarity on the High Wire," *Business Week,* September 4, 1989, p. 26.
87. "AFL-CIO Convention Welcomes Walesa; Polish Leader Appeals for U.S. Aid," *Daily Labor Report,* p. A-12.

CHAPTER 16

Applying the Labor Relations Process to Professional Sports, Health Care, and Agriculture

"If you looked at that list, you'd say labor was doomed in Gompers' time. . . . The horse-collar makers' union and the harness makers' union were doomed. We lose parts and we gain parts, and when you're going through these transitions, you have to adapt, re-examine your methods and look at your structures."

Lane Kirkland, President of the AFL-CIO, quoted in David Shriebman, "Hard Labor," *The Wall Street Journal*, April 11, 1989, p. A-8.

This chapter is intended to pose for the reader a very real challenge—the application of the text material to three areas of labor-management relationships: professional sports, health care, and agriculture. The three sections in this chapter are independent, but they should be read with two issues in mind: (1) the extent to which these areas show similarities and differences and (2) their respective applications to the elements in the labor relations process portrayed in Exhibit 1.1 (Chapter 1).

Professional Sports

Professional sports leagues (football, baseball, hockey, soccer, and basketball) differ in several respects: the nature of the sport; its potential appeal; the number of teams per league; the number of players per team; the number of games per season; and the marketability of the sport to a national versus a regional following.[1] However, these sports share a significant similarity: a very select unionized work force that generates the American public's interest far beyond the number of employees involved. Estimates have suggested that one out of every 4,000 high school baseball players will start in the major leagues, one out of 5,000 high school football players will start in the National Football League, and one of 12,500 high school basketball players will make the starting five on a pro basketball team.[2] These select individuals generate intense audience enthusiasm. For example, anyone who has been to a professional baseball stadium has experienced the excitement of the game:

> The lack of violence but the sense of menace in the thrown ball, the slashing spikes, the swing of the bat; the sudden splendid bursts of action—a runner going from first to third, or even home, on a single, sliding in inches ahead of or behind a perfect peg; the suspense of pitcher vs. hitter in a late-inning rally, with the winning runs on base; . . . the power and the glory of an overwhelming pitcher in his prime; the art and cunning of an experienced pitcher past his prime; the swagger of a big hitter at the plate.[3]

Behind-the-scenes union-management relationships seldom are as exciting as on-field action; yet a consideration of these unique activities can serve as an interesting application of the labor relations process. This subject is divided into three areas, which represent differences between unionized sports and other industries.

Direct Involvement of Additional Participants

Labor relations activities in professional sports involve more participants than those listed in the inner circle of Exhibit 1.1 in Chapter 1.

Commissioners Commissioners have an uncertain, confusing status in professional sports. The commissioner is supposed to coordinate managerial policies and actions affecting the teams in the league; however, the commissioners of at least three sports (hockey, football, and baseball) have fined some owners for various infractions, such as indicating the team should finish last in order to receive a top draft choice.

Equally uncertain is the commissioner's role in collective bargaining. Most union officials regard this individual as a paid management representative instead of a third-party neutral. However, the commissioners of baseball and football were criticized in some quarters for not helping to resolve various baseball and football strikes. The commissioner of baseball exerted a major influence on the 1985 and possibly subsequent negotiations when he ordered the owners to open their financial books to the union when the owners claimed they could not financially meet the union's bargaining proposal.

Agents Agents negotiate contracts and provide financial counseling for selected athletes. The actions of agents can complicate the traditional union-management relationship. Indeed, a rash of successful contract negotiations conducted by the independent agents can result in players' questioning the value of union membership.

Media The media component of the influence of community composition and attitudes (Exhibit 1.1 in Chapter 1) is more directly involved in professional sports labor relations through reporting collective bargaining and strike activities. Professional sports seem to receive a disproportionately large amount of media coverage in bargaining efforts, given the rather small number of employees and minor impact on the economy. A comment made by a disgruntled union member about poor union leadership receives little media attention in most industries; however, an entire newspaper article or television interview might be given to a professional athlete-celebrity who expresses the same attitude. Marvin Miller, former head of the Major League Baseball Players' Association (MLBPA) and a former official with the Steelworkers Union made this comment during one baseball strike:

> The steelworkers' union negotiations always had a far greater impact on the economy of the country than the baseball negotiations. But it probably got 5 percent of the attention that the baseball strike has received. I'm well aware of the kind of focus and artificial spotlight that is placed on baseball.[4]

Some media financially sponsor various sporting events. Recent national television contracts have provided owners in professional baseball $1.46 billion (1990–1993); in hockey, $34 million (1988–1989 through 1990–1991); in basketball, $600 million (1991–1994); and in football, $3.6 billion (1990–1994).[5]

Some of these arrangements allow each team to negotiate local television rights as well for most of its games. For example, the New York Yankees recently received a 12-year cable TV agreement worth $500 million. These large revenue sources increase management's costs to disagree with the union in collective bargaining and help account for rather substantial athlete salary averages (currently, $220,000 in hockey, $300,000 in football, $500,000 in baseball, and $750,000 in basketball).[6]

Wage Bargaining: Behaviors and Criteria

Sports unions negotiate minimum salary levels for their appropriate bargaining units; their members then negotiate salaries on an individual basis. This task is neither pleasant nor easy for the athletes. Even two Hall of Fame baseball players, Joe DiMaggio[7] and Mickey Mantle, reportedly had difficulty in negotiating contracts. Management indicated that Mantle's wife might become familiar with private investigator reports of his late-night experiences if he did not agree with management's salary offer.[8] Also consider Jim McMahon's first year's negotiating experience with the Chicago Bears football team, whose owner made the following observation:

> Young man, we're offering you more money than we've ever offered a rookie. . . . If it was up to me, you should go to Canada to play pro football. . . . If we give you two hundred bucks a game, you're overpaid. You've got a bad arm, a bad eye, bad knees, and you're too small.[9]

Union and management officials in professional sports do not rely on compensation differences (education and apprenticeship training, job classification, and seniority, for example) commonly found in other labor-management relationships. They instead rely on a wide variety of performance-based statistics such as passes completed, number of tackles, and earned run averages.

Sometimes a hired athlete is associated with a sharp increase in fan attendance and revenues. For example, hockey legend Wayne Gretzky has a 10-year contract worth $31.3 million that will expire at the end of the 1998 season. Gretzky's team owner noted in the contract announcement that his club lost $5 million in 1987–1988, the season before signing Gretzky, and made $6 million in 1988–1989.[10]

Yet several studies have suggested that the relationship between player salaries and team performance (both athlete and financial) is weak or inconclusive.[11] This situation might be due to owners' egos. Ewing Kauffman, once owner of the Kansas City Royals, and his counterpart George Steinbrenner of the Yankees believe that they and all other owners are "ego maniacs." Other owners, including Ray Kroc and Marvin Davis, have admitted that their teams were their hobby. Sports owners are typically rich; for example, a recent *Forbes* magazine list of the 400 richest Americans listed 28 individuals who owned at least a 30 percent share of a professional sports team.[12] Most of them also draw their largest revenues from enterprises unrelated to their teams.

Therefore, owners might acquire or retain a particular player for publicity reasons and agree to a player salary higher than merited by the player's performance. It also appears that unions representing baseball and basketball players have obtained some collective bargaining advantage when they have dealt with owners, who for the most part do not share common business concerns.

The relationship between pay and performance is further distorted when athletes and owners (and sometimes, in baseball, an arbitrator)[13] consider salary period (a 1-year contract versus a multi-year contract with deferred income, for example) and specific performance criteria. These considerations create the complications discussed here.

Performance Statistics Based on Subjective Judgments Many "hits" and all "errors" are determined by an official scorer, while umpires subjectively determine "balls" (leading to possible "walks"), call "strikes" (leading to strikeouts), and judge the difference between fair and foul balls.

Variable Interpretation of Performance Statistics Some baseball statistics are difficult to interpret in positive or negative terms. For example, does a high number of double plays mean that the pitcher has good control in getting the batter to hit a ground ball to an infielder? Or does it mean that a pitcher has poor control, and has given up too many hits and walks to let runners get to base? A seemingly negative statistic, fielding errors, might be viewed in positive terms. A very fast and capable fielder might get a glove on more balls than less skilled players, and have more fielding chances and therefore more errors.

Interdependence of Performance Statistics Performance statistics are influenced by other players and factors. One player's offensive statistics, such as runs scored and runs batted in, depend on the player's place in the batting order and the ability of other players to get on base and move the player to home. Other team players also affect a pitcher's ability to win games, a situation that Jim Bouton described for Yankee pitcher Diego Segui. According to Bouton, Segui pitched "lousy" for two games (giving up four runs in six innings), but received two victories. The press thought Segui was pitching better because of the results. Bouton believed that legendary pitching coach Johnny Sain summarized this situation by saying, "The world doesn't want to hear about labor pains . . . it only wants to see the baby."[14]

There are also many varied playing conditions that can affect players' performance statistics. For example, a player's batting average can be affected by each ballpark's unique characteristics, such as visibility, foul territory, the weather, the altitude, the playing surface, and ground maintenance.[15]

In some cases individually negotiated salary contracts result in unique incentive clauses (extra payment for games won or 50 cents for each fan admitted over a pre-set figure, for example) and large financial arrangements. Consider, for example, the $50 million salary, broken down as follows, for an Atlanta Braves relief pitcher, guaranteed as long as he promised to stay in "first-class physical condition and pledges himself to the American public":[16]

- $1.375 million signing bonus ($1 million of which was deferred).
- $1.5 million for the years 1986 to 1990 (half deferred annually and invested at about 13 percent).
- $1.196 million a year in interest for the years 1991 to 2021.
- $9.2 million principal in the year 2021.

Shoulder injuries cut this player's career short, although he managed to have 40 saves for the club. Individually negotiated, large salary contracts can cause some athletes to become indifferent, even hostile, toward their union and toward related activities such as a strike. These players might feel that the union does not get involved in their most significant working condition, pay.

Professional Athletes' Career Concerns: Mobility and Longevity

Most professional athletes do not have complete flexibility in selecting their employer because they enter employment through a "draft," in which only one team offers employment. Once on a team, players are restricted in moving to another team. This situation has been described by a former baseball player:

> A salesman reluctant to transfer from one office to another may choose to seek employment on the sales force of a different firm. A plumber can reject the dictates of his boss without relinquishing his right to plumb elsewhere. At the expiration of one contract, an actor shops among producers for the best arrangement he can find. But the baseball monopoly offers no such option to the athlete. If he elects not to work for the corporation that "owns" his services, baseball forbids him to ply his trade at all. In the hierarchy of living things, he ranks with poultry.[17]

Baseball's first reserve clause likely occurred over the price of a uniform. A player angry that his team was too cheap to pay for his uniform signed with another team. In the intervening century, players have been "sold for as little as 25 cents and traded for a bulldog, a bird dog, a turkey, and an airplane."[18]

Unions have attempted to remove some of these restrictions. The Major League Baseball Players' Association negotiated perhaps the strongest contract provision regarding player rights to move from one team to another (after an arbitrator ruled in the union's favor on this matter). In essence, a baseball player with 6 years of service who has not executed a contract for the next succeeding season can become a "free agent" (negotiate with other teams for his services) after notifying his club.

Several empirical studies have demonstrated that free agency has been associated with increased player salaries in baseball.[19] Professional football players, however, have not fared so well under free agency, a situation prompting an NFL quarterback to make the following comment:

> The way the NFL is, there's no reason to spend money because there's no incentive to win. Whether you win the Super Bowl or win one game all year, it's all pretty much the same because of revenue sharing. The 28 teams in the NFL all get the same huge sum from the TV networks at the start of the year, so why pay to have better players if it doesn't matter? Unless you're really committed to excellence, why spend money? Just finish 8–8 every year and turn a profit. Walter Payton could tell you better than anybody about the system. He became a free agent a few years ago, meaning he was supposedly available to sign with any team. But no other team bothered to offer him a contract; no other team even called. After all, he's only the all-time NFL rushing leader. Who could use him?[20]

Athletes' employment mobility concerns are tempered by short playing career concerns. One study found the average career for professional athletes was 7.5 years in hockey, 7 years in basketball, 4.5 years in football, and 4 years in baseball.[21] Short careers can affect union leader-member relationships and the union's ability to achieve certain collective bargaining gains as well. An executive director of the NFLPA observed,

> Football players are young, but they have limited careers. It's harder to get them to fight for causes that may not bring them immediate benefits. They're playing now; what do they care about the rights of players in the future?[22]

The 1987 football players' strike illustrated career issues and other collective bargaining considerations. Football players struck to achieve free agency provisions as they wanted many team owners bidding for their services. Yet, they also realized that a strike over free agency could reduce, even eliminate, an already short career. This situation is further illustrated in the "Labor Relations in Action."[23]

Health Care Employees

There are at least three ways in which labor relations in health care differ from those in professional sports or agriculture: (1) several different job classifications, (2) unique labor legislation (the Taft-Hartley amendments in 1974 and public-sector legislation), and (3) unique bargaining issues and concerns.

Legislative and Administrative Influences on Health Care Bargaining

Legal Guidelines Prior to 1935 the health care industry was relatively unaffected by labor legislation. The Wagner Act of 1935 did not specifically exempt hospital organizations; thus, the NLRB and the courts determined whether certain hospitals came under its coverage. In 1947 Section 2(2) of the Taft-Hartley Act exempted voluntary, nonprofit hospitals from federal labor relations laws. Employees working in veterans' hospitals of the federal government were eventually granted organizational and collective bargaining rights under the 1962 Executive Order 10988 (discussed in Chapter 15) and are now covered under the Civil Service Reform Act of 1978. Employees working in state-administered hospitals (for example, mental institutions) usually had to rely upon applicable state statutes in attempting to engage in collective bargaining activities (discussed in Chapter 14).

Because voluntary, nonprofit hospitals constitute the largest single sector of the health care industry in terms of number of hospitals, admissions, payroll expenses, and union activity, their omission from federal labor legislation coverage greatly blunted collective bargaining prospects in the industry for many years. Unions seeking to organize these hospitals could not rely on procedures found in the National Labor Relations Act due to the industry's exemption. Therefore, rights to form unions had to be found in state statutes. And most state statutes either prohibited collective bargaining in hospitals or had no provisions regarding the subject.

This situation changed in 1974, with the Taft-Hartley amendments extending federal labor relations coverage to all private-sector hospitals, including convalescent hospitals, health maintenance organizations, health clinics, and nursing homes.

These amendments recognized that strikes could cause serious problems in the health care industry, and therefore established unique collective bargaining and strike guidelines. Management and/or union officials in health care (unlike their counterparts in other private-sector industries) have the following requirements:

- Both must submit a notice to modify or terminate existing labor agreements to the Federal Mediation and Conciliation Service (FMCS) 60 days before the expiration of the existing labor agreement (a 30-day notice is required in other industries).
- Union representatives must submit a 10-day intent-to-strike notice in writing to the hospital and FMCS specifying the exact date and time the strike is to occur.
- Both must be involved in a fact-finding procedure through a Board of Inquiry (BOI) that can be appointed by the director of the FMCS if a threatened or actual strike or lockout affecting a health care operation would substantially interrupt the delivery of health care in the local community. The reports of the BOI range from a detailed assessment of bargaining issues to a simple statement that "we met, we bargained, we settled."[24]

Thus, strikes are legal in the private health care industry but only after complying with several unique legislative provisions.

The passage of the 1974 amendments caused a substantial increase in union organizing activities and employee representation elections. There are now 44 national and international unions that have organized health care employees. Unions that represent the largest number of hospital employees include Service Employees International Union, District 1199 National Union of Hospital Health Care Employees, American Federation of State, County and Municipal Employees, and the Teamsters.

The success of many union organizing drives at hospitals depends on the hospital's characteristics. For example, unions appear to be more successful in larger hospitals and less successful in church-related and other nonprofit hospitals. Also, higher voter turnout usually reduces chances of a union election victory.[25]

In 1984 the New York chapter of District 1199 (consisting of some 80,000 members) remained with the Retail, Wholesale and Department Store Union (RWDSU) while 65,000 other members formed the National Union of Hospital and Health Care Employees (NUHHCE), another AFL-CIO affiliate.[26] However, the NUHHCE was subsequently "sanctioned" by the AFL-CIO for seeking to organize employees who were members of the American Federation of State, County and Municipal Employees. This rarely invoked punishment means that other AFL-CIO unions will be free to recruit any NUHHCE members with the AFL-CIO's support.

Fourth and Plenty: The Free Agency Issue and the 1987 Football Players' Strike

Seventeen negotiation sessions between football players and management were not successful as the collective bargaining agreement expired August 31, 1987, with no replacement. Gene Upshaw, the union's chief negotiator, announced player representatives had voted to establish September 22 as a strike date. Management's chief negotiator, Jack Donlan, countered that the NFL owners had voted unanimously to field teams with "whatever players we can get" if a strike occurred.

There were several unresolved bargaining issues such as minimum salaries, guaranteed contracts, random drug testing, and pension plan contributions. However, Gene Upshaw contended that the major unresolved issue was free agency, or the movement of players once their contracts expired. Management proposed to continue the practice of the player's old club having the right of first refusal (matching the new club's salary offer) and to lower the compensation (in rounds of draft choices) the new team signing the free agent would give to the player's old team.

The union wanted no first refusal rights or compensating draft choices for players having 4 or more years of service; and first refusal rights but no draft choice compensation for players having fewer than 4 years service. Upshaw attached moral significance to this issue. "Free agency cannot be summed up in terms of dollars. It's not about money, it's about dignity and freedom. It's about who you work for." Players indicated they would support a strike, not because of free agency (felt to benefit only a small percentage of the players), but because they felt the strike would not last long.

On September 22, two weeks into the season, the NFL players went on strike for the second time in 6 years. Upshaw informed the players to expect a long strike, even though he maintained that if management cooperated, a settlement could be reached in 3 days. He also predicted that management's attempts to have players cross the picket lines would create dysfunctional tensions among players even after a settlement was reached: "Any roster player who does cross the picket line is going to cut his career short. He'll never be the same again. His teammates won't like him, the bitterness will be there. You never forget the guy who tried to stab you in the back. And this is not the type of game that you need added incentive for anyone."

Games were not played the first week after the strike (September 27 and 28). Owners estimated they lost $40 million in revenues. Most of the 1,585 football players went to the picket lines, with some physical altercations resulting when strike replacements crossed those lines. The players showed surprising solidarity for 3 weeks—over 90 percent of them stayed out during this period. The owners imposed an October 14 deadline on players to return if they wanted to be paid for the games that weekend. On October 12, 1987, the striking NFL players agreed to end their walkout "if management agreed in writing to submit the dispute to a combination of mediation and arbitration." If accepted by management, the union would send the players back to work immediately while a federal mediator assisted both sides in reaching an agreement. If this attempt failed after 6 weeks the dispute would go to binding arbitration.

Upshaw initially attached finality to this proposal, "I would say, if the owners decline this, then we're out for the duration, out for the year." This position quickly softened. The NFLPA held a conference call on October 13 to persuade the 28 teams' player representatives to keep their players from defecting before this deadline. One player representative recalled,

> Reps started yelling at each other from one side of the country to the other. . . . Then Chicago rep Mike Singletary called time out and offered to lead a prayer. All across the United States players were praying. That's when I realized the strike was over, that we were doomed.

The Washington Redskins, the only team not having a single player defector to date, voted to return en masse on October 15, and other teams followed suit. Owners, however, indicated they would neither need nor pay the players for the upcoming weekend games (again played with replacements) as they had missed the 1:00 p.m. reporting deadline. Many felt that the owners used replacements for the third week to teach the regular players a lesson. The owners claimed they wanted to make sure the players were in shape to avoid possible game injuries. Whatever the reason, management made more profit each week football was played with strike replacements. The average weekly team revenues during the strike were reduced, but the expenses—particularly player salaries—were also lower. Each team increased its weekly profit by approximately $120,000 during the strike. Players and the NFLPA were widely labeled "losers" during the strike as they did not receive even one of their bargaining proposals, and the NFLPA also experienced a sharp drop in dues payments. Management discontinued the dues checkoff when the strike started and only one-fourth of the members paid their annual dues of $2,000, a $3 million annual loss to the union. Players lost approximately $80 million in wages during the strike, with the average paid player losing $15,000 per week and the Buffalo Bills quarterback, Jim Kelly, who admitted not knowing what the bargaining issues were, losing more than $250,000.

Many blamed the NFLPA for this strike loss, contending that the organization made several tactical errors:

- It picked a rallying point issue, free agency, that did not immediately inspire the members. The NFLPA once had free agency in the mid-1970s but bargained it away to gain a union security clause and dues checkoff. Players were therefore being asked to sacrifice an average of $15,000 in weekly salary to obtain something they once had. Many players would have preferred to receive an immediate, larger share of the resources.
- It could not resolve the members' often deep collective bargaining differences on many teams. The NFLPA was engaged in frequent, publicized intraorganizational bargaining—quelling player or team threats to cross the picket line, for example. On the other hand, the NFL Management Council's executive committee kept a tight rein on its members, which enabled management to speak with one voice.
- It treated the media like they were agents of the owners. There were few if any successful NFLPA efforts to inform the public of the players' and union's perspective. Few football players and union leaders engaged in attitudinal structuring such as appearing on television or radio talk shows in the months before negotiations began.
- It did not recognize and therefore attempt to meet management's financial power. The NFLPA apparently underestimated the owners' financial revenues from televised strike replacement games. Owners also obtained a $100 million line of credit in case revenue losses occurred during the strike. The union did not have a corresponding strike fund to supplement members' lost income during a strike. It could also have struck later in the season, thereby giving players more income to offset lost game wages if the strike were called.

Upshaw contended that management, not the union, was responsible for dismal bargaining behaviors and results:

> I don't know if there's anything that would have forced management to negotiate with us. Their positions never changed. . . . Management had one objective in mind and that was to bust the union. It was not free agency. It was not the issues we had out there.

The NFLPA expressed this sentiment by charging management with violations of good faith bargaining and antitrust laws. The unfair labor practice charge has not yet been resolved.

In July 1988, U.S. District Court Judge David Doty denied injunctive relief to 284 unsigned veteran National Football League players who sought to become

(continued)

(continued)

unrestricted free agents. He invoked the Norris–La Guardia Act, which denies federal courts jurisdiction to issue injunctions in cases involving labor disputes. Doty noted,

> Collective bargaining involves agreements on and tradeoffs among a broad range of different items affecting the terms and conditions of employment. For a court to align itself with one of the parties by, in effect, eliminating from bargaining one of the major items in the bargaining mix, would work a wholesale subversion of the collective bargaining process.

Doty's decision does not mean that management is innocent of antitrust violations. In fact, Doty considered it "probable that the players will prevail" in the antitrust trial and that some players "are likely to sustain irreparable harm" if they are prevented from signing with other NFL clubs after this decision was issued.

The decision prodded management to implement a free agency system, "Plan B," on February 1, 1989. In essence, teams can protect a maximum of 37 players and the remainder can become unrestricted free agents with no compensation or first refusal rights for the old team. The first year of Plan B saw 229 out of the 619 unprotected players changing teams and their average salary increasing from $141,000 to $198,000.

One player beneficiary was Mike Tice, formerly Seattle's tight end. He made $210,000 last season but signed a 3-year, $1.1 million contract with the Washington Redskins. Tice had previously blasted Upshaw for his emphasis on free agency during the 1987 strike. "I told him, 'Bunk on your free agency. We don't care about free agency, we want benefits. We don't want to leave Seattle'. . . . So guess who was the first guy on the bus."

However, players' gains from free agency have not automatically transferred into a vote of confidence for free agency and Gene Upshaw. Only 19 percent of the respondents believed that liberalized free agency should be "the union's first bargaining priority"; the vast majority (71 percent) instead called for "improved benefits." A subsequent *Sports Illustrated* poll of 617 NFL veterans asked, "How do you assess Gene Upshaw's performance as executive director of the NFL Players' Association?" The responses were 51 percent "favorably," 39 percent "unfavorably," and 19 percent of the respondents had no opinion.

In November 1989, a two-to-one decision issued by the Eighth Circuit Court of Appeals disagreed with Judge Doty, contending instead that management's

NUHHCE's 1987 convention delegates voted to seek affiliation with a larger labor organization. A deep division within the executive board followed, with some officers preferring affiliation with the Service Employees International Union (SEIU) and others, including the union's president, Henry Nicholas, wanting to join AFSCME.

Eventually, NUHHCE members voted on a geographically determined district basis on whether to join the AFSCME or SEIU union. Thirteen districts (51,430 NUHHCE members) voted to join SEIU while five districts (25,200 NUHHCE members) including Nicholas's home district, Philadelphia, voted to join AFSCME.[27]

Administrative Considerations of the NLRB Representation elections in the private sector health care industry are conducted by the NLRB, which has unique legislative and administrative considerations regarding election solicitation and bargaining-unit determination.

"Plan B" free agency provision was a result of collective bargaining, a product of a labor-management relationship, and therefore did not constitute a violation of antitrust laws. This decision, subsequently affirmed by a seven-to-two vote of the Court of Appeals, suggests that various antitrust claims filed by the NFLPA against the owners would not be supported by the courts. The NFLPA has appealed this decision to the Supreme Court (status uncertain at this book's printing). It also informed management that it would voluntarily decertify itself and no longer represent the players for collective bargaining purposes.

The union's decertification tactic was taken to pressure management into serious collective bargaining efforts. The NFLPA reasoned that owners without a union and related labor agreement provisions could not invoke the antitrust exception granted by the Court of Appeals. Thus, according to this reasoning, management would no longer be able to implement free agency or the college draft (restricting a college football player to seeking employment with one team or even a few teams), because these actions would violate antitrust laws.

Many owners, as well as the commissioner of football, have acknowledged that this tactic could hinder management's traditional controls over player entry and mobility, possibly making related activities such as "Plan B" free agency illegal. Indeed, this alteration of the labor relations process between the NFLPA and the owners represents a unique situation, in which the union could strengthen and increase its bargaining power (raising management's cost of disagreeing with the union) by removing itself from the relationship.

The NFLPA's decertification also means that some 200 previously filed player grievances would not be processed by the NFLPA; also, previously obtained player benefits (salary minimums, pension and severance payments, and health and life insurance, for example) and player access to information about other players' salaries would revert to the pleasure of management. Moreover, the voluntary decertification without a member vote means that a rival labor organization does not have to wait a year to seek player representation.

Will the NFLPA decertify itself? Will there be collective bargaining resulting in a labor agreement? Can management continue its traditional limitations on player entry and mobility in the NFL? The labor relations process in professional football entered the 1990s rife with uncertainties.

Source: Derived from material and sources in Lisa Davis, "The 1987 NFL Strike and the Issue of Free Agency."

A current problem concerns areas in the hospitals where unions may solicit employees. Some hospital managers initially maintained that unions should be barred from seeking employee votes in any hospital area accessible to patients. The Supreme Court (*Beth Israel Hospital* v. *National Labor Relations Board*) indicated that there was no congressional intent in the 1974 amendments to restrict solicitation. It further indicated that a broad rule prohibiting solicitation is likely unreasonable, and that union solicitation can occur in areas where patient care will not be jeopardized. However, specific solicitation areas at particular hospitals often rest on contradictory interpretations of related evidence by the NLRB, lower courts, and the Supreme Court.

The NLRB has also been engaged in a multi-year series of court challenges over its determination of appropriate bargaining units (ABUs) in the health care industry. These proposals eventually specified eight units—physicians; registered nurses; all other professionals; technical employees; skilled maintenance employees;

business office clerical employees; all other nonprofessionals; and guards – in large acute-care hospitals and four units, including a combined professional unit, in smaller hospitals.[28] The NLRB would no longer have to decide hospital union questions on a case-by-case basis if the regulations became effective.

Health care managers objected to these guidelines, contending,

> Not only will health care providers be faced with a multiplicity of organizing campaigns, contract negotiations and grievance and arbitration administration, but the potential for disruption of services occasioned by strikes and work stoppages will increase. Furthermore, the carving out of separate units, e.g., for physicians and for registered nurses, will severely impact the ability of management to change the way in which health care will be provided to patients in the future.[29]

Managers were also concerned that the NLRB's uniform approach to ABUs would impede the board's ability to respond to rapid industrial changes at one or many hospital facilities. Union representatives have been generally favorable toward the NLRB's appropriate bargaining unit determination.[30]

Collective Bargaining Activities by Hospital Employees and Related Bargaining Issues

Nurses The American Nurses Association (ANA), though it has less than 30 percent of all employed nurses as members, is the major organization representing nurses. Since its inception in 1897, the ANA has been concerned with economic protection of its members. The organization avoided direct involvement with collective bargaining; however, in 1946 it encouraged state nurses' associations to actively implement collective bargaining programs aimed at economic benefits and participation of nurses in the planning and administration of nursing services. Under this arrangement, the state nurses' associations negotiate with employers when authorized to do so by the membership. The ANA believes that its state affiliates have more direct knowledge about actual and desired working conditions, and it will not become involved in a dispute from a financial or advisory standpoint unless requested to do so by the appropriate association.

This program has continued, although it was modified in 1950 when the ANA adopted a no-strike policy and formulated a *nurses-in-dispute policy,* which contended that because nurses have direct legal and ethical obligations to patients, they should take a neutral position if their facility is involved in a labor-management dispute. Hence, the ANA emphasized that nurses were not to strike; instead, they should tend to their patients during employee-employer negotiations.

Union activity of nurses increased dramatically in the 1960s and 1970s with several significant strikes and other collective action taking place in California, Ohio, Minnesota, Iowa, and Connecticut. Nurses have received a surprising amount of public support during their strike activities. Few people directly blame them for dislocations during a strike. In most strike situations, ample time has been given to transfer already admitted patients or to stop accepting patients for elective surgery. Also, the public has begun to view hospitals as big business concerns rather than charitable institutions.[31]

Nurses' collective bargaining issues reflect both professional and economic issues such as

- Control over the scope and exercise of duties.
- Some control in selecting work hours.
- Ability to decide what constitutes "safe working conditions."
- Training.
- Compensation in line with education and responsibility.[32]

House-Staff Employees Labor relations concerns arise over the working conditions that house-staff employees (residents, interns, and fellows) face—for example, low wages and extensive working hours, averaging in some cases 100 a week, often for consecutive periods ranging from 36 to 72 hours. Additionally, training necessary for certification makes house-staff officers particularly vulnerable; they are subject to arbitrary actions by medical supervisors. In some cases, the training program is designed to eliminate a specified number of employees before completion. Those completing the program still have to depend on the good will of their supervisors and other hospital administrators for further hospital privileges and recommendations for other positions.

However, the NLRB determined in its *Cedars-Sinai* decision that the 1974 Taft-Hartley Amendments did not apply to house-staff who were regarded as students primarily involved in attaining education necessary for practicing medicine, not employees who are earning a living. Currently, house-staff unions have no recourse to the NLRB or to the courts. Yet, they can obtain recognition by management either on a voluntary basis or possibly through strikes.[33]

Physicians Apart from house-staff employees, there are at least 26 organizations committed to some form of collective bargaining for physicians. This situation contradicts rather strong antiunion positions taken by the American Medical Association and American Dental Association. However, physicians have become more militant because of declines in their incomes in recent years and increases in legal challenges and malpractice suits.[34]

The president of the largest doctors' union (Union of American Physicians and Dentists, which represents some 43,000 members in California and in other states) says that most physicians "have lost the ability to set their own fees, to determine freely the nature and number of units of service they can render and even to decide where the service may be rendered."[35] A recent survey found that nearly 40 percent of the doctors interviewed said that based on their current knowledge about careers in medicine they would not have become a doctor if they had a career choice to make again.[36]

Many doctors might not consider joining a union because inevitable strikes would result, and strikes run counter to the profession's code. A countering argument, however, is that strikes include provisions for emergency or even urgent care. Further argument states the following:

> Although deferring routine or elective activities might temporarily inconvenience some patients, we are convinced, because of our firm belief that there is a total consonance of interest between doctors and patients, that such a short-term incon-

venience would be compensated for in the long term by our winning from our paymasters improvements in the standards of patient care.[37]

The NLRB has determined that full-time staff physicians and dentists employed by a health maintenance organization (HMO) are managerial employees because they serve on committees that make and carry out the employer's policies. These individuals are therefore excluded from labor organization protections under the Taft-Hartley Act.

Union Impact on Health Care Work Rules

Unions have historically been associated with wage increases in the hospital industry. Two studies[38] have shown that:

1. Union officers representing hospital nonprofessionals tend to obtain higher wage gains than union officers representing nurses.
2. The union's impact on wages increases with the length of time collective bargaining has been in effect in hospitals.

The first finding seems reasonable in view of the historically non-militant stance of the American Nurses Association, which has stressed professional issues instead of economic job actions such as strikes. The second finding can be partially explained by a shift in union goals over time. Unions, after winning a representation election, first concentrate on union security issues, then in subsequent negotiations focus on economic issues.

A third study has found that wage increases have been higher than corresponding productivity gains, although this figure represents a very small proportion (5 percent) of increased hospital expenditures.[39]

Farm Workers

This section will emphasize agriculture labor relations activities in California, since this state has experienced significant union activity and has farm working conditions similar to those throughout the United States. This state has also witnessed a comprehensive labor relations law as well as the emergence of a charismatic union leader, Cesar Chavez. Finally, Chavez's union, the United Farm Workers, provides vivid examples of problems and prospects that all farm worker unions face.

Overview of Farm Laborer Working Conditions and the Rise of Cesar Chavez

Statistics on farm workers often vary because of widespread mobility among these individuals. Currently there are approximately 2.6 million farm workers in the United States including some 217,000 migrant farm workers.[40] The National Safety Council indicated in 1987 that farm workers suffered 160,000 on-the-job injuries and 1,600 deaths. Migrant working and living conditions have often been described as brutal,[41] characterized by four unique and unpleasant working conditions:

1. **"El Cortito"** The dreaded, common piece of equipment, "El Cortito," or "the short hoe" used in crop tending, has a handle less than 3 feet long. The migrants have to stoop in the fields to use it, so that their backs are practically parallel

Cesar Chavez, the powerfully charismatic leader of the United Farm Workers, has successfully organized migrant workers to gain wage increases and contracts. His nonviolent approach, based on worker loyalty to "La Causa," usually relies on boycotts of products.

Source: Photo by Paul Fusco, Magnum.

to the ground. This equipment is outlawed in California and Arizona, although its use continues in other states.

2. **Transitory Nature** Another unpleasant aspect of this job is its transitory nature, necessitating frequent relocations to find work. Cesar Chavez's recollection of his typical work year is presented in the "Labor Relations in Action," and illustrates a representative work schedule.

3. **Employer Attitudes** It is, of course, impossible to identify the growers as having a common attitude regarding their employees. Yet the following quotations from growers illustrate employment philosophies ranging from indifference to paternalism to racism:

> The class of labor we want is the kind we can send home when we are through with them.
>
> It wasn't fair for Chavez to strike my ranch. . . . My workers were simple people, good people, and I liked them and took good care of them. If a man and his family worked hard, I gave them a low-rent room and sold them groceries at only slight markups. Once, I even paid for the funeral of the daughter of one of my workers.

Cesar Chavez's Recollection Regarding His Work Year

We did not pick the same crops every year, but there was a pattern. Most winters we spent in Brawley where there were carrots, mustard, and peas. I did cabbage and lettuce in January, picking or working it, tying or loading it on a trailer. Then a little later we capped cantaloupe and watermelon, putting a wax paper over the plant to keep it from freezing and to keep the ground warm, just like an individual hothouse for every plant. When it got warmer, we came back, took the cap off, worked the ground around the plants, and thinned them, using a short-handle hoe.

Probably one of the worst jobs was the broccoli. We were in water and mud up to our necks and our hands got frozen. We had to cut it and throw it on a trailer, cut and throw, cut and throw. We slipped around in the mud, and we were wet. I didn't have any boots, just shoes on. Those crops were in December through March. In January to March there also were the cauliflower, mustard greens, onions, carrots, cabbage, and lettuce.

Then we worked in the watermelon, just picking up the vines which grew in the irrigation ditches and training them away from the ditches. The melons started in May, and I would work in the sheds for a labor contractor who was related to us.

In late May we had two or three options, Oxnard for beans, Beaumont for cherries, or the Hemet area for apricots, places that no longer have much or any of those crops. I think we did all at one time or other. Most of the time my dad would leave it up to us. "Do you think you'll like it?" he would ask.

We started making the apricots in Moorepark where they pick them up from the ground, just like prunes. In San Jose, on the other hand, we had to climb a ladder.

That would be the early part of summer. From there we had all kinds of options. We never did asparagus, and we only did figs once. The milk of the fig eats through your skin like acid. Some people put grease on their hands, but we couldn't do that. It was just awful.

We worked in lima beans, corn, and chili peppers, picked fresh lima beans for fifty cents a basket. Then in August we had grapes, prunes, cucumbers, and tomatoes. Those go into September and part of October. We would go before those crops started and wait in a camp until they were ready. For example there were raisin grapes about ten miles beyond Fresno. We had to be there at least a week in advance, or we couldn't get a job. That was a week of lost time, sometimes more, with no pay whatsoever.

Then we did cotton from October through Christmas. I just hated it. It was very hard work, but there was nothing else. After the cotton, just like ducks, we usually went back to Brawley to start with the crops in January.

Source: Selection is reprinted from *Cesar Chavez, Autobiography of La Causa,* by Jacques E. Levy, with the permission of W. W. Norton & Company, Inc.

> These people were made to suffer; some of them even enjoy the work. God made the Mexicans with stubby legs and greasy hair. So, you see, they can lean low and tolerate the sun in the fields. Chavez made those people think they're something better.[42]

4. **Exemption from Labor Relations Laws** Finally, agricultural employees continue to be specifically exempted from federal labor relations laws, and this lack of federal labor relations coverage has made it most difficult for farm

workers to organize. Without federal legislation, legal emphasis shifts to appropriate state laws and judicial interpretations of legal organizing and collective bargaining tactics (for example, picketing and boycotts of farm products). Only seven states (Arizona, Idaho, Kansas, Michigan, California, Wisconsin, and Hawaii) currently have laws covering farm workers,[43] with California having the most extensive coverage.

It should be noted that at least one farm workers' union has reservations about being included under the National Labor Relations Act. Under this act, most migrant workers could be denied voting rights in union elections since employers could request elections during the off season, when a handful of steady, company-dominated workers would decide the representation issue for the majority of seasonal workers. Only the California Agricultural Labor Relations Act guarantees peak season elections.

Early Organizational Attempts In 1905 the Industrial Workers of the World attempted to organize farm workers; however, union-organizing successes until 1962 were sporadic because of the lack of membership base and labor legislation.

Another major obstacle to union organization has been the *bracero program,* which allowed legal importation of Mexican farm workers *(braceros)* under war emergency agreements between the United States and Mexico during World War II. Almost overnight, the haphazard system of recruiting farm labor was replaced by a highly organized recruiting process. This method ensured growers a plentiful supply of cheap labor, while allowing Mexico to send its restless unemployed to another country. The two countries continued this program after World War II until Congress officially terminated it in 1964.

The ending of the bracero program may have helped farm worker organizing, as unions might have had a more stable base of potential members. However, some research has shown that the program's elimination has neither significantly reduced the number of foreign farm workers nor increased the wages of domestic farm workers. These findings might be due to increases in the number of alien workers illegally crossing the border.[44]

Chavez's Formation of a Union Forming a union in 1962 enabled Chavez to approach the farm worker's employment conditions more directly. Exhibit 16.1 illustrates how this approach has been directly translated into current labor agreement provisions. He believed that union activities should be nonviolent in order to obtain favorable public opinion. Nonviolence also has a pragmatic value; for example, a boycott of a supermarket hurts the employer economically, while a violent act (such as arson) enables the employer to collect insurance and receive a refund on taxes.

The first strike conducted by Chavez occurred in the rose fields in the spring of 1965. This dispute lasted 4 days, with employees receiving a wage increase but no labor agreement. The growers were eager to resolve the dispute since skilled rose grafters were in short supply.

The most publicized activities of this union were the 1965 Delano strike and the grape boycott. These efforts were initially successful in that longshoremen re-

Exhibit 16.1 **Major Provisions of Standard UFW Contracts**

1. **Union Security and Management Rights**
   - Recognition of UFW as sole bargaining agent for farm workers
   - Union shop (employees must join union after 5 days of work)
   - Dues checkoff (employer forwards 2 percent of worker pay to union)
   - Union health and safety committee to advise on work practices
   - Successor clause (agreement is binding on new owner)
   - Management rights (all rights not stated in agreement are management rights)
2. **Wages and Related Provisions**
   - Hourly or piece-rate wage structure and how it is to be adjusted
   - Piece-rate incentives and end-of-season bonuses
3. **Hours of Work and Overtime Pay**
   - Overtime pay after 8 hours
   - Reporting pay, e.g., 4 hours pay for each day the employee reports as instructed but there is no work
   - Premium pay for working at night
   - Travel pay for time spent riding to and from the work site
   - Rest periods, e.g., 15 minutes for every four hours worked
4. **Paid and Unpaid Leave**
   - Vacations: 2 to 4 percent of gross earnings
   - Paid holidays: five to seven holidays for workers employed the day before and after the holiday
   - Leaves for union duty, jury duty, etc., without loss of seniority
5. **Employee Benefits**
   - RFK Medical Plan—employer contributes $.75–$1.25 for each hour worked
   - JDLC Pension Plan—employer contributes 15–20 cents for each hour worked
   - MLK Fund—employer contributes 5–15 cents for each hour worked
   - Jury, bereavement, and witness pay—employer pays at average rate
   - Citizen Participation Day—employer pays workers at their average rate for first Sunday in July
   - Housing: what access and cost if provided
6. **Seniority and Hiring**
   - Employer maintains a seniority list on the basis of hours worked
   - Union shall maintain a hiring hall to supply new workers
   - All new employees have a 5-day probation
7. **Job Security**
   - Notify union of subcontracting necessary if workers do not have required equipment or skills
   - Mechanization: employer shall notify the union and bargain; union can call a strike if settlement is not reached.
8. **Dispute Settlement**
   - Grievance procedure: multi-step appeals to settle differences of opinion over what the contract means
   - No strikes and lockouts during agreement

Source: Review of 250 UFW contracts in Philip L. Martin, Suzanne Vaupel, and Daniel L. Egan, *Unfulfilled Promise: Collective Bargaining in California Agriculture* (Boulder, Co.: Westview Press, 1988), p. 54.

fused to load "scab" grapes on ships. However, the boycott became somewhat difficult when the growers increased the number of different labels from 6 to 100, thereby confusing the pickets. Thus, the boycott was enlarged to include all California-grown grapes.

The grape boycott received national attention, particularly in the 1968 presidential campaign, during which it was endorsed by candidates Kennedy, McCarthy, McGovern, and Humphrey. On the other hand, Nixon denounced the boycott while eating grapes at a press conference in Fresno, California. The Nixon administration later gave more tangible support to the grape growers during the Vietnam War. The Defense Department countered reduced consumer interest in grapes by increasing 1968 to 1969 grape shipments to the troops some 350 percent (2.5 million pounds) over the previous year.[45]

Five years after the initial dispute, the Delano growers agreed to the principle of collective bargaining and signed labor agreements that raised economic benefits and established grievance procedures. Delano could be termed a success for the farm workers, yet the labor settlement increased jurisdictional battles among unions for the right to represent farm workers.

Jurisdictional Problems among Farm Worker Unions

The union formed by Cesar Chavez was originally independent from the AFL-CIO, although it received an AFL-CIO charter in 1972. This union, after numerous name changes, became the United Farm Workers (UFW).

Teamster-UFW Conflict While jurisdictional problems were somewhat peacefully worked out with the AFL-CIO, serious problems remained with a then independent union, the Teamsters. A discussion of these disputes helps explain the internal problems of the UFW and the emergence of related labor legislation and also enables an examination of a rather rare impediment to the contemporary labor relations process—intense union rivalry for the same employees.

Although at least one Teamster local provided assistance to the UFW during the grape boycott, cooperation between the two unions was the exception rather than the rule. The 1970 UFW victory in Delano heightened jurisdiction problems, for it prompted other growers to resolve labor relations expediently. In fact, 170 labor agreements were signed with Salinas and Santa Maria growers 1 day before Chavez announced the Delano settlement.

The UFW intended to switch its attention to the lettuce and vegetable fields of the Salinas and Santa Maria valleys after the Delano settlement. Growers in these valleys realized that unions were inevitable, and their concern shifted to minimizing their losses. They had previously approached the Teamsters, who were initially reluctant to break a 1966 to 1967 jurisdictional treaty with the UFW. Yet a Teamster-grower settlement was reached when Teamster drivers, who were on a brief strike, agreed to return to work only if their jobs were not disrupted by field hand strikes. This rationale prompted the Teamsters to push for (and quickly receive from the growers) extension of truck driver agreements to include the farm workers.

The UFW was predictably outraged by this turn of events, charging that the Teamsters had "sweetheart contracts" with the growers and the agreements were secured without asking the employees to vote for their union preference. The UFW countered with a strike (involving some 10,000 employees) to put pressure on the growers; violence often occurred between UFW and Teamster employees. Although this effort and the related lettuce boycott hurt the growers, problems continued to exist between the Teamsters and the UFW.

The Teamsters made huge inroads into the UFW's bargaining victories. In 1973 the UFW held agreements with approximately 300 growers, involving some 60,000 employees. In 1974 this number was reduced to 12 agreements covering only 5,000 employees, while the Teamsters held some 350 collective bargaining agreements with the growers. A large part of this turnaround was due to the eager reception given to the Teamsters by the growers. To be sure, employees under these sweetheart arrangements were not able to vote their union preference. When this situation changed in California, many of the farm workers indicated their preference for the UFW.

Yet there might be other reasons for the Teamsters' success, as illustrated by the following remarks of a farm worker on Chavez's "La Causa."

> La Causa is good, and its time will come again. When I hear the cry of 'Huelga' I want to, you know, walk out of the fields, to screw the grower right at Harvest time, to help Cesar in this hard time he has. But look around you at all these open mouths to feed. We will keep thinning the lettuce because we need the dollars. I like the Chavez union most, but they made some mistakes. The Teamsters are not as bad as he says. They helped me get food stamps in January when there was no work.[46]

The Teamsters' traditional approach to collective bargaining clashed with the UFW's broader social goals. The Teamsters' use of much greater financial resources and of skilled staff employees in their collective bargaining efforts may have raised doubts among some farm workers as to the appropriate method of union representation and the most efficient method of attaining these goals.[47] Many farm workers still revere Chavez as a hero; however, their concerns are shifting to bread and butter issues.

Part of the tactical difference between the unions is due to Chavez's formulation of the UFW as a social movement:

> I once said you couldn't organize farm workers in conventional ways. . . . It has to be a movement. . . . What happens is the people get to feel that the idea, the movement, belongs to them. It's theirs, not ours. No force on earth, including the Teamsters and the growers can take that away from them. The more the people get beaten, the more they'll fight. The more persecution, the more strength they have. . . . When you learn about your movement, . . . you get to love it.[48]

Viva la huelga! can be roughly translated as meaning "strike"; yet its Spanish meaning carries a much more social connotation, particularly when associated with the UFW flags symbolizing hope, aspiration, and sacrifice. The movement for which the cry is the catchword has also had strong religious overtones since its inception—religious officials of many denominations have historically lent their efforts to farm workers in general.

Chavez has always considered loyalty to the movement a prerequisite for participation. Most of the UFW's staff have been volunteers, paid $5 a week. The lack of full-time, experienced employees placed the UFW at a disadvantage to the Teamsters. The administration of the UFW became somewhat haphazard—terms and records of negotiations were either slipshod or nonexistent. Also, with few exceptions, negotiators could not make binding agreements with the growers on even routine matters without Chavez's personal approval. Turnover among volunteers further added to haphazard administration.

The California Agricultural Labor Relations Act In addition to continuing organizing activities and administering the UFW, Chavez also pressed for farm labor legislation. After years of lobbying efforts and negotiations with legislative officials, the California Agricultural Labor Relations Act (CALRA) went into effect on August 28, 1975. This act has several provisions that strengthen farm worker unions in general[49] and the UFW's position relative to the Teamsters in particular. Two major provisions of CALRA require secret-ballot elections before union certification at times when the employer's payroll reflects at least 50 percent of the peak agricultural employment. Also, elections are to be held within 7 days after the receipt of the election petition. Under the law, a union may not conduct a secondary boycott against an employer that handles the products of a company where the union has lost an election conducted under the Act. However, consumer boycotts of a particular struck product remain legal. Recently, CALRA has adopted a make-whole remedy for employees when the employer has been found not to have bargained in good faith. The AFL-CIO has long desired that this remedy for bad faith bargaining be included in the National Labor Relations Act; however, they have to date been unsuccessful.

In the first 5 months after the CALRA was passed, over 32,000 farm workers voted in 429 elections. The pro-union sentiment of these elections was evident (84 percent of the workers voted for union representation), as was the pro-UFW sentiment. The UFW once again became the major bargaining representative, winning 198 elections during this 5-month period.

The implementation of the CALRA and the voting results prompted the UFW and the Teamsters to resolve their jurisdictional differences. On March 10, 1977, the unions signed a pact. It was agreed that the UFW would organize all employees in elections conducted by CALRA's Agricultural Labor Relations Board, and the Teamsters would organize all employees in NLRB elections. In essence, the UFW would represent the field workers, and the Teamsters would represent cannery workers and most agricultural truck drivers. This pact was not renewed in 1984, and the Teamsters might resume their organizing activities of farm workers.

The Future of Unions for Farm Workers

The future of unionized farm workers depends on the ability to successfully meet the challenges of innovative bargaining structures, illegal aliens, working conditions, and various political administrations.

Bargaining Structures Farm workers in Ohio and Michigan have long attempted to obtain collective bargaining with independent tomato and cucumber growers. Campbell Soup Company has been the major target, since this organization essentially sets farm workers' employment terms when it indicates how much it will pay growers for tomatoes before the first seed is planted.

The Farm Labor Organizing Committee, in affiliation with the UFW, along with civil rights and religious groups, conducted an 8-year boycott against Campbell Soup. This action resulted in a tripartite labor agreement that included pay raises, union recognition, agency shop, a 48-hour grievance resolution procedure, and the establishment of joint committees to study working conditions.

Illegal Aliens These individuals are often difficult to organize into a union; indeed, they may represent a lower cost employee alternative to the growers. As illegal immigration continued in the 1970s and early 1980s, farm wages stabilized or fell and farm worker unions lost many of their contracts.

The passage of the Immigration Reform and Control Act (IRCA) of 1986 was intended to curtail this employment alternative by imposing sanctions or fines on employers who knowingly hire illegal alien employees. Growers, fearing increasing immigration restrictions and loss of crops because of resulting labor shortages, objected to this legislation. These concerns have not been realized, however, as an exception to IRCA was made for seasonal farm workers who had an amnesty time period to apply for permanent resident status. Approximately one million individuals used this option, and the number of available agricultural workers has not yet been reduced.[50]

Working Conditions: Mechanization and Pesticides Mechanization represents a major challenge to farm worker unionization. For example, Libby, McNeil and Libby countered a successful union-organizing drive of Wisconsin cucumber workers by mechanization. Within 1 year of the union's *(Obreros Unidos')* successful election, harvesting machines rendered the bargaining unit nonexistent.[51] In view of mechanization advances, farm worker unions will face a difficult dilemma: do they fight mechanization as a job destroyer, or do they attempt to win higher wages for a smaller number of workers? The UFW appears to favor the first approach:

> The taxpayer pays twice for state-supported farm research. He pays, first, when public funds are used to develop the machines with no thought for the men and women whose jobs are wiped out; he pays again when these once gainfully employed workers turn to the state for support and the public is forced to absorb the social costs of mechanization.[52]

Pesticides represent another farm worker concern.[53] In 1984 the UFW conducted a grape boycott to protest the growers' use of five pesticides claimed to pose serious health risks to farm workers and their subsequently born children and the consumers. However, this boycott did not reduce nationwide grape sales. It also did not strengthen union representation. In 1973 the UFW represented 83 percent of the table-grape workers; the UFW now has none of these employees under contract.[54] Chavez augmented the grape boycott with a 36-day water-only fast in 1988. He noted,

> Many events . . . precipitated the fast, including the terrible suffering of farm workers and their children, the crushing of farm-worker rights, the denial of fair and free elections and the death of good-faith collective bargaining in California agriculture.[55]

Political Administrations The preceding quotation suggests the boycott and fast was also aimed at enhancing the union's existence and operations. California unions did gain when CALRA was first implemented, winning over 90 percent of the 687 elections (624 union certification, 63 no unions) conducted during the first 7 years of the act. Fortunes changed after a new California governor was elected in 1982 and began to replace members of the Agricultural Labor Relations Board. Unions won less than half of the certification elections (59 out of 121) conducted in the fiscal years 1982/1983 through 1986/1987. UFW membership statistics are also currently between 12,000 and 30,000 depending on the selected estimate, down from a peak membership of over 100,000 in the 1970s.[56]

Mr. Chavez contends that this situation reflects government suppression of union organization. Some, however, counter that this situation reflects Chavez's inability or unwillingness to transform an initial social movement into a traditional labor organization.

Summary

Labor relations activities in various professional sports are markedly different from corresponding activities found in other occupations, particularly concerning wage determination.

Until recently, collective bargaining in health care organizations has been hindered by a lack of labor legislation. This situation changed in 1974 with the Taft-Hartley amendments that extended federal labor relations coverage to all private-sector hospitals. Yet subsequent labor relations activities (such as union organizing and strikes) are differentiated from other occupations because of the critical nature of work in the health care fields. Similarly, nurses, house-staff, and physicians often modify their collective bargaining concerns with the concept of "professionalism."

While many of the conditions found in the agricultural industry are described as "brutal," collective bargaining in this sector was virtually nonexistent until 1962, when Cesar Chavez founded a union (subsequently called the United Farm Workers). This union faced several obstacles, such as rival union activity, opposition from the growers, absence of federal labor legislation, alien employees, mechanization, and different collective bargaining structures.

Discussion Questions

1. Considering the variables shown in Exhibit 1.1 (Chapter 1), discuss two differences that professional sports, health care, and agriculture each have when compared to labor relations in other occupations. (Discuss six differences.) Also indicate two general similarities of all three sectors, qualifying your answer when appropriate.
2. Select one nontraditional sector and present a detailed discussion of how this sector relates to all of the variables in Exhibit 1.1. You might have to engage in some speculation and outside research to complete this question.

References

1. Robert C. Berry, William B. Gould IV, and Paul D. Staudohar, *Labor Relations in Professional Sports* (Dover, Mass.: Auburn House, 1986), p. 3.
2. "Scorecard," *Sports Illustrated,* June 16, 1986, p. 10.
3. Tom Wicker, "Baseball," *Esquire,* December 1975, p. 135.
4. Gary Pomerantz, "Marvin Miller," *Times Union and Journal,* June 28, 1981, p. D-3.
5. *The Sporting News,* December 11, 1989, p. 60; "NBC Pays $600 Million for NBA Rights," *USA Today,* November 10, 1989, p. 1-C; and "TV Contract Seen as Triumph for Tagliabue," *Miami Herald,* March 10, 1990, p. 3-D.
6. Hal Bock, "Decade Will Be Known for Its Soaring Salaries," *Miami Herald,* January 4, 1990, p. 9-D.
7. Roger Kahn, *Joe and Marilyn: A Memory of Love* (New York: William Morrow and Company, Inc., 1987), pp. 130–149.
8. Mickey Mantle, *The Mick* (New York: Doubleday and Company, 1985), pp. 144–145.
9. Jim McMahon and Bob Verdi, *McMahon!* (New York: Warner Books, 1986), p. 107.
10. "Gretzky Has Deal Worth $31.3 Million with Kings," *New York Times,* February 3, 1990, p. 33.
11. See, for example, Marshall H. Medoff, "On Monopolistic Ex-

ploitation in Baseball," *Quarterly Review of Economics and Business* 16 (Summer 1976), pp. 113–121. For an approach to this problem and discussion of related research, see Gerald V. Scully, "Pay and Performance in Major League Baseball," *American Economic Review* 64 (December 1974), pp. 915-931. For an earlier conceptual approach to wage determination, see Simon Rottenberg, "The Baseball Players' Labor Market," *Journal of Political Economy* 64 (June 1956), pp. 242-258.
12. "Funds and Games," *USA Today,* October 11, 1989, p. 2-C.
13. For some insights into baseball salary arbitration, see Peter Seitz, "Footnotes to Baseball Salary Arbitration," *Arbitration Journal,* June 1974, p. 100; Raymond Grebey, Jr., "Another Look at Baseball's Salary Arbitration," *Arbitration Journal* 38 (December 1983), p. 25; Marvin J. Miller, "Arbitration of Baseball Salaries: Impartial Adjudication in Place of Management Fiat," *Arbitration Journal* 38 (December 1983), p. 34; and James B. Dworkin, "Salary Arbitration in Baseball: An Impartial Assessment After Ten Years," *Arbitration Journal* 41 (March 1986), pp. 63–70.
14. Jim Bouton, *Ball Four* (New York: World Press, 1970), p. 10.
15. Noel Hynd, "Giant-Sized Confession: A Groundskeeper's Deeds," *Sports Illustrated,* August 29, 1988.
16. Mark Mayfield, "Two Who Deferred to Security," *USA Today,* November 13, 1985, p. 1C.
17. Curt Flood, *The Way It Is* (New York: Trident Press, 1970), pp. 14–15. See also *Curtis C. Flood* v. *Bowie Kuhn et al.,* 407 U.S. 258 (1972). For additional details regarding this decision, see Phillip L. Martin, "The Labor Controversy in Professional Baseball: The Flood Case," *Labor Law Journal* 23 (September 1972), pp. 567–571.
18. Thomas M. Boswell and Richard B. McKeown, "From Trial by Law to Trial By Auction," *Journal of Contemporary Law* 4 (1978). For detailed accounts of the early history of the reserve rule see Harold R. Seymour, *Baseball: The Early Years* (New York: Oxford University Press, 1960), pp. 106–115; James B. Dworkin, *Owners Versus Players* (Boston: Auburn House, 1981), pp. 41–62; Lionel S. Sobel, *Professional Sports and The Law* (New York: Law-Arts Publishers Inc., 1977), pp. 81–89.
19. James B. Chelius and James B. Dworkin, "Free Agency and Salary Determination in Baseball," *Labor Law Journal* 33 (August 1982), pp. 539–544; Paul D. Staudohar and Edward M. Smith, "The Impact of Free Agency on Baseball Salaries," *Compensation Review* 13 (Third Quarter 1981), pp. 46–55; Paul M. Sommers and Noel Quinton, "Pay and Performance in Major League Baseball: The Case of the First Family of Free Agents," *Journal of Human Resources* 17 (September 1982), pp. 426–436; James Richard Hill and William Spellman, "Professional Baseball: The Reserve Clause and Salary Structure," *Industrial Relations* 22 (Winter 1983), pp. 1–19; and Henry J. Raimondo, "Free Agents' Impact on the Labor Market for Baseball Players," *Journal of Labor Research* (Spring 1983), pp. 183–194.
20. McMahon, *McMahon!* p. 123.
21. *Face Off,* September 1971, p. 2.
22. Bob Rubin, "Dolphin's Disinterest? Maybe It Was the Sun?" *Miami Herald,* June 5, 1977.
23. For further insights into this issue, see Daniel H. Kruger, "The Crisis of Player Mobility: The NFL Strike of 1982," *Labor Law Journal* 38 (January 1987), pp. 48–62; Paul D. Staudohar, "The Football Strike of 1987: The Question of Free Agency," *The Monthly Labor Review* 3 (August 1988), pp. 26–31; Cynthia L. Gramm and John F. Schnell, "Crossing the Picket Line: An Analysis of Player Choice during the 1987 National Football League Strike," (unpublished paper).
24. Lucretia Dewey Tanner, Harriet Goldberg Weinstein, and Alice L. Ahmuty, "Collective Bargaining in the Health Care Industry," *Monthly Labor Review* 104 (February 1980), p. 50. For additional details and implications of these requirements, see John G. Kruchko and Jay R. Fries, "Hospital Strikes: Coping with NLRA Notice Requirements," *Employee Relations Law Journal* 9 (Spring 1984), pp. 566–579.
25. John Thomas Delaney, "Union Success in Hospital Representation Elections," *Industrial Relations* 20 (Spring 1981), pp. 149–161; see also Gregory E. Huszczo and Bruce J. Fried, "A Labor Relations Research Agenda for Health Care Settings," *Employee Responsibilities and Rights Journal* 1 (1988), pp. 73–74.
26. Leon Fink, "Bread and Roses; Crusts and Thorns: The Troubled Story of 1199," *Dissent* 33 (Spring 1986), pp. 179–188.
27. "Majority of Hospital Union's Members Vote to Affiliate with SEIU," Bureau of National Affairs Inc., *Daily Labor Report,* no. 103, May 31, 1989, A-8, A-9.
28. "NLRB Publishes Final Rule on Hospital Bargaining Units," Bureau of National Affairs Inc., *Daily Labor Report* 76 (April 21, 1989), pp. D-1–D-11.
29. "Hospital Group Members Urged to Oppose Proposed NLRB Rules," Bureau of National Affairs Inc., *Daily Labor Report,* no. 150 (August 6, 1987), p. A-2.
30. "Selected Statements on Appropriate Health Care Bargaining Units Delivered at NLRB Hearing, August 17, 1987," Bureau of National Affairs Inc., *Daily Labor Report,* no. 158 (August 18, 1987), pp. F-1–F-5.
31. Philip D. Rutsohn and Richard M. Grimes, "Nightingalism and Negotiations—New Attitudes of Health Professionals," *Personnel Journal* 56 (August 1977), p. 399.
32. Karen A. O'Rourke and Salley Reynolds Barton, *Nurse Power: Unions and the Law* (Bowie, Md.: Robert J. Brady Co., 1981), pp. 6–7. For additional insights into nurses' bargaining issues, see Allen M. Ponak, "Unionized Professionals and the Scope of Bargaining: A Study of Nurses," *Industrial and Labor Relations Review* 34 (April 1981), pp. 396–407; and Joan R. Bloom, G. Nicholas Parlette, and Charles A. O'Reilly, "Collective Bargaining by Nurses: A Comparative Analysis of Management and Employee Perceptions," *Health Care Management* 5 (Winter 1980), pp. 25–33.
33. Susan D. Caswell, "The Movement that Died: Housestaff Unionization in The Private Sector," *Labor Law Journal* 37 (June 1986), pp. 332–339.
34. Alice A. Oberfield and Pamela S. Tolbert, "Physician's Work," *ILR Report* 26 (Spring 1989), p. 8; see also "Doctors Organize Battle to Reduce Malpractice Suits," *New York Times,* February 15, 1985, pp. 1, 11; and John A. Klover, David B. Stephens, and Vincent P. Luchsinger, "Contemporary Perceptions of Unionization in the Medical Profession: A Study of Unionized and Non-Union Physicians," *Journal of Collective Negotiations in the Public Sector* 9, no. 2 (1980), p. 108.
35. Sanford Marcus, "Trade Unionism for Doctors: An Idea Whose Time Has Come," *New England Journal of Medicine,* December 6, 1984, pp. 1509–1510.
36. Lawrence K. Altman, "Changes in Medicine Bring Pain to Healing Profession," *New York Times,* February 18, 1990, p. 1.
37. Marcus, "Trade Unionism for Doctors."
38. Sloan and Steinwald, Hospital Labor Markets, pp. 105–121; and Richard Feldman and Richard Scheffler, "The Union Impact on

Hospital Wages and Fringe Benefits," *Industrial and Labor Relations Review* 35 (January 1982), pp. 196–206.
39. Frank A. Sloan and Killard W. Adamache, "The Role of Unions in Hospital Cost Inflation," *Industrial and Labor Relations Review* (January 1984), pp. 252–263.
40. Philip L. Martin, *Harvest of Confusion* (Boulder, Colo.: Westview Press, 1988), p. 53.
41. Dianna Solis, "*On the Move:* From Farm to Farm, Migrant Workers Struggle to Survive," *The Wall Street Journal,* May 15, 1985, pp. 1, 18; and a three-part series on these conditions in *The Orlando Sentinel,* March 26, 1989 through March 28, 1989.
42. Sam Kushner, *Long Road to Delano* (New York: International Publishers, 1975), p. 95; Winthrop Griffith, "Is Chavez Beaten?" *New York Times Magazine,* September 15, 1974, p. 24. © 1974 by The New York Times Company. Reprinted by permission.
43. For additional insights into these laws, see Karen S. Koziara, "Agricultural Labor Relations Laws in Four States—A Comparison," *Monthly Labor Review* 100 (May 1977), pp. 14–18; Harold C. White and William Gibney, "The Arizona Farm Labor Law: A Supreme Court Test," *Labor Law Journal* 31 (February 1980), pp. 87–99; and Ronald W. Haughton, "The Influence of Labor Management Relations on the Settlement of Agricultural Disputes," *Arbitration Journal* 35 (June 1980), pp. 3–7.
44. Lamar B. Jones and G. Randolph Rice, "Agricultural Labor in the Southwest: The Post Bracero Years," *Social Science Quarterly* 61 (June 1980), pp. 86–94. For a more thorough discussion of the history of farm workers' collective actions as well as the bracero program see Linda C. Majka and Theo J. Majka, *Farm Workers, Agribusiness, and the State* (Philadelphia: Temple University Press, 1982).
45. Dick Meister and Anne Loftis, *A Long Time Coming* (New York: Macmillan, 1977), p. 157.
46. Griffith, "Is Chavez Beaten?" p. 18.
47. For an example of this consideration, see Joel Solkoff, "Can Cesar Chavez Cope with Success?" *New Republic,* May 22, 1976, p. 14.
48. Griffith, "Is Chavez Beaten?" p. 18.
49. Sue Eileen Hayes, "The California Agricultural Labor Relations Act and National Agricultural Labor Relations Legislation," in Robert D. Emerson, ed., *Seasonal Agricultural Labor Markets in the United States* (Ames, Iowa: The Iowa State University Press, 1984), pp. 328–370. See also Walter Fogel, *California Farm Labor Relations and Law* (Los Angeles: Institute of Industrial Relations, 1985).
50. Peter Applebome, "Farm Law Abused by Illegal Aliens," *New York Times,* November 17, 1988, pp. 1, 17.
51. Phillip L. Martin, "Harvest Mechanization and Agricultural Trade Unionism: *Obreros Unidos* in Wisconsin," *Labor Law Journal* 28 (March 1977), pp. 166–173.
52. Cesar Chavez, "The Farm Workers' Next Battle," *Nation,* March 25, 1978, p. 331.
53. Linda C. Majka, "Labor Militancy among Farmworkers and the Strategy of Protest: 1900–1979," *Social Problems* 28 (June 1981), pp. 533–547.
54. Katherine Bishop, "Chavez Takes a Smaller Union Into A Decade of Fights," *New York Times,* June 18, 1989, p. E-7.
55. "Crosses Mark 25 Days of Chavez's Fast to Aid Grape Boycott," *Dallas Morning News,* August 11, 1988, p. 9-A.
56. Phillip L. Martin, Suzanne Vaupel, and Daniel L. Egan, *Unfulfilled Promise* (Boulder, Colo.: Westview Press, 1988), p. 39.

EPILOGUE

Future Considerations and Issues Affecting the Labor Relations Process

Predicting the specific direction union-management relationships will take in the 1990s would be risky; however, the material presented in the preceding chapters does give us a basis for comment.

The possible relationships between external influences, management, and union officials' negotiation of work rules in the 1990s are presented first. Next, possible issues and implications of two other important groups, government and employees, are discussed. Readers are then encouraged to apply this information, as well as material from previous chapters, to Case 4.1 about Eastern Airlines and the Collective Bargaining Negotiations Exercise: QFM Company and IWU.

All subject matter in this book is based on our model of the labor relations process formulated in Chapter One. This model is again illustrated and discussed in abbreviated form here.

External Influences on the Labor Relations Process

Public opinion generated through the media will continue to influence employee attitudes toward unions and their subsequent decisions to unionize and/or participate in various collective bargaining activities such as strikes. The extent of this external influence on union and management participants has not been accurately measured and is probably small. With these provisions in mind, a shift in media portrayal of unions and collective bargaining appears to be taking place. The unions involved in the recent Eastern Airlines and Pittston coal miners' strikes were portrayed as "underdogs" fighting for a principle against financially questionable managerial practices. During at least one stage of the 1990 professional baseball players' strike, management was portrayed as being more greedy and unreasonable than the players.

Elements in the Labor Relations Process

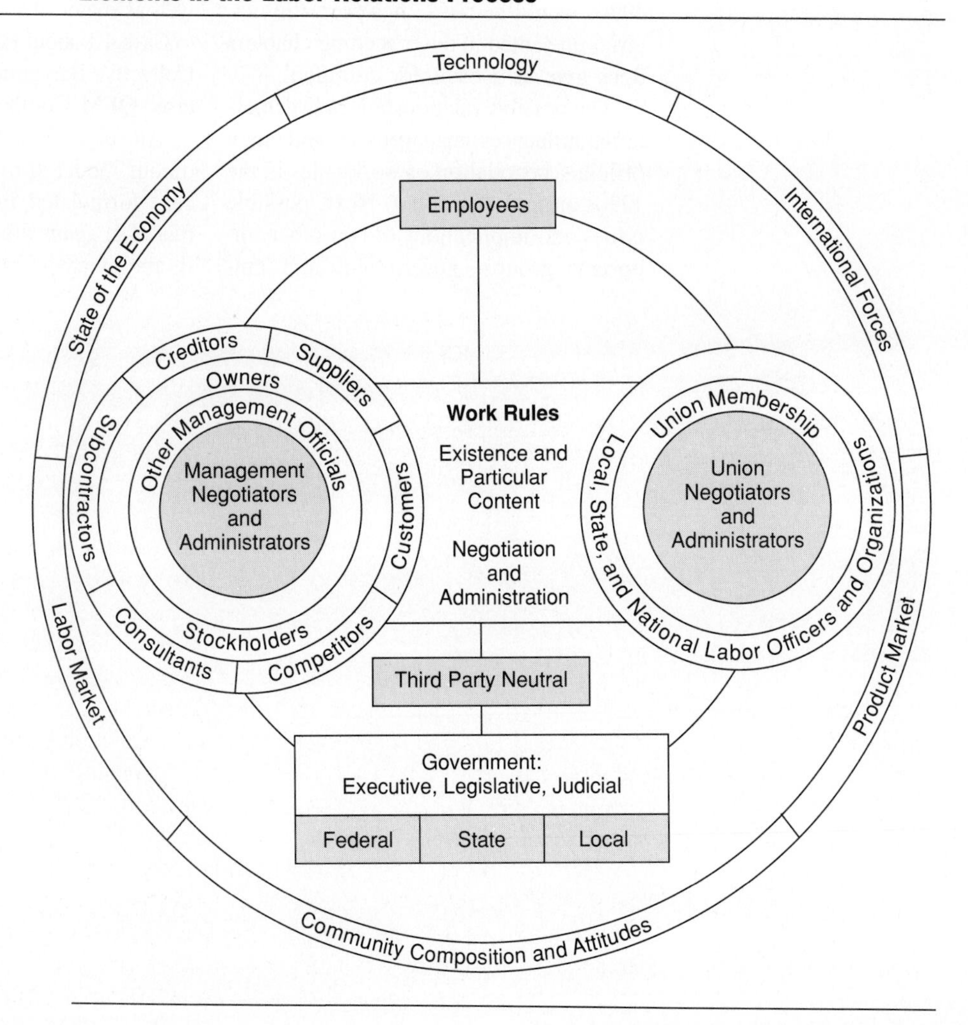

However, public opinion was not firmly placed in either party's camp due to the players' average salaries of about $500,000 per year and the owners' lucrative TV contracts combined with their refusal to make their economic situations public. On the other hand, violence that occurred during the Pittston and Greyhound strikes, as well as allegations of corruption within the Teamsters, did nothing to endear the public to the unions.

Other external influences will exert more direct and significant pressure on the labor relations process. These influences, which are largely interrelated, will constrain and limit negotiations of wages, economic benefits, work rules, and other noneconomic subjects. The realization of a global economy, coupled with the continuing trade deficit problems (foreign imports being greater than U.S. exports), high capital costs for investments in new technology, the state of the economy, and a work force that is unprepared for a modern workplace creates challenges as well as opportunities for the participants in the labor relations process. The recession of the early 1980s with its decline in gross national product, increase in unemployment, and closing of plants, resulted in wage and work rule concessions in many industries; caused a "reality check" on unions, managers, and employees; and resulted in re-negotiations of many labor agreements. The prosperity of the later 1980s brought about an increase in the gross national product, lower unemployment, and economic expansion, and unions were again able to negotiate attractive wage increases to regain most of the conceded benefits from earlier days of "give backs" or "take backs."

Although the 1990s have begun during the longest period of economic growth in U.S. history, even the most optimistic forecasters do not predict that economic prosperity will continue without some peaks and valleys. Consequently, the participants in the labor relations process will have to adjust to the changing climate. They must continue to respond to financial and competitive pressures within the United States and from foreign manufacturers and businesses by developing and producing better products at competitive prices.[1] For the United States to achieve this goal, it will require investments in new technology to regain its competitive status in certain industries and to maintain its competitive position in others. (See Exhibit 1 for a listing of the United States' status in various industries.)

External influences will continue to be translated into management and union collective bargaining objectives during the 1990s. Management will strongly seek labor agreements that increase its freedom to direct floor operations (such as fewer job classifications), contain or reduce costs (possibly health insurance and payments for time not worked), and directly relate compensation to the organization's financial results (perhaps lump sum bonuses).[2] Unions will focus on external influences' impact on job security. Labor agreement provisions for employment guarantees, advance notice of layoffs and technological change, restrictions on subcontracting, and job retraining and relocation services will all be important issues. Attempts will also be made to increase compensation for learned skills commensurate with technological innovations.

Unions will be reluctant to use strikes to obtain their bargaining objectives. The number of employee days lost due to this bargaining alternative in the 1990s will remain as low or lower than comparable figures for the 1980s. Seventy-seven percent of recently surveyed employers indicated they would consider replacing employees if they went out on strike.[3] As indicated by recent strikes at American Tele-

Exhibit 1 **Examples of U.S. Manufacturers' Competitive Edge**

Industries Where the U.S. Has Lost Its Competitive Edge	Industries Where the U.S. Has Retained Its Competitive Edge
General industrial machinery	Drugs
Household appliances	Bakery products
Leather tanning and finishing	Dairy products
Toys and sporting goods	Pulp and paperboard mills
Knitting mills	Metal cans and shipping containers
Women's and misses' outerwear	Aircraft bodies and parts
	Household audio and video equipment
	Communication equipment

Source: "U.S. Manufacturers Advised to Boost Competitiveness through Better Technology," *Daily Labor Report,* March 12, 1990, p. A-1.

phone and Telegraph, NYNEX, Eastern Airlines, and Greyhound, management can continue operations during a strike through technological features in the workplace and/or strike replacements of even skilled employee categories.

Some companies will also consider tactics used by International Paper and Greyhound to increase pressure on the unions and their members prior to negotiations. International Paper advertised for replacement employees and had the new applicants line up outside the employment office within viewing distance of the mill workforce so the present employees would be aware of its intentions in the case of a strike. Greyhound started hiring and training replacement drivers in anticipation of its need in case of a strike by the union.

In response to the "hard-ball" tactics of employers, unions will increasingly resort to corporate campaigns as an alternative to strikes. Unions will wage these campaigns on many fronts, making it difficult for management to plan a response as is possible in preparation for a strike. Corporate campaign tactics will include adverse publicity about the employer, consumer boycotts, targeting financial institutions that do business with the employer, political lobbying, and putting pressure on shareholders.[4] Unions will also increase their use of informational picketing and tele-picketing (calling potential customers by phone) to advise shoppers to avoid patronizing nonunion retail establishments.[5] In the next decade, unions will play an ever-increasing role in the financial arena. In Chapter Four, we mentioned that unions are learning to use their financial clout by purchasing stock or participating in corporate takeovers. In Chapter Thirteen, we discussed union participation in employee stock option plans (ESOPs). The AFL-CIO has established the Employee Partnership Fund (EPF) for which it hopes to raise $200 million for small and medium-size financial deals. The EPF will be used for investments and will sell shares to employees or the public. As we have already seen in the 1980s, with the Eastern Airlines declaration of bankruptcy and the takeover efforts of United Airlines and others, unions will play a major role in major financial activities.[6]

Key Participants in the Labor Relations Process

The bargaining approaches that will be used by management and union officials in the 1990s are far more difficult to predict. At first glance, it would appear that external influences will generate parallel goals for these participants; namely, the business's survival that is necessary for revenues, returns to shareholders, and employees' jobs. This situation could result in more integrative, problem-solving contract negotiation and administration, an approach that is strongly advanced by the Bureau of Labor-Management Relations and Cooperative Programs of the U.S. Department of Labor in the "Win-Win" approach to collective bargaining. The "Win-Win" approach includes principles bargaining, collaborative bargaining, integrative bargaining, and mutual gain among its advocated practices.[7] However, several conditions are necessary for labor-management cooperation to occur on a wide-range basis. First, management, union officials, and employees must clearly recognize a payoff for their efforts. Union members might find it difficult to cooperate if their efforts resulted in higher productivity and fewer jobs. They might also forget their motivation for and related maintenance of cooperation in good times.[8]

Adequate mechanisms for cooperative efforts also need to be established. In various employee input programs, for example, a two-way communication mechanism needs to be established so employees can voice opinions without fear of managerial retaliation and union officials do not have to worry about their organization and positions being subverted by the process. Problem solving also relies on the sharing of sufficient, perhaps even previously "confidential," information such as financial and production data, sales, and/or revenue projections between management and unions so both may be informed participants.

Information exchange relates to a third cooperation prerequisite—sound interpersonal relationships. Some research has indicated that this condition will be more important than economic pressures of the 1990s in implementing successful cooperative programs. Union and management officials will need to trust each other and cooperation will be more likely to occur in situations where at least some management officials have also experienced the "shared hardship" of reduced wages and benefits and/or layoffs.[9]

In some situations, unions will have difficulty trusting management because of management's previous behavior. For example, at one rubber plant, the union accepted wage and work rule concessions as a cooperative effort to help the company cut its costs and meet its competition. Later, during a representation election at a nonunion plant, company officials told employees that the union had "sold out its members by taking concessions." The plant has remained nonunion. Likewise, employees find it difficult to accept management's requests to control wage demands and/or accept wage reductions when they read about executive pay levels and raises. For example, a 1990 salary survey reported that U.S. executives earn on average 50 percent more than Japanese executives with comparable positions and 90 percent more than comparable executives in Germany and the United Kingdom. In addition, considering the spending power of their salaries, U.S. executives have three times the spending power of Japanese executives and twice that of their German counterparts.[10] In a March, 1990, speech before the National Economists Club in Washington, D.C., Dr. Rudolph Oswald, Director of Research for the AFL-CIO, reported that executive pay rates had more than tripled between 1980 and 1988, whereas factory employee wages rose only 44 percent. After adjusting for inflation, he disclosed that factory employee pay rates remained approximately constant.[11] In addition, as reported in Chapter Fifteen, U.S. employee earnings in real wages (buying power) are less than those in Belgium, Denmark, Germany, the Netherlands, Norway, Sweden, and Switzerland.

Much antagonism has occurred between unions and employers because of their various organizational activities. The present legal procedure for establishing representation rights for unions is essentially designed to lead to an adversarial relationship, especially in the first negotiations. The organizing campaign typically includes unpleasant, perhaps degrading, statements and brochures about the opposite party. If the union is successful, these negative statements are carried over to the negotiation table. In addition, both parties spend enormous amounts of time, money, and resources in the campaign, all of which could be spent on ways to make the organization more productive and competitive. Other countries have different approaches to these steps in the labor relations process. The Canadian procedure, for example, relies on card signing by employees to certify the union and third-party arbitration of the first contract if the two parties are unable to negotiate it on their own.

ETHICS

Current law allows for extensive delays and minor penalties for violating the laws, both of which raise not only legal but ethical questions. For instance, as discussed in Chapter Five, the extensive delays allowed by present law not only frustrate employees who want representation rights but provide the means by which employers may forestall unionization and employee representation at the bargaining table. Moreover, with such small penalties, some employers build legal violation into their labor relations strategies.

In the 1990s there will be a closer examination of some of the legal concepts that have been basic to the labor relations process in the United States. Our public policy makers might easily examine labor relations processes in other countries and consider those concepts that work. For example, in the United States supervisory employees are excluded for union representation rights. After a leveraged buyout or plant closing in the 1980s, these jobholders were frequently the first ones to be adversely affected. In addition, with the changing nature of the workplace, there is frequently a thin line between a supervisor and an employee.

Another concept that should be examined closely is the union obligation to represent bargaining unit employees who do not (financially) support the union. Is it fair for union members to pay bargaining representation and contract administration (including arbitration) expenses for the non-paying bargaining unit employees? In cases where the employees want union representation but are unable to achieve a majority, should there be some mechanism by which these employees can be represented or obtain some form of recognition rights for associate members?

In the 1990s our public policy makers should re-think the role of labor unions, their place in history, and their role in balancing the counteracting interests of the major actors in society. As has been learned so many times in other countries (consider Eastern Europe with government-dominated unions for so many years and the weakened unions in Latin and South America, Asia, and Africa), labor unions help to balance the interests between governments, business, and other groups. A key question is: Can the United States afford to allow the number of labor unions to shrink to such a small percentage that they no longer serve effectively as a balancing force? Do the nonunion employees not realize the "spill-overs" they receive from the labor agreements negotiated between unions and employers in the unionized sectors?

The 1990s will not see an end of adversarial relationships. One leader of a national union suggests that noncooperative relationships will remain, at least at some locations, because American managers "can't clobber us with your right hand and try to shake hands with your left."[12] At present, there is little reason to think that government at the federal or state level will substantially change the content and direction of existing labor legislation, preferring instead not to intervene in union-management relationships.

The additional success of union representatives' efforts will depend on various characteristics/predispositions of employee participants. A related consideration during the 1990s will be the extent to which unions will convert previously reluctant employee classifications into significant union membership categories. For example,

> [First] . . . as women become increasingly committed to the labor force they may become less and less satisfied with their traditional jobs, and so more prone to the argument of comparable worth and to unionism. This may be the case especially in white-collar factories, such as banks and insurance companies, where heavy layoffs occurred in the recent recession. Second, as the South becomes increasingly industrialized, both racial tensions and anti-union sentiments may decline. Third, unions may win converts among college-trained members of the "baby boom generation." Only a fraction of this group can be accommodated in professional and managerial jobs; tremendous frustrations may develop as their occupational aspirations become thwarted. Conceivably, unions could take advantage of these frustrations, although doing so may require substantial changes in organizing strategies and bargaining goals.[13]

Unions also have to satisfy employee concerns if they are to be successful in the remaining two steps of the labor relations process: negotiating and administering the labor agreement. Many of these concerns can be grouped into two general employee preference categories: 1) short-run, measurable, and material improvements in workplace conditions and 2) long-run, broad improvements affecting employees' off-job life.

Some maintain that unions will self-destruct in the 1990s because they will continue to focus on the first employee preference category to the exclusion of the second. One industrial relations observer contends,

> Unions are dead in the water. . . . They're victims of a completely inefficient and bureaucratic leadership that has pursued narrow self-interest, and bought into the corporatist system, instead of building a strong labor movement to oppose it. The labor movement in the United States is not a labor movement at all, but a collection of insurance companies parading as unions.[14]

This contention might be supported by no less than the founder of the AFL, Samuel Gompers. His classic "more" has been assumed by many to pertain exclusively to the first employee preference category; yet Gompers's following statement where "more" was uttered covered elements of social reform as well.

> We want more school houses and less jails, more books and less arsenals; . . .
>
> More learning and less vice, more constant work and less crime, more leisure and less greed, more justice and less revenge.
>
> In fact, more of the opportunities to cultivate our better natures, to make manhood more noble, womanhood more beautiful, and childhood more happy and bright.[15]

Proscriptions made by academics and labor union officials while provocative are not decisive. The AFL-CIO's Executive Council has noted, " . . . the labor movement exists to advance the interests of workers as workers see their interests. . . ."[16] Employees will continue to assess their union's success on the first preference dimension, not the second. Unions, in attempting to achieve this success, will likely experience more intraorganizational bargaining during this time period.

Probable divisions will occur among employees particularly between the younger and older union members. In some cases the traditional benefits of seniority (layoff protection and eligibility for promotions) have been weakened by large layoffs and managerial bargaining pressures for fewer job classifications. Additional bargaining over benefit cost containment (insurance coverage and pension plan) will likely exacerbate these differences.

Hopefully, the reader will apply much of this book's subject matter regardless of the labor relations process's direction in the United States. Some topics such as negotiations, bargaining power, and correction of an individual's behavior should apply to career and personal situations beyond the field of labor relations. But the book's emphasis on interpersonal relationships, resolving conflict, and cooperation through attitudes (such as respect) and activities (such as face saving) should have general applicability as well. Above all, the reader should appreciate the best answer to a labor relations question ("When will a particular strike be over?") is a thoroughly explained "It depends."

References

1. "An Interview with Jerry Jasinowski," *Labor Relations Today,* January/February 1990, p. 4.
2. *BNA Special Report: Employer Bargaining Objectives, 1990,* (Washington, D.C.: Bureau of National Affairs Inc., 1989), p. 2.
3. *Ibid.*
4. "Lawyers Predict Corporate Campaigns Will Remain Popular as Strike Alternatives," *Daily Labor Report,* March 7, 1990, p. A-11.
5. "Ohio UFCW Local's Aggressive Approach to Picketing Is Model for Other Locals," *Daily Labor Report,* March 16, 1990, p. C-1.
6. Aaron Bernstein, "Soon, LBOs May be Union-Made," *Business Week,* February 26, 1990, p. 91.
7. Jerome T. Barrett, "A Win-Win Approach to Collective Bargaining: The Past Model," *Labor Law Journal* 41 (January, 1990), p. 41.
8. Jack Barbash. "Do We Really Want Labor on The Ropes?" *Harvard Business Review* 63 (July/August 1985), p. 12.
9. Gary N. Chaison and Mark S. Polvnick, "Is There A New Collective Bargaining?" *California Management Review* 28 (Summer, 1986), p. 59.
10. "U.S. Senior Executives Highest Paid in World, Report Indicates," *Daily Labor Report,* December 28, 1989, p. A-6.
11. "High Executive Pay Is Not Product of Market Forces, Union Official Says," *Daily Labor Report,* March 7, 1990, p. A-12.
12. "Future of Labor Unions Focus of Debate at Management Conclave at Wharton School," Bureau of National Affairs Inc., *Daily Labor Report* 189 (October 2, 1989), p. A-5.
13. George Strauss, "Industrial Relations: Time of Change," *Industrial Relations* 23 (Winter, 1984), pp. 12–13.
14. Karen J. Winkler, "Precipitous Decline of American Unions Fuels Growing Interest Among Scholars," *Chronicle of Higher Education,* November 12, 1986, p. 16.
15. "Statements on Collective Bargaining During the Next 50 Years," Bureau of National Affairs Inc., *Daily Labor Report,* Number 134 (July 7, 1985), p. D-1.
16. *The Changing Situation of Workers and Their Unions,* (n.p.: AFL-CIO, 1985), p. 17.

Case for Part 4

CASE

4.1 Eastern Airlines' Participants and Strikes in the Labor Relations Process

The machinists' strike at Eastern Airlines (EAL) was probably the most publicized labor relations event of the late 1980s. It generates many insights into the labor relations process.

A brief summary of EAL's labor relations activities under Frank Borman (1975 to 1984) is given first, followed by Frank Lorenzo's labor relations involvement before the machinists struck on March 4, 1989.[1] The strike occupies the majority of this case, and readers are encouraged to analyze this material for its implications.

Labor Relations Background

Borman's Years at Eastern

Mr. Borman became president of a financially burdened Eastern Airlines in 1975. He quickly implemented cost reductions affecting both salaried and union employees. More salaried than union employees were removed in an initial layoff and some costly benefits formerly given to managers were eliminated. Borman also refinanced inherited financial debt on more favorable terms, largely because he convinced Eastern employees to accept a wage freeze in 1976 followed by an 8 percent wage increase in 1977, coupled with a 5-year profit-sharing plan, the Variable Earnings Program (VEP).

Borman was basically involved with three unions, representing the pilots (Airline Pilots Association or ALPA), machinists and baggage handlers (International Association of Machinists or IAM), and flight attendants (Transport Workers Union or TWU). An ALPA spokesman indicated that the unions cooperated over these pay innovations because Mr. Borman, unlike other Eastern management officials, solicited employees' opinions instead of taking arbitrary action.

Profits were observed for 1977 through 1979, and employees received twice as much as they contributed to VEP. However, Eastern did not experience profits for the next 6 years. Mr. Borman said in 1983 that additional wage concessions were needed or Eastern would file for protection under the Federal Bankruptcy Act. ALPA agreed to $100 million in wage reductions

[1]For more specifics on this case, including quotation sources, see either pages 6 through 10 of the third edition of this book; "Union Management Tumult at Eastern Airlines: From Borman to Lorenzo," *Transportation Journal* 28 (Summer 1989), pp. 13–27; or "Peripheral Collective Bargaining at Eastern Airlines," *Transportation Journal* 29 (Spring 1990), pp. 4–19.

(averaging 22 percent) in 1983, and the IAM and TWU agreed to 18 percent wage reductions in 1984.

Borman proclaimed that unions and management had put their past confrontations behind them. However, union leaders reacted strongly to Borman's unilateral extension of employee wage concessions into 1985. For example, Charles Bryan, president of Eastern's machinists' union, commented, "This treacherous act by Frank Borman represents a total absence of credibility and the ultimate betrayal of the trust of our members and your union leaders."

The pilots and flight attendants accepted wage cuts in 1985 and 1986, but the machinists did not. Bryan said that his members would accept a 15 percent pay cut if Borman agreed to resign. Borman responded by announcing his intentions to sell EAL to Texas Air and its chairman, Frank Lorenzo, who had a reputation for union busting because he voided labor contracts when he took Continental Airlines into Chapter 11 bankruptcy reorganization in 1983. Bryan did not see how Lorenzo could be any worse than EAL's present management: "[Lorenzo] is a businessman . . . we'll probably be able to work together."

Lorenzo's Limited Labor Relations Involvement

On November 25, 1986, the government approved EAL's sale to Texas Air. Mr. Lorenzo publicly indicated that EAL's labor relations approach would not reflect Continental's bankruptcy experience. Indeed, he could not "imagine a set of circumstances that would produce Chapter 11 for Eastern."

Lorenzo could not legally use bankruptcy to break Eastern's existing labor agreements when he arrived at the organization. However, he eliminated Borman's past practice of having union officers on the Board of Directors. Some of Lorenzo's newly hired managers set about disciplining or firing employees for minor rule infractions. Starting in 1986, mechanics were watched by video camera hanging above their work areas, and 840 mechanics, including 39 union stewards, were fired. Lorenzo and EAL's new president, Philip Bakes, also stressed that previously negotiated salaries were a "concern" and needed reduction. Charles Bryan, still president of the machinists' union, stated, "This isn't union-busting 101. . . . This is advanced union-busting."

Lorenzo appeared to have a calm attitude toward pending labor negotiations with the machinists. He felt that there would be labor peace by 1989 because members would reject their leaders' ideological pleas in favor of jobs. Lorenzo further noted,

> If the employees like the jobs they have today . . . they had better respond because those jobs are not going to be guaranteed in the future. Eastern cannot survive the way it is currently constructed economically. There is nobody around that's going to fund it.

Negotiations over a new labor agreement began in October 1987 and extended beyond the old agreement's expiration date of December 31, 1987. The company suffered $182 million in net losses in 1987, and EAL felt that wage cuts were particularly necessary from the IAM because the prior EAL management had obtained a 20 percent pay cut from all unionized employees except the machinists. The IAM had instead received an 8 percent increase, thereby creating a 28 percent wage discrepancy with other unionized employees.

This discrepancy created hard feelings between EAL and its two other unions, the ALPA and the TWU, whose contract was amendable December 31, 1988. Both unions expected that Lorenzo would show appreciation toward their efforts. However, the ALPA's president indicated that Lorenzo instead "started pushing all of us and wouldn't let up. . . . He gave us no hope."

Initial Strike Considerations and Efforts

In September 1988, an overwhelming majority of the IAM members voted (81 percent) and rejected (99 percent) Eastern's bargaining proposal. This vote, however, could not result in a strike. Federal labor law covering the airlines first requires that the National Mediation Board (NMB) declare an impasse and release the parties from its jurisdiction. Then management would be free to impose its last contract offer on the union, and the union would be free to strike.

This situation was eventually realized on March 4, 1989 when the machinists did not return to work and established picket lines at 102 airports across the country.

Impasse Issues

Wage and benefit concessions were the impasse issues. Yet, personalities and ideologies were even greater bargaining concerns. Alfred Kahn, former Civil Aeronautics chairman, maintained that Bryan and Lorenzo were "like two scorpions in a bottle . . . the hatred is so great that they seem prepared to ruin the airline." Noted labor practitioner Theodore Kheel maintained that all Eastern unions believed Lorenzo "is out to destroy them and that collective bargaining represents a battle for survival. . . . Now they are on a collision course. The unions want to get rid of Lorenzo and Lorenzo wants to get rid of the unions." Bargaining behaviors and impasse therefore reflected mutual hostilities, distrust, and brinkmanship instead of rational attempts to resolve bargaining differences. Union members maintained that Lorenzo was a "money" man, not an "airlines" man, and some of Bryan's fellow negotiators believed that Bryan was "so worried about being betrayed by management that he's virtually incapable of reaching an agreement."

Personality clashes reflected and enhanced a broader ideological bargaining issue, namely, who would run the airline? This issue stemmed from job characteristics of some union members, and a 5-year pattern of collective bargaining activities and results. Pilots have traditionally performed some management functions, such as determining which approach path will save the most fuel. Mechanics also regularly made independent judgments "that can add up to enormous profit or loss margins in the micro-managed economy of daily airline operations." Many of these employees believed their "managerial" efforts had been ignored or unrewarded over the years. Indeed, they had had to take wage concessions to compensate for major managerial blunders, such as equipment purchases made by top executives. They also realized that management sought wage concessions even though its third quarter 1988 labor costs as a percentage of operating revenue (35.4 percent) were close to standard for the industry (34.1 percent).

Much of the publicized picket line acrimony was directed at Frank Lorenzo, who was perceived as symbolizing management neglect of employee contributions and sacrifices. The three unions shared a nearly unanimous attitude that the strike was necessary to end Lorenzo's liquidation of Eastern, a rationale typified by the following ALPA advertisement of their collective bargaining concerns,

> In the three years since this outsider, Lorenzo, has come on the scene he has drained Eastern of its finest assets, upstreamed Eastern cash to his private holding company, intimidated thousands of loyal employees into leaving, attempted to compromise safety with maintenance cut-backs, failed to bargain with his employees in good faith, and then blamed the employees for the lack of profitability the company has been experiencing.

Unions' Strike Solidarity Efforts

Bryan could not be completely sure of his members' support of the strike. The IAM's resounding strike vote in September 1988 did not automatically ensure membership solidarity in March 1989, as many members had since left Eastern and many of the remaining members might be reluctant to risk wage losses or loss of employment.

The IAM did take steps to ensure that members would not cross picket lines during a strike. Members were paid $100 a week for picket-line duty, an almost symbolic reward since many previously earned this amount working one day at Eastern. The IAM also publicized suspensions and fines, as well as liens on members' homes and automobiles if they crossed a picket line.

The machinists also sought the pilots' essential support in their strike efforts. EAL could likely continue operations by replacing striking mechanics, but many thought the organization could not replace 2,000 pilots if they honored IAM's picket lines.

Pilots have not honored picket lines of other airlines' unions in the past and have had previous, severe collective bargaining differences with the IAM. For example, the IAM effectively scuttled a bid by the Airline Pilots Association to buy United Airlines through an employee stock ownership plan. One ALPA official commented about a month before the machinists' strike, "There's a lot of people who haven't forgotten that one. . . . I don't think you'll find anybody at United who'd back anything the IAM is doing." Also, as previously noted, ALPA had made more wage concessions at Eastern than the machinists had.

EAL pilots would also risk much if they supported the machinists. They could lose their jobs and, even more important, their seniority. The most senior pilots were eligible for the best routes and pay. Eastern pilots averaged $70,000 a year, with entry-level pilots making $25,000 and senior captains earning $120,000 or more. Pilots obtaining similar employment at another airline would lose their seniority, start on probation, and possibly earn an initial $18,000 a year.

Eastern management no doubt realized the pilots' vulnerable collective bargaining situation and attempted to settle its labor dispute with the pilots by offering a bargaining proposal 3 days before the machinists' strike that would be guaranteed by Texas Air if Eastern was forced into a Chapter 11 bankruptcy filing. The proposal promised no furloughs of active pilots, a fleet size of 222 aircraft, no transfer of international routes, and an automatic 20 percent pay increase if Eastern breached the furlough or minimum fleet size proposals. The offer called for a 3 percent wage increase in 1992 and 1993.

Pilots' union leaders rejected this offer, claiming that it asked for an unprecedented $64 million in new concessions from their members. This rejection and subsequent honoring of the machinists' picket line severely curtailed Eastern's contingency strike plan to operate at 20 percent of capacity (only 4 percent of capacity was maintained during the first 3 weeks of the strike). It also earned publicized respect from Bryan, who contended, "The real heroes and heroines are the invincible men and women from the Airline Pilots Association and the Transport Workers Union, representing the pilots and flight attendants, who recognize our common cause and stand together in solidarity in this classic confrontation between good and evil."

The pilots' union exhibited the most extensive rewards and sanction program to keep its members from returning to work. The national ALPA established a $37 million strike fund that would pay Eastern pilots an average of $2,400 in monthly strike benefits. This fund was generated by ALPA members who were working for other airlines contributing 3 percent of their earnings. ALPA also established interest-free loans for members who did not receive March 15th paychecks because of EAL's bankruptcy petition. This fund, arranged by an assessment of $300 a month from other ALPA members, could yield loans of $2,000 for captains, $1,500 for first officers, and $1,200 for second officers. The national ALPA also attempted to strengthen EAL pilots' job security by pledging that its local unions would not fly planes or routes previously owned by EAL unless Eastern pilots received new jobs with the seniority they had accumulated at Eastern.

The pilots' union also maintained an active telephone hot-line to encourage pilots to keep honoring the picket line. There is, however, a thin line between encouragement and intimidation. One pilot indicated that he answered telephones and persuaded other pilots not to cross picket lines because this activity "Saves the most souls. When a pilot crosses the line, that's a soul lost, a friendship ended." He also informed a pilot who called in and was wavering, "If you cross the line, you will be committing professional suicide."

More direct tactics were taken by members of the ALPA against Eastern pilots who crossed the picket line. Examples included picketing strike-breakers at their homes and jamming their takeoff communications with the air controllers with strike-breaker epithets. National ALPA criticized these intimidation efforts; however, there is a tradition of bitterness when a group of pilots has worked during a strike. For example,

> At United, lingering bitterness from a 1985 strike still pits older pilots against younger colleagues, who came to work for lower salaries. A letter from a group calling itself "Professional United Pilots" was posted in crew rooms and reads:
>
> "By accepting this job [at lower wages], you announced to the world what you are worth. You aren't educated, talented or capable enough to make a decent living. You have been flying night cargo and air taxi, wearing blue jeans, drinking beer."

The flight attendants also honored the machinists' strike. Mary Barry, president of Eastern's flight attendants' union, did not establish a strike fund, but indicated that any member who crossed the picket line would be fined $500 plus a day's pay for every day worked. Barry's rationale for this sanction: "Solidarity is essential to union survival."

By April 12, 1989, the AFL-CIO had raised $1 million in contributions from member unions for a flight attendants' strike fund. The AFL-CIO also established a relief fund available to Eastern union members for "emergency" purposes. It contributed $100,000, which was matched by the Communication Workers of America and the American Federation of State, County, and Municipal Employees. The United Auto Workers and the United Steelworkers union each added $50,000 to the fund.

These efforts were probably associated with few members of any Eastern union crossing the picket lines. Three months into the strike only 250 of 3,600 EAL pilots had crossed the picket line, and only 200 out of 2,000 ground employees were working. Five months into the strike 342 pilots had resumed work with Eastern.

Management's Initiation of Bankruptcy Proceedings

EAL management considered two basic responses to the strike: filing for bankruptcy and selling organizational assets. Bankruptcy represented a seldom-publicized management alternative throughout negotiations with the IAM. However, union negotiators were well aware of Lorenzo's successful use of bankruptcy when he acquired Continental Airlines. More specifically, in January 1984, a federal bankruptcy court judge supported Lorenzo's decision to seek bankruptcy at Continental, cancel collective bargaining agreements, and reduce labor costs, maintaining that Continental did not have any other reasonable recourse by which to keep the airline in business.

As noted earlier, Lorenzo disclaimed the bankruptcy option; yet, EAL filed for bankruptcy on March 9, 1989. Lorenzo claimed this action was prompted by the pilots' refusal to cross the picket lines of striking mechanics, a situation that he claimed imposed daily losses of $4 million on the company. Phil Bakes, president of EAL, noted that the company was not insolvent. EAL's debts at the time equaled about $2.5 billion. Even when unfunded pension liabilities ($320 million) are figured in, the firm's assets exceeded its liabilities by over $1 billion.

From the onset of the bankruptcy proceedings, the company expressed intent to reorganize and emerge as a smaller operation. A full-page ad, "Down, But Certainly Not Out," in *The Wall Street Journal* noted:

- Unions forced bankruptcy because of the strike and previous drawing and destabilizing of the company's financial health over the past decade.
- Bankruptcy, while painful, offers the opportunity to rebuild and restructure the airline through "a small but growing team of professionals of extraordinary pride and dedication—sharing common goals and a common spirit of an underdog fighting back to the top of the industry."

The unions wanted U.S. Bankruptcy Judge Burton R. Lifland to remove the Lorenzo management team and appoint a trustee to run Eastern. A spokesman for the machinists' union contended, "Lorenzo has proven that he does not know how to run an airline. . . . Two airline bankruptcies in five years should be proof enough for anyone."

Removal of Lorenzo would offer the unions two advantages. The unions could quickly return to work without a negotiated settlement claiming a bargaining victory in Lorenzo's removal. Also, a trustee would have the authority to accept an offer for the airline. Under bankruptcy proceedings Lorenzo could reject all prospective purchases if he so desired.

Judge Lifland did not appoint a trustee, although he indicated that he could still use the trustee option at any time during the proceedings. Lifland instead appointed David L. Shapiro to serve as an examiner. Lifland said that Shapiro's role was to serve as a "head banger" and "facilitator" to conduct a process that eliminated "hidden agendas" and get the planes flying. An examiner listens to the parties and reports whether there is an impasse or whether labor and/or management is being irresponsible. Related duties included

- To investigate asset sales that Eastern made to its Texas Air Corp. parent.
- To mediate disputes among management, labor, and other factions.

- To keep in contact with all involved and report information to Lifland.

The judge stressed "I do not intend to string this out," because he maintained that the public interest would be best served by ending the dispute quickly.

Potential purchasers of Eastern gave Judge Lifland and examiner Shapiro chances to operationalize their roles. Peter Ueberroth, former commissioner of professional baseball, attempted to purchase EAL some 5 weeks into the strike when EAL was operating 110, or 10 percent, of its pre-strike flights with 4,500 of the 30,000 pre-strike employees on the payroll.

Ueberroth stressed that his proposal was premised on full cooperation with Eastern's unions. However, the machinists were concerned that Ueberroth was not specific in the areas of profit-sharing in return for wage concessions and job security issues.

The machinists eventually agreed in principle to $160 million in wage concessions while the pilots agreed to a small wage reduction. Changes in medical insurance plans and a freeze in pension plan contributions would account for most of the remaining $210 million in concessions sought by Ueberroth.

An attorney for the ALPA stressed that "the parties don't need to focus on litigation. . . . We need to focus on the process of getting Eastern's planes back flying as soon as possible." Yet the pilots did not completely heed this advice, as they insisted that they would only agree to the wage concessions if Lorenzo was replaced by a trustee at the time the sale was struck.

The pilots feared that the sale might not be eventually approved. Working under Lorenzo would then probably continue because it would be nearly impossible to get the pilots to leave Eastern and honor the picket lines a second time.

Ueberroth agreed with this condition. Lorenzo, however, would not accept a trustee, and some indicated that he intimidated both Lifland and Shapiro with his obstinacy, since both could have labeled Lorenzo's action irresponsible, thereby enabling a court-appointed trustee for Eastern.

Ueberroth then withdrew his offer citing unspecified hurdles to the purchase. He affixed no blame contending, "I'm not throwing any stones." However, a spokesperson for the IAM indicated, "Our people are very mad and very disappointed." Lorenzo blamed "totally unreasonable and unworkable union demands" for the collapse of Ueberroth's proposal and reiterated his intentions to restructure Eastern as a small airline.

Eastern's Reorganization Plan and the Labor-Backed Ritchie Alternative

EAL management responded to the withdrawal of Ueberroth's offer by submitting an informal reorganization plan. The reorganized airline would be a low-fare carrier with some 50 to 60 percent of its pre-strike operation. The fleet would drop from 255 to 157; cities served would drop from 102 to 77; and total employment would be about 17,000 including 1,700 pilots, down from a pre-strike employment figure of 30,000. According to this plan, Eastern would have 79 flights to 27 cities by June 9th, and 221 flights (one-third of the completed plan) to 52 cities as of July 2nd. A spokesperson for ALPA immediately expressed skepticism about this plan. "It's all smoke and mirrors . . . It's just another one of Frank Lorenzo's unfilled promises that he made."

The company also indicated that the rebuilt airline would be facilitated by selling one-third ($1.8 billion) of its assets and become fully operational by December 1989. Some of the sold assets would be used to repay $914 million of Eastern's $2.4 billion debt by January 1990.

Related "belt-tightening" occurred June 1st when EAL announced that non-contract employees (all but about 300 of the 3,000 people now working for the company) would take wage and benefit cuts. Top management increased its previous 10 percent cut to 20 percent through 1989. Other employees were expected to work 10-hour days instead of 8-hour days, with reduced benefits and no vacations through 1989.

The three unions' roles in this reorganization plan were unclear. Lorenzo realized that unsettled labor agreements would likely result in Eastern's passengers walking through picket lines, saying, "We remain very interested in negotiating with the unions. . . . But if we have to build the company back with picket lines, then that's how we will build it back." Regarding the pilots, Lorenzo said, "Eastern can . . . rebuild substantially, without one pilot returning." He also said that he sometimes called the Airline Pilots Association "OPEC-ALPA," because like the oil cartel, the union was creating a false impression of all demand and no supply. "There are very significant numbers of pilots who are out there who are dying to work for commercial airlines. . . . This line that there's a pilot shortage and that we can't get qualified pilots is wrong."

Lorenzo's position did not deter potential Eastern buyers. By May, interest was expressed by Joseph Ritchie, Carl Icahn, William Howard, and Jay Pritzker. A lawyer for Eastern summarized some, if not all of these offers, "They're outrageous. . . . They are poorly thought out. People are coming in to try to steal the company and gratuitously risking [Eastern employees'] jobs." Bankruptcy examiner David Shapiro seemed to express the same attitude, "It's time to either put up or shut up—I would like to see at least $100 million (in cash) at risk. . . . This airline cannot be purchased with mirrors."

On May 25th, Judge Lifland added more certainty to Eastern's financial picture when he approved the sale of a profitable Eastern asset to Donald Trump, who indicated that he would continue to employ some 171 ALPA pilots and 600 IAM machinists and TWU flight attendants in this venture. Trump's acknowledgement of the unions had to reflect his obtaining an additional 21 planes above his pre-strike offer at no additional cost. Trump maintained that the additional planes were appropriate compensation for subsequent strike uncertainties and a possible related drop in the number of shuttle passengers. An ALPA spokesperson responded, "We're happy to [let the shuttle's 21 planes leave EAL's jurisdiction] as part of a new unionized airline."

Eastern's unions then turned their attention to Joseph Ritchie, a Chicago commodities trader, and helped formulate a plan to purchase Eastern. Ritchie informed Lifland and Shapiro that this plan had the requisite $100 million in cash. Half of this amount would come from a multi-employer health and pension fund run by union and management representatives not involved with Eastern, $25 million from Ritchie's funds, and $12.5 million each from the IAM and ALPA.

The unions also repeated their previous wage concession pledge of $210 million and agreed to another $175 million to $200 million during the 6 months it would take to implement Ritchie's plan. The new concessions would be implemented if Eastern's losses under Ritchie's ownership amounted to more than the $291 million in losses projected under the proposed plan. Eastern's creditors would then not have to absorb the losses. The minimum pay cut per employee would be approximately $7,200 if these concerns were realized.

This proposal, along with others, was subject to the approval of Eastern's parent company, Texas Air, and its CEO, Frank Lorenzo, who subsequently refused Ritchie's offer. Shapiro, who raised Ritchie's required cash commitment from $100 million to $200 million, indicated that he would not respond to this refusal by appointing a trustee for Eastern's operations because he found the Ritchie plan financially defective. Shapiro strongly preferred Eastern's reorganization and downsizing efforts and hoped that "Eastern's unions will come to accept this reality."

Court-Ordered Collective Bargaining and Subsequent Results

Lifland and Shapiro under Section 1113 of the Bankruptcy Code ordered collective bargaining between Eastern and its three unions to resolve potential wage grievances and other issues. The unions were concerned and angry about this bargaining development. Machinist officials believed the examiner's attempt to get the pilots to settle with Lorenzo was an attempt to break the machinists' strike. This attitude was perhaps best reflected by an IAM spokesperson, who indicated the union would meet with management to show "good faith" even though Lifland and Shapiro had no authority over the union's bargaining with Eastern, and they were skeptical that management would sincerely attempt to resolve the bargaining impasse.

The unions may have been correct in their assessment. Frank Lorenzo, on the eve of the first court-appointed negotiation sessions, indicated the striking pilots' diminished, even nonexistent role at Eastern,

> We're not dependent on the pilots by any means. . . . The real game is being played out with the consumers, with the traveling public. . . . Eastern is re-emerging as a quality airline.

These comments were enhanced by others Lorenzo made during this time period. For example, in a July issue of *Business Week* he opined, "Three months ago, there was a lot of talk about using Eastern as a symbol of union power. . . . It was the last place they should have made Custer's last stand." He also predicted that by November 1989, "the labor movement is going to be running 90 miles an hour away from the Eastern Airlines situation."

Yet, union and management officials did respond to bankruptcy court initiatives. For example, there were 23 days of increasingly vigorous bargaining between EAL and the pilots with some sessions lasting until 3 a.m. A major obstacle was the inability of the company to provide employment for the striking pilots, given the replacements EAL had hired. Nearly half of the EAL pilots were at least 50 years old; therefore, at least some of the discussions during this bargaining period probably focused on ways to encourage many pilots to retire.

A bargaining settlement was not reached during these negotiations. The airline pilots did reject an airline proposal that would return 1,200 to 1,700 of the striking pilots to employment at Eastern. Some reports indicated that ALPA wanted a guaranteed return of 2,400 striking pilots. The union did not deny this situation; instead, it indicated that the major issues were "the transfer of assets, the stripping of our airline, and the long-term survivability of the airline."

Another ALPA and IAM issue concerned the strike replacements' qualifications and airline safety. ALPA had continually stressed the passengers' need for experienced pilots, "not pilots that have to be shanghaied from some fly-by-night training school in Rhode Island." By July, Eastern had employed 527 new hires for its pilots' training program. EAL's minimum requirements included an FAA-certified commercial pilot's license and 1,200 hours of flight time. Some pilots left this program claiming the hiring situation was unsafe. One pilot notes, "it takes more than a few years flying a corporation jet to become a pilot on a Boeing or an [A-330] Airbus." Pilots maintained that Eastern would encounter another safety problem when the organization's increased flight schedule would make it difficult to have at least one extensively experienced pilot on each aircraft.

ALPA suggested that a third safety problem occurred with replacement mechanics. For example, it bought an ad in *USA Today* to assert that Eastern secretaries, reservations clerks, sales representatives, and lawyers weren't qualified to replace machinists on strike. All of these allegations were rejected by management and by the Federal Aviation Administration, the government organization charged with monitoring airline safety.

Through August, lawyers represented the only group posting gains over the collective bargaining impasse. Lawyers' fees—other than those paid by the unions, which do not have to be disclosed in bankruptcy court—totaled approximately $7.4 million. This amount, to be paid out of Eastern's assets, applied to some 135 lawyers at rates ranging from $70 to $375 an hour. David Shapiro, the special examiner appointed by Judge Lifland, applied for $236,100 at an hourly rate of $300, while 14 other attorneys at his firm applied for an additional $507,698. David Simon, the lead attorney for the pilots' union, indicated that he would "happily accept" only 25 percent of Eastern's legal fees contending, "Bankruptcy is a trough and all of the animals in the barn feed in it. . . . Especially in a bankruptcy context, the fees that are paid typically are outrageous."

Bargaining Divestment

The Strike at 6 Months

ALPA and the other EAL unions had not experienced any notable success by Labor Day. Large numbers of EAL pilots did in fact reaffirm their strike solidarity by attending meetings in seven cities and overwhelmingly voting not to cross picket lines established against Eastern. However, some 300 pilots had crossed picket lines the second week in August after some national and local ALPA officials suggested that members think about ending their strike.

Jack Bavis, the chairman of Eastern's ALPA, was one union official who raised the possibility of pilots returning to the limited positions remaining at Eastern. Union members and officials criticized Bavis for his stance. They countered that the pilots' strike sacrifice would be for nought if they accepted work under Lorenzo's direction.

Bavis paid for his position. He lost a vote of confidence from his union's executive board and was replaced by Skip Copeland, a 27-year Eastern pilot, labeled a "hard charger," "hawk," and "gladiator," who would add "vim and vigor" to the union's bargaining impasse. Asked whether the EAL pilots would have anything to show for their efforts, Copeland said,

"They've got one thing—dignity. They can still look in the mirror when they shave in the morning, and they can get money somewhere else." Eastern now had 670 pilots who had returned to work (including 220 pilots who had returned the first week of the strike). This figure, coupled with 300 new hires who completed training and 730 enrolled in training, enabled Eastern to stop hiring pilots and meet its intended 390 flights.

Eastern's pilots' union encountered further dissension when the national union did not support its request for a nationwide seniority system enabling striking EAL pilots to continue wages and benefits if another organization employed them. National ALPA also ignored the EAL pilots' request for a nationwide "suspension of service" to prompt legislative investigation into Frank Lorenzo's continuing fitness to operate both Eastern and Continental Airlines. One spokesperson for Eastern's union pilots suggested surprise and anger when the national union snubbed both requests,

> We didn't think it was a long shot. . . . We feel betrayed. ALPA is not acting in a way that resembles a traditional labor union. . . .
>
> We have a whole lot of Eastern pilots who are extremely . . .disappointed. . . . We see a tremendous lack of leadership, a lack of guts, a lack of moral fiber.

Meanwhile, Charles Bryan, whose machinists initiated the picket lines, admitted the EAL management was putting on a "brave and very good front." Yet, EAL did not have much trouble subcontracting ramp employees at a rate ($5 to $6 an hour) one-third of that earned by former unionized employees.

Fourth-Quarter Difficulties for Unions and Management

ALPA, IAM, and TWU entered October realizing that Eastern did not appear to need their members to continue airline operations. Eastern's management experienced full employment levels for its smaller reorganization during this period. Eastern's post-strike employment of 1850 pilots was filled in part by 600 to 870 of Eastern's ALPA members (some 3,600 before the strike) who had crossed the picket lines. About 1,075 of the 5,000 flight attendants who struck Eastern were again working at the company, which then had 4,000 of these employees, and approximately 300 of the 9,000 IAM members (mechanics, baggage handlers, and ramp workers) crossed the picket line to join 2,100 new employees in these classifications. The airline was also not under any economic or legal pressure to resolve bargaining differences with any of its unions. Indeed, EAL and the bankruptcy court appeared far more interested in financial resurgence than in collective bargaining settlements. Union attention turned toward congressional intervention, which appeared to represent the only hope for bargaining impasse resolution.

At the onset of the strike, President Bush declined the National Mediation Board's request for a presidential board to investigate the impasse and make recommendations. Mr. Bush did not view the Eastern strike as a national emergency and contended, "It would be inappropriate for the government to intervene and impose a solution." He maintained that the dispute should instead be resolved through the free collective bargaining process. At least one news analyst, Jack Anderson, believed President Bush's rationale was associated with Lorenzo's recent $100,000 contribution to the Republican party.

In October, the Senate reconsidered an earlier bill (HR 1231), passed by the House on March 15, 1989, that would require President Bush to appoint a presidential emergency board under the Railway Labor Act. This bill had been postponed indefinitely in April. Legislators and even the unions thought that active discussion of HR 1231 would discourage potential purchasers of Eastern. There was also some congressional concern at the time that there were not enough votes to override a threatened veto by President Bush.

However, there were no likely purchasers of EAL in October, and impasse resolution by the parties appeared dim. Both the Senate and the House passed HR 1231, which was in turn vetoed by President Bush in late November. Bush maintained that new legislation such as HR 1231 would only disturb the legal charge of the bankruptcy court to protect the overall interests of the concerned parties in an even-handed fashion. Frank Lorenzo complimented Mr. Bush for his "clear vision . . . judgment, and political courage." Lorenzo further commented, "The 20,000 members of the Eastern family thank you with all the special gratitude that people who have put their hearts, their lives, their careers and their beliefs into rebuilding this company can convey."

The AFL-CIO responded that Bush's veto sent a strong message to every working American that the president is not on their side because he backed Frank Lorenzo, a symbol of the worst type of American employer. Henry Duffy, president of the ALPA, further contended that Bush demonstrated his support of the "scorched-earth policies" of Lorenzo and Texas Air, who used "bankruptcy as a bludgeon against their employees."

Skip Copeland, president of Eastern's pilots' union, no doubt agreed with the union antagonism over the veto. However, he indicated on November 22, 1989 that the pilots' strike against EAL had ended with an unconditional return to work,

> We did everything within our power to win a just war against a greedy and insensitive management. The time has come now to get back, help rebuild Eastern and get on with our lives and our professions.

Copeland and other union leaders knew that the day of his strike cessation announcement was the deadline for pilot bidding for new flight assignments commencing in March 1990. Perhaps union leaders feared that if the return to work was not ordered, more pilots would cross the picket lines to ensure that they would fly choice flights at convenient times. This decision also enabled EAL pilots and flight attendants to become eligible for Florida unemployment insurance benefits. This amount, equivalent to half of the average weekly wage for a 1-year base period, can reach a maximum of $200 a week for 26 weeks. Florida law does not provide unemployment benefits for employees who are striking or honoring picket lines.

The TWU local representing the flight attendants quickly joined the pilots in abandoning their strike against Eastern. Mary Barry, president of this organization, said that giving up on the strike was "a very difficult decision but one made in the best interests of the flight attendants."

EAL management accepted these decisions in a noncommittal fashion. One EAL official responded to the two unions' announcements that they would return to work by saying, "You know what they say about 'he who hesitates.' " Management indicated that the strikers could place their names on a waiting list and predicted that there would not be any employment vacancies for flight attendants until 1990. Under the Railway Labor Act, the pilots' contract, which was amendable in July 1988, and the flight attendants' contract, which was amendable in January 1988, remained in effect until a new collective bargaining agreement could be reached.

These actions left the machinists alone in continuing the strike. IAM President George Kourpias said following a meeting with IAM District and Local Eastern strike leaders that the 8,500 striking workers were determined to stay on the picket line until Eastern workers received "fair and just treatment on the job" from EAL chairman Frank Lorenzo. Kourpias further noted,

> Frank Lorenzo's style of employee relations is a cancer that must be stopped at Eastern or it will spread to virtually every industry in the nation. If other employers see that they can fatten their corporate treasuries on the backs of the men and women whose sweat made those profits, every worker in America is in trouble.

Most, if not all, of the IAM members were not angry at the pilots and flight attendants for deciding to end their strikes. They instead appreciated the financial sacrifices ALPA and TWU members had made on their behalf.

Eastern management also had some setbacks as the end of fourth-quarter 1989 approached. The airline, which originally planned to emerge from bankruptcy protection on September 1, 1989, had to request a third extension for its reorganization plan. By the end of December, EAL operated 829 flights daily at 50 percent capacity. Airlines typically require traffic at 60–65 percent just to break even. Eastern's 1989 losses were estimated at $850 million ($284 million of which occurred in the fourth quarter), and a management representative explained, "It is easy to forget that we were still in the midst of a campaign to recover traffic lost in the strike. . . . That does not happen overnight."

AFL-CIO President Lane Kirkland claimed that this situation meant management as well as the union lost in the Eastern strike.

> We cannot say that the strike has been a success for labor because its objective, a fair and decent solution, has not been achieved. . . . But I do say there's been

no victory for the employer. Clearly his objective was to operate at substandard rates, gaining an advantage on other airlines.

The Strike at 1 Year

Almost 1 year to the day of the strike, management received another setback when the appointed bankruptcy examiner, David Shapiro, released a 300-page report indicating that there was substantial evidence in 12 out of 15 cases that Texas Air transferred $285 to $403 million worth of assets (planes, gates, and landing slots, for example) from Eastern without adequately compensating the airline.

Shapiro noted that Texas Air agreed to settle the claims by paying Eastern $280 million and that this settlement was not an admission of liability by Texas Air. ALPA, TWU, and the IAM contended that this report vindicated their strike positions against Lorenzo's "Robber Baron" approach toward upstreaming Eastern's assets. However, Shapiro continued to contend that Eastern did not need a trustee to guide the organization out of bankruptcy.

Management contended that this action, coupled with an earlier agreement with its unsecured creditors, would enable Eastern to emerge from bankruptcy by July 1, 1990. A few weeks later, however, management revised its loss estimate to $300 million for 1990, some $185 million larger than its January estimate for the year.

This revision indicated that management needed to extend beyond the July 1 date to emerge from bankruptcy. The revision also prompted management to ask unsecured creditors such as the unions and manufacturers of aircraft and jet engines (Boeing and General Electric, for example) to settle for 25 cents on the dollar, revised downward from 50 cents on the dollar proposed in January 1990 and full payment with interest proposed in July 1989.

The unsecured creditors refused this offer and asked U.S. Bankruptcy Judge Burton Lifland to appoint a trustee to sell the airline. On April 18, 1990, after hearing four days of testimony, Lifland concluded that EAL management was not competent to operate the airline. Related evidence included EAL's financial losses ($1.2 billion) since filing for bankruptcy in March 1989, and the inability of EAL management to make reliable forecasts even over the short run.

Lifland appointed Martin Shugrue to manage EAL, a move applauded by the unions, which had attempted to remove Frank Lorenzo and his Texas Air corporation from the direction of Eastern's operations. Shugrue, a former president of Continental Airlines, from which he was ousted by Lorenzo, has enjoyed good relations with labor unions.

Charles Bryan of the IAM welcomed Lifland's appointment of Shugrue as trustee. Bryan indicated that the machinists' strike would continue until a labor agreement was negotiated and acknowledged that striking employees may not have their jobs back until 1995. Eastern management did not appeal Lifland's action in U.S. District Court. Philip Bakes resigned his $325,000-a-year position as president of EAL within two days of Shugrue's appointment as trustee, contending that

> Marty Shugrue, the court-appointed operating trustee, will assume all duties normally associated with the position of chief executive of Eastern Airlines. . . . I am leaving Eastern Airlines. I have no current plans at all. . . . I am going to sit on the sidelines and cheer Eastern on.

Eastern still faces an uncertain future, although Lifland is likely to urge Shugrue to continue to operate the airline instead of slowly liquidating it. Unionized employees might have a significant impact on Eastern's future even if they are not working for the organization. Passengers are still wary of the airline's lack of dependability and adversarial union-management relationships. Picket lines are ongoing at airline terminals. Moreover, if Texas Air is not held responsible for Eastern's employees' pension fund obligations (estimated at $900 million) the possibility of finding a buyer for Eastern is diminished.

Assignment

Formulate and explain three implications or conclusions that EAL's bargaining experience might have for the labor relations process in other organizations.

Collective Bargaining Negotiations Exercise: QFM Company and IWU

Learning Objectives

1. To gain an understanding of negotiation preparations, actual negotiations, and assessment of negotiations outcomes.
2. To develop an appreciation for the psychological interactions and the realism of contract negotiations.
3. To learn the mechanics of give-and-take, compromise, and trading issues and to practice the art of negotiation.
4. To familiarize the participants with the issues in collective bargaining and the difficulty of writing provisions to the satisfaction of both parties.
5. To realize the importance of and problems associated with teamwork in a bargaining situation.
6. To gain an appreciation for the application of bargaining theories to negotiations.

Rules of the Negotiations Exercise

1. Participants must not discuss the exercise with anyone except team members.
2. Each participant will be assigned a role (organization position) by the instructor.
3. The negotiations must take place within the framework of the *present* company and union at the St. Louis plant. Creativity is encouraged, but a realistic and pragmatic approach is recommended.
4. Data, materials, and information used for each position or argument on behalf of a proposal should not be falsified.
5. Each team may have as many meetings *outside* class as are needed and desirable.
6. Team members must follow the instructions of their respective team leaders.
7. All activities of team members should be directed toward negotiating an agreement that is mutually acceptable and that the parties can live with, survive, and prosper.

Instructions to the Participant

1. Each participant will be assigned to either the management or the union team. An organization position will be assigned to each person.

2. The team leaders – the presidents of the Industrial Workers United (IWU) and the AFL-CIO and the industrial relations director of Quality Furniture Manufacturing Company (QFM) – will call separate meetings to discuss and prepare for the upcoming negotiations and anticipate each other's proposals. Major issues for negotiations should include:
    a. Union security, dues checkoff, union shop
    b. Wages, job classes, premiums
    c. Management's rights
    d. Promotions and layoffs (use of seniority)
    e. Grievance procedure and arbitration
    f. Affirmative action plans
    g. Pension plans
    h. Supplemental unemployment benefits
    i. Vacations
    j. Holidays
    k. Sick leave
    l. Other issues allowed by instructor
3. In the preparatory meeting, each team will study the present agreement, identify its problems and items needing change, and gather materials, data, and information to justify the team's proposals and positions.
4. Based on study, analysis, strategy, and plans, each team will complete the first four columns of Form 1 and give it to the instructor. (The form is not to be shown to anyone else.)
5. The union president and the industrial relations director and their respective teams will meet at a time specified by the instructor for the purpose of negotiating a new agreement. The union will present its proposals first and explain the need for each proposal. Then management will present its proposals and/or counterproposals and justify each.
6. Actual negotiations will begin after the proposals are exchanged and will continue until a new agreement is negotiated and signed or the present contract expires. (The instructor will specify time periods.)
7. Upon completion of the negotiations, each team will determine the total annual costs (anticipated) of the new agreement. If directed, the teams will submit a written agreement.
8. Additional instructions will be given the participants by the instructor.

Sources of Materials for Preparation

Government publications: U.S. Department of Labor, Bureau of Labor Statistics, *Area Wage Surveys, Employment and Earnings, Handbook of Labor Statistics, Monthly Labor Review, Characteristics of Major Collective Bargaining Agreements.*

Binder services of Bureau of National Affairs Inc. (BNA), Commerce Clearing House, and Prentice-Hall. Especially helpful is the BNA *Collective Bargaining Negotiations and Contracts.*

Business Publications: *Business Week* and *The Wall Street Journal.*

U.S. Department of Commerce, *U.S. Industrial Outlook* (published every year).

Form 1

Bargaining Priority (1 = Most Important, 2 = Second Most Important, and so on)	Subject Area for Negotiations (Brief Description)	Proposals to Other Party (First Day)	Realistic Objective for Negotiations	Actual Accomplishment (to Be Completed after Negotiations)

Professional industrial relations journals: *Arbitration Journal, Employee Relations Law Journal, Industrial and Labor Relations Review, Industrial Relations, Industrial Relations Law Journal, Journal of Collective Negotiations in the Public Sector, Labor Law Journal, and Monthly Labor Review.*

Proceedings: Industrial Relations Research Association, Labor Law Developments, National Academy of Arbitrators, and NYU Conference on Labor.

Labor agreements between companies and labor unions (as available).

Furniture Manufacturing Industry

The furniture industry can be characterized as a "highly competitive, nonintegrative industry composed largely of small and medium-sized family-controlled business."[1] Although the industry consists of about 1,200 companies, only 50 are publicly held, and most of the others are family operated. The latter showed little inclination to adopt efficiencies already common in other manufacturing industries. Furniture manufacturers still operate only one shift and remain highly labor-intensive. High-quality workmanship and craftsmanship have been their goal, and much of the work is still done by hand to give the products their distinctiveness.[2]

While plants are scattered throughout the United States, two-thirds are located in the Southeast, the Middle Atlantic, and the Great Lakes regions. Since the Pacific Coast has an ample supply of softwood and hardwood, more plants are currently locating there. Manufacturers using plastics and metals (rather than wood) in their furniture are able to locate more closely to their markets and have therefore spread throughout the country.

Products are distributed over fairly wide geographic areas, and 70 percent of the output is sold directly to retailers. Brand names and product line identity are important to some of the larger manufacturers, but there are problems of design copying and enormous pressures for frequent restyling.[3]

The demand for high-quality furniture, such as the "Eagle" brand for Quality Furniture Manufacturing Company, has been recession-proof. In view of the past 8 years of economic expansion, a business downturn within a year or two is likely. Furniture shipments are expected to increase over the next few years at an annual rate of only 0.5 percent, after adjustment for inflation. The demographic forecast is favorable for the furniture industry, however, because the baby boom generation is aging. The total spending for furniture by adults age 35 and over will increase at a rate of about 2.5 percent per year, while total spending by adults under age 35 will remain level.

Furniture imports increased in 1988 to $3.8 billion, an increase of only 3 percent above 1987, and down from an average annual rate of 27 percent between 1983 and 1987. Two-thirds of the U.S. imports came from Taiwan, Canada, Italy, Mexico, and West Germany. With improvements in Mexico's economy and the free-trade agreement between the United States and Canada, the prospects for increasing exports are favorable. (Tariffs will be phased out over the next 5 years. Current Canadian tariffs are 12.6–15.3 percent, and U.S. tariffs are 2.5–9.6 percent.)

The value of household furniture shipments reached $18.5 billion in 1988, an increase of 0.8 percent in constant dollars, and substantially slower than the 1987 growth rate of 5.9 percent. Interest rates in 1989 for personal purchases ranged around 9 percent, and mortgage rates were just a little higher. These high rates adversely affected home buying and purchases of household goods, including furniture.

While production, sales, and exports increased, employment in the furniture industry declined in the 1970s and 1980s. Employment reached its highest level in 1973 with 327,000 employees; by 1988, employment had dipped to 267,000. More of the labor-intensive types of furniture were being produced by foreign manufacturers and were being imported.

The QFM Company and the Union

QFM Company began in 1820 in Laconia, New Hampshire, as a family-owned and family-operated furniture manufacturer. It was headed by Herman Sweeny, one of the early settlers in Laconia. The company grew to 30 employees by 1920, but at that time B. F. Sweeny, Herman's son, decided to move the firm to St. Louis, Missouri—a location more central to the firm's market. Barely surviving the 1930s depression, QFM was one of the first companies to convert its manufacturing processes to the production of war materials. The company prospered during the war, and afterward Sweeny decided to expand, sell stock publicly, and focus on producing metal and plastic-laminated furniture. With the production experience it had gained during the war and with its location some distance from the predominantly wood-furniture manufacturers, QFM Company launched a new era for itself in 1946.

By 1970 the St. Louis plant of Quality Furniture Manufacturing Company had 1,300 employees and was producing 450 dinette sets, 200 sets of lawn tables and chairs, and 300 bar stools and miscellaneous furniture daily. Then came the 1971 to 1973 furniture boom, with its expectations of continuous growth. QFM's new president, Gerald Brooks, decided that a new, modern plant and more diversity in the product line were necessary to meet the expected demand. Taking into consideration location, material supply, transportation, markets, labor situations, and other factors, Brooks decided to build the new plant in Dallas, Texas. This plant was to specialize in the new product lines, and the St. Louis plant was to concentrate only on dinette sets. In 1972, 200 employees were transferred from St. Louis, and another 200 were hired from the Dallas–Fort Worth area. The Dallas plant started with no union and 400 employees. By 1989 it had grown to a 900-employee work force, still with no union. It pays its Dallas employees at least $1 less per hour than it pays the St. Louis workers in comparable jobs. The St. Louis plant continues to produce 450 dinette sets per day, mostly for chain retailers, and employs about 1,000 workers. No new product lines have been added at the St. Louis plant, and its employment level is the same as in the pre-1970 days. The Dallas plant has started producing a new product line–dinette sets under the Eagle brand name. Consumer response has been positive, and the Dallas plant's future looks very promising.

Throughout its history, QFM Company has prided itself on being a progressive employer; however, recent events–building the Dallas plant, increasing employment in Dallas while lowering it in St. Louis, paying QFM workers in St. Louis less than comparable area wages–resulted in an NLRB representation election for the Industrial Workers United Union in St. Louis in 1975. After a heated campaign by both management and the union, NLRB investigations of unfair labor practices, and challenged ballots, the union lost the election by a vote of 497 to 481. Two years later, the union returned and won the election by a vote of 611 to 375. The election campaign was bitter, and the negotiations that followed were even more bitter. After a 6-week strike, a labor agreement was signed. There have been six negotiations since 1977, and no strikes have occurred. However, the current agreement is close to expiration. Although the company officials now express a commitment to return to the era when management and labor trusted each other, worked cooperatively, and shared mutual goals and benefits, the union leaders are reacting by waiting to see their deeds. The upcoming negotiations will determine the company's commitment. The union believes it is strong, with 80 percent of the bargaining unit now union members.

References

1. Wickham Skinner and David C. D. Rogers, *Manufacturing Policy in the Furniture Industry,* 3d ed. (Homewood, Ill.: Richard D. Irwin, 1968), p. 1.

2. "Why Furniture Makers Feel So Comfortable," *Business Week,* July 30, 1979, p. 76.

3. Skinner and Rogers, *Manufacturing Policy,* pp. 2–12.

4. John Harris, "Household Consumer Durables," *1989 U.S. Industrial Outlook* (Washington, D.C.: Government Printing Office, 1990), pp. 42-1 to 42-10.

Exhibit 1 **QFM Company Balance Sheet, 1990**

Assets	
Current Assets:	
Cash	$ 1,818,678
Notes and Accounts Receivable	42,053,211
Inventories	53,133,326
Prepaid Expenses	696,573
Total Current Assets	$ 97,701,788
Fixed Assets	
Land	8,470,000
Buildings	21,175,000
Machinery and Equipment	16,634,402
Total Fixed Assets	$ 46,279,402
Total Assets	$143,981,190
Liabilities and Stockholders' Investment	
Current Liabilities:	
Notes and Accounts Payable	$ 13,982,952
Accrued Payroll	5,590,200
Taxes (local, state, federal)	44,891,000
Total Current Liabilities	$ 64,464,152
Stockholders' Investment:	
Common Stock (common @ $20 per share)	33,880,000
Earned Surplus	45,637,038
Total Stockholders' Investment and Earned Surplus	$ 79,517,038
Total Liabilities and Stockholders' Investment	$143,981,190

Exhibit 2 **QFM Company Income Statement**

	1989	1990
Net Sales	$162,635,782	$178,899,528
Cost of Goods Sold:		
Production (labor, materials, overhead, etc.)	131,115,806	136,975,594
Administrative	11,113,639	11,875,618
Sales	5,420,800	7,114,800
Other	1,375,888	1,560,852
Total Cost of Goods Sold	$149,026,133	$157,526,864
Income before Taxes	$ 13,609,649	$ 21,372,664
Taxes (local, state, federal)	3,953,796	5,271,728
Net Income	$ 9,655,853	$ 16,100,936

Exhibit 3

QFM Company Net Sales and Income

	Net Sales	Net Income
1988	$153,429,984	$ 2,274,398
1989	162,635,782	9,655,853
1990	178,899,528	16,100,936
1991 (estimated)	185,960,048	22,467,799

Exhibit 4

Number of QFM Production and Maintenance Employees by Seniority in St. Louis and Dallas Plants

Years	St. Louis	Dallas
0–1	5	100
1–2	15	150
2–3	40	160
3–4	45	150
4–5	45	158
5–10	205	115
10–15	200	25
15–20	105	20
20–25	120	10
25–30	152	10
30 or more	78	2
	1,010	900[a]

[a]Includes those transferring from St. Louis.

Exhibit 5

Number of QFM Employees in Each Job Title, by Wage Grade

Wage Grade	Job Title	St. Louis	Dallas
1	Janitor	10	9
2	General Laborer	30	32
3	Materials Handler	45	48
4	Packer	36	35
	Machine Operator–B	120	120
	Utility Worker	38	20
	Interplant Truck Driver	16	18
	Sander	40	40
	Assembler	295	319
5	Welder	16	10
	Machine Operator–A	120	62
	Electrician–B	5	7
	Maintenance Worker–B	11	12
	Gluer	56	40
6	Mechanic	10	8
	Spray Painter	43	35
	Cutoff Saw Operator	25	18
7	Electrician–A	15	8
	Maintenance Worker–A	11	8
	Inspector	26	18
8	Tool Grinder–A	5	5
9	Tool and Die Maker–A	12	8
10	Leadman	25	20
		1,010	900

Exhibit 6

Average Hourly Earnings, Excluding Overtime for All Manufacturing Employees

	July 1988	July 1989
Total Manufacturing	$10.17	$10.48
Durable Goods	10.67	11.00
Lumber and Wood Products	8.66	8.93
Furniture and Fixtures	7.99	8.25
Stone, Clay, and Glass Products	10.53	10.74
Primary Metal Industries	12.22	12.41
Fabricated Metal Products	10.20	10.51
Machinery, Except Electrical	10.98	11.36
Electric and Electronic Equipment	10.24	10.36
Transportation Equipment	13.19	13.64
Instruments and Related Products	9.96	10.29
Miscellaneous Manufacturing Industries	7.98	8.30
Nondurable Goods	9.46	9.76
Food and Kindred Products	9.56	10.02
Tobacco Manufacturers	15.78	16.31
Textile Mill Products	7.31	7.65
Apparel and Other Textile Products	6.03	6.28
Paper and Allied Products	11.72	12.05
Printing and Publishing	10.48	10.87
Chemicals and Allied Products	12.70	13.11
Petroleum and Coal Products	14.93	15.31
Rubber and Miscellaneous Plastic Products	9.15	9.45
Leather and Leather Products	6.19	6.53

Source: U.S. Department of Labor, Bureau of Labor Statistics, *Employment and Earnings, September 1989* (Washington, D.C.: Government Printing Office, September 1989), pp. 83–93.

Exhibit 7

Mean Hourly Earnings of Manufacturing Plant Employees in Dallas and St. Louis

Job Titles	Dallas, Tex.	St. Louis, Mo.
Carpenter	$14.01	$14.39
Electrician	16.03	16.55
Painter	14.28	15.30
Machinist	15.77	15.75
Mechanic	15.04	13.78
General Maintenance	8.48	9.62
Tool and Die Maker	15.19	NA
Truck Driver	9.63	13.04
Shipper	9.33	8.04
Receiver	9.79	8.04
Warehouse Worker	10.34	11.60
Order Filler	7.34	NA
Packer	6.38	9.17
Material Handler	7.91	10.64
Forklift Operator	10.80	12.51
Janitor	9.48	11.39

Source: U.S. Department of Labor, Bureau of Labor Statistics, *Area Wage Survey: Dallas–Ft. Worth, Texas Metropolitan Area, December 1988* (Washington, D.C.: U.S. Government Printing Office, 1989), pp. 22–23: U.S. Department of Labor, Bureau of Labor Statistics, *Area Wage Survey: St. Louis, Missouri–Illinois, Metropolitan Area, March 1989* (Washington, D.C.: U.S. Government Printing Office, 1990), pp. 20–23.

Exhibit 8

Consumer Price Index for Urban Wage Earners and Clerical Workers and Percent Changes, 1967–1989

Year	Index	Percent Change
1967	100	–
1968	104.2	4.2
1969	109.8	5.4
1970	116.3	5.9
1971	121.3	4.3
1972	125.3	3.3
1973	133.1	6.2
1974	147.7	11.0
1975	161.2	9.1
1976	170.5	5.8
1977	181.5	6.5
1978	195.3	7.6
1979	217.7	11.5
1980	247.0	13.5
1981	272.3	10.2
1982	288.6	6.0
1983	297.4	3.0
1984	307.6	3.4
1985	318.5	3.5
1986	323.4	1.5
1987	340.4	5.3
1988	354.3	4.1
1989	377.6	6.6

Source: U.S. Department of Labor, Bureau of Labor Statistics, *Monthly Labor Review* 113 (February 1990), p. 90.

Exhibit 9

Average Gross Hours and Earnings of Manufacturing Production Workers and Furniture Production Workers, 1978–1989

	Manufacturing			Furniture		
	Weekly Earnings	Weekly Hours	Hourly Earnings	Weekly Earnings	Weekly Hours	Hourly Earnings
1978	$249.27	40.4	$ 5.91	$167.91	38.7	$4.35
1980 (Dec.)	315.70	41.5	7.40	268.77	39.7	6.77
1982 (Nov.)	337.90	39.5	8.62	246.77	38.2	6.46
1985 (Aug.)	384.35	40.5	9.49	253.99	38.6	7.20
1986 (Aug.)	391.15	40.2	9.73	255.98	37.7	7.44
1987 (Aug.)	403.27	40.7	10.39	311.92	40.3	7.74
1988 (July)	413.92	40.7	10.13	310.81	38.9	8.25
1989 (July)	424.44	40.5	10.48	318.45	38.6	7.99

Source: U.S. Department of Labor, Bureau of Labor Statistics, *Employment and Earnings,* September 1989, pp. 82–83.

Exhibit 10

Average Hourly and Weekly Earnings for All Private Workers and for Manufacturing Workers

	July 1988	July 1989
Hourly Earnings		
Total Private	$ 9.24	$ 9.63
Manufacturing	10.17	10.48
Average Weekly Earnings		
Total Private	$324.32	$338.01
Manufacturing	413.92	424.44

Source: U.S. Department of Labor, Bureau of Labor Statistics, *Employment and Earnings,* September 1989, pp. 82–83.

The Labor Agreement between Quality Furniture Manufacturing Company (QFM) and Industrial Workers United (IWU), AFL-CIO

This agreement is entered into on ____________________ by the Quality Furniture Manufacturing Company (QFM), located in St. Louis, Missouri, and Industrial Workers United (IWU). This agreement covers employees at the St. Louis plant only.

Article I

Recognition The company recognizes the IWU as the sole and exclusive collective bargaining agent in all matters pertaining to rates of pay, wages, hours of employment, and other conditions of employment for all production and maintenance employees, excluding professional employees, storeroom employees, office clerical employees, guards, and supervisors, as defined in the National Labor Relations Act.

Article II

Union Security The company agrees not to interfere with the right of employees to join the Union and will not discriminate against employees who are Union members. Employees in the bargaining unit are completely free to participate in the affairs of the Union, provided that such activities do not interfere with their work duties and responsibilities.

While no employee will be required to join the Union as a condition of employment, union dues will be deducted from any bargaining unit employee's pay check, provided proper written notification is given to the Company. At the end of each pay period, the Company will forward the collected dues, minus a 5 percent administrative fee, to the Union.

Article III

Management Rights All management functions of the enterprise that are not specifically limited by the express language of this agreement are retained by the Company. The functions and rights listed here are examples of the exclusive responsibilities retained by the Company and are not intended as an all-inclusive list: to manage the manufacturing operations and methods of production; to direct the work force; to decide what work shall be performed in the plant by subcontractors or by employees; to schedule working hours (including overtime work); to hire, promote, demote, and transfer; to suspend, discipline, and discharge for cause; to relieve employees due to lack of work or for other legitimate reasons; to create and enforce reasonable shop rules and regulations; to establish production standards and rates for new or changed jobs; to introduce new and improved methods, materials, equipment, and facilities; to change or eliminate existing methods, materials, equipment, and facilities.

Article IV

No Strike and No Lockout The company agrees that during the life of this agreement there shall be no lockout of bargaining unit employees.

The Union agrees that during the life of this agreement there shall be no strike, work stoppage, slowdown, work refusal, delay of work, refusal to report for work, or boycott.

Article V

Hours of Work The normal workweek shall consist of eight (8) hours per day, forty (40) hours per week, for a five (5) day week, from Monday to Friday. The starting time shall be made by the Company, and it can be changed by the Company to suit varying conditions of the business. Such changes in working schedules shall be made known to the Union representative in the plant as far in advance as possible. Employees shall be notified by a written bulletin or other communications medium.

Article VI

Grievances and Arbitration Procedures Grievances arising out of the operation and interpretation of this agreement shall be handled and settled in the following manner:

- *Step 1.* The aggrieved employee and/or shop steward shall discuss the grievance with his or her supervisor.
- *Step 2.* Should the answer provided by the supervisor not produce a satisfactory solution to the grievance, the grievance shall be reduced to writing and

shall state the provision of the agreement which has been violated. The department head shall arrange for a meeting of the aggrieved employee, the shop steward, the supervisor, the employee relations supervisor, and himself or herself for the purpose of discussing the grievance. The department head shall provide a written answer to the grievance after the close of the meeting.

- *Step 3.* If a satisfactory conclusion is not reached, the grievance can be referred to the plant manager by the Union. The plant manager shall schedule a meeting to discuss the grievance with the Union. The local Union can bring in a representative of the international Union at this step, and the plant manager can bring in anyone who he or she feels may aid in the resolution of the grievance.
- *Step 4.* If a grievance is appealed to arbitration, the Company and the Union shall attempt to select an arbitrator. If this attempt fails, the Company and/or Union shall ask the Federal Mediation and Conciliation Service to submit a list of seven (7) arbitrators. Each party shall eliminate three (3) names from the list by alternately striking one name at a time, and the person whose name remains shall serve as the arbitrator.

The arbitrator shall render a decision in writing that shall be final and binding upon the parties.

The arbitrator to whom any grievance is submitted shall have the authority to interpret and apply the provisions of this agreement, and the arbitrator's decision must be in accordance with and based upon the terms of this agreement or of any written amendment thereto. But the arbitrator shall have no jurisdiction or authority to add to, subcontract from, or modify any of the terms of this agreement.

The Company and local Union shall each pay its own expenses incurred in connection with the arbitration and one-half of the expenses and fees of the arbitrator and the facilities used in the arbitration hearing.

Article VII

Seniority "Seniority" as used in this agreement shall be the period of continuous service in the job or plant from the date of the employee's appointment.

"Probationary employment" consists of a period of one hundred twenty (120) days of employment.

Layoffs shall be made in the following order:

a. Probationary employees
b. Other employees in order of job seniority

Recall shall be made in the following order:

a. Employees in order of job seniority, given equal job ability
b. Probationary employees

Promotions shall be made on the basis of qualifications, merit, and seniority. Promotions out of the bargaining unit remain management's prerogative.

An employee who quits or is discharged for cause shall lose all seniority rights.

If the Company decides to terminate any operation or job and the employees remain on layoff for a period of twelve (12) months, the employees shall be considered to have been terminated for cause at the expiration of said twelve (12) month period.

Article VIII

Wages and Classifications Job classifications and a wage schedule setting forth the rates of pay of the various classifications are included in Schedule A and are hereby made part of this agreement.

If and when the Company creates a new job classification or modifies, alters, amends, or combines existing jobs, or revises the skills and responsibilities of a job, job descriptions will be drawn and a wage rate assigned. The Union shall have a maximum of five (5) working days to examine the job description to determine whether it accurately describes the principal functions and whether the pay range is consistent with established job classification pay ranges.

If the Union takes exception, it can review both factors with the Company. If the issue cannot be resolved, the Union can take the issue through the grievance procedure.

Job classifications are for pay purposes only and do not pertain to whoever might perform the work in that classification—unless modified by the terms of the agreement.

Article IX

Insurance An employee who has completed ninety (90) days of employment is eligible for enrollment in the company group insurance programs on the monthly premium date for each particular insurance coverage that next follows the completion of ninety (90) days of employment.

1. *Group Life Insurance*

Group Life Insurance	Accidental Death and Dismemberment
$10,000	$10,000

2. *Accident and health insurance.* One-half of the employee's weekly pay up to a maximum of $150. It is understood and agreed that the cost of the hospitalization, medical and health insurance, major medical insurance, accident and health and life insurance will be borne 50 percent (50%) by the Company and 50 percent (50%) by the employee, when subscribed to by the employee. It is understood and agreed that in the event that the Company wishes to change carriers, there is no obligation to negotiate with the Union prior to instituting the change.

Employees on medical leave for a period in excess of ninety (90) consecutive days may continue to be covered under the group insurance program after the first ninety (90) days, providing the employee pays the total insurance premium.

Article X

Pension Plan A pension plan for bargaining unit employees of the Company is hereby incorporated as a part of this agreement.

As of October 6, 1977, the normal retirement benefit for all years of service continues to be $18 per month per year of service.

Article XI

Holidays All employees, after completing six (6) months of service with the Company, shall be paid seven (7) hours' pay for the following holidays:

- New Year's Day
- Independence Day
- Labor Day
- Thanksgiving Day

- Day after Thanksgiving Day
- Christmas Eve Day
- Christmas Day

To be eligible for holiday pay, the employee must have worked the days immediately preceding and following the holiday. Legitimate excuses for absences will be considered.

Article XII

Vacation Employees shall qualify for vacation with pay in accordance with the following (determined June 1 of each year):

Continuous Service	Vacation with Pay
More than 1 but less than 5 years	1 week
More than 5 but less than 10 years	2 weeks
More than 10 but less than 20 years	3 weeks
More than 20 years	4 weeks

Vacation pay shall be computed on the basis of each employee's average weekly earnings from June to June. Payment will be made on the work day prior to the vacation period.

Article XIII

Sick Leave A full-time employee is eligible for sick leave after completing six (6) months' service with the Company. An eligible employee will accumulate sick leave at the rate of one-half day per month of service from date of hire. Sick leave will not be carried over from one year (January 1 to December 31) to the next, and it can be used only for personal illness not covered by workers' compensation. The Company retains the right to require a doctor's certificate as proof that absence was due to a legitimate injury or illness.

Article XIV

Duration of Agreement This agreement shall become effective as of ____________, and shall continue in effect until 11:59 P.M., ____________. Thereafter, it shall renew itself for yearly periods unless written notice of termination is given by one party to the other not less than sixty (60) nor more than ninety (90) days prior to the expiration date.

Schedule A Wages and Classifications

Wage Grade	Job Title	Wage Rates
1	Janitor	$ 7.65
2	General Laborer	8.50
3	Materials Handler	8.60
4	Packer	10.20
	Machine Operator–B	10.20
	Utility Worker	10.20
	Interplant Truck Driver	10.20
	Sander	10.20
	Assembler	10.20
5	Welder	11.00
	Machine Operator–A	11.00
	Electrician–B	11.00
	Maintenance Worker–B	11.00
	Gluer	11.00
6	Mechanic	11.90
	Spray Painter	11.90
	Cutoff Saw Operator	11.90
7	Electrician–A	12.70
	Maintenance Worker–A	12.70
	Inspector	12.70
8	Tool Grinder–A	13.50
9	Tool and Die Maker–A	14.40
10	Leadperson	15.20

Glossary

Ability. Measure usually accompanying seniority; includes some combination of skill, knowledge, attitudes, behavior, performance, production, and talent.

Absorption. The merging of two unions where the larger union takes over the smaller union.

Ad hoc arbitrator. An individual hired by union and management officials to resolve a dispute on a case-by-case basis.

Administrative law judges. Persons employed by the National Labor Relations Board (NLRB) who conduct hearings involving unfair labor practices and render decisions to the Board (NLRB) in Washington.

Agency shop. Provision requiring employees to pay the union a sum equal to membership dues to defray bargaining and grievance costs, but not requiring them to join the union.

Alienation. A mental sense of estrangement from work where the employee cannot derive meaning from the work tasks or products.

Ally doctrine. A doctrine used by the NLRB to determine how closely allied an apparent secondary employer is to a primary labor dispute.

Amalgamation. The merging of two or more unions into one.

American Federation of Labor (AFL). A labor organization formed in 1886 by Samuel Gompers and others to improve the short-range, material, and decentralized goals of union members; a forerunner of the AFL-CIO.

American Plan. A movement by employees in the 1920s and 1930s that stressed the principles of "rugged individualism" and the right of employees to not join unions.

Apprenticeship programs. Formal, supervised programs of training and experience, often supplemented by off-the-job instruction.

Appropriate affirmative action. An NLRB order to an employer or union requiring the granting of relief to a person whose Section 7 rights have been violated.

Appropriate bargaining unit. A grouping of jobs or positions in which two or more employees share common employment interests and conditions (community of interests); the NLRB designates that holders of these jobs would qualify to vote in union representation elections.

Arbitration. The terminal step in most grievance procedures where the arbitrator resolves the grievance by making a binding decision.

Arbitration hearing. A meeting with the grievance participants and the arbitrator wherein evidence, exhibits, and testimony are presented and these provide the basis for the arbitrator's decision.

Arbitrator. A third-party neutral employed by union and management officials to make a binding decision on an employee's grievance.

Attitudinal structuring. Involves activities aimed at attaining a desired relationship between the parties that will in turn affect the negotiation process and subsequent administration of the labor agreement.

Attrition. A reduction in employment without any layoffs; it usually comes in the form of not replacing those who retire or leave voluntarily.

Automation. Technological change in which machines perform tasks formerly performed by humans, and the human operator is replaced by automatic controls.

Bargaining power. A union or management negotiator increases bargaining power by increasing the other party's disagreement costs or reducing the other party's agreement costs.

Bargaining ranges. A multitude of negotiation issue priorities for union and management officials that is bounded by upper and lower bargaining limits.

Blacklist. A list of union activists maintained by employers and exchanged with other employers; it was declared an unfair labor practice in 1935.

Bona fide occupation qualification. A legitimate qualification necessary to perform a job task.

Boulwarism. A collective bargaining approach once used at General Electric and found violative of good faith bargaining because it focused on the employees instead of the union.

Boycott. The refusal to purchase or to handle products involved in a labor dispute.

Bumping. An employee who is more senior or more skilled replaces a less senior or less skilled employee, who is then laid off, or "bumps" another employee.

Business agent. A full-time union administrator, usually of a craft union, who is responsible for the union hiring hall, serves as the "watchdog" over the local labor agreement, and leads the local negotiations.

CAPS. A term used to describe the height to which wages may be adjusted upward.

"Captive audience." Employees who have been required to attend a meeting to hear a presentation by the employer during a pre-election campaign.

Cease and desist order. An order to stop certain activities by the National Labor Relations Board directed toward violators of the National Labor Relations Act.

Centralized bargaining. Collective bargaining covering more than one appropriate bargaining unit, such as single employer–multi-plant bargaining , multi-employer bargaining.

Chilling effect. The result of the belief that one or both parties may get a better settlement in arbitration than in negotiation, leading to a lack of effort at reaching an agreement in negotiations.

Clinical approach. A desirable but not always attainable grievance resolution attempt to uncover all of the causes of the employees' grievances and have these causes influence the remedy.

Closed shop. Currently illegal labor agreement provision that requires an employee to be a union member in order to obtain a job.

Co-determination. A concept used in several European countries in which unions and employers co-determine designated policies and procedures.

Codified relationships. Relationships that occur in contract administration when first-line supervisors and union stewards behave according to some established norm or code, such as the labor agreement.

COLA (cost-of-living adjustment) (escalator) clause. A clause written in a labor agreement that adjusts wages in accordance with some predetermined formula.

Collective bargaining structure. Employee/employer groupings that can affect the collective bargaining outcome and/or be subject to the provisions of the negotiated labor agreement.

Collective bargaining. An activity whereby union and management officials attempt to resolve conflicting interests in a manner that will sustain and possibly enrich their continuing relationships.

Common law (case law). Court decisions that are made in the absence of statutory laws; these decisions stand until they are overturned by a higher court or changed by legislation.

Common law of the shop. A major influence on the arbitrator's decision that refers to the labor agreement language, intent, and past practices of the union and management officials at a particular industrial facility.

Common situs picketing. Picketing by construction unions of an entire work site even though the labor dispute may have involved only one union and one employer.

Company union. Illegal union that receives financial help from the company.

Compulsory arbitration. The type of arbitration required by law.

Concession bargaining. Occurs when management obtains from unions reduced wage levels and/or modification or elimination of work rules (combining job classifications, for example) to increase managerial discretion.

Conference boards. Organizations within national unions that discuss issues pertaining to the union and a particular company.

Congress of Industrial Organizations (CIO). A labor organization (federation) formed in 1938 to unionize employees on an industrial basis; it eventually merged with the AFL in 1955 to form the AFL-CIO.

Consumer Price Index (CPI). An index that helps to determine the relative cost of living, such as CPI of the Bureau of Labor Statistics.

Contingency union shop. A labor agreement provision in right-to-work states that indicates that the union shop provision will apply if and when the state's right-to-work laws are appealed.

Contract bar doctrine. NLRB rule specifying that a valid, signed agreement for a fixed period of 3 years or less will bar any representation election for the life of the agreement.

Convention. Supreme governing body of a national union, held annually or biennially.

Cost-of-living adjustments (COLA). Improvement of wages during the life of the contract to compensate for the effect of inflation on real wages.

Craft union. A union composed of members who have been organized in accordance with their craft or skill, such as bricklayers and electricians.

De facto bargaining. Bargaining that takes place in the public sector that is not authorized by legislation.

De minimis. Used when arbitrators dismiss a technically correct but trivial grievance on the grounds that an award in the grievant's favor would encourage more trivial grievances, thereby damaging the labor-management relationship.

Decertification. An NLRB procedure that is available for employees when they believe, usually as the result of election, that the union no longer represents the interests of the majority of the bargaining unit.

Deferred wage increase. A wage increase deferred to a later date or to the occurrence of some specific event, such as when the company becomes profitable.

Distributive bargaining. Bargaining that occurs over some issues (wages, for example) where one party's goals conflict with those of the other party, so each party tries to keep the upper hand.

Due process. Procedural aspects in discipline cases, such as following time limits proscribed in the labor agreement, providing union representation, and notifying the employee of the specific offense in writing.

Dues checkoff. Not a union security provision in the strict sense of the word, but it does allow the union members to have their dues automatically taken out of their payroll checks (as for any other payroll deduction) and transferred to the union.

Economy. The system of production, distribution, and consumption of goods and services.

Employee Representation Plans. Company-established unions in the 1920s and 1930s that were instituted as an alternative to the more autonomous, independent labor organizations.

Employee stock ownership plans (ESOP). Plans giving employees an opportunity to become shareholders in the company by providing discount prices on shares or by matching employees' payment for stock.

Employment at will. A legal doctrine meaning that an employee can quit his or her job for any reason at any time and the employer can discharge the employee for any reason at any time.

End-run bargaining. A term used to describe an action on the part of a union to bypass the employer negotiators and to attempt to bargain directly with the decision makers.

Enterprise union. A union within one company or enterprise.

Ethical Practices Committee. AFL-CIO committee established to control corrupt practices and racketeering in its member unions.

Exclusive recognition. A designation of labor unions by the federal government that indicates that the union has been selected by secret ballot by employees to be the exclusive representative of a group of employees.

Exclusivity doctrine. A legal doctrine meaning that only one union exclusively represents a group of employees and that the employer may bargain with only this union (certified by the NLRB as the exclusive bargaining representative).

Executive Order. An order given by the chief of the executive branch of government—for example, the president of the country or governor of a state.

Fact-finding. The type of third-party involvement in which a neutral party gathers facts, organizes them, and presents related recommendations either privately or publicly.

Fair representation. The union's legal obligation to represent fairly all of the bargaining-unit employees, union members and nonmembers alike.

Featherbedding. Payment for work that is not needed; workers working at reduced speed; workers duplicating the work of others.

Federal Service Impasse Panel (FSIP). Committee within the Federal Labor Relations Authority that investigates any negotiation impasse presented to it and takes any action it considers necessary to settle the dispute.

Final-offer selection (FOS) arbitration. The type of interest arbitration that gives the arbitrator the authority to select one of the proposals presented by the parties with no compromised settlement allowed between proposals.

Good faith bargaining. Negotiators' obligation from the National Labor Relations Act to demonstrate a sincere and honest intent to consummate a labor agreement and exhibit reasonableness in their bargaining positions, tactics, and activities.

Grievance. Any employee's concern over a perceived violation of the labor agreement that is submitted to the grievance procedure for eventual resolution.

Haymarket Riot. A protest over the eight-hour work day on May 4, 1886, that resulted in the deaths of several participants and turned public opinion against labor as well as the Knights of Labor.

Homestead Incident. A sharp wage cut coupled with replacement employees at the Carnegie Steel Works in 1894 that resulted in prolonged union violence and elicited somewhat favorable public opinion for organized labor.

Hot-cargo agreement. An agreement stating that union members will not be required to handle goods made by nonunion labor and/or workers at a struck plant.

Industrial union. A union composed of members who have been organized on an industry basis, such as steelworkers and autoworkers.

Industrial Workers of the World (IWW). A loosely knit organization formed in 1905 by Big Bill Haywood and others to "emancipate the working class from the slave bondage of capitalism."

Informational picketing. Attempt by a union to inform the public that a labor dispute exists.

Injunction. A court order that restricts or requires certain activities.

Integrative bargaining. An approach characterized by trust and openness when both parties attempt to resolve a common problem or concern to their mutual benefit.

Intent. Refers to what union and management officials had in mind when they negotiated the labor agreement or engaged in an action that resulted in a particular grievance.

Interest (or contract) arbitration. A type of arbitration in which the arbitrator makes a final and binding decision on issues that will be included in the labor agreement.

Intra-organizational bargaining. Refers to activities employed by management and union negotiators to achieve consensus within their respective organizations or bargaining teams.

Job evaluation. Process of determining the relative importance of each job to the organization to help in understanding occupational wage differentials.

Job-security work rules. Provisions that attempt to make jobs more secure, such as spreading the workload by placing limits on the load that can be carried, restricting the duties of employees, limiting the number of machines one operator can tend, prohibiting modern tools or equipment, and requiring standby crews.

Joint councils. Groupings of local unions that have common goals, employers, and interests.

Journeyman. A highly skilled worker who has normally completed certain training and experience requirements.

Just cause. Places the burden of proof on management to prove that its discipline was logically derived from the nature of the employee-employer relationship, contract provisions, proper rules of conduct, and/or established and accepted practices.

Knights of Labor (KOL). The first large labor organization in the United States, formed in 1869 and dedicated to long-range, social reform goals.

Labor market. An external influence on the labor relations process that pertains to skills and wage levels of employees in the local community.

Laboratory conditions. NLRB doctrine in which an attempt is made to conduct union election campaigns in conditions as nearly ideal as possible, to determine the uninhibited desires of the employees.

Labor relations process. Process in which management and the union jointly decide upon and administer terms and conditions of employment.

Language analysis. Occurs when union and management negotiators interpret the others' remarks along three dimensions: how specific is the statement; how final is the statement; and what are the consequences associated with the statement?

Leapfrog. An action by a union to use a settlement with one company as a base from which to gain a better settlement with another.

Lifetime employment. An arrangement in which an employee is guaranteed employment for as long as he or she wants or until he or she retires.

Lockout. An act by an employer when it shuts down its operation during or before a labor dispute.

Lump-sum pay adjustment. A one-time payment made to adjust wages; the amount is not included in the base pay.

Maintenance of membership. Contract requirement that those employees who decide to join a union must remain a union member for a certain period of time.

Mandatory bargaining issues. Topics related to wages, hours, and other conditions of employment that must be bargained; however, failure to reach agreement does not automatically constitute a bargaining violation.

Med-arb (mediation-arbitration). The type of third-party settlement in which the neutral serves first as a mediator and, if unsuccessful, serves as an arbitrator.

Mediator. A third-party neutral, often a federal government employee, who has no binding authority but nonetheless assists union and management officials in reaching a collective bargaining settlement.

Mitigating circumstances. Considerations (such as an employee's long and good service work record and/or management contributing to the problem, for example) that influence the arbitrator to reduce or eliminate management's initial disciplinary action.

Multinational corporation (MNC). A corporation that does business or has operations in more than one country.

Narcotic effect. An addiction to arbitration as a result of experience with the consequences of arbitration in bargaining impasses.

National consultation rights. A designation granted labor unions in the federal government that indicates that the union is the representative of at least 10 percent of the workers and allows the union to be notified of proposed substantive changes in the conditions of employment.

National emergency dispute. A strike or lockout resulting from a negotiation impasse in a major industry that creates a national emergency.

National War Labor Board. A panel of union, management, and public representatives established during World War II that arbitrated some 20,000 disputes and publicized arbitration's potential benefits.

Negotiating unit. The employees who will be bound by the negotiated labor agreement that can (1) be identical to the appropriate bargaining unit, (2) include more than one appropriate bargaining unit, or (3) represent a combination of the preceding arrangements depending upon the particular bargaining issue.

Oral warning. A rather mild form of discipline representing an informal effort to correct and improve the employee's work performance.

Outsourcing. Cost-cutting strategy of shifting work away from a plant to lower-cost producers and purchasing parts needed in production from these producers, often eliminating union jobs.

Parole evidence rule. Holds that evidence, oral or otherwise, cannot be admitted for the purpose of varying or contradicting written language recorded in the labor agreement.

Past practice. Represents a specific and identical action that has been continually employed over a number of years to the recognition and satisfaction of both parties.

Pattern bargaining. A collective bargaining settlement at one company or one segment of an industry that strongly influences the bargaining objectives and/or results at another company or segment of an industry.

Permanent arbitrator. An individual employed by union and management officials to resolve disputes during the life of the labor agreement.

Picketing. The outside patrolling of the employer's premises for the purpose of achieving a specific objective.

Power relationships. Relationships that occur in contract administration situations where the first-line supervisors and union stewards pursue differing interests or goals.

Preferential treatment clause. A negotiated labor agreement provision that indicates union members will be given employment preference over non-members when a new facility is opened.

Premium pay. Pay that is an addition to the base wage rate.

Prepaid legal plans. An arrangement where employees (union members) may obtain counsel of a lawyer for a certain period of time for legal counsel as an employee benefit.

Prevailing wage. A wage rate prevailing within a particular area or labor market.

Price list. Cites specific rules and furnishes uniform penalties for single or repeated infractions for a number of possible disciplinary offenses.

Product or consumer picketing. Attempt by a union to persuade customers to refuse to purchase products from the employer with whom the union has a labor dispute.

Product market. An external influence on the labor relations process that indicates where the company either sells its product or purchases key elements for its manufacture.

Progressive discipline. Refers to increasingly severe penalties corresponding with repeated, similar offenses (violations) committed by an employee.

Promotions. Personnel changes within an organization that advance the employee to a position of more responsibility, usually accompanied by a wage increase.

Pullman Strike. A nationwide, unsuccessful strike of the American Railway Union (led by Eugene Debs) against unilateral wage cuts and layoffs at the Pullman Company in 1894.

Quasi-union shop. A union shop provision in right-to-work states that is obscurely nullified later in the labor agreement.

Recognitional picketing. Attempt by a union to gain recognition from employees of the union as their bargaining representative.

Red-circled wage rate. A wage rate paid to an employee that is greater than that assigned by the job evaluation plan.

Referendum. A direct vote by citizens or by union members to approve or reject terms of a newly-negotiated labor agreement.

Reserve gate picketing. Picketing at a gate designated by the employer for entry by employees not involved in the labor dispute.

Reserved rights doctrine. States that management's authority is supreme in all matters except those it has expressly conceded in the collective bargaining agreement and/or restricted by law.

Right-to-work laws. Laws found in twenty-one states that have implemented 14(b) of the National Labor Relations Act and prohibit union membership (and related union security clauses) as a condition of employment.

Scarcity consciousness. Employees' belief that they are living in a world of limited opportunity and that unions can help them in achieving more job security.

Secondary employers. Employers who are not directly involved in the labor dispute with a union or unions.

Seniority. Length of an employee's continuous service.

Severance pay. Payments made to employees who sever their relationship with their employer either by layoff or retirement (not discharge).

Shop steward. The elected representative of the employees in a particular unit who represents its members at local union meetings, handles grievances at the first level, and collects dues.

Sovereignty doctrine. A doctrine stating that the legislative body cannot delegate its authority to make decisions.

State of the economy. An external influence on the labor relations process that can be broadly defined as an absolute or relative movement among such quantitative indicators as inflation, unemployment, and productivity, or it can be defined in more narrow terms pertaining to a specific industry or organization within that industry.

Statutory law. Laws that are passed by legislative bodies such as Congress and city councils.

Strike. A temporary stoppage of work by a group of employees for the purposes of expressing a grievance or enforcing a demand.

Strike insurance. Payments made to union officials by management to keep the union from going out on strike.

Strike benefits. Payments made to union members on strike from funds set aside by the national union.

Strikebreakers. Employees who continue to work during a strike and are willing to cross the union picket line; the term also refers to others who are hired for the specific reason of working during a strike.

Struck work. Work done during a strike that is normally done by those employees on strike.

Subcontracting. An employer action taken when the employer determines that it cannot perform all the tasks or some of the tasks necessary to operate its business successfully and arranges for another firm to perform those tasks. The employer may also subcontract tasks that can be performed elsewhere at a lower cost or higher quality.

Successor employer. An employer who takes over a facility having an already established labor organization; this employer might be obligated to continue the previously negotiated labor agreement.

Sunshine laws. Laws that make public many meetings by government officials, such as negotiations with union officials.

Superseniority. A privilege granted in a labor agreement that entitles a union officer or highly skilled employee to be the last person laid off.

Supplemental unemployment benefit plans (SUB). Benefits made to supplement payments that are already received, such as unemployment benefits.

Supreme Court Trilogy. Three Supreme Court decisions in 1960 that gave considerable prestige and discretion to the arbitrators in resolving employee grievances.

Suspensions. Disciplinary layoffs without pay given by management to impress upon the employee the seriousness of the offense.

Sweetheart contracts. Where the union official settles for less than he or she could have obtained if he or she had not "sold out" to management.

Sympathetic relationships. Relationships that occur in contract administration between individuals when each is aware of the other's situation and is guided by an understanding and appreciation of that situation.

Technological change. Changes in the production process that result from the introduction of labor-saving machinery and changes in material handling and work flow.

Technology. A most significant influence on work rules; it affects the pace and scheduling of work, characteristics of the work environment, and tasks to be performed.

Tenure. A form of job security that protects faculty rights to express their opinions and means that faculty generally cannot be terminated except for cause.

Third and one-half step. An informal grievance step where union and management representatives meet to discuss and trade grievances.

Totality of conduct doctrine. NLRB doctrine to guide interpretation of unfair labor practice behavior, stating that isolated incidents such as campaign speeches must be considered within the whole of the general circumstances of the campaign and with the possibility that other specific violations have occurred.

Transfer. Personnel change from one position to another with relatively equal authority, responsibility, and compensation, determined by seniority and ability.

Union hiring hall. A place that operates as a clearinghouse for the placement of union members, usually in the construction trades.

Union instrumentality. Employees' perception of whether the union will function to attain desired outcomes such as higher wages, improved working conditions, job security, and protection from arbitrary treatment by management.

Union security clause. A labor agreement provision that makes it easier for the union to enroll and retain members.

Union shop. Contract requirement that once hired, an employee has a certain time period to become a union member in order to keep his or her job.

Vesting. An agreement that the employee's pension is guaranteed, regardless of whether the employee remains with his or her present employer.

Wage indexation. Wages are adjusted in accordance with the Consumer Price Index.

Wage package. The total amount of compensation, including wages, premium pay, incentives, and so forth.

Wage reopener. A clause written in a labor agreement to allow the parties to negotiate wages during the life of an agreement.

Whipsawing. Actions on the part of a union to put pressure on employers when it strikes one or more employers of a multi-union bargaining group in hopes of getting a better settlement from those employers not struck or from those that are struck.

Wildcat strike. Work stoppage involving the primary employer-employee relationship that is neither sanctioned nor stimulated by the union, although union officials might be aware of it.

Work preservation clause. A clause written in a labor agreement to preserve a certain amount of hours of work or number of employees covered by the labor agreement.

Work rules. The focal point of labor relations; they can relate to compensation or to employee rights, and they reflect the dynamic and sometimes vague aspects of the labor relations process.

Work scheduling. Regulating shifts and fixing the workday or work week.

Written warning. Summarizes previous oral attempts to correct the employee's behavior and is entered in the employee's work record file.

Yellow-dog contract. An agreement between the employer and employee stating that the employee will not join a union or assist in organizing a union as a condition of employment.

Name Index

Subject Index

Danbury Hatters case, 63
Decertification procedures, 150–152